CH01370064

THE UNIVERSITY OF CAMBRIDGE IN
THE AGE OF ATLANTIC SLAVERY

In this powerful history of the University of Cambridge, Nicolas Bell-Romero considers the nature and extent of Britain's connections to enslavement. His research moves beyond traditional approaches which focus on direct and indirect economic ties to enslavement or on the slave trading hubs of Liverpool and Bristol. From the beginnings of North American colonisation to the end of the American Civil War, the story of Cambridge reveals the vast spectrum of interconnections that university students, alumni, fellows, professors, and benefactors had to Britain's Atlantic slave empire – in dining halls, debating chambers, scientific societies, or lobby groups. Following the stories of these middling and elite men as they became influential agents around the empire, Bell-Romero uncovers the extent to which the problem of slavery was an inextricable feature of social, economic, cultural, and intellectual life. This title is also available as open access on Cambridge Core.

NICOLAS BELL-ROMERO is a Postdoctoral Research Fellow for the Tulane History Project at Tulane University in New Orleans. From 2020 to 2023, he was one of the two lead researchers for the University of Cambridge's Legacies of Enslavement Inquiry.

THE UNIVERSITY OF CAMBRIDGE IN THE AGE OF ATLANTIC SLAVERY

NICOLAS BELL-ROMERO

Tulane University, Louisiana

CAMBRIDGE UNIVERSITY PRESS

CAMBRIDGE
UNIVERSITY PRESS

Shaftesbury Road, Cambridge CB2 8EA, United Kingdom

One Liberty Plaza, 20th Floor, New York, NY 10006, USA

477 Williamstown Road, Port Melbourne, VIC 3207, Australia

314–321, 3rd Floor, Plot 3, Splendor Forum, Jasola District Centre, New Delhi – 110025, India

103 Penang Road, #05–06/07, Visioncrest Commercial, Singapore 238467

Cambridge University Press is part of Cambridge University Press & Assessment, a department of the University of Cambridge.

We share the University's mission to contribute to society through the pursuit of education, learning and research at the highest international levels of excellence.

www.cambridge.org
Information on this title: www.cambridge.org/9781009652544

DOI: 10.1017/9781009652582

© Nicolas Bell-Romero 2026

This publication is in copyright. Subject to statutory exception and to the provisions of relevant collective licensing agreements, with the exception of the Creative Commons version the link for which is provided below, no reproduction of any part may take place without the written permission of Cambridge University Press & Assessment.

An online version of this work is published at doi.org/10.1017/9781009652582 under a Creative Commons Open Access license CC-BY-NC 4.0 which permits re-use, distribution and reproduction in any medium for non-commercial purposes providing appropriate credit to the original work is given and any changes made are indicated. To view a copy of this license visit https://creativecommons.org/licenses/by-nc/4.0

When citing this work, please include a reference to the DOI 10.1017/9781009652582

First published 2026

Front cover illustration: Universal Images Group/Getty Images

Printed in Great Britain by CPI Group (UK) Ltd, Croydon CR0 4YY

A catalogue record for this publication is available from the British Library

A Cataloging-in-Publication data record for this book is available from the Library of Congress

ISBN 978-1-009-65254-4 Hardback

Cambridge University Press & Assessment has no responsibility for the persistence or accuracy of URLs for external or third-party internet websites referred to in this publication and does not guarantee that any content on such websites is, or will remain, accurate or appropriate.

For EU product safety concerns, contact us at Calle de José Abascal, 56, 1º, 28003 Madrid, Spain, or email eugpsr@cambridge.org

CONTENTS

List of Figures　　*page* vi
List of Tables　　vii
Acknowledgments　　viii
List of Abbreviations　　xi

　　Introduction　　1

1　'The principal ingredient necessary to form a good planter': Education and the Making of a Transatlantic Elite　　19

2　'The Highe Priest hath banished you forth': Missionary Protestantism and the Origins of the British Empire　　49

3　'The Glory of their times': Natural Philosophy, the Law, and the Spoils of Empire　　76

4　'Several University Gentlemen, who have quite altered their Tone': The Problem of the British Slave Trade　　104

5　'Those who wish to see the Slave System decline, and at length gradually and safely': The Ambitions of Cambridge Abolitionism　　138

6　'We presume that its influence is nowhere greater than in the Universities': Ending and Defending American Slavery　　164

　　Conclusion　　202

Appendix A: Cambridge Families and the Transatlantic Economy　　206
Notes　　210
Bibliography　　294
Index　　371

FIGURES

1.1 Lease for 13 and a half years of Triall plantation, 1762, Church Mission Society Unofficial Papers. Cadbury Research Library, University of Birmingham.   *page* 33
1.2 Unknown, *Burch Hothersall*, oil on canvas, unknown date. Emmanuel College, University of Cambridge.   34
1.3 Robert Edge Pine, *Ralph Wormeley V*, oil on canvas, 1763. Virginia Museum of History and Culture.   35
3.1 The Coffe[e] Tree, print from Richard Bradley, *A Short Historical Account of Coffee* (London: EM. Matthews, 1715). Royal Society.   84
4.1 Charles Farish, 'A Summary of the consequences of the abolition of the slave-trade', 1798, Letters, Papers, and Domestic Correspondence of George III. National Archives, Kew, London.   107
5.1 Election broadside on behalf of George Pryme to the Electors of the Town of Cambridge, 11 June 1832, Collection of Election Broadsides, Handbills, and Squibs. Cambridgeshire Archives.   149
6.1 An Offering from English Churchmen to the American Bishops. Towards the Re-Establishment of their University for the South and South-West Dioceses, Charles Todd Quintard Papers. Sewanee: University of the South.   167

TABLES

1. Student Birthplaces *page* 206
2. Familial Involvement in the Atlantic Economy 208
3. Student College Ranks 208
4. Colleges Attended 209

ACKNOWLEDGMENTS

The last four years were a rather peculiar time to write about the so-called "peculiar institution." Two unconnected events occurred in March 2020: I began work on this topic after being appointed as one of the two Research Associates for the University of Cambridge's Legacies of Enslavement Inquiry, and the United Kingdom enforced the first lockdown for the COVID-19 pandemic. The fact that this book exists at all, therefore, should also be credited to the assistance and support of numerous colleagues, friends, and family.

I want to first thank colleagues who have been integral to the Cambridge inquiry from its inception to completion. Sabine Cadeau, who, along with this author, were the lead researchers for the project, has been a wonderful friend and collaborator throughout the trials and tribulations of the inquiry. Martin Millett, the fearless Chair of the Advisory Group, has many gifts: sage wisdom, kindness, patience, and a magical ability to make things happen in the tangled bureaucratic webs of Cambridge. Bronwen Everill and Nick Guyatt have bravely persevered through sections or offshoots of this book and have been an incredible source of support and encouragement throughout, as they have been for so many early career researchers before me. Sujit Sivasundaram and Peter Mandler were generous with their time and patience as a text on around two-dozen colleges and multiple centuries of Atlantic history glacially took shape. Sarah Pearsall shared her wisdom at the early stages of the project, and her guidance has helped me to find my voice as a historian. From the Cambridge Advisory Group, I also want to thank Ash Amin, Adam Branch, Mark Elliott, Toni Fola-Alade, Mónica Moreno Figueroa, Mark Purcell, Ángel Gurría-Quintana, Sharon Mehari, Priscilla Mensah, Toby Green, Meleisa Ono-George, Olivette Otele, and Diana Paton. Stephen Toope, Cambridge's former Vice-Chancellor, generously supported the research. At Caius College, I have a debt of gratitude to Annabel Brett, Melissa Calaresu, James Cox, Michelle Ellefson, Michael Joseph, Pippa Rogerson, and Ted Tregear.

Beyond the Advisory Group, I was inspired by the expertise and advice of numerous academics from near and far. From the start of the project, Sabine and I were lucky to meet William Whyte and Mishka Sinha at St John's College, Oxford, and compare findings on institutional connections to enslavement and colonialism with colleagues from the "other place." I received much-welcome words of encouragement during my "fifteen minutes" of academic fame from Corinne Fowler and Michael Taylor. I also want to thank Laura Channing, Kate Ekema, and Joseph La Hausse de Lalouvière for the many coffees and expert advice that they have provided over the years (in Laura's case, many years!). Towards the end of the writing process, I was lucky to (virtually) meet Christopher Jeppesen and benefit from his expertise on Jesus and Trinity colleges. The September 2022 'Envisioning Reparations' conference provided an opportunity to present the research findings and meet with international experts on enslavement and reparations – and I want to thank Sabine and Nicki Dawidowski for their heroic efforts in ensuring that the event was such a great success. At the conference, I met Michael Banner, the Dean of Trinity College, and I have learnt a great deal from his findings on student connections to enslavement. The early career research network of historians working on the history of enslavement and its afterlives, which had its inaugural meeting at the University of Hull in November 2022, was another wonderful moment to engage with scholars in the field – and provided Sabine and I the opportunity to share notes about our experiences of working at Cambridge. Although a career opportunity in New Orleans has sadly curtailed my involvement in that organisation, I want to thank Cassandra Gooptar and Isabel Robinson for doing the impossible and building a community during a pandemic. At Tulane University, I want to thank Marcia Walker-McWilliams and Cécile Yézou for their continued support and encouragement.

This institutional history of enslavement has (surprise, surprise) benefitted from the generosity of numerous institutions both within and beyond Cambridge. First, I cannot thank enough the many archivists and external researchers who were integral to the project and are the lifeblood of the profession, including Robert Athol at Jesus College, Rupert Baker at the Royal Society, Anna Crutchley at Trinity Hall, Tom Davies at King's College, Adolphus Depass at the National Library of Jamaica, Tim Evenden at the East Sussex Record Office, Katy Green at Magdalene College, Joseph Hettrick, Evie Stevenson, and Hannah Cliel at the Bank of England, Jayne Hoare at the Cambridgeshire Archives, Philippa Hoskin at Corpus Christi College, Roger Hull from Liverpool, Asma Iftikhar at the Cadbury Research Library in Birmingham, Mandi Johnson at Sewanee, Gaye Morgan at All Souls College, Jonathan Smith and Diana Smith at Trinity College, Lucy Thomas at Christ's College, and Hannah Westall at Girton College. Many of these institutions kindly allowed me to reproduce images from their collections in the text. At the Cambridge University Press, I am indebted to Michael Watson, Rosa Martin, and the two anonymous peer-reviewers who have helped to transform what was a shorter institutional report into a book manuscript.

I could not be where I am today without my friends and family. From Caius, I am so grateful to Helen, Martin, Lander, Nik, and Amelia who have been with me since I started my doctorate. I want to also thank Lewis, Sarah, Sam,

Lindsey, Megan, and Ali. They have made my time in Cambridge so special. The five-a-side-football lads – including Kris, Tim, Erik, Michael, Niall, Hugh, Caleb, and Blake – have kept me (almost) sane and distracted – and generously tolerated my fondness for long-range shots and passes that I should not be attempting. Though separated by lockdowns and geographic distance, my family in Australia, the United Kingdom, and the United States have been supportive when the world was in such turmoil. I always enjoyed sitting down and chatting to my parents on the phone or, when they were finally able to visit the UK, sharing a pint at the pub. They were always able to place everything in perspective, whether personal matters or the research, and put me back on track when I was close to (what felt like) a mental breakdown.

Returning to where I started, in March 2020, I should mention another much more important and noteworthy life moment than a multi-year pandemic or an esoteric academic project: I first moved in with my then partner and now wife, Evelyn Strope. Her love inspires me every day. I want to thank her with all my heart.

ABBREVIATIONS

ASC	All Souls College, University of Oxford
BE	Bank of England, London
BL	British Library, London
BOD	Bodleian Library, University of Oxford
CA	Cambridgeshire Archive, Ely
CCA	Clare College Archive, University of Cambridge
CCC	Corpus Christi College Archive, University of Cambridge
CCMR	Christ's College Muniments Room, University of Cambridge
CRL	Cadbury Research Library, University of Birmingham
CUL	Cambridge University Library
ES	East Sussex Record Office, Brighton, UK
GCA	Girton College Archive, University of Cambridge
GCC	Gonville and Caius College Lower Library, University of Cambridge
GSU	Genealogical Society of Utah, Salt Lake City, Utah
HJ	*The Historical Journal*
HL	Houghton Library, Harvard University, Cambridge, Massachusetts
JC	Jesus College Archive, University of Cambridge
JJBL	John J. Burns Library, Boston College, Massachusetts
KCA	King's College Archive Centre, University of Cambridge
LA	Lancashire Archives, Preston, United Kingdom
LARC	Louisiana Research Collection, Tulane University, New Orleans
LHC	Louisiana Historical Center, Louisiana State Museums, New Orleans
LPL	Lambeth Palace Library, London
LRO	Liverpool Record Office, Liverpool, UK
MC	Magdalene College Archive, University of Cambridge
NatWest	NatWest Group Archives, Edinburgh, UK
NLJ	National Library of Jamaica, Kingston
NRO	Norfolk Record Office, Norwich, UK
NYCRO	North Yorkshire County Record Office, Northallerton, UK
NYPL	New York Public Library, New York
QC	Queens' College Presidential Lodge, University of Cambridge
RA	The Royal Society, London
RS	The Royal Archives, Windsor Castle, Windsor

LIST OF ABBREVIATIONS

SHC	Somerset Heritage Centre, Taunton, UK
TH	Trinity Hall Archive, University of Cambridge
TNA	The National Archives, Kew, London
VMHB	*The Virginia Magazine of History and Biography*
VMHC	Virginia Museum of History and Culture, Richmond
WL	Wren Library, Trinity College, University of Cambridge
WLC	William L. Clements Library, University of Michigan, Ann Arbor
W&M	Earl Gregg Swem Library, College of William and Mary, Williamsburg
WMQ	*The William and Mary Quarterly*
WRL	William R. Laurie University Archives and Special Collections, University of the South, Sewanee, Tennessee

Introduction

This is the story of an East Anglian market town and university in the age of Atlantic slavery, and what that colourful history suggests about the nature and extent of Britons' involvement in and connections to enslavement. From the rise of chattel slavery in the early seventeenth century through to its abolition in North America more than two centuries later, the University of Cambridge's students, alumni, fellows, professors, and benefactors held a multitude of personal, cultural, economic, and political ties to enslavement. They owned or leased plantations and invested in colonial, slave-trading, and antislavery organisations. They counted prominent (and not-so-prominent) enslavers as friends and family members. They educated, tutored, mentored, and debated with the sons of slaveholders, merchants, and slave-traders. Cambridge men mounted powerful legal, philosophical, and religious defenses for colonial companies, lobby groups, and individuals involved in these enterprises. They engaged in collecting and scientific work, with the assistance of enslaved Africans and enslavers alike. They facilitated donations and benefactions from men with investments in the slave economy. Furthermore, Cambridge members voiced their opinions on the problem of enslavement, whether they were abolitionists, proslavery activists, or, indeed, occupied a middle ground on the issue. Far from a black and white tale of plantation owners and abolitionists, Cambridge's past illuminates the vast spectrum of associations that Britons, including those who lived outside of the major metropolitan urban centers, had with a transatlantic empire that was integral to the social, economic, intellectual, and cultural worlds of the colonies and metropole.[1]

There are several reasons why Cambridge provides such a valuable lens into Britain's participation in enslavement. First, Cambridge was a vibrant, cosmopolitan town and gown community where students, fellows, benefactors, and residents from all corners of Britain and the empire met and debated, and formed new associations, friendships, and connections; and, second, the market town provides a window into the multi-faceted legacies of enslavement in the interior of the country, as distinct from emerging or established mercantile and financial centers – such as Liverpool, Manchester, Glasgow, and London – that have received more historical attention. Numerous questions have motivated this study: were university students, alumni, and fellows connected to slavery and the propagation of racist thought? Why did people hold these connections and how did these linkages manifest themselves and evolve over time, including after emancipation? What do these histories suggest about the abolition and proslavery movements? And what does this history tell us about the many connections that Britons held to the transatlantic slave economy and colonial slave societies? Utilising archival records from Britain, the United States, and the Caribbean, the book is, at its heart, a study of "intellectual culture": the social, political, and intellectual relationships, networks, and institutions that underpinned and enabled slavery, anti-Black racism, and colonisation. Building upon traditional intellectual methodologies, the text examines slavery and race-making in a variety of written and material sources, including stock books, letter collections, benefaction papers, bursar account books, plantation ledgers, wills and testaments, silverware, portraits and paintings, pamphlets, newspaper records, and legal memoranda. Though white middling and elite men have left most of these published and archival records, Cambridge's history contributes to a growing literature examining the multiplicity of different connections that Britons had to the Atlantic world, even for those who did not live on the seacoast.[2]

Despite a recent explosion in institutional histories of enslavement in both Britain and the United States, the methodologies that underpin such studies are decades old, indeed. Historians on both sides of the Atlantic Ocean have long conducted community studies that have examined what more localised spaces suggest about broader shifts in society, culture, and the economy. Aside from villages, towns, and cities, community histories have broadened to include transatlantic mercantile trading partnerships and guilds, religious groups, plantations, universities, and families. By thinking small, scholars have thought anew about wider regional, national, and imperial webs of commerce, politics, war, and religious belief. Regarding universities, Lawrence Stone wrote some decades ago that academic institutions neither served as a superstructure, an ideological justification, for events beyond their metropolitan, parish, or national borders – nor did they reflect radical changes in Britain and its empire. He called for further research on the academy's connections to wider society, noting that a university's most significant dichotomies were between its 'own built-in conservatism' and the 'pressures' to 'adapt to new external conditions'.[3]

Students were a pillar of this community, yet the book will primarily focus on fellows (senior academic members of a college), masters (college heads), and professors (who provided lectures and led their fields in particular subjects). These men had long-term (and often life-long) connections to Cambridge. In integrating the enormous and growing field on slavery and its afterlives with community studies, the history of singular academic institutions can make significant claims concerning the economic, social, cultural, and intellectual processes of Britain and its slave empire, particularly – in the case of Cambridge – how those connections helped to shape people's lived experience. By focusing on the interconnections between an educational institution (and the surrounding local community) and the Atlantic world, the narrative works within a longstanding historiographical tradition in imperial history of highlighting how the 'histories of the colonisers and colonised' were 'inextricably linked'.[4]

Newspapers, diaries, and pamphlets receive their due, however there is much to be said for the significance of personal and collegiate financial records for uncovering the thoughts and opinions of individuals, families, and institutions toward the Atlantic enslavement system. If an investigation into a nation's taxation and fiscal mechanisms reveals the 'skeleton of the state stripped of all misleading ideologies', then account books, subscription lists, investment accounts, and probate records provide – alongside other sources – a similar insight into Britons' many entanglements with enslavement. Subscription lists, which record investments in colonial enterprises and political causes, have been particularly helpful as they show that Cambridge men were financial supporters of antislavery and slave-trading organisations in the absence of correspondence records. Issues abound with such sources, of course, as with other traditional intellectual material. Historians are often unable to uncover whether intellectual support or the pursuit of profit (or both concerns simultaneously) drove their investments, and, again, these sources are skewed towards middling and elite Britons (men who, respectively, worked in businesses and the professions, or those who wielded political power), who possessed the surplus resources to fund imperial endeavours, whether those goals included the Christian conversion of enslaved people or the expansion of enslavement. These problems are not insurmountable though: financial manuscripts can be placed in conversation with other written records and material culture to discern people's opinions, and a concern with the middling and elite men, who at one time or another were educated at or employed at Cambridge, is a sensible point of focus given that the University's existence was, increasingly, predicated on fostering a class of gentlemen who were able and willing to lead and forge the nation in a variety of professional fields.[5]

Histories of the University of Cambridge have long ignored its connections to enslavement. If Atlantic slavery appears in histories of the colleges or universities, scholars have concentrated on abolitionism (and, even then, on opposition to the slave trade, not plantation slavery). That approach appears, at first glance, rather sensible. After all, abolitionists pivotal to the movement for the ending of the slave trade and emancipation, such as Thomas Clarkson, Peter Peckard, and William Wilberforce, once called Cambridge home. The University Senate, too, sent antislavery petitions to the House of Commons in January 1788 and then once again in March 1792, and individual colleges (as we shall see in Chapter 4) donated money to the Society for Effecting the Abolition of the Slave Trade, which Clarkson and eleven other men formed on 22 May 1787.[6] Cambridge has long remained isolated from the growing historical trend to reconsider enslaving and slaveholding connections from an institutional perspective, rather than just a focus on the individuals, businesses, or families involved in these enterprises. Caius, Christ's, Emmanuel, Homerton, Jesus, King's, Pembroke, Queens', St Catharine's, and Trinity colleges have joined other British academic institutions – including All Soul's, Christ Church, Exeter, and St John's colleges in Oxford, and the universities of Bristol, Dundee, Edinburgh, Glasgow, Liverpool, London, Manchester, and Nottingham – in investigating their complex histories. Numerous American universities have conducted such projects too, such as Brown, the College of William and Mary, Georgetown, Harvard, Johns Hopkins, Princeton, and Yale universities. Though these studies concentrate on the economics of enslavement, this book argues that a more holistic historical focus on the social, political, and intellectual life of a town and gown population can better illuminate the vibrant texture of local and regional connections to enslavement and empire, even in predominantly rural and urban areas that were not established along the coastline of the Atlantic Ocean.[7]

Cambridge's past allows one to reconsider, too, how universities made and remade empires. 'The academy', Craig Steven Wilder notes, 'never stood apart from American slavery – in fact, it stood beside church and state as the third pillar of a civilization built on bondage'. Despite recent historical efforts, institutional histories of slavery, empire, and its afterlives are often narrated in passive language, with university fellows, lecturers, and students either being the beneficiaries of imperial advancement in white-dominated colonial societies or colluding with enslavers and colonisers to reap profits from plantations, resource extraction, and Indigenous dispossession. The extractive relationships of British universities to land, with Oxford and Cambridge benefitting from aristocratic land grants, were reproduced in the Americas, Australasia, South Africa, and Canada. Universities did far more than benefit from enslavement or government land grants. Cambridge men were, like many university-connected individuals, agents of empire who propagated, defended, and often challenged a violent Atlantic slave imperium. Imperial activities, in turn, enabled university figures to enrich themselves, their families, their institutions, and their intellectual reputations – as fellows and professors highlighted their statuses as distinguished thinkers to make their claims heard both at home and abroad.[8]

Universities, as spaces of interaction for the middling and elite classes, therefore, provide an interesting vantage point on enslavement and its afterlives – a historiography that has grown exponentially in recent decades. Historians have stressed that both the abolition and proslavery movements emerged due to concerns about the state of the British Empire following the American Revolution, with abolitionists fearing that Britain's defeat to the United States, finalised in the Treaty of Paris on 3 September 1783, was a providential sign that the nation was corrupted because it had kidnapped and trafficked African men, women, and children. On the powerful forces that antislavery activists fought against, scholars have highlighted the influence of the enslaver class, who had the money, connections, positions, and educations to protect their perceived right to human property – and those slaveholders included members of the landed aristocracy, clergymen, college fellows, and merchants. Those historians who have discussed slavery and its legacies often distinguish between *indirect* and *direct* connections to enslavement when considering the extent of Britons' linkages to slavery – between those subjects who purchased slave-made goods, and those individuals and organisations who owned plantations. From the vantage point of Cambridge and its history, Britons' many encounters with enslavement encompassed a more complex and colourful spectrum of local, national, and imperial associations and interconnections, from dining halls to tobacco shops to legal chambers to companies to antislavery and pro-slavery lobby groups.[9]

Since its founding in the Middle Ages, the University of Cambridge has shaped (and been moulded by) events beyond the parish borders – both in England and abroad in continental Europe. Seeking refuge from hostile townsfolk in Oxford, scholars fled that university for the thriving market town of Cambridge in 1209. Whilst situated in a commercial entrepôt, Cambridge had humble beginnings – the first scholars congregated in hostels with a Master. By 1226, the scholars had established a Chancellor and, five years later, King Henry III provided his protection through a royal charter, but with the condition that students enrol under a Master if they were to live in Cambridge.

Operating as small academic communities (a *civitas*), academic studies had two principal international models to draw upon in forming a *stadium generale* (or university): southern Europe's focus on law and medicine at universities like Padua, Siena, and Bologna, or Paris's proclivity for philosophy and theology. The latter model largely won out, and the fourteen- or fifteen-year-old students undertook a broad academic programme including grammar, logic, rhetoric, music, arithmetic, and astronomy which was heavily dependent on Aristotle (or Aristotle as interpreted in Christian commentaries, such as those by the Dominican theologian Thomas Aquinas). From a foundation in the "arts," students could become doctors in divinity or canon and civil law.[10]

As undergraduate studies took form and function, academic officials and systems of governance were institutionalised. The system of matriculation was invented (so called because students were entered on a master's *matricula* or roll), caps and gowns differentiated degrees, Proctors were appointed to safeguard the University's accounts, valuable treasures, and books and manuscripts, and graduation ceremonies took form. Universities had a unique position in England. Robert Anderson argues that since 'state and church were often in conflict, the universities could carve out space between them… not subject to the direct control of the local bishops, whilst in the secular world they enjoyed autonomy and privilege as property-owning corporate bodies with their own legal rights' – rights that 'lasted well into the nineteenth and early twentieth centuries'.[11]

Economics, not just academics, enabled Cambridge's rise to prominence and pre-eminence in England. Derived from the Middle English for "passage" or "ford," Cambridge (or Granta Bridge, as it was once known) was a major centre of communications in the Kingdom of England and a clearing house for corn, fish, poultry, cheese, reeds, and oils. The Cam was a major arterial route – so much so that one public orator in 1620 called it 'our river… [the] means of which we enjoy the wealth of the neighbouring country'. The draining of the fens, though resisted by many surrounding farmers and townsfolk, did not significantly harm the region's significance because of its geographical position (though Christians had severely damaged the town's social fabric centuries prior when the Christian inhabitants had expropriated, murdered, and expelled Cambridge's Jewish population after 1275). Of the four trade fairs, Stourbridge Fair was perhaps the largest and most famous in Europe and attracted traders ranging from cabinetmakers to milliners to perfumers. The fairs were a riotous occasion, with music booths established performing operas and instrumental compositions – but the fair's attendees were safe in the knowledge that the charters of 1268 and 1382 had instituted two aldermen, four burgesses, and a mayor and bailiff to keep the peace (subject to annual elections). After the festivities, the town market provided another avenue for dealers to sell their wares, including book traders who congregated around the Church of St Mary the Great, the University's Church (and the host for academic meetings and debates before the erection of the Senate House in 1730). The population grew in line with the trader's profit margins – from 6,490 inhabitants in 1587 (including 1,500 University members) to 7,778 in 1728 (with 100 college servants and 1,499 full University members). From 1801 to 1951, the population exploded again from 10,087 people to an estimated 91,170 residents. Granted in 1575, the coat of arms of the City of Cambridge paid tribute to the region's trading connections, with three ships with furled sails on a river.[12]

Medieval and early modern Cambridge were far from insular ivory towers, therefore. Few students from abroad initially attended, but the University remained committed to educating the servants of the state from its inception, including lawyers, priests, and schoolteachers. After Henry VIII's excommunication from the Catholic Church, the Renaissance prince required conformity and loyalty from the universities (as he did his chief ministers) – and that policy necessitated dramatic changes to the curriculum. The Queens' College fellow Erasmus inspired enthusiasm for classical humanism, or the *studia humanitatis* – with Aristotle now taught amongst a wide range of ancient authorities (such as the Roman statesman and philosopher Marcus Tullius Cicero) in languages ranging from Hebrew to Latin to Greek. Alongside welcome changes to the curriculum, sixteenth-century Cambridge experienced equally intense shifts in its academic structure, with canon law, the medieval church authorities, and the rule of the masters the targets of Henry's ire. Bending the University to his will, Henry created five "regius" professors from civil law to medicine (and thereby challenged the Master's rule).

Universities were also fertile ground for new investigations into natural philosophy and modern languages. The liberal arts were ascendant, and the universities became finishing schools for the upper classes, providing a common language of discussion and debate for England's elite. Though the universities would be reformed in the nineteenth century (and enrolments fell precipitously in the eighteenth century), the political economist Adam Smith, an alumnus of the universities of Glasgow and Oxford, judged the two ancient English universities too harshly. He commented that the 'present state of degradation and contempt' with which universities were regarded had much to do with professors, lecturers, and tutors, who, rather than 'being paid by voluntary contributions, which would urge them to increase the number, and to deserve the gratitude of their pupils, the Oxford professors are secure in the enjoyment of a fixed stipend, without the necessity of labour, or the apprehension of control'. Edward Gibbon was more scathing, writing that the 'schools of Oxford and Cambridge were founded in a dark age of false and barbarous science; and they are still tainted with the vices of their origin'. That declension narrative, which historians have since challenged, ignores the vibrancy of academic thought in this era.[13]

Given Cambridge's national and regional significance, it was almost inescapable that the University's intellectual life would become intertwined with England's slave empire. At first, English colonisation was essentially outsourced to companies that sought to acquire resources with the assistance of investors. Chartered by King James I on 10 April 1606, the Virginia Company of London was one of two companies, alongside the Virginia Company of Plymouth, that controlled the North American coast. The first would settle all land that stood between 34- and 41-degrees latitude (from Cape Fear in modern-day North Carolina to the Long Island Sound near contemporary New York), and the second occupied the territory between Nova Scotia and the upper Chesapeake. Yet the Virginia Company was joined by other such enterprises: arriving on 14 May 1625, the colonisation of Barbados was financed by Sir William Courten, a City of London merchant, with the colony exporting goods worth almost £285,000 – twice that of other English colonies – forty years later. Whether they travelled to Barbados or Virginia, the first white colonists were company men, but the original "planters," who were tasked with growing and producing goods that could be sent back to Europe, outlived and outgrew their fledgling employers.[14]

From the mid 1640s in Barbados, the growing population of landed enslavers developed a new system of *integrated* plantation management that dwarfed the *latifundium*, the Roman agricultural estates that depended on enslavement for the production and harvesting of wine, olive oil, and grain in antiquity. Designed as intricate forced labour camps, the plantations had all the components of the supply chain – from the growth of sugar and tobacco (the two most profitable crops in the British Atlantic) to its processing and sale – situated on the estate, rather than dividing these activities into separate operations. The estates had systems of double-entry bookkeeping and carefully tabulated records on debts, produce, and the names, ages, and occupations of the enslaved workforce. The plantations had to be organised because their activities were complex, time consuming, and uncertain given that tropical storms, earthquakes, fires, enslaved uprisings, or European conflicts regularly impacted regional and transatlantic supply chains. Sugar, for instance, had to be grown, planted, harvested, transported to mills where it would be processed, and then processed and distilled into rum or other byproducts.[15]

To hedge against these uncertainties, enslavers engaged in both vertical *and* horizontal integration: the accumulation of rival plantations and capital by a growing slaver aristocracy, and that merger movement precipitated an extraordinary transformation in plantation life. By 1774, a white Caribbean colonist was, on average, ten times richer than that of mainland North America; and in Jamaica (the richest British colony), the average wealth of its free residents was three times that of the average Englishman or Welshman. Alongside the growing numbers of European colonists who searched for fame and fortune in Britain's twenty-six American colonies, the enslavers brought enslaved Native Americans and, in greater numbers, West Africans to labour on the plantations. Whilst free white and Black Jamaicans were on a parity in 1673, enslaved Africans constituted around ninety per cent of the population less than a century later. Extraordinary fortunes could be earned on the American mainland too. For instance, over the course of his life, the Virginia-born George Washington, the first President of the United States, owned 45,000 acres of prime real estate in Indian country, a plantation, and had investments in land and canal companies.[16]

Colonists supplied the land, and transatlantic traders in enslaved Africans, whether state-backed companies or independent partnerships, provided the labour. At first, the Empire's labour supply was predicated, in part, on Native American enslavement, with the colonies of New England, Virginia, and South Carolina dependent on enslaving Indigenous captives, who were traded or captured in colonial conflicts, such as Metacom and Weetamoo's War (1675–78), where many Wampanoag were forced into slavery following their defeat (including Metacom's nine-year-old son who was captured and trafficked to the Caribbean). The status quo of Indian enslavement soon shifted, however, as rampant diseases, such as smallpox, and conflict turned the slave-traders' avaricious gaze to West Africa's shores. Estimates are often updated to account for new information and archival findings; still, historians estimate that 12.5 million Africans were kidnapped and trafficked, and 10.7 million men, women, and children survived the journey from their capture in regions such as Senegambia and west-central Africa to their arrival in the "New World." Marched overland from the African interior to coastal ports and forts, slave-traders stripped people of their clothing, which ranged from woven robes or gowns to sarongs and loincloths, and (just as forcibly) their names and identities.[17]

The English and then, following that kingdom's union with Scotland in 1707, the *British* Empire joined the Dutch West India Company in establishing powerful monopolistic slave-trading companies. The Royal African Company (RAC) was the most prolific transatlantic slaving enterprise in world history, trafficking 186,286 Africans to the Caribbean – and the relentless pursuit of profit sparked regional conflicts, with the Komenda Wars fought between 1694 and 1700 as the English and Dutch struggled for supremacy over trading rights (conflicts where African kingdoms, like the Equafo, acted as kingmakers). The RAC was not alone: founded in 1600 to trade from the Cape of Good Hope to west of the Straits of Magellan, the East India Company (EIC) trafficked between 10 and 13,000 Madagascans across the Indian Ocean from its inception to 1834, when it was forced to end the practice after the controversial firm had been found to be illegally trading West Africans. The British did not start the transatlantic trade, yet they had more than made up for lost time in becoming one of the leading traders in enslaved Africans.[18]

The South Sea Company (SSC) was particularly notable because of the predilection of students, fellows, and colleges for purchasing its securities (as Sabine Cadeau will prove in her forthcoming systematic analysis of Cambridge's finances). Established by Robert Harley, the then-Chancellor of the Exchequer, in 1711 to restructure the national debt and expand Britain's trading empire, the Company realised its ambitions in the 'Negro trade' after the 1713 Treaty of Utrecht granted Britain a monopoly to operate in the Spanish Americas. From its inception, Harley and his allies marketed the Company to prospective investors as a slave-trading firm, and, from 1714 to 1740, the SSC transported more than 75,000 enslaved people from Africa and the British Caribbean to the Spanish Americas. Planning for strong returns from slaving and mercantile trading, the SSC's trading stock (and, later, annuities, which were essentially government bonds) were an immensely popular security with private and institutional investors, including monarchs, the Church of England, colleges, universities, hospitals, and other charities. For a prospective British investor, the SSC appeared to be a sure bet: the Company had an element of risk diversification built into its structure because the government paid the firm a fee each year for managing a portion of the national debt, and investors would share slave-trading profits if that ambitious venture was successful. To some, Helen Paul argues, the purchase of Company stock was 'akin to buying a lottery ticket with the small chance of winning a large jackpot'. The jackpot, investors believed, was considerable: the 'lessening of Public Debts', officials acknowledged, would be achieved through the South Sea enterprise

'Ingaging in Sundry Trades', one of which included the 'Advantages that may arise to Great Britain by the Assiento for Negroes' – a sum that was (fancifully) estimated to be around £455,000 a year for 'import[ing]' 4,800 enslaved people. The South Sea enterprise was more than a case study the dizzying animal spirits of the stock market (at one point the price rocketed to £1,050 at the end of June 1720 before crashing). The firm was integral to Britain's ambitions of a slave-trading empire.[19]

Whether South Sea, Royal African, or East India Company vessels, the conditions on slave ships were appalling, with men, women, and children separated and forced to crouch or lie down below deck so that the ships could be packed with captives. Secured by irons, the heat was unrelenting and unbearable, food scarce, and diseases such as dysentery and smallpox were commonplace. Insurrections were a particular threat to the sailors: in 1729, African captives aboard the *Clare* drove the crew from the vessel, landing and liberating themselves near Cape Coast Castle on the Gold Coast (in modern-day Ghana). Mutinies resulted in fires or explosions – the captives, it appeared, were determined to drag their floating prison to the ocean's depths rather than face a lifetime in bondage. Just as often, enslaved people chose death by suicide, with many captives strangling or stabbing themselves, refusing medicine, or jumping overboard to escape their bondage. In a rather futile and desperate effort to control their captives, white traders distributed tobacco – called 'refreshment' – to their captives. One French slaver even devised a weekly schedule of when the tobacco would be distributed, how much was to be provided, and who was to receive that product. The business of slave-trading, as Nicholas Radburn has shown, was profitable and adaptable, even to antislavery efforts to ameliorate conditions – in fact, the Dolben Act of 1788, which Parliament instituted to curb overcrowding on slave ships halved death rates and thereby 'improved the efficiency of slave traders' businesses'. Though dehumanised as property, Africans smuggled jewellery, pipes, musical instruments, and gaming materials to the plantations, and maintained their families, languages, cultures, and religious traditions.[20]

Resistance to racial enslavement, whether on slave ships or in contemporary writings, predated the late eighteenth-century abolition movement. Christianity, Islam, and Judaism have debated slaveholding, more broadly, for millennia. (Gregory of Nyssa asked: 'But if God does not enslave what is free, who is he that sets his own power above God's?') The debate escalated after racialised distinctions started to become more pivotal in the New World in defining who was enslaved or free in the early modern era. From the sixteenth century, Spanish theologians from Salamanca, such as Bartolomé de las Casas and Francisco Vittoria, denounced Native American enslavement, which colonists had justified on the grounds of paganism (a legal principle that the great Elizabethan jurist Sir Edward Coke utilised in drafting the *Lawes of Virginia* for the Virginia Company). English colonists and missionaries, including Morgan

Godwyn, George Keith, and Samuel Sewall, also attacked African enslavement in sermons and pamphlets from the end of the seventeenth century. European pamphleteering is a limited understanding of antislavery activism, though. Since Euro-American colonisation began, Africans and Native Americans have resisted captivity, petitioned religious organisations such as the Vatican to end the slave trade, published treatises calling for African nations to be recognised as sovereign countries, and engaged in more localised forms of protest – running away, breaking tools, poisoning and killing enslavers and overseers, and interfering with crops – or they have triggered larger enslaved uprisings, with one of the earliest recorded revolts taking place in Santo Domingo in 1521.[21]

Christians did not monopolise writings on enslavement either – in 1614, the Berber writer Ahmad Baba al-Timbukti argued that neither Muslims nor the subjects of Muslim states could be enslaved, and especially not on racial grounds. The Berber scholar, who favoured enslavement predicated on religious belief, recognised the pernicious radicalism of racial slavery: that the belief that one's skin colour and ethnicity was a strict determinant of one's enslavement and freedom was a recent innovation in the seventeenth century. Though religion determined enslavement in the Islamic Middle East and was there more of 'sociocultural significance' than a mechanism for profiteering, the European model of racial enslavement created what historian David Brion Davis calls 'the most extreme and systematic form of personal domination, dishonor, dehumanization, and economic exploitation, a form of domination and exploitation that became a model, in the eyes of successive generations of liberationists, for all Western and white male imperialism'.[22]

Branding was integral to the process of transforming human beings into racial capital that could be transported, purchased and sold, or bequeathed in wills and marriage contracts. The act of branding to indicate ownership or punish resistant enslaved people was practiced in antiquity, yet as enslaved individuals moved between slave-traders, mercantile agents and shipowners these American enslavers added additional brands, identifying, for instance, whether export duties had been paid. Branding had become an important tool in the transmutation of human beings into a marketable commodity. On the West African coast, many of those enslaved by the Royal African Company were marked "DY" for James II, the Duke of York – an indelible tie between the monarchy and enslavement. The South Sea Company proposed branding to discourage theft of their valuable captives awaiting transportation. Their Court of Directors wrote that 'The Mark A' – after *Assiento*, the name for the monopoly contract that the Company had with the Spanish Crown – 'we approve of, and hope it will answer the ends proposed'. They specified that the enslaved be marked 'on the left shoulder, heating the mark red hot and rubbing the part first with a little palm or other oil' – a rather gruesome and unimaginably painful practice common amongst European enslavers.[23]

Branded as property, the enslaved were treated as such on the North American and Caribbean plantations. Thomas Thistlewood, a white Jamaican enslaver who regularly sexually assaulted and tortured his workers, was no outlier – he was a well-respected Briton living amongst whites who responded to small infringements, such as starving enslaved people eating sugar cane, with floggings and humiliating punishments. For more significant acts of resistance, enslaved Africans were burnt at the stake, had their arms cut off for raising 'it against a white person', and were quartered and had their corpses chained to trees for killing overseers. Those forms of 'spectacular terror' helped to enforce white enslaver rule over Black majority populations.[24]

Enslavers justified their treatment of Black people through a complex amalgamation of racial ideas. By 1603, when William Shakespeare penned *Othello*, English peoples had access to numerous sources of information on the African continent and its inhabitants that, Virginia and Alden Vaughan argue, 'portrayed African skin as unattractive and, in some texts, as the stigma of divine punishment'. Shakespeare had made Othello the hero, but still compared him to whites – 'Your son-in-law is far more fair than black' – and had other characters denounce him as 'an old black ram' or 'the devil'. Travel narratives, stories and fiction, and the Bible, therefore, were as significant as scientific discourse – at least for poorer enslavers who did not have access to such tomes – in marking Black people (and Native Americans) as degenerated "savages" and evil "heathens," who the European colonists were justified in conquering and enslaving en-masse. As one female American observer commented, slavers 'sought their code of morality in the Bible, and there imagined they found this hapless race condemned to perpetual slavery'. Religious justifications for enslavement became intertwined with more powerful racial attack on Africans, as white colonists erroneously associated the Biblical Curse of Ham myth (see Chapter 3 for further details) with Black skin and thereby argued that Africans were condemned to enslavement from birth.[25]

Enslavers also published literature defending their racial attitudes regarding the African people that they denigrated as "negroes" and "negresses." In Edward Long's 1774 *History of Jamaica*, he maintained that Africans were 'savage[s]' who must 'be managed at first as if they were beasts; they must be tamed, before they can be treated like men'. One Saint-Domingue plantation manual, published in English in 1798, also stated that the "negroe" is 'docile and timid, and because he never thinks of a better condition than what he actually enjoys, unless the thought, as well as the means of attaining, is forced upon his observation… [a] creature whom we are forced to keep in his *natural* state of thraldom, in order to obtain from him the requisite services'. It was the planter's obligation and duty, the manual read, to 'exact from the negroe all the work he can reasonably perform, and use every means to prolong his life'. Whether they assumed that racial difference was environmental (derived from differences in temperature and climate) or inherited (due to differences in blood, anatomy, or skull shape), many whites agreed that that Black people were naturally subservient and therefore naturally suited to their perpetual enslavement.[26]

From weights and scales to chiming bells, the enslavers transformed innocuous objects into powerful tools to stigmatise people as property. Enslaved people were weighed when they were bought or sold at the slave market. Olaudah Equiano, a formerly enslaved man and a leading British abolitionist, remembered that he had 'often seen slaves… in different islands, put into scales and weighed; and then sold from three pence to six pence or nine pence a pound'. Sold by the 'lump', as Equiano described these auctions, husbands were taken from wives (and vice versa), and children from their parents. Timekeeping was crucial to controlling these gang labourers. If you were transported to the seventeenth, eighteenth, and nineteenth century North American plantations, you would hear the ringing of bells that were used to regulate the dawn-till-dusk workday. Charley Williams, who laboured on a Louisiana cotton plantation, remembered: 'you can hear an old bell donging way on some plantation a mile or two off, and then more bells at other places and maybe a horn… Bells and horns! Bells for this and horns for that! All we knowed was [to] go and come by the bells and horns!' St. Catharine's College, Cambridge, owned one of these bells, inscribed 'DE CATHARINA 1772,' which was donated by a former student who had found it on a sugar estate in British Guiana. Drums were another instrument of plantation timekeeping, though white enslavers heard that sound with a degree of trepidation as its distant rumble often signalled an enslaved insurrection.[27]

Slavery and colonialism underpinned Europe's prosperous consumer economies, even as enslaved people often starved on the plantations in times of drought or war. To keep up with demand, enslavers dedicated vast tracks of land to mass plantation agriculture, devastating soil and vegetation to make room for their estates and livestock. The British Atlantic's 'ghost acres' – the sugar produced in the Caribbean, the timber from Canada and Sierra Leone, meat and dairy from Ireland, and cotton from the southern United States – allowed Britain and other European empires to consume, produce, and grow in population far more than the meagre size of their metropolitan territorial landholdings would suggest. Slavery alone did not alone drive Britain's long term economic growth, yet the historians Maxine Berg and Pat Hudson argue that enslavement was 'formative in the timing and nature of Britain's industrial transition'. Aside from cotton, tobacco, indigo, sugar, and rice, mahogany furniture – "mahogany" being derived from the Yoruba word "M'Oganwo" – was produced with enslaved-harvested wood. Trade goods and sundries such as sugar, tobacco, and mahogany found their way into the University's dining halls and living quarters. In October 1762, Thomas Chapman, the Master of Magdalene, left an extensive inventory of his college lodge, which recorded numerous mahogany tables, chairs, and basons. Upon entering the dining room, the guests also enjoyed 'four Tea and Sugar Canisters'.[28]

The age of revolutions did not halt these slaving operations in the Americas. The American Revolution had a Janus-faced impact on slaveholding, with at least thirty-eight slaveholders signing the Declaration of Independence from Britain. In fact, Robert Parkinson argues that wartime consensus building for white Americans was, in part, based upon fear of enslaved African Americans and Native Americans. On the other hand, though, Black and white abolitionists also took advantage of the revolutionary moment to abolish enslavement in all states north of Maryland between 1777 and 1804. The Haitian Revolution, whose Black participants demolished the plantation regime, expelled the enslaver class, and defeated the numerous imperial armies (including the British), had unintended consequences. The United States purchased Louisiana in 1804 (with Napoleon Bonaparte using that money to fund his European conflicts), thereby fulfilling Thomas Jefferson's dream of creating an 'Empire of Liberty' in the south and west. Though Jefferson and his contemporaries thought that enslavement would die of its own accord, that hope was unfortunately misplaced. After Eli Whitney invented and patented the "cotton gin" in 1794 (a wooden drum with interchangeable parts that efficiently cleaned seeds from that crop's fiber), the deep south became a "cotton kingdom" – a vast, immensely profitable territory that stretched from Alabama to Texas.[29]

Whitney had created the "gin" (or engine) as a labour-saving tool for the enslaved, but the device facilitated a dramatic expansion in slavery – and US congressmen soon struggled to reconcile the question of western colonisation with whether these new, fledgling states would be free or enslaver societies. The cotton empire was America's 'second slavery', and there were noticeable continuities with the first European plantations: the cotton estates were as commercialised as the original tobacco farms, which were gradually replaced due to increasing costs and degrading soil. This world was governed, in part, by the cotton scale. Weighing time was filled with anxiety as enslaved people tried to avoid the wrath of a whip-wielding overseer. An ordinary day's work was measured at 150 pounds a day. A survivor of slavery stated: 'No matter how fatigued and weary he may be – no matter how much he longs for sleep and rest – a slave never approaches the [cotton] gin house with his basket of cotton but with fear. If it falls short in weight – if he has not performed the full task appointed him, he knows that he must suffer'. To meet their workload, the enslaved replaced their baskets with others already weighed, and discreetly added cotton or dirt and rocks to their baskets. Despite their efforts at subterfuge and sabotage, the overseers made them 'try it over several times and weighing what cotton they pick every night, the overseer can tell just how much every hand can pick. He then gives the present to those that pick the most cotton, and then if they do not pick just as much afterward they are flogged'. If enslavers were not present for this spectacle, these weights were a constant reminder of their presence and the demands that whites placed on the enslaved. It was this world that the Confederate States of America defended in the American Civil War.[30]

The "age of abolition" was, of course, beset with complications and contradictions too. The abolition of the slave trade did not herald the downfall of plantation slavery, as some abolitionists had hoped – indeed, some plantation owners welcomed abolition. In an April 1818 missive to his sister, a Jamaican enslaver acknowledged that he was 'no friend to the slave trade, it is certainly an infamous traf[f]ick – the Negroes here, are on the whole a happy people, and since the non-importation of Africans, they are greatly improved, more intelligent, more domesticated. – They have also in great measure got rid of that religious fanaticism, which at one time overwhelmed & evinced them'. Slavers hoped that abolition would reinvigorate the plantation system, and the writer proudly observed that his family were 'now very anxious to purchase a Property here, and all his friends are actually on the look out for him'. (The rising price of sugar was another cause for optimism.) The Slavery Abolition Act of 1833 did not end coerced labour, with enslaved people below the age of six freed and the rest designated as "apprentices," who were abused until these schemes were abolished in stages from 1 August 1838.[31]

That process came to an end throughout the British Empire in 1843 (the East India Company was initially excluded from the law ending apprenticeships). Having raised £20 million through borrowing or investments in government stock, the British compensated former slaveholders and plantation mortgagees, including Cambridge fellows, masters, and alumni. These compensation claims were awarded around the same time as English merchants and mining companies entered the Brazilian market, with British enslavers operating there until abolition in 1888. To restock their colonies with labourers, however, Britons also relied on new forms of coerced labour to work the sugar plantations that had enslaved Black labourers. Derided as "coolies," Britain trafficked and transported around 2.5 million indentured workers of South Asian or East Asian descent to colonies including Jamaica, Guyana, Malaya, New South Wales, and Fiji, with that system – which many historians call "neo-slavery" – persisting from 1838 until 1922. This system was not unprecedented within the Americas, with many free African Americans – liberated after the Thirteenth Amendment – imprisoned and forced work as convict labourers. The much-heralded age of abolition was an era of forced labour and mass-enslavement too.[32]

The thematic chapters that follow explore the University of Cambridge's entanglement with Atlantic slavery, colonialism, and the plantation system. The first chapter begins from the bottom-up, looking at undergraduates and their personal connections to the fellowship (fellows being the senior administrative and academic members of colleges). Students, the men (at this time) who made the University function, are the perfect place to start a story concerning Cambridge's connections to slavery because their experiences illustrate the fact that slaveholders, far from operating at the peripheries, were prominent (and sometimes pre-eminent) in the halls and rooms of one of Britain's most prestigious intellectual institutions. Cambridge fellows, in turn, facilitated these transatlantic connections for the betterment of the University and Britain. The story begins with the backgrounds and motivations of enslavers for sending their children abroad for a costly and (potentially, given the dangers of smallpox and hard drinking) deadly education. Following this discussion, the chapter examines the close relationships between fellows and students, with enslavers appointing chaperones – or "superintendents" – as go-betweens for colleges and the young attendees. Although the students examined did not all come from vast fortunes, the discussion will focus on the wealth streams that flowed into Cambridge, as these students spent significant sums on the trappings of metropolitan life. The impact of American independence will then be assessed, proving that, although horror stories about students run amok in Cambridge convinced some to avoid a British education, men with connections to the transatlantic economy continued to see the universities as a necessary pathway to joining the imperial elite.

Turning from the undergraduate community to the fellows, lecturers, and masters, the following two chapters detail how the Cambridge-educated professional classes – the clergymen, natural philosophers, and lawyers – helped to develop the ideological underpinnings of the English and British Empires. Inspired by the colonisation of Ireland, Cambridge fellows served on, invested in, and defended the Virginia Company and its offshoots. From New England to Guinea, Cambridge men promoted the empire through sermons, corporate charters, pamphlets selling these enterprises to potential investors, and legal documents. The University of Cambridge soon became a hub of missionary Anglicanism, with fellows supporting, through their purses and pamphlets, the Society for the Propagation of the Gospel in Foreign Parts and its efforts to Christianise enslaved Africans. Natural scientists soon followed the clergymen. Cambridge botanists, geologists, and astronomers, including John Woodward (who did not attend the University but donated his sizeable geological collection to establish the Museum of Earth Sciences), had longstanding connections to slave-traders and depended upon North American and Caribbean slave societies for a significant proportion of their foreign collections. Cambridge men received donations from Caribbean enslavers who used enslaved Africans to collect plants, rocks, and other flora and fauna – ensuring that the University's rich scientific past had an unrecognised linkage to enslavement. At the same time, Cambridge-educated lawyers and jurists, including Sir Nathaniel Lloyd – a judge advocate, the King's legal advisor and a significant benefactor – and Professor Thomas Rutherforth, were involved in the day-to-day legal operations of slavery and the articulation of its theoretical and ideological foundations in the law.

The fourth and fifth chapters explore how Cambridge students, fellows, and alumni sought to defend, reform, or demolish outright the foundations of Britain's slave empire. In the historical literature and public memory,

Cambridge remains associated with abolitionism, particularly the work of Clarkson, Peckard, and Wilberforce. Still, this approach is limited for numerous reasons: it idolises three men (whilst forgetting the numerous white and Black activists who advocated for change); that simplistic history ignores the abolitionists' arguments, which were arrayed along a spectrum of competing approaches to ending or reforming the slave trade and enslavement; it forgets the significant role of Cambridge men, such as the former Trinity fellow Stephen Fuller, in the proslavery lobby; this story omits the personal and familial relationships of abolitionists to the plantation regime, with a number of antislavery activists either being descended from slaveholders or financially benefitting from the institution; and histories of Cambridge focus on abolishing the slave trade, with no attention paid to how the activism of fellows or undergraduates continued, shifted, or ended once the debate over the slave trade changed to a much broader conversation over the abolition of slavery. From reading pamphlets, newspapers, subscription books, broadsides, letters, and petitions, Cambridge was neither a bastion of human rights nor a breeding ground for proslavery activists – it was a community and academic institution as torn as any in Britain or North America over whether to abolish, ameliorate, or defend slavery, and Cambridge abolitionists were divided over whether the paths of immediate or gradual abolition should be taken to halt the plantation machine. Given the deep personal, economic, and intellectual connections between these Cambridge men, histories of abolitionism, amelioration, and proslavery cannot – and should not – be understood as separate movements – each were born from a deep commitment to preserving, spreading, and defending British imperial rule.

On 1 August 1838, freedom was granted to formerly enslaved people in the British Caribbean, but, as the sixth chapter argues, Cambridge men remained committed to either abolishing or defending the plantation regime and the planter class in the United States. From the Jesus fellow Edward Strutt Abdy to the Queens' alumnus Alexander Crummell, the University educated prominent abolitionists who worked within and with American antislavery organisations and Black missions in Sierra Leone and Liberia. Nevertheless, Abdy and Crummell's enslaver opponents remained powerful within and beyond Cambridge. As with the abolition of British slavery, then, Cambridge was no outlier on the question of African American enslavement – town and gown reflected Britain's politics and prejudices. Pro-Union observers who travelled to the University learned that fact upon arrival. On hearing lectures and student debates, Americans were worried about the strength of pro-Confederate opinion there given that Cambridge was an educator of Britain's governing class – a fact that the white-supremacist Confederates were keenly aware of at the time. Confederate propagandists, such as Henry Hotze, targeted Cambridge students and fellows – many of whom had parents or family members with previous ties to the plantations – as potential recruits to spread Southern opinion in Britain. Even after the guns fell silent and peace was negotiated between the generals Ulysses S. Grant of the Union and Robert E. Lee of the Confederacy at Appomattox Court House in Virginia on 9 April 1865, Cambridge educators facilitated the safe arrival of former Confederates and donated to institutions predicated on defending white rule in the South. The story of American slavery and freedom at Cambridge illuminates the enduring significance of university men to imperial discussions and debates. As Britain's slave empire fell, Cambridge men became committed to defending a southern empire predicated on white rule and cotton plantation agriculture.

1

'The principal ingredient necessary to form a good planter': Education and the Making of a Transatlantic Elite

The painter Benjamin West called them "The Cricketers." Finished between 1763 and 1764, this little-known conversation portrait depicted five young Americans: James Allen and Andrew Allen of Pennsylvania, Ralph Wormeley V of Virginia, and Arthur Middleton and Ralph Izard of South Carolina. In the painting, the men sit at leisure, engaged in polite conversation with the River Cam visible in the background (or the Cam as West imagined it, as he had never visited the town). Though the two Allen brothers did not attend Cambridge (they completed their legal educations at the Inns of Court in London), the remaining three cricketers were undergraduates there. The five tourists shared another connection: they were descended from wealthy and politically powerful slaveholding and slave-trading families. The Allen family, who were West's chief benefactors, enslaved Africans, rented their forced labourers to mercantile partners, and advertised recent arrivals of slave ships. Ralph Wormeley's family had 102 enslaved persons on their tobacco plantation, "Rosegill." Middleton, too, would be a signatory to the Declaration of Independence, and both he and Izard possessed huge estates that together numbered close to 8,000 acres and more than 200 enslaved persons.[1]

A snapshot in time, this painting illuminates the presence of men with connections to the transatlantic slave economy at the University of Cambridge. The sons and relatives of plantation owners, merchants, financiers, and slave-traders attended Cambridge from the rapid expansion of North America's slave societies in the seventeenth century through to British slavery's abolition in August 1838. Using John Venn and John Archibald Venn's extensive list of students from the foundation of the university to 1900, University College London's *Legacies of Slave-Ownership* database, and other primary and secondary sources, a sample of 850 students with families and family members actively engaged in the transatlantic slave economy have been uncovered. As the first expansive social history of enslaver students at a British or American university, exploring their birthplaces, student class, and colleges of choice, the backgrounds and experiences of these Cambridge students illuminate the banal personal connections between enslavers and fellows, and presents an important methodological lens to consider the historic emergence of a transatlantic elite that used their educations and wealth to elevate their status in the British

Empire. In fact, college fellows helped to garb these students with respectability, thereby identifying them as members of the British ruling classes. The University also stood to benefit from admissions. At a time when Cambridge was at its lowest point in admissions and at risk of institutional decline, all colleges benefitted – some to a greater degree than others – from enrolling many rich and well-connected students. In so doing, the chapter illuminates how casually slaveholding was woven into the fabric of British life from the bottom up and top down, and how university educations helped to construct and reinforce the power of an Atlantic economic elite.[2]

Students with families that were involved in the transatlantic economy arrived from Britain's twenty-six American colonies and only increased in number as the plantations and slave societies expanded throughout the Americas (see Table 1). The three largest sources of Caribbean students were from Barbados (with 140), Jamaica (113), and Antigua (46). The mainland North American colonists – befitting their relatively poorer status compared with the Caribbean sugar magnates and the growing number of domestic colonial colleges providing a suitable tertiary education – sent fewer students to Cambridge. The next three largest colonies of origin were Virginia (33), South Carolina (17), and Bermuda (14). Regardless of birthplace, the pattern was consistent in the data: if you went to Cambridge and you were from North America, your family was more likely than not involved in enslavement.[3]

Students with transatlantic ties called Britain home too. The three largest counties for student admissions were Middlesex (132), Lancashire (76), and Somerset and Yorkshire (20) (see Table 1). These locations made sense given the prominence of London, Liverpool, and Bristol as major ports and financial centres for the chattel slave economy and the growing number of landed estates in Britain owned by absentee slaveholders in counties such as Somerset, Denbighshire, Yorkshire, Norfolk, Kent, and Essex – an expression of the self-confidence and power wielded by the *nouveau riche*. The Bevan family, who were involved in provisioning the Caribbean colonies, acquired Riddlesworth Hall in Norfolk, the Salusbury's owned Lleweni Hall in Denbighshire (amongst their other landholdings which included plantations in Saint Kitts and Nevis, which were sold in 1776), and the Harford banking family owned a castle – Blaise Castle near Bristol. Enjoying the fruits of their colonial riches in Britain, the fortunes of the rapidly growing Atlantic economy were intertwined with the numbers of students coming to Cambridge from the North American colonies. As slaveholders grew their coffers, Cambridge benefitted from a growing influx of eager students.[4]

As a result of the incredible wealth that could be gained from chattel slavery, the students with connections to the Atlantic world who arrived in Cambridge originated from families deeply enmeshed in the slave economy – from financiers to merchants to slave-traders to cotton manufacturers to plantation owners (see Table 2). Most of these men were born into families that owned plantations (630), yet many counted merchants involved in the provisioning trade that supplied the Caribbean with material goods (52), slave-traders (44), and bankers and financiers (25), who underwrote the complicated insurance and debt arrangements that facilitated the system, amongst their family. Families were involved in multiple parts of the supply chain that underpinned the enslaved economy, and the student admission sample reflects that complicated reality: many students were from families involved in both the merchant trade and had landed estates (47), owned plantations and participated in the slave trade (17), and some student families were involved in both banking and the plantation economy (12). The professions of these student families reflected the entangled nature of slaveholding and the immense wealth that could be gained from these enterprises. Great wealth resulted in greater spending – and the enslaver class spent significant sums on carriages, cutlery, clothing, portraits, and books to stock their bulging libraries from suppliers in Europe. In time, they invested their money in another enticing, intangible commodity: a British education, which was an avenue of social advancement, particularly for those interested in the law or church or politics, for which an education at European universities helped one establish vital personal and professional connections that paid dividends in later life.[5]

Slaveholders valued an education from a university as globally prominent as Cambridge. That education was quite comprehensive: at this time, a person's course of study combined a moral as well as intellectual education and focused on instilling the qualities of a refined gentleman. A focus on refining a 'polite gentleman' in the eighteenth century was replaced in the following century, however, with a greater focus on stoicism, hard work, and 'inner moral worth'. The Virginian slaveholder Nathaniel Burwell certainly agreed that education did not just involve tutorials and lectures (even as Cambridge undergraduates received a comprehensive education in Latin in the trivium of grammar, rhetoric, and logic alongside the Quadrivium of music, arithmetic, geometry, and astronomy). To Burwell and his contemporaries, education helped to form a proper gentleman. If he did not concentrate on his studies, Burwell worried, his brother would be 'unfit for any Gentleman's conversation, & therefore a Scandalous person & a Shame to his Relations, not having one single qualification to recommend him[.]' Education, for Burwell, made the man, stripping away perceived colonial manners and mannerisms, and would transform his brother into a respectable British subject. According to two Virginian parents, a British education was essential because it placed one above the 'common level & drudgery of Life' accorded to the 'lower Class', helping to 'preserve you in the same Class & Rank among mankind'.[6]

Hoping to avoid such shame and 'scandal', enslavers stipulated in their wills that their children would receive the best education possible, making clear in these documents whether their offspring were to be educated at home or sent abroad to Europe – the latter option becoming increasingly popular for British Americans because their growing wealth did not match the poor schooling which they received in the colonies. Robert Carter of Virginia ensured in his will that his son 'George be kept at school at the College of Wm. & Mary [the college in Virginia] two years longer & that then he be Sent to the University of Cambridge for an education… & if my ex'tors his Brothers See it is so fitting that he… may be entered first at the Inns of Court, that if his inclination & capacity Lead that way he may be bred to the Law'. Enslavers planned their children's education in minute detail, from the colleges and schools that they attended to the subjects that they studied. For instance, Robert Carter decreed that one of his sons, Landon, was to become a 'perfect master' in Latin, Greek, and Hebrew. With some of their personal finances invested in the same South Sea, Royal African, and East India securities as the Cambridge colleges and fellowship, the enslavers claimed that an expensive education – an "English education," as it was called – at the public schools, ancient universities, and legal Inns of Court in London – would establish their children amongst the aristocratic governing classes who ruled the British Empire.[7]

The Antiguan slaveholder Samuel Martin identified education as the basis for white planter dominance. Perhaps remembering that his father had been killed by Akan enslaved persons on their plantation, Martin was particularly preoccupied with the qualities that were needed to become an effective plantation owner. He determined that an English education was one avenue to achieve this skillset, despite the risks of sending children overseas, whether from the dreaded smallpox virus or common colds, which forced students to ocassionally flee to the coast for 'sea air'. First admitted to Trinity College in 1711, Martin's *Essay upon Plantership* was immensely popular, running to seven editions after its original publication in the 1750s, and it was also featured in Arthur Young's *Annals of Agriculture*. Written for the 'instruction of a young planter', Martin dismissed metropolitan charges, according to one historian, of 'crudeness, lack of education, corruption of morals, materialism, alcoholism, and cruelty' that were aimed at the colonists, who had been 'de-anglicize[d]' in the colonies. Rather, he argued that plantation owners were the equal of Roman farmers who had 'captivated all the renowned legislators, patriots, soldiers, orators, and poets of antiquity, who gladly devoted their hours of retirement to this admirable Instructress, and her industrious filter Experience'. Listing the enviable traits of a worthy "planter," Martin concluded that 'A liberal education is undoubtedly the principal ingredient necessary to form a good planter, who ought at least to know the rudiments of all the sciences, if he attains not the mastery of them[.]' For Martin, education made landed enslavers the equal of aristocrats and patriotic intellectuals, soldiers, generals, and legislators.[8]

To the chagrin of some fellows who favoured religion, enslavers such as Martin particularly valued Cambridge's expertise in mathematics and sciences. From the Welsh mathematician Robert Recorde's development of the equals sign ("=") in the sixteenth century to Isaac Newton's laws of universal gravitation at the end of the following century, Cambridge was renowned for mathematics and "natural philosophy," as the sciences were then called. Enslavers understood this fact, and it was unsurprising that they were interested in numbers given that, as plantation managers, they depended upon sophisticated accounting principles and calculations. As Morgan Godwyn, a minister in Virginia and Barbados, wrote in 1680, the 'Planters chief deity' was 'Profit'. On 25 May 1756, Stephen Fuller (an important figure throughout this story) wrote to Benjamin Newton of Jesus College introducing Samuel Alpress. Alpress (who, like Fuller, will appear later) was born in Jamaica, and Fuller noted that 'As Mathematicians are of more use in that Island than any other sort of People, I would have him immediately initiated in that Kind of Knowledge and conducted in it as far as 'tis possible wishing that and Natural Philosophy to be his Principal Studys'. Mathematical laws, for Fuller, were a tool to perpetuate enslavers' authority and wealth, and the surviving records reflected the significance of mathematics, the oldest tripos course on offer at Cambridge, with the Virginia-born Robert Beverley's surviving Trinity College notebooks detailing his efforts to understand complex algebra and mathematical logic.[9]

Fuller and others were secure in the knowledge that a university education was not intended to challenge anti-Black or proslavery orthodoxies. Anti-slave-trade activists, such as Peter Peckard, the Master of Magdalene, however, argued that Cambridge fellows were not doing enough to combat the 'fashionable' education that justified slavery and the slave trade. Instead, Peckard called for a 'firm and conscientious adherence to the rules of Virtuous Education' based on the 'Natural Equality of the human race'. Peckard's words carried a degree of truth: a classical education at Cambridge did not undermine an undergraduate's pre-conceived belief in Black or Indigenous inequality. Greek and Roman philosophers alike, such as Aristotle and Cicero, the two most popular classical authors, argued that some were slaves by nature – an idea, known as "natural slavery," that again gained traction in the sixteenth century to defend the enslavement of Native Americans in the Spanish colonies. The college libraries were no less ambivalent on the question of slavery. If administrative records are to be believed, colleges were in no rush to purchase abolitionist tracts, even at the height of the abolition movement.[10]

If they willed it, enslavers confronted few barriers to sending their children to Cambridge besides wealth and assent to the Church of England. Dissenters were excluded. Until the mid-nineteenth century, there was no standardised admissions exam (unlike the University of Paris). Rather than anxious about whether their children would gain admission into the university, rich parents were often concerned that their sons would waste their fortunes on drinking, dining, and frivolities in Cambridge, London, and other British metropolitan centres. To combat this tendency, family members turned to their vast networks of social contacts, many of whom either owned plantations or were involved in the transatlantic slave trade, to chaperone their children whilst in England, inform their tutors of the student's plans, manage their finances, and report back on issues. (Stephen Fuller quipped that this role was a 'superintendancy'.) The Virginian tobacco merchant John Norton informed on student progress to friends and family, reporting to his son, John Hatley Norton, in April 1770 that 'Your Cozen [John] Baylor is at Cambridge'. That was where the good news ended because Norton then complained that 'I hope it may answer tho' I think he has not capacity to make a scholar & had better contented himself with learning the grammar in his Mother tongue properly, & reading history instead of attempting Greek Authors'. The personal relationships between chaperones and the fellowship were vital to the attendance of overseas-born students.[11]

Fellows and educators imposed few barriers to the attendance of enslavers – in fact, they encouraged their admission. After all, the Atlantic was a competitive educational marketplace where fellows and masters sought out the sons, brothers, and nephews of enslavers as students. Far from being appalled by conditions in American slave societies, university and college officials wrote pamphlets to convince the colonists' wealthy children to attend their institutions. The popularity of British universities, which at that time included Cambridge, Oxford, Glasgow, Edinburgh, and St Andrews, was evident in how the colonial colleges responded to their dominance. John Witherspoon, the President of the College of New Jersey (now Princeton), pleaded with the Caribbean colonists to attend colonial colleges because the climate, distance from their homes, and reputation for focused study (not frivolity) were more dependable there. He deferentially addressed his fellow British colonists, arguing that they were persons in the 'highest ranks of life' and industrious landholders whose 'own activity and diligence' had seen them 'rise to opulence'. The Scotsman was probably aware of students using his College as a preparatory school for Cambridge. A plantation tutor noted that one Virginian, a 'Boy of Genius and application is to be sent to Cambridge University', but not before undertaking 'a course either in Philadelphia or Princeton College first'. Whatever Witherspoon's complaints, some begged to differ with his approach. One of Witherspoon's critics responded that the British universities were supplied with 'numerous, honourable and learned body of Fellows, for the Purposes of Instruction and Discipline', unlike the American colleges where 'one Person, besides the Superintendance and Government of the whole, is oblig'd to teach Divinity, and Moral Philosophy, as well as Rhetoric,

Chronology and History[.]' No maligned minority, universities courted the transatlantic economic elite.[12]

William Byrd II, a Virginian slaveholder, dined with the most illustrious Cambridge men. Byrd had studied at the Middle Temple and was elected to the Royal Society of London for Improving Natural Knowledge (or "Royal Society") thanks to the patronage of Sir Robert Southwell, a friend of Byrd's father (who owned the 1,200-acre Westover Plantation in Virginia). Three years after his appointment as the London agent for the Virginia Governor's Council in 1698, Byrd, then aged twenty-six, undertook a fourteen-week tour of England to introduce the eighteen-year-old Sir John Perceval, Southwell's nephew, to Britain's most eminent religious, mercantile, and cultural figures. To that end, they visited Cambridge. John Colebatch, a Trinity fellow and later Professor of Moral Theology (1707–1744), was the tour guide for their Summer visit, and Byrd reported to Southwell that they had been 'surveying the University' alongside 'a man of distinction for learning and knowledge of the world, and we had the happiness of having abundance of his Company'. Enjoying the sights of Cambridge, Byrd and Perceval then 'din'd yesterday [on Sunday] at Mr Vice-Chancellour's [Richard Bentley], where Philosophy flew about the Table faster than the wine', and Byrd was happy to note that 'Sir John begins to make good discoverys of himself in Company', Perceval made good, too, on Byrd's introductions to distinguished men of the kingdom, such as Bentley (the most famous English classicist of the age). Perceval supported a college in Bermuda, and served as the president of the Georgia Trustees, a governing body that established the American colony of the same name. As for Byrd, he enjoyed esteem and infamy in equal measure – being remembered as much for his wealth and writings as for his multiple extramarital affairs and proclivity for sexual violence against the enslaved maids who ran his household.[13]

Thomas Gooch, the Master of Gonville and Caius College, illustrates the close relationships between enslavers and fellows as well. Gooch advised his brother William – who was Virginia's governor from 1727 to 1749. For many years, Thomas facilitated the arrival of Virginian students at Cambridge, utilised his access to Thomas Pelham-Holles, the Duke of Newcastle and Cambridge's ever-meddling Chancellor, to aid William's policies, and interceded with the Archbishop of Canterbury to find a new president for the local College of William and Mary. As a testament to their close relationship, William thanked Thomas in April 1728 for 'several Letters with the Hints & Advice for which I thank you; and I hope whenever you write you'l[l] continue the same method, which may always be of use to me, especially if we should have Peace, or War should be proclaimed'. Gooch's patronage network was particularly helpful in passing Virginia's Tobacco Inspection Act in 1730. In fact, Thomas's 'close relationship' with Newcastle made William's position much more 'secure', one historian notes, as the governor implemented new laws that aimed to improve the quality of Virginia's tobacco. In July 1733,

William wrote to Thomas hoping for 'your opinion of things by the first ship the next Winter, for I shall call an Assembly in the Spring, and would willingly be at some certainty with regard to [British] politicks'. The Master utilised his academic and clerical status to assist his brother's governorship in the halls of political power. That support was both personal and official in nature – and the Goochs discussed the frustrations of being a colonial official in regions where the governor's authority was contingent upon the power of the dominant planter class. Much of their correspondence concerned the new governor's expenses in purchasing enslaved people. In one letter, William elaborated on the enormous costs that a new governor, desperate to impress his fellow plantation owners, incurred on becoming the leader of an American slave society: he had to purchase 'Horses, Cows & Slaves and a constant grand expense of Housekeeping' and organise a celebration for the king's birthday. After airing these complaints, the governor commented that one of the enslaved persons, who may have worked in the kitchens and household or tended the palace gardens, was a 'little black boy' and that he had 'named him Caius'. From his letters, Thomas did not protest his younger brother's effort to name an enslaved man in Caius College's honour.[14]

Though silent on the enslaved "boy" named Caius, the two men spilled much ink discussing students who went to Cambridge from enslaver backgrounds. Thomas had met with wealthy Virginian slaveholders and merchants, most notably John Randolph and Robert Cary (who would later become George Washington's tobacco trader), at the George and Vulture, a London inn – and William hoped that Thomas would wine and dine his Virginian friends. For instance, in June 1731 William informed his brother that a 'very pretty young Gentleman… was coming over to your Colledge'. Two years later, Thomas received another filial missive, which addressed another new arrival: the 'Son of Col. Carter's, late President of the [Virginia's] Council' who was coming 'to your University, but goes to Trinity where his eldest Brother, now his Guardian… was brought up himself'. Unlike some of his undergraduate contemporaries, Carter was no dunce or drunkard – William acclaimed Carter as a 'sober youth and a very good scholar' and he 'entreat[ed] the favour of you to encourage him by your Countenance and Invitation sometimes to Dinner'. After two months had passed, William again pestered Thomas, noting that the 'eldest son to Col. Grymes… comes to Trinity Hall in your University to study the law'. As with the other Virginian luminaries, William hoped that he would be invited to 'dinner with you, and drinking our healths, and let me have a paragraph in your letters concerning' him and Carter's son to 'shew their relations'. Even as the master of a college with no familial connections to these men, the transatlantic ties that bound friends and superintendents worked to Cambridge's benefit as they brought Virginians and other colonists to Britain's shores.[15]

Aside from their acceptance of slaveholders, college fellows had a close and enduring connection to enslavers because many Cambridge men either owned plantations or were related through blood and marriage to slavers. Junior and senior fellows with slavery connections were numerous in number and present at most colleges. For example, Benjamin Bosanquet, whose Huguenot father was a prominent banker and director of London Assurance (which provided, amongst other services, maritime insurance to slave traders), became a fellow of Trinity in 1733; the Reverend Richard Smith part-owned the mortgage on Mapps Plantation in Barbados whilst a fellow at Trinity from 1791 to 1804 and was twice Junior Dean (1798 and 1800–1801); and Robert Pedder Buddicom, the scion of a slave-trading family from Liverpool, was elected a Queens' fellow in 1807. Thomas Tenison was apparently a slave-trader before being elected a fellow of Trinity Hall, holding the latter post from 1725 to 1728. The son of Edward Tenison, the Bishop of Ossory and cousin of the more prominent Thomas Tenison (the Archbishop of Canterbury), the young Thomas was provoked by a 'just correction' at his school in Sevenoaks to set off for Bristol, a port city that, by the middle of the eighteenth century, transported nearly half of the 20,000 enslaved Africans sent to the Americas from Britain. Leaving Bristol, he served on a slave ship bound for Guinea, where, as a contemporary chronicler wrote, 'by his good behaviour, he [eventually] rose to be Superintendant of the slaves, during their voyage to Barbadoes'. Tired of life as a slaver and 'common sailor', Tenison returned to complete his education at Cambridge, becoming a fellow at Trinity Hall upon the recommendation of the Master, Sir Nathaniel Lloyd, and served as the chestkeeper for the college's funds.[16]

Apart from individual fellows, enslaver and colonial connections went to the top of the University hierarchy. Christopher Monck, the 2nd Duke of Albemarle, Cambridge Chancellor (1682–1688), and benefactor who provided £100 for the construction of Trinity's Wren Library (construction for which was completed in 1695), was, at the same time, one of the Lords Proprietors of the Carolinas and the Bahamas and later became Jamaica's governor; Dr George Sandby the Master of Magdalene from 1760 to 1774 and Vice-Chancellor, had a lease on the 300-acre Triall Estate in Jamaica through his wife (see Figure 1.1); and the Hon. George Neville Grenville, Master of Magdalene from 1813 to 1843, was the son of Richard Griffin, 2nd Lord Baybrooke. (Indeed, his father, who was the Provost-Marshal of Jamaica until the end of the Napoleonic Wars, appointed George to the position because the Baybrookes were the hereditary visitors to the College and thus had the right to select the Master.) Family connections entailed substantial economic benefits, too, and Grenville was a trustee via a marriage settlement to Hope Estate in Jamaica, worth an estimated £20,000. Fellows without discernible links to the plantations became close to enslaver families as well, and the strained and underfunded nature of tuition at Cambridge in the early modern period may have cemented relationships between slaveholders and academic tutors, as teachers were forced to take on multiple family members. At Trinity, Thomas Postlethwaite, the future Master, taught numerous members of the Hall family from Jamaica, including two sons of Thomas Kirkpatrick Hall; and James Backhouse, a tutor, instructed two sons of John Campbell, who owned New Hope plantation in Jamaica.[17]

Sibling relationships provided a support network for students far from home. Walter Pollard was the second son of a Barbadian doctor and had entered Emmanuel as a pensioner in October 1772 after his schooling at Eton and Harrow. Walter's university letters do not survive, however his elder brother John's missives from Oxford discuss the trials and tribulations of young men at college. Writing from Queen's College, Oxford, in November 1772, John missed his sibling and complained that he 'was much disappointed at not having heard from you once while you continued in London, not for so long a Time after your settlement in College'. He mentioned, too, that their father had 'expressed some disapprobation at your neglect in writing'. When they did write, the brothers broached topics such as the (in)adequacy of 'Tutor & Rooms', the pitfalls of a 'large acquaintance' of friends, the 'Study of Logick', John Locke's *Essay on Human Understanding*, a course that John attended on 'Experimental Philosophy' with Thomas Hornsby (the Savilian Chair of Astronomy) that had caused him to feel 'my own insufficiency sometimes', the illness of 'our ever honoured Father', and his anxieties concerning their 'considerable' college expenses. For his part, Walter was a successful student, acclaimed for his 'ingenuous temper, his sportive humour, his sprightly manners, his virtuous principles, and his literary attainments' – qualities that earned him the friendship of John James Hamilton, the 1st Marquess of Abercorn, Charles Manners-Sutton, the later Archbishop of Canterbury, and William Pitt the Younger, who was admitted to Pembroke on 26 April 1773. Unfortunately for Walter, his time at Cambridge was cut short after a 'fatal hurricane', as the young Emmanuel student remembered, had laid 'our properties in the dust, the hard earnings of the past, the hopes of the rising generation'. After securing his father's lands in Barbados and Virginia, Walter returned to England, earning an appointment from his old friend Pitt as the Comptroller of the Exchequer.[18]

Cambridge, then, was a family affair. Cambridge counted some of the most powerful enslaver families amongst their number: the Carters and Baylors of Virginia, the De Lancey's and Livingstone's of New York, the Izards and Lynchs of South Carolina, the Fullers and Longs of Jamaica, the Martins and Byams of Antigua, and the Husbands and Mayers of Barbados. The Fullers were a particularly prominent family at the University. Numerous Fullers attended Trinity, including the brothers John (1723), Henry (1732), Rose (1732), and Stephen (1734). The family had had a swift rise to power. Originally, Dr Fulke Rose had moved to Jamaica from Mickleton in Gloucestershire; however, by 1670, he possessed 380 acres and had a substantial interest in the Royal African Company. The catastrophic 1692 earthquake in Port Royal, Jamaica, disrupted the Rose-Fuller family's operations, but it did not shake their ascent to financial prominence. The doctor's grandson, Rose Fuller MP, owned the plantations of Grange Pen, Hoghole Estate, and Knollis along with a workforce of 290 enslaved Africans. The Fullers soon diversified and developed a significant financial interest in the ordinance trade. Given the continued struggle for imperial supremacy in the Caribbean between Britain, France, Spain, and the Dutch, the gun trade was incredibly lucrative. From their Weald iron forges, the Fullers expected an annual income of between £500 and £1,500 a year from the production of cannons and firearms for the British army. A 'King in Brightling', John Fuller (the father of the brothers listed above) purchased a 242-acre estate in Sussex, later named "Rose Hill" after his wife, expanding their landholdings so that, by 1777, they controlled extensive property in both England and Jamaica. The patrons of painter J. M. W. Turner and sponsors of the Royal Institution, the Fullers were representative of the cultural, political, and financial power wielded by participants in the Atlantic slave economy.[19]

The prominence of enslaver families resulted in a greater degree of familiarity between students and fellows. Stephen Fuller was a significant go-between for students and the Cambridge fellowship. Having completed his expensive schooling at Charterhouse, Stephen was a scholar at Trinity in 1735, took his BA in 1739, and was 'Chosen Fellow' of the College in 1741. That year, in September, his father John Fuller sent Stephen's report of a 'violent hurricane' in Huntingdonshire to the Royal Society (of which his father and brother, Rose, were also Fellows). Fuller also corresponded with college fellows, including Stephen Whisson, Trinity's Bursar. In March 1756, Whisson responded to Fuller's 'friendly offer; for I think the proposals such as some young men would be glad to accept of, and there was a time when I could have recommended one very amply qualified for that business[.]' The nature of this "business" was not discussed, but Whisson had 'thought of two others, both [of] which wou[l]d have done us credit and they both seemd pleasd with the prospect; when the affair was first mention'd; but after long consideration and consulting their friends, they have declin'd it'. The College refused Fuller's proposition because of 'the fears of mothers and remote hopes of small pittances at home prevailing against the prospect of immediate advantage abroad'. Fuller's attempt to recruit Trinity men for opportunities overseas had not met with opposition from the College – the students' families had stopped him. Whisson's rejection did not damage their friendship. Two months later, in May 1756, Stephen Fuller introduced the Bursar to his nephew John and hoped that he would 'defray the Expences of his admission &c. draw upon Mr. Thos. Fuller Merchant in St. Clements Lane London ten days after date for your reimbursement'. Planning his nephew's academic future, Fuller hoped that 'As soon as he is admitted my Brother would have him return to his Master again, & he shall go down & reside in October next. When I will give you further Instructions in addition to his studies'. Only John's success at Cambridge, Fuller admitted, would 'entitle him to be look'd upon as one of the Family'. Like the Burwells, the Fullers took their educations seriously as the mark of a true gentleman.[20]

Cambridge's acceptance of chattel slavery offered more than social connections – it provided a not-insubstantial income stream for the colleges. Though the average number of colleges and universities grew in the British Atlantic world, the late seventeenth, eighteenth, and early nineteenth centuries were the most difficult period in the University's turbulent history. After the education boom of the sixteenth and early seventeenth centuries, the legacy of which can still be seen in the extensive building work and professorships founded in that era, Cambridge experienced a precipitous fall in its student population. For some years of the eighteenth century, 300 students were in residence. John Venn has argued that 'anyone, who in 1760, endeavoured to infer the future from observation of the past [student enrolments] might well have come to the conclusion that in another century Cambridge and Oxford would be nearly extinct'. It is not difficult to see why, then, wealthier students, including young men with ties to the transatlantic economy, were welcomed at the struggling colleges.[21]

There were many reasons for the collapse in student numbers. The university experienced numerous scandals as the indolence of Cambridge fellows and lecturers became more apparent, with some arguing that the colleges exploited students for money, silver plates, tankards, and benefactions – and the college silver collections still bear the names of students from enslaver backgrounds, some of whom were expected to spend fifteen to twenty pounds on plate upon arrival. The role of a college fellow was, to all intents and purposes, a prestigious yet comfortable position. Fellows had few necessary duties other than dining at hall and attending service in chapel, but some did not even rise to these meagre duties. As Peter Searby notes, 'many were lax in attendance, and some were wholly non-resident'. Most did not teach. In 1788, one frustrated polemicist called for the reform of Cambridge because the 'enormous, and enormously increasing, Expence in the Education of young Men in this University, has been, is, and always must be Matter of very serious Concern to the Kingdom in general'. To that writer, the 'great Influx' of wealthy men to the colleges, perhaps referring in part to the relatives of enslavers, had corrupted the college fellowship, particularly the richest colleges.[22]

Cambridge's critics had a point: families and students spent vast fortunes on their educations, and, facing increasingly competitive oral and (from 1772) written examinations, young men turned to private tutors – raising the cost of their educations. From 1720 to 1830, a year's tuition at Cambridge, including board, increased from around £30 to £250, with Rose Fuller alone spending perhaps £570 at Cambridge and Leiden in the Netherlands. Student money impacted the local Cambridge and wider British economies too. If their ancestors came to the Caribbean poor in the seventeenth century, as the poet William Davenant mused, the children of enslavers returned to England rich a century later. One pamphleteer in 1701 estimated that enslavers in England invested around £50,000 per annum in the mother country on land, expensive educations for their children, and the other "baubles of Britain."[23]

Student expenses, in turn, enabled them to project an aristocratic self-image to their peers. For these men, the sum of 200 pounds for a year's expenses (perhaps £28,870 today) was a pittance. (Fuller advised one parent that 200 pounds was sufficient.) A disgusted Cambridge fellow noted that 'the number of... West Indians have done infinite hurt by their lavish way of spending both money and their time'. Horse racing was a popular (and expensive) component of student leisure, as it was in Virginia and the other North American colonies, as a means of projecting gentility. By 1740, the number of races had grown to such an extent that government regulation was required, as racing became 'an integral part of the fashionable social scene'. In an August 1756 letter to Rose Fuller, one slave-holder 'begg[ed]' his favour to 'see how his [son's] best Suit of Cloaths is and likewise whether He has any Breeches or Shoes fit to be seen in at ye Races' at the town of Lewes in East Sussex and, if he 'wants new Cloaths', Fuller would 'order a suit to be made, I shall bring shirts &c with me'. The Ascot and Newmarket races were popular student diversions, especially with Virginians. John Baylor of Caius was such a frequent attendee of the Cambridgeshire racetracks there that he later named his Virginian plantation "Newmarket" in that town's honour.[24]

Students found excitement in Exchange Alley too. A cursory examination of the South Sea records reveal that many Cambridge men owned securities. Richard Roderick of Queens', the son of Dorothy and the Reverend Dr Richard Roderick, was provided with £1,410 in annuities by his parents whilst completing his Bachelor's degree in September 1728, and he later became a fellow at Magdalene in 1742. John Mandeville of Corpus also owned £500 of annuities. The rising tide of wealth in the collegiate university drove some fellows to distraction. Amid the South Sea Bubble, Zachary Pearce, a Trinity fellow, complained that the 'old thirst for sciences seems to have been somewhat quenched here already' because 'our men are generally rich rather than educated men'. The 'desire for silver', he wrote, outweighed scholarly endeavours. Fellows sought to profit from investments in the slave trade: for instance, Richard Loving of Trinity owned £100 of Royal African Company stock, and Richard Monins, a St John's fellow, held £122 of South Sea stock. Perhaps reflecting on his colleagues and students, Richard Bentley, the Master of Trinity, identified a true intellectual as someone who 'lives inglorious or in want, To college and old books confin'd; Instead of learn'd, he's call'd pedant, Dunces advanc'd, he's left behind: Yet left content a genuine stoic he, Great without patron, rich without South-sea'. Bentley, who provided his Greek manuscripts to Trinity's Wren Library, had a secret though: he had £4,250 in South Sea stock around the Bubble, expanding his holdings in annuities to £5,500 by March 1725. (According to his journals, he later lost around £4,000 in 'the South Seas'.) Bentley was a man rich and poor in South Sea, indeed.[25]

Even at study, the relatives of slavers spent vast sums of money. John Fuller's expenses at Trinity and later at the Inns of Court, though frugal (in comparison to others), provide an insight into exactly what wealthier students purchased and the wider commercial economies in Britain that were bolstered through their expenditure. Families assisted the students wherever possible, providing money (and, in John Baylor IV's case, a hamper of hams, cider, brandy, and wine), yet their expenses frightened even the proudest and most trusting parents, forcing Fuller to assure a worried relative that 'I am of Opinion that boarding in some sober family will be the best Method [for his holiday] as I shall by that means be less liable to fall into any temptations: as to chumming I think it must on many Accounts be disagreeable & inconvenient[.]' On the subject of 'chumming', John assured Rose Fuller that 'it shall be my constant Endeavour by my future Discretion & diligent application, to render myself deserving of the Confidence you repose in me'.[26]

If John was frugal, then that is some indication of the significant incomes that these men drew upon in Britain. From March to mid July 1761, he spent more than seventy pounds on board, stockings, tea, sugar, handkerchiefs, gloves, wine, a journey to Maidstone, various books (including Sir Edmund Plowden's legal reports), pens, ink, paper, the rent of chambers, breakfast, shoes, and a mirror. He also hired the services of numerous workers, including a milliner, laundress, hosier, and landlady. These expenses did not include his tuition nor the significant amounts of alcohol and coffee that students consumed at coffeehouses in Cambridge, such as "Clapham's" or "Greek's" (named after its Greek proprietor). One visitor witnessed 'chief professors and doctors' amongst the patrons reading 'papers over a cup of coffee and a pipe of tobacco, and converse on all subjects; and thus you can make their acquaintance'. At these establishments, students and fellows traded news and formed friendships that endured following university, whether they remained in the metropole or returned to the colonies.[27]

Cambridge alumni donated to their colleges too. Burch Hothersall, the son of a Barbadian slaveholder, was admitted at Emmanuel College as a fellow-commoner in 1672, took an MA that same year, and later donated more than £120 for a new chapel organ (see Figure 1.2). (The college account books noted that a payment was made for 'Entertaining Mr. Hothersall and his Lady Joice at dinner who gave the organ… and [there] wine then [served]'.) Resplendent in a red gown, his portrait is still held by the college. William Long, the son of the Caribbean merchant Beeston Long, gave 100 pounds to Emmanuel, after a college fire in 1811 damaged the Westmoreland Building. Furthermore, in 1870, funds from Richard Burgh Byam's earlier £200 bequest to King's College (he had been a fellow there from 1807) was used in 'erecting two brass standards for lights at the East end of the chapel'. The standards were inscribed with Byam's name as a tribute to his generosity.[28]

Some students spent far more than Burch Hothersall or Richard Burgh Byam. Unsurprisingly given its reputation for educating the social elite, Cambridge reflected Britain's prevailing class hierarchies (see Table 3). The noblemen and fellow commoners (sometimes called 'Gentlemen Commoners'), 203 of whom were from enslaver families, were perched atop of the University's social pyramid. They were entitled to miss lectures, take plain exercises for the bachelor's degree, and dine at high table with the fellows. In return, these students provided plate to the college and paid higher fees. These students were highly esteemed – Dr William Savage, the Vice-Chancellor (1724–1725), acclaimed the fellow-commoners

EDUCATION AND THE MAKING OF A TRANSATLANTIC ELITE 33

for adding 'a great Lustre to our University' and he wanted them to appear in clothing 'proper to their Quality & Station; which, by distinguishing them from all other Scholars, would be both an Honour to ye University, & also a means of procuring that greater Degree of Respect to themselves, which is due to Persons of their Quality & Fortunes'. Dressed in gowns trimmed with gold, the fellow-commoners were marked out at the University as members of the gentility.[29]

Below the exalted fellow-commoners stood the pensioners who paid for their board and lodgings and, at the bottom of the hierarchy, the sizars, who worked as college servants or received scholarships to afford tuition (see Table 3). The pensioners were overrepresented within the student sample because the University class system was reformed in the nineteenth century. Still, student admissions reflected the power and wealth of families with ties to the transatlantic economy: 571 entered as pensioners and only twenty-seven commenced as sizars. These figures should not be taken at face value, however. Some students were admitted as sizars, but these students often acted as servants to their elder siblings at the college, and some changed their class multiple times whilst at university. Fourteen of the sampled individuals started as pensioners and ended their time at Cambridge as fellow-commoners, and some young men went through more dramatic changes in social status: Arthur Holt from Virginia underwent an educational odyssey, beginning life at Christ's as a sizar, rising to become a pensioner, and then finished his college residence as a fellow-commoner.[30]

Figure 1.1   Lease for 13 and a half years of Triall plantation, 1762, Church Mission Society Unofficial Papers. Cadbury Research Library, University of Birmingham.

Figure 1.2 Unknown, *Burch Hothersall*, oil on canvas, unknown date. Emmanuel College, University of Cambridge.

Lewis Burwell IV from Virginia was one such fellow-commoner. Born in Gloucester County, Virginia in 1710, Lewis's maternal grandfather was Robert "King" Carter, who bequeathed to his family more than 300,000 acres and enslaved around 3,000 African men, women, and children upon his death. The young Burwell's father also owned a plantation named "Fairfield." Lewis had a tumultuous time at Caius College, which he attended because his cousin Sir James Burrough, a fellow, donor, one of the architects of the Senate House, and later Master, was a prominent figure at that institution. Burwell appears in the Caius

Figure 1.3 Robert Edge Pine, *Ralph Wormeley V*, oil on canvas, 1763. Virginia Museum of History and Culture.

Bursar's Books in 1729 for a minor expense, and the elder Carter worried that his grandson did not have the qualities of a 'Scholar' and 'Gentleman'. That same year, Carter wrote that Burwell was 'under the care of Dr. Gooch our Governors Brother supposing him to be endowed with the same noble Qualitys that our Governour… whose temperate & Gentlemanly behaviour among us worthy render him a fit Pattern to us all to square our Morals by who have the honour to be frequently in his conversation[.]' Gooch's guidance had little effect. On his

'Scholarship', Carter complained that his grandson's head (and purse) was 'not to be turned to make any large improvements... what good the conversation of the University will do you I shall not prognosticate but I think I may fairly suppose you will come into your own country [Virginia] very indifferently equipped with talents proper to govern your affairs here'. The following year Carter denied Burwell another £170 to fund his expensive lifestyle, and the Virginian planter lamented to Micajah Perry, a London tobacco merchant and chaperone who had likewise tried to constrain Burwell's finances, that 'if this is to be the Effects of an English Education I don't know who will venture their Sons thither[.]' Burwell's trials had not ended years later. In a July 1734 letter to his old tutor Burrough, Burwell complained of his efforts to find a marriage partner, his painstaking efforts to study the law, and economic difficulties following his mother's death. At the end of the letter, he paid his respects to 'the Master [Thomas Gooch], Mr. Simpson [Robert Simpson, a fellow at Caius], & the rest of my worthy acquaintance[s] in your College'. Burwell had not endeared himself to his relatives, but his friendships with men such as Gooch, Burrough, and Simpson (a South Sea investor) persisted beyond Cambridge.[31]

From their class rank at Cambridge, the students had already been earmarked as an aristocratic class because of their education at English public schools. A Cambridge education was a package deal: an enterprising family would typically send a child over to England for an "English education" that involved schooling, university, and, if they were to be trained for the law, the Inns of Court in London. That context explains why only around half of sampled students graduated, as Cambridge was one stop on a student's longer educational journey. Lewis Burwell was one of many who were educated at Eton (142), and other public schools represented included Westminster (59), Harrow (51), and Charterhouse (39). At these schools, students would have found common cause with teachers, some of whom were prominent investors in the East India and South Sea companies. For example, Dr Henry Godolphin, the Provost of Eton and Dean of St Paul's, had £1,000 in East India securities in April 1694, and later owned £2,140 in South Sea stock in the early 1720s, continuing to hold his investments at the time that Burwell attended school. Godolphin was the namesake of "Godolphin House" at Eton, in part because he funded chapel repairs and erected 'at his own expense' the copper statue of the College's founder, Henry VI, which remains a prominent feature of School Yard.[32]

Slaveholders also drew upon family and friends for advice on where to send their sons. The South Carolinian merchant Ralph Izard contacted a friend, advising him that 'Harrow bears a very good character' and would 'be as proper a place for him [the son] – as any – until he arrives at age'. Yet Izard also recommended 'two or three years residence at Geneva' and, 'If he is sent to Cambridge – or Oxford', he 'must have a considerable degree of judgment and discretion – if his time – and money – are not thrown away – to very little purpose'. After all, these children were investments, and their education reflected the value that their family placed on a British schooling. Simon Taylor, a Jamaican plantation owner and one of the richest men in the Empire, offered advice too. He treasured his time at Eton, holding on to his 'Eton buttons', but reflected that he was a 'better scholar' when he arrived in 1755 than when he left, writing that 'a person may as well send his child to the devil at once, as either Oxford or Cambridge' – and he complained that students often ruined themselves through overspending and joyriding in carriages. Acknowledging these temptations, families often banded together to choose schools for their sons, with students from enslaver backgrounds attending the same elite institutions. At Eton, Ralph Wormeley V was friends with Izard, Daniel Dulany of Maryland, and John Randolph Grymes, a fellow Virginian. There they mixed with the *crème de la crème* of England, with Wormeley counting the future parliamentarian and abolitionist Charles James Fox, and Robert D'Arcy, the 4th Baron Hildyard, amongst his youthful companions.[33]

The colleges that these students attended reflected their attempts to attain social capital at Cambridge. To varying degrees, almost every college admitted these students; still, the three largest institutions of attendance from the student sample were Trinity (329), St John's (160), and Trinity Hall (53). After those three colleges, the students were more dispersed, with Christ's (40), Peterhouse, Pembroke, and Queens' (35) the other leading institutions in popularity (see Table 4). Slavers made a logical choice in Trinity and St John's, two of Cambridge's most prestigious seats of learning. In the latter half of the eighteenth century, half of England's peers and sons of peers matriculated at Trinity and 151 men who entered there between 1790 and 1820 became parliamentarians. Students formed enduring friendships with members of the British elite. (Henry Goulburn, who attended Trinity and whose father owned a sugar plantation, became friends with Henry John Temple, the 3rd Viscount Palmerston and future Prime Minister, at Cambridge.) Trinity's prestige accounts for the fact that, between 1710 and 1838, men with familial connections to the transatlantic economy constituted around five per cent of total admissions there. This figure rose to almost ten per cent around the middle of the eighteenth century and did not fall below five per cent until the 1820s.[34]

Student portraits were another component of the aristocratic self-presentation that enslavers projected at home in the Americas and abroad in Europe. The students provided ample opportunities for portraitists, such as Benjamin West and the Welsh painter John Downman, to further their careers in Cambridge. Dressed as the dutiful student, mortarboard resting atop a powdered wig and one hand in his waistcoat (a sign that the sitter was a member of the gentry), John Baylor IV of Virginia was painted soon after his arrival at Caius. Ralph Wormeley V also sat down for a personal portrait the same year as West painted "The Cricketers" (see Figure 1.3). Wormeley employed the services of no less than Robert Edge Pine, who painted George II and George

Washington, to memorialise Wormeley's education and, as a result, his promising future as a leading political figure in Virginia. Wearing the black and gold gown of a fellow-commoner, Wormeley held his mortarboard in his left hand as the entrance to Trinity Hall lay in the background. Upon leaving Cambridge, students again took the opportunity to have a portrait completed. John Carter, the future secretary of the Colony of Virginia, posed for a portrait attributed to Sir Godfrey Kneller – a Royal African Company investor and the court painter for Charles II and George I. The use of royal painters helped to cement an aristocratic image to their fellow British subjects, whether in the colonies or in Britain, and made these men stand apart as potential leaders.[35]

These glittering portraits bely the fact that the sons of enslavers often used violence, both against fellows and college servants, to prove their superiority. Charles Crawford of Antigua was one such belligerent student. Baptised at St John's Church on 28 October 1752, he was the son of Alexander Crawford of Evansons plantation. His brother received the estate in Alexander's will, but Charles was granted a legacy of £2,000 and an annual income of £150. With too much time (and money) on his hands, Crawford gained a reputation as a violent drunk at Queens' College, Cambridge, where he matriculated in November 1768. Hearing that Samuel May, a Pembroke senior fellow, had impugned the character of several ladies in Crawford's company, he entered May's rooms and forced him to sign a recantation or suffer defenestration. Queens' eventually expelled the Antiguan on account of 'having been drunk, and for assaulting and beating a waterman in the town, and for making a riot'.[36]

That judgment was not the end of the matter – the College made two further futile attempts to eject Crawford from Cambridge: the first he ignored; and, when Queens' barred his dormitory door, he hired a local blacksmith to break the locks. Following his forced removal, Crawford returned to the dining hall where he resisted the efforts of servants to 'take him out', threatening them that if 'they had any regard to self-preservation' they were 'not to touch him'. Cambridge fellows, students, and servants were not the sole objects of Crawford's ire: he threatened to strike Michael Lovell who, as was 'usual for West India merchants', had been 'consigned' to his care – an altercation that the London-based Caribbean merchant attributed (using the environmentalist discourses of the time) to 'young West-Indians' being 'less discreet' and 'more expensive' than British subjects from 'colder climates'. Queens' soon filed a lawsuit to remove Crawford, who seems later to have mellowed, becoming a poet in Pennsylvania and an abolitionist, freeing his enslaved workers in his will. Five years after Crawford's matriculation, a newspaper wondered whether his change in habits had shown that the 'Mind of a Creole may be enlarged, and how much the Language be originally learnt amongst his Father's Slave-Drivers may be refined by a Residence at *Queen's College, Cambridge*'.[37]

Alongside class structures, Cambridge reflected the wider racial prejudices in Britain at the time. Historians estimate that there were perhaps 10 to 15,000

EDUCATION AND THE MAKING OF A TRANSATLANTIC ELITE 39

Black people in Britain during the eighteenth century. There may have been Black attendees at Cambridge too. Born around 1700 to John and Dorothy Williams, a newly freed Black couple in Jamaica who were slavers, Francis Williams was the youngest of three sons. His father John was an energetic figure in Jamaican society, arguing before the Assembly in 1708 and 1716 to ensure that his family had the 'customs, and privileges of Englishmen'. From childhood, Francis was academically gifted and, as a result, John Montagu, the 2nd Duke of Montagu, the governor of Saint Lucia and Saint Vincent, decided to send him to England to be educated. Montagu's charity was replete with prejudiced stereotypes of Black inferiority, however. The governor had used Francis as an experiment to see whether Black men prospered in academic settings and, predictably, Williams excelled and, if accounts are to be believed, attended Cambridge. (No archival evidence exists of his attendance but given the paucity of records such a gap in the historical record is not unusual.) In England, Williams was often greeted with exclusion and derision though. The philosopher David Hume mocked the poet, recalling that they 'talk of one Negro as a man of parts and learning; but it is likely he is admired for slender accomplishments, like a parrot who speaks a few words plainly'. Later in May 1771, the *Gentleman's Magazine* described how he was 'dressed like other gentlemen in a tye, wig, and sword' and was 'admitted to the meetings of the Royal Society', but was ultimately 'rejected solely for a reason unworthy of that learned body, viz. on account of his complection'. It was further reported that Williams was admitted a member of Lincoln's Inn on 8 August 1721. Given his treatment in England (not to mention the costs of such an overseas adventure), few free Black students followed his example.[38]

Despite the relative scarcity of source material on early Black Cambridge students, the presence of African-descended servants or enslaved persons in the town of Cambridge cannot be dismissed. A record exists from 4 February 1710 mentioning the baptism of a 'Negro Christian' at Conington Hall near Cambridge, and Black persons were used as servants for the aristocracy and were featured in portraits as a status symbol for the landed nobility. Cambridge newspapers featured several advertisements for Black servants in the eighteenth and nineteenth centuries. In November 1797, Elizabeth Bigland advertised the services of 'A Black Servant' (who was probably formerly enslaved) in a Cambridge newspaper to 'Any Lady or Gentleman that is in want of a sober steady Man Servant, twenty-six years of age, and in good health'. Bigland further stated that the man had been in her service for three years, and 'previous to which he lived with her son [Edward Bigland] in [Westmoreland] Jamaica, with whom he conducted himself with the greatest propriety from a state of infancy'. More than fifty years later, another article advertised for 'a black servant – a post as a footman or Butler'. Some students, whose families donated to Cambridge, had enslaved people working on their British estates. John Yorke, an enslaved man from the Fish River plantation in Jamaica, was brought to

Britain when his enslaver's daughter, Elizabeth Campbell, married a white man named John Yorke. By 1772, Yorke was enslaved to John Hutton, the owner of Marske Hall in Yorkshire and an alumnus of Christ's. As local researchers have shown, the parish register described Yorke as a 'a negro servant belonging to John Hutton' – a young man 'supposed then to be about 17 or 18 years of age and could say his catechism in a tolerable way'. Freed after saving a gamekeeper's life in a moor fire, Yorke was provided with a cottage where he married a Yorkshire lady, Hannah Barker, in 1799 and they together had seven children. As for Hutton, his sons John and Timothy donated 100 pounds to the University Library fund and their extensive Arabic and Persian manuscripts to Christ's.[39]

Students certainly utilised the services of enslaved people whilst they lived in Britain. In 1770, John Faucheraud Grimké matriculated at Trinity College. The son of a prominent South Carolinian enslaver, Grimké depended upon Henry Laurens, the future President of the Continental Congress, as his benefactor. Laurens was a rice planter and partner in the largest slave-trading firm in North America, facilitating the enslavement and trafficking of more than 8,000 Africans in the 1750s alone. In 1772, Laurens was in London on business and attended by "Scipio," who later changed his name to Robert Scipio Laurens. In an October 1772 letter, Laurens informed Grimké's father that they were travelling to Geneva, and that they would 'fill a Genteel hir'd Coach & be attended by an interpreting Servant & my Black Man'. The trip would be 'preparative', Laurens argued, before Grimké made a 'more extensive tour' of Europe – a grand tour to expose young, wealthy men to the continent's polite society, music, and art. Before and following the 1772 Somerset Decision, which made enslavement illegal on British soil, undergraduates undoubtedly encountered Black Britons in Cambridgeshire.[40]

Enslavers' efforts to cultivate an aristocratic image through education led, in time, to more tales of prodigals gone astray in Britain. Samuel Alpress, who later served on the Jamaica Assembly, attended Cambridge. Born in January 1739, Samuel's father owned a 125-acre estate in Clarendon, Jamaica, and 51 acres in Vere Parish with 273 enslaved workers in total. George Alpress, who also managed one of the Fuller plantations, chose Jesus College to continue his son's education, writing to that institution in July 1754 with a letter of recommendation from his former schoolmaster. Along with Stephen Fuller's cover letter (or 'Doct Fuller', as he was called), Alpress Snr'.s introduction stated that he had 'already expended a Considerable sum of money upon his Education it will give me the greatest Satisfaction in this Life to have him reap the benefit of it'. He hoped that a Cambridge education would 'qualify him to make a figure in this Island as a Barrister at Law wch Profession I would in that prefer I am willing to bring him up to one other most suitable to them'. During his stay at Jesus, Samuel relied upon Thomas Fuller, a London merchant, for the necessary funds to finance his expenses and tuition, and Stephen Fuller set out in chapter and verse Alpress's education to Benjamin Newton, a Jesus fellow: 'He is intended for the Law, and is admitted of the Temple, but we shall probably let him take a Bachelor's degree with you. When his Education is finish'd, he is to go to Jamaica, where he is to get his Bread by his Profession'. Alpress's conduct disappointed his family and friends, especially Fuller.[41]

Admitted as a pensioner, Alpress matriculated in 1756 and soon after his financial problems began. In only his second term, the young man had exceeded his yearly allowance, forcing him to beg Fuller for more money and permission to learn 'to Fence an hour an afternoon'. In January 1758, he sent another letter appealing for more funds, which was revealing of the kinds of social networks and friendships that these students made at Cambridge. Alpress recounted that, after matriculation, he 'knew one or two young Gentlemen of Fortune in the University, I was introduced into a great deal of Company, (and without any Vanity to some of the best, of Men of Fortune may be so stiled) wch. naturally led me into a vast Expence, & I at that Time not considering, that they had large Estates to support them in it, & I none'. Alpress was caught in a bind: having little money, he worried that he was 'engag'd in a large Circle of Acquaintance, [and] to drop them all at once my false Modesty wou'd not permit me, as they wou'd naturally have inferred something bad, from so sudden a Transition, as that of a general Acquaintance, to that of none'. Fearing social embarrassment, he borrowed extensive sums of money, around £140 in total, and 'Having got ready Money I went often to Taverns, and as I commonly herded with my Fellow-Commoners my Credit was established upon, that Accts'. Friendship with the fellow-commoners drew the ire of his creditors, and he sought refuge in London for three months to avoid repayment.[42]

Returning to Cambridge, Alpress made little effort to improve his studies. Before the end of his freshman year, college fellows were determined to see the back of him. William Hawes, a fellow, complained to Fuller that 'Mr Alpress seems to have ye Misfortune of thinking himself born to an independent Fortune, & that therefore all application to Business is unnecessary'. Such self-delusion, Hawes worried, meant his 'staying at College will be of no service to himself, tho' a great Expence to his Friends'. By mixing with the rich, Alpress had become an embarrassment to Jesus College. Fuller's problems were further compounded because he had numerous plans for his future and had expectations of positions above his fortune – a situation perhaps exacerbated by his longstanding friendships with wealthier Cambridge students. Learning that the Church may be a suitable profession, Alpress complained that a 'Curacy of 40£ p. ann. Is what I dare say, Hond. Sr. you yourself will think a very scanty sustenance, as a Clergyman is suppos'd to keep good Company, & appear as a Gentleman, which I'm sure such an Income would not permit now, as my Fathers Intention is that I shd. Provide for myself'. (Rose Fuller had offered Jamaica's 'best living'.) Alpress preferred a commission in the army before commencing his curacy – yet further evidence of the posts that were available to the enslaver class.[43]

As the end of Alpress's time at Cambridge drew near, his debts mounted, and his profligacy served as a warning to future undergraduates. Fuller refused to answer the young man's letters, so Alpress implored Benjamin Newton at Jesus for money to pay his creditors. According to him, 'Mr Newton says he cant let me have any more therefore should be very much oblig'd to you if you woud send me some'. In February 1759, Alpress participated in a riot in Ely, with Newton writing that the Jesuan and his friends had taken 'a days pleasure on the water with several other Scholars, according to an annual custom', but he was remanded in the Justice of the Peace's home on a £100 bail. Soon his debtors returned: a clergyman requested reimbursement for having paid ten guineas to the local barber whose house Samuel had robbed, and four guineas to clear his expenses at an inn after a 'drunken frollick'. In May, the fellows informed him that he had 'in general behaved so very ill, & particularly so last week, that they can by no means suffer him to continue here any longer, there being no hopes that he will do himself any good, and the reputation of the College suffering daily from his irregular Behaviour'. Alpress was unrepentant. Leaving for London, he believed he had kept enough terms and had 'Friends enough in the College to get the Society to give me leave to admit at any other University to keep the other Term for a Degree'. Alpress never got his wish – he returned to Jamaica to embark on a successful political career, passing away in 1784.[44]

Alpress's conduct and that of other students served as a warning to future undergraduates and confirmed the attitude of some Americans that Cambridge was not worth the expense. Virginians had tired of sending their prodigals abroad. William Nelson, the future Governor of Virginia, sent his son Thomas to study at Cambridge, and his decision was widely lauded, with one correspondent arguing that his education – though 'expensive' – had 'proved a Foundation for him to build a Stock of manly Sense on; I believe he has as good a Heart as any Man living; his morals are sound; his Conduct steady, uniform & exemplary; & in point of Fortune, which necessarily gives a Man an Independency of Spirit, he is inferior to very few'. Thomas's father was less confident – in February 1768, Nelson mentioned to John Norton, who had offered to look after his children in England, that he would not send his son Hugh to Cambridge because 'the Temptations to Expence & Dissipation of Money & Time are too great for our Estates here; especially as the Improvements of our youth are Seldom answerable to Such great Expences as they often incurr'. Landon Carter echoed these sentiments. He remarked, perhaps with a chip on his shoulder (he had not attended a British university), that 'everybody begins to laugh at [an] English education the general importers of it nowadays bring back only a stiff priggishness with little good manners as possible'.[45]

The American Revolution and the rise to prominence of the former colonial colleges, such as Harvard, Princeton, and Yale, further drained students away from Cambridge. Even before American independence, a newspaperman declared that local schools would inculcate 'Patriotick Principles' and instil the 'True interests of *their* Native Country'. Still, southerners did not disregard their expensive educations – those who attended the English schools and universities took great pride in their prestigious educations in comparison to their fellow countrymen in New England. 'Before and just after the Revolution', the US Attorney General Hugh Swinton Legaré wrote, 'many, perhaps, it would be more accurate to say most, of our youth of opulent families were educated at English schools and universities'. He proudly continued: 'There can be no doubt their attainments in polite literature were very far superior to those of their contemporaries at the North, and the standard of scholarship in Charleston [South Carolina] was consequently much higher than in any other city on the continent'. Similarly, Dr Samuel Miller of the Princeton Theological Seminary argued in 1808 that classical learning was more developed in the middle and southern states, such as Pennsylvania, Maryland, Virginia, and South Carolina, than in New England. 'The reason', he maintained, 'is, that owing to the superior wealth of the individuals in the latter States, more of their sons were educated in Europe, and brought home with them a more accurate knowledge of the classics'. In time, the planters travelled to universities in Scotland, France, and Germany. Southerners, then, took great pride after leaving Cambridge, in their superior educations compared to the men that they called "Yankees" in the north.[46]

Following American independence in July 1776, the influx of students with enslaver backgrounds from Britain and the Caribbean showed no signs of abating. Instead of student numbers declining, the descendants of Liverpool slave-traders arrived in force (see Table 2). Seventy-three students with families involved in slave-trading came to Cambridge, using the university – alongside their marriages into landed wealth – to join the British elite. John Collingwood Tarleton, who matriculated at St John's as a fellow-commoner in 1810, was one of these students. The name "Tarleton" was infamous at the time, both for General Banastre Tarleton reportedly massacring a group of surrendering American soldiers during the Revolutionary War and for the family's slave-trading operations. John Collingwood's father (also named John) was a prosperous slave-trader and a leader of the proslavery lobby. (Writing to his brother in February 1788, John Tarleton had 'minutely gone thro' [with William Pitt] the whole detail of the situation and nature of the African commerce' and convinced him that the 'prohibition of a further importation of negroes' would produce, in the colonies, 'a rapid decline in the two latter, and total ruin, & impending destruction'.) After his father's death in 1815, John Collingwood inherited a Northumberland property, a London warehouse making £300 per annum, an estate worth £23,000, and the family's Demerara plantations. The abolition of the slave trade did little to damage these families or their fortunes.[47]

Enslavers continued to attend as the plantation's wealth and power survived the age of revolutions. The Berney family were proof of this. Numerous members of that extended family attended Caius, but three men were especially significant. Hanson Berney, the son of Sir Thomas Berney of Kirby Bedon, Norfolk, had matriculated as a fellow-commoner in 1738, and then was elected to a junior fellowship from 1743 to 1756. Furthermore, John Berney, Hanson's cousin, a Caius fellow and bursar, donated £200 to support a scholarship fund upon his death in 1782. Sir John Berney, who attended the same college in 1776, also maintained a strong personal connection to his alma mater, convincing the Caius philologist Robert Forby to become a tutor to his sons and provided him with a living (that was until the family ran into financial difficulties). The Berneys owned the plantation Hanson's in Barbados, which was featured on a survey of Barbadian landholdings between 1717 and 1721. The family became involved on the island because Sir Thomas had inherited the plantation through his wife, Elizabeth Folkes. (The estate was mentioned again in 1766, when Hanson was identified as owning 'land in St. George's… formerly in tenure of Samuel Hanson [Elizabeth's father]'.) The Berney's owned and managed this estate until the early nineteenth century whilst they maintained close personal ties to Cambridge, and it was likely that other college members were aware of the plantation when they conversed with Sir Hanson and elected him to such a junior fellowship. Thomas Gooch had close ties to the family and was perhaps instrumental in attaining that position for Sir Hanson.[48]

Situated on a road between the capital Bridgetown and the Board Hall sugar plantation, Hanson's consisted of a main plantation house, two "negro yards" (where the enslaved had their dwellings and grew their own crops, poultry, and livestock), two mill fields, a hog pen, cotton, gardens, and other parcels of land. The "yards" were imperative for enslaved subsistence given the shortage of food in Barbados. In the House of Commons inquiry into the slave trade, an enslaved man 'of the same Sir Hanson Berney' was 'employed to carry the rum of the estate to market and sell it, and to make bargains for small supplies, with the traders in town'. The Berney estate also included '383 acres of Land… 46 of which are not contiguous to the Sugar works but near enough to plant corn[.]' Following Hanson Berney's death in 1778, his son, Sir John, and the executors struggled to sell the property to defray the family's debts. (Helped, in no small part, by John Berney, the Caius fellow, who bequeathed the 'principal part' of his fortune to his similarly named relative.) Time was of the essence. As one observer noted, the sugar price had shown 'considerable advance the price of the produce has also tended to enhance the value of Land and property in this Island'. They cautioned that this 'local advantage' was 'temporary, [the price rises] arising… from the repeated failure of Crops in several of the Islands for 3 or 4 years past'. Furthermore, the land had to be sold because of 'the unhappy disturbances in the French sugar colonies and particularly the late dreadful and ruinous effects of the revolt in St. Domingo'. Far from depress the price of sugar,

John's legal representatives claimed (or hoped) that the Haitian Revolution was an opportunity to be exploited, as it would take a number of years for the French plantations to return to 'peace and concord' and that 'in the mean time… the present very great price of sugar and other West Indian produce should tempt many to speculate in buying here, and of course advance the price of Estates also[.]' The Berney trustees' confidence in France's ability to maintain control over that slave society was misplaced. By 29 August 1793, the revolutionaries controlled more than a third of the island and had forced the French Assembly to abolish racial slavery (though the French colonists intended on replacing enslavement with a system of indentured servitude). Sir John's opinions on the morality of Black enslavement, however, are complicated – he was listed as a subscriber to Olaudah Equiano's 1789 memoir. The sale took much longer than expected (the newspapers featured no fewer than nine sale or lease notices in one year); still, in 1810 the Berney family managed to sell the 316-acre plantation, and its workforce of eighty enslaved persons – around the lower third of Barbadian plantations in terms of the size of their labour force.[49]

Slaveholders, such as the Berneys, maintained their plantations in the age of abolition, and Black students attended Cambridge in greater numbers too, including the Afro-Polish violinist George Polgreen Bridgetower, who performed with (and impressed) Ludwig van Beethoven and took a Bachelor of Music from Trinity Hall in June 1811. Bridgetower's success was due to his prodigious talent and his father's enterprising ability to get his son noticed by the English aristocracy, as most talented African musicians were condemned to forge professional careers at the fringes of the social scene. Bridgetower's father, Friedrich de August, may have been an enslaved man of African and European descent and travelled to Europe from Barbados, perhaps taking the name "Bridgetower" after his birthplace's largest town 'Bridgetown' (and most likely his point of escape from enslavement). Arriving in Europe, Friedrich married Mary Ann Bridgetower and fathered George, who may have been born in Baila, Poland, in either February or October 1778. At the age of ten, Bridgetower was a renowned musician, performing for the British royal family at Windsor and at the Bath Assembly Rooms, which were frequented by King George III. He was also acquainted with Dr Charles Hague, Cambridge's Professor of Music. Bridgetower's life at Cambridge is somewhat obscure, but during his degree he composed and performed with a full band at Great St Mary's Church before the Chancellor and the Duke of Gloucester, who were visiting the University. *The Times* reported that the 'composition was elaborate and rich; and highly accredited to the talents of the Graduate'. As the church echoed with the rich sounds of Bridgetower's composition, the performance was more significant because Cambridge's musical tradition owed a debt to men with slaving connections: the siblings of Thomas Tudway (1704–1726), a long-tenured Cambridge Professor of Music, had been Royal African Company merchants and master mariners in the Antiguan trade – a trade in men and women who looked like Bridgetower.[50]

Mixed-ethnicity students who were the sons of enslavers also attended Cambridge at this time. Thomas Hopkinson from British Guiana was admitted at Trinity College on 26 June 1819 after attending Anstey School in Hertfordshire. In a later court case in 1828, the press reported that Hopkinson was a man of colour and property owner in Demerara. (His education at Cambridge was significant because mixed-ethnicity family members were often shunned and deemed as threats to prevailing racial hierarchies and white dominance.) Little is known about Hopkinson's mother, however Thomas's father, John Hopkinson, was well-known on Demerara. Indeed, 'any nobleman or gentleman connected' with that colony apparently knew the family. John Hopkinson was mentioned as taking a leading role in suppressing the 1823 Demerara revolt. After the Lieutenant Colonel John Leahy and his militia fired into a crowd of 2,000 enslaved people, killing 200, he gathered his men at John and Cove plantations belonging to Hopkinson. Forcing their enslaved men, women, and children to remain on the plantation, Leahy, Hopkinson and the other landed enslavers tried Dublin, the supposed ringleader of the revolt, amongst the hundreds of rebels who were executed for their resistance to colonial power. Nevertheless, the execution of the Reverend John Smith of the London Missionary Society, a 'freeborn native Englishman', increased British antislavery sympathy as white Britons protested the execution of a freedom-loving (and white) Christian.[51]

Alongside Black or mixed-ethnicity students, the student body's complex relationship to slavery became evident in the white students who had enslaved relatives. Robert Collymore matriculated at Trinity in 1811. He was the nephew of Robert Collymore, a Barbadian enslaver resident in St George, and Amaryllis Collymore, who Robert had manumitted in 1784. She soon became 'the richest free woman of color in pre-emancipation Barbados', and, in 1824, she was bequeathed "Lightfoots" estate and several enslaved persons in Robert's will. Her will was worth an estimated £10,000 to family members, and included sixty-seven enslaved persons provided to various relatives, with an estimated property value of £3,000, silverware, furniture, houses, and land at Haggatt Hall and Bridgetown worth £7,000 to her descendants. Yet Robert, Jr., his cousin, who had the same name, was born an enslaved man – a fact he may have felt compelled to hide at Cambridge. He would have certainly found it difficult to hide his slaving background. At a dinner, a Trinity student joked that he had been at a college formal with 'Sugar Bichard' (Alexander Grant, the son of a Jamaican planter).[52]

Private tutors guided the steady stream of students from the Caribbean to Cambridge. Slave societies, indeed, often spent significant sums on education because of the growing number of educated men who wandered the colonies and the consolidated plantations in search of pupils, placing advertisements for their services in newspapers such as *The Barbadian*. The Reverend William Browne, an alumnus of St John's, was one of their number. In a May 1825 edition of that newspaper, alongside advertisements for saddles, draft horses, and sacks of flour, Browne proposed, for forty dollars a quarter, 'instructing a limited number of young Gentlemen from the age of 14, in the GREEK and LATIN CLASSICKS, MATHEMATICKS and ALGEBRA' – with 'Gentlemen prepared for either of the Universities, and read with for Ordination'. The same notice was printed more than seven times, offering Barbadian families a path to educational success. The English education system, then, continued to attract white families, many of whom feared the social and cultural stigma of living amongst enslaved people. James Scarlett of Jamaica, later the 1st Baron Abinger, reflected in his memoirs that his parents 'were sensible of the corruption of morals' in a slave society. They feared 'contamination' from social 'intercourse either with slaves' or with anyone 'whose dialect was touched with the broken English of slaves'. Such racial anxieties ensured that Scarlett was hurried along to Trinity College before a successful legal career.[53]

British-born students with enslaver parents who followed that path to Cambridge continued to make a name for themselves – but not as their parents would have wished. Admitted to Trinity College in October 1816, Lawrence Dundas was the second son of the Hon. Lawrence Dundas, the later 1st Earl of Zetland, who made a career as a wine merchant and army contractor before purchasing two plantations in Dominica and Grenada. The younger Dundas would not leave Cambridge alive, however. A victim of his vices, the Dundas incident drove the Reverend Frederick Herbert Maberly of Chesterton to write *The Melancholy and Awful Death of Lawrence Dundas*. According to Maberly, the lamentable incident began on 5 February 1818 when Dundas met with five students, among them Keith Alexander Jackson, a fellow-commoner at St John's (and the nephew of Joseph Jackson, a Jamaican enslaver, and the heir of Sarah Woodruff, who died the previous year and had one enslaved person in Port Royal), and William Thellusson, a Trinity undergraduate (and the third son of Peter Isaac Thellusson, the 1st Baron Rendlesham and a banker and heir to a Grenadian estate). Meeting at Jackson's property, the men dined for four hours before they set off for Barnwell, a ward of Cambridge infamous for being a 'resort of women of the town', but Dundas never made it that far. So inebriated that he was unable to put on his gown, the Trinity student 'tumbled into a muddy ditch' on Parker's Piece, and 'after stripping everything off, saving his pantaloons and his stockings… he fell to rise no more; for he was found dead on Friday morning in a sitting posture in the ditch… he does not appear to have been drowned, but to have perished from the inclemency of the weather'. Driven to despair, Maberly denounced undergraduates for their 'evil nature' and for behaviour more suited to a 'glutton and drunkard' than scholars.[54]

Though acknowledging the risks, the Caribbean colonists continued to send potential undergraduates to Britain. Wealthy enslavers from British Guiana, the Bahamas, and Trinidad soon added new revenue streams for the colleges. The Dickinson family from Somerset, who were Bristol merchants and Jamaican plantation owners, were one such example. On his death in 1799, Stephen Fuller left £10,000 to his grandson, William, who followed his father into Parliament, and William's children, Francis and Edmund, both attended Trinity in 1831 and 1838. Francis, whose correspondence survives, was simultaneously involved in the wider Cambridge community and the proslavery lobby. In June 1838, the Secretary of the Oxford and Cambridge University Club in London informed Dickinson that he was being elected a member of that exclusive society, and he corresponded with George Peacock, the Lowndean Professor of Astronomy at Cambridge, concerning college matters. (Thomas Lowndes, who had endowed that professorship, was Provost-Marshal of South Carolina and, at his death in May 1748, he authorised his executors to sell 'all my estate in Carolina'.) At that time, Dickinson was also a member of the Association of Jamaican Proprietors. Following abolition, the Proprietors depressed Black wages because, in their words, 'a great proportion of the labouring population refuse to work at all, while others will only work for a rate of wages that is impossible for the planters to pay without absolute loss'. The enslavers, then, did not fall into obscurity and poverty following abolition. Rather, they maintained their positions in the wider Cambridge community.[55]

Historians of enslavement have increasingly devoted attention to the students who attended colleges and universities, and this chapter has shown the importance of such an approach to our historical understanding of the material and cultural benefits that educational institutions and the students derived from enslavement, and the significance of education to the formation of a transatlantic economic elite. For colleges, the slow trickle and sudden influx of students – many of them fellow-commoners, the propertied elite – in the seventeenth, eighteenth, and nineteenth centuries provided a source of revenue and prestige given the political prominence of these men with ties to the colonial economy. These linkages go beyond the material, however. College fellows and tutors were involved in plantation operations and even those who were not slaveholders forged close connections with undergraduates involved in the slave economy, dining with them at high table, providing money for debts, and keeping in touch with alumni long after they had left. Far from innocent and unaware bystanders or abolitionists waiting to convince these students of their misdeeds, the college fellows accepted and nurtured these undergraduates who, after Cambridge, often returned to the colonies to run their estates and take leading roles in governing slave societies. In educating students with transatlantic economic ties, Cambridge men helped to bolster imperial racial hierarchies.

2

'The Highe Priest hath banished you forth': Missionary Protestantism and the Origins of the British Empire

Beyond Cambridge, past and present fellows ministered to and baptised enslaved persons in North America and West Africa and defended the institution of racial chattel slavery. Thomas Thompson, formerly a fellow and the Senior Dean of Christ's College, was one of their number, joining the Society for the Propagation of the Gospel in Foreign Parts (SPG), a Church of England missionary organisation, on the recommendation of the Reverend Thomas Cartwright, a college fellow and the Archdeacon of Colchester. Thompson was first sent to Monmouth County, New Jersey, and later published a letter in 1756 and travel narrative in 1758 about his Atlantic missionary adventures. After five years in North America, Thompson next travelled to West Africa. Arriving in February 1752, he was less than enthused about his prospects for 'saving' souls, deriding West Africans as lazy, drunk, idolatrous, and superstitious 'Barbarians'.[1]

For almost four years, Thompson resided at Cape Coast Castle, one of around forty fortresses that lined the West African coastline. First home to the Swedish Africa Company, who traded in timber and gold, the British RAC used the Castle's dark, cramped dungeons to imprison Africans awaiting transportation to the Americas. Whilst Thompson tried in vain to convert the locals, he became the Castle's chaplain – recalling that the 'Castle, which formerly had a Chaplain, being now without one, I was permitted to officiate in the Place of Chaplain. By Favour of the Governor I had a convenient Chamber allowed me, was often invited to his Table, and he was in every Respect very kind and civil to me'. Whilst civil in public, the governor, Thomas Melvil, who led the Castle after the RAC was reorganised into the African Company of Merchants, privately dismissed Thompson's efforts to 'convert the Negroes' and argued that the former fellow depended on 'the old Prophets & super-natural aid' to save Africans from Satan.[2]

Melvil was correct: Thompson's mission was unsuccessful – he brought back only three young West Africans, among them Philip Quaque, the son of a local chief and slave trader, to train as Anglicans – but he earned enduring fame (or infamy, depending on the audience) for the proslavery pamphlet he published just a year before his death. Thompson dedicated the text to William Devaynes, the five times chairman of the East India Company, a member of the African

Company of Merchants, and a vocal proponent of colonisation in Sierra Leone. Understandably, Thompson was not shy about his Cambridge connections – he displayed his credentials on the frontispiece as 'THO. THOMPSON, M. A. SOMETIME FELLOW OF C. C. C. [Christ's College, Cambridge]'. Projecting intellectual authority, Thompson made several arguments in the piece: that African leaders did the enslaving; that enslavement was legal according to established writings of the day, including the laws of nations and war and the teachings of the Bible, and was not contrary to the laws of nature; and that the wrongs of slavery were due to individual cases of sadistic masters, rather than an indication of how enslaved people were treated throughout the British Caribbean.[3]

These intertwined arguments underpinned Thompson's conclusion: that the slave trade and plantation economy rescued West Africans from the oppressions that they suffered in their homelands. Slavery, according to Thompson, halted the much greater despotisms that the local population suffered because of the practices 'among the natives themselves'. As with plantation owners, Thompson appealed to political economy and commerce to prove the legality of "man-stealing." To him, slaveholding arose from a 'necessity of supplying our *West India* and *American* colonies with the fittest hands for plantation-work' – the phrase "fittest hands" indicating that Europeans enslaved Africans for their apparent proclivity for hard labour, expertise for cultivating some crops, such as rice, and supposed resistance to tropical weather and diseases. Enslavement, to him, was a necessary evil.[4]

Abolitionists, including Granville Sharp and Anthony Benezet, challenged Thompson on his conclusions and readings of scripture. Criticising Thompson's arguments as an effort to defend enslavement, Granville's Sharp's 1773 *Essay on Slavery* was dedicated to refuting the Christ's man. Intending to highlight slavery's *Inconsistency with Humanity and Revealed Religion*, Sharp, who had a profound influence on Cambridge antislavery activists, attacked Thompson's claims. 'I have not leisure to follow this author methodically', Sharp wrote, 'but will, nevertheless, examine his ground *in a general way*, to prevent any ill use that may be made of it against the important question now depending before the judges'. The court case he may have been referring to was *Somerset v. Stewart* (known as the "Somerset Decision") which, at the time of writing, was still before William Murray, 1st Earl of Mansfield. As a committed Christian, Sharp hoped that men of the cloth, like Thompson, would display charity to the enslaved. The gospel, he declared, 'destroys all *narrow, national partiality*; and makes *us citizens of the world*, by obliging us to profess *universal benevolence*…whatever "the *worshipful* committee of the company of merchants trading to *Africa*", may think of it, or their advocate, the reverend Mr. Thompson'. Sharp appealed to Thompson's Christian beliefs to question the Cambridge man on the veracity of his claims regarding the slave trade. As for Thompson, his residence in West Africa damaged his health, and the SPG reported that the 'fatal Distemper there, the Flux, and other sharp

Sicknesses' had forced him to return to England. Claiming a small, yet generous, 'Benefaction' from Christ's to aid him after the expense of his passage home from Africa, Thompson died in 1773.[5]

Advertising his status as a former Cambridge fellow, Thompson's writings and reception illustrate the importance of academic status, even as the ancient universities were challenged for the inadequate educations that they sometimes provided to their young charges and prodigals. As an institution predicated, in part, on providing the British Empire with clergymen, missionary Protestantism was one of the principal avenues through which Cambridge fellows and benefactors became agents in the expanding empire, helping to reinforce slaving ideologies, and fund imperial religious organisations and educational institutions. More recently, historians, such as Travis Glasson, have highlighted the SPG's ownership of the Codrington plantations in Barbados and proslavery efforts, and the present chapter extends these claims to the seventeenth century, with many Anglican missionaries struggling to claim ownership over the global marketplace of souls from Catholics, Baptists, and Quakers. The chapter first charts the involvement of Cambridge men in the Virginia Company and associated imperial companies in New England, Bermuda, the Bahamas, and Guinea. The focus will then turn to the eighteenth century and the emergence of the Society for the Propagation of the Gospel and the Society for the Promotion of Christian Knowledge, which counted prominent Cambridge founders, donors, and supporters amongst its number.[6]

Cambridge men were involved in North American colonisation from its inception. St John's College educated many of these men, and that institution's significance to the colonisation of Virginia mirrored Emmanuel's importance to the Puritan expedition to New England. Cambridge men took a leading role in the Company: Robert Gray, who matriculated around 1589, wrote a sermon in support of emigration as a solution to England's problem of overpopulation; Thomas Morton, who graduated in 1586 and later became a fellow and lecturer in logic, defended the Colony's legality; Gabriel Archer, an officer at the Colony's first settlement in Jamestown, was at St John's for two years; and Samuel Purchas, the 'most vigorous and prolific promoter' of the Company, once called Cambridge home. William Crashaw (who was a fellow from 1594) wrote much of the Company's propaganda and his collection of 200 books, which were so substantial that their storage necessitated the construction of the Old Library at St John's, were delivered to that institution thanks to Henry Wriothesley, the 3rd Earl of Southampton (who was also a member of the Virginia Company).[7]

Crashaw was a Company shareholder and advocated that 'We give the Savages what they most need. 1. Civilitie for their bodies. 2. Christianitie for their soules'. The first tenet would 'couer their *bodies* from the shame of the world' and the second objective would 'couer their *soules* from the wrath of God'. For Crashaw, colonisation would transform "savage" Native Americans into useful English subjects – in fact, the Company 'will make them richer than we finde them. For he that hath 1000. acres, and being a *ciuill* and *sociable* man knowes how to use it, is richer than he that hath 20000. and being a savage, cannot plow, till, plant nor set, and so receives no more profit then what the earth of it selfe will yeelde by nature'. To that end, he proposed endowing 'Schooles and colledges' for the 'Children of the He[a]then' where they were to be educated in 'Civilitye and Christianitie' and the English language. For colonial promoters such as Crashaw, profit and religion were two sides of the same coin, with the struggle for Native American souls a motivating factor for colonisation.[8]

The St John's men joined other Cambridge luminaries who sought to colonise North America. Educated at Trinity, Alexander Whitaker had a close connection to St John's (his father, William Whitaker had been the master there from 1586 to 1595). Yet the Ferrar family were the most significant enthusiasts for the Company. Born in London, Nicholas Ferrar, the Company's Secretary and Treasurer was one of the youngest children of his father, who was also named Nicholas. Sent away to boarding school, the younger Nicholas later entered Clare Hall as a fellow-commoner, took his BA in 1610, and was elected to a fellowship that year (and he held that fellowship for more than two decades). For the Ferrars, the Virginia Company was a family affair, and they often enjoyed the company of Sir Walter Raleigh and became associated with Sir Edwin Sandys, who later designed the headright system in Virginia, which granted land to colonists. Nicholas and his family had endless ambitions for England's new colony. The first colonists had fallen victim to starvation, disease, and war with the local (and powerful) Powhatan, but Nicholas considered establishing iron works in the colony and his niece, Virginia, drew up plans for a silkworks. Furthermore, Ferrar planned to establish a college in Virginia for the conversion of Native Americans (as per his father's will and legacy of £300) and he negotiated tobacco contracts with the government. Ferrar's position as a Cambridge fellow was perhaps a significant part of his political appeal. Whitaker, in his pamphlet *Good News from Virginia*, 'let all men know' that as a 'Scholler, a Graduate, a Preacher, well borne, and friended in England' such fellows were not self-interested and should therefore be trusted for their opinions.[9]

The colonisation of Ireland inspired these educated men. Cambridge had long and enduring connections across the Irish Sea – a proving ground for the political, legal, and ethical language of English conquest. Oliver Cromwell, an alumnus of Sidney Sussex, remains infamous for his efforts to re-conquer Ireland after the successful Catholic rebellion of 1641, and his deportation of 'tens of thousands' of Irish prisoners as indentured servants to colonies such as Barbados and Virginia. Cromwell was not the first Cambridge connection to Ireland, however. The first Master of Gonville Hall (now Gonville and Caius

College), John Colton (c. 1320–1404), left that position to become the Lord Treasurer of Ireland in 1373, earning further posts as the Lord Chancellor from 1379 to 1382 and the Bishop of Armagh in 1383. In Ireland he commissioned the *Visitation of Derry*, an account of a ten-day tour intended to assert the English colonists' power over that region, and he also diligently worked to forge peace between the O'Neill clan and King Richard II. With the Irish cast as a 'sacrilegious and ungovernable people, hostile to God and humanity', a people who required a 'crusade' for the 'wellbeing' of Christianity – a 'just war against those evildoers' – more Cambridge men followed Colton in the following two centuries, including William Bedell, a pensioner at Emmanuel and later fellow in 1593, who was the Provost of Trinity College, Dublin, from 1627 to 1629 and the Bishop of Kilmore and Ardagh for thirteen years, supervising the translation of the Old Testament into Gaelic. Moreover, Sir Thomas Bendish, England's ambassador to the Ottoman Empire and a donor of around fifty books on subjects ranging from mathematics to anatomy to St John's, invested £400 in the Adventurers for Irish Land, which speculated in confiscated Catholic estates and aimed to replace these inhabitants with English colonists. Francis Ash, a goldsmith, East India Company shareholder, and Governor of the Muscovy Company (which held a monopoly trading contract with Russia), also speculated £250 with the Adventurers. Ash donated forty books to the University Library and endowed ten scholarships at Emmanuel College.[10]

Sir Thomas Smith was a more significant connection still between Cambridge and Ireland. The second son of an Essex sheriff, Smith ascended the University ranks after took his BA degree at Queens' around 1530. Elected a fellow of the same college, he held that prestigious position for seventeen years and, whilst navigating the academic ladder, gained a legal degree at Padua, a Regius Professorship of Civil Law in 1542, and the Vice-Chancellorship from 1543 to 1545. Following a seven-year posting as the provost of Eton College, Smith, an early Protestant, benefitted when Edward VI, the first monarch to be raised Protestant after his father Henry VIII left the Catholic Church, ascended the throne. After the young King's untimely death, Edward Seymour, the 1st Duke of Somerset and brother to Edward's mother, Jane Seymour, seized power – and Sir Thomas was gifted further postings as the Secretary of State and knighted for his diplomatic services. Though he lost favour following Mary's accession, her death and Elizabeth I's rise to power marked the beginning of another golden age in Smith's political career.[11]

Smith's connection to Irish colonisation began in 1571. In the intervening thirteen-year period after Elizabeth's accession in November 1558, Smith had entered Parliament (as the Member for Grampound in Cornwall and then Liverpool), been appointed the ambassador to France, and had established a friendship with Sir William Cecil, the Queen's chief advisor. As a reward for his service (and in a rather brazen attempt to subvert the authority of the local O'Neill clan), Elizabeth provided Smith with 360,000 acres of East Ulster land.

Smith supported Elizabeth's unsuccessful military programme in Ireland, the "Enterprise of Ulster," where wealthy English colonists were provided with land grants to subdue the Irish, a 'wicked, barbarous, and uncivil people'. According to Hiram Morgan, Smith had two goals for the region: 'the enrichment of himself and his son, and the simultaneous strengthening of England's position in Ireland'. For Smith, patriotism served profit, and vice versa.[12]

Founding a joint-stock company to finance his endeavours, Smith launched three campaigns between 1572 and 1575 to establish his Irish estates. Hoping to recreate English society on Ireland's shores, Smith foresaw new settlements where the Irish would live 'in the godly awe of [the] lawes of England'. Indeed, 'playnting' Ireland with 'Englyshe laws' and religion, he argued, would reform Irish 'barbarity', providing in turn a significant 'profite' to the 'estate of England'. Smith, a contemporary of the humanist Sir Thomas More (who authored *Utopia*), joked that he was establishing a '*Eutopia*', and his understanding of colonisation was partly rooted in readings of his student Richard Eden's translation of Peter Martyr d'Anghiera's *Decades of the new worlde or west India*, which justified American colonisation and bondage because it freed Indigenous peoples from their cannibalistic rulers. For agents of empire, including Smith, the objective of colonisation was to transform the social and cultural landscape of early modern Ireland – converting pagan "savages" into productive, civilised subjects – and that paternalistic attitude was evident in Virginia too.[13]

Before his involvement in Ireland, Smith contributed to a growing literature that debated and planned the development of an English empire. His *De Republica Anglorum: the Manner of Gouernement of Policie of the Realme of England*, was first published in 1583 but written between six to ten years before his Irish enterprises began. It justified Elizabeth's rule at the head of a Protestant English empire. In *De Republica Anglorum*, Smith wrote an entire chapter on the nature of enslavement. Basing his conclusions on Roman law, he equated villeins, who were feudal tenants that offered their services in return for land, with the enslaved, or *servi*. The *servi* were those purchased with money, seized in war, or 'left by succession, or purchased'. *Servi* would not form part of the commonwealth because he defined such a community as being of 'free men collected together and united by common accord & covenauntes among themselves' in peace and war. The enslaved would be viewed as 'instruments' in the same manner that a husbandmen understood his 'plow, the cart, the horse, oxe or asse'. The Elizabethan councillor, some historians suggest, may have also been responsible for the short-lived (and, in practice, unenforceable) Vagrancy Act of 1547, which condemned destitute people unwilling to work to enslavement. Smith, however, would not live to see his magnum opus's publication. He passed away at his Hill Hall estate in Essex on 12 August 1577, leaving his Latin and Greek manuscripts to Queens' College.[14]

Cambridge's Irish connections ensured that early Virginia Company officials had precedents to draw upon when planning American colonisation.

Aside from its ideological underpinnings, University men helped to establish the institutional groundwork for slavery in the Americas. In 1615, Ferrar helped to found the Somers Island Company, which administered the colony of Bermuda for more than sixty years. African enslaved persons were brought to the island from 1616 for pearl diving and there were an increasing number of enslaved Native Americans, particularly after the Pequot War in 1636 and Metacom's War from 1675 through to 1678. Indigenous slavery inspired much debate amongst Cambridge alumni. Emmanuel Downing, a scholar at Trinity Hall in 1602, had emigrated to Salem in the Massachusetts Bay Colony, and was elected a Deputy to the General Court of Massachusetts, a Magistrate in the Quarterly Court at Salem, and Recorder of Deeds. In the Summer of 1645, Downing advocated long before the outbreak of the conflict with Metacom that if a 'Just warre' began in the region it would 'deliver them [Narragansett peoples] into our hands, wee might easily haue men woemen and Children enough to exchange for Moores, which will be more gaynefull pilladge for us than wee conceive, for I doe not see how wee can thrive until we get into a stock of slaves suffitient to doe all our buisines[.]' According to Wendy Warren, colonisation drove enslavement (and vice versa), with 1,300 Native Americans enslaved in New England alone.[15]

The scale of Indigenous enslavement led the Reverend John Eliot, a Jesus alumnus, to protest this situation. In August 1675, he attacked the policy of 'sending away such Indians' to become 'perpetual slaves' in the Caribbean. The English, he continued, must convert Native Americans – not seek to 'extirpate nations'. Warning the governor against selling Indigenous peoples, a 'dangerous merchandise', Elliot condemned 'the abject condition of the enslaved Africans' whose lives had been purchased through the sale and labour of Native enslaved people. The English were hypocritical, he protested, if they condemned the Spanish for 'destroying men and depopulating the land' whilst they engaged in these same atrocities. Eliot's more diplomatic vision of Euro-Native American relations found few allies even amongst those at home who questioned the means and ends of England's empire. Joseph Mede of Christ's College wished the colonists 'well as anybody' in May 1634, but he differed 'in the grounds they go upon'. He feared that, rather than converting 'barbarous nations' and the servants of Satan, 'good [Protestant] Christians' would become as corrupted as the Catholic servants of 'Christ our Lord': those 'Mastives the *Spaniards*', whom God, Mede wrote, had been sent to 'hunt' and 'worry' in a 'hideous manner' the Indigenous peoples of South America. Mede feared nothing less than a combined 'Army of *Gog* and *Magog*', with Native Americans and corrupted Europeans marching (or, more likely, sailing forth) under Lucifer's infernal banner, from the Americas 'against the Kingdom of Christ'.[16]

Eliot's entreaties, it appears, also fell on deaf ears in both New England and Virginia. More infamously, in August 1619 '20. and odd Negroes' arrived at Point Comfort in Virginia. Taken from a Portuguese slaver, the São João Bautista, and transported to North America through an act of piracy, these Black indentured servants were originally transported from Luanda, the centre of Portugal's slave trade in Angola. Six months later, the presence of thirty-two Afro-Virginians was noted in a Virginian census. John Pory, a secretary of state of the colony (and a Caius graduate), mentioned their arrival and how the ship was 'victualled and manned... anew, and sent her with the same Commission to raunge the Indies'. He was aware of that ship's cargo. Twenty years earlier, Pory, publishing as a scholar 'lately of Gonevill and Caius College in Cambridge', translated al-Hasan Muhammad al-Wazzan's *A geographical historie of Africa*. The translation elaborated on the problem of racial difference. On Blackness, he wrote that 'Negros or blacke Moores' are 'thought to be descended from *Ham* the cursed son of *Noah*'. Moreover, in a subsequent passage, race was considered a 'hereditary qualitie transfused from the parents, then the intemperature of an hot climate, though it also may be some furtherance thereunto'. Pory's translation was such a success that it reportedly influenced the creation of William Shakespeare's titular character in *Othello*.[17]

After 1619, the year 1622 was another significant milestone in the Company's involvement in slavery. The newly established General Assembly in Virginia had restricted colonists from expanding their tobacco operations, but the Powhatan had other plans. On the four-year anniversary of Chief Powhatan's death, that nation surprised the English in the Great Assault of 22 March 1622, killing at least 347 colonists, almost one-third of the colony (including the Reverend Samuel Maycock, a plantation owner and Caius alumnus). The leaders of the Company were infuriated. Although a subject of some debate, some historians argue that 1622 was a turning point in which Native American enslavement and extermination, rather than baptism, became a principal goal for the colonists there. Edward Waterhouse, the Company's secretary, certainly argued that this massacre had relieved the English of a moral quandary: how to colonise Virginia and convert Indigenous peoples without violence. Waterhouse wrote that the English were now justified in the 'way of conquering them is much more easy then of civilizing them by faire meanes, for they are a rude, barbarous, and naked people' – advocating that they be chased with 'our horses, and blood-Hounds to draw after them, and Mastives to teare them, which take this naked, tanned, deformed Savages, for no other than wild beasts'. Instead of a proud 'Nation', Waterhouse denounced the Powhatan as 'wilde and Savage: yet as Slaves, bordering rebels, excommunicates and outlaws'.[18]

Waterhouse was not alone. The mathematician Henry Briggs, a former fellow of St John's, Cambridge, and Oxford's Savilian Professor of Geometry, annexed a pamphlet, discussing a northwest passage to the South Seas through the 'noble Plantation' of Virginia and the Hudson Bay to spread religion and commerce to benefit 'these poore ignorant Heathen people' for the 'publique good of all the Christian world'. (Briggs owned two shares in the Company.) Furthermore, an October 1622 letter, signed by Nicholas Ferrar, urged the Governor to execute 'a sharp revenge upon the bloody miscreants, [by] ... rooting them out for being [no] longer a people upon the face of the Earth'. The Company men were true to their word. Native American enslavement, which had begun soon after colonisation, continued until the early nineteenth century.[19]

Likewise, John Donne, who may have been awarded an honorary Doctor of Divinity from either Cambridge or Oxford in 1615 and later the Dean of St Paul's and chaplain to James I, helped to articulate the Company's exclusionary labour regime. Donne had tried to become the Company's secretary in 1609 but was appointed an honorary member of the council on 3 July 1622. He did not contribute money to the Company, which was already in great financial difficulty, yet he offered writings and sermons in service to that enterprise, some of which, as Thomas Festa makes clear, helped to establish the 'theoretical basis for future forms of enslavement'.[20]

Donne set out the purpose of the colonies: they were to be workhouses where vagrants, Native Americans, Black servants, and "undesirable" English subjects would be transported and worked on tobacco plantations for the benefit of Virginia's growing white colonial elite. He wrote that the 'Plantation' would 'redeeme many a wretch from the Jawes of death.... It shall sweep your streets, and wash your dores, from idle persons, and the children of idle persons, and imploy them'. Virginia would be a 'such a Bridewell [a London prison], to force idle persons to work'. As a result of ideas such as Donne's, the Company sent hundreds of impoverished children, ranging in age from eight to sixteen, who were forcibly transported to Virginia by the City of London from 1617 to 1622. In fashioning America's exploitative labour system, university-educated men were amongst its intellectual vanguard.[21]

At Trinity College, the lecturer and naturalist John Ray (or Wray) advocated for the seizure of Native American property. The venue for his anti-Indigenous discourse was the morning divinity exercises delivered in the chapel, which Ray later had collated and published (with further additions and notes from respected authorities). The Trinity fellow claimed that nature and its resources were a gift from God – a gift that had to be exploited through 'Improvement' and 'Industry'. The alternative to his 'civilised' ideal – a 'civil and well-cultivated Region' where naturalists 'enrich[ed] thy Country' through their discoveries, and English subjects leveraged the natural world for the good of 'Trade and Merchandise' – was a 'barren and desolate Wilderness'. The exemplars of such a "savage" culture which he proposed to Trinity students were ancient Scythia and the 'rude and unpolished *America*' – a continent where 'slothful and naked Indians' lived 'in pitiful Hutts and Cabans, made of Poles set endways' in a manner consistent with 'brute Beasts'. Ray's claims mirrored Virginian colonial rhetoric, which often infantilised Native warriors as indolent "savages" who turned prime agricultural estates into wastelands.[22]

The now-Faculty of History was a significant beneficiary of men such as Wray. Two prominent figures, Fulke Greville, 1st Baron Brooke, and Sir

Henry Spelman, an English antiquary, provided funds to support History lectureships. In 1628, the Baron Brooke, a shareholder in the Virginia Company, provided lands and £100 per annum 'for the founding of an History Lectureship in the University of Cambridge'. Spelman, who donated funds from a Middleton rectory and manuscripts for the formation of an Anglo-Saxon lectureship, had the support of the VC, Dr John Cosins, to become the MP for the University on account of this benefaction (but only seventy votes were cast in his favour), and he 'induced' a friend, Sir Ralph Hare, to donate to St John's College. Spelman was a founding member and treasurer, from 1627, of the English Guinea Company. The Guinea enterprise, whilst involved in enslavement, also had trading ambitions in ivory, gold, redwood, hides, and pepper grains in the Indian and Atlantic oceans, with voyages made from 1618 along the Gambia River. University benefactors were far more antagonistic towards Christian captivity in the Mediterranean. North African corsairs trafficked people from Italy, Portugal, Spain, England, France, and Hungary (with captives forced to labour until they were ransomed), and European states, in turn, seized Ottoman and Moroccan rowers for service on their galleys. The Craven Scholarships for two poor scholars at Cambridge (and another two at Oxford), which John Craven, 1st Baron Craven of Ryton, endowed in 1647, contained a clause assigning the residue of the fund 'for the redemption of English Christian captives and prisoners in algiers, or in any other places under the domination of the Turk'.[23]

The Atlantic trade in goods, such as tobacco, was neither a theoretical concern for the University nor merely a matter for personal consumption. By the seventeenth century, the University Court was a court of record, and the Vice-Chancellor presided over trade in the marketplace and issued licenses to taverns, vintners, and tobacco shops. In these stores, tobacco was cut into small pieces and sold by weight to eager consumers, who understood that product's origins. Europeans celebrated how 'The noble herb tobacco... journeys to us from afar across the seas from Mexico and Peru... it comes from wild people... [and] Makes for romping and sozzled and wild people'. John Swan, publishing as a former Trinity student, outlined the novel medicinal 'verteus' of tobacco from the 'West *Indies*': it eased headaches and 'helpeth' the pain of 'bitings' from 'mad dogs' (diseased canines were a common fear of English townsfolk). University officials, however, were worried at the traffic in a mind-altering product, especially after a Caian was caught in 1611 'puffing tobacco in Mr. Vice-Chancellor face when he came into the shop', and Trinity's Dean threatened expulsion from the fellowship for the consumption of tobacco in hall. Twelve years later, the Vice-Chancellor established rules for university members which regulated lecture attendance, dress, speech, and tobacco consumption. From 1635, at least seven Cambridge tobacconists were authorised to trade in heavily restricted amounts, but the court records are filled with cases of unlicensed retailers undermining the University-issued patents and selling to eager domestic consumers who coveted that drug as eagerly as they later did sugar, coffee, mahogany, and cotton goods.[24]

The Virginia Company's visions of empire, though, were a mirage. Beset with debt, dependent on lotteries to function, riddled with factionalism, and with the colony struggling to survive after the 1622 massacre, the Company was dissolved, and James I asserted royal rule over Virginia – a colonial structure that persisted in one form or another until American independence in 1776. The Somers Island Company remained a viable prospect, but investors suffered substantial losses (and they would not be the last from the era of company colonisation). Nicholas Ferrar owned £50 of stock in the Company. There were other investors who had university connections. George Montaigne, a former Queens' fellow from 1592 to 1611 and the Bishop of Lincoln, held ten pounds and twelve shillings worth of securities. He appeared on two lists of subscribers in 1618 and again in 1620, though the exact date of his initial investment remains unknown. The year that Montaigne first appeared as a subscriber he purchased property in Cambridge to endow two scholarships at his former college. Neither Ferrar nor Montaigne lost out as much as William Herbert, the 3rd Earl of Pembroke. Herbert, who along with James I helped to found Pembroke College, Oxford, remains immortalised in statue in front of the Bodleian Library. Along with East India Company money and his involvement in the Guinea Company, the former Chancellor of Oxford held £400 in Virginia stock and served on the king's council for the Company – a significant investment that resulted in a division of Bermuda being named in his honour. Herbert was said to have obtained a grant in Bermuda, yet his attempt at imperial riches was revoked on 6 April 1627 because of a previous claim by James Hay, 2nd Earl of Carlisle.[25]

Following the Virginia Company's dissolution, Cambridge men helped to establish the laws and religious structures of power that enabled slavery to grow and persist in New England. The first shipload of eighteen enslaved Africans arrived in that "city upon a hill" in 1638, barely eighteen years after the *Mayflower* landed at Cape Cod. The minister John Cotton had a profound role in shaping the laws governing New England. The son of a Derby lawyer, Cotton matriculated as a lowly Trinity sizar in 1598, then moved to Emmanuel, a puritan college, to finish his BA in 1603, and MA three years later. Accepting a fellowship at Emmanuel, he studied there for five more years, earning a reputation as a scholar and local preacher. His skills were in such demand that he preached the funeral sermon for Robert Some (or Soame), the Master of Peterhouse, and he soon left Cambridge to become a vicar of St Botolph's Church in Boston, Lincolnshire. A supporter of the French-Genevan theologian John Calvin and an even fiercer opponent of Catholicism, Cotton was forced to leave England after the accession of Charles I, who distrusted ardent Protestants. On leaving for North America, Cotton gave an impassioned address supporting colonisation, exalting the English 'to plant a colony' because their home was overcrowded, and he approved of those who wanted to leave for 'merchandize and gaine-sake' – arguing that God sanctioned the profit motive. He implored colonists to 'Arise then, this is not your rest'. The exodus included fellow Cantabrigians such as Thomas Hooker, the former Dixie Fellow at Emmanuel, and Roger Williams, who took his degree at Pembroke, and the leading lawyer John Winthrop, whose father was an auditor at Trinity College.[26]

Ministering in Boston, Massachusetts, until his death in December 1652, Cotton assisted in establishing a colonial charter that legalised slavery in New England. In the 1641 Massachusetts Body of Liberties, a legal code which Cotton helped to devise along with Nathaniel Ward (another Emmanuel alumnus), the text read that 'There shall never be any body slaverie villinage or Captivitie amongst us, unles it be lawfull Captives taken in just warres, and such strangers as willingly belie themselves or are sold to us'. The document read that 'those [persons] shall have all the liberties and Christian usages which the law of god established in Israell concerning such persons doeth morally require. This exempts none from servitude who shall be judged thereto by Authoritie'. That statute was not an antislavery clause – for one, it legally established that Indigenous people captive in war could be enslaved, and that "strangers," meaning African-descended peoples, were enslaved if obtained through exchange or purchase. King James II replaced the Body with a Provincial Charter in 1691, yet the code had legalised the Native American and African slave trades that were underway in North America. Predating the Barbados, Virginia, and Connecticut statutes on enslavement, Cotton's Charter had helped to legalise slavery in the English Americas.[27]

The governmental influence of Cambridge members and major benefactors was not restricted to statutes: William Sancroft, the-then Archbishop of Canterbury, designed the seal of Jamaica in 1661. Sancroft, a former Emmanuel master (1662–1665) and distinguished donor upon his death in 1692 of over 5,000 volumes to its library (which doubled in size thanks to his generosity), was well-acquainted with England's growing Atlantic empire. The moderate royalist was friends with Tobias Rustat, who served on the court of assistants to the RAC. In fact, Sancroft, who maintained his connections to Cambridge and its constituent colleges following this departure, appears to have 'helped to smooth the path of Rustat's gift' to the ancient universities: £1,000 to establish a fund for the University Library, the same amount to St John's, Oxford, and two fee-farms to Jesus College to support scholarships for the sons of deceased clergymen. Sancroft's seal for Jamaica had the king 'seated on his Throne, with two *Indians* [Native Americans] on their knees, presenting him *Fruits*, and two Cherubins aloft, supporting a Canopy'. On these administrative seals, Europeans depicted the 'barbarousness' and submissiveness of Indigenous peoples to justify their "civilising" mission in the Americas. Underneath Charles II's feet, the motto read: 'How sweet the fruit the hard rind yields'. The reverse of the seal featured a shield 'Bearing a Cross charged withe five Pines; two *Indians* for the *Supporters*, and for the *Crest* an *Alligator*'. There was a solemn prayer for a Christian empire: 'Behold the cross hath spread its arms into another world and beareth fruit'. Delivered to Jamaica's incoming governor Sir Charles Lyttleton, the seal's motto was ominous in tone: 'The Indians twain shall serve one Lord'. The depiction of Native Americans as royal vassals was, of course, at odds with the reality of well-organised Indigenous resistance to English colonialism in the Americas and the self-confident diplomatic missions that various Indigenous communities, sovereign nations, and confederacies made to the European continent.[28]

The "puritans," as their enemies called them, soon colonised the Bahamas. In the aftermath of the Civil War, the royalists banished Bermuda's religious dissidents to the Bahamas, which had been claimed in 1629 but remained uncolonised. Enter John Mapletoft. At fourteen years old, Mapletoft matriculated as a Trinity College pensioner, graduating with a Bachelor's degree around 1652, entering the fellowship in 1653, and gaining a doctorate in divinity in 1690. A friend of the philosopher John Locke, he was the Physic Professor at Gresham, and a diplomat to Denmark. It was perhaps through these political and academic connections that he became a signatory to the Articles of Association of the Company of Adventurers to the Bahama Islands in September 1672. Holding £100 in stock, an investment which Locke later took possession of, Mapletoft's fellow subscribers claimed a thirty-one-year lease on 12,000 acres in New Providence (modern-day Nassau), with rights and royalties on resources ranging from gold to gems, ambergris to pearls, and whales to shipwrecks. At the time, the population of the Bahamas included 403 enslaved people (almost half of the total) and investors intended on founding colonies. Sir Peter Colleton, an investor, noted that 'planting is my trade and I thinke I may without vanity say I understand it as well as most men'. Although unsuccessful (like many of these imperial schemes), the Bahamas Company was merely another imperial enterprise that Cambridge-educated religious men turned to their economic benefit.[29]

Soon, Cambridge alumni, fellows, and lecturers became fervent evangelists to this growing empire from the Atlantic to the Indian oceans. The Church's support for imperial activities made sense given that church men were integral figures in the British establishment. Cambridge Anglicans bolstered the monarchy, political state, and the hierarchical social order. The Church helped to forge a distinctive Protestant British national identity – a religious culture of nationalism that sought to combat the Catholic powers of France and Spain. With the twin pillars of the May 1662 Act of Uniformity in public prayers and sacrament and the Book of Common Prayer in place, the 'Anglican establishment' became more impregnable in the reign of Queen Anne, with Dissenters marginalised and excluded from office and from teaching or running schools

(Jewish people, too, remained without equal rights). In time, the 'Church upheld the natural hierarchy of mutual obligations which were thought to provide social cohesion, and the State protected the legal establishment as the appropriate agent of benevolence and public morality'. Due to its prestige, the clergy were increasingly drawn from gentile families; indeed, in one parish the number of elite incumbents more than doubled between 1683 and 1730, though historians have also suggested that this shift in social class perhaps had as much to do with expanding meanings of the term "gentlemen" at that time. These sons – some of them from enslaver backgrounds – took degrees at Cambridge, to the extent that at the beginning of the eighteenth century seventy-eight per cent of graduates were ordained. With their educations and backgrounds, these alumni took up fellowships and, if they had the right connections, parish positions and bishoprics. These esteemed clergymen increasingly saw the future of Protestantism abroad.[30]

Anti-Catholicism, the perception that Catholics posed a clear and present danger to the nation's internal and external security, provided added impetus to these missionary efforts. Catholics were demonised in this era as idolatrous, cruel, traitorous, and, importantly, 'anti-English' fanatics who were intent on forging a religious empire. England's anti-Papist stance was rooted, in part, in real or imagined plots, including the unsuccessful effort to blow up the House of Lords on 5 November 1605, and the fabrications of that 'great dunce', Titus Oates (who attended Cambridge but did not graduate). Oates whipped the kingdom into a three-year frenzy (1678–1681) due to his false claim that the Pope's adherents were plotting to assassinate Charles II. Spanish atrocities in the Americas also mobilised the English against Catholics. Thomas Taylor, who had been a fellow and tutor at Christ's, preached in 1612 against the 'Romish Wolves': the 'effusion of blood, which the Popish Spaniards have made among the poore Indians [Native Americans], under the pretence of converting them to the faith'. Taylor reported that Hispaniola had seen its 'seven and twenty millions of People… destroyed', with its Taíno indigenous inhabitants 'throwne downe from the top of a steep mountaine 700 men together' – atrocities that had led 'poore men' to 'hang themselves with their wives and children' and the women to 'dash their owne childrens braines against the stones' to avoid falling into Spanish hands. Nevertheless, England's criticisms of the Spanish must be tempered with the realities of their empire, as white Virginian colonists waged wars against their 'deadliest enemies', the Native Americans, with reports that the children of one chief had been thrown 'overboard and shoteinge owtt their Braynes in the water'.[31]

Cambridge's inhabitants were party to this anti-Catholic fervour after William, the Prince of Orange, landed with his Dutch forces at Torbay, Devon, on 5 November 1688. English aristocrats had invited the Protestant Prince to rule following the birth of James II's son, James Francis Edward (which seemed to portent a new Catholic dynasty), but the town and gown population were intent on discovering potential enemies. On the night of 13 December, ten days before James abandoned the country (with James's army abandoning him first), the Cambridge Alderman recalled that '2 *or* 300 (*many scholars among them*)' were rioting under the 'pretence to seeke for papists' and their allies, with houses 'ransack[ed]' for 'armes'. The crowd were driven into a frenzy because of reports that '5 or 6000 of the Irish' had sacked nearby Bedford and 'cutt all their throats' and were now on route to Cambridge to perpetrate similar atrocities. In the confusion, candles were lit in solemn prayer, some fled town to 'escape the danger', and others took revenge on their neighbours. Fear of the 'Irish beasts', as one Cambridge fellow had earlier labelled Catholics across the Irish Sea, was a potent motivating force in local and national politics.[32]

Aware of the Catholic threat, Cambridge men were in the vanguard of missionary Anglicanism, hoping to bring the light of Protestantism to the "pagan" world. The various companies appealed to senior scholars and doctors at the University to find 'godly minister[s]' with offers of money and lodging. As Captain Roger Wood, the governor of Bermuda wrote to one Cambridge graduate in the 1630s, appealing for him to come and 'help us': 'It pleased God in his providence to guide your tongue unto such a strayne at Cambridge that swept you out of all your former imaginations and dreames of lyving at ease in Syon and for to make you more sensible off it the Highe Priest hath banished you forth of his jurisdiction'. For that reason, Cambridge men enthusiastically proselytised on behalf of the East India Company too. The Company, which had been first formed on 31 December 1600, soon expanded, establishing a foothold in Gujarat and its first factory in Machilipatnam in modern-day Andhra Pradesh.[33]

Cambridge men arrived in the early stages of South Asian colonisation with the aim of proselytising to the local population (and forming a bridgehead against Catholic evangelism). Richard Elliott joined the Company in 1677 after a successful academic career at Eton, where he was a King's Scholar, and at Eton's sister institution King's College, Cambridge, where he was a fellow from 1669 and provided more than £1,681 for the purchase of three advowsons. Missionary enthusiasm had its limits, however. Some clergymen in the Caribbean despaired at the white colonists' hesitancy to 'Propagate the Gospel among either Blacks or Whites'. One writer observed in 1730 that he was acquainted with 'near Thirty Gentlemen, Natives of the *Leeward-Islands*, who had their Education at *Oxford*, *Cambridge*, or *Trinity-College*, where of some profess the Law, and some Physick' – but 'none of them' had thought to 'study Divinity, or enter into Holy Orders, that they might supply the Churches of their Native Country'.[34]

Financial support for the EIC and other imperial enterprises partly underpinned the collegiate religious mission. In the March 1736 will of John Craister, the Trinity fellow provided £400 of funding so that the College could purchase a 'perpetual advowson' (the right to recommend someone to a vacant position in the clergy), but in time, he preferred that the sum be laid out in 'such Security'. Trinity's Senior Bursar, the Reverend Dr John Paris (who later funded a prize for the best Latin declamation), received £550 from Craister's executors, which he then used to purchase 'five East India Bonds of £100 each purchased with pt. of the £550 lodged in the hands of the Coll on July 5, 1738'. From 1739 to 1742, the India stock earned more than £80 in interest.[35]

More colleges followed suit: Magdalene helped to fund repairs to its chapel with East India money, and Jesus and Trinity Hall fellows showed a particular predilection for that investment. At Jesus, Dr Charles Proby, who had a benefaction fund in his name (part of which was invested in South Sea stock), had £400 invested. At Trinity Hall, George Oxenden's donation of £150 was used to purchase East India bonds, which were then sold to finance another donation; the fellow Charles Pinfold (who would go on to become the Governor of Barbados), supported Dr John Chetwode's scholarship fund with £250 in India securities; and John Andrews, whose benefaction was never received by the college due to legal problems, had £1,000 invested in the Company. Furthermore, Exton Sayer, a South Sea investor, fellow of the College from 1714 to 1724, and later a Whig Parliamentarian, helped the East India enterprise politically, leading the government in its efforts to stop an opposition attempt to end the Company's monopoly.[36]

Samuel Blythe's benefaction to Clare was more significant than all these investments in shaping a college. Doncaster born and bred, Blythe (or Blyth) did not come from great wealth – he rose due to his prodigious abilities to take a BA by 1656 (matriculating as a sizar), an MA in 1659, and his DD in 1679. In between his first and third degrees, Blythe became a fellow at Clare, the Vice-Chancellor in 1684–1685, and Master from 1678 until his death on 19 April 1713. As he ascended the academic ladder, Blythe was also a deacon in Ely, the vicar of Everton in Huntingdonshire, and a rector of Newton in the Isle of Ely. Blythe provided almost the entirety of his estate, besides smaller bequests, to Clare, worth around £6,000, for the purchase of advowsons. As scholars attest, Blythe was 'a great benefactor', the College's 'principal benefactor', and a Master whose bequest 'guaranteed its [Clare's] continuing success and prosperity'.[37]

The college records reveal that Blythe used a small part of his significant wealth to fund colonial endeavours. In November 1699, he purchased £400 of East India Company stock – securities which were provided to Clare and were intended to purchase a parsonage in Duxford. The Duxford purchase did not occur until March 1869; still, the College made over £271 from the stock's interest between 1713 and 19 April 1716. The great benefactor was no stranger to the empire in North America. In 1673, his account book made note of a 'Henry Perrott born at Rapahanocke in Virginia' on a 450-acre plantation, who was 'admitted by Mr. [Charles] Alston in my absence under my [Blythe's] care'.[38]

Hoping to make a tidy profit, Clare sold the EIC stock in 1716. They valued the four securities at £576, yet they received a windfall of £592, which was then used to purchase Bank of England stock to support the benefaction (by 1723, the College had £3,500 laid out in that security). Blythe was deceased and therefore had no involvement in the transaction, but in October 1719 Dr Richard Laughton and William Grigg, the Master, invested £500 from the College chest in South Sea bonds. After receiving £20 in interest, the bonds were sold for £300 Bank of England stock on 4 April 1723 and the surplus given to Grigg. In effect, both these investments – the East India and South Sea money – continued, through the Bank of England purchases, to buttress Clare's finances, cementing Blythe's legacy as the College's most significant and generous benefactor.[39]

Cambridge fellows can even be found on the founding documents of successor organisations to the original East India Company. Bartholomew Wortley, a fellow and lecturer at Caius, appears to have invested at least 500 pounds in new East India Company shares in 1698 and, as a result, was named on their foundation charter. The son of a humble plumber from Fakenham, Norfolk, Wortley took his BA in 1676, MA in 1679, and held a Caius fellowship until 1706. The plumber's son displayed such an aptitude for classical languages that he was elected to a lectureship in Hebrew from 1690 until 1696. His EIC investment would have been consistent with his religious attitudes and economic hopes for profit, given that he would have expected to receive dividends from the Company's imperial activities that its founders assured could be 'devise[d]' in one's 'last Will and Testament'.[40]

The new EIC was created, in part, in response to well-founded criticisms of the original firm: that it had monopolised trade and restricted it from "interlopers," and that it had not endeavoured to spread Protestant Christianity abroad and limit the global spread of Catholicism. That cause was one that Wortley, given his later religious position as a parish clerk in Bratton Fleming, Devon, would have wholeheartedly supported. The enterprise's mercantile founders planned to maintain a minister and schoolmaster in their garrisons and factories whilst providing 'a decent place for divine service'. The founders of the new East India Company instructed missionaries 'to learn the Portugueze and Hindoo languages, to enable them to instruct the Gentoos &c in the Christian religion[.]' Enslavement was also mentioned in the Company charter (unsurprisingly given that the EIC had traded in Madagascan enslaved persons and had tried to establish a slave society in St Helena in the South Seas based on 'a Barbados discipline'). The document ordered local ministers to 'instruct the Gentoos, that shall be the Servants or Slaves of the Company, or of their Agents in the Protestant Religion'. Wortley's interest appears to have ended with his signing of the charter, as the old and new Companies, which had no measurable competition, decided in 1708 to merge and form the "United Company of Merchants Trading to the East Indies," more commonly known as the "Honourable East India Company."[41]

Wortley continued to invest in colonial companies, holding £160 in South Sea trading stock. By the end of his long life, Wortley owned around £437 in South Sea shares and annuities. He loathed the Company's 'Villain Directors' – an insult that suggests that Wortley had been an investor in the firm before the stock Bubble burst – and he mentioned that his original shareholding 'was all reduced' to £500 because it had in part been paid 'of ye principle' and 'part Annihilated of the Annuities'. William Barbor, one of Wortley's tireless executors, struggled to judge the size or significance of these securities, informing Sir Thomas Gooch that he had unfortunately found 'as yet no Papers for ye S S Stock'. In total, Wortley's benefaction of over £7,000 funded two fellowships, £400 towards casing the east and west sides of Gonville Court and in rebuilding the north side, five pounds spent annually on a Commemoration Feast on 23 February, and advowsons in Beachampton in Buckinghamshire, and Kirstead in Norfolk – with most of these expenses involving dividends from his original SSC investments.[42]

In striving for religious conversion in the English colonies, Wortley had company within his college. After his schooling in Ely, Owen Stockton then proceeded to Christ's College, but soon migrated to Caius where he was elected a junior fellow, senior fellow, Hebrew lecturer, steward, and a catechist (a teacher of Christian principles). Following his death, Stockton expressed a desire to extend those Christian principles to the North American colonies. Amongst his other bequests, which included £500 and his book collection to Caius, he promised a donation of £140 (or £20 per annum for seven years) to Harvard's Indian College, established around the 1640s, so that Native Americans could be converted and trained to preach the gospel in their language. The clause in the will, which was never carried out (it was predicated on his daughter passing away at an early age), stipulated that if the convert 'do so long reside in the said Colledge and at the End of every Seven Years or sooner, vacancy by Death or otherwise a new one to be chosen'. (He was not alone in his enthusiasm for Harvard's mission: John Lightfoot, the Master of St Catharine's, also donated his Old Testament books and 'oriental literature' to that college upon his death, which were later destroyed in a 1764 fire.) For the English, the Christianisation of Native Americans was seen as an effective method of transforming Indigenous peoples into loyal subjects (though the reality was that Indigenous peoples who did convert to Christianity often used their faith to build strategic alliances with the colonists on their own terms). After a protracted legal process in which the Court of Chancery vested Stockton's £500 donation in South Sea securities, the money entered Caius's possession. From 1727 to 1739, the College made more than £300 from annuities dividends.[43]

None of these investments were novel: Cambridge investors in colonial companies had likeminded friends further north in Scotland. The Company of Scotland Trading to Africa and the Indies, which aimed to establish a commercial empire on the isthmus of Panama, depended upon significant defenders from Edinburgh University, amongst other institutions. The Company's investors included James Gregory, the Professor of Mathematics, George Mosman, a bookseller and library donor, Thomas Young, the city magistrate and donor, Sir Robert Sibbald, the first Professor of Medicine, Archibald

Pitcairn, a Professor of Medicine, Sir Archibald Stevenson, a Doctor and Professor, Sir Robert Chiesly, the Lord Provost, and Alexander Rule, Professor of Oriental Languages. Furthermore, William Scott, the Regent of Humanity (a position overseeing teaching and administration), and David Gregory, a Professor of Mathematics, published in support of Scotland's empire, with the former organising a harangue (or lecture) in defense of colonisation, declaiming that the 'Isthmus of Darien is ours by well-merited right' and 'this Colony of ours will be able to stand four-square against the unjust attacks of them [the Spanish] or of any others, for Scots today, even as of old, are as brave in defence of their gains as in the making of them'. Cambridge, then, did not hold a monopoly over the phenomenon of universities committing their ideas and purses to colonisation – Edinburgh men were similarly invested in the Atlantic imperial project.[44]

When not investing in trading companies and colonial colleges, Cambridge fellows were heavily involved in missionary organisations. Founded in 1701 by the Reverend Thomas Bray, the SPG and the Society for the Promotion of Christian Knowledge (SPCK) had numerous adherents in Cambridge. The SPG was a plantation owner after a charitable bequest from Christopher Codrington, the former governor of the Leeward Islands, in 1710 to fund and support what became Codrington College in Barbados. On an individual basis, the list of college fellows who subscribed to the SPCK was extensive: John Mapletoft, Thomas Chapman, the Master of Magdalene, John Reepe of King's, John Green, Master of Corpus, Stephen Whisson of Trinity, the Reverend Robert Leman of Caius, and Henry Hubbard of Emmanuel, to name just a few. Multiple colleges donated money to the SPG and SPCK – small benefactions that assisted organisations with connections to the Caribbean. The Bursar Books and Council Minutes show that Caius made three donations of five pounds, ten pounds, and fifteen pounds respectively to the SPCK in 1727 (principally so that the New Testament could be translated into Arabic) and the SPG in 1743 and 1752. Corpus Christi provided money too. In Michaelmas term 1743, the College donated ten pounds and ten shillings 'to the Society for propagating Xtian knowledge', and, seven years after the first recorded donation, Corpus provided the same amount for the 'Propagation of the Gospel'. On both a personal and institutional level, Cambridge men were clearly committed to missionary enterprises.[45]

The SPG owned the Codrington estate, yet the SPCK's operations intersected, too, with imperial and plantation operations in both hemispheres of the British Empire. Henry Newman, the Society's secretary, conversed regularly with Jamaica's political class. In January 1723, he contacted the Governor of Port Royal, hoping that 'you live very elegantly and get a vast deal of money, at which all your Friends here rejoice', though he regretted the 'Bubble' for the 'Mine Adventure' in Jamaica. Supported with investments from, among others, Benjamin Hoadly, a former fellow at St Catharine's (1697–1701) and chaplain to George I, and Henry Bland, a late King's College fellow, the Adventurers had made abortive efforts to mine gold in the colonies. Newman's letters to Jamaica contained news about Cambridge as well. The newspapers, he noted to Jamaica's governor, Henry Bentinck, 1st Duke of Portland, 'give me leave only to mention that the new Institutions of 24 Preachers of Whitehall selected by the Bp of London from both Universities, and the New Professorships erected by the king in each University for Modern History & Languages has had a wonderfull Effect on some of the Clergy to dispose them to a better temper for his Majesty's Govermt. than they seem'd to leave when yr. Grace left the Kingdom'.[46]

Aside from the new Professorship of Modern History, Cambridge-affiliated men displayed their "temper" for the king's government through imperial enterprises in India. In 1709, the SPCK organised for a printer to travel to Tranquebar to translate the Bible into Tamil, and missionaries soon followed. The missionary expedition was funded with the assistance of Cambridge men. Two years later, the SPCK's India accounts mention 'Cash received of the University of Cambridge by Mr Chamberlayne' – around £20 in total. (A donation that was supplemented with individual subscriptions, including from William Ayerst, the Canon of Canterbury and former Queens' fellow.) South Sea investments underpinned these operations – with Elizabeth Chamberlyn's 1724 donation to the SPCK including £300 in capital stock and £700 in annuities. The treasurers who organised these donations and the finances of the SPCK had connections to the ancient universities, too, with John Denne – the Archdeacon of Rochester and tutor and fellow of Corpus – helping to purchase £4,000 in South Sea annuities to support the missionary enterprise. Given their extensive involvement in college finances, fellows made prudent treasurers.[47]

Cambridge fellows also assisted the Associates of Dr Bray, a philanthropic group established to educate enslaved African Americans. Funded with the assistance of a Dutch associate, Abel Tassin d'Alonne, a private secretary to the English monarchy, Bray and his four Associates began their work on 15 January 1724, hoping to use D'Allone's generous £900 donation to build Black schools in the colonies. After sending twenty missionaries to America, Bray's Associates allied with James Oglethorpe's convict colonisation project in Georgia, supported by university luminaries such as John Helsop, a Sidney Sussex fellow and Proctor, and Edward Waring, the Lucasian Professor of Mathematics at Cambridge, who was included on a list of men making 'Provision for Parochial Libraries, and for Instructing the Negroes in the British Plantations'.[48]

Matthias Mawson, the Master of Corpus from 1724 to 1744 and the legatee of property to fund twelve scholarships at that college, assisted the Bray Associates too. On behalf of that enterprise, he distributed eighty copies of Erasmus's *Ecclesiastes* to the colleges, which, though published in 1535, continued to shape the practices and role of preachers. Mawson, of course, recognised the significance of the American economy to British prosperity, preaching in 1743 of his desire to convert 'those poor miserable People the Slaves, from whose Labours and Toil arises so great a Part of the Wealth of this Nation'. The Georgia enterprise enjoyed Corpus Christi's generous patronage following Mawson's Mastership. In the College accounts for Michaelmas 1751, the College provided ten shillings and six pence 'To the Governor of Georgia', William Stephens, who led a colony that maintained a ban on slavery until four years later, in 1755 (though the rules and regulations on the prohibition of enslavement had been lifted since 1751).[49]

The stakes, to Cambridge men, were high in their American colonies. Religion was a competitive marketplace – and Anglicanism was not the only belief system available to white colonists, Native Americans, and enslaved Africans. The Governor of North Carolina, Charles Eden, desperately wrote recommending Thomas Gale of Trinity College as a missionary because 'our Tedious Indian Warr has reduced the Country so lowe' that without the 'Nursing Care' of religion the people would be 'wholly lead away by the Quakers'. In that struggle for religious supremacy, Mawson, who had invested £250 of the college's funds in the South Sea Company around the Bubble, and other prominent Cambridge Anglicans were eager supporters of missionary efforts.[50]

Across the Irish Sea, George Berkeley, the Bishop of Cloyne in the Church of Ireland, benefitted from the largesse of Cambridge members too. In 1725 Berkeley, who remains famous for his philosophical contributions to human knowledge and vision, accelerated plans to establish a college in Bermuda that trained evangelists to Native Americans – a 'reservoir' of 'learning and religion, and streaming through all parts of America… purging away the ill manners and irreligion of our Colonies, as well as the blindness and barbarity of the nations round them'. Cambridge men aided his ambitious project: Henry Finch, the Dean of York and former Christ's fellow (who also gave £100 for redesigning the College hall's interior), and his brother Daniel, the 2nd Earl of Nottingham, provided £300; and Dr Edward Pelling, an alumnus and former Trinity fellow, donated £100 before his death. Given that Sir Matthew Decker, the former governor of the SSC and the-then Director of the EIC, donated money, the scheme was not averse to racial chattel slavery – and Berkeley illustrated that point when he moved to Rhode Island with his wife, Anne Forster (the daughter of the Chief Justice of the Irish Common Pleas), and purchased "Whitehall" plantation where he enslaved between three and five Africans. Finding secure employment in North America, Berkeley had less success with his proposal for a Bermuda college – and, when Parliament's promises of a grant proved illusory, a disenchanted and frustrated Berkeley returned to London in 1732.[51]

These imperial connections included more than financial muscle – Cambridge men were closely involved in organising, facilitating, and spreading the SPG's mission. Thomas Tenison, who graduated from Corpus Christi in 1657 and was elected a fellow two years later, helped to establish the SPG as the Archbishop of Canterbury. Tenison was involved in the Codrington plantations in St John's parish in eastern Barbados and served on its organising committee, which spent much of its time managing the estate, approving expenditures, and buying and selling enslaved people, who were later branded with the word 'SOCIETY' to 'mark ye Negros'. Aside from ensuring the 'keeping up the full number' of the around 300 enslaved labourers on the Society's two sugarcane plantations, the committee debated whether the 'Plantation may be purged of such Negroes as are Burthensome to it'. The Cambridge-connected churchmen who joined Tenison on the committee at various points included Sir William Dawes, who served as chair on some occasions whilst he was the Bishop of Chester and Master of St Catherine's College (1697-1714), Thomas Gooch, who also attended whilst he was both a fellow and then the master of Caius, John Moore, Bishop of Ely and Visitor of Trinity College, and Lionel Gatford, who funded two exhibitions at Jesus College.[52]

As a testament to his American missionary zeal, Tenison became the Vice-Chancellor of the College of William and Mary and later bequeathed £1,000 for the American episcopacy along with books to establish a proposed college in Barbados. In his generous will, Tenison donated another £1,000 for mortgaging land to Corpus Christi College – the profits devoted to the augmentation of scholarships, and the residue to supplementing the fellows' income. Cambridge men were inspired by Tenison to travel to the Caribbean, but with often deadly results. In December 1745, William Bryant of St John's, Cambridge, returned 'his hearty Thanks to the Society for choosing him their Professor in Philosophy and in Mathematicks for Codrington College' and he hoped that the committee would hold the position until 'the latter End of January to finish the Course of Lectures, which he is at present engaged in Reading in that university.' The climate and the regular, rampant outbreaks of smallpox and yellow fever there did not agree with his health, and Bryant died soon after his arrival.[53]

Thomas Sherlock, the Master of St Catharine's following Dawes's tenure, was an adherent to the SPG and a member of the Barbados Committee, too, and like Thomas Thompson maintained that the Christian Gospel did not interfere with civil property – property being defined to include enslaved Africans. Sherlock enjoyed successive positions as the Bishop of Bangor in 1728, then of Salisbury in 1734, and then of London from 1748. The St Catherine's man was mistrusted, however, in Hanoverian circles for his expansion of church powers – and, given his interest in appointing chaplains for the East India Company and unsuccessful proposal to provide English bishops with the power over the colonial church (ecclesiastical responsibility for the overseas church was then concentrated with the Bishop of London), these administrators had some cause for concern. Sherlock penned strong opinons on ancient and more modern forms of enslavement and shared them with readers during a rancorous pamphlet debate which escalated after Benjamin Hoadly, the-then Bishop of

Bangor, questioned in March 1717 the biblical justification for church government. Writing from a High Church position a year later, Sherlock, then Master, rebutted Hoadly's assertion that the 'Example' of Jesus Christ was '*much more peculiarly fit for Slaves than to Subjects*' as the former, like their crucified Lord, were forced to suffer arbitrary authority without revenge or rancour. The Master argued, however, that slavery was not the most degraded condition one could experience. 'It was never true in Fact', he wrote, 'that *Slaves* were in virtue of their *constant Condition the lowest and most helpless sort of Mankind…* in every Countrey many Subjects were in a more *distressed* and *low* Condition than the better sort of Slaves'. Furthermore, he accused his opponent of gaining 'all his intelligence about slaves from the West Indies' and had thereby conflated the '*Slaves* of Antiquity' with '*Negroes*' – indeed, Sherlock may have been somewhat anxious at the prospect that the enslaved Africans were treated as people who could, as a result of their status, particularly understand and follow Christ's example relative to whites.[54]

Cambridge-educated clergy also debated whether the Christianisation of enslaved persons made them free, as enslavement for African-descended persons was, in part, predicated on their "heathen" status. William Fleetwood, the future Bishop of Ely and King's fellow from 1678 (and another enthusiastic South Sea investor), addressed the SPG at Mary-le-Bow in London on 16 February 1711 to reassure slaveholders that enslaved conversions did not lead to freedom. To assuage their concerns, he pleaded that there was 'no fear of losing the Service and Profit of their Slaves, by letting them become *Christians*… [enslavers] are neither prohibited by the Laws of *God*, nor those of the *Land*, from keeping *Christian Slaves*; their Slaves are no more at Liberty after they are Baptized, than they were before'. He claimed that there were 'People in St. *Paul's* time, that imagin'd they were freed from all former Engagements by becoming *Christians*; but St. *Paul* tells them, this was not the Meaning of *Christian Liberty*; the Liberty wherewith *Christ* had made them Free, was Freedom from their Sins'. The rights of liberty, he observed, originated from being '*English-Men*', not Christians. Finishing his sermon, he noted that 'If therefore it be lawful in our Country, to have or keep any Slaves at all, it is equally lawful to have or keep them so, tho' they are *Christians*'. Progressively, race, not religion, determined enslavement and freedom.[55]

Early SPG missionaries, in time, discussed what Travis Glasson calls 'ethnic theology': the religious debates, which relied on Genesis, over whether Africans were natural slaves. The debate concerned the Biblical Curse of Ham, where Noah had cursed Canaan, the child of Noah's son Ham, after Ham had seen 'the nakedness of his father'. The passage reads: 'Cursed be Canaan! The lowest of slaves will be his brothers'. Never mind that the curse was more of an omen, Cambridge theologians debated the meaning of this passage and how it related to Africans. To Richard Kidder, a former Emmanuel fellow and Bishop of Bath and Wells, Africans were the descendants of Ham. In his 1694 *Commentary*, he noted the 'servile and base condition of *Canaan's* Race. And *Canaan* shall be his servant'. Simon Patrick, the Dean of Peterborough and a Queens' College fellow, similarly concluded that the 'Four Sons of *Ham* and their Children, had all *Africa* for their Portion… and no small part of *Asia* which fell the share of *Cush* and *Canaan*'. More than half a century later, Thomas Newton, the Bishop of Bristol, dean of St Paul's Cathedral, chaplain to George II, and Trinity fellow, extended these arguments. Drawing upon Augustin Calamet's *Dictionary of the Holy Bible* (who himself relied upon the Persian writer al-Tabarī's *Ta'rīkh*), Newton argued that the 'whole continent of Africa was peopled principally by the children of Ham' and the sons of Ham were the 'servant of servants'. The debate on the suitability of Africans as slaves, it must be remembered, coincided with a period when Cambridge alumni and professors, such as the Caian graduate Adam Elyott and Simon Ockley, the Adams Professor of Arabic, published captivity narratives about themselves and others. After graduating, Barbary pirates captured and sold Elyott into slavery – his escape from which he publicised in a later pamphlet. Anti-African prejudice, therefore, flourished at a time when knowledge about that continent (not to mention the realities of racial enslavement and white Christian captivity) were at their height.[56]

The SPG's conciliatory approach to slavery was emblematic of how many Cambridge fellows tolerated and facilitated Britain's slave empire. David Humphreys, a fellow at Trinity from 1719 and Secretary to the SPG, defined the Society's goals in his 1728 history of the organisation. With Native Americans and West Africans having become accustomed to the English language, Humphreys believed it was a 'great Reproach to the Christian Name, that so many Thousands of Persons should continue in the same State of *Pagan* Darkness, under a Christian Government, and living in Christian Families, as they lay before under, in their own Heathen Countries'. Humphreys worried, however, that the SPG may have done more harm than good. 'Many Planters', he complained, 'allow them one Day in a Week [Sunday], to clear Ground and plant it, to subsist themselves and Families'. In effect, the enslavers had used rest days for Christian services to further work their exhausted labourers and force them to provide provisions for their families. Humphreys wrote that the SPG had to contend with anti-Black prejudice, with some enslavers arguing that '*Negroes* had no souls', or 'that they grew worse by being taught and made Christians'. Humphrey did not challenge these statements – rather, he pointed to the Christian school in New York, which ministered to the city's population of African and Native American enslaved persons, as civilised institutions for "heathens" in the New World. To illustrate the benefits of conversion, he referred to the enslaved revolt in New York City on the night of 6 April 1712, when twenty-three Akan enslaved people set fire to an outhouse in the East Ward, with the flames providing an opportunity to ambush and kill the white colonists who had arrived to put out the conflagration. Hit-and-run tactics and efforts to weaken the enemy through sporadic, targeted fighting, rather than through more drawn-out set-piece engagements (as was common in European warfare), were a feature of some West African military cultures. Nevertheless, the revolt failed, and Humphreys was eager to inform his readers that 'the Persons, whose *Negroes* were found to be the most guilty, were such as were the declared Opposers of making them Christians'. In the face of suspicion about their motives, he recognised that enslavers – the 'Masters of Families' – needed to be made allies if missionary efforts were to succeed.[57]

Cambridge men soon argued that Christianisation would render enslaved people more docile workers for their white enslavers. As a result, Christianity became a tool for perpetuating and defending slavery. The SPG had to rebut the enslavers' fearful claims that Christian belief resulted in enslaved rebellions, such as the September 1739 Stono Revolt in South Carolina and the New York slave conspiracy in 1741. The minister Anthony Ellys's solution to these revolts was Christian conversion. He had entered Clare College as a pensioner in 1709, becoming a fellow in 1714 and took his doctorate in divinity at Cambridge in 1728. In a February 1759 sermon, Ellys noted the 'advantage of making good Christians, even of the Negro-slaves, will also be very worthy of consideration'. The advantages of Christian instruction, he thought, were many: 'For in proportion as their obstinacy, sullenness, and eagerness for revenge shall come to be abated and altered by religion, they will make better servants'. Ellys's hopes went further still. He claimed that Black Christians would discipline and police the plantation. Black people, he wrote, 'may become guards and defenders of their masters; and there will be no longer any such revolts and insurrections among them as have sometimes been detrimental, if not even dangerous, to several of the colonies'. Further emphasising the ties between slavery and colonisation, Ellys hoped that Black conversion would make these Americans more 'firmly attached to our national interest' and a firm 'barrier' against 'the assaults of the heathen savages who lie farther behind them[.]' Missionaries were thinking strategically in moulding arguments that would appeal to the enslaver class, and the notion that enslaved Black men, in particular, could act as auxiliaries and a buffer against Native American raids or African slave revolts would, he believed, convince wary colonists to aid the SPG.[58]

Not all missionaries, it should be remembered, agreed on the issue of enslavement. The yearly sermons before the Georgia colony's governing Trustees – addresses which often supported those colonists who aimed to propagate slavery there – expressed some discomfort with this important issue. George Harvest, a Magdalene fellow, agreed, of course, with the utility of the colonies, arguing that, rather than depopulate nations (as some contemporaries argued), colonists were useful auxiliaries in the service of the colony of Georgia, which, as a bulwark against the Spanish colonies in East and West Florida and French-controlled Louisiana, was 'the *Gibraltar* of AMERICA'. He supported, too, the Trustees' commercial ambitions, noting in his 1749 address that 'the Fitness of the Land for Cultivation has been fully attested' in such goods as silk, an 'industrious Worm [that] lives a Lesson to the Sluggard… [by] inviting both Young and Old, Women and Children, and even the Aged Impotent, to employ their gentle Labour to improve and bring it to Perfection'. Unlike Virginia, his dreams of an empire of silk had some basis in fact – the first Seal of the Trustees featured a silkworm egg, and, at its peak, women were being paid between twenty to twenty-five pounds per annum to train their fellow colonists in the art of silk-making, with the work of 500 women being estimated to produce silk worth over £28,125. (The dream ended with the advent of enslavement and widespread rice cultivation, which had labour demands at just the time of the year when labourers were needed for silk harvesting and production.) The Magdalene man took a more sombre tone on the problem of enslavement. 'That profane Plea against the baptizing *Negroes*', he argued, 'namely, that they are thereby released from their Slavery; I designedly pass over, as being of no possible Weight with *Christians*'. Furthermore, Harvest rebutted that the 'free Constitution' of Georgia 'abhors Slavery' and he was confident his audience would 'all agree with me, that Slaves ought to be made *thus free!* May the Spirit of the Lord prevail among them, that they may have this blessed Liberty! May that Master, whose Service is the most perfect Freedom, make them *free indeed*! And, by his Grace, emancipate them from their State of Pagan Bondage, into the glorious Freedom and Liberty of the Sons of God!' Harvest, a long-forgotten fellow, articulated his vision of a Christian path to freedom through religious conversion.[59]

That possible avenue to freedom was closing in Georgia. Buoyed by the relaxation of antislavery laws, the population of white colonists there increased from 500 in 1741 to 2,381 in 1753, and the number of enslaved Africans grew exponentially from 600 in 1751 to 15,000 in 1775. Thomas Francklin, a Trinity College fellow, preached his 1750 sermon in Westminster to the Trustees as the colony was on the cusp of a such a profound shift in its social and economic makeup. He lauded the Georgia colonists because they had established the colony without 'Force and Violence' – 'no Property was invaded, no Blood spilt' – and, he maintained, there was 'originally design'd that there should be no such Thing as Slavery in *Georgia*'. The colony was established on a principle of 'general Equality', and that was why Francklin was not concerned that the Trustees had 'found themselves under the Necessity of introducing Negro-slaves into the *Colony*'. The preacher argued that enslavement in Georgia would be predicated on 'Prudence and Humanity', and he therefore trusted that 'if these unhappy Beings [the enslaved] must eat the Bread of Slavery, they shall at least eat it in Peace and Quiet, that their Chains may not gall them'. The system of enslavement that Francklin envisioned in the Americas would be based on a rather perverse social contract: 'we use their [Black] Bodies for our Support and Happiness, their Souls may be refreshed; and that for their Service here to us, we may bestow on them, by our Instructions, the glorious Opportunity of securing to themselves eternal Happiness hereafter'. The exchange of earthly labours for eternal life was, to a true Anglican believer such as Francklin, the bargain of a lifetime.[60]

Missionary debates over slaveholding continued, with Cambridge men in the vanguard of these debates. East Apthorp, the son of Charles Apthorp, a

Bostonian merchant and slave-trader, and Grizzel Apthorp, the daughter of a Jamaica merchant, was educated at Boston Latin School, and then completed his studies at Jesus College, winning the Chancellor's Medal and receiving a BA in 1755, an MA in 1758, and a fellowship from 1758 to 1761. Apthorp never forgot his Cambridge roots, publishing as a 'late Fellow of Jesus College in the University of Cambridge', and took up residence in a New England town also bearing that name: Cambridge, Massachusetts. Returning there after his father's death, wealthy merchants invited him to become the SPG's minister. Refusing the £20 per annum salary, Apthorp used a significant inheritance from his father, a renowned slave-trader and catcher, to build a mansion which remains a part of Harvard University today. After travelling to old England in September 1764 in the wake of a religious controversy, Apthorp disagreed with the ameliorative stance of some British missionaries. In 1786 at Lincoln's Inn, he declared: 'The System of African slavery is a powerful obstacle to the humane business of conversion'. 'A distinguished prelate [Edmund Keene, who had been the Master of Peterhouse and Bishop of Chester]', he continued, 'hath excited the public compassion to *mitigate* its horrors: but a politic and peaceful sect have set the example in their own district of *abolishing* it'. He approved that the missionaries had 'freed their slaves, and allowed them wages for their labour' – contrasting that progressive approach with Keene's amelioration.[61]

For almost two centuries (and long afterwards), Cambridge clergymen and nonconformists were prominent defenders and propagators of Atlantic colonisation efforts. Supporting, whether through funds or deeds, colonial schemes ranging from the Virginia Company to the Society for the Propagation of the Gospel to Berkeley's aborted efforts to establish a Bermuda college, clergymen did not just benefit from colonialism and slavery – they were actively involved in directing and shaping those coercive and exploitative systems and institutions. The lives of these men illustrate the significance of university thought at a time when institutions such as Oxford and Cambridge provided an illustrious sheen to colonial endeavours. Consequently, the support of Cambridge fellows for enslavement – as illustrated in Thomas Thompson's *African Trade* pamphlet – was vital to selling these operations to the English and British middling and elite classes. It would be wrong, however, to isolate this story to the upper ranks of society. If the experiences of Owen Stockton (a fourth son) and Bartholomew Wortley (the son of a plumber) are indicative, Cambridge fellows who supported these activities originated from wide-ranging backgrounds, yet, whatever their ranks, many were prominent Protestant agents of empire. As England's Atlantic imperium took shape and form, Cambridge natural scientists and legal thinkers entered the breach, utilising their networks and ingenuity to shape and profit from empire – helping, in many cases, to define the nature of racism and Black enslavement, and ensuring that the spoils of empire and conquest returned home to Cambridge.

3

'The Glory of their times': Natural Philosophy, the Law, and the Spoils of Empire

Dr Thomas Townes, a physician and the son of a Barbadian enslaver, is not a household name. Nevertheless, the Christ's alumnus was an early proponent of innatism: the notion that the differences between white and Black persons were derived from interior biological phenomenon – an idea contrary to the more popular theory of environmentalism. Born and schooled in Barbados, Townes rose through the academic ranks after matriculating at Christ's in 1664, took his BA around 1668, M.B. a year later in 1669, and MD in 1674. There he may have met Martin Lister, a St John's fellow, and one of the foremost English naturalists. A fellow of the Royal Society and Royal College of Physicians, Lister was familiar with the plantation system, as the former organisation had invested in the East India and Royal African companies. In fact, Lister was a member of the Royal Society's influential governing council from 1683 to 1685, when it received dividends on its £200 investment in the African Company.[1]

After graduating, Townes returned to Barbados – and Lister was involved in that decision as well. In a letter, Townes reported that he would 'goe shortly to the Barbados, where of I can serve your curiosity of inquiring after any thing, that is rare to these Northern parts, you may command me'. The letter advised Lister that, if he wanted to 'send your commands to me', they should be addressed to Edward Lascelles, a tobacco merchant in Threadneedle Street. Arriving in Barbados, Townes got to work and sent a letter in March detailing some of the experiments which he had conducted on the enslaved population. 'It wil[l] not be unwelcome perhaps', he informed Lister, 'if I tel[l] you that the blood of Negroes is almost as black as their skin. I have seen the blood of at least twenty both sick and in health drawn forth, and the superficies of it al[l] is as dark as the bottome of any European blood after standing a while in a dish'. The humoral balance – the Roman and Greek physician Galen's notion that blood, if it did not properly circulate, stagnated, and thereby caused sickness – was still an article of scientific faith at this time.[2]

Townes used that idea to different ends than most physicians, though. Rather than seeing blood as shaped by climatic conditions, Townes reported to Lister that 'the blackness of Negroes is likely to be inherent in them, and not caused (as some imagine) by the scorching of the Sunne'. Consequently, the blood of Black people, he argued, was different to 'creatures here that live in the same Clime and heat with them, have as florid blood as those that are in a cold Latitude viz: England'. Townes's project of human experimentation may have cost the lives of his victims, who were weakened through sickness, malnutrition, and overwork on the colonial plantations.[3]

Townes's experiments were taken seriously in the Royal Society. Lister, a prominent Cambridge fellow (who had been elected to that position by mandate from the king), informed Henry Oldenburg, the Society's secretary, that 'A correspondent of mine at Barbados, the learned Thomas Townes has lately furnished me with an observation or two, which I shall transcribe for you'. Lister soon informed John Ray of Townes's findings. In a short note in July 1675, he wrote: 'Blood of negroes black'. These observations were debated in the Royal Society's global correspondence networks, with Lister hearing that an 'Ingenious' physician named Thomas Glover had 'lately come from our American Plantations' in Virginia and Barbados. There he had also 'let many Negros blood, and always observ'd it as florid and red as any Europeans blood, and that he never saw any of a black or dark color, as is represented by the latter, you received from that island'. Glover was receptive to Townes's findings, however, arguing that he would inquire into 'other places, where Blacks inhabit' concerning the 'truth of this observation'. In turn, Lister was defensive of his Barbadian protégé and correspondent, complaining that Glover had not conducted the same 'Experiment' as Townes and thus the Royal Society would have to embark on more research to confirm his findings in Barbados.[4]

Natural philosophers and, as we shall see, lawyers were intimately connected, both personally and intellectually, to the propagation of the British Empire. Whether considering the theoretical and philosophical foundations of race, accepting collections from slave-trade investors, travelling to slave societies to conduct research, or assisting in the governance of Britain's slave empire, Cambridge men were dedicated agents in imperial processes, and their experiences further illustrate the spectrum of interconnections between Britons and their empire. Though seemingly unconnected stories, the growing professionalisation of the natural science and legal fields was inextricably intertwined, as historians have shown, with Britain's slave empire. In turn, Cambridge fellows ensured that the spoils of imperial conquest, whether plants or book collections, would return to the University and Britain writ-large, and be laundered in scientific collections and college buildings. The chapter will explore these processes, looking first at natural scientists and then at lawyers and jurists who, following on from the Virginian and New England missionaries, enforced rules, laws, and legal philosophies that codified the heavily contested racial fiction that white Europeans could enslave African children from birth. The legacies of these ideas would be felt far beyond the county borders of Cambridgeshire.[5]

With the rise of England's Protestant empire, natural scientists – like Townes – were some of the first men who benefitted. For natural philosophers, their acceptance of slavery was born, in part, out of a self-interested desire to access and profit from the colonial spaces where they could make new discoveries and then bring these specimens home to Britain. As Kathleen Murphy writes, recent works on the global history of science have 'expanded the practitioners of Atlantic science to include enslaved and free Africans (as well as Native Americans and white women) alongside more familiar figures such as Benjamin Franklin, Alexander von Humboldt, and Charles-Marie de La Condamine'. That story was true at Cambridge too. For the enslaved were pivotal to many of the discoveries that have been attributed to important men of science in Cambridge's history.[6]

University fellows and former students, in turn, donated to collections. John Covel, the Master of Christ's (1688–1722), provided Sir Hans Sloane, a plantation owner in Jamaica through his marriage to the heiress Elizabeth Langley Rose (Fulke Rose's widow), with 'A manati strap for whipping the Negro slaves in the Hott W. India plantations'. Covel, who had previously served as the Chaplain to the Levant Company, which exported trade goods such as silver, pepper, nutmeg, wool, and cotton from the Ottoman Empire, gave £100 for altering the college chapel and organised a subscription to raise money for construction efforts (which Sir Isaac Newton provided nineteen guineas towards). The Christ's College Commemoration Books record that Covel generously 'built the Tower of the Chapel and furnished it with a Clock and Bell'. Sloane also commissioned George Lewis, a Queens' alumnus, Chaplain to the EIC in Madras, and skilled Persian linguist, to collect shells, butterflies, and nuts – with Lewis's extensive collection of literature from the Levant and Asia donated to Cambridge University Library.[7]

Colleges cultivated extensive collections of natural and human specimens too. The Benin Bronzes have justifiably received much attention, yet it bears remembering that the institutional acquisition of treasured possessions has a centuries-long history. After Captain James Cook's three-year voyage (1768–1771) on the HMS *Endeavour* to observe the transit of Venus, he brought back numerous 'Weapons, Utensils and Manufactures' from the Pacific Islands and New Zealand. John Montagu, the 4th Earl of Sandwich (and namesake of the Sandwich Islands, which was the European name for Hawai'i), donated these items to his alma mater, Trinity College. The inventory included paddles, clubs, a battle axe, edge tools, necklaces, dresses, fishhooks, and a bottle of an 'elastic Gum' from South America. The Cook treasures joined Trinity's other oddities: the piece of a mummified Egyptian, a 'magick cup' from Egypt, a Rhinoceros horn, a 'Quiver containing seventeen Poison Darts used by Indians', Samuel Morland's speaking trumpet (an early megaphone), and the heart of Daniel Malden, a sailor who had broken out of Newgate several times and had then been executed in 1736 for stealing linen. Trinity's collecting also extended to flora. Under the supervision of Richard Walker, the Vice-Master of Trinity, John Harrison, the college gardener, expanded upon John Ray's botanic garden that had been kept since the 1660s, with '*Banana*, Coffee-shrub', 'Torch-thistle' (so named because some Native Americans used the stems of that species of cacti as torches), and 'the Red Jessamine of the West Indies'. The age of discovery was an era of imperial collecting, and colleges (and college men) were at the forefront of this endeavour – receiving rarities from Africa, Asia, and the Pacific.[8]

Despite the efforts of these hobby collectors, a working definition of "science" and "scientists" was somewhat elusive. Samuel Johnson, in his 1755 *Dictionary*, defined the sciences in five ways: as 'Knowledge'; 'Certainty grounded on demonstration'; 'Art attained by precepts, or built on principles'; 'Any art or species of knowledge'; and 'One of the seven liberal arts, grammar, rhetoric, logick, arithmetick, musick, geometry, astronomy'. Science, then, was defined through its methods – the scientific method of reasoning, experimentation, and deduction that led to an empirical conclusion. There were no science departments and scientists were treated as theoreticians alongside philosophers, rhetoricians, and men of the cloth as thinkers struggling to pursue knowledge about the world, both material and spiritual. Theology and religion were not at all separate; the questions that natural scientists explored often revolved around divine phenomena or Biblical stories, such as proving the creation in Genesis or Noah's Flood. The Royal Society was not the sole preserve of scientific researchers either, with the Fullers and other members of the landed gentry holding positions of authority. Scientists, especially in medicine, were considered trained professionals but it was not until the early nineteenth century that gentleman amateurs, such as Stephen Fuller, were replaced with university-educated specialists.[9]

Born 1 May 1665, John Woodward never attained an undergraduate degree; still, he was one of the most significant of these natural scientists in Cambridge's history. Despite his limitations in education, Woodward rose from an apprenticed linen draper to an apprentice in medicine to Dr Peter Barwick, Charles II's physician. Benefitting from Barwick's patronage, he became the Gresham Professor of Physic in 1692 and then, a year later, a Royal Society fellow. Woodward's connections to Cambridge began that year too, as Thomas Tenison made Woodward a Doctor of Medicine – though it was the latter's death and benefaction that had a real effect on university life. When he died on 25 April 1728, Woodward's executors disposed of his 'ready money, my money in the South Sea Company, all Debts owing to me, all money due to me on mortgages, on Bonds, Bills, notes, or other securities and my said Household Goods, Books, Antiquities jewels, plate, and all my other personal Estate herein' to purchase lands that would then be donated to Cambridge and used to support a lectureship in his name, the Woodwardian Professorship of Geology.[10]

Woodward's South Sea assets were a noteworthy component of his generous benefaction. In the aftermath of the Bubble, Woodward's executors owned £820 of stock, which was divided into £410 of stock and the same amount in annuities, with the sum in the latter security increasing to around £700 on his death. These investments complimented his personal ownership of £500 in Royal African stock in 1720. Given Woodward's wealth, the Woodwardian Professor enjoyed some luxuries: they were paid £100 a year and were only required to read four lectures on a topic mentioned in his 1695 work, *Natural History of the Earth*, where the donor had, in the later enlarged version of the text, posited that Native Americans, Africans, and Europeans differed in 'Stature, Shape, Features, Hair, and Complexion' due to climate, soil, and diet. Those environmental determinants, Woodward argued (and students and fellows would have heard in the lectures), explained why Indigenous 'Americans' were more akin to the 'early Inhabitants' of Europe in that they 'knew Nothing of Letters, of Coyn'd-Money, of Iron, of the Plough, or of Horses'.[11]

As an aside, Woodward's calculations of the profits that he might have gained from these South Sea and Royal African securities owed a significant debt to mathematicians. Finance and the financial calculations of annuities and compound interest had started to pique the interest of Cambridge fellows and their interlocuters, most prominently Isaac Newton at Trinity College. Their studies were essential for the national interest as the rise of the South Sea and East India companies and the government's efforts to finance the public debt with securities in these trading firms necessitated investigations into the viability of these assets for private and public investors and the fiscal-military state. Newton's South Sea holdings increased exponentially from £1,000 in 1712 to at least £10,000 in 1717 to £16,275 in June 1721 and, a year later, to £21,696. He made profits on this investment before the Bubble but suffered greatly in the crash. Newton's interest in finance began fifty years earlier in 1670, when he wrote to John Collins, an accountant and mathematics instructor. Their letters concerned annuities and Newton's efforts to determine, through logarithms, the expected interest rate from assets. William Jones (c.1675–1749), a friend of Newton's who purchased Collins's papers, deposited several notebooks with the University containing his calculations of simple interest, compound interest, pension annuities, and accounts of a tabulation of imports and exports, which reveal the interest of contemporary Cambridge mathematicians in financial matters.[12]

Woodward and his *Natural History* owed a significant debt as well to enslaved Africans. The collection of fossils that he bequeathed to Cambridge – contained in two large oak cabinets – included material from slave societies, including Virginia, Maryland, Barbados, and Jamaica. Together, these specimens contributed to Woodward's grand theory that the Biblical Deluge had produced fossils, as these were the creatures contained in the 'promiscuous Mass of Sand, Earth, Shells and the rest, falling down [due to gravity] and subsiding from the water'. The Bible, for him, provided the answers to scientific questions – and, to answer those hypotheses, he encouraged natural scientists to use enslaved collectors. In his *Brief Instructions for Making Observations*, he wrote that the '*gathering* and *preserving* of Insects, Shells, Plants, Minerals, &c. *may be done by the Hands of Servants;* and that too at their spare and *leisure times:* or in *Journies*, in the *Plantations*, in *Fishing, Fowling, &c. without Hindrance of any other Business*, the *things* herein desired being *common*, and such as (one or other of them) *occur in almost all Places*'.[13]

Enslavers and natural scientists obliged. They followed Woodward's detailed instructions, sending numerous specimens for his research. Much of this material was undoubtedly attained with the explicit help or assistance of enslaved persons. Since at least the sixteenth century, the enslaved were used as fishermen and pearl haulers in the Caribbean and mainland Americas, trawling the Atlantic's oyster beds, so their labour was essential if various specimens had to be drawn from the ocean floor. On the teeth of marine life, Woodward noted that one specimen 'is found on the Coasts of *Jamaica*, *Barbadoes*, and other Parts of the *West-Indies*'. On a particular species of sea urchin, Woodward wrote that such a specimen could be 'found on the Shores of *Barbadoes*'. In his records of Virginian specimens, Woodward noted the existence of numerous species – the 'Bottom Shell of an Oyster' or the 'upper Valve of a small Oyster' – that were, more likely than not, discovered and collected by enslaved Africans.[14]

Woodward relied on the Royal African Company for his scientific work too. He was not alone in pleading for the slave-trading company to support his passion for collecting: the Virginian naturalist John Banister requested that they 'bestow on me 4 or 5 guinny negros' to assist him on scientific expeditions. In his published *Collection*, Woodward had gold from Guinea, which he 'had of the *Royal African* Company, and was inform'd they once had a Lump that weigh'd somewhat above 3 Ounces'. Charles Hayes, a mathematician, geographer, slave-trader, and sub-governor of the Company, had sent that valuable specimen. Woodward recalled that Hayes 'in his Letter from *Cape-Coast* in *Guinea*, 7 Feb. 1704, mentions one he saw there that weigh'd 4 Ounces… and that he had accounts of much larger found in those Parts'. From this information, Woodward speculated whether torrential rains had managed to disperse gold from the mountains. Aside from Hayes and Woodward, numerous scientific luminaries and fellows were involved in the RAC. Dr John Arbuthnot, the Scottish physician, director of the Royal Academy of Music, and inventor of the famous "John Bull" satirical image, held £2,000 in stock; Dr John Freind, whose estate helped to fund a College Readership in Chemistry at Christ Church, Oxford, and an Anatomy School, held the same amount of stock; Dr Thomas Pellett, the President of the Royal College of Physicians and alumnus of Queens', Cambridge, had £1,000 invested; and Dr William King, the principal of St Mary's Hall, Oxford (now Oriel), had £1,000. Men of science and education were intimately and financially connected, then, to the most prolific global slave-trading enterprise.[15]

Woodward also depended for his specimens on the intrepid work of other Cambridge fellows in the American colonies, who required the acquiescence of enslavers and their enslaved labourers. Woodward's *Natural History* refers multiple times to a '*Mr. Vernon*' – William Vernon, a fellow of Peterhouse. Much of Vernon's intrepid life remains shrouded in mystery, but he was born in Hertford and entered Peterhouse in 1685, graduating with a BA in 1689. At Cambridge, he befriended John Ray who invited the young naturalist into the Royal Society's prestigious circle. Elected a college fellow in 1692, Vernon was granted leave and funding to 'improve his Botanick studies in the West Indies', lest he marry or pass away there – the former unlikely given Vernon's overt fondness for mosses and Lepidoptera, and the latter much more likely given the Caribbean's high mortality rates. Several years later, Vernon was sent to Virginia because William Byrd II and Sloane sought his expertise for a natural history of the colony. Travelling throughout the Chesapeake, Vernon sent numerous specimens to Woodward, including pieces of bone, shells, and teeth. Though the Peterhouse fellow died in 1711 in obscurity, Woodward and Vernon had cemented the university's reputation for natural history.[16]

Cambridge's slaving connections did not end with Woodward. The first Woodwardian Professor, Conyers Middleton, had financial investments in the slave trade in the form of South Sea stock. The sale document for these investments was signed, sealed, and delivered in the presence of Thomas Crosse, the Vice-Chancellor of Cambridge, and John Mickleburgh, the Minister of St Andrews Church and Professor of Chemistry in Cambridge, on 29 September 1721. Born in Richmond, North Yorkshire, on 27 December 1683, Middleton entered Trinity College in March 1699, graduating with a BA degree in 1703, and was elected to a fellowship in 1705. He received his Doctorate in Divinity from no less than George I. After his first wife, Sarah Morris, passed away in 1731, Middleton reinvented himself from a controversialist (often locked in petty collegiate squabbles with Richard Bentley) into a natural philosopher. In his inaugural lecture, he observed that the study of fossils may help prove the historicity of Noah's Flood. Though Middleton made few statements on enslavement, his 1745 *Letter from Rome* mentioned that the face of a saint he saw there was 'as black as a *Negro*'s; so that one would take it rather for the representation of a *Proserpine*, or *infernal Deity*, than, what they impiously stile it, of the *Queen of Heaven*'. Middleton was no innovator in these prejudicial remarks – Black people and Black skin, amongst many early modern white Britons, were associated with sinfulness, savagery, and bondage. Isaac Barrow, the Master of Trinity College and Newton's mentor and predecessor as Lucasian Professor, preached that 'Nature coveteth good success to its designs and undertakings… therefore was he put to water dry sticks and to wash *Negros*; that is, to instruct a most dull and stupid, to reform a most perverse and stubborn generation'.[17]

Continuing the studies of these Cambridge luminaries, the Reverend Charles Mason, the Woodwardian Professor of Geology for twenty-eight years and, like Middleton, a fellow of Trinity, was looked upon – like the Cambridgeshire landscapes which he traversed and mapped with precision – as 'rather unhewn, rough, and unsociable'. Despite his obtuseness, Mason developed networks of correspondence and knowledge production that stretched to the Caribbean. One such correspondent was the Reverend William Smith, the Rector of St John's Parish in Nevis, whose *Natural History of Nevis, and the Rest of the English*

Leeward Charibee Islands in America was dedicated in 1745 to Mason and the island's 'Worthy Gentlemen', who he hoped would benefit from the 'spiritual Blessings of Heaven[.]' Having maintained a record of the region's climate and wildlife, Smith presented his work to Mason, who encouraged him to write the treatise. In any case, many of Smith's observations involved enslaved African assistants. He noted how the enslaved collected cockles on the shore, gathered the bark of dogwood trees and used its juice for fishing, and the dangers of collecting poisonous sea creatures. Searching for shells, Smith and his companions 'ordered my Negro Man *Oxford* to strip, dive, and unloose it [an object at the bottom of a pond]', and "Oxford" managed to pull 'Roots and Branches' from the water which convinced the Reverend that the 'vast *Atlantick* Ocean… might abound at [the] bottom with large growing Trees, and smaller bushes, as well as with Weeds, or Grass'. After arriving in Cambridge, Smith presented his collection of roots and shells to Mason, another enduring example of how the hidden labour of enslaved Black people shaped scientific thought at Cambridge.[18]

Alongside the Woodwardian Professors, Cambridge botanists supported colonial enterprises. Richard Bradley, who had a similar non-university background to Woodward, rose from a journeyman interest in gardens and botany to a professorship after the publication of his 1710 work *A Treatise of Succulent Plants* earned him notice from Sir Hans Sloane and the naturalist and apothecary James Petiver, who worked with traders in enslaved Africans to collect specimens. After a visit to the Netherlands, which stimulated his imagination for horticulture (and for the medicinal effects of coffee to cure the plague), Bradley became the first Cambridge Professor of Botany in 1724.[19]

Holding the chair until his death in 1732, Bradley intervened in subjects ranging from infectious diseases to tulips – and, in these studies, he regularly conversed with men such as Sloane. Compiling his lectures, which he claimed would 'bring me in a good sum of money', Bradley wrote to Sloane around 1727 hoping to 'have the opportunity of seeing your History of Jamaica. It would do me great service in what I am about'. Like Woodward, Bradley's research interests utilised Caribbean collections, particularly Sloane's displays. His 1721 treatise *A Philosophical Account of the Works of Nature* mentioned in exhausting detail how in 'the *West Indies* there is another sort of *Flying Lizard*, different in the Colour, and Make of its Wings' (with the coloured plates for this discussion taken '*from my own Collection: the same is in Sir Hans Sloan's Cabinet*', and that in '*Suriman*, and some other Parts of the *West Indies*, there is a large *Fly*, which they commonly call the *Lanthorn Fly*' – a specimen found 'likewise in *Sir Hans Sloane's Collection of Rarerities*'. His *History of Succulent Plants*, which appeared in five editions from 1716 to 1727, contained a wealth of detail on White Torch Thistles 'in the West-Indies, *growing among the Rocks, and shooting forth its Pillar-like stems upright to a great Heighth*'. Bradley's research into Caribbean flora and fauna, from flying lizards to bats that 'were as large as a *Rat*', owed a significant debt to the colonists who discovered these specimens.[20]

Figure 3.1 The Coffe[e] Tree, print from Richard Bradley, *A Short Historical Account of Coffee* (London: EM. Matthews, 1715). Royal Society.

Bradley was a much-publicised botanist, but he was not content to collect oddities – he considered his chosen profession as an avenue to improve the empire. Bradley had considered erecting a *'Physick Garden at* Cambridge'. Four decades later, the generosity of Richard Walker brought this plan to fruition, yet Bradley had greater ambitions for the garden than the 'Wisdom and Goodness of God'. He compared it to Amsterdam's Garden which had received 'Plants, from several Parts of the World; which, as the Governors see Occasion, are transmitted to some of their own Plantations, the least distant from them, and thereby advantage their Trade'. The coffee tree was the perfect example, to him, of the positive externalities generated due to a public garden (see Figure 3.1). At first, the Dutch cultivated the tree in Batavia 'till' they imported many Tun Weight from thence of their own Growth and brought Trees of it to Amsterdam; where, after a little Time, they raised several Hundreds and sent them to Surinam and Curasau in the West Indies, from whence I am told, they receive a good Freight of Coffee every year'. The project was such a success for the Dutch, he claimed, that 'they may gather Coffee enough in those Plantations to supply the greatest Part of Europe'. Reflecting upon the 'State of our American Plantations, and our extensive Trade', he thought that it was imperative that they send 'many Plants of Use, which will grow freely there, and may be collected and prepared for them, in such a Garden as I speak of'. Given that, between 1767 and 1789, coffee exports from Saint-Domingue had quadrupled, Bradley's enthusiasm for that produce was well-founded.[21]

Understandably, Bradley's obsession with coffee, particularly its medicinal qualities, continued unabated. A regular of the Grecian coffeehouse in Devereux Court (a place for refreshment frequented by Sloane, Petiver, and Newton), the Professor again discussed coffee trees in the 12 September 1727 edition of his successful *The Weekly Miscellany For the Improvement of Husbandry, Trade, Arts, and Sciences*. Running for over two decades, the Botanist published a letter that he had received from a "J. Wickliffe" in Bristol applauding his *Short Historical Account of Coffee* that had 'pleased me and the Company where I was'. (Presented to the Royal Society on 28 April 1715, the *Account* celebrated coffee's medicinal and mercantile qualities.) The reader, perhaps a merchant, supported growing coffee in the North American plantations and remembered that he had been in Barbados where 'I saw a good Number of Coffee-Trees growing very well… It is a new thing in that Island; but as it is new, it will ask some Time before the Barbadians will come into it; for they were not, when I was there, fond enough of it to set heartily about improving it'. Nevertheless, the Bristol correspondent acknowledged that it 'grows well' in Barbados and given that they had seen 'great Plantations' in Surinam and Curaçao exporting the product, Barbadian enslavers should be 'encouraged' to produce coffee that was 'much fresher and cheaper' than elsewhere, owing to the shorter voyages between England and the Caribbean plantations. Bradley agreed – and he replied that a 'parcel' of coffee trees had been delivered from Barbados to the

Royal Gardens at Hampton Court to encourage production. Relating information from his distinguished contacts, including Dr Antoine Laurent de Jussieu, the Professor of Botany in Amsterdam's Botanical Gardens, Bradley noted that the trees must be 'raised by laying the tender Shoots in Earth, which may be an Instruction to those in Foreign Countries' – providing a more detailed method of growing and raising coffee trees in his *Gardiner's Calendar*.[22]

Natural science was, as with so many other aspects of Cambridge life, a family affair. Both John Martyn and his son Thomas succeeded Bradley as the Professors of Botany – and their appreciation of the world beyond Britain's shores perhaps came naturally: John's father (and Thomas's grandfather) was a Hamburg merchant and John had married a daughter of Claude Fonnereau, a Huguenot 'merchant prince' who had a significant fortune in the linen trade, including to East India (a sizeable fortune that was reinvested in land and, in part, in EIC and SSC stocks). Following his election to the Royal Society in 1727 after lecturing on botany in London, John, alongside his influential mentor Sir Hans Sloane, worked with travellers to attain specimens from the Caribbean, including from William Houstoun, a Scotsman who had been employed on board the *Assiento* as a slave ship's surgeon with the South Sea Company. Martyn mused in a 1731 letter to Houstoun, who depended upon Indigenous and enslaved African collectors for his specimens, that he had 'done enough already to stir up the jealousy of any man who has not been before you in the West Indies; and, if I am not grievously mistaken, you will soon make it difficult for any one to have success who comes after you'. Their connection continued after Martyn's appointment to the Professorship at Cambridge, and in October 1732 Martyn and his fellow Society members supported Houstoun's application to be admitted as he had set out for Georgia, with the support of the Bray Associates, 'in Search of the Plants & Drugs of that Country'. Martyn and Sloane also proposed that Rose Fuller, a 'Gentleman well Skill'd in all parts of the Mathematicks, Natural and Experimental Philosophy, & most branches of Curious & Usefull Learning; being desirous of becoming a Member of this [Royal] Society'. The findings of these men, including fourteen seeds from Spanish America and specimens from Barbados, Dominica, and Jamaica, were documented in Martyn's *Historia Plantarum Rariorum*.[23]

The later Professor's linkages to enslavers also extended to his other hobbies, among them his editorship, alongside the clergyman Richard Russel, of the satirical *Grub-Street Journal* from 1730 to 1733. On 25 May 1732, the same year that Martyn was appointed as Professor, the *Journal* published a notice of 'a Negro-BOY, Named SCIPIO' who had '*Went away from his Master*' and had not 'been heard of since'. The "master" in the advertisement was Andrew Smith, an attorney in King Street, Cheapside, and the document was one example of a wider genre of such advertisements in Britain and the North American colonies that aimed, Simon Newman argues, to 'commodify those who dared elope'. The text read that Scipio 'had on a blue Livery, a small Sleeve to his Coat, turn'd up with yellow Plush, trim'd with white Metal Buttons; his Coat double-breasted to the Waste; the Buttons of his Breeches plain and flat, made of white Metal'. The dressing of the Black enslaved in somewhat garish outfits was part and parcel of middling and elite white efforts to display their manservants to a gawking public as symbols of the master class's wealth and social status. In a city with ports and other methods of escape, the master in this case, Smith, hoped that Scipio, a 'Strong made Boy', would not travel far as he 'talks bad English' (perhaps indicating that he was recently enslaved from West Africa). Scipio's fate does not appear in the record, however John Martyn's publication of that advertisement in the *Journal* was another example of the complex range of interconnections between academic knowledge-seekers and the individuals and families, from the more prominent Fullers to the attorney Andrew Smith, that benefitted from Britain's slave societies.[24]

Thomas, who held the Professorship for more than sixty years (1762–1825), was a far more prolific author than his father, though. Elected to a Sidney Sussex fellowship after graduating from Cambridge, Thomas contributed numerous works from a translation of Jean Jacques Rosseau's *Letters on the Elements of Botany* in 1785 to an Italian travel guide to illustrations of the Swedish naturalist Carl Linneaus's botanical system. Martyn's impressive publishing record coincided with a period of turbulence in the Cambridge botanical world. Charles Miller, the first Curator of the botanical garden, left the University in 1770 for Sumatra to cultivate nutmegs, spices, and other vegetables which 'might prove advantageous objects of commerce'. Observing the garden's dwindling finances, Martyn stepped into the breach and assisted as Curator alongside his other duties. The Cantabrigian had an interest in the gardens, but he did not show a similar proclivity for teaching – and he returned to London after 1796 (though he still held the Professorship for the rest of his long life). The time away from the classroom, however, enabled Martyn to improve and expand upon Philip Miller's already monumental *The Gardener's Dictionary*.[25]

Thomas's two volume *Dictionary*, which was published in 1807, had an obvious debt to the Black population in the Caribbean and the significant knowledge that they had gained in medicine and construction methods through their inventive efforts to survive slavery. The *Dictionary* mentioned how the people that he labelled "negroes" used certain plants and glutinous barks as diuretics, to stimulate menstrual flow, or to treat roundworms; he claimed that the enslaved used Jamaican cabbage trees for mats in slave huts and the seeds as feed for wild hogs; he recognised their attachment to papaw trees because they 'render the air healthy, and therefore plant them near their houses'; and he informed readers that the enslaved and poor whites utilised the shells of the Cucurbita (a relation of the pumpkin) as 'water-cups' and the pulp was 'employed in resolutive poultices'. Martyn was clear throughout about the significance of local Black knowledge in the publication, and he recognised in one passage on Jamaican hibiscus that 'Its common name there is *Congo Mahoe*; the negroes affirming that it came originally from Africa'.[26]

The *Dictionary* was intended for application to plantation economies. That emphasis is clear in a section on indigo production, where the Cantabrigian introduced new passages that were not in Miller's original published version. For context, Elizabeth Pinckney, who was born in Antigua and moved to South Carolina with her family in 1738, started running her father's plantations at the age of sixteen and sought to perfect the cultivation of indigo as a dye for the transatlantic textile market. Her entrepreneurial efforts paid dividends as that product became the colony's second most profitable cash crop after rice (leading, in turn, to the growing popularity of that good beyond the Carolinas). The production and sale of indigo crossed imperial lines, with prominent French Louisiana enslavers such as Julien de Lallande Poydras trading that commodity to London and holding insurance contracts there on the produce that they shipped across the treacherous Atlantic Ocean.[27]

Martyn had some words of advice for these colonists. Like Samuel Martin's plantation manual, the Cambridge scholar established in detail how to grow, develop, and reap this crop. 'The culture of Indigo', he wrote, 'has been greatly neglected among the English colonists, though no part of the world affords a better soil, or more commodious situations for that purpose than Jamaica'. Thankfully, 'they have begun however to plant there of late years'. He continued: 'Seventeen negroes are sufficient to manage twenty acres of Indigo: and one acre of rich land, well planted, will, with good seasons and proper management, yield five hundred pounds of Indigo in twelve months: for the plant ratoons and gives four or five crops a year: but must be replanted afterwards'. The Cambridge Professor advised that the planters not leave the crop too long before it was to be cut, and that 'some experiments in the culture and management of indigo' would allow them to reap that produce 'whilst young and full of juice'. Martyn recognised that 'labour being dear in the West Indies', so he advised the use of drill ploughs to sow the seeds and a hoe plough to keep the crop free of weeds and ensure also that the stalks would be stronger and therefore resistant to insect outbreaks. From the size of the enslaved labour force and plantation grounds to the technologies required for cultivation, Martyn's expertise was dedicated, in no small part, to assisting landed enslavers in their efforts to expand imperial commerce.[28]

If some Cambridge men were content to stare at the ground, others found knowledge and wisdom in the heavens. Nevil Maskelyne, the fifth Astronomer Royal and Trinity fellow, had connections to imperial and slaveholding enterprises. Though Maskelyne was a keen physicist and mathematician, his early life was more grounded – the unfortunate passing of his father at the age of twelve left his family in dire straits, though his education at Westminster School coincided with the eclipse of 14 July 1748 (a seminal event in his life). Entering St Catharine's College in 1749, Maskelyne – despite being the seventh wrangler – initially considered a career in the church and was ordained as a minister in 1755 and was elected to a Trinity fellowship a year later.[29]

The East and West Indies shaped Maskelyne's life and fortunes. His elder brother, Edmund, was an administrator and soldier in the East India Company, and his younger sister, Margaret, married Robert Clive on 18 February 1753 (and Clive later employed Edmund as his aide-de-camp). Clive (or the 1st Baron Clive) was twice Governor of Bengal and had earned a vast colonial fortune. The baroness longed for his return home, however, writing to Edmund from Berkeley Square in May 1766 that he had been 'an instrument of so much good to Bengal & the India Company, that it quite disordered me, & my rejoicing was beyond all description', hoping that 'there will be no occasion for my Lord to stay in India longer than December, although the Directors of course ask him to stay another year'. Nevil benefitted from his East Indian familial associations, and, that same month, he sent a letter to Edmund being 'greatly obliged to you for your kind intention expressed in your letter of making me a present of 500£ India stock; tho' I must own I am not so surprised at so great a testimony of regard from a brother of so generous and affectionate a disposition'. Less than twenty years later, Nevil gained significant financial benefits from the Caribbean. In 1784, he married Sophia Pate Rose, whose father, John Pate Rose, owned an estate in Northamptonshire and another in Jamaica, named "Mount Hindmost," which produced rum and sugar.[30]

Nevil's courtship with Sophia was neither his first nor last association with the Atlantic world. His involvement there began in July 1760, when the Royal Society sent him to St Helena in the South Atlantic Ocean to observe the transit of Venus. ('Some Members of the University of Cambridge' had, that very same year, also lobbied for and succeeded in making the EIC open 'any of their Settlements' and 'divers Factories' in Sumatra, Batavia, and Madras to scientific minds interested in observing the Transit, though the firm admitted that it possessed only one set of tools for that endeavour.) The trip was a failure owing to poor weather, which obscured his vision of the celestial event, yet Maskelyne took advantage of his time there to use the moon to determine longitude. Having published his lunar-distance method in the *British Mariner's Guide* (utilising the work of the German astronomer Tobias Mayer), and thereby establishing his reputation in the calculation and tabulation of nautical travel, the Board of Longitude next sent Maskelyne to Barbados in 1763 to determine the capital Bridgetown's coordinates via the observation of Jupiter's moons. (The Board had hoped to send their educated observer to Jamaica, but a deadly fever there had scuppered these plans.) Springing into action, Maskelyne had to get his affairs in order with little time to spare, writing to his brother that he had 'taken 100£ on Portugal specie with me which I am inform'd is the best method of supplying myself', and asked whether he could collect his college rents from Trinity, which along with his other funds would be sufficient 'for 8 months at Barbadoes'.[31]

Sailing from Portsmouth, Maskelyne's arrival in Barbados six weeks later was 'saluted with 15 Guns' from Needham's Fort. The friendly welcome continued whilst he was on the island: 'Since my arrival here', he noted to his brother in December 1763, 'I have passed my time much more agre[e]ably, to which the great civilities I have received from the gentlemen of this place have not a little contributed'. He established his observation point on Constitution Hill; still, he had plenty of time – whilst enduring a heat that was 'somewhat too great for an European Constitution' – to traverse the island, commenting that the colony was 'very pleasant in general, & as green if not greener than in England, but not with Grass, but with India Corn, Guinea Corn, & Sugar Cane plants; the first of which is chiefly used for sustaining the poultry & sometimes also the cattle, & the second is the chief food of the negroes'. He made few remarks on enslaved labourers in the letters (though he pondered in his journal whether 'workmen' in the observatory had moved his instruments). Lodging with a Bridgetown attorney, Maskelyne reassessed his prejudices against the colonists, observing that this important 'Island is reckon'd the Garden of all the West Indies, & is indeed very pleasant, very different from the Idea we commonly form of this part of the world in England'. That visit – the research from which he published as a '*Fellow* of Trinity College, Cambridge' – and his wife's Jamaican connections may have made a lasting impression. As the slave trade was debated four decades later, Maskelyne purchased Jesse Foot's 1804 *Observations principally upon the Speech of Mr Wilberforce*, which challenged the 'black accusations' that had been cast at enslavers.[32]

Sir Nathaniel Lloyd, the Master of Trinity Hall from 1710 to 1735, was a significant agent in the British Empire, providing legal advice on slavery-related cases and assisting benefactions connected to the plantations. Born on 29 November 1669, Nathaniel followed in his father, Sir Richard's, footsteps from cradle to grave. He was educated at Oxford, and, like Lloyd senior, he was elected a fellow of All Souls. Nathaniel trod another well-worn familial path – becoming an advocate in the Doctors' Commons, a society of Doctors of Law with educations at Oxford and Cambridge practising civil (particularly probate and maritime issues) and canon (or ecclesiastical) law in London, which his father had done as the Dean of Arches. Though classified as an honourable and 'masculine office', Britons were rather torn in their opinions concerning barristers, who specialised in common law, or the advocates. For some, the law was an 'Laudable and Honourable' profession – one 'worthy of a Scholar and a Gentleman'; and, to other observers, lawyers were 'fusty, musty, dusty, rusty, filthy, [and] stinking'. Legal careers, the historian David Lemmings notes, were 'attractive' to families who had enough financial standing to support their son's careers but did not have the provincial landed estates or 'national standing' to attain high political offices for their children.[33]

Lloyd's familial wealth and status certainly had its limits. Although a Member of Parliament for the City of Durham, his father was a younger son, and he did not inherit the family seat, Aston Hall, in Oswestry on the Welsh border. Consequently, Nathaniel's inheritance included a dozen silver plates, the lease of his father's legal chambers, and books and funds to support his legal career. Lloyd was intelligent and hardworking, however – and he needed those traits because English law before the publication of William Blackstone's *Commentaries* in 1765 was dry and complicated. Still, the rewards of that 'worthy' office were compelling, as the Commons' advocates, many of whom had specialist knowledge in international law, found ready employment in the Church, the admiralty and vice-admiralty courts, and in diplomatic service.[34]

Lloyd's lifelong involvement in the Doctors' Commons brought him into contact with Britain's slave empire. Founded in 1511, the Commons maintained close institutional ties to Trinity Hall, which at times earned an average yearly rent of £63 from their ownership of its rooms. This monetary linkage between Trinity and the Commons members, many of whom were involved in Atlantic trading companies, meant that the college earned an economic benefit from individuals involved in the empire. Humphrey Henchman, the grandson of the more famous Bishop of London, possessed £3,500 in stock after the Royal African Company launched another issue of securities in 1722. Imperial companies also hired the Commons as council to manage issues of maritime law. After taking a Doctorate at Trinity Hall, Sir Thomas Penfold was hired as council to the Hudson's Bay Company, which operated the North American fur trade, for one guinea. The size of the Commons was never large – indeed, between 1512 and 1856 'only 462 advocates were admitted (or a little over one a year)' – but the civilians had an outsized influence because 'the study of civil law' was thought to 'cultivate the art of statesmanship'. Together, Lloyd and his colleagues shaped the nature and extent of Britain's sovereignty over the oceans.[35]

Few of these advocates, who provided their rents to Trinity Hall, matched Charles Davenant in stature. Davenant, a parliamentarian since 1685 and a former student at Balliol College, Oxford, defended joint-stock organisations against individual traders seeking to challenge their monopolies. An advocate for the EIC, Davenant, who had a stable living as the Commissioner for Excise, earned around £1,000 a year for three years, writing a "Memorial on the East-India Trade" in February 1696 and an *Essay on the East India Trade*, which argued that 'the Wealth England had once, did arise chiefly from Two Articles: First, Our Plantation Trade. Secondly, Our *East India* Traffick'. No better statement could be made for the importance of imperial rule to England's finances, and Davenant sought to prove his point further in subsequent publications hoping to resume the RAC's monopoly, which had effectively ended in 1689. Davenant argued that a free trade in enslaved Africans had led to the 'Planters complaining extremely of the great scarcity of, and extravagant Advance upon the Price of Negroes[.]' Company rule would, he claimed, address this chaos. Far from impartial lawyers adjudicating on cases, therefore, the civilian lawyers were active participants in imperial companies, and Trinity Hall stood to gain financially from their imperial and slaving activities in chamber rents.[36]

Whilst at the Doctors' Commons, Lloyd ascended the legal ladder. On 15 November 1701, he was appointed a deputy admiralty Advocate, a position that his father had held, replacing Dr Henry Newton for a time as the 'advocate Generall for all matters Ecclesiastical, Maritime, & Foreign, relating to the Crown', earning £20 an annum for this position. Five years after being knighted in May 1710, Lloyd became George I's legal advocate, advising government officials negotiating a treaty with France to lower trade duties (negotiations which the French swiftly nullified). As an expert on admiralty law, many of his cases around this time involved Atlantic slavery. Lloyd contributed to the law of contraband – an important issue given that the Atlantic had a budding illegal trade in an assortment of smuggled goods, including human beings, to avoid imperial taxes. A manuscript survives detailing his approach to the adjudication of prizes from the United Provinces of the Netherlands, which were involved in the slave trade in both the East and West Indies, prohibiting the delivery of victuals and manufactured goods to 'any port of the state of the United Provinces, or into any of their territorys, lands, plantations, or countries'. In crippling European enemies who relied on their transatlantic trade, Lloyd perhaps hoped to undermine Dutch slave societies, such as Curaçao and St Eustatius, which were largely dependent – like the British colonies of Barbados and Jamaica – on foodstuffs and mercantile goods to survive.[37]

Lloyd adjudicated on plantation estate cases as well. Cornelius O'Kelly was one of several Irishmen and Irish families, including the Walshes, Skerrets, Stapletons, and Rourkes, who moved to Saint-Domingue to exploit France's fastest growing colony. (John Stapleton and his wife Helen Skerret were one of the most prominent emigrants and used their newfound wealth as plantation owners and slave merchants to purchase an estate in Nantes.) On 20 March 1712, Lloyd dealt with a case concerning Hughes O'Kelly, whose 'late Brother Cornelius O Kelly Dyed in 1704 at St Domingo, under the French Government, Leaving an Estate of about 30000 Livres Tournois, which he Had, by Deed of Guilt in his Life-time, settled on the Petitioner, Pursuant to the Laws of France[.]' The French government had not honoured the will, though. 'That notwithstanding', the petition continued, 'the French have possessed themselves of the said Estate, and by a judgment obtained by surprize, Doe still detain the same[.]' Known as Queen Anne's War, the death of the childless Charles II of Spain had precipitated a transatlantic struggle for the Spanish American colonial possessions between Britain and the French and Spanish – and the colonial government perhaps confiscated O'Kelly's estate due to the war. Taking that context into account, Lloyd suggested that O'Kelly had a just case against the French government and that he should receive assistance from British ministers to find a conclusion to the case – 'according as the Laws and Practice of France shall permit' – that suited his interests. Lloyd had a role, too, in the aftermath of the English capitulation of Nevis to the French in 1706, when he advised the government a decade later to round up 'all the negroes' who had at that time 'fled' the plantations to the woods and mountains, and he provided advice on the legality of the French forces under Pierre Le Moyne d'Iberville holding hostages after Britain's defeat.[38]

Lloyd's jurisdiction as the Advocate General and legal counsel went to other prominent issues related to enslavement. Alongside the contraband trade, Lloyd adjudicated on piracy cases and had a role in defining the laws concerning the treatment of pirates. The Treaty of Utrecht in 1713 had ended the War of the Spanish Succession, yet peace had put large numbers of privateers out of work. Forced to explore new opportunities for profit, these privateers attacked ships transporting silver, foodstuffs, gold, and slaves. In 1720, Lloyd gave an opinion along with Philip Yorke, 1st Earl of Hardwicke, on whether legal officers could try and execute pirates at sea. This issue remained a significant point of contention because judges sought to provide colonial authorities with the ability 'within your Majesty's colonies or plantations for trying of pyrates there'. They recognised the importance of that issue for imperial and regional security, 'considering how much the seas have been infested with pyrates', but they could find no such precedent for a trial in this manner.[39]

Such a trial would soon emerge, however. In January 1723, Lloyd adjudicated on a case involving a Royal African Company slave ship, the *Gambia Castle*, and John Massey, who along with a group of soldiers had been sent to protect the vessel and regarrison a Company fort. The crew were mutinous from dysentery, malaria, and scurvy due to severe malnutrition – and they had subsequently turned to piracy alongside the first-mate George Lowther. Massey returned to England, but the Company had other plans, arguing that he should be 'fairly hanged' (a sentence duly carried out). That was not the end of Lloyd's dealings with West Africa. Two years later, he empowered 'the commander of his Majesty's ship the Kinsale, in conjunction with the principal agents belonging to the African Company at their settlements abroad, to try and execute such pirates as may happen to be taken on the coast of Africa[.]' As the Crown's legal counsel, Lloyd perhaps understood his role of defeating piracy and bolstering a slave-trading enterprise as intertwined objectives.[40]

The Master of Trinity Hall soon confronted the pirates of the Caribbean in the courtroom. On 8 March 1718, Lloyd committed a pirate to Newgate who had travelled to that infamous prison to visit 'some of his Acquaintance[s]… with whom he had committed several Piracies in the West Indies'. More than four years later, in October 1722, Lloyd also sat in judgment on a Council of the Admiralty, which was deciding on a case involving Robert Lowther, the Governor of Barbados. The report in the newspaper read that on 12 February 1719 a vessel sailing into 'Carlisle-Bay in Barbadoes, was known to be a Pirate Ship whereupon Application was made to Capt. Whorwood, and Capt. Smart, Commanders of two of His Majesty's Men of War, viz. the Rye-Galley and

Squirrel'. Whorwood had fought pirate vessels in the Chesapeake Bay after the War of the Spanish Succession and had petitioned for more powerful ships and military support, but his activities opposing piracy were soon impeded. After capturing the vessel in Carlisle Bay, Lowther had demanded to have the 'Pirate Ship deliver'd to him, alledging an Act of Parliament', yet Whorwood insisted on his 'Right to dispose of the Prize, pursuant to His Majesty's Gracious Intentions, and produc'd his Orders from the Board of Admiralty to take, burn, sink, or otherwise destroy any Pirate Ships, or Vessels, &c'. The debate escalated quickly – Lowther detained Whorwood and deemed his seizure of the pirate vessel 'a Criminal Article'. In the commotion, the accused pirate appealed to the governor, arguing that he was, in fact, travelling to Barbados to 'sell his Slaves'. The accused pirate escaped custody – providing merely another reason for the Council to terminate Lowther's controversial governorship.[41]

Lloyd provided legal counsel for the South Sea Company too. Aside from slave-trading, the landmark *Asiento* contract, which Britain had acquired from Spain in 1713, had granted one vessel of 500 tons a year of duty-free merchandise to the great trade fairs at Portobello and Veracruz. Britain had formed a bridgehead in the Spanish Americas. The first ship, the *Royal Prince*, was scheduled to leave in 1714, but had only left port in 1716 – in consideration, the Spanish raised the tonnage of the next ten ships to 650. In 1722, the Company contacted Lloyd to advise them as they disputed the Spanish calculations of the relative tonnage of their vessels. They implored the advocate to consider whether the Company could 'Legally send out their annual ship this year, by virtue of the aforesaid Treatys' without 'measurement or otherwise' and sell their goods in Veracruz. Lloyd eased their concerns – he mentioned that the treaties ensured that the vessels could leave for the Spanish colonies – and he advised that the Company must stay within the policies stipulated in the Treaty. 'Indeed', he observed, 'there are a clause or two, as The Compa[ny] are Desirous to avoid *Henceforwards*: and, Frauds will be avoided which might redound to Prejudice, by the Entry *of these ships*. Which seems to Carry, a Like Rule for other annual ships'. 'This', he continued, 'I Conceive that the Secure way will bee, for the Company to Keep up to the Treaty and Convention, and not trust to the accounting for any Excesse'. To remain profitable, the SSC's trade in manufactured goods could not be curtailed – and Lloyd's legal advice helped to preserve its commercial activities.[42]

Alongside advising the South Sea and other companies, not to mention acting as the Master for Trinity Hall, Lloyd was a major investor in imperial enterprises. In 1707, he came into possession of his parents' stock in the East India Company, amounting to £230, which they appear to have held since at least 1684. (Dame Elizabeth had £112 in 1691 and Sir Richard retained £100, and they increased their collective holdings to £230 eight years later.) Lloyd seized the opportunity to acquire more securities, and, in 1720, he appeared twice on a list of SSC stockholders, with his assets amounting to around £4,000 some of this stock being held with Jacob Sawbridge, a London banker and a director of the Company. Holding that same amount in stock in 1720, Lloyd increased his share to at least £6,000 in the whirlwind of speculation around the Bubble, indicating that he was one individual amongst many who had unwisely bought into a bull market. As noted in the Chapter 2, in 1723 the company's assets were divided into stocks and annuities to stabilise the firm, and Lloyd was not cautious following the Bubble. He increased his stake – owning £12,080 in annuities before lowering that amount to £9,158 in annuities by 1733 – but Lloyd maintained an active interest in the Company's trading stock, with over £600 in securities held on his death.[43]

Besides his South Sea holdings, Lloyd – like his father, Richard – owned a stake in the Royal African Company. In 1720, he appeared on a *List of Names of the Adventurers* with £3,000 stock – a substantial sum that qualified him to be chosen governor, sub-governor, or deputy-governor. He was not the only university grandee or benefactor on that list: the Reverend Joseph Smith, the provost of Queen's College, Oxford, who facilitated a £1,000 donation from Queen Caroline to that institution, had £500 invested in the RAC; and James Brydges, the 1st Duke of Chandos, Chancellor of the University of St Andrews, possessed £30,000 of stock and used £1,000 of his fortune to endow the Chandos Chair of Medicine and Anatomy there. He was also listed as benefactor of £500 to the construction of the Cambridge Senate House, which was completed in 1730. Chandos had spearheaded a new infusion of capital at the time of Lloyd's investment to remove the Company's debt burden and 'reinvigorate' (in one economic historian's words) its slave-trading activities. The RAC's quadrupling of the number of shares issued and outstanding propelled the Company into a relatively successful era: a new fort was constructed in Angola (and others were repaired), ships were outfitted, and money and goods flowed into its depleted warehouses. Still, with the Company perhaps not matching the expected return on investment, Lloyd decided to dump his stock, with the final £2,000 sold in 1722.[44]

Ever shrewd with finances and administration, Lloyd turned his hand to managing Christopher Codrington's benefaction. Colleagues since their appointment as fellows at All Souls, Lloyd was awarded 100 guineas in Codrington's generous will, which the lawyer had in his possession, after the colonial administrator died on 7 April 1710, his health irretrievably damaged after leading a failed invasion of French Guadeloupe. Lloyd mourned his friend, who had given £10,000 to build and stock a new College library. He begged the College Warden for the 'acceptance of Mr Codringtons Picture, for yr. Hall: The Image of One Dead, to live again, among my Surviving Friends[.]' However, with Codrington's chief beneficiary, his cousin Lieutenant Colonel William Codrington, refusing to pay out the legacies to All Souls, Lloyd's first act on Codrington's behalf was to provide the SPG's committee members with Christopher's will, which 'bequeathed some of his [Barbadian] plantations' to them – and the Barbados Committee retained Lloyd as legal counsel. Lloyd, for his part, was a subscriber to both the SPG and SPCK for much of his life.[45]

Codrington's cousin started to transfer the legacies three years after the benefactor's death, and Lloyd was one of the overseers of the planned Codrington Library's construction and managed the benefaction fund for the College. As the money trickled in in 1713, he facilitated the transfer of funds to the College, and signed off on the accounts. One of those balance sheets on 2 June 1714 mentions Dr Peirce Dod's purchase of £2,300 of South Sea stock on the College's behalf. Dod was an interesting figure in his own right: a later investor in the Royal African Company, the Oxford man had a controversial medical career, writing pamphlets dismissing the science of smallpox inoculation. For All Souls', however, Dod was an exceptional servant to the college – and, although Dr Edward Kynaston, another fellow, travelled by coach to South Sea House on Threadneedle Street in London, the College ordered the 'Stock to Continue in Dr. Dods name'.[46]

Retrieving the investment before the Bubble burst, Dod continued the South Sea investing that Lloyd had first supervised. After Lloyd's fellowship ended, Dod held £6,220 in South Sea securities in June 1723, which was then split into £3,110 in annuities and the same in stock. By 21 November 1728, Dod managed to acquire £5,100 in annuities under "The Wardens Colledge of All Souls in Oxford." (An institution-level investment in such government debt securities was not unusual: Wadham College, Oxford, owned SSC annuities as well.) Dod assured the Warden that 'The Interest arising from the Annuities is now in my hands & ready to be paid whenever I shall be drawn upon[.]' Between 1725 and 1743, the most that the College made each year from the interest in these annuities was £664.[47]

Although he managed Codrington's money, Lloyd mobilised his own funds to support the project. That investment was essential because, as John Smail argues, credit markets were in their infancy. Bonds and loans were emotive in the eighteenth century – they were bonds of trust and not just commercial instruments. In November 1718, Lloyd wrote to the Bursars to assure them that 'all the Clear Profitts, which shall accrue to mee from my Fellowship, after All Souls Day 1718, and for soe long time, as I shall Continue Fellow... for the use aforesaid, to the Bursars yearly, shall bee their sufficient Discharge, against mee my Executors, or Administrators'. Lloyd acted as a personal lender of last resort to the College – a position to which he could dedicate his energies seeing as he had resigned his position as the King's Advocate and from the Doctors' Commons in October 1726. He provided two bonds to the College, one for £1,000 which All Souls paid £25 half yearly for, and another for £1,200 at £30 half yearly. Writing to the Warden in July 1729, he noted that 'I will as a Common Creditour, Lend the College £1000 at 5 p cent upon their Common Seal payable by them To mee, my Executors, or Administrators'. He did not want this money, he informed All Souls, 'taken as any Benefaction by them, nor is it so intended by mee'. The money that he donated through his fellowship, two bonds, and later bequest for £1,000 were integral to the construction of the library, Hall, cloister, buttery, and quadrangle. For these efforts, he was immortalised with a bust that peers down at readers in the Codrington Library and a portrait by Thomas Gibson.[48]

Lloyd's legal expertise was used to the benefit of another substantial benefaction in Oxford aside from Codrington – one which also had ties to British imperial interests in South Asia and the Americas. Lloyd was well placed to assist John Radcliffe's executors. A doctor by trade, Radcliffe amassed significant wealth from property; yet, like Lloyd and so many other elites, he had also invested in imperial ventures. In 1688, he joined with nine others to fund the recovery of shipwrecked treasure in St Helena – an interest in the South Seas that continued until the end of his life when he invested in the SSC in 1711 (holding £12,500 in trading stock before selling his securities two years later). Contributing £5,000 to the Helena enterprise, Radcliffe also funded three East India ships, the *Antelope*, *Adventure*, and *Wolfaire* between 1696 and 1705, and was an investor in that Company's stock. He provided '£50 a year for ever', too, to the Society for the Propagation of the Gospel. Upon his death on 1 November 1714, Radcliffe was worth around £140,000, with £40,000 provided to Oxford for an additional library (named the Radcliffe Camera, which was partly funded with South Sea money), £5,000 to his alma mater University College (money that was used for building two sides of a new quadrangle), four scholarships, travelling fellowships, and a prize fund for a medical science thesis. In June 1725, Lloyd provided legal guidance on choosing the Library Keeper for the Camera. He noted that the 'Founder' had not 'presented any method or form of choosing' that position, except for a stipulation that they be a 'Master of Arts' in Physick. Nor, Lloyd continued, did Radcliffe 'Direct any Examination, As to their Proficiency and Learning to be made[.]' The importance of his advice was highlighted by its recipient: Charles Townshend, 2nd Viscount Townshend, who assisted his brother-in-law, the Prime Minister Robert Walpole with Britain's foreign policy.[49]

As for Lloyd, he departed the mortal coil on 30 March 1745 leaving generous bequests to multiple colleges in both Oxford and Cambridge. The recipients included the University of Cambridge (providing £500 to the library and the same sum for University repairs along Regent's Walk), All Soul's (as mentioned above), Lincoln College, Oxford (who he gave £500 to remodel the library's bookshelves, and was featured in the *Oxford Almanack* as one of its principal 'Founders & Benefactors'), Trinity College, Oxford (his alma mater), and he saved his most generous bequest for Trinity Hall. He provided an initial £1,000 in return for an annuity of £50 to redevelop the Front Court, donated £3,000 to remodel the Hall and extend its grounds to the River Cam, and helped with extensive repairs to the chapel, 'so as to be almost rebuilt'. The monumental building work in the chapel included new marble flooring, wainscoting, iron work and glass for the windows, lead piping, a communion table, and doors and dressings. Trinity Hall did not receive Lloyd's South Sea securities – these went to establish a charity fund for the poor of Oswestry and Whittington, a market town and village on the English side of the Welsh border – but the college purchased £2,660 in South Sea annuities four years before Lloyd's death, which earned more than £63 in dividends the first year (though the Company was no longer involved in slave-trading). Buried in the college chapel, Trinity Hall recognised Lloyd as their most generous benefactor – establishing a memorial to the man who had shaped the college's 'fabric'.[50]

Trinity Hall's connection to the Atlantic world did not end with Lloyd. Sir William Wynne, a specialist in probate law and later Dean of the Court of Arches (1788–1809), contributed to several slavery-related cases, even as the University debated the efficacy of slaveholding. Wynne's life revolved around the collegiate system, with his father, John Wynne, serving as the Principal of Jesus College, Oxford. The Welshman instead chose to attend Cambridge – arriving at Trinity Hall in 1746, taking his Doctorate in 1757, and holding a Fellowship from 1755 until his death.[51]

Wynne was involved in imperial matters after American independence. As Dean, he adjudicated on cases related to US merchants, since that nation's newfound independence from Britain meant that they were aliens – citizens of a foreign country – and therefore unable to trade within the Empire under the Navigation Acts, which restricted trade to British ships – a damaging development for Caribbean colonists who relied on the American carrying trade for goods (often around forty per cent of goods leaving some New England ports were destined for the Caribbean). One query considered whether a register could be granted to ships constructed before independence. Wynne answered that vessels constructed before the Revolution could trade because 'such vessels could not be said to belong to any Colony or Plantation [belonging] to his Majesty', and if British subjects had purchased ships from the beginning of the war until the ratification of the Treaty of Paris, these purchases were rendered 'illegal' because the trade had happened with 'revolted colonies'. He also advised that customs officers could seize vessels from American citizens built and purchased by Britons after 1776 'trading to from or in any British Island or Plantation, or to any Part of this Kingdom or other [of] his Majesty's Dominions'.[52]

Three decades later, Wynne ruled on another American vessel, the *Washington*. Intended to be 'employed in a slave-trade adventure on the coast of Africa' before the abolition of the slave trade in the United States (and then turning to gun running and trading near the Congo River), Wynne and two other judges, Sir William Scott and Sir John Nicholl, refused to release the ship which had been impounded in Barbados. An adjudicator on imperial cases, Wynne followed Lloyd in making benefactions to his college too. After claiming the Mastership in 1803 (at the second attempt), Wynne donated 252 volumes to the library over nine years.[53]

Though Lloyd and Wynne were involved in day-to-day legal matters, natural law and the natural rights of enslaved Africans caused significant philosophical debate within Cambridge. Thomas Rutherforth (also spelled "Rutherford") was the most prominent (and undiscussed) Cambridge interlocutor in that debate. The son of a Cambridgeshire rector, Rutherforth was admitted as a sizar at St John's College in April 1726, and he rose to become a Royal Society fellow in 1743 and the Regius Professor of Divinity in 1745 (and was thereby elected a Doctor of Divinity at Cambridge). Like Lloyd and Gooch, Rutherforth had powerful friends and became a chaplain to Frederick, the Prince of Wales (and George II's heir apparent before the former's untimely death in 1751), and he later ministered to Frederick's wife, the dowager Princess Augusta, after his passing.[54]

Rutherforth's personal connections extended to the mercantile classes. In a letter to Peter Burrell, included in his *Two Sermons Preached Before the University of Cambridge* in 1747, the professor commended the former sub-governor of the South Sea Company and investor in the Royal African Company for 'placing your son under my care' and hoped to provide that student with 'that virtue and regularity' which 'had been laid before by your instructions, and by the example, which he saw at the head of his own family'. Rutherforth would reveal his commitment to prominent merchants and enslavers, such as Burrell, through publications as well as his teaching.[55]

Rutherforth's two volume magnum opus, *Institutes of Natural Law*, published at Cambridge in 1754, was a popular treatise amongst prominent American statesmen, including James Madison and Alexander Hamilton. The text was a commentary on the Dutch humanist Hugo Grotius's 1625 *On the Law of War and Peace*, which was a plea for law and order after the Thirty Years' War devastated much of Europe. The text extended Grotius's discussion of the ethics of enslavement. Rutherforth was a committed paternalist, arguing that enslaved people were children whom enslavers had a duty to civilise. 'The good of the child is the end, to which the authority of the parent over the child is directed', Rutherforth declared in the treatise, 'and the good of the master is the end, to which the authority of the master over the slave is directed'. He went on to concede, however, that the 'parent has no right to command the child', still he maintained that 'the master has a right to command the slave to do such actions, as are for the masters' benefit'.[56]

Rutherforth's *Institutes* defended the natural inequality of human beings. Though people were not natural slaves, they remained a 'slave from his birth' because 'Nature has indeed made a difference between the parts and capacities of mankind'. Some were able to 'judge for themselves, and to pursue their own good' yet others had to be 'directed'. Consequently, in rejecting natural slavery, Rutherforth established enslavement on the grounds of humanitarian action and the common good – that enslavement was an 'obligation' for individuals to be directed in their actions by enslavers 'in view to their benefit, who direct him'. Next, the Regius Professor turned to the legal doctrine of *partus sequitur ventrem* ("that which follows the womb"). Originally passed in Virginia in 1662 after a mixed-ethnicity woman Elizabeth Kay Grinstead had successfully sued for freedom because she had a white English father, the law mandated that children followed their mother's legal status. In resolving the question of whether the children of sexual violence between enslavers and the enslaved were free, the law allowed slaveholders to profit from their children, as Thomas Jefferson did with his six children to Sarah "Sally" Hemings. Rutherforth reconciled himself to this doctrine even though he opposed natural slavery. 'Since liberty is the natural state of mankind', he queried, 'it may be asked whether the children of slaves are free?'[57]

To answer this fraught question, he constructed four justifications for enslaving children: an act of the parents (who placed their children into slavery), a person's consent, criminal guilt for committing an offense, and debt peonage. The Professor turned to debt as a reason why the children of enslaved mothers should be enslaved. 'The original debt', he wrote, 'is indeed encreased by its maintenance during its infancy'. He continued: 'For the loss of her work and the extraordinary expence, which the child occasions, during the time of gestation and birth, fall upon the master of the mother and not upon the master of the father'. The extent to which enslavers relied on debt as a justification to enslave their offspring is difficult to answer, but Rutherforth's text certainly provided legal and ethical cover for enslavers in the courtroom and remained a central tenet of gradual abolition schemes that determined that enslaved people had to work to a certain age to relieve themselves of their "debt" to enslavers.[58]

Rutherforth's argument about the efficacy of childhood enslavement, which echoed the German jurist Samuel von Pufendorf, was controversial though. The Professor of Moral Philosophy at the University of Glasgow, Francis Hutcheson, rubbished this claim in his *A System of Moral Philosophy*, which his son published one year after Rutherforth's *Institutes*. Hutcheson accepted that when 'one maintains the child of a stranger, whatever prudent expences are made may justly be charged as a debt, where the contrary is not declared', but he was wary of how nations committed 'to the natural rights and liberties of mankind' had used this principle to enslave 'equally innocent children of captives in war, or of men of a different complexion… for ever, with all their posterity, upon no other pretence of right than this claim upon them for their maintenance'. If the debt was paid, Hutcheson rebutted, then the enslaver had no right to hold that child in bondage, and the enslaved minor had 'plainly a right to choose that labour by which he can soonest discharge the debt'. The Scotsman had attacked the notion that one set of natural rights existed for whites and another for Black British subjects.[59]

Rutherforth's support for childhood enslavement was contested in Cambridge as well. Fellows were aware of (and commented upon) the horrors of enslavement – in fact, comparing people's actions to an enslaver was fast becoming a punchline. Thomas Gilbert, a Peterhouse fellow, wrote a poem in 1738 questioning why someone acted 'Like *Christian* tyrants to the Negro slaves?' Edward Christian – the Downing Professor of the Laws of England (1788–1823), Professor at East India Company College (1806–1818), and elder brother of Fletcher Christian, a leader of the mutiny on the *Bounty* – wrote a popular response to William Blackstone's *Commentaries on the Laws of England* from 1793 to 1795. Innocent people, he wrote, including children, retained the 'power of action' even under threat from 'barbarous laws' and, in another passage, Christian attacked the idea that 'the master's right to the service [of the enslaved] can *possibly* continue' under the writ of habeas corpus because 'the negro in a state of slavery is incapable of entering into [a contract] with his master'. Christian rejected the possibility of children being indebted for their birth.[60]

Slavery was again central to the second volume of Rutherforth's *Institutes*. Unlike servitude, Rutherforth maintained that slavery had ramifications for a person's citizenship and rights within the community. Freedom was necessary to be the member of a civil society, and, consequently, Rutherforth claimed that 'a slave is incapable of being a member' of such a community because they were beholden to enslavers and must therefore 'act for his master's benefit in all things, according to the judgement and will of his master'. Incapable of acting for the 'general security' through wartime service or public employment, enslaved Black persons were denied a pathway to citizenship through patriotism, as many Black soldiers claimed in the British Empire. That theory anticipated, in some respects, the South Carolinian congressman David Ramsay's 1789 *Dissertation on the Manner of Acquiring the Character and Privileges of a Citizen of the United States*, where he argued that 'Negroes are inhabitants, but not citizens. Citizenship confers a right of voting at elections, and many other privileges not enjoyed by those who are no more than inhabitants'. Rutherforth also prescribed how much power the state had over enslaved people's treatment on the plantation. According to him, as the enslavers' property and persons considered outside of civil society, the enslaved could be treated however slaveholders wished since the broader community had no 'authority over the master for the benefit or security of his slaves'. There is evidence of this doctrine in practical use and for Rutherforth's influence on slave laws in the antebellum United States. For instance, in the North Carolina case *State v. Mann* in 1829, the judge Thomas Ruffin used Rutherforth's *Institutes* to argue that enslavers were not liable for a grievous harm upon enslaved persons because such an act was for the 'good of the child'.[61]

Rutherforth was certainly not the only St John's academic to write on slavery and natural law. A contemporary of Rutherforth, John Taylor, received his BA in 1725, and, after practicing with the Doctors' Commons he was appointed as a college fellow and as a tutor to the children of John Carteret, the

2nd Earl of Granville, a Secretary of State under George II. Published in 1769, Taylor's *Elements of Civil Law* echoed many of Rutherforth's claims in the *Institutes*. Regarding the doctrine of *partus sequitur ventrem*, Taylor argued that children were enslaved at birth because the 'offspring of a slave, through its own impotency, can provide nothing for the state of its infancy; and... the future service of its life is due to the owner, as a debt of education'. Taylor viewed the enslaved as inhuman, comparing them to horses and other property; still, he also expanded on Rutherforth's original arguments, particularly on whether enslaved persons should be soldiers in service to the empire. 'The Romans never made soldiers of their Slaves', Taylor wrote, for two reasons: 'the honour of the profession', and 'the secret was, they durst not trust them with arms, their number so considerable; which is now the steady politics of our West India colonies, and for the same reason'. Together with Rutherforth, Taylor's writings show a strain of Cambridge intellectual thought existed that defended enslavement at birth.[62]

As with the *Institutes*, Taylor's *Elements* spread beyond Cambridge, finding its way into the libraries of Thomas Jefferson and other elite enslavers and abolitionists. In fact, the text's afterlife overshadowed its author: proslavery activists utilised its commentaries on the consistency between Christianity and enslavement and the natural basis of coerced labour within the 'little Empire of a private family', where 'children' were subordinate to their parents, to defend the plantation system. Abolitionists, too, seized upon Taylor discussion of the treatment of the enslaved as 'no persons' and 'beasts' under Roman law to illustrate the '*cruelties*' and '*diabolical injustice[s]*' that enslaved African Americans lived under. In 1852, the eight members of two enslaved families were met by a free man on board a ship whilst travelling with their Virginian enslavers, Jonathan and Juliet Lemmon, to New York and subsequently freed – with the help of local abolitionists – under a writ of habeas corpus. The lawyers who supported the enslaved in the so-called Lemmon Slave Case (named after the enslavers), which established the right of personhood for the enslaved, drew upon Taylor's work, amongst other authorities, to claim that enslavement 'originates in mere predominance of physical force, and is continued by mere predominance of social force or municipal law', and was therefore an 'active violation of the law of nature'. The findings in the case illuminate the long-reach and malleability of Cambridge legal texts.[63]

Having discussed the Cambridge professional classes – the clergymen, natural scientists, and lawyers – in the preceding chapters, one can see the active involvement of fellows, lecturers, and benefactors in imperial processes. Though wealth and academic thought are often separated, the two were inextricable – especially so if Cambridge figures wanted to use their hard-earned funds to support imperial endeavours, as they did with most schemes and enterprises that historians have drawn attention to in the seventeenth and eighteenth centuries. From the Guinea Company to American courtrooms, the thoughts and cashbooks of Cambridge intellectuals had a lasting influence, shaping the origins and nature of the English and British empires. Their experiences disprove Prime Minister William Gladstone's assertion concerning the 'antagonism which is offered to wealth by mental cultivation [at universities]'. Soon, the antagonisms within Cambridge grew between fellows, students, and alumni who attacked the slave system and those who sought to consolidate and defend the plantation machine.[64]

4

'Several University Gentlemen, who have quite altered their Tone': The Problem of the British Slave Trade

On 28 March 1798, Charles Farish, a Queens' fellow, sent a dramatic petition to George III calling for the end of the transatlantic trafficking of enslaved Africans. The Georgian King, it should be noted, had a complex personal relationship to enslavement. His grandfather, George I, had invested tens of thousands of pounds in the SSC, George II had served as its governor, and the latter's son, Frederick Louis, owned stock too. Furthermore, George III's son William, the Duke of Clarence (later William IV), was in the proslavery camp, principally because he claimed that abolishing the slave trade would greatly weaken Britain's maritime strength, and the king himself was concerned during the American Revolutionary War with the defense of the British Caribbean, particularly Jamaica. On the other hand, George III's nephew, the Duke of Gloucester, was an abolitionist voice in the House of Lords and the monarch had written in his youth between 1755 and 1758 "Of the Laws relative to the Nature of Climates." In his antislavery commentary on the Baron Montesquieu, George attacked the notion, subscribed to by, among others, Thomas Rutherforth, that 'a person rearing a poor helpless Infant acquires a dominion over him[.]' In fact, the radical, youthful royal observed, 'this can only hold while it [the enslaved child] is incapable of earning its own livelyhood[.]' Given these familial politics, Farish's petition arrived at a critical moment because the royal family were torn on the problem of enslavement. Intent on converting the king to abolition, Farish wrote an extensive, yet long-ignored, remonstrance to convince him to pressure Parliament and end the slave trade.[1]

Alongside the philosopher William Paley, whose ideas are alluded to in the petition, Farish had an intellectual debt to William Henry Coulthurst – and they travelled in the same evangelical circles at Cambridge. Coulthurst was the son and heir of a Barbadian merchant and he later appeared in the slave compensation records as the co-owner of a plantation in Demerara. An alumnus of St John's and a tutor at Sidney Sussex from 1788 to 1791, Coulthurst was a committed opponent of the slave trade but a defender of enslavement writ-large. He argued that by a 'humane Treatment and a well[-]regulated Police' of the enslaved their 'Population' would 'be sufficiently upheld and preserved without such Importations from Africa, and by Improvements in the Mode of the Agriculture the Estates would to all intents and Purposes be equally as beneficial as at present'.[2]

Farish's petition echoed many of these statements. After a deferential preamble, the Queen's fellow highlighted the 'happy effects' which would follow the abolition of the slave trade. It is worth quoting this passage in full: 'War', he wrote to King George III, 'will be deprived of half its horrors, and peace of all its fears. Suspicion and the dread of captivity will no longer interrupt domestic quiet. Half the causes of contention and bloodshed will be done away. The voice of complaining will scarce be heard in the land. Commerce will spread her sails. The rude savage will by degrees learn the useful arts and mild manners of civilized life. And Religion will no longer hesitate to open her lips on that benighted shore, when there shall be no Christian Slave-merchants there to shame her cause'. 'When this stone of offence is removed', he concluded, 'the Ministers of the Gospel may hope to win over many souls… to their Master, and a people whom he hath not known shall serve him'. His long-ignored "Summary of the consequences of the abolition of the slave-trade" (see Figure 4.1) sought to promote a virtuous cycle where the end of the slave trade would lead, inexorably, to the gradual abolition of enslavement. Free Africans could then, he concluded, labour in the British Caribbean and transform the region into a new Eden – a Christian empire.[3]

'Like the touch of the son of Mary', Farish claimed in the petition, the abolition of the slave trade would achieve more than laws or regulations to ameliorate slavery. It would halt what Farish called 'those dreadful mutinies' – referring to slave revolts, such as in Haiti – because those uprisings were inspired by 'freshly-imported slaves'. Abolition, he maintained, would also 'make it the *unquestionable* interest of the Master not to be cruel to his slave, or to lay upon him a greater burthen than he can bear'. Without the incentive to starve, torture, or murder their replaceable enslaved labour force, Farish argued, the 'balance of profit' would favour the humane treatment of the enslaved and inspire enslavers to introduce the plow and other labour-saving technological innovations to their plantations. If abolition was enacted, West Africans would 'bear their lot with patience, and even with cheerfulness; till Government shall… reach out to them a protecting hand: and by wise provisions of law gradually accomplish their emancipation'. Abolition would reform the British Empire – it would be, in his hopeful words, an 'act of national justice and repentance' that would expunge the sin and guilt for enslavement and rescue Britain's traders in enslaved people from a 'baleful commerce, which destroys their health and taints their minds'. He pondered a horrifying alternative to abolition: letting enslaved Africans, if they survived the conditions of the Atlantic middle passage, 'loose on their country fleshed in blood, and prepared to do any deed of violence?'[4]

Cambridge abolitionism, therefore, was far more complicated than the conventional wisdom, usually promulgated in histories and public forums, of university-educated abolitionists such as Thomas Clarkson and William Wilberforce striving for Black freedom. University fellows, students, alumni, and their interlocutors occupied a wide spectrum of opinions regarding the slave trade and the abolition of slavery writ large, with many arguing that if slavery was reformed then it would not have to be confronted directly, with the chattel economy dying over the course of one or two decades. At the same time, Stephen Fuller, a former Trinity fellow, was one of the leaders of the proslavery lobby and urged the universities to empathise with enslavers. Such complexities were particularly evident in African exploration and colonisation, which Cambridge men helped to support and fund. The following chapter discusses abolition, proslavery, and colonisation in turn, thereby showing how universities were neither abolitionist nor proslavery – Cambridge was, like the royal family, riven with intergenerational conflict and debate, with the opinions of undergraduates often outpacing those of the fellowship, many of whom remained committed to "moderation" in the debate over the potential end of the slave trade. Together, these men shared a higher goal and purpose in the renewal of a humiliated and divided empire following Britain's disastrous defeat in the American Revolutionary War.

The politics of enslavement were personal to Cambridge men. Charles Farish's maternal uncle was a doctor and plantation owner in Grenada, and – after schooling in Carlisle – Farish went to Hawkshead Grammar School in Lancashire, an institution frequented by the slave-trading and mercantile classes. While there he befriended William Wordsworth, the later poet laureate and abolitionist, and may have also stayed at Hugh and Ann Tyson's boarding lodge. The Tyson boarding house was close to a Quaker meeting house where, given that the Society of Friends formed the vanguard of radical abolitionism, slavery would have almost certainly been discussed. Though no equal of Wordsworth, Farish wrote poetry – and it is from his early writings that we can see his opinions developing on the slave trade. In June 1784, whilst an eighteen-year-old student at Cambridge, he wrote a thoughtful poem on 'Sunburnt Nation's... Where direful Slav'ry with her ruffian bands Waves her black banners o'er the wretch'd land And drags the Captive [Slave] from afar: Plunging his Country in the woes of War[.]' The undergraduates, not the fellows, it appears, were the more radical generational undercurrent for anti-slave-trade opinion. Although Charles matriculated at Trinity College in 1784, graduated as fifteenth wrangler in 1788, and held a fellowship at Queens' from 1792 until his death in 1824, he remains more well-known for his opposition to the enforced celibacy of the fellowship than his antislavery activism. After his dramatic petition, the College's records do not reveal any determined effort on his behalf concerning the slave trade within that institution but tell rather of his efforts as a fellow dealing with mundane activities such as debts, the purchase of coal, the appointment of chapel clerks, and an expulsion.[5]

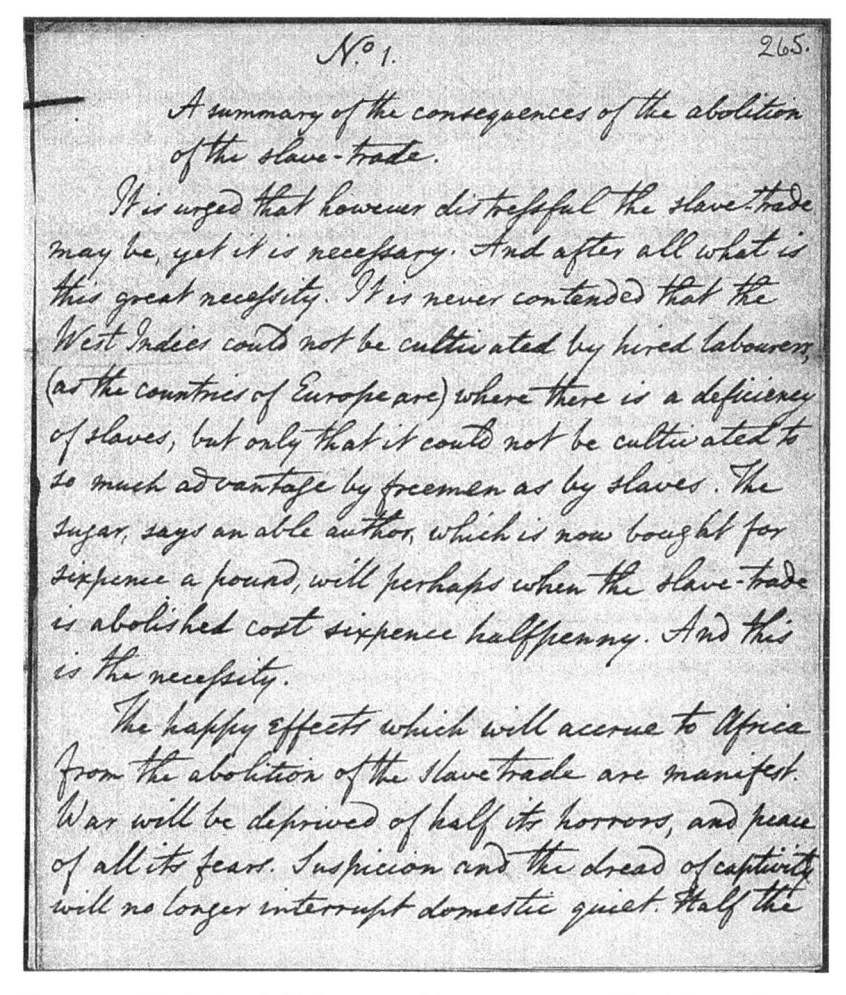

Figure 4.1 Charles Farish, 'A Summary of the consequences of the abolition of the slave-trade', 1798, Letters, Papers, and Domestic Correspondence of George III. National Archives, Kew, London.

The American Revolution galvanised opinion on the slave trade, as British observers, such as the lexicographer Samuel Johnson, dismissed the revolutionaries for crying liberty when they were the 'drivers of negroes'. That was true amongst the wider Cambridge community, too, as the imperial crisis over "taxation without representation" shifted after American independence into a continental war. The Lieutenant General Sir William Draper won a scholarship and fellowship at King's College, later donating the colours he captured from the Siege of Manilla in October 1763 to his alma mater – a donation 'hung up in that beautiful Chapel, with a proper solemnity, and the conqueror was rewarded with a red ribband'. Draper, who had negotiated a sizeable ransom from the Spanish after the Siege, was similarly ruthless with the Americans – proposing in 1774 (at the height of the North American imperial crisis) that, in response to colonial resistance, the British should 'Proclame *Freedom* to their Negroes; then how long would they be a people? They would soon cry out for pardon, and *render unto CÆSAR the Things which are CÆSAR's*'. John Hinchcliffe, the Master of Trinity from 1768 to 1788 and Member of the House of Lords, commentated on enslavement as well, but from a more moderate perspective than Draper's call for a British-inspired enslaved rebellion. A committed disciple of Granville Sharp's 'Spanish Regulations', Hinchcliffe wanted to 'soften and gradually reduce the Slavery in the West Indies' through similar policies to the Spanish colonies, where the enslaved were able to work one day a week besides Sundays to receive the '*wages of a freeman*' – an 'encouragement to industry' so that enslaved Africans could earn their freedom. Predicated on paternalistic assumptions of African indolence and aversion to family life, Hinchcliffe and Sharp's proposals were intended to provide 'strength' and 'security' to slave societies that were under threat from enslaved revolts.[6]

After the Revolution, antislavery ideas dominated debate at Cambridge, with Hinchcliffe and Richard Watson, a Trinity fellow, Regius Professor of Divinity, and Bishop of Llandaff, inviting Granville Sharp to the university to discuss the amelioration of slavery in the Spring of 1781. Amelioration – the reform of slavery, not its abolition – was the limit of much white antislavery thought, however. Often, Cambridge intellectuals were in like mind with men such as Edmund Keene, the Master of Peterhouse, who understood enslavement as an imperial opportunity. He had declared before the SPG in 1757 that 'Civil Authority' over the Americas had presented missionaries with an 'Opportunity of doing religious Service, by instructing the native Indians [Native Americans] and transplanted slaves' – a process further assisted by Europeans' 'Vicinity and Connection' with Native peoples and the 'Dependence and Subserviency' of Africans. If they intended on reforming slavery, many middling and elite Britons understood that issue as one amongst a host of social problems plaguing British society, including poverty, drunkenness, and the corruptions of commercial society.[7]

Peter Peckard, the Master of Magdalene, was one of the most significant and radical of these Cambridge antislavery polemicists. At St Mary's Church on 30 January 1784, he faced his congregation, many of whom probably had connections, both personal and financial, to enslavement – a context that made his words more significant. He attacked chattel slavery as an affront to humanity and the Christian God. 'The treatment which in general man experiences from man', he preached, 'is to the last degree ungenerous, oppressive, and cruel'. Giving his lesson from the Gospel of Peter, which encouraged Christians to 'honour all men', Peckard deplored the 'horrid instances of uncountrouled despotism exhibited in the overgrown empires of the world'. He condemned the popular white belief that a 'great part of the human race' must be enslaved solely because their 'external complexion' was 'different from our own, but who are formed of the same blood with ourselves'. In his powerful invective against the slave trade (one of the first of his many forthright efforts), Peckard attempted to undermine the ideologies of race – particularly that of blood – that had enabled Thomas Townes and other enslavers to justify holding Black people in bondage for more than a century.[8]

One of Peckard's most momentous antislavery acts occurred three years earlier, however, when he set an essay question after conversations about the choice of topic with John Hinchcliffe. Following their discussions, Peckard acted. Prompted by the *Zong* massacre in 1781, where 133 Africans, en route from the Gold Coast to Jamaica, were thrown to their death from a slave ship to preserve supplies of drinking water (their murder compared to 'just as if horses were kill'd'), Peckard set an essay question in Cambridge's Latin dissertation competition in 1785. He chose '*Anne liceat invitos in servitutem dare?*' – "Is it lawful to make slaves of others against their will?" Thomas Clarkson was willing to take on Peckard's academic challenge. Born in nearby Wisbech in 1760, Clarkson was around twenty-five years old – and a recent graduate of St John's – when he entered the competition. Drawing upon first-hand accounts of the slave trade, the works of the Quaker activist Anthony Benezet, and travel narratives, Clarkson won the essay prize (with Robert Heslop of Sidney Sussex the runner-up). His academic successes (and a spiritual awakening on the arduous road from Cambridge to London) convinced Clarkson that abolitionism was a lifetime calling from God.[9]

After translating his Latin essay into English, Clarkson published the dissertation, *An essay on the slavery and commerce of the human species, particularly the African* in 1786. It was an almost instant success. He argued that the slave trade was not only immoral and an affront to a nation the 'basis of whose government is *liberty*' – enslavement was counterproductive because it undermined the political economy of the British Empire. 'Nothing can be more clearly shewn', he claimed in the *essay*'s preface, 'than that an inexhaustible mine of wealth is neglected in *Africa*, for the prosecution of this impious traffick'. If Britain developed colonies in West Africa, Clarkson wrote, 'the revenue of this country might be greatly improved, its naval strength increased, its colonies in a more flourishing situation, the planters richer, and a trade, which is now a scene of blood and devastation, converted into one, which might be prosecuted with *advantage* and *honour*'. For Clarkson, the end of the slave trade would be an avenue to create a more moral empire in Africa, based on "civilising" and Christianising Africans.[10]

Neither Clarkson nor Peckard should be seen in isolation though. Black Britons profoundly shaped Peckard's education in Britain's greatest moral, political, and social problem: the problem of slavery. As Michael E. Jirik has shown, Black British antislavery activists are conveniently forgotten in histories of Cambridge abolitionism. Along with the growing influence of rational dissent at Cambridge stressing religious and civil liberty, Black Britons formed much of the vanguard against the slave trade. Born in 1745 in Eboe in Benin, Olaudah Equiano – who had been captured in Africa, purchased his freedom, and then published an influential autobiography detailing his experiences – was a key figure in the Cambridge antislavery movement. Equiano visited the town in July 1789 and there he met with Peckard and other local abolitionists, praising the 'Gentlemen of the University' who had shown him 'true civility without respect to colour or complexion'. (Peckard even helped to advertise his *Interesting Narrative*.) Before his arrival, Clarkson introduced Equiano to Thomas Jones, a Trinity tutor, who volunteered to sell copies of his slave narrative to cover Equiano's travel expences – and this formerly enslaved man perhaps helped to radicalise Peckard's abolitionism. Six months after Equiano's visit, Peckard gave another sermon in January 1790, which extended his criticisms against the transatlantic trade to plantation slavery, calling for Britons 'to give liberty to the captives, to loose the bands of wickedness, to undo the heavy burthens, to let the oppressed go free, to break every yoke'. That was a radical argument for many white antislavery activists. Opposition to the slave trade did not, at this time, necessarily result in calls for the immediate abolition of enslavement.[11]

Peckard may have gone further though in his anonymously-published 1788 treatise *Am I Not a Man? and a Brother?* – a document, often attributed to the Magdalene man, that drew its name from the modeller William Hackwood and ceramicist Josiah Wedgwood's design for a kneeling enslaved man who would be emblazoned on a seal promoting the London-based Committee for the Abolition of the Slave Trade. (The Master chose to remain anonymous even as he mentioned a 'Dr Peckard', and said that 'I freely declare myself of the same opinion'.) Peckard objected that human law had to accord with the 'Commands of God, and the Common Rights of Human Nature' – with the 'Traffick in the Human Species... destructive of the one, and contradictory to the other, and therefore... not justifiable by an Human Institution'. Labelling the enslaved as 'Brutes', the author informed his reader that 'the benevolent spirit of religion teaches us that a truly righteous man is merciful to his beast'. Questioning the notion that Black people were an 'inferior race' (despite the writer's equation of the enslaved with "beasts"), he pondered 'how are we to determine with precision who is or is not black?' given the 'gradations in human complexions', referring to Jefferson's writings on the mythical '*White Negroe*' (an African nation with white skins) in his 1787 *Notes on the State of Virginia*. Mocking Jefferson's argument that Africans 'secrete less by the Kidneys, and more by the skin, which gives them a disagreeable odour', he called for some semblance of human equality and dismissed the natural scientific basis for racial enslavement.[12]

For this treatise and his powerful attacks against the slave trade, Peckard was admired in the local newspapers. In the *Cambridge Chronicle*, three poems appeared that implanted in readers' minds images of suffering Africans and children torn from their parents. The first, published in February 1788, asked 'Shall thus the Sons of Freedom's blithe domain, Thus barter man and Basely Rob for Gain?' The poet called for Britons, inhabiting a land for persons who would "never be slaves," to 'turn from rapine – see the patriot Band [of abolitionists] Arrest thy course, and seize thy guile – fraught hand'. The first poet lauded Peckard as the equal of Wilberforce and as a 'patriot of the world', yet the second poem was less emotional in tone. Though difficult to say for certain, the author may have been James Moore, a Magdalene undergraduate. If he did author the poem, Moore's approach to slavery focused – much in line with abolitionist thought at the time – on labelling traders in enslaved Africans as 'Christian butcher[s]' who 'laugh[ed]' at the 'groans' and 'shame' of enslaved people.[13]

Published in March that year, the third poem, "The Slaves: An Elegy," made pointed criticisms of both the slave trade *and* plantation slavery. Naming himself "Della Crusca," the poem may have been the work of Robert Merry, the grandson and son of highly influential members of the Hudson's Bay Company and an alumnus of Christ's, where he studied before living in Florence and joining the Florentine Academia della Crusca (founded in 1583 to guard the purity of the Italian language, and the source of his well-known epithet). 'Lo!', he declared, 'where to yon PLANTATION drooping goes The SABLE HERO of Human kind, while near Stalks a pale DESPOT, and around him throws The scourge that wakes – that punishes the tear'. Through vivid imagery, Merry asked his audience to consider whether 'Drops of Blood the HORRIBLE MANURE That fills with luscious Juice, the TEEMING CANE? And must our Fellow-Creatures thus endure, For Traffic vile, th' Indignity of Pain?' Merry, whose maternal grandfather was the beneficiary of a trust in an Antiguan plantation, viewed enslavement as an embarrassment for an empire that claimed that no Briton would be slaves.[14]

Academic support for abolition was also monetary in nature. After the Society for Effecting the Abolition of the Slave Trade (SEAT) was established in May 1787, the University of Cambridge occupied an entire section of donors. Four students subscribed to the Society: Robert Parker of Sidney Sussex, Richard Moore of Peterhouse, George J. Legh of Christ's, and James Scarlett of Trinity. The most prominent Cambridge colleges provided money to SEAT, too, including Caius, Catharine Hall (now St Catharine's), Corpus Christi, Christ's, Emmanuel, Magdalene, Peterhouse, Sidney Sussex, St John's, Trinity, and Trinity Hall. In total, Cambridge colleges, fellows, tutors, and students donated £137 and 10s in 1787, with that impressive figure increasing to around £161 and 19s in 1788, six per cent of SEAT's budget (due, in part, to a surge in donations from St John's).[15]

These sums were facilitated through correspondence networks between resident college fellows and the members of the Committee for the Abolition of the Slave Trade, with William Frend of Jesus, James Lambert and Thomas Jones of Trinity, and the Reverend Coulthurst of Sidney Sussex sending letters of advice or support. Lambert communicated 'some important Questions relative to the slave trade' and the 'state of the unhappy slaves in the islands, which he had transmitted to a friend, who had resided in them, to answer'. The influence of Lambert and Jones was critical to the election of reformist fellows including John Tweddell (a student of the latter), who was appointed after a November 1790 address in Trinity Chapel supportive of the French Revolution and critical of the 'english barbarity' and 'legalized piracy' that had torn enslaved people from the 'sweets of life'. The strength of these networks ensured that Cambridge was the most prominent donor to the anti-slave-trade movement amongst the British universities.[16]

Some caution – and context – is required, however, when assessing the significance of these donations relative to Cambridge's other charitable endeavours. Since colleges were generous donors before the eighteenth century, a donation to a body such as SEAT was far from unusual. Three months after the first of their two donations to end the slave trade, Caius gave ten guineas – the same amount as both their anti-slave trade donations combined – 'to the Poor of the Town of Cambridge, viz. seven Guineas from the College, & three Guineas from the Allocation Fund, on Account of the Severity of the Weather'. Following the French Revolution and the Catholic Church's disestablishment, five guineas were provided for the 'relief of the French Refugee Clergy & laity'. Four fellows at Corpus Christi donated four pounds and four shillings to SEAT, but the College also provided five pounds and five shillings toward printing Arabic psalms and New Testaments for 'Eastern Christians', twenty-one pounds in 1759 for relieving the British army fighting France in Germany, and ten pounds to French emigrant clergymen fleeing the Revolution. When a French invasion seemed imminent in 1798, the university and its constituent colleges and members provided £7,000 for the war effort. The donations, then, suggest anti-slave-trade sympathies, but, as with most middling and elite Britons, the colleges did not consider enslavement worthy of special attention compared to other causes, such as poverty reduction, military support, and missionary Anglicanism.[17]

Subscriptions to pamphlets and dramatic plays provided another avenue for Cambridge men to highlight their abolitionist credentials. Equiano's publicization efforts depended upon subscription lists, which were a form of self-promotion for an author and an opportunity for publishers to inflate the 'number and status' of their supporters. Abolition presented some challenges to this model as subscribers, many of whom paid half in advance for book production costs and the other half on delivery, were perhaps fearful of their opinions becoming known on such a contentious subject, with one author noting that the subscribers' names were 'omitted', in part, for 'other speculate' reasons. Weathering the potential storm of criticism, numerous Cambridge fellows subscribed to Thomas Harwood's 1788 play, *The Noble Slave: A Tragedy* – an example of the anti-slave trade literature that flourished at this time. (Indeed, James Plumptre, a Clare Hall fellow, later remarked that stage productions, such as Harwood's, had influenced 'the public mind with respect to the state of the *Negroes*, and the infamous traffic of the *Slave-trade*'.) The subscribers included twenty fellows and students from King's, thirteen from Jesus, and ten from Trinity. The most prominent men were the Reverend Francis Barnes, Vice-Provost at King's, and Sir Griffith Boynton, a Baronet from Trinity. Harwood, 'Late of University College, Oxford', followed the story of Alcander, a 'noble slave', who saved a woman, restored a king, and became a loyal counsellor to prove that whatever the 'laws of fate ordain', no one could 'encroach' on the 'rights of man'.[18]

Undergraduates at Cambridge, it appears, were particularly forthright in their attacks against the slave trade. From makeshift debating societies to Greek poetry, antislavery thought and activity was as rich in Cambridge as elsewhere in Britain. In December 1796, a Magdalene student's diary mentioned a meeting of a mock 'House of Commons', where he 'moved for the consideration of his Majesty's (Thomason's [Thomas Truebody Thomason, a Queens' student and later fellow and East India Company chaplain]) message about dissolving the House. He moved the abolition of the slave trade'. Six years earlier, Wilberforce's first abolition bill had been comprehensively defeated by 163 votes to 88 – and the student debate perhaps betrayed a sense of frustration at parliamentarians' conservatism, or a student politician's wily effort to head-off an effort to dissolve their makeshift chamber by introducing such a divisive measure.[19]

Away from such discussion groups, students devoted their pens and speeches to the abolition effort. Samuel Taylor Coleridge's 1792 Greek ode *Against the Slave Trade* was awarded a Gold Medal and recited 'publickly in the Senate House' on commencement day. As stipulated in the Medal's rules, Coleridge wrote in imitation of the Greek poet Sappho, denouncing 'slavery's evil', which was 'richly fed by the groans of the wretched'. Tripos verses, an antiquated tradition of two undergraduates constructing a Latin poem for various "Tripos days" during the year, also discussed enslavement, with one unfavourably comparing 'the labours of the Africans' to the mercy and clemency one usually expected upon being conquered.[20]

Cambridge students soon entered the popular lecture circuit to make their voices heard. Following his graduation from Cambridge (and joining the example of other lecturers such as Thomas Clarkson, who travelled across Britain with his campaign chest of African crafts to convince Britons to support a free and commercial continent without enslaved people), Coleridge lectured his audience about the slave trade on 16 June 1795 at the Assembly Coffee House on Bristol Quay. Costing one shilling for admission, Coleridge's talk was advertised as from a graduate of 'Jesus College, Cambridge' – an opportunity for his audience to hear from England's rising generation of cultural and political leaders. According to Coleridge, Britain's vices stemmed from its consumer economy – from the corrupt desire to cure 'artificial Wants' with the purchase of sugar, rum, cotton, coffee, and mahogany. Though perhaps a risky proposition at a coffee house, the Jesus alumnus argued that these goods were not 'useful' and were rather picked and produced under a brutal labour system that tortured the enslaved through 'savage Punishments', and that – far from the 'nursery for Seaman' – the slave trade condemned white sailors to death at sea or to become 'shadows in their appearance' after becoming embroiled in that commerce. Condemning both the Duke of Clarence for his 3 May 1792 maiden speech opposing abolition and William Pitt, the prime minister, for being recalcitrant and cautious in his efforts to abolish the trade, Coleridge declared that the enslaved, as in Tacky's April 1760 momentous revolt in Jamaica, were more than justified in rebelling against their white oppressors.[21]

Charles Farish was stirred by Cambridge's anti-slavery literary flair too. His petition to George III included a "Reverie on a Benguelinha or Angola Linnet, which was caught in Africa and carried successively to Brazil, to Botany-bay, to England, twice to the West-Indies, & finally to England again." Farish may have attached great meaning to this sentence: slavers usually dismissed anti-slavery pamphlets and ideas as reveries (or daydreams); the choice of bird, a Linnet, was perhaps symbolic as a finch from Angola was called a *Negral*, perhaps an allusion to enslaved "negroes" (who were captured and caged as animals); and the bird travelled to Brazil, the largest slave society, Botany Bay, a convict colony in Australia (or Van Diemen's land, as it was then known), and to the West Indies, plantation societies that required no introduction to the king. Farish's dreamscape was more of a nightmare, with the fictional enslaved dreamer imagining 'pleasant fields' and then waking to find 'his dead yokefellow chained to his side himself afflicted by a painful disease, his bruised and naked body lying on a bare and loathsome board: his allotted space not broader than a coffin'. The still night was punctuated with the 'noise of corpses plunging into the sea', perhaps an allusion to the *Zong* massacre. In criticising European colonisers as the 'depopulators of continents', Farish also observed – like Thomas Thompson – that Africans were partly responsible for these crimes, as 'it is not uncommon for a Chieftain, when oppressed with debts contracted for Gunpowder or destructive liquors, to betray a part of his people into the hands of their Oppressors, & this often not without bloodshed'. Furthermore, he distinguished between enslaved Africans born in the colonies, who could be held in bondage, and those kidnapped and trafficked to the Americas. 'Whatever right the West India Planters may have to the Slaves which they have bought with their money or which have been born under their roof and fostered by their care', he noted, 'they can have none to the people of

Africa'. Enslavers did not feed Africans 'with the milk of their bosom', 'tend him in the wayward freaks of childhood', or 'teach him to handle the javilin, and instruct him in the simple arts of savage life'. Enslaved people born on the plantations, he implied, owed some of their intellectual and physical development to the white enslaver class.[22]

Most of their number had never visited a plantation, yet Farish and his fellow Cambridge men understood the stakes of the slavery struggle and the debates in Parliament. Andrew Burnaby, a Queens' alumnus and clergyman, had published his travels through North America in 1775 and again in 1798 (where he criticised the 'cruel and oppressive' system of enslavement); and several Cambridge men were listed as subscribers, including the Trinity fellow Henry Hinchliffe, to the former customs officer William Eddis's *Letters from America*, which informed interested British readers about the important geographical distinction between the relatively 'scarce' number of the enslaved in New England and the slave societies of the Carolinas where 'they [the enslaved] considerably exceed the number of white inhabitants'.[23]

News concerning the (often vitriolic) antislavery debate was also spread through private correspondence networks. William Smyth, the son of a prominent Liverpool banker, a Peterhouse fellow (and later Regius Professor of Modern History), understood the significance of this historical moment, so he decided to travel to the House of Commons 'with an Intention of hearing the Debate on the Slave Trade' but was too late given the public's interest in 'this important subject'. He was unwilling to be defeated in his goal – he intended to 'retreat to Day' since the subject was adjourned, and he would make sure, he informed his correspondent, to be at Parliament by 10 o'clock sharp the next morning so that he could hear the speakers. Smyth's interest may have been further stimulated because Cambridge had joined the debate. The University had petitioned the House of Commons against the slave trade, arguing that 'A firm belief in the Providence of a benevolent Creator, assures them that no system founded on the oppression of one part of mankind, can be beneficial to another'.[24]

College fellows ministered in urban centres that were dependent on the enslaved economy. That activism occurred in Liverpool, which, between 1801 and 1807, had invested perhaps £2.6 million in the trafficking of enslaved people, and further north in Hull, a site for the importation and re-exportation to the Baltic of American-grown tobacco and the production and distribution of cotton goods and wrought iron (of which the Caribbean took 63 per cent and mainland North America perhaps 34 per cent). Gilbert Wakefield, a Jesus fellow from 1776 to 1779 (and, at the same time, a Liverpool vicar), and Thomas Clarke, a former Clare fellow who returned to minister in his local Hull, attempted to guide their flocks to abolitionism.[25]

Having hoped to establish a day-school in the area, Wakefield's congregation was thrown into a state of uproar as the American Revolutionary War, in which France intervened on the colonists' side, had led to hundreds of prisoners being brought to Liverpool, the 'grand mart' and '*head-quarters*' of the African slave trade. The Jesuan's antislavery views crystallised in this three-year period as he observed the malnourished and ill-treated prisoners. Lecturing from the pulpit, he argued that the city's residents were 'aggravating the calamities of war by the rapine and injustice of private hostility' to prisoners – an immunity to human suffering that they had developed because they were 'so habitually immoral' through their participation in the '*African* slave trade and privateering in that war!' The '*thunder*' of his lecture may have 'agitated' an attendee's nerves; still, Wakefield argued that such an awakening was necessary after he heard from one captain that he had repeatedly 'knockt' the head of an enslaved infant against 'the side of the ship, and threw it into the sea'.[26]

The Reverend Thomas Clarke from Hull published his February 1792 sermon *On the Injustice of the Slave Trade*. The address was given in the Holy Trinity Church (or Hull Minster) before a congregation that may have included merchants and traders. Publishing as a 'Late-Fellow of Clare-Hall' (until 1856, Clare was known as "Clare Hall"), Clarke proclaimed that enslavement was contrary to the Christian golden rule: to do unto others as you would have them do unto you. Dedicated to Granville Sharp and pleading the 'Cause of Mercy and of Justice', the Hull vicar understood that abolition was a 'Test' for the British nation – an assessment of that empire's commitment to 'Humanity and Justice'. Neither skin colour nor complexion, as he understood it, justified how Europeans treated the enslaved, even if 'Labourers are wanted to cultivate the West India Islands, the Produce of which is consumed in this Land, and the Profit of that Produce enjoyed by Englishmen'. In an interesting passage (and perhaps in a nod to his audience), Clarke mentioned the inextricable ties between Britons and the slave-grown produce that was 'moistened with Blood'. The former fellow stopped short of calling for a nonimportation and nonexportation movement of slave-grown produce, but he made several other proposals on the question of abolition: first, he argued that a Christian awakening in West Africa would draw out their 'Seeds of Intelligence' and thereby lead to a 'rapid Improvement' in their lives and conditions; and, second, he observed that the abolition of the transatlantic trade was but the first battleground in a wider offensive against the 'glaring Evils' at home and abroad, such as naval impressment (perhaps 250,000 British seamen were impressed over the eighteenth and early nineteenth centuries), and in opposition to the 'Ravager[s] of INDIA'. Unfortunately, Clarke's ambitions were controversial. He recalled that many Hull residents had refused to sign the town's abolition petition because 'our domestic Evils ought first to be redressed'. The principle that enslavement was a "foreign" crime, out of sight and mind, was a constant source of contention for antislavery activists.[27]

Newspapers were, of course, crucial to the propagation of information as well. Cambridge was home to Francis Hodson's *Cambridge Chronicle* (which was strongly against the French Revolution and Parliamentary reform) and

Benjamin Flower's more radical *Cambridge Intelligencer*, which, although it only lasted a decade (1793–1803), was nationally syndicated. Flower published debates and letters on the slave trade, examples of slave advertisements, and abolitionist literature. Gilbert Wakefield, the Jesus alumnus, had a letter published disputing whether the gospels permitted slavery. In another issue, Flower's featured a Jamaican slave advertisement from April 1796, with the first line reading: 'FOR SALE, 353 Choice young Angola NEGROES, Imported in the Ship Enterprize, Captain John Heron from the River Congo'. He distributed a poem, too, titled "The Willing Slave," which described the experiences of 'an AFRICAN WOMAN, whose favourite Boy was kidnapped by the Crew of a Boat'. It lamented 'OH! HENRY didst thou hear in vain, The moving tale the Captain told? – Go, then, and reap the sordid gain. And sell thy fellow Men for Gold!' Interestingly, the paper propagated fears about enslavers in local politics, reporting that John Tharp, a Jamaican proprietor (and Cambridge's High Sheriff), had subscribed £1,000 to the local militia movement. The paper noted that 'Gratitude to ministers for their encouragement of the *Slave Trade*, has doubtless influenced this gentleman [in his donation], who is well known for his large property in the West Indies, and his partiality to the above traffick'. Never before had slavery been so prominent in British provincial papers, and Cambridge was no different in that regard, with papers prosecuting their arguments to an eager and increasingly literate population (indeed, as early as the late seventeenth century, even poor Cambridgeshire children were being taught to read at home or by village school-dames).[28]

Philosophical treatises taught at Cambridge, which students read (though perhaps less enthusiastically than the newspapers), voiced the complications and conflicts around slavery in the British Empire. William Paley's *Principles of Moral and Political Philosophy*, though published in 1785, arose from a series of Cambridge lectures on the moral philosophy of Samuel Clarke, Joseph Butler, and John Locke conducted whilst he was a fellow at Christ's from 1766. A Christian utilitarian (an ethic that saw religion and religious belief as the surest path to individual and collective happiness), Paley's lectures, which were a set text at the University of Cambridge and elsewhere, defined enslavement as 'an obligation to labour for the benefit of the master, without the contract or consent of the servant'. Slavery, he believed, acted 'consistently with the law of nature' on three grounds: for crimes committed (though slavery had to be 'proportioned' to the crime), from captivity, and from debt (the second and third of which had to end as soon as 'the demand of the injured nation, or private creditor is satisfied'). Paley was a determined opponent of the slave trade, arguing that it 'excited' Africans to war, and slavery was exercised 'by the *English* slave holder... with rigour and brutality'. Rejecting the claim that enslavement was cheaper than free labourers working for wages or that the institution was founded in Christian scripture, Paley called for gradual abolition 'carried on by provisions of law, and under the protection of civil government'. Christianising the enslaved, he maintained, and its 'mild diffusion of light and influence' was to be preferred over an immediate end to the system.[29]

The Reverend Robert Robinson's 1788 sermon reveals the extent to which some Cambridge residents were prepared to attack Britain's connections to the slave trade and the companies that had profited from that traffic. Robinson, a steadfast supporter of religious freedom and toleration, was the most 'prominent' and popular dissenting preacher in Cambridge, and he often addressed 600-strong congregations. Preached at the Baptist Church and Congregation of Dissenters at Cambridge on 10 February, Robinson's sermon, *Slavery inconsistent with the Spirit of Christianity*, attacked the South Sea Company. Robinson had numerous friends at Cambridge, including John Randall, the Professor of Music, who would have been aware of South Sea investments at the University. As a result, his criticisms of the Company may have been personal to his listeners. Robinson implicated the SSC in contracting 'with foreigners for an annual supply of negro slaves to work their [the Spanish] gold and silver mines'. Calling for the use of free labour in the mines and plantations, Robinson argued that the Company had been engaged in gratifying 'the ambition and avarice of a few at the expence of the general prosperity of commercial kingdoms, and the natural rights of millions of the human species'. Addressing a captive audience, whose families and collegiate institutions had bought and profited from these securities, Robinson attacked Englishmen for propagating the Atlantic slave trade.[30]

Forming the Cambridge Society for Constitutional Information, which, together with the *Cambridge Intelligencer*, was a lightning rod for dissenting and parliamentary reformist opinion in the town and University, Robinson wrote perhaps the first anti-slave-trade opinion that was presented to Parliament. Drawn up with the support of Cambridge freeholders and dissenters, the petition attacked the trade without disparaging the plantation system. Reform, not immediate abolition, was their tactic regarding racial chattel enslavement. 'Your petitioners are aware', the document read, 'that Britain derives innumerable benefits from her plantations, and that the plantations depend upon the labours of negroes; but they are not convinced, that a slave trade is necessary to a supply of labourers'. Claiming to 'abhor slavery in every form', they hoped that an abolition of that hated commerce would stop the 'cruelty necessary to the safety of the slaveholders'.[31]

Cambridge antislavery activists, such as Robinson, had friends in London, who congregated around Clapham Common. That community grew after the Reverend Henry Thornton purchased Battersea Rise near the homes of prominent banking families, including the Barclays and Deacons. 'Thornton's 'Clapham system', Roshan Allpress argues, 'was therefore ideally positioned to interact with and recruit from among Britain's commercial elites'. Aside from commercial interests, many Clapham men were from the ancient universities. The curate Henry Venn was educated at St John's and Jesus colleges, and later became a Queens' fellow in 1749. (His grandson, also named Henry, lobbied Parliament to order the Royal Navy to patrol the coast of West Africa to stop the slave trade.) Still, the most famous Cambridge figure in London was William Wilberforce, the Member of Parliament for Yorkshire from 1784 until 1812. Despite being immortalised in statue at his former college, St John's, Wilberforce showed about as much interest in his Cambridge studies as Samuel Alpress – that is to say, little at all.[32]

The friendships that Wilberforce made at the University, particularly with William Pitt the Younger, served him well in public life, however – and the social connections that he brought to the Clapham community ensured that the philanthropic sect had both 'credibility' and 'political influence'. One Cambridge man changed his life: Isaac Milner, the evangelical President of Queens' and the Lucasian Professor of Mathematics. Milner was pivotal to Wilberforce's conversion around 1784–1785, stirring the latter's opposition to the slave trade as an un-Christian and morally bankrupt activity. The Cambridge philanthropists, who had deep ties to the Clapham community, included the King's fellow Charles Simeon (Wilberforce's friend, a leading evangelical, and a donor to the African Institution, which administered the Sierra Leone colony) and the St John's fellow and missionary William Jowett. (Jowett would publish in favour of a bishopric in Sierra Leone and against the 'bodily sufferings' and 'spiritual violence' meted out to enslaved Africans.) Although abolition would take over twenty more years to accomplish, Cambridge fellows, students, and alumni with different moral perspectives and visions of how to create an empire without the slave trade were at the forefront of this movement.[33]

Nevertheless, Wilberforce's opponents were wealthier, formidable, and equally committed to enforcing their vision of the British Empire. Stephen Fuller, the former Trinity fellow, was one of the most impactful proslavery activists. Historians call him 'the chief broker in orchestrating the West India interest', whose qualities included 'persistence and amenability' and a talent 'to argue a case and to avoid confrontation'. Fuller provided the movement with 'direction and energy' and, according to another scholar, 'much of the hard work' was done by him alone. In fact, Fuller complained that the Jamaica legislature had 'left him too much to himself'. The agent for Jamaica in London for thirty years (1764–1794), Fuller had free reign to conduct his lobbying efforts, amassing expenses of between £3,000 and £4,000 in 1779, almost the annual budget for a small Caribbean colony.

As with British abolitionism, the foundations for the proslavery lobby were established in the era of the American Revolution. The London Society of West India Planters and Merchants was founded in 1780 and Fuller was an enthusiastic early member of that powerful organisation. Throughout the Revolutionary War, he petitioned George III and Parliament to ensure that the British sugar islands remained defended upon the entry of Spain and France into the war with the United States, emphasising the importance of the sugar trade to the nation's finances. Fuller, who had never visited Jamaica, manipulated patronage networks and his connections to the military, church, education, and politics throughout Britain to gain support for the proslavery cause. He recognised that emphasising the exorbitant wealth from the plantations would not stem the tide of antislavery's moral arguments alone; the enslavers had to communicate to their fellow Britons why it was both economically necessary and morally justifiable to enslave people on the basis of racial distinctions.[34]

Fuller deployed several arguments to halt anti-slave trade opinion in Britain – and, as an agent, Fuller ensured that the people who spoke these words were British military heroes. Fuller was, of course, committed to proving that slavery was the basis of imperial economic strength. Reporting in February 1788 to the Jamaican Committee of Correspondence, Fuller recalled that three petitions had been sent from Bedford, Hull, and York calling for the end of the slave trade as 'contrary to the common Rights of Humanity'. Utilising his connections to Thomas Townshend, the 1st Viscount Sydney and the former Home Secretary, Fuller collected 'materials' to convince Parliament and these dissident urban areas of the 'impossibility of abolishing Slavery; and if we do not avail ourselves of the labour of Slaves, our Enemies will, to our own undoing'.[35]

Collecting statistics and signed memoranda, Fuller assembled comrades to counter abolitionist opinion in the newspapers and in Parliament. George Brydges Rodney, 1st Baron Rodney, the hero of the naval Battle of the Saintes against France in 1782 (a battle which had saved Jamaica from French occupation), was an ally because of his years of service in the Caribbean. Rodney had rescued the Caribbean at the Saintes, and Fuller implored the celebrated admiral 'to do it a second time… by giving yourself the trouble of appearing for five minutes at the Plantation Office, and relating what your Lordship knows of the general behaviour of the Planters in that Island to their Negroe Slaves, and of the nature of their labour, compared with that of the Labourers in England'. Rodney did as he was told – leading a group of prominent men from the Royal Navy who supported the enslavers. Buoyed by the assistance of these men, Fuller argued that it was the abolitionists who were immoral since they ignored the suffering of the white labouring classes.[36]

Enslavers had, they believed, a persuasive case, as they moulded a transatlantic, imperial version of Britishness that extended to the Caribbean. They ensured that Britons in the metropole defined abolitionism as the forced seizure of *British* property, rather than an action against an overseas-born enslaver class. Slaveholders appealed to anti-African racism, too, framing the transatlantic traffic in enslaved people as a liberation from 'tyrannic' and 'savage' West African chiefs, and enslavement as a positive good and civilising tool for African-descended peoples. Furthermore, enslavers also argued that antislavery activists were abridging their rights to due process as Britons, as outlined in Magna Carta, and thereby aligned abolitionists with subversive revolutionary forces in France – the women and men who stormed the Bastille on 14 July 1789, who had confiscated estates and property in the name of their ideals, and executed suspected traitors in the Terror. In equating British antislavery activists with French radicals, enslavers understood Britain's prevailing Francophobic mood, as 412 recorded burnings of the republican polemicist Thomas Paine effigies took place across the country from 1792 to 1793, and William Pitt the Younger's government arrested thirty radicals for sedition.[37]

The storm of anti-radical reaction buffeted Cambridge. The outbreak of the French Revolutionary Wars in April 1792, which Britain entered a year later in April 1793 in opposition to the newly established French Republic, polarised town and gown politics. By December 1792, locals were attacking a dissenting meeting house – their efforts to 'burst open the doors' stopped thanks to the intervention of 'some Masters of Arts' from St John's College. The Reverend George Whitmore of that College was unimpressed (with the dissenters and brave graduates, that is). The Riot Act was read to the locals, but he deemed the outburst of patriotic fervour 'A Laudable Ebullition of Justifiable Zeal!!!' Pitt, who had been a reluctant supporter of the war, counted on much support in the town. Associations were created that denigrated reformists and dissenters as dangerous and traitorous 'Republicans and Levellers' – terms that aligned reformists with English Civil War radicals. Sir Busick Harwood, then the Downing Professor of Medicine, had a creative response to the legal maxim of the presumption of innocence: 'every Dissenter', he noted, 'should be considered a rogue, until he had proved himself to be an honest man'. The situation escalated further: a Paine effigy was burnt on Market Hill, and another effigy of a local grocer named Gazam, who had apparently uttered seditious comments, was carried around town – those who did not support this procession were considered disloyal. Gazam, it appears, could not count on the support of Emmanuel College – when the effigy was 'exhibited' at the college gate, Richard Farmer, the Master, gave the rioters five shillings as encouragement. Gazam fled to the United States, and some fellows likewise faced persecution and banishment from Cambridge. William Frend, who attacked the Anglican religious establishment, was exiled from the Jesus fellowship (despite the support of undergraduates, with graffiti appeared in town proclaiming 'Frend for ever!!!' and 'LIBERTY' and 'EQUALITY'). Frend likened his persecution to the system of 'outrageous violence… exercised on the coasts of Africa', but he escaped the worst of these trials. The Queens' fellow Thomas Fyshe Palmer, who supported universal suffrage, was expelled from the fellowship and transported across the world to Botany Bay. Palmer's banishment led an incredulous George Dyer, publishing as a student "Late of Emmanuel College, Cambridge," to declare 'FAMINE AND SLAVERY, THE PUNISHMENT FOR SEDITION'.[38]

With their opponents under political pressure, Fuller's argument hinged on the Consolidated Slave Laws of 1788. Amelioration (the reform of enslavement, rather than its abolition) was a powerful weapon in the proslavery arsenal, and helped slavers identify as "moderates" compared to "radical" abolitionists.

Fuller's skill, however, was in codifying the reforms and spreading that message to Britons in the corridors of power. On 2 April 1788, he wrote to the Jamaica Committee, informing them that '*My Code Noir* consists of a short abstract of all our Jamaica Laws relative to the Government of our Negroe Slaves, beginning with the Act of 1696 in the first column, and the melioration of that, and all the rest of our Laws'. His proposal to create an alternative to France's *code noir* (King Louis XIV's 1685 decree establishing the laws of enslavement) was enumerated in two pamphlets: the *Notes on the Two Reports from the Committee of the Honourable House of Assembly of Jamaica* and *The New Act of Assembly of the Island of Jamaica* (both published in 1789). In these volumes, Fuller contrasted the "isolated" instances of anti-Black violence with how the enslaved were treated following the Consolidated Law, which provided vague protections for the enslaved from extrajudicial murder, an annual clothing allowance, and additional time for Black families to work plots of land for food.[39]

These laws had a monthly inspection process; that being said, Fuller was not particularly concerned about the enforcement of these regulations – his goal was to offer a philanthropic fig-leaf to Jamaican enslavers. The Consolidated Laws were his, rather successful, attempt to wrest the mantle of humanitarianism from the abolitionists. He made his intentions clear in the preface to the *New Act*, contrasting the '*theoretical* philanthropy' of the antislavery cause with the 'present Act', which had 'exhibited a specimen of *real practical* philanthropy, as well as legislation, not to be paralleled perhaps upon the face of the globe'. Many white, elite Britons, it appears, fell for Fuller's bait as the proslavery lobby transformed the title of "abolitionist" into an epithet denoting fanaticism, 'theophilanthropic enthusiasm', and 'revolutionary' politics.[40]

Aside from Parliamentarians, Fuller lobbied Oxford and Cambridge universities. After all, proslavery activists recognised that opinion-leaders, including fellows and professors, would help to sway the British populace and its youth. In 1610, Sir Edward Coke had declared that the universities (namely Oxford and Cambridge) were 'the eyes and soul of the realm, from whence religion, the humanities, and learning were richly diffused into all parts of the realm'. Eager to sway the souls of influential university men toward favouring his efforts at amelioration, in June 1788 Fuller proposed to Lord Hawkesbury, the President of the Board of Trade, that 'six or seven hundred' copies of the Consolidated Act be distributed to 'the Lords & Commons, and if your Lordship thought it proper, or worth while, to the two Universities, and such corporate bodies as have presented Petitions to Parliament'. Hawkesbury vetoed the idea, since he believed that the masters and fellows would 'all purchase it when it is published & will thereby be sufficiently known without the Formality of circulating to them, which might have a bad Appearance'.[41]

Fuller's lobbying continued for over a year, and, in May 1789, he wrote that he had met 'several University Gentlemen, who have quite altered their Tone, and upon the whole I think that the investigation, as far as it has gone at present, has done us no sort of harm, but a great deal of good'. Who were these "Gentlemen"? It is significant that we need to ask that question given the close relationships between enslavers and the Cambridge fellowship. Regardless, both the *Notes* and *New Act of Assembly* can be found in Cambridge's Library as part of the collection bequeathed by the successors of the Reverend James Yorke, the Bishop of Ely (1781–1808), whose father Philip Yorke had in 1729 determined the legality of African slavery on the basis that they were pagans. If Fuller is to be believed, he convinced some university graduates and fellows to make his cause their own.[42]

Abolition-era novels attest to the often-intense debates at the ancient universities concerning enslavement. Published in 1827, the Reverend John Riland's *Memoirs of a West-India Planter* was a fictional portrayal of a 'Jamaican creole', the son of a 'planter turned abolitionist' who attended Christ Church, Oxford. Riland was not an heir to a Jamaican fortune, but the Reverend and his fictional subject had begun their intellectual journeys at the same time: he had attended St Edmund Hall, graduating with a bachelor's degree in 1800. Novels should not be dismissed as historical sources, however – they were, the contemporary novelist Clare Reve argued, a 'picture of real life and manners' – and pictures, rather than revealing a whole story, provide a specific perspective on reality (a world where Oxford men debated enslavement in poems, histories, and public debates). After arriving at that university, Riland's fictional protagonist received a letter from his father ordering him to return to Jamaica via Liverpool and West Africa. His classmates were incensed, and one student argued 'that a planter's son was only a kind of domestic slave; and must expect to hear the whip crack even in orders signed by "I am your most affectionate father."' To Riland, Black enslavement undermined sentimental white familial relationships. Consoling himself with a copy of Bryan Edwards's *History of Jamaica*, which the Bodleian librarian had pulled as a 'special favour' to remind the fictional student of his colonial home, the young prodigal found a network of support amongst his Oxford friends. Hearing that he was travelling abroad on a slave ship, the fictional Jamaican's friends, referring to him as 'massa George', declared that 'the accounts of the middle passage have been villa[i]nously exaggerated – in fact, it is quite a party business – and as to the whistling of Granville Sharp and Clarkson, and fifty such fellows, why it might be as well if they would lay aside a little of their transatlantic charity, and practice some at home: for, to my certain knowledge, there are some of your philanthropists among us, who will absolutely turn a beggar from the door, and deny even a poor man his evening comforts at the alehouse, and then give their ten guineas each' to the antislavery cause.[43]

That conversation, which the narrator records occurred while Cambridge petitioned against the transatlantic trade, continued between fellows and students who were relatives (such relationships being common, of course, at Cambridge). The novel described a conversation between a Magdalene fellow and the Jamaica-born student, with the former being a 'maternal relation'. The college fellow worried that the 'fanatical' antislavery activists had convinced the public that 'slavery is not sanctioned by the sacred writings'. The Magdalene man claimed that enslavement was familiar to Jesus of Nazareth, and that 'slaves, agricultural and domestic, surrounded him wherever he went'. In the novel, a Pembroke student also appealed to commerce, reminding the protagonist that enslavement was 'so necessary a branch of commercial interest', and that to 'abolish a *status* which in all ages God has sanctioned and man has continued' would be an act of 'robbery' against British subjects and of 'extreme cruelty to the African savages' who, as a result of their enslavement, had been saved from 'massacre' and 'intolerable bondage' in West Africa. Riland's Oxford was a site of profound debate and contestation over Black enslavement.[44]

Francis Randolph was one non-fictional Cantabrigian who supported the continuation of the transatlantic trade in enslaved Africans. Having resigned his King's College fellowship barely a year earlier, Randolph's 1788 published letter to then-Prime Minister William Pitt – a pamphlet which advertised his credentials on the title page as a 'Late Fellow of King's College, *Cambridge*' – defended the trade on the grounds of pragmatism. Regarding African enslavement, reformation, not revolution, was his mantra. As the son of a Bristol doctor who had extolled the 'Medicinal Virtues of Bristol Waters' and a relation of Thomas Randolph, the former President of Corpus Christi College, Oxford, and Vice-Chancellor, the young Francis's upbringing in Bristol, a slave entrepôt, may have reinforced his attitudes concerning slavery. Acknowledging that Britain's 'Exigencies' were 'so dependent upon the Planters Wealth', Randolph suggested that 'Undoubtedly there would be no Difficulty in cutting off the Abuse at once by an immediate Abolition of the African Trade, but I am afraid such a Law would have an Operation widely different from the End proposed. – To restrain and to amend seems to be all that can be done at present, and the Difficulty will lie in the Mode and Manner of it, so as to render it at the same Time humane and salutary'. He accepted the cruelties of enslavement but pondered whether 'the Disposition of the Planter may sweeten the Bitterness of Servitude' and he observed that the Africans' 'Condition' was 'in general much more eligible, it is said, than their own Country'. To this Cambridge man, Randolph supported the enslavers' claim that bondage in the Caribbean was to be preferred over freedom in West Africa.[45]

Debating James Tobin, the Nevis proslaver, Ramsay, and the Reverend John Newton (a slave-trader turned abolitionist), Randolph set out towards the end of the pamphlet several ameliorative policies. The clauses included: that transatlantic traders had to sell to the British colonies; that Africans should be purchased after a certain age (perhaps with a 'free Negro' working on the slave ship to explain 'to them the Nature and Terms of their Captivity, and so render the servitude wholly voluntary'); the enslaved would work fixed hours and take

Sundays off except if punished for misdemeanours; and emancipated slaves would have their freedom 'suspended' if they had committed a crime.[46]

Sixteen years after this pamphlet's publication (and three years before the abolition of the slave trade), Randolph's proslavery attitudes had deepened. Writing as "Britannicus," he hoped that Pitt would not accede to the demands of anti-slave-trade "fanatics" who aimed to destroy 'perhaps the very *political existence* of this country'. Noting that he was neither a slaveholder nor a slave-trader, Randolph criticised abolitionists for misusing religion to attack the nation's economic foundations. He asked: 'Must Great Britain, then, be essentially injured in order *to improve Africa, and prevent the negroes from gratifying their taste for eating each other?*' He argued that the Bible justified enslavement because Abraham, the 'father of the faithful', had 318 enslaved people. More to the point, he claimed that the 'toleration and use of slavery is *a principle implanted in our nature*, as is evident from its maintaining throughout mankind in all ages, in all countries, in every stage of barbarity or refinement'. Narrating the history of slavery through the Bible, Greek epics, and Roman law, Randolph refuted the claim that '*to Europeans only, the African slave trade is indebted for existence*'. This argument underpinned much of the pamphlet. If Britain was to give up this 'beneficial commerce', then they would merely open the door to other European and North American empires, including the United States, to lay a further financial claim to the enormous profits due from the 'Slave Commerce'. In fact, he made the astonishing calculation that 18 million pounds in revenue from slavery-related activities annually 'go into the pockets of Englishmen, and circulate in the country'.[47]

Some Cambridge men were more torn about the continued existence of the slave trade and plantation slavery. The son of an apothecary who was the future physician to George IV, Samuel Hallifax had a distinguished career – attaining a fellowship at Trinity Hall in April 1760, a professorship in Arabic, and then a Regius Professorship of Civil Law for twelve years from 1770 to 1782. In a course of his Cambridge lectures on Roman law, Hallifax claimed that the 'Revival of Domestic Slavery in America affords no proof, that the introduction of a new Slavery into England is now lawful' – in other words, he supported Lord Mansfield's finding in Somerset vs. Stewart that enslaved people could not be removed from England. Assuming his new position as the Bishop of St Asaph, Hallifax's 28 May 1789 sermon before the SPG, however, detailed his approach to domestic slavery in the Americas. To him, conversion had two interrelated goals: '*civilizing* and *saving*' – and the Codrington plantations had failed to 'propose an example of lenity to the owners of other plantations, and to shew to them and to the world, by the manner of providing for the accommodation of our own slaves, that we are not unmindful of the equality of our common condition'. For Hallifax, the Codrington estates had the potential to become a shining beacon to other enslavers on how to run a plantation on the grounds of amelioration, cultural refinement, and religious conversion.[48]

Consequently, Hallifax agreed with Charles Farish and, to some extent, Fuller's policies on slavery: that amelioration and 'Mitigation' were the soundest course of action. Although Hallifax did not foresee the slave system continuing (as Fuller had proposed), he argued that there was a possibility for reform – and Fuller and his allies may have exploited this middle ground in convincing college fellows that moderation was a legitimate third option to resolve the problem of slavery. Reading his sermon, Hallifax subscribed to much of the SPG's gospel on enslavement: like Thomas Thompson, he wrote that 'no sober believer' accepted the proposition that 'Christianity and Slavery are incompatible' because that was 'more than the authority of Scripture will warrant us to affirm'; as with Thomas Sherlock, he minimised the violence of Caribbean slavery, claiming that 'the very worst and most arbitrary system that ever was practiced in any one of the European Colonies, has never exceeded, or even equalled, in severity that established by the Roman Code'; and, akin to William Fleetwood, he proclaimed that it was critical that, in order to Christianise enslaved Africans and 'gain an entrance into any plantation but our own', the Society build alliances with enslavers and ensure that they understood that baptism was not a 'virtual Manumission'. Finishing this line of argument, the Bishop maintained that the Society should acquiesce to the colonial legislatures, who, he hoped, would accept 'the rights of human nature, to the interests of the planter and of the slaves, to the national commerce, and the national honour'. He prayed that the laws governing slave societies would be 'altered or annulled', thereby paving the way for 'its future and complete Abolition'. No avid defender of Britain's slave empire, Hallifax's writings were further proof of the significant influence of ameliorative policies, particularly for middling and elite Cambridge, that perpetuated the plantation economy.[49]

Away from the pulpit, the abolition debate also played out in the courtroom – and a Cambridge man was a significant actor in that drama: Sir James Marriott, a fellow (1756–1764) and, subsequently, the Master of Trinity Hall (1764–1803). Sir James accrued numerous positions during his career: Vice-Chancellor, King's Advocate, Judge of the Admiralty Court, and MP for Sudbury on two occasions (where he supported Pitt's faction). The decorated jurist, as was the case with Sir Nathaniel Lloyd, had engaged in multiple discussions and cases regarding the empire, from issues as mundane as over whether to enforce a residence requirement on a Barbadian clergyman to the much more gripping topic of taxing the American colonists without their consent, which he supported because (in a speech that was greeted with 'much merriment') the Americans were represented in Parliament '*by the knights of the shire for the county of Kent*'. Marriott's interest in North American affairs also extended to Québec, where he devised a plan of a code of laws in 1774.[50]

The issue of the slave trade placed his name in the public spotlight, however. In October 1791, a Bristol captain named John Kimber was master of the *Recovery*, which had been sailing for over a month on route from New Calabar in West Africa to Grenada in the British Caribbean. His original cargo included 300 enslaved people, of which twenty-seven died from the horrendous conditions on board. The ship and its captain would be little remarked upon if not for what happened next. Six months later, the *Recovery* became a cause célèbre after William Wilberforce mentioned in a parliamentary speech that Kimber had whipped, suspended by one leg, and, as a result of this torture, had caused the death of a fifteen-year-old enslaved girl because she had refused to dance on deck (the enslaved were often forced to dance, under threat of being lashed, in a futile effort to keep the captives healthy on the disease-ridden ships). Though Kimber refuted the charges in the newspapers (and had the support of the Bristol mercantile community), the Scottish satirist Isaac Cruikshank depicted the Bristolian slave-trader as a gluttonous, immoral, and inhuman figure – an exemplar of the 'Dealers in human flesh' – who abused the African woman because of her 'virjen modesty'.[51]

In June 1792, Kimber was tried in London for the murder of two enslaved women, with Marriott the presiding judge (and with notable figures in attendance, including the future William IV). The trial lasted five hours, with the defence quickly gaining the upper hand after it was discovered that of the five witnesses, two were prejudiced against Kimber and three were supportive of the captain. In his instructions to the jury, Marriott also reminded them that a 'ship is a little government' and that, as a result, there could be no 'hope of security' on board without 'absolute power, placed in one man' – in fact, he argued, the 'passions of human nature operate there in their full violence, and all on board of a ship is too often nothing but one scene of misery and terror, disorder, disobedience, confederacy, resentment and revenge'. These statements, Nicholas Rogers suggests, appealed to a 'propertied jury' that viewed the revolutions in France and Saint-Domingue with a mixture of suspicion and terror. Marriott soon stopped the trial as it became evident that the witnesses had been discredited, and, having urged the jury to find Kimber not guilty, the captain's peers agreed. The trial was a setback for Wilberforce, who was accused of misleading Parliament – though the abolitionist and his supporters were convinced that Marriott and his peers had merely questioned the veracity of the witnesses rather than the merits of the case.[52]

Sir James's legal work continued, however. He presided over another slave ship case that same month after the mariner George Hindmarsh repeatedly clubbed the captain Samuel Burnie Cowie to death on board the *Eolus*, which was 'one league from Annamboe, on the Coast of Africa', and then threw the body overboard. (Hindmarsh was convicted and executed.) Marriott's will showed that he was clearly intimate with the colonial enslaver class. He provided £5,000 in three per cent consolidated annuities in the Bank of England to Sophia Ricketts, the 'widow of the late George Poyntz Ricketts late Governor of Barbados' along with a set of valuables including a 'blood stone Box'. Sir James also made bequests to Sophia's daughter and son (Marriott's godson), which included his prints and book of prints to the former and 100 pounds to purchase a sword sabre for the latter if he joined the army or navy. Governor Ricketts was born on Jamaica and had inherited Midgham plantation from his father Jacob (who had sired a 'free Mulatto James' and had a child expected with another enslaved woman named Ancilla).[53]

Cambridge men enthusiastically assisted the West India Lobby too. Altogether, twenty members of both Houses of Parliament, who were actively involved in the proslavery lobby between 1780 and 1796, were educated in whole or part at Cambridge, including Sir Patrick Blake (St John's), Sir Charles Davers (Trinity), Sir William Young (Clare), Brownlow Cust (Corpus Christi), and John Warren, the Bishop of Bangor (Caius). Proslavery activists mentioned Cambridge in their writings too. Gilbert Franklyn, a partner with Anthony Bacon in a slave-trading firm and the owner of three plantations in Tobago, was one such author. In attacking Clarkson for his writings, Franklyn did not blame Cambridge for the campaigner's arguments. Like Fuller, his 1789 pamphlet contrasted the practicality of the enslavers' approach to amelioration with the utopianism of abolition. Dismissing Clarkson's pamphlet as an 'academical exercise', Franklyn argued that the Cambridge 'judges' of such a competition were not 'competent to decide upon' whether 'Mr. Clarkson's pen was guided by truth or fiction', and that such a concern 'did not necessarily enter into their consideration' because 'the members of the University of Cambridge possessed no such ocular evidence of African or West Indian slavery'. Given the involvement of Thomas Thompson and other former and current fellows in North America, India, and West Africa, this was an erroneous assertion; nevertheless, Franklyn suggested that the enslavers' superior educations – their 'minds more enlarged, and manners more refined' by the 'education which their youth receive in England' – had 'softened' their approach to enslavement.[54]

The economic and moral arguments put forward by men such as Randolph and the legislative wrangling of Fuller through the Consolidated Slave Laws ensured that, from the creation of SEAT in 1787 until the abolition of the slave trade in 1807, the antislavery struggle took two long, bitter decades. Witnessing the British public's response to the Laws, Fuller was jubilant. In December 1788, he reported to John Grant, the Chief Justice of Jamaica, that 'the Consolidated Act, has done more towards the opening of the Eyes of this country, than every thing that has been hitherto written or said upon the subject of Slavery, and it will convince the whole world that you neither stand in need of the instruction of the mother country, nor the stimullation of an impertinent set of Fanatics to do, what your own humanity & feeling has prompted you to do already'. Fuller was certain (incorrectly, as it turned out) that the enslavers had won the battle to defend the transatlantic slave trade.[55]

Over the following years, Fuller propagated the news about Jamaica's amelioration measures to the British public. He printed 1,200 copies of the policies to send to the press, both Houses of Parliament, the cabinet, prominent Church figures, including the Archbishop of Canterbury and Bishop of London, and to the towns petitioning for the end of the slave trade (Cambridge included). The Saint-Domingue revolt inspired Fuller to increase his lobbying efforts to avoid enslaved uprisings in the British colonies. Fuller wrote that he was 'struck with Horror at the accounts of the insurrections of the Negroes in St Domingo', and believed that the 'seeds of the rebellion' had germinated in London's antislavery community. These anti-Haitian claims had both adherents and opponents at Cambridge. In 1800, Herbert Marsh, a St John's fellow, had discussed the 'insurrection… among the negroes' there, which had been 'so dreadful in its effects' that the French colonists were 'reduced to a state of despair'. On the other hand, William Burdon, a radical Emmanuel fellow and Newcastle coal mine owner, celebrated the Haitian leader Toussaint Louverture for 'nobly' defending the island from France – indeed, the 'black General', though 'bred a slave', had 'put to shame the most enlightened Europeans' and the French Emperor Napoleon Bonaparte, who, in his efforts to reconquer and re-enslave Saint-Domingue, was a 'bloody tyrant' and a 'disgrace on human nature'.[56]

Using the fear of a servile insurrection to weaken anti-slave-trade resolve, Fuller successfully transformed proslavery campaigners into the victimised party, not enslaved Africans. In May 1791, Fuller claimed, with some justification, that his success in defeating Wilberforce's motion against the slave trade was owed, in part, to 'the weight & solidity of our Consolidated Act'. Fuller's final written effort in support of proslavery, his *Colonisation of the Island of Jamaica*, published in 1792, was again intended to illuminate the reciprocal benefits of slavery. Accumulating statistics from Jamaican districts on enslaved births and deaths, he argued that the colonies had founded a 'grand system' of reciprocal 'benefits' and 'privileges and restraints' – and the 'mother-country' had drawn numerous 'advantages' from its western empire, 'advantages so various, and so important to her navy, her manufactures, trade, commerce and active industry, of every species (to say nothing of revenue), as [to] surpass all the powers of calculation'.[57]

Nearing the end of his colourful life, Fuller's personal copy of Robert Norris's 1789 memoirs of the King of Dahomey contained detailed calculations of the numbers of enslaved people required to "stock" the Caribbean plantations. As he observed, 'Jamaica requires a supply of 12,000 slaves annually' to complete its cultivation of sugar. Calculating Africa's population at 106 million people, or "Negroland" as it was called in the pamphlet, Fuller estimated that slavers could transport, at minimum, 26,500 Africans annually to the plantations. He also highlighted Norris's estimate that the export of British manufactures to Africa and the Caribbean colonies amounted to 3 million pounds – a figure that would be 'reduced to nothing' if the abolitionists succeeded in Parliament. Fuller died in 1808, but the former Cambridge fellow had helped to stall abolition for a decade – and his commitment to the cause had few equals.[58]

Moving from the metropole to West Africa, the exploration and colonisation of that continent illustrates the immense challenges of converting abolitionist discourse into reality. In 1786, Londoners believed action was required to alleviate the numbers of "Black Poor" in the East End who had been brought to Britain through the Atlantic slave trade. Following the American Revolutionary War, in which thousands of free and enslaved Black people fought with the British to attain their freedom, the population of these refugees swelled. On 5 January 1786, a baker named Mr Brown advertised that he would provide 'a Quartern Loaf to every Black in Distress, who will apply on Saturday next between the Hours of Twelve and Two', including a subscription form at the end of the piece so that Black Londoners could sign up for assistance. These individual, localised efforts grew into a popular movement, with the Committee for the Relief of the Black Poor identifying '250 Persons, who are objects of the Charity'.[59]

With prominent financial supporters including Samuel Thornton, a director of the Bank of England, the Committee financed a settlement in Sierra Leone called Granville Town, but the enterprise was a failure – with some colonists captured and enslaved – so the eager antislavery activists founded St George's Bay Company in 1790 and then the Sierra Leone Company on 11 March 1792. Inspired by Granville Sharp's call for a *Free English Territory in Africa*, numerous Cambridge fellows and professors invested in 1792. These men included: the Reverend William Farish (£100 investment); the Reverend William Frend, the former Jesus fellow (£50); Henry Greene, a former Peterhouse fellow (£200); Arthur Atherley Hammond of St John's (£50); the Reverend Thomas Jones, Equiano's publicist, Trinity's junior dean from 1787–1789, and a college tutor (£100); the Reverend Dr Joseph Jowett, the Professor of Civil Law at Cambridge and Trinity Hall fellow (£200); Beilby Porteus, a former Christ's fellow and the Bishop of London (£50); Peter Peckard (£100); the Reverend Thomas Postlethwaite, the Master of Trinity (£300); and Francis Wollaston, the Jacksonian Professor of Natural Philosophy (£100). From the beginning, the Company, Bronwen Everill argues, was predicated on a 'desire for humanitarian intervention', which 'promoted an "imperialistic" expansion of colonial and metropolitan resources in West Africa'.[60]

The prophesised free utopia in Sierra Leone was an illusion, however. Whilst the second influx of 1,190 colonists, most of them Britain's Black allies during the American Revolution, arrived from Canada on 15 January 1792, the third group of arrivals were the 99,000 men, women, and children that the Royal Navy's anti-slavery squadron captured at sea and transported to Freetown between 1808 and 1863. According to the 1807 abolition act, enslaved people were entered 'into His Majesty's Land or Sea Service, as Soldiers, Seamen, or Marines' or bound 'whether of full Age or not, as Apprentices, for any Term not exceeding Fourteen Years[.]' Abolitionists proposed apprenticeship for the 35,000 Black children who arrived in Sierra Leone, precipitating an 'age of child enslavement'. The unpaid labour of Black children was supported by colonial officials, such as Zachary Macaulay, the Governor, as it "trained" liberated

Africans to become free labourers – those who tried to escape their newfound "freedom" were clapped in irons.

Thomas Perronet Thompson, a twenty-five-year-old Lieutenant and Queens' College alumnus and fellow, was appalled and launched an investigation after succeeding Macaulay as Sierra Leone's Governor in Spring 1808. Upon his arrival, he discovered that Africans were 'sold within the colony' from a cattle pen, and that a gaoler had announced to spectators that 'no person is to take away any of the slaves without paying the sum of twenty Dollars[.]' In August 1808, he was recalled – with Wilberforce's acquiescence – after attempting to outlaw apprenticeships. Thompson accepted Wilberforce's excuses (the latter did not want to jeopardise the fight against plantation slavery when apprenticeship was on the table), but he implored the Directors of the African Institution, which helped to run the colony until 1823, that 'slaves are *apprentices*. Their purchases redemptions. Surely this contemptible system needs only to be exposed to cease to exist'.[61]

West Africans would, in time, endure the arrival of other European abolitionist and colonising projects. The Bulama (or Bolama) Association was one of the lesser well-known projects on the coast, but it equalled some of the more disastrous aborted efforts at British colonisation in that region. Led by Philip Beaver, the President of the Association's council, and Richard Hancorn, the 275 colonists were inspired by the ideas of Malachy Postlethwayt and John Fothergill, who argued that British imperialism on the African continent was a humanitarian solution to the transatlantic slave trade. Hoping to promulgate 'humane, civilized commerce' on the continent, the original memorandum of the association offered sixty pounds per 500 acres for absentee colonists and thirty pounds for the same arrangement for subscribers who braved the journey to the African continent. The Association enjoyed the beneficence of numerous Manchester merchants, and university alumni and officials such as Sir John Riggs-Miller, who attended Trinity Hall (though he did not graduate), and Adam Afzelius, a SLC-supporting Botany Demonstrator at Uppsala University in Sweden and a donor to its ethnographical collections. Though the Association was quite radical in its ideals – establishing freedom of religion and prohibiting enslavement – the plan was unrealistic from the start, and the ships did not even know where the island that they intended to colonise was located. First arriving in May 1792, injuries, deaths, and diseases ensured that – a year later – six survivors including Beaver were left as a grim testament to the difficulties of transforming abolition rhetoric into a colonial reality in another new world.[62]

Seeking to avoid death from disease and misadventure, Europeans realised that greater knowledge was required about West Africa and the continental interior. The Association for Promoting the Discovery of the Interior Parts of Africa hoped to end white colonisers' ignorance about the continent. Founded by Sir Joseph Banks, one of the foremost naturalists of the eighteenth century (and a man famed for travelling with Captain James Cook on the *Endeavour* to

Australia), the African Association benefitted from the support of metropolitan elites, including Richard Watson (the Bishop of Llandaff and the Cambridge Regius Professor of Divinity), Sir Busick Harwood, William Wilberforce, Dr Thomas Gisborne (a three-time President of the Royal College of Physicians and senior fellow who donated much of his library to St John's College), Thomas Gray Comings, a Trinity fellow, Dr Luttrell Winne and Brownlow North (both of whom were fellows of All Souls), and George Cecil Renouard, the Almoner's Professor of Arabic at Cambridge.[63]

The Association was another example of a centuries-long interest in geography at the University, which had excited the minds of students and fellows about the potential profits and obvious horrors of a commercial empire. St John's College Library stocked Samuel Purchas's *His Pilgrimage*, which was published from 1613 and deemed Virginia 'the fittest place for an earthly Paradise', and the Welsh Reverend Griffith Hughes's *Natural History of Barbados*, a 1750 work that justified the slave trade because Africans were 'little better than Slaves in their own Country'. Cambridge locals were involved in these geographical discussions and debates too. Thomas Salmon, who had run a coffeehouse in Cambridge and compiled much of his work there (some of which was recommended to undergraduates), published a popular work of descriptive geography in 1739, entitled the *Modern History, or Present State of all Nations*.[64]

Salmon was a vehement critic of slave-trading more than four decades before that attitude was fashionable in Britain. He wrote that 'Young Blacks at full growth and in their prime, under three pounds a head, and boys and women in proportion; and these poor creatures are pack'd as close as Herrings, 7 or 800 of them in a ship, where they are forced to lie double, almost the whole voyage, and kept with no better food than horse-beans'. Salmon appealed to the merchants and their pocketbooks. The 'profit, one would think', the coffeehouse owner complained, 'should induce the Merchants to use them well; for a slave, that is purchased for three or four pounds at Angola, is worth twenty or five and twenty in America'. The *Modern History* detailed the horrors of the middle passage and how the enslaved 'jumped overboard, rather trusting to the mercy of the sea, than their white masters, from an apprehension… that they are to be fatted for slaughter, and devoured by white men'. The fear of white cannibalism – of European enslavers killing and consuming their captives – was a common feature of enslaved testimony, including Equiano's *Narrative*, and such stories convinced Salmon that, given the choice between the 'cruel Spaniard' and their silver mines or the 'English Planters' who 'don't use their slaves much better', there was little wonder that enslaved Africans chose death rather than bondage.[65]

Though abolitionist in principle, the Association utilised the trans-Saharan trade routes or the Gambia River to send explorers into the interior. The underlying motivations for this mission shifted as much as the arduous terrain that these explorers aimed to navigate. At the Association's inception on 9 June

1788, which Watson served on as a committee member until 1805, the founders planned to enlighten Europeans' geographical understanding of the interior – an area of the map that remained a 'wide extended blank' – and utilise that stock of "useful" information on the Niger, Senegal, and Gambia rivers to enlarge the 'fund of human knowledge'. Pleading for government assistance and funds after one of their members, the Irish former army officer Daniel Houghton, was robbed and perished before he reached the Niger (further than any European had travelled before), the Association argued that such "useful" geographical knowledge could be gained through another avenue: an 'extensive and lucrative Trade' in 'European goods' to the interior – a trade that might net Britain 'a Million Sterling per annum', and perhaps open another imperial frontier that could be as lucrative as the 'East Indies'. Planning a consulship and 'Fort and Settlement' in Senegambia, these metropolitan elites hoped to establish a bridgehead for London's 'Mercantile Houses' in gold, which the Association argued had been inefficiently harvested by 'ignorant Savages'. The commercial intercourse and planned fort would 'assert by arms' Britain's right to possession of this territory over 'Rival Nation[s]' in West Africa and Europe.[66]

The Association's potential success was predicated on collaborations with European enslavers. Houghton, who had been unsuccessfully employed to find the cities of Timbuktu and "Houssa" (the equivalent, for misinformed Europeans in West Africa, of the magical El Dorado), had been the fort-major of Île de Gorée in Senegal, which traded around 500 enslaved per year alongside peanuts, gum, and ivory. That military position and his experience as an adventurer, the Association acknowledged, had provided the Irishman with 'knowledge of the [Gambian] Negro Nations'. Following his death, the Association relied on the expert geographical knowledge of military men and the slave forts that they commanded – outposts which acted as 'conduits' for European goods and enslavement, and as regional hubs of commercial activity for African mercantile elites who transported goods (including cloth, metals, beads, and weapons) and people to the slave ships and from fort to fort. With Houghton's approval, Fattatenda was considered an ideal location for the establishment of a base of operations on the Gambia, due to it being 'free' from 'noxious effluvia and stagnant air' and thus 'formerly occupied by a British factory'. The Association maintained close ties to the African Company of Merchants and the governors of slave forts in Calabar, who were contacted to see 'whether any of them have the reputation of being curious and likely to promote the wishes of the Society'. From its dealings, the Association's 'Geographical Missionary' expeditions were beholden to both white and African enslavers – in fact, the Society acknowledged that an explorer who 'wish[es] to make friends with the… Traders as well as the great Men [is] obliged to be very profuse with my Rum as this class of men are those who go farthest up the Country and can give me the most information'.[67]

European universities were integral to the Association's mission in the African interior. After Houghton's death, the Association, with Watson on the committee, searched for and found a new enthusiastic potential recruit named Friedrich Conrad Hornemann, a native of Hildesheim in Lower Saxony. On 4 May 1796, Johann Friedrich Blumenbach, an expert in comparative anatomy who argued that all ethnicities had originated from a single ancestor (a theory known as monogenism), forwarded Hornemann's proposal to the Association and recommended that he attend the University of Gottingen in Hanover for instruction in natural history, mineralogy, geography, mathematics, astronomy, medicine, and Arabic.[68]

At Gottingen, Hornemann enjoyed the tutelage of Europe's finest professors: Christian Gottlob Heyne, the First Librarian; Blumenbach, who was a professor of medicine and natural science; the historian Arnold Hermann Ludwig Heeren; and Thomas Christian Tyschen, who was later celebrated for his 1823 *Grammatik Der Arabischen*. Blumenbach despised enslavement because it limited the capacity for Africans to achieve their full potential, and Heeren also critiqued the "peculiar institution," pondering whether ancient slavery, in raising free Greeks to a 'sort of nobility' where they could live 'by the labors of the other' and produce cultural achievements, had been a price 'too dearly purchased by the introduction of slavery'. Regardless, the months of academic instruction at Gottingen did not spare Hornemann on his ill-fated voyage, and he died in Niger after delivering information from the western Sahara and central Sudan.[69]

Hornemann perished on his travels; still, the Association did not fail for want of trying – they enlisted powerful African traffickers in enslaved people, who were called "slatees," to aid white explorers. Europeans utilised slavers to collect intelligence, send post, and for transport and guidance. The merchants were particularly powerful on a continent that, in parts, was characterised by 'warlordism' and the inability of states – including Muslim polities, who had long debated the efficacy of enslaving the subjects of Islamic states – to maintain monopolies of governance over large extended territories, ensuring that such authorities were often unable to safeguard personal liberties or property. From 1600 to 1800, the five Hausa states of Gobir, Kano, Katsina, Zamfara, and Zassau fought almost as many conflicts as they made alliances, and mass kidnappings and enslavement were the consequences of that power vacuum, leading to close to 20 million Africans being trafficked west to the Americas and east to the Islamic lands.[70]

Before his untimely death, Hornemann was instructed to inquire into the 'Slave Trade' on his travels, and the Association soon received detailed reports concerning how local warlords and sultans alike earned bribes and taxes from raids to enslave captives – indeed, for some leaders in the interior the revenue from these expeditions rivalled land taxes (gold that was then used to finance the purchase of firearms and weaponry from European empires). The Association were candid about their reliance on African slave-traders, and the Committee in June 1797 hoped that Gambian 'Slave Dealers' would 'render opportunities frequent of receiving Letters or Dispatches from' Hornemann. Later, the Treasurer and Secretary contacted the African Company of Merchants to ascertain the goods that would be required for 'remuneration of any Slatee or Slave Merchant who should be induced to conduct and safely reconvey from the interior' their adventurers. The personal associations between Company traders and African merchants were well known as some Calabar traders had travelled to Liverpool to 'learn English' (in fact, it was suggested that the Association's explorers leave that English port for Calabar because of these economic networks). Three years before the abolition of the transatlantic slave trade, the Committee agreed to 'conciliate' Calabar's 'three principal Slatees or Negroes traders'.[71]

European explorers also purchased enslaved people, thereby participating in the African and trans-Saharan slave trading economies. Both the Swiss traveller Johann Ludwig Burckhardt and Edward Daniel Clarke shared a close friendship, Cambridge educations, and a spirit for adventure. Burckhardt was celebrated for becoming the first European to see Petra, Jordan, since the Crusades and the temples of Abu Simbel in Egypt. Clarke's adventures began at Jesus College – launching a balloon from the college grounds – and his more earthly travels took the Jesuan alumnus through Northern and Eastern Europe, and Africa. Arriving in Shendi in the Sudan, Burckhardt recollected that he sold his 'merchandize' and 'bought a slave boy about fourteen years of age', in part to have a 'useful and constant companion', but also because he 'afford[ed] me an ostensible reason for going in the direction of the Red Sea, where I might sell him with profit'. The Swiss adventurer traded enslaved people in the port city of Suakin on the Red Sea. Slave sales helped him afford his expenses there and Burckhardt, then in Jeddah, complained that he was forced to 'sell my slave' for forty-eight dollars – a 'faithful and useful companion' – to 'defray my daily expenses'. He lamented that, 'although I have since had several other slaves in my possession', he had 'never found one equal to him'. Clarke, who became the first Professor of Mineralogy at Cambridge, also travelled through Suakin, where he persuaded a customs officer that he was not a Mamluk (former slaves who had become a powerful military class) so that he would not lose a 'faithful slave, the only thing of value left to me'. These transactions took place at a moment when Europeans were beginning to highlight and oppose the purchase and treatment of the enslaved in Egypt and the Sudan. After their travels, Clarke and Burckhardt donated to Cambridge: the former his minerals and a series of ancient Greek sculptures which he had "removed" and transported to the University (the statues forming one of the 'two principal divisions' of the Fitzwilliam's antiquities collection), and the latter bequeathed more than 300 Arabic manuscripts.[72]

Bryan Edwards succeeded Sir Joseph Banks as the Association's leader in 1797, and that powerful slaveholder – with Watson, a Cambridge Professor, on the Committee – shaped the group's publications. That influence was particularly felt in the case of the Scottish explorer Mungo Park, the Association's most successful adventurer, who, on his first trip from 1795–1797 along with six African assistants, travelled to Ségou in the Bamana Empire and then, on his second expedition, reached Timbuktu, one of the Association's long-term goals. Park was close associates with Edwards, yet the intrepid Scotsman despised the transatlantic trade – and it could not be otherwise considering he met with one group of enslaved who had asked, such was the Europeans' desire for African labourers, whether their countrymen would be eaten once they crossed the 'salt water'. (After all, almost none of their countrymen or women had ever returned from the Americas.) The bestselling work extended to three editions and was translated into German and French; however, Edwards, the MP for Grampound, took advantage of Park's silence on the morality of the slave trade to revise the manuscript before it hit the printing press, leading the enslaver George Hibbert to argue that the 'tenor' of the *Travels* did 'not lead to a conviction that we shall better their condition by abandoning the trade'. The government's takeover of the Association's functions and the final merger with the Royal Geographical Society in 1831 ended another chapter in the long association of European explorers with enslavement.[73]

One year after the publication of Park's *Travels*, Watson advocated the amelioration and gradual abolition of the transatlantic traffic, arguing that enslaving a family in perpetuity (in essence, from childhood) was more of a crime than slavery for an individual. The professor contacted Pitt to consider how the slave trade could be abolished – and the profit motive was central to his argument. The Cambridge man argued that a duty on the importations of all enslaved persons would make it cheaper for slavers to 'rear slaves than to buy slaves, and the trade will in a few years cease of itself'. Favouring the emancipation of enslaved people at a certain age, he noted – in reference to an unnamed slaveholder associate – that if they lowered the mortality rate the enslavers would have more enslaved labourers than if they worked them to death on their sugar, rice, and coffee estates. The reform of *partus sequitur ventrem*, which Watson referred to in an 1807 address, echoed the Virginian planter and William and Mary professor St. George Tucker's proposals for a gradual abolition where the enslaved worked to compensate enslavers for their freedom. As Watson argued, 'the labour of the man should recompense the master of his parents for the maintenance of the child, is a just principle' – and once the enslaved had reached the age of 'twenty-one, of twenty-five, or thirty years' it may 'be reasonably calculated that by their labour, as adults, they have repaid the masters of their parents, for the risk and expertise attending their rearing and education'. Slavery had become an election issue (a reality which Wilberforce exploited in 1806 to bring abolitionist MPs into politics), and Watson's opinions showed that as the slave trade bill passed 283 votes to 16 – in part because the suppression of that traffic would serve the war effort against France – the people's pens had turned to abolition writ-large.[74]

The curtain had come down on the first act in a long war over enslavement at Cambridge, yet the slave trade debate had exposed fissures within the universities concerning how to end, reform, or protect the slave trafficking and plantation systems. Though historians focus on the antislavery activities of Peckard, Clarkson, and Wilberforce, this chapter has shown that, in truth, men such as Charles Farish were more illustrative of the ameliorative nature of much anti-slave trade thought. If Cambridge fellows were willing to consider ending the slave trade, then those beliefs did not necessarily constitute an attack on slave societies or the planter class. From the slave trade onwards, undergraduates, to a certain degree, appeared far more radical than the fellowship on these issues and debates – and there is therefore a case to be made for historians to see universities, like so many other British towns and communities, as divided on the question of slavery. On the other end of the spectrum, Stephen Fuller and the proslavery activists have received growing attention from historians, but these men lobbied beyond Parliament – turning their attention to thought-leaders in the universities. Fuller calculated that, by influencing the eyes and soul of the kingdom, slavers could impose their power on all sectors of British society. Their power would then be unassailable. As a new century dawned, the second act of the antislavery struggle began: a debate on how to end African enslavement.

5

'Those who wish to see the Slave System decline, and at length gradually and safely': The Ambitions of Cambridge Abolitionism

Seven years after the abolition of the slave trade, the 'Chancellor, Masters and Scholars' of Cambridge drafted another antislavery petition urging the British Parliament to take decisive action on one of the most pressing issues of the day. On 4 July 1814, the situation appeared no less critical. In the Atlantic Ocean, the first years of the abolition act had revealed Britain's measures to be a paper tiger – smuggling continued in the face of potential fines – so Parliament introduced the Slave Trade Felony Act in 1811, which denounced slave-trading as 'contrary to the principles of justice, humanity, and sound policy' and made that practice a 'capital felony'. Across the Channel in France, it had been more than a decade since Emperor Napoleon Bonaparte had sent an army to crush the Saint-Domingue revolutionaries and re-establish enslavement in Guadeloupe, French Guiana, and the wider French Caribbean (costing the French thousands of troops, treasure, and the life of Napoleon's brother-in-law Charles Leclerc, who led the expedition and died from yellow fever). The work of abolition was far from over.[1]

Alongside the cities and towns of York, Scarborough, London, and Bedford, the University – in a petition that has never been studied – called for the 'total Abolition of the *African* Slave Trade'. Applauding the 'wise and benevolent measures, which have been carried on for the Abolition of the African Slave Trade', the petitioners 'looked forward with a confident hope, to the prospect of its complete Annihilation'. The politics in the Senate House had, at times, spilled out into the open, and William Chafy, the Master of Sidney Sussex, had previously tried in vain to block an address calling for more action in abolishing the slave trade – not, it must be noted, because he was a fervent proslavery activist, but rather because of his support for Robert Jenkinson, the 2nd Earl of Liverpool's anti-abolitionist administration (Liverpool's father was a trustee for a plantation). Claiming to be acting in the absence of another pro-Liverpool man – Philip Douglas, the Master of Corpus Christi – Chafy's efforts were in vain, and the petition passed by two votes. Thankfully, this time the abolitionist petitioners avoided another political contest (in fact, the members of the Senate noted that Prince William Frederick, Duke of Gloucester, had won the electoral contest for University Chancellor in 1811 on account of his entrenched opposition to enslavement). In the petition, the Senate also congratulated Parliament on inducing 'Foreign Powers to imitate the noble Example which it has displayed', however they 'beg[ged] to express their regret at the very different prospect now held out on the part of the Government of France'. The Cambridge men were concerned for 'the African Settlements [in Senegal] and West Indian Colonies [of Guadeloupe and Martinique] now restored to France, [with] the most serious consequences to the general Cause of African liberty and Civilization'. In supporting British colonisation in West Africa and the Caribbean as the 'Guardians of Learning and Religion', they expressed their 'abhorrence' of France's colonial activities in the Atlantic world and hoped to 'express those Sentiments' that had been 'foremost to avow and inculcate; and which, as they humbly hope, they have been instrumental in promoting'. The Cambridge Senate had again brandished its anti-slavery credentials after a period of public silence on the issue following its earlier petitions to Parliament.[2]

The 1823 petition went further, proposing measures to end enslavement. The Senate proclaimed that the 'existence of Slavery is inconsistent with the Principles of British Legislation, of Sound Policy, & of Justice; and contrary to the feelings of Humanity and to the Spirit of the Christian Religion'. The petitioners condemned the British Caribbean colonies for having taken 'no effectual measures… for the Gradual Termination of Slavery & the preparing of the unfortunate Subjects of it for Freedom; or even to the mitigating of their wretched Condition'. They hoped for an end to a system that had practiced 'Arbitrary & Debasing Corporal Punishments' – an end to violent slave societies where 'Enfranchisement is so greatly discouraged, where Marriage is infrequent, & where Religious Instruction & the Duties of the Sabbath are nearly altogether precluded'. Under attack for these sentiments from some slaveholder members of Parliament, Cambridge pushed for the 'mitigation' of enslavement, with further legal 'Provisions' advised if the Caribbean colonies complied – with the express hope that, 'eventually', these policies would result in its 'final and Complete Termination'.[3]

If many Cambridge fellows and students agreed that enslavement had to end, that was where the consensus on its termination or reformation ended. For more than thirty years, Cambridge-affiliated men invested in and propagated almost every abolition measure, from the promotion of slave-free commerce to the Christianisation of enslaved Black people. These gradual measures, however, stood at odds with the immediatism that was more popular in Black and white radical circles. Furthermore, as with the slave trade debate, there were numerous Cambridge intellectuals and alumni who either operated in a middle ground, supporting the plantation regime in the belief that Christianising Africans would produce more docile workers, or they supported the proslavery lobby in its efforts to attain compensation. Examining each of these approaches in turn, the chapter follows the stories of abolitionist activists in Cambridge, overseas missionaries and ameliorationists, and proslavery campaigners to illustrate how Britons were continuing to think through and develop their positions on enslavement.

Over the course of the more than three decades between the abolition of the slave trade and the end of slavery in 1838, proslavery campaigners and antislavery activists, many of whom formed the Society for the Mitigation and Gradual Abolition of Slavery Throughout the British Dominions in 1823, again fought for political and intellectual supremacy. The abolitionists' ambitious goal was to hasten the end of enslavement. Cambridge alumni and fellows, as was often the case, occupied all sides of the debate. As with the Cambridge Senate, white abolitionists such as William Paley and William Wilberforce were supporters of gradualism – that slavery should gradually end once enslaved people had reached a certain age or after a period of apprenticeship to their former masters to teach them how to work and live as free labourers. Although not involved in the day-to-day running of the Society (he had resigned from Parliament in 1825 due to ill health), Wilberforce was a co-founder. Clarkson, however, was frustrated at the pace of change. In 1824, he admitted that the end of the slave trade had not 'materially improved' the conditions of the enslaved, and he called for abolitionists to '*resume their labors*'. He understood radical Britons' impatience for slavery's immediate termination, writing in in his diary that 'Everywhere People are asking me about *immediate abolition*, and whether that would not be the best'.[4]

Radical abolitionists, such as the Quaker schoolteacher Elizabeth Heyrick, attacked white Britons for their conservatism. The same year as Clarkson's pamphlet, Heyrick's *Immediate, not Gradual Abolition* mocked the Anti-Slavery Society for its 'slow, cautious, accommodating measures' toward enslavers. 'We make slow progress in virtue', she frankly observed, 'lose much time in labour, when, instead of going boldly forward in its straight and obvious path, we are continually enquiring how far we may proceed in it without difficulty and without opposition'. Heyrick regretted that abolitionists, through their cautiousness, had helped to delay and forestall the end of racial slavery.[5]

Samuel Taylor Coleridge was emblematic of the tensions amongst white antislavery activists concerning slavery, abolition, and race. As we have seen, Coleridge had condemned slave-traders and hoped that they would receive 'burning punishment' for their crimes, and he maintained that Britain's wrongs in West Africa would result in divine retribution. (Coleridge even aimed to turn his words into deeds – he had proposed a new colony, "Pantisocracy," on the banks of the Susquehanna River in Pennsylvania without distinctions of class or rank.) Still, he advocated African religious conversion, rather than the more ambitious goal of raising Black people to the status of white Europeans through the immediate end of plantation slavery. In an 1812 Lecture on Shakespeare, Coleridge revealed his opinion of Africans, arguing that Othello had to be a 'Moor' because 'negroes were not known except as slaves' and could not possibly rise to the position of a general. 'I utterly condemn your [abolitionist's] frantic practice of declaiming about their rights to the black themselves', he wrote on abolition. 'They [the enslaved] ought to be forcibly reminded of the state in which their brethren in Africa still are, and taught to be thankful for the providence which has placed them within the reach of the means of grace'. In a similar fashion to many abolitionists, Coleridge believed in the civilising and disciplining potential of the plantation regime.[6]

Youthful opposition to the transatlantic trafficking of enslaved Africans, of course, did not naturally result in an overwhelming condemnation of enslavement later in life. For instance, William Lamb, the 2nd Viscount Melbourne, who as a Trinity undergraduate had delivered a prize-winning December 1798 sermon in the college chapel which was printed and distributed (and which Charles James Fox had quoted in the House of Commons). In the sermon, Lamb hoped that the cause of improving human knowledge would 'civilize the rude millions of Africa' and 'strike the fetter from the galled limbs of the supplicating slave'. After attaining the Prime Ministership in July 1834 (a position that he held on two occasions in 1834 and from 1835 to 1841), however, he described abolition as a 'great folly' and he dismissed Sir Thomas Fowell Buxtons's pleas to establish 'posts in the interior of Africa' as a bridgehead to 'civilising that continent' through the spread of a legitimate trade in goods and the end of the slave trade. He was not alone: Thomas Robert Malthus, a former Jesuan fellow and author of *An Essay on the Principle of Population* (a landmark 1798 treatise which had been used by both abolitionists and proslavery activists to prosecute their case), opposed the slave trade but his pen was notably silent on the issue of abolishing racial chattel slavery. In truth, George III, the Viscount Melbourne, Malthus, and Coleridge had thought through their positions on enslavement and racial justice over the course of many decades – and, on numerous occasions, Britons arrived at more conservative and prejudicial positions concerning the rights of enslaved Black people than their youthful exuberance would suggest.[7]

Financial funding from Cambridge for abolitionism underwent a significant transformation too. Colleges had provided important (and noteworthy) sums to SEAT, yet Cambridge institutions were not as generous to the African Institution and Anti-Slavery Society. From 1822 to 1828, the Cambridge subscribers included the Reverend Henry Godfrey, the President of Queens' (£10.10 donation), the Reverend William Mandell, a Queens' fellow (£10.10 donation), John Stevens Henslow of St John's (£1.1 subscription), James Plumptre, (£10 10s. donation), William Whewell of Trinity (£1.1 subscription), William Farish (£3.3s subscription); and the Reverend Henry Venn of Trinity (a £2.2s donation and £1.1s annual subscription), who was a prominent committee member of the Anti-Slavery Society. Aside from the gown-wearing population, the Banker, MP, and thirteen-times mayor John Mortlock provided £500 and audited the Institution's accounts. From the university, the most generous sum arrived from an 'Association among the Undergraduates' (£22.17), proving that undergraduates were (once again) at the forefront of the debate within the university. The subscription lists do not mention if the colleges contributed their funds, suggesting that Cambridge had concluded much of its institutional financial support for abolition.[8]

At Cambridge, the university members and donors had numerous opinions on how to end slavery. Abolitionism continued to be a contentious issue at the dawn of a new century, even as the colleges were no longer actively involved in donating to or financing antislavery organisations. William Woodis Harvey, though, had prior experience of a post-emancipation society before matriculating as a Queens' sizar in March 1824. Born in Penzance, Harvey was one of the many Wesleyan preachers who travelled to Haiti after it had successfully declared its independence on New Year's Day 1804. Heralding a new 'State of Haiti', the Declaration inspired its Black citizens to 'deny the inhuman government that for long has held our minds in humiliating thralldom any hope of reenslaving us'. 'In short', Jean-Jaques-Dessalines' secretary, Louis Boisrond-Tonnerre, wrote, 'we must live independent or die'. Arriving in 1818, Harvey formed the crest of an Anglican wave that sought to drive French Catholicism from the island of Hispaniola. The young man's experiences in Haiti were far from auspicious, however – and his visit to the island may have coloured his writings on the new nation and its post-emancipation life. Though wielding a prized letter of introduction from Wilberforce, Haitians were not rushing to attend his sermons and the archbishop, who Harvey dismissed as an 'infidel' that was motivated solely by profit, stopped children from attending and singing at his morning service. The Cornishman was fortunate he just had to deal with one disgruntled dignitary: a Wesleyan missionary in Port-au-Prince claimed that he was forced to hold his meetings in private because of the 'violence of the mob'.[9]

Returning to Britain, Harvey enrolled at Cambridge with the encouragement of the Reverend Charles Valentine Le Grice, a college fellow and Paley critic. There, he joined other students in questioning the efficacy of slaveholding or the other contentious political and social problems of the day. At the Cambridge Union Society, founded in 1815, undergraduates debated global issues ranging from Spanish American to Greek independence (with the Union donating £20 to the latter cause) to Irish colonisation to the morality of Black enslavement. On the latter topic, the student debaters were well-informed: the Society, at various points, subscribed to or owned copies of the *Jamaica Chronicle* newspaper, the Oxford alumnus George Wilson Bridges' proslavery *A Voice from Jamaica*, the treatise *An Appeal on Behalf of the Sugar Slaves of the West Indies*, the pamphlet *Stephens on the Condition of Negro Slaves*, and Zachary Macaulay's *Negro Slavery*. Activists may have also mined the college archives for resources on the history of enslavement. In one antislavery pamphlet, a polemicist mentioned that, from the records of our 'Saxon ancestors' in England, 'several entries' of 'manumissions exist in a MS. of the four evangelists in the library of *Corpus Christi*, or *Bennet* College, Cambridge'. The records were used as evidence that Britain's ancestors in Anglo-Saxon and Medieval England were committed to ameliorating slavery before it was 'unhappily again revived' through the 'discovery of America'.[10]

The slavery question was, unsurprisingly, a contentious subject for students debates, and in March 1824 the Society discussed whether 'the condition of slaves in the West Indies previous to 1800, such as to entitle the planters to the support of Parliament'. With the planters defended by, among others, the former Union President, John Job Rawlinson, and the slaves by seven students, the motion was defeated with 78 in favor of the slaves and 55 for the enslavers. Two years later, in May 1826, the Union debated another motion: 'Has the conduct of the Legislative Assemblies in the West Indian Colonies up to the year 1806 been such as to entitle them to the approbation of the Country'. Again, the result was 11 in the affirmative and 51 in the negative, an indictment of the white colonists' treatment of the enslaved. Students, as with the slave trade, were, once again, in the vanguard of radical white opinion concerning the end of enslavement.[11]

The Union papers are light on details concerning these debates, but the *Cambridge Chronicle* reported a sensational 1825 Town Hall meeting on the abolition of chattel slavery. The meetings, which also took place in other cities such as Birmingham, provided an opportunity for residents to pressure their local representatives to support abolition. The Reverend James Scholefield, the evangelical Regius Professor of Greek (and a passionate supporter of the Sierra Leone mission), and William Farish were two such attendees. Scholefield was an experienced political combatant: two years earlier, he was a member of a Cambridge committee that supported Greece's more than eight-year revolution against the Ottoman Empire – a cause, the committee declared, 'for the Greek against the Barbarian, for Liberty and Oppression, for the Cross against the Crescent'. For the Reverend, abolitionism and Greek independence were conjoined struggles between liberty and oppression. He thundered that Britons had 'borne the burthen and shame of sanctioning the [slave] system quite long enough, and he trusted they were now determined to tell the Government, in firm but respectable language, that they would tolerate it no longer'. In advocating for a 'speedy abolition', Scholefield was rather isolated at Cambridge in his proposal for immediatism. Though a bitter pill to swallow, Scholefield suggested that the 'burthen' of compensating slaveholders might 'bring about this desirable measure'. The Professor saved most of his invective for Britons, like Stephen Fuller, who claimed that the white poor lived in worse conditions than West African slaves, attacking them as men of 'slavish minds' who 'deserved to be hooted out of society as not possessing common English feeling'. Farish concurred with Scholefield. Giving a vote of thanks to the mayor, he remembered that a previous Vice-Chancellor, Peter Peckard, and Thomas Clarkson had 'been one of the first persons who called attention to this subject', and he recalled Peckard's sermon 'upon the cruelty of the system &c. that the pamphlet came out with a black border round the pages, similar to the newspapers on melancholy public occasions'. As the meeting was dissolved, Farish and Scholefield had tried to ensure that town and gown were united in their opposition to enslavement.[12]

The question remained *how* and *when* to abolish that system, however. Having spent almost six years in Haiti, Harvey, in his *Sketches of Hayti*, was convinced that gradual abolition was the wisest course of action. For the Queens' man, the Haitian Revolution presented Britons with a unique opportunity to witness how a 'people newly escaped from slavery' were 'still suffering and exhibiting in their character, its pernicious and demoralizing effects; gradually returning from scenes of confusion and bloodshed, to habits of industry, peace, and order; steadily aiming, amidst frequent reverses, to establish a regular and independent government'. From Cap-Français, the capital of the autocratic Henri Cristophe's new Kingdom of Haiti, Harvey reported that Haitians had struggled 'to improve their agriculture, to repair an exhausted population, to form commercial connexions, and to introduce a knowledge of the arts and sciences'. Harvey identified the source of these social, economic, and intellectual ills: he blamed the Revolution's 'excesses and cruelties' on French legislators, who had 'contended for *immediate* emancipation; forgetting, in the heat of their zeal, the unfit state of the negroes at this period to value and improve the advantages of freedom; and thus overlooking the propriety and necessity of a gradual method of liberating them'. No disinterested narrative of Haitian politics, the *Sketches*, which Harvey wrote and published whilst a student, warned white Britons about the effect of immediatism – the laying 'waste the plantations', the destruction of property, and the 'massacre' of 'unprotected proprietors without distinction'. Such a scene of anti-white bloodshed, which he blamed on Dessalines (referring to the 1804 massacre of between 3,000 and 5,000 white and mixed-ethnicity French inhabitants), had occurred because 'uneducated, barbarous' and 'uncivilized' Haitians were incapable of self-rule. If enslaved Africans were emancipated in a 'gradual manner, in which the British government proposes to liberate the slave of the West India colonies', their situation, the Cambridge member claimed, would be far 'superior'. The *Sketches* was a handbook on how *not* to end slavery.[13]

Four years later, in 1831, another "Member of the University of Cambridge" published their *Suggestions on the Abolition of Slavery in the British Colonies; or, Slavery Gradually Starved to Death Upon a Low Diet*. They promoted East India sugar and an end to the Caribbean monopoly over that product. As monopolies, they argued, diverted industry from more profitable activities, officials had to mitigate enslavement to make producing Caribbean sugar dearer – 'to treat, feed, and clothe them better' – and thereby convince enslavers to employ free labour. The 'invasion' of the Caribbean's monopoly, with close to 60,000 tons of Jamaican sugar exported in 1798, would 'absolutely constrain them to adopt measures of gradual emancipation'. Avoiding the 'violent and convulsive consequences… under any other system of abolition', the "Member" confidently claimed, was 'best calculated both morally and intellectually to prepare the slave for the reception and fruition of freedom, to instruct him, in fact, in the rudiments of liberty… he would be most cordially reconciled to his master, being united to him by the threefold bond of gratitude, affection, and mutual voluntary dependence'. The plantation system and bonds of dependence between Black and white colonists could then continue.[14]

British antislavery activists had tried to propagate East India sugar for decades, and the pamphlet was similarly attached to market-based solutions to the plantation's abuses. With more than 70,000 copies published, William Fox's *Address to the People of Great Britain, on the Propriety of Abstaining from West India Sugar and Rum* helped to inspire women-led boycotts of Caribbean sugar in Britain. Images and cartoons displaying the 'Barbarities of the West Indies', with enslaved people being boiled in sugar vats, which further defined a link between sugar-production and violence. Such activism had been going on in Cambridge, too. Thomas Musgrave, the Professor of Arabic, held meetings at his house where the attendees pledged to not use articles produced by enslaved people.[15]

Building on these nonimportation measures, the "Member" implored the government to take decisive action on the 'Slave Question' – an issue that continued 'wantonly to exasperate the country… a country, provoked by innumerable parliamentary abuses, and, above all, smarting under the painful conviction, that their voice is unheard by Government, their wishes uncompiled with, their complaints disregarded, and their wrongs unredressed'. Domestic political corruption and transatlantic enslavement were interconnected vices. Enslavers had purchased rotten boroughs to disenfranchise Britons and supplied them with '*luxuries*', ensuring that the disreputable title of 'Slave owner' had become an honourable distinction in public life. To counteract the enduring power of the planter class, the "Member" pondered how to end slavery 'with the least expenditure of life, happiness, and property' – a panacea to 'England [being] enslaved by her own colonies'.[16]

The abolitionist ignored the realities of East India Company rule, which Edmund Burke and other parliamentarians had pilloried for corruption, violence, and avarice – with "Nabobs" returning to England to enjoy their riches. In fact, Caribbean slaveholders, such as Francis Buchanan, claimed that East India enslavers were committing abuses there too – and the slavers had some truth to their claims of antislavery hypocrisy: the government had banned the export of enslaved people from Calcutta on 22 July 1789 and had halted the importation of slaves into Bombay in 1805, but the East India Company was more hesitant to challenge plantation or domestic bonded labour systems.

Bonded labour was 'reproduced and even reinforced' and adapted in colonial British law, and forms of hereditary debt bondage, called *al-amanji*, were 'appropriated and modified by the new colonial rulers'.[17]

Applauding the East Indian sugar growers, the anonymous "Member" nevertheless argued that an end to the Caribbean sugar duty would provide for the moral and political regeneration of Europe. Drawing upon the work of the political economist Adam Smith, and travel narratives from Poland to Mexico, the author denounced slavers' reliance on duties and taxes to thwart the importation of superior East Indian sugar. If economic profits and prosperity depended on the rate of demand for a product, as the author claimed, then the welfare of free people of colour would increase in turn as they were loosened from their shackles and enabled to produce more (assuming, of course, that the enslaved were less efficient than free labourers). Criticising the 'passion for absenteeism' amongst British Caribbean slaveholders and the policy of a 'mitigated' state of slavery, the "Member" was careful to inform his readers that Black people were not degraded by their enslavement. 'Are the emancipated blacks of Hayti', he noted, 'a slothful and inactive race? are they such in Sierra Leone? in the United States? and, above all, are they such in our own colonies (the liberated Negroes I mean)?' Stoking fears of political corruption, the enemy from within, the pamphlet was also addressed to the planter class, who would, in the absence of enslavement, 'begin to think of economizing, not only in the cultivation of his sugar plantations, but in all his domestic arrangements and expenses' employing cattle, engaging in crop rotation, and introducing technological advancements to improve their apparently unproductive estates. In truth, the annual profits on Caribbean sugar production were sometimes as high as £1.7 million (and agricultural profits from that region could rise up to £2.5 million including other staples).[18]

The end of slavery, the author implied, would also unravel the tangled financial webs of mortgages and debt that financed the plantations. Far more than the 'opiate' of 'melioration', which he believed the government had propagated to 'stupify the public mind', the author dreaded the 'volcano' of immediate abolitionism. Angered by abuses and usurpations, the suddenly-free labourers would, he predicted, descend like 'some bedlam of maniacs, or some caravan of wild beasts' to commit 'carnage, plunder, outrage, and devastation' in the colonies. The abolitionist shared the enslavers' fear that immediatism would unleash a 'confederacy of lawless savages' upon the colonies. Alongside racialised fears about Black majority rule, the author's qualified support for East India rule would have appealed to his Cambridge contemporaries. University luminaries continued to invest in India stockholdings, such as the King's fellow, Dean, and former Cambridge Vice-Provost, Martin Thackeray (who bequeathed his extensive library and £1,000 to fund a college prize in mathematics for Eton alumni).[19]

George W. Craufurd, a prominent King's fellow, protested the 'Impolicy of the Slave Trade' as well. Craufurd had familial connections to slavery – his grandfather, Sir Alexander Craufurd, owned Grenville Estate in Jamaica and, through his wife, he mortgaged Heart's Ease in the same colony. (Grenville was left to George's father, also named James.) George's two elder brothers joined the British army, and the eldest, Thomas, was killed in action at the Battle of Waterloo in June 1815. George, however, remained at Cambridge after his education as a King's Scholar at Eton and at King's College in 1820. A fellow for nineteen years, two as Bursar and another seven as a Divinity Lecturer, he was ordained in the Church and held a chaplaincy with the EIC. Both an abolitionist and the inheritor of a fortune tied to slave wealth, Craufurd donated £1,000 to King's and another £1,000 upon his death two years later to support a Divinity Lectureship. The involvement of abolitionists in the plantation economy was not unusual at Cambridge, though. The Reverend Adam Sedgwick was a Professor at Cambridge and was commemorated and acclaimed as the namesake of that university's Natural History Museum. The natural scientist was 'disgusted' that the parliamentarians had accepted 'slave-grown sugar' – and he mentioned to his contemporaries that he had 'sucked in a hatred of slavery from my mother's breast and learnt it from my father's knee'. Coincidentally, Sedgwick was co-trustee to a Jamaican plantation, an estate which was awarded £3,783 in compensation for 174 enslaved.[20]

Craufurd directed his energies to abolishing slavery – yet he admitted in 1832 that the 'greater part of mankind are very little moved, except by motives of SELF-INTEREST', so he identified several economic arguments against enslavement. For one, the expense of furnishing the enslaved 'liberally with food and raiment' was an unnecessary cost to production if the labourers were free and fed and clothed themselves (in reality, enslaved people fed and clothed themselves whilst working small plots of land on plantations). Appealing to consumers, he argued that such an 'ADDITIONAL CHARGE' was a 'direct tax' levied on Britons that need not be paid if East India sugar was purchased instead. Furthermore, he observed that slavery was a loss to the British economy from interest payments for purchasing the enslaved (£84,000), insurance (£42,000), the inferiority of enslaved labour (£70,000), and accidents on the plantation (£14,000). The total loss from slavery over seven years was £1,540,000. Given this financial burden, Craufurd asked 'How many more years shall this wretched system continue, and be actually SUPPORTED by us?' Craufurd's consideration of statistics appealed to readers because the British Association for the Advancement of Science had founded a "Statistical Section" at Cambridge in June 1833 in the rooms of Richard Jones, a Trinity political economist, who had lectured on the 'Evils attendant on slavery in all its forms'. Abolitionists made their cause an issue of statistics – and their calculations found the rationale for enslavement wanting.[21]

Britain's slave empire was on the ballot. In the wake of the Reform Act, which abolished smaller, unrepresentative districts and gave representation to male smallholders and artisans (expanding Cambridge's electorate to 1,400 voters), the 1832 Cambridge election was another battleground in the national debate on African slavery. In the organised chaos of Britain's election system, Oxford and Cambridge often held elections for county, borough, and the university all at the same time (with the electors for the latter restricted to MAs and doctors). The contested elections of the nineteenth century were a welcome change from the relative monotony of eighteenth-century local politics (the Whigs had held that seat uncontested for almost forty years, from 1737 to 1774). The contest for the two-member seat was between Charles Philip Yorke, a Tory who had served as the MP for Cambridgeshire (1790–1810) and Home Secretary, Lord Chancellor Brougham, Francis Jeffrey, the Lord Advocate, Thomas Spring Rice, 1st Baron Monteagle of Brandon, and George Pryme, an abolitionist and Cambridge's Professor of Political Economy. Pryme's lectures had considered 'Whether [the] labor of [a] slave is dearer than that of a freeman?', concluding that the Romans had suffered due to the 'scarcity of capital' amongst the middling farmers, which meant their 'great landed proprietors were… compelled to cultivate their own estates by the labor of captive enemies reduced to slavery' – ensuring that Rome, reduced to 'plunder and extortion' as the 'chief sources of wealth, they neglected all others'. The Whig supporters Pryme and Rice were victorious in the election, but the contest soon divided and embittered the Cambridge electors as Yorke's champions cried foul to the voting public that their man had been defamed as a proslavery activist.[22]

Publishing broadsides, Yorke's beleaguered supporters denounced the Whigs for their scurrilous accusations. Using pseudonyms such as "Fair Play" and "An Abolitionist," they noted that Yorke 'declares his abhorrence of Slavery, and avows his determination to vote for *its abolition*'. Pryme, who became a prominent abolitionist voice in Parliament and sceptic of slaveholder compensation, argued that he had 'ever been anxious for measures to improve the condition of the Slave, with a view to the early and complete abolition of Slavery'. The "Abolitionist," however, considered Yorke as 'true a FRIEND to the SLAVE' as these men, and, to prove the point, published excerpts from all the candidates, including Pryme's address at the Red Lion inn on 11 June (see Figure 5.1). The charges dogged Yorke's campaign, and he belatedly republished his 13 September speech at the Eagle Inn as a broadside declaring his credentials as a 'friend to humanity' who detested enslavement and prayed for the introduction of measures which, 'consistently with common justice, and the well-being of the slaves themselves, will bring about the extinction of the slave system'. These charges would not disappear in the Cambridge political cauldron.[23]

The one saving grace for Yorke was that he did not own a plantation, as that issue had become a millstone for candidates in the 1830s. Henry John Adeane, the successful Whig candidate for the 1830 election, had defended claims that, since he was a trustee for an uncle's plantation (and therefore had an 'interest in the continuance of slavery'), he could not be 'sincere' in his support for gradual abolition. Eager to distance himself from that stigma, Adeane tried to convince

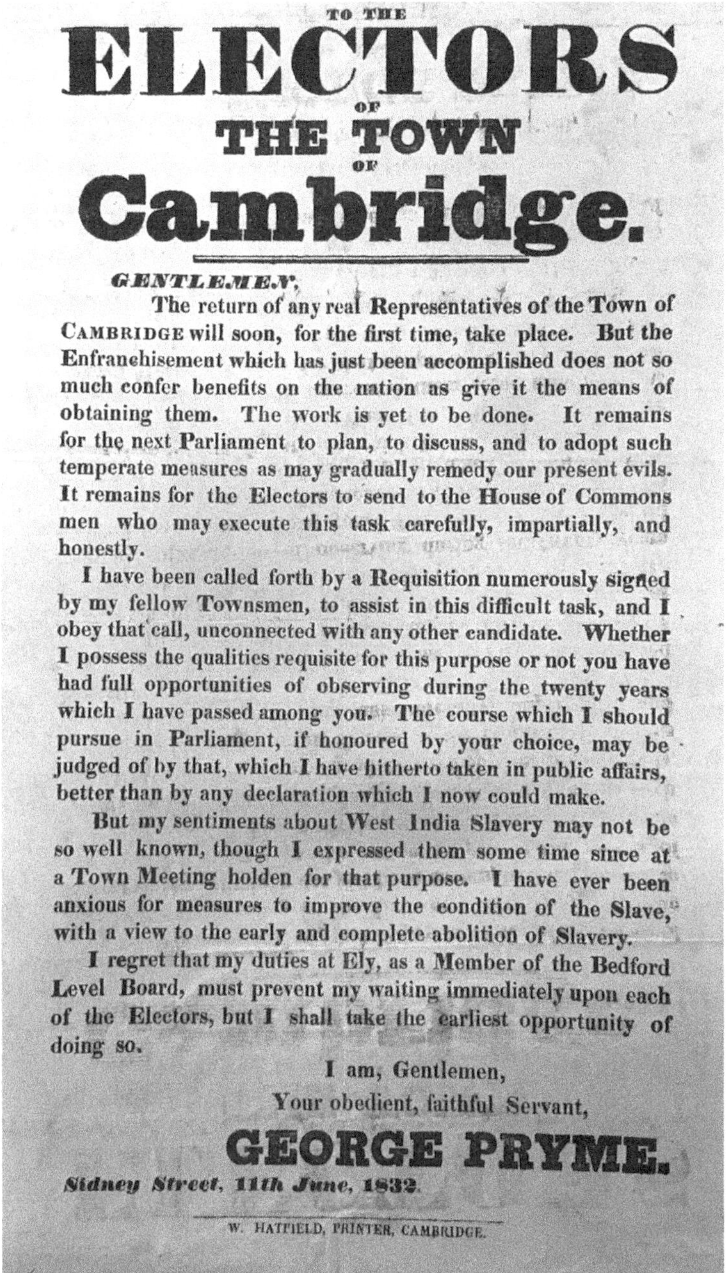

TO THE ELECTORS OF THE TOWN OF Cambridge.

GENTLEMEN,

The return of any real Representatives of the Town of CAMBRIDGE will soon, for the first time, take place. But the Enfranchisement which has just been accomplished does not so much confer benefits on the nation as give it the means of obtaining them. The work is yet to be done. It remains for the next Parliament to plan, to discuss, and to adopt such temperate measures as may gradually remedy our present evils. It remains for the Electors to send to the House of Commons men who may execute this task carefully, impartially, and honestly.

I have been called forth by a Requisition numerously signed by my fellow Townsmen, to assist in this difficult task, and I obey that call, unconnected with any other candidate. Whether I possess the qualities requisite for this purpose or not you have had full opportunities of observing during the twenty years which I have passed among you. The course which I should pursue in Parliament, if honoured by your choice, may be judged of by that, which I have hitherto taken in public affairs, better than by any declaration which I now could make.

But my sentiments about West India Slavery may not be so well known, though I expressed them some time since at a Town Meeting holden for that purpose. I have ever been anxious for measures to improve the condition of the Slave, with a view to the early and complete abolition of Slavery.

I regret that my duties at Ely, as a Member of the Bedford Level Board, must prevent my waiting immediately upon each of the Electors, but I shall take the earliest opportunity of doing so.

I am, Gentlemen,
Your obedient, faithful Servant,

GEORGE PRYME.

Sidney Street, 11th June, 1832.

W. HATFIELD, PRINTER, CAMBRIDGE.

Figure 5.1 Election broadside on behalf of George Pryme to the Electors of the Town of Cambridge, 11 June 1832, Collection of Election Broadsides, Handbills, and Squibs. Cambridgeshire Archives.

the electors that he was little more than a 'faithful servant' in the 'management' of the estate on St Kitts, which had fifty-eight enslaved workers. The Reverend Maberly (who we met in the first chapter) remained unconvinced, claiming before a cheering local audience that Adeane had 'used the common argument of the West India Planters, and others that were opposed to the emancipation of the slaves, that their minds were not prepared, that they were not sufficiently enlightened for the reception of liberty'. Local candidates had attempted to avoid the issue of abolition (some had advocated that the 'white slavery' of British labourers be eliminated first), but abolitionist opinion alongside the agricultural distresses of the winter of 1829–1830 in a rural constituency had inspired distrust of rich landholders and slaveholders who claimed political independence whilst holding material interests in enslavement.[24]

Craufurd soon interrogated Yorke on the question of enslavement. Alongside prints depicting a slave ship and the horrors of the plantation, the King's man was driven to write his polemic after seeing placards in town that celebrated the Tory grandee's abolitionism. Denouncing the self-proclaimed 'friend to the slaves', he labelled Yorke as one of their '*most effectual* enemies' because he was committed to 'delay[ing] to an *indefinite* period their emancipation'. Furthermore, Yorke – calling himself a 'plain sailor' – had supported gradualism and claimed that the enslaved were 'so far BETTER OFF' than white English labourers. A 'sudden emancipation', Yorke claimed, was 'fraught with danger to the colonies, and misery to the slaves themselves'. Whilst the candidate was committed to emancipation 'on principles fair and equitable to the proprietors of Colonial property, and with safety to the commerce of our country', Craufurd detailed the murders, torture, and abuse that enslaved Africans, treated 'as *brute cattle*' – worse than a 'farmer's dog' – received on the plantations. Forced to grow and market their own produce, Craufurd argued that enslaved workers had shown through their '*incredible industry*' that they were prepared for freedom. It was not the first or last time the Cambridge electors were confronted on slavery or forced labour regimes, as printers published numerous pamphlets addressed to town and gown electors throughout the nineteenth century.[25]

Cambridge abolitionists and ameliorationists had an impact beyond their university. Beilby Porteus, a Christ's fellow and major benefactor and the Bishop of London, illustrates the persistence of ameliorationist thought in the Caribbean. The Atlantic slave economy was a constant feature of Porteus's life. His father Robert was a Virginian enslaver who had inherited a 692-acre plantation on the York River – a property named "New Bottle" that was a gift from Richard Lee I, a member of the Virginia House of Burgesses (the colony's legislative assembly) and owner of a 4,000-acre property with ninety African enslaved persons. Robert had had a successful career in Britain's oldest North American slave society. The then-governor Alexander Spotswood appointed him to the ruling

Council of State in 1713, and he only moved back to England because of ill health and to better educate his children. Beilby, the youngest son, was a beneficiary of his father's wealth and sound decision-making, earning his bachelor's degree in 1752 and his doctorate in 1767. Elected a college fellow the same year that he graduated, Porteus's reputation was further enhanced after his poem, *Death: A Poetical Essay*, won the prestigious Seatonian Prize for claiming that human beings were responsible for their sins.[26]

Ordained as a priest in 1757, Porteus then became the chaplain to Thomas Secker, the Archbishop of Canterbury, in 1762, was appointed a chaplain to King George III, and was then nominated the Bishop of Chester fourteen years later in 1776. Porteus was not an immediate convert to the antislavery cause. William Knox, the Archbishop's advisor, claimed that Porteus had argued, in a letter to Benezet that was attributed to Thomas Secker, that the SPG could not condemn slavery because it would make enslavers 'more suspicious and cruel' and ensure that slaveholders were 'more unwilling' for Africans to 'learn Christianity'. Knox, a former plantation owner, wrote: 'Had proper attention been shown to what they recommend [in] respect [to] the treatment of the negroes in the Colonies, much of the present outcry against the slave trade would have been prevented, and it is a little extraordinary that the present Bishop of London [Porteus]' had asserted proposals for reform given that he had maintained the status quo. Slavery was not high on Porteus's list of priorities. In the House of Lords, his legislative contributions included bills against Sunday evening social clubs – indeed, he instructed the clergy to bring about a 'reformation of manners among the common people' – and he feverishly worked with William Wilberforce in 1787 to secure a proclamation from George III condemning vice and immorality in Britain.[27]

Defeat in the American Revolutionary War, not a profound religious awakening, motivated Porteus to reconsider the 'means and ends of empire'. Inspired by James Ramsay's invocation to proselytise to enslaved persons, who were, in his view, held in spiritual darkness without respite from despotic enslavers, Porteus claimed that American independence was divine judgement on Britons for failing to create a Protestant empire. Porteus's February 1783 annual sermon to the SPG was the moment when he pushed his fellow clergymen to consider dramatic action. Drawing upon Ramsay's plan for a spiritual awakening in the Caribbean, he declared: 'If there are any human creatures in the world who concentrate in themselves every species of evil here enumerated, who are at once poor and broken-hearted, and blind, and captive, and bruised, our Negro-slaves are beyond all comparison those creatures'. He condemned their treatment as 'mere machines and instruments to work with, as having neither understandings to be cultivated nor souls to be saved'. Without any 'knowledge of a Creator or Redeemer', Caribbean enslavers had ensured that the enslaved were 'heathens, not only in their hearts, but in their lives; and knowing no distinction between vice and virtue, they give themselves up freely to the grossest immoralities, without so much as being conscious that they are doing'. His solution: mass conversion and a new code of laws, modelled on France's *code noir*, that facilitated their 'improvement'.[28]

"Improvement" was the operative word for Porteus's project. He had little interest in ending chattel slavery (despite such views being aired by some of his contemporaries) – rather, he hoped to develop a new generation of enslaved Christian Africans who remained 'uncorrupted by those heathenish principles and savage manners with which the constant importation of fresh slaves from Africa has never failed to infect them[.]' Beginning with the SPG's Codrington plantations in Barbados, the Bishop planned a reformation of manners, with a new code of laws making the enslaved populace amenable to the 'blessings of society and civilized government' and therefore to Christian conversion, thereby transforming "rebellious" slaves into dutiful workers without the 'smallest injury to the rights, the property, or the emoluments of the planter[.]'[29]

Porteus was committed to Christianising enslaved Africans. In 1788, he published another call for the instruction of enslaved people, arguing – in language reminiscent of Anthony Ellys's SPG sermon – that 'the best Christians make the best servants'. Ending the slave trade, as he had advocated five years earlier, would ensure that "savage" Africans were not transported to the Caribbean and corrupt "seasoned" enslaved people in the Americas. (Along with Henry Dundas and Lord Hawkesbury, the President of the Board of Trade, he had served on the committee of enquiry established on 11 February 1788 to investigate 'the present State of the Trade to Africa, and particularly the Trade in Slaves'.) Porteus soon put words into actions. Acquiring the Brafferton estate, which the English scientist Sir Robert Boyle's executors had purchased to fund the College of William and Mary's Indian School, Porteus founded the "Society for the Religious Instruction and Education of the Negro Slaves in the British West Indies" in 1794. Under a royal charter, the Society was committed to amelioration and paid stipends to ministers in the Caribbean to inspire them to educate and proselytise to enslaved Africans.[30]

The Society soon published a Bible for the instruction of the enslaved population, with the sections on slave rebellion in the Book of Exodus carefully removed. Cambridge efforts to propagate the Bible amongst the enslaved continued: in Surinam, a 'C. A. Austen, Esq. of Queen's College, Cambridge' assisted the British and Foreign Bible Society (which Wilberforce and the Welsh clergyman Thomas Charles founded in 1804) in publishing an 'edition of the New Testament in the Negro-English'.[31]

From its inception, enslavers were integral to the Society, with ex-officio members including the clergies of London and Westminster, the President of the Board of Trade, the Secretary of State for the Home Department, the Lord Mayor, three London aldermen, and four representatives of Caribbean planters and merchants. Aside from providing oversight, the merchants and plantation owners were the largest donors to the Society, with three organisations – the West India Planters and Merchants of London, Liverpool, and Glasgow –providing £1,200 in funds by 1824. University men were on the list too: Richard Burgh Byam, the King's fellow and benefactor, was a prominent enslaver donor; and John Ireland, the Dean of Westminster, who established the Dean Ireland's Professorship of the Exegesis of the Holy Scripture at Oxford, subscribed £20.[32]

One year before his death, Porteus published another pamphlet in 1808 imploring the *Governors, Legislators, and Proprietors of Plantations* to Christianise the enslaved. In that letter, he recapitulated how his 'official connexion' to the Caribbean had led him to bring the 'blessings of Christianity to Heathens inhabiting his Majesty's dominions'. Applauding abolition in 1807, Porteus hoped that it would encourage enslavers to maintain 'the stock of slaves sufficient for the cultivation of your lands' and facilitate 'the natural increase of the Negroes at this time in the islands'. Still, Porteus did not identify the violence on the plantations as a reason why Africans died in such wretched conditions. To him, Christianity was a check on the 'most fatal [of] obstructions': the '*promiscuous and unbounded illicit commerce of the two sexes*, in which the Negro Slaves are permitted to indulge themselves without any check or restraint'. Bound by the 'moral restraints' of marriage, the bishop foresaw a population explosion in the Caribbean, and proposed that schools be established in Britain's colonies there. The funds, he proposed, should be raised from enslavers to fund Christian education because the "proprietors" would undoubtedly 'reap all the benefits of the institution, in the increase of their native Negroes, and will consequently save all the enormous sums formerly expended in the importance of fresh slaves from Africa' – a benefit, he wrote, which they 'cannot, I think, reasonably object'. Porteus, a former Christ's fellow and benefactor, had laid the groundwork for a plantation enterprise that would attempt to control Africans' bodies and souls.[33]

Porteus's passing did not end his dream of a Christian empire. Several Cambridge men hoped to Christianise Africans – and Richard Burgh Byam was one of their number. On 4 December 1820, he wrote to the Bishop of London, William Howley, recounting his experiences in the Caribbean assisting 'with the Improvement of the lower classes of the Inhabitants there'. The most pressing topic – an attitude that he shared with the Cambridge petitioners in the opening anecdote – was the 'Marriage of the Slaves'. He recounted the experiences of two mixed-ethnicity enslaved people who wanted to marry, and he envisioned – along the same lines as Antigua – that a more 'enlightened and liberal understanding… may become familiar among the white Inhabitants than have been ever hitherto admitted in favor of their ignorant and degraded Brethren'. Antigua, he argued, had achieved more in the 'moral Improvement' of its 'working classes' than any Caribbean colony, and he prayed that a spirit of "improvement" would proliferate throughout the region.[34]

The Reverend John Hothersall Pinder, an alumnus of Caius, also published sermons on enslaved African morals. Following university, he was ordained as a deacon in 1818 and a priest the following year. Returning to Barbados, he was appointed the chaplain of Codrington plantation from 1818 to 1827 and then Codrington College's principal from 1829 to 1835. The Cambridge alumnus was at home: following its founding, men from the ancient universities occupied the College's highest positions of authority, such as Mark Nicholson of Queen's College, Oxford, who was recommended for the post of Schoolmaster in 1797 by his Provost and the Dean of Christ Church. Pinder also had family nearby, and he intended on using their estates as a laboratory for his moral mission in the Caribbean. He planned to visit his father's plantation – around two miles from the College – 'to instruct his Slaves' on the 'afternoon allotted [for religious instruction]' and there 'make the young Negroes commit to memory the Creed – The Lord's prayer – & ten commandments – then use a selection of the Common Prayer, with a portion of Scripture – and conclude with a lecture'. To achieve that end of religious conversion, he published in 1822 his paternalistic *Advice to Servants*. Pinder proclaimed: 'It is the duty of the master to establish the worship of God in his family, where thanksgiving, prayer for blessings, and confession of sin may daily be offered up to the Almighty by all the members of the family'. Listing the duties of masters and the enslaved, Pinder mentioned that their obligation was 'to *advise* a servant, when they see any bad or faulty habit creeping on upon them; if advice is neglected, they must reprove; if their reproof is set at nought, they must use other means'. Pinder's reference to "other means" required no elaboration, either to enslavers or enslaved.[35]

Byam, writing from Cambridge in 1825, made another significant contribution to ensuring that the 'Slave System decline[d]', which he claimed could 'at length *gradually* and *safely* become extinct'. Praying for moderation in the slavery debate, the fellow ensured that his readers understood that he was a clergyman, '*Owner of West India Property*', and member of Barbados's governing council. Crusading for the 'Improvement of the Condition of the Negroe Population', he proposed that free labour was both more practicable and profitable than enslaved labour. For four years, he conducted religious experiments on his plantation which gave him the 'amplest opportunities… of studying the Negroe character, and of fitting it for the reception of freedom, if ever the power of setting such an example should be within his reach'. Unlike many of his fellow planters, he felt that there were 'no evil consequences' from emancipation, and that his plantation, which had a parish church nearby, could set an example to his more recalcitrant landed neighbours. There was a significant legal roadblock to his moral revolution: enslaved Africans formed 'a part of the *Security* to Merchants in England, for money advanced under the repeated depressions of Colonial interest'. To achieve abolition, he proposed establishing a sinking fund to free 250 enslaved people with each of the shares costing £100 pound (in total, around £25,000 to fill the share allotment) – with the securities held in Goslings and Sharpe Bank. The banking scheme's records did not survive, but Byam's renewed call for 'greater Moderation' in the abolition debate resonated beyond Cambridge.[36]

Henry Nelson Coleridge, the nephew of William Hart Coleridge, the Bishop of Barbados, propagated these ameliorative opinions to the British public. Following an exemplary education at Eton and Cambridge, where he received two Browne Medals for Latin and Greek poetry, the younger Coleridge was awarded a fellowship at King's from 1821 to 1829. In 1825, the distinguished scholar departed the familiar surroundings of college life for a six-month Caribbean tour alongside his uncle, who was a fervent advocate for Black education and the reorganisation of Codrington College. The voyage, which he published anonymously as *Six Months in the West Indies*, would be more educational than another tour of France, Italy, Switzerland, or a 'Polar expedition', he argued, because it allowed him to consider, from a supposedly "impartial" perspective, whether 'men set down as fanatics or tyrants' were worthy of those epithets given their financial, political, and social status as imperial subjects. From the first word to the last, Coleridge wanted the public to view him as a moderate mediating between the polemics of the African Institution and the 'Planters'. The Cambridge man's claim of impartiality was spurious at best (he later argued, concerning Trinidad, that 'If ever I turn planter, as I have often had thoughts of doing, I shall buy a cacao plantation'). Moreover, in a later edition, he argued that the 'Abolitionists' had precipitated an 'awful crisis' that had 'hacked' at Britain's colonial power – a species of 'domestic treason' that was unprecedented in the annals of the British Empire.[37]

Depicting the Caribbean as a Little England, Coleridge's sympathetic narrative, which he later publicised as from a 'Late Fellow of King's Coll., Cambridge' (though he undertook the voyage whilst a fellow), presented the plantation regime shorn of its violence or the realities of living in Black majority societies. The narrative was, in essence, a literary counterpart to James Hakewill's 1825 painting *Harbour Street, Kingston* showing Jamaica's wide boulevards, maintained buildings, gleaming redcoat soldiers, and disciplined inhabitants carrying goods to market – a genteel English town on America's shores. In truth, European visitors were struck by the vibrancy of colonial marketplaces – spaces that were, to an extent that concerned white colonists, dominated by the enslaved and free people of colour. Women carried goods to market, spending most of their Sundays, which was the only day they had free from the backbreaking work on the plantations, selling the produce whilst their husband and children tended the plots and harvested enough produce for the family's consumption. By land or coasting vessels, the enslaved sold provisions and 'a few course manufactures, such as mats for beds, bark ropes of a strong and durable texture, wicker chairs and baskets, earthen jars, etc. for all which they [found] ready sale'.[38]

As his ship came into port and docked in Barbados, Coleridge certainly feared the 'mass of black faces' and their 'violent feelings', and, in turn, he complimented the "planters" on their lineages, patriotism, educations, gallantry, 'feudal' hospitality, technological innovations, and refinement – with Bridgetown alone boasting two literary societies and an agricultural society dedicated to sugar, that 'noble plant'. Far from a 'carceral landscape', punctuated with the sounds of whips and bells (and with the severed heads and rotting corpses of executed Black enslaved people often left in the sun as a warning to the enslaved), he described the Caribbean as a 'sublime', 'lovely', 'verdant', 'beautiful', and 'delightful' environment where planters' houses, windmills, and churches punctuated a landscape of picturesque valleys and tilled fields. Clearly, in tone and argument, the King's fellow followed other British travellers to the Caribbean, including Nevil Maskelyne, who had become more supportive of the planters following their visits, with many comparing the lives of its Black inhabitants favourably to white labourers. To Coleridge, the Caribbean slave societies were rustic 'country villages in England'.[39]

Cunning and obsequious, the enslaved and free Africans who populated these societies were, to Coleridge, figures of distrust or disgust. The nakedness of enslaved women particularly shocked the Cambridge fellow, and he commented on how the immodest exposure of their bosoms was the 'most disgusting thing in the manners of the West Indian slaves'. Coleridge argued that it was the enslavers' responsibility to 'correct' the attitudes and morals of the enslaved – without whites, he countered, Africans would resort to debauchery and violence. Frustratingly for Coleridge, the enslaved did not embrace white generosity – as with the Trinidad governor providing money to children (who he called 'naked niggerling[s]' and compared to a 'sucking pig') – with 'pleasure' or 'gratitude'. Amongst their racial "betters," he complained, the enslaved did not know when to remain silent – 'every passion', he argued, 'acts upon them with strange intensity; their anger is sudden and furious, their mirth clamorous and excessive, their curiosity audacious, and their love the sheer demand for gratification of an ardent animal desire'. The enslaved were, to him, the very opposite of refined British subjects, yet Coleridge enjoyed his newfound power – indeed, he found 'nothing more delightful' than to be greeted by 'negro girls' with 'How d'ye, massa?' He advocated for the improvement of enslaved conditions, but he acknowledged that the Black inhabitants performatively embraced European policies and then they 'relapse[d] with certainty the moment the external compulsion ceases'. Interestingly, enslaved clothing – not just the lack thereof – was a particular focus of his writings. He advocated for Africans to purchase and wear fashionable clothing, such as hats, because 'new comforts' through conspicuous consumption would stir within people a fear of losing such possessions, which would provide a 'stimulus to industry' and a 'spur to improvement'. Black opinions did not figure in Coleridge's arguments concerning the means and ends of their improvement.[40]

Storming the 'Castle of [Black] Indolence', the Cambridge man recognised that the planters were integral to his civilising project. Coleridge fervently believed that slavery's ills were owed to the 'different education' and 'different tempers' of the master class (in fact, he considered it unlikely that a youth educated at 'Oxford or Cambridge' could become 'monsters' once they landed in Carlisle Bay in Barbados or St John's Harbour in Antigua). Defending slaveholders, he observed that Black butlers or ladies' maids were 'scarcely beneath' the same class of white English workers – they received no wages and were condemned to a lifetime of bondage, he carefully admitted, but under 'their masters' protection' they enjoyed all the necessities of life (he even noted that some had even refused freedom when offered). The crimes of slavery, in his opinion, either occurred because white smallholders did not have the means to support their workers, the enslavers had become excessively "familiar" with their slaves, or because the Caribbean constitutions governed these colonies 'on the model of England' when they were, in fact, more akin to Athens or Sparta – city-states where there was a similar 'equality amongst the free' and a 'restlessness of spirit'. To Coleridge, anti-African violence was the result of such modern white Athenians and Spartans being exasperated about British 'interference' and 'tyranny'. Establishing the religious and constitutional legality of enslavement (the latter of which, in 'every age of its existence' had authorised slavery), Coleridge asked his readers to resist the 'spirit of the times' and admit an inconvenient truth: African slavery was not an 'exception to the general freedom of mankind' – it was rather like that practiced in Egypt, Greece, Rome, and Russia. Coleridge, of course, conveniently ignored the fact that those states and empires had not predicated their slave systems on racial difference.[41]

Amelioration, not immediate emancipation, was his ambition for the 665,000 enslaved Africans who lived in the British Caribbean in 1834. Aside from clothing, Coleridge advocated for a raft of measures, including the modernisation of prisons. On Saint Vincent, he criticised the existing legislature for spending an enormous sum on churches but did not think to raise funds for a 'tread-wheel'. Prison treadmills were introduced into English prisons in 1779 to transform obstinate prisoners into industrious labourers – and Coleridge, amongst other plantation reformers, advocated for that device's usage in Jamaica, arguing that a 'chained slave' did not perform the work of one hour of a British labourer but there was the potential for further efficiencies 'on the steps of the Brixton staircase'. He feared that there were threats to his plans from within, however – and the potential scourge, in his mind, of Methodism inspiring slave 'insurrections' was another obstacle to reform. To mend that potential schism, Coleridge advocated the expansion of Church of England membership and attendance in the colonies because 'negros are a very curious and observant race, and after they have learnt that there is a God' they had discovered 'that their master does not worship in the same manner'.[42]

Towards the end of the narrative, in a chapter entitled 'Planters and Slaves', Coleridge addressed the African Institution with his ameliorative proposals, noting that enslavement should 'hardly at present' be abolished. Concluding that both abolitionists and ameliorationists wanted to raise the enslaved to 'an equality' with the 'rest of the citizens of the empire', he differed over the means to achieve that vision. His *'moral* cause' was founded on several objectives: education, particularly the provision of Bibles and prayer books; the enacting of colonial codes for the 'protection' of slaves (including the abolition of Sunday markets and freeing women from corporal punishment); and allowing freedom to be purchased at 'market price' on the Spanish plan. In avoiding the 'sudden revolution[s]' seen in Haiti, Coleridge's understanding of emancipation was predicated on the notion that the enslaved must prove themselves 'fit to be free'.[43]

Henry had travelled to the Caribbean to treat his rheumatism (and to distract from an engagement to his first cousin); still, the travel account overshadowed the trip's humble origins and became an almost-instant sensation. Favorable reviews were featured in the newspapers, excerpts were published in print, the work was sold as far afield as the colony of New South Wales, and the essayist and antiquarian Charles Lamb, in a March 1826 letter to Samuel Taylor Coleridge, applauded his 'excellent sense' on the question of slavery. The pamphlet and its author had their detractors, however. One Birmingham writer condemned Coleridge for ignoring the 'horrible licentiousness' of the plantations – indeed, in condemning the young traveller for his *School-boy Conceptions of Rights and Wrongs*, the polemicist argued that if he had reported 'but one tenth part' of this 'filthy subject' then 'his readers would have been tolerably convinced, that to talk of making good moral characters of the Negroes, while you keep them in bondage under the present system, is just as wise, as to talk of making a dandy of a chimney-sweeper, while you insist that his soot-bag shall never be taken off his back for an instant'. Coleridge's family were also unimpressed with their youthful relative, and their opinions illuminate the tensions within families concerning enslavement and abolition. Henry's cousin, the poet Hartley Coleridge, pointedly argued that there was a 'flippancy' and 'vulgarity' about the work since it did not communicate 'sufficiently the moral enormity of the slave system'.[44]

Cambridge proslavery activists were similarly passionate about their chosen cause. Their number included Peter Borthwick of Jesus and Downing colleges, John Pollard Mayers of St John's, the Reverend Richard Bickell of Sidney Sussex, and the Reverend Stephen Isaacson and Ralph Bernal of Christ's. Denouncing the abolitionists as zealots intent on crippling the empire, Bernal advocated for amelioration, not abolition, to be British imperial policy. He claimed before the House of Commons in May 1823 that the 'general body of Planters' were in favour of 'any real amelioration of the condition of the negroes; but at the same [it] must be traced out slowly and cautiously, and, in order to produce certain and beneficial effects, must be undertaken with a due regard to the capability of the negroes for receiving those advantages which it might be proposed to confer on them'. Amelioration, for proslavery activists, was again replete with racial stereotypes – that the enslaved were unready for freedom or for unsupervised labour. If reform was achieved in haste, Bernal worried, the British colonies would suffer the same fate as '*St. Domingo*'.[45]

Following the example of Coleridge and other contemporaneous British polemicists, Bernal and Stephen Isaacson maintained that instances of violence on the plantations were rare. After arriving in the Caribbean, Isaacson argued in August 1832 that he had seen 'the crowded churches of the West Indies – the happy, intelligent countenances of the slaves, as they crowd to the courts of the Lord's house, eager to catch the glad tidings of salvation, and drink of the fountains of living waters'. Coleridge and Isaacson had a common vision of the plantation. Comparing the 'peasantry' in England to the enslaved, Isaacson noted that Black people were in a 'prosperous state' and that Britain had been the 'last' to enter the slave trade and the 'first' to abolish it – and that cause, he claimed, was driven by reformist enslavers, who had civilized their Black workers.[46]

Unlike his fellow alumni, the Reverend Richard Bickell advertised his membership at Cambridge in his pamphleteering. His 1825 book *The West Indies as They Are; Or A Real Picture of Slavery* listed his illustrious titles: 'A Member of the University of Cambridge, Late Naval Chaplain to Port-Royal [Jamaica], Sometime Curate of that Parish, and Previously of the City of Kingston, in the Aforesaid Island'. The frontispiece highlighted his reputation as a five-year resident of Jamaica and learned gentleman, who was admitted a pensioner at Sidney Sussex on 13 October 1817. Two years later, there is a record of a "Rev. Bickell" having married Elizabeth, daughter of John Anderson, who owned Clifford's Plantation in Jamaica; and Bickell came into the ownership of two smaller properties on that island, including "Whitecroft" with around twenty-three enslaved African labourers.[47]

Bickell had established his credentials, and he used that position to advocate for amelioration. 'Let every Saturday be given to the Negroes for working their grounds and carrying their surplus provisions to market', he wrote, '[…] Let the Sabbath be kept holy: Let none but magistrates have the power of flogging: Let them encourage marriage among their overseers, and lessen the power of overgrown and rapacious attorneys'. On Christianising Afro-Jamaicans, Bickell had some experience (the Jamaican parish registers record him as having baptised 'a free quadroon', a 'free mulatto', and the daughter of two persons of colour). To Bickell, amelioration was in the planters' self-interest, ensuring that the plantation would 'return a handsome income to the proprietors of estates and merchants; and would be a happy and favoured home to the then improved and grateful Negro; who, in a few years, instead of being the untutored and grovelling savage he now is, and the revengeful one he is inclined to be… would become a contented and virtuous servant'. If the enslavers wanted to maximise profits, then Bickell pressured them to envision amelioration as the continuation of enslavement by more profitable means.[48]

On occasion, Cambridge fellows were caught in the proslavery crossfire. In a June 1828 newspaper, "A West Indian Proprietor" lambasted John Lamb, the Master of Corpus Christi and associate of the abolitionist Professor Scholefield, for organising, along with the Mayor of Cambridge, another antislavery Parliamentary petition. 'Had you, Reverend Sir', the "Proprietor" declared, 'given your sentiments with a due consideration to truth – and had you not… [thrown] utter abuse and slander against a respectable portion of British subjects, in violation, of that holy religion, the badge of whose sacred order you have been invested with, this letter would never have been addressed to you'. Turning Lamb's words against him, the "Proprietor" quoted the Master's statement that emancipation was 'calculated as much for the benefit of the Master as the slave… these West Indian proprietors – these slave drivers are unchristianized, brutal, and cruel, and so long as they have slaves to command, as long will they remain so'. Rejecting these accusations, the slaver maintained that his compatriots had 'received liberal educations in Great Britain' from schools and universities with 'two thirds' of proprietors having 'never visited the West Indies' – perhaps warning Lamb not to bite the hand that had fed Cambridge. In the future, as a 'Master of a College', the polemicist hoped that he would preach 'a spirit of peace and good-will' rather than an 'unfounded calumny' against his fellow British subjects.[49]

Britain's continued sweet tooth might have been one reason for the author's indignation against John Lamb. Sugar from both the Caribbean and Morocco remained a valuable British import – the most valuable until 1820. In Cambridge's case, Corpus Christi mentioned 'Barbary sugar' from North Africa in leasing arrangements relating to the College's tenement on Bene't Street (now the site of the world-famous Eagle pub). From 1609 to 1838, the leases included a cash payment and one pound of 'good Barbary sugar merchantable at audit time' – a testament to the value of a good that was celebrated in a Thomas Gresham play. Though North African enslavement had little of the systematised and financially sophisticated plantation, mercantile, and insurance economies visible in North and South America, Moroccan sugar was predicated upon enslavement. The Moroccan sugar economy greatly expanded during the reign of Sultan al-Mansur, who along with his brother defeated a Portuguese army at the Battle of Ksar-el-Kebir and thereafter reigned from 1578 to 1603. Following his victory, writers reported that the Sultan constructed 'sugar refineries like pyramids' in the south and, with the gold and enslaved Africans which he had acquired from his military campaigns in the Sudan, enlarged Morocco's sugar industry (with much of that produce making its way to England because of an alliance between both nations). European dominance in the sugar market (thanks to the Caribbean trade) dampened al-Mansur's ambitions, but the linkage between sugar cane cultivation and enslavement on Moroccan plantations continued until abolition. Thanks to these tenement arrangements, the fortunes of the largest slaveholding society in the Maghreb and the lives of Cambridge's humble urban tenants were intertwined.[50]

Cambridge men were involved in other forms of proslavery literature besides pamphlets and published speeches, however. Cambridge-educated enslavers wrote poetry to propagate the image of benevolent slaveholders. The Scottish doctor James Grainger, enjoying the patronage of a Trinity undergraduate, published his famous *Sugar Cane* in 1764; still, M. J. Chapman's 1833 poem *Barbados* was a significant, yet often unrecognised, contributor to proslavery literature too. The preface illustrated the anti-Black intentions of the poem, with Chapman intending to 'stop the current of frantic innovation, that threatens with almost instant ruin both colonies and empire'. Chapman, a Trinity alumnus, contrasted the happiness of enslaved Africans with the death and destruction reaped through a servile revolt. Referencing Haiti, Chapman painted an apocalyptic image for his readers: a 'sea Of blood and battle wade to liberty! Hence comes the plot, the agony of strife, The toil of treason, and the waste of life; The sound of battle, rushing through the trees; The hurried tramp of frantic savages! The slave, infuriate, pants for Freedom's smiles, And Hayti's fate attends our Eden-isles'.[51]

Black sexual violence against white women figured prominently in his account, and, to control those passions, Chapman outlined how enslavers had civilised African-descended peoples, arguing that 'Polygamy has now nearly ceased among the slaves; and the authority of the marriage-sanction is generally recognised by them', further propagating the racist myth of the promiscuous, polygamous slave. The charge of polygamy, Sarah Pearsall notes, was 'shorthand for societies lacking law and religion' – an indication that Black people were 'unfit for freedom and full citizenship'. Similarly, Chapman used the fear of enslaved revolts, African sexual deviancy, and the image of the civilising plantation to counter the abolitionist drive for gradual or immediate emancipation.[52]

Cambridge alumni lobbied government to preserve slavery. By 1830, the enslavers and their representatives in Parliament had ensured that no government measure had been passed to end enslavement. A large part of their success was due to one man: John Pollard Mayers, Barbados's agent in London. Having matriculated at St John's in 1794, he went on to the Middle Temple and was called to the Bar in 1799. Using his skills of negotiation and conciliation, Mayers – like Fuller and the multitude of Cambridge men who supported the West India Lobby before him – accumulated oral testimonies and statistics from Barbadian enslavers to establish the humanitarian nature of plantation management, and ensured that compensation was both realized and that enslaved had control over the process. Yet, in his efforts, he was undermined by enslavers, who did not want the government prying into their affairs and were reluctant to provide such information to Mayers. Facing down the proprietors' intransigence, he negotiated with the government to provide enslavers with a golden parachute. He urged them to accept wage payments for Black apprentices and, when emancipation appeared a near-certainty, he assisted Caribbean slavers in attaining as much monetary compensation as was conceivable from the government. In February 1833, he contacted Viscount Goderich at the Colonial Office and convinced him that, since land was held individually in Barbados, the slaveholders would have to be paid a much larger indemnity than previously thought. Though Mayers was not instrumental in providing around 20 million pounds in compensation to Caribbean enslavers, he emphasised Britain's complicity in slavery to shame Parliament into providing slaveholders with reparations that allowed them to survive emancipation with their fortunes largely intact.[53]

The end of enslavement in the Caribbean was greeted with contrasting opinions in Cambridge. Joseph Romilly, a Trinity fellow, both voiced these sentiments and witnessed them firsthand. In April 1834, Romilly wrote a very revealing passage in his diary that indicated his position on the question of slavery. 'Finished Monk Lewis's account of his slaves in Jamaica', he quipped, 'the book is charming: shows its author in a very amiable point of view: his banishing the whip, giving the Slaves *every* Saturday, making a grand quarterly feast for them, distributing prizes to the deserving, is all excellent – Would that many Planters had been like him[.]' The volume in question was Matthew Gregory Lewis's *Journal of a West India Proprietor*, which was written between 1816 and the latter's death at sea in 1818 and eventually published in 1834. Well-connected in literary circles, "Monk" Lewis, as he was then known, had been educated at Christ Church, Oxford, and had been in feverish correspondence with Wilberforce about whether to free the 500 enslaved persons that Lewis had inherited on his father's Jamaican plantations.[54]

Though Romilly saw enslavers as redeemable proprietors, a Cambridge election that he observed in June 1841 revealed that the politics of slavery remained paramount. Sir Alexander Cray Grant, an alumnus of St John's who received almost £14,000 in compensation for his plantations, ran for a parliamentary seat in Cambridge. Observing the race, Romilly reported that there was 'A great deal of excitement on Parkers Piece from a Banner being carried about representing a Planter flogging a black; the Planter was a strong likeness of Sir A. Grant'. Whether a member of the town or gown waved this banner, slavery remained at the forefront of Cambridge life, and many students, alumni, and fellows were committed activists in this debate. Grant was ultimately successful in his efforts to unseat a local Whig MP, with a local paper denouncing the former slaveholder, in a rather revealing passage, as 'a most respectable representative of the Tories, lay and clerical, gown and town, voters and non-voters, bullies, burghers, and bigots'. The papers soon turned against each other, with the *Cambridge Independent Press* denouncing the *Cambridge Chronicle* for its defence of a former enslaver who held property in 'human flesh'.[55]

The successful election of Grant was more feared because the Caribbean sugar duties were being debated in Parliament, and it was likely that Sir Alexander would attempt to enforce the planters' 'monopoly' through the imposition of an 'extravagantly dear price' on 'foreign sugar'. The issue of monopolies had become a bitterly debated issue in Britain and Cambridge, with Thomas Perronet Thompson, publishing as a "Member of the University of Cambridge" more than a decade earlier, likening the Corn Laws (a set of tariffs which maintained high prices for barley, wheat, and oats to the benefit of rich landowners) to enslavement. The Queens' man argued that there 'is a unity of principle; both systems being founded on the oppression of the weak for the advantage of the strong'. The Sugar Duties Act of 1846 were passed at the same time as the repeal of the Corn Laws, ensuring that there would be no preferential treatment for British colonists (and thereby flooding the British market with cheaper Cuban and Brazilian slave-grown sugar). Slavery had ended, but the politics and power of slaveholders remained a fraught question in both rural and urban Britain.[56]

For much of the university's history, Cambridge has been associated with the struggle for abolition and anti-racism – and for good reason. Numerous luminaries of that humanitarian struggle were educated within its wood-panelled rooms and, in many cases, developed their antislavery beliefs in conversation with professors and fellows. Rather than an outlier, however, Cambridge remains an instructive case study about the varieties of political experience and opinion concerning enslavement and the slave trade. Amongst gradual abolitionists and ameliorationists, the age of abolition was an era of experimentation when fellows debated how best to end the slave system without a revolt or revolution on the Haitian model. In the process, these men, whether students or college fellows, targeted the perceived symptoms of enslavement – the violence, lack of clothing, educations, and religion, for instance – rather than the racial foundations of a plantation system that its proponents had every intention of continuing and protecting after abolition.

6

'We presume that its influence is nowhere greater than in the Universities': Ending and Defending American Slavery

On 8 June 1868, the Reverend Dr William Hepworth Thompson, the Vice-Chancellor, received a welcome letter. William Mercer Green, the first Episcopal bishop of Mississippi and one of the founders of the University of the South (or "Sewanee"), thanked Thompson and Cambridge for donating thirty books to help found Sewanee's library. The volumes included a Bible, the Gospel according to Saint Matthew, a philosophical study of the Trinity of Plato and Philo Judaeus and its impact on early Christian ecclesiology (perhaps a suggestion from Thompson, a famed classical scholar), the volumes of *Astronomical Observations made at the Observatory of Cambridge*, a catalogue of specimens at the Cambridge Anatomical Museum (which mentioned three 'skulls of Negroes' presented by 'George Budd, MD [and fellow of] Caius College'), multiple editions of the catalogue of Cambridge manuscripts, and an index of printed books preserved in the library. The donation distilled Cambridge's numerous contributions to literary, scientific, religious, and philosophical thought over the preceding centuries. Green recognised the enlightened collection as such: 'I take pleasure', he wrote, 'in conveying to you the thanks of our "Board" for the liberal donation of Books which your honourable University has, through the Bishop of Tennessee, made to our infant Institution'.[1]

The "Bishop" mentioned therein was William Quintard. Hailing from Stamford, Connecticut, Quintard moved to Memphis, Tennessee, to continue his medical practice but soon gave up this profession for the priesthood after meeting James Hervey Otey, the first Episcopal bishop of Tennessee. Otey was the son of a Virginian slaveholder, and he envisioned a 'literary and theological seminary' – a dream that became the University of the South, (a white supremacist institution, as Otey intended, to train a white 'native' ministry). From the beginning, as Sewanee's research into its history has shown, the University was intended to add cultural and religious lustre to the Southern enslaver class, allowing them to 'go forth [bearing] a tone that shall elevate the whole country'. Between 1857 and 1859, the Sewanee Mining Company, which derived a significant proportion of its early profits from leasing Black convicts, donated 10,000 acres of land that the University stands upon.[2]

The American Civil War, which lasted for four years and devastated the southern plantation economy, threatened these plans – and, in turn, the enthusiastic founders of Sewanee sought to defend the Confederate states. The first three Chancellors of Sewanee, Otey of Tennessee, Polk of Louisiana, and Elliott of Georgia were Confederate enslavers, and Quintard – despite initial pro-Union sympathies – served as a regimental surgeon and helped to compile *The Confederate Soldier's Pocket Manual of Devotions*, which offered blessings to 'Thy servant, the President of the Confederate States [Jefferson Davis], and all others in authority; and so replenish them with the grace of Thy Holy Spirit, that they may always incline to Thy will, and walk in Thy way'.[3]

After the Civil War, Quintard made five trips to England to request donations for the fledgling institution, hoping to put Sewanee (quite literally) on the map. The Confederate sympathiser was amongst friends: according to the historian Richard Blackett, thirty-nine out of forty-four clergymen identified as Confederate supporters were Anglicans, many of whom had deep ties to the universities. Having preached at the Cambridge University Church and received an honorary doctorate from that university, Quintard returned to Sewanee with £2,500 raised from the leaders of the Anglican church (see Figure 6.1). Joining Oxford University, who provided £150 for books, Cambridge donors included the Vice Chancellor (£5.5), William Selwyn, the Lady Margaret Professor of Divinity (£10.10), and his brother George Selwyn, the Bishop of New Zealand and namesake of Selwyn College, Cambridge (£10). The committee organising the donations also depended on the expertise of William Emery, a former Dean and Bursar at Corpus, and Alexander Beresford-Hope, a Confederate sympathiser (and the recipient of a Cambridge honorary doctorate). At Sewanee's re-opening in 1868, Quintard hoped that the 'first-class Church university' would 'in some degree do for our country what the Universities of Oxford and Cambridge have so well done for England and the civilized world, the University of the South has begun its work for God and our land'.[4]

For Green, Quintard, and their comrades, therefore, the Cambridge gift, was a message of solidarity in the cause of spreading and defending white "civilisation" in the southern United States. The donation was more than an eclectic collection of religious, scientific, and philosophical works – Green considered it 'as something more than a disinterested contribution to the cause of Religion and Learning'. It was a token of 'National and Christian good-will' and Green hoped that Cambridge's generous gift would 'draw more closely together two people who ought ever to be One in love and good works, as they are One in Faith, and in Tongue, and in the enlightened pursuit of civilized life'. He concluded: 'As the descendants of Englishmen, the great mass of our people [Southerners] take pride in those two great lights of the "Mother Country" – Oxford and Cambridge; and will ever rejoice in their welfare'.[5]

For Sewanee, Britain's ancient universities were a reference point: the satin ermine of the Sewanee vice-chancellor's gown was appropriated from

Cambridge's attire; Cambridge-educated men, such as Professor Caskie Harrison, took up tenured positions at the University of the South; and its Gothic architecture was an inspiration for southerners. In 'redeeming' Christianity and maintaining through the 'portals of slavery, an inferior, subject, dependent and necessary race, on which his whole order of civilization is based', Sewanee claimed that they were in common cause with Cambridge.[6]

Slavery had ended in the British Atlantic, yet Cambridge's connections to Sewanee reveal that the problems of American slavery and American freedom remained pivotal to British intellectual life. After abolition, Cambridge members were actively involved in discussions and debates concerning enslavement in the United States. As with the preceding decades and centuries, the University reflected the complex racial views of British society writ-large, with some students and fellows – notably Edward Strutt Abdy and Alexander Crummell – actively opposed to the southern "slave power". Still, pro-Confederate intellectuals provided monetary and ideological support for those southern enslavers during the Civil War. The first section follows the efforts of students, alumni, and fellows to challenge the cotton economy that was a mainspring of Britain's growing industrial sector. Crummell, an early pan-Africanist, is well-known in both scholarly and public histories, but Abdy remains a more marginalised figure in histories of British abolitionism. Following these antebellum abolitionists, the discussion will turn to students and fellows' involvement in spreading pro-Confederate or pro-Union opinions, with Cambridge as divided as most British urban centers on whether the slaveholding South were fighting a just war of independence against the North, or whether they deserved opprobrium as tyrannical enslavers. In the Cambridge Union, lecture halls, student societies, and private correspondence and pamphleteering, the problem of African American slavery was another front in the often-uncivil war of words over enslavement in the British Empire.

Edward Strutt Abdy was at the forefront of these debates. The fifth son of a local Essex church man, Abdy was educated at Felsted School and then at Jesus College, where he was elected a fellow after finishing his bachelor's degree in 1813. Abdy's extended family was connected to chattel slavery: Sir William Abdy, the Seventh Baronet, earned around £13,404 from two Antigua plantations and one estate in Saint Vincent in the 1833 settlement; and Edward was also related to Thomas Rutherforth, the long-deceased Regius Professor. Abdy, however, dedicated his life to the abolitionist cause in the United States. Abdy's radicalism on race relations – he was a supporter of interracial marriage, for instance – has perhaps ensured that the Jesuan fellow alongside his firebrand forbears, including the radical Peter Peckard, have been forgotten in histories which have often privileged more gradualist figures such as William Wilberforce in the pantheon of Cambridge abolitionism.[7]

CONTRIBUTIONS.

	£	s.	d.		£	s.	d.
The Archbishop of Canterbury,	25	0	0	Oxford University, for Books,	150	0	0
The Archbishop of York,	10	0	0	The Duke of Buccleuch,	25	0	0
The Archbishop of Dublin,	10	0	0	The Marquis of Lothian,	25	0	0
The Bishop of London,	10	0	0	The Earl Beauchamp,	50	0	0
The Bishop of Winchester,	10	0	0	The Earl of Dartmouth,	15	0	0
The Bishop of Oxford,	10	0	0	The Earl Stanhope,	5	0	0
The Bishop of Ely,	20	0	0	The Earl of Harrowby,			
The Bishop of Lincoln,	10	0	0	The Earl Nelson,	10	0	0
The Bishop of Chester,	10	10	0	The Earl of Shaftesbury,	5	0	0
The Bishop of Salisbury,	10	0	0	The Earl of Carnarvon,	15	0	0
The Bishop of Bangor,	10	0	0	Lord Redesdale,	50	0	0
The Bishop of Cape Town,	20	0	0	Lord Rollo,	25	0	0
The Bishop of Gibraltar,	10	0	0	Lord Cranborne, M.P.	10	0	0
The Bishop of Derry,	10	0	0	Lord Wharncliffe,	10	0	0
The Bishop of Barbados,	5	0	0	Lord Lyttelton,	3	0	0
Bishop Smith, late of Victoria,	1	0	0	Lord Berwick,	5	0	0
The Bishop of Exeter,	10	0	0	Ven. Lord Arthur Hervey,	5	0	0
The Bishop of Worcester,	10	10	0	Rev. Lord Charles Hervey,	12	10	0
The Bishop of Bombay,	5	0	0	Lord John Manners, M.P.	5	0	0
The Bishop of St. Asaph,	20	0	0	Viscountess Downe,	5	0	0
The Bishop of Rochester,	10	0	0	Lady Helena Trench	5	0	0
The Bishop of Llandaff,	5	0	0	Rt. Hon. W. E. Gladstone, M.P.	10	0	0
The Bishop of Moray and Ross,	3	3	0	The Right Hon. G. Hardy, M.P.	10	0	0
The Bishop of Perth,	5	0	0	Sir W. Farquhar, Bart.	10	0	0
The Bishop of New Zealand,	10	0	0	Rev. Sir F. Gore Ouseley, Bart.	5	0	0
The Dean of Durham,	10	0	0	Sir P. Keith Murray, Bart,	1	0	0
The Dean of Ely,	2	2	0	Vice-Chan: Sir W. Page Wood,	10	0	0
The Dean of Salisbury,	5	0	0	A. J. Beresford Hope, Esq. M.P.	10	0	0
The Dean of Norwich,	25	0	0	J. A. Shaw Stewart, Esq.	50	0	0
Mrs. Meyrick Goulburn,	5	0	0	W. Perry Heyrick, Esq.	10	0	0
The Dean of Chester,	3	3	0	J. G. Hubbard, Esq.	10	0	0
The Dean of Ripon,	1	1	0	R. E. E. Warburton, Esq.	10	0	0
The Dean of St. Andrews,	5	0	0	G. Richmond, Esq.	10	0	0
The Dean of Bocking,	1	1	0	Robert Bayman, Esq.	25	0	0
The Dean of Edinburgh,	1	0	0	W. H. Pole Carew, Esq.	10	0	0
Vice-Chancellor, Oxford,	10	0	0	Admiral Ryder,	5	0	0
Vice-Chancellor, Cambridge,	5	5	0	W. S. Lindsay, Esq.	5	0	0
Rev. Canon Selwyn,	10	10	0	N. Clode, Esq.	5	0	0
Rev. Prebendary Ford,	5	0	0	Miss Hargreave,	10	0	0
Rev. Canon Thomas,	5	0	0	H. T. Boodle, Esq.	5	0	0
Hon. and Rev. R. Liddell,	10	0	0	Philip Cazenove, Esq.	10	0	0
Hon. and Rev. Graham Colborne,	1	10	0	Part Collection at Ely Cathedral,	15	0	0

Figure 6.1 An Offering from English Churchmen to the American Bishops. Towards the Re-establishment of their University for the South and South-West Dioceses, Charles Todd Quintard Papers. Sewanee: University of the South.

In 1834, Abdy travelled to the United States to study New York's Auburn Prison, widely seen as a model of prison reform. Alexis de Tocqueville, the French aristocrat, had journeyed there three years earlier, and Abdy began a grand tour encompassing New England, Washington, D.C., and several western and southern states. Unlike de Tocqueville, Abdy spent much of his time in free Black communities. Published in 1835 with the assistance of John Murray II (the member of a prominent family of travel publishers), his three-volume *Journal* was far more radical than most contemporary white abolitionist pamphlets. With his Cambridge collegiate credentials highlighted on the title page, he attacked Americans and American slavery on all fronts. He criticised New Yorkers for paying Black teachers less than whites for work in African schools, and he condemned the treatment of free Black people in the northern states. Visiting Hartford, Connecticut, Abdy spent time listening to the opinions and experiences of the town's beleaguered Black residents, who told him it was 'hardly safe' to walk the streets at night, or else be showered with stones and racist epithets. Abdy also witnessed America's longstanding tradition of anti-Black racial violence in New York City on 7 July 1834, when a mob attacked an antislavery meeting at the Chatham Street Chapel, precipitating further rioting that month.[8]

Abdy's travels convinced him that white Americans were collectively responsible for enslavement. Observing the nation's capital of Washington, D.C., Abdy wrote with disdain that a slave pen was visible from the Capitol Building. Arriving at Robey's Tavern, a slave market, he described it as a 'wretched hovel' that was 'surrounded by a wooden paling fourteen or fifteen feet in height' to prevent escape, and the pen had exposed 'both sexes, and all ages' to the sweltering heat and biting, freezing temperatures of winter, noting that some had 'actually frozen to death'. Enraged, Abdy derided America's religious communities, including Quakers, for their 'disgraceful servility' to enslavers; and, regarding the so-called planters, Abdy mocked their 'chivalry' and denounced them as 'bandits' and 'pirates' whose "property" was 'defended by violence' – 'heartless oppressor[s]' who he hoped might be attacked in the future by 'some sable Spartacus or some colored Kosciuszko'. Abdy noted that the US was 'in debt to outraged humanity. She has enriched herself by plunder and oppression'. Combining letters, testimonies, and diary entries, the *Journal* was a witness statement against enslavement in the antebellum United States, a nation that he (correctly) predicted was on course for a 'civil or a servile war'.[9]

Abdy's commentary then turned to American university intellectuals, especially proslavery European immigrants in the southern states. These migrants included Thomas Hewitt Key, who, after coming up to St John's and Trinity colleges, was recruited as the founding Professor of Pure Mathematics at the University of Virginia – an institution which later received $250 worth of books from Cambridge University Press because of the generosity of W. Gordon McCabe, a Confederate officer. (It was not the last Virginia-bound donation: Robert Potts, a Trinity mathematics tutor, sent money to the College of William and Mary in 1859 after a fire gutted its main building.) Key also enslaved Sally Cottrell, who had laboured for Ellen Randolph Coolidge, Thomas Jefferson's granddaughter. George Long, whose publications often credited him as a 'late Fellow of Trinity College, Cambridge', also emigrated to Virginia to become a professor of languages. Long married a local widow and, when they returned to England, they had a 'black friend' as a companion: the formerly enslaved manservant Jacob Walker. Long, a founder of the Royal Geographical Society, published his *Geography of America* in 1841, which characterised African Americans as in a 'degraded condition' that 'produces in most of them its natural effect of making them mean, timid, lying, and thievish'. According to Long, the enslaved were a subservient race who had been reconciled to their condition due to 'a sense of the natural superiority of the whites'.[10]

Meeting Charles Follen, a Harvard University Professor of German and chair of a committee for the New England Anti-Slavery Society Convention, Abdy contrasted that professor with these university enslavers. 'The professor', he recalled, 'who had been driven across the Atlantic, by the enemies of political liberty in his own country, had not, like too many exiles from Europe, attempted to conciliate the friends of personal slavery in the land of his adoption, by open advocacy or servile indifference'. Abdy, an honorary life member of the Massachusetts Anti-Slavery Society – which was dedicated to the immediate abolition of enslavement and the liberation of 'unrighteously oppressed' slaves – praised Follen's work with that organisation, acclaiming him for his 'pure love of freedom, a sincere conviction that the happiness of every one is the happiness of all'. Professor Follen's lectures appealed to his students to envision Africa as the cradle of human civilisation, and he often raised the example of Egypt in his lectures to highlight the wonders of Black civilisation. It was more frustrating to Abdy, then, that Follen had suffered the 'obloquy' of Harvard – the funders for Follen's professorship, which included the merchant and former slave trader Thomas H. Perkins and Chinese shipping mogul Samuel Cabot, Jr., had forced him to resign on account of his activism and strident criticisms of the university administration.[11]

The three-volume *Journal* enjoyed rave reviews on both sides of the Atlantic. The text received warm, generous appraisals from *Leigh Hunt's London Journal*, the *Monthly Review*, *Westminster Review*, *Monthly Repository*, *Quarterly Review*, and the *Baptist Magazine*. The Library Company of Philadelphia purchased the volumes and excerpts were featured in *Liberty* and in a later 1857 compendium titled *The Legion of Liberty!* Abdy was compared favourably to other travel writers on slavery, too, such as R. R. Madden's *Twelvemonth's Residence in the West Indies* and Charles Joseph Latrobe's *The Rambler in North America*. The *Monthly Review* complained that, although 'Another tour' in the United States had been published, like so 'many very ordinary publications belonging to the same field, a very tiresome work', Abdy was 'no ordinary writer' and a man who 'rises with his antagonist, and we think is triumphant'.[12]

Abdy had Scottish supporters too. The *Journal* was published when the Glasgow and Edinburgh Anti-Slavery Societies and their Church of Scotland allies were protesting the floggings and abuses that were still being inflicted upon freed Black "apprentices" on Caribbean plantations. On 2 September 1835, Abdy thanked William Tait, an Edinburgh publisher, 'for the flattering manner in which you have spoken of a work that I felt had little to expect beyond a passing notice in a short review'. Though the initial silence around the work had 'wounded' his vanity, he hoped that 'the book must make its way as well as it can – and I trust the importance of the cause will not be lost in the demerits of the advocate'. Abdy's vanity was not the sole issue at stake – he was anxious that the book sold because the 'question' that it addressed concerned the 'welfare' and 'very existence of the republican union'.[13]

Abdy's *Journal* was an influential political tool for American abolitionists. Antislavery activists noted that northern publishers, such as Harper & Brothers, had refused to publish the text, and some criticised the editors for their dependence on the "slave power." The American Anti-Slavery Society's 1835 annual report included a letter from Harpers mentioning that since Abdy was 'an abolitionist' they 'would [therefore] have nothing to do with him'. In the war of words over enslavement, the politics of publishing Abdy's volumes became a potent weapon against the 'friends of the South'.[14]

Whilst in the United States, Abdy debated the historian William Ellery Channing, convincing him that racial prejudice, not scientific fact, accounted for Black poverty. Rejecting Channing's policy of educational segregation as the tool to end racial tensions, Abdy derided it as a plan intended 'to destroy a distinction by continuing it'. Five years later, he again confronted scientific racism in his writings. His 1842 *American Whites and Blacks in Reply to a Germany Orthodermist* argued that America's racial "problem" – the coexistence of white and Black Americans – was, contrary to Thomas Jefferson (an American President who feared a race war), an overblown concern. Rather, he thought that racial mixing and intermarriage was the ideal solution to ignorance and distrust, and he criticised the widespread immigration of Europeans to the cotton plantations in the Mississippi, calling racism the 'aristocracy of the skin'. He determined that racism was set in 'defiance' to the 'sentiments of common courtesy, the dictates of sound policy, and the precepts of pure religion'. Skin colour, he argued, was not a scientific fact – it was an accident of birth.[15]

Abdy was not opposed to phrenology – the pseudoscience of observing the skull to determine an individual's physiological and psychological attributes – in principle, however. In New York City, he visited St. Philip's Episcopal Church in lower Manhattan, whose graveyard was the final resting place of that metropolis's Black luminaries. In a section of the *Journal* titled 'Africo-American craniology', Abdy, upon noticing the skulls in the graveyard, commented that 'it may fairly be assumed' that they were the 'remains of native Africans' as they were 'both thicker and more depressed in the front than those of recent internment'. The former Cambridge fellow distinguished between the intellectual and physical development of 'native Africans', people who had been trafficked through the slave trade, and African Americans, a people who whites thought had been "civilised" through their interactions with Euro-Americans.[16]

These attitudes reflected developing phrenological opinions in Cambridge. In 1826, Dr Johann Gaspar Spurzheim visited Cambridge, and his lectures were 'received with very marked respect' and 'attended very well by the resident members, and by most of the tutors and lecturers of Colleges'. Born near Trier in Germany, Spurzheim, who had studied medicine at the University of Vienna, lectured widely in Europe and the United States on his *The Physiognomical System*. The enthusiastic attendees of his seminars on phrenology in the Cambridge 'botanical lecture-room' – a 'favor never conferred on any who are not members of the establishment' – 'increased as the course advanced; till, towards the close, it amounted to 130, among whom were 57, partly professors, partly tutors, and fellows of different colleges'. The lectures included lessons on doctrine and live dissections of brain matter, and Cambridge men feverishly discussed his theories. *The Phrenological Journal* reported in 1837 that diligent students were 'perusing' Spurzheim's work and attempting to 'attack the strongholds of metaphysical dogmas, even in the bosom of an University'. The *Journal* could not contain their enthusiasm, gushing that within ten months 'one of the leading characters in the University' had made a failed proposal to hold the *Journal* at the local Philosophical Society, and that a 'rising generation' of men, who were more interested in medical and scientific pursuits than religion, had started to collect casts and skulls and had made phrenology a 'favourite theme of discussion'. One college member reportedly had seventy to eighty casts of living members of the University.[17]

Abdy's writings were predicated on such civilising language, and he called for the 'blessings of civilisation to Africa': the gospel and the virtues of commercial society. Yet Abdy also advocated for the recognition of Haitian independence, an immediate end to American slavery, and his belief that violence – not conciliation with enslavers – may be required to end the slave power. He sombrely concluded that a 'war for America will be a war of freedom; and the blood of Africa will "lie heavy on her soul" on the day of battle'. A friend of William Lloyd Garrison and the Black Philadelphian abolitionist James Forten, and a man who helped to form the American Anti-Slavery Society and donated to British abolitionist causes, Abdy exemplified both the limits (in regard to his phrenological opinions) and radicalism of white abolition. Abdy died on 12 October 1846, but the unmarried fellow left his entire estate, estimated at £500, to American antislavery organisations.[18]

Cambridge educated other radical individuals in the battle against American slavery, among them free African Americans who studied at the University. Alexander Crummell was the most notable among them. Born in New York on 3 March 1819 to Charity Hicks, a free woman of colour, and Boston Crummell, a former enslaved man, Crummell grew up on one of the frontlines of abolition politics. New York owed much of its wealth to the booming cotton trade, and it was there that Crummell's parents and other abolitionists struggled against the enslavers who grew, spun, and sold that "white gold," which when Alexander was born accounted for forty per cent of that city's exports. The Crummell family home was the assembly point for the organisers of the first African American owned newspaper, the *Freedom's Journal*, and Alexander's education at the African Free School and from his father instilled in him a lifelong sense of belonging to an African diaspora that encompassed the homelands of his ethnic Temne people in Sierra Leone and Guinea.[19]

Forced to travel abroad to Britain after he was refused entry to General Theological Seminary in New York and then in a Philadelphia congregation on account of his race, Crummell travelled to England in 1847. During a speaking tour, Crummell captured the attention of white abolitionists, including Wilberforce, who helped him afford living expenses of around £200 annually at Queens', attending a university famed in American abolition circles for educating Peckard and Clarkson. White charity served Crummell's grander purpose: a Black man with an education at Oxford and Cambridge (two prestigious universities which he considered far 'superior' to the fledgling American colleges) would, he admitted, have a 'lively and startling influence among the prejudiced and proslavery at home', who considered African Americans as intellectually and morally degraded. Crummell hoped that the 'standard of learning' amongst his Black countrymen would be raised, and the influence of an educated clergyman of colour could have '*permanent* advantages' for 'my people and my race in America'. The New Yorker excelled considering his inexperience in Latin, passing his final exams after two attempts, and continuing his lecturing tour throughout England, spreading his Pan-African vision: that one's African identity should be embraced to enable Black solidary in the Atlantic world.[20]

American slavery was a much-debated topic in Cambridge. Public lectures and seminars, Anna Roderick suggests, helped to foster a 'knowledge-based culture' in the Victorian era that did not shy away from national discussions over suffrage and education, or international debates concerning military affairs, empire, and slavery. The-then mayor Richard Foster organised anti-slavery meetings in the Town Hall where residents heard from white abolitionists like the Reverend Elon Galusha, the New York representative of the American Anti-Slavery Society, and Edward Barrett, a formerly enslaved Jamaican who tactfully stressed to his audience that he had undergone (thanks to the 'instrumentality of Missionaries') a Christian conversion and that he did not take part in the Baptist War, an eleven-day failed revolution of 60,000 enslaved people against white rule. Barrett's omission of his involvement was revealing. The slavers' brutal suppression of the revolt (lasting from Christmas Day 1831 until 5 January 1832) and the execution of Samuel

Sharpe, a Black Baptist, had inspired abolitionist opinion in Britain. Barrett perhaps diplomatically tailored his life story to the white audience, who wanted to hear more about his 'heartfelt gratitude' for being 'rescued' from his 'fetters by British liberality' due to the Slavery Abolition Act, rather than being confronted with a Black revolutionary who had taken up arms against colonial rule.[21]

Barrett was not the last Black lecturer to inform the Cambridge freeholders about his past. The extraordinary success of the American abolitionist Harriet Beecher Stowe's novel *Uncle Tom's Cabin*, which was published in two volumes in 1852 and sold perhaps a million and a half copies in England alone, further increased demand for first-hand accounts of slavery. On 15 September 1855, the Cambridge audience heard a 'thrilling' lecture from Ellen and William Craft, two formerly enslaved people who had managed to escape because 'Mrs. Craft' had disguised herself as a white slaveholder (with her husband 'the slave in attendance'). Following the discussion, a collection was made at the door, part of which was to be 'added to a fund for buying the freedom of the mother of Mrs. Craft, who is still in slavery'. The effort to free Ellen's mother, Maria, from bondage in Georgia – which echoed the experiences of Frederick Douglass, whose freedom was purchased for £150 thanks to the tireless efforts of Quaker abolitionists – succeeded after the American Civil War. The next lecture took place almost a year later on Sidney Street in the heart of Cambridge. The speaker was William Watson, 'late of King's College, London', who regaled his audience on the importance of a slave's education through a short history of his life – a history of enslaver violence that, he and the newspaper publicist both believed, would 'bear testimony to the authenticity of "Uncle Tom's Cabin."' The speakers after the publication of Stowe's novel continued to provide more proof, if any was needed, of the veracity of her claims. George Panell, an 'escaped' enslaved person, delivered a June 1858 talk, too, on the 'cruelty he had undergone while a slave, and how he escaped'. With slave narratives becoming ever more popular, Black lecturers travelled throughout Britain to maintain antislavery fervour in one of the epicentres of abolition.[22]

Aside from these more cerebral meetings, musical and theatrical performances informed audiences about enslavement. Victorians enjoyed a dramatic expansion in the number of theatres that catered for the British masses, including working people, with more than 300 imperial-themed plays being performed that informed viewers about incidents in India, South Africa, the Sudan, and Australia. On 22 March 1854, the Theatre Royal in Cambridge (the town's first permanent theatre, which was built in 1816) presented 'a Series of PANORAMIC SKETCHES, ENTITLED *Negro Life! in Freedom and in Slavery*' conducted by Henry Russell. The songs included "The African Village" – with its lyrics regaling audiences of a continent 'Where the lonely Negro village rears its rude and rustic eaves; Where the untaught savage bows to his idol in its shrine' – "The Chase of the Slave-Trader by a British Cruiser," and "The Slave

Sale – Come who bids?" It would take two decades, though, before Black performers sang in Cambridge.[23]

On 13 June 1876, the Cambridge Guildhall hosted the Fisk Jubilee Singers. An African American acapella group formed to raise funds for Fisk University, a historically Black college in the United States founded ten years prior, the group communicated a 'culture of opposition' where Black transatlantic performers, including anti-lynching campaigners like Ida B. Wells, used their performances to attack white American racism. That evening the Jubilee singers delivered 'a SERVICE of SONG consisting of THE QUAINT HYMNS AND MELODIES, Sung by them in their Days of Slavery', with the proceeds 'to be devoted to the EDUCATION OF FREE SLAVES AT FISK UNIVERSITY, U.S.A'. The Singers' performance of spirituals such as "Swing Low, Sweet Chariot" and "Wade in the Water," the music echoing throughout the halls, told a 'tale', the abolitionist Frederick Douglass had written regarding such music on a separate occasion, 'which was then altogether beyond my feeble comprehension; they were tones, loud, long and deep, breathing the prayer and complaint of souls boiling over with the bitterest anguish'. The spirituals affected audiences with the music of the enslaved.[24]

Examinations provided another opportunity for students to ponder the moral, legal, and economic underpinnings of enslavement. Public exams were more unusual at the beginning of the nineteenth century, however more meritocratic "middle-class examinations" were becoming standard practice at Oxford and Cambridge – and the Royal Commission of 1850, charged with inquiring into the labyrinthine organisation and finances of the two ancient universities and its constituent colleges, had introduced the natural sciences and moral sciences Tripos. From the era of reform onwards, when the Anglican stranglehold over the universities was loosened, undergraduates, it appears, were instructed in the moral foundations of North American slavery. Students in the 1832 Bachelor of Arts examinations discussed Paley's maxims on enslavement, including whether there was 'any argument in favour of Slavery, that it is no where condemned in the Scriptures?', to 'Define Slavery, and shew from what causes it can arise consistently with the law of nature', and state from 'what causes' slavery 'may arise'.[25]

Fifty years later, the moral sciences and political economy examinations presented students with more ethical quandaries to consider. Candidates debated whether it was 'always wrong to act against one's conscience, though not always right to follow it... Is it [therefore] right for one who believes slavery to be wicked to assist a slave to escape against the laws of the country?', and 'What circumstances tend to determine the average rate of profit in a country? Why is it, generally speaking, low in a country where there is a large population of *slaves*?' – an effort to make students question the economic viability of enslavement. Following Clarkson's example, students also applied to and won prize competitions with poetry, essays, and treatises that considered the singular importance of Christianity to the abolition of slavery in medieval England and on the numerous international laws that sought to restrict the African slave trade.[26]

After taking in the sights in Cambridge (or strenuously preparing for his exams), Crummell made friends with college fellows. One was Charles Clayton, who had a long career at Caius. The son of a Cambridge fishmonger, Clayton was admitted as a pensioner and scholar at the College after attending the local Perse School (which Stephen Perse, a Caian physician and fellow, had founded in 1615 as a collegiate feeder school to mend town and gown relations). Awarded the Browne Medal in Latin and Greek Poetry, Clayton held a fellowship from 1838 to 1866, with shorter stints as a Hebrew (1842–1844) and Greek Lecturer (1842–1846). His diary mentions their meetings. On 7 April 1848, he scrawled 'Mr. Crummell, from New York, arrived'. That same month he had also brought Crummell along to tour several local schools, as Clayton was involved in religious education. Apart from attending missionary meetings (where Crummell sometimes addressed the audience), dining and walking with the Crummells, and bringing him along to meet other Cambridge academic luminaries, he also mentioned their attendance at 'the boat-races'. As with enslavers and fellows, therefore, personal and familial relationships between Black abolitionists and white Cambridge missionaries were vital to antislavery networks both within and beyond that market town.[27]

The Caius man's evangelicalism was the foundation of his friendship with Crummell. In his diary, Clayton commented that 'A Missionary must have a thorough knowledge of religions, of the nature of man, & must be entirely devoted [to] his cause'. He was a member of the Church Missionary Society (CMS) and Secretary of the Church Pastoral Aid Society, which aimed to 'carry the Gospel, by means of the Church, to every's man's door'. Slavery was discussed in these missionary meetings. In November 1836, the CMS heard of one twenty-two-year-old evangelical's struggles to convert the Māori, with a 'Chieftain wishing to kill his slave, afterwards converted by this slave'. To make matters worse, an 'old man' had interrupted the 'white mens' prayers' and sermons exclaiming 'tis a lie'. The conversion of Afro-Caribbeans following emancipation continued to be one of the principal goals of the CMS. Professor James Scholefield claimed that with £64,000 in income the Society could maintain its 'ten stations' in 'Western Africa; the Mediterranean; the West Indies; (in the East Indies) Calcutta, Madras, Bombay; Ceylon; North[-]West America; New Zealand; China[.]' Missionary Anglicanism had met with its share of problems, with the 'Climate very unhealthy; many have died; Miss[ionar]y band thus very much reduced[.]'[28]

Clayton was a committed abolitionist. He attended meetings of the Anti-Slavery Society and, at one time, contemplated missionary work in Sierra Leone. At one such meeting in the Guildhall at Rochester, Clayton heard from New York abolitionist figures such as Henry Brewster Stanton, a writer for

Garrison's *Anti-Slavery Standard* and *The Liberator*. According to Clayton's diary on 18 August 1839, Stanton – though there was regrettably 'no religion however in his speech' – spoke of slavery's 'cruelties', the attacks on 'whigs' by 'Anti-Abolitionists', and the 'tongue-tie of ye Press & pulpit[.]' From 1849, Clayton had a growing interest in leaving Cambridge for Sierra Leone, which was then in the process of appointing its first bishop, and he eagerly felt that 'men's minds are turning to Africa'. He met with a merchant from West Africa, and Henry Venn even mentioned that he would 'probably be offered the see' in the colony.[29]

Though Crummell visited Liberia, the Caius man was too attached to life in Cambridge to leave. Elizabeth Melville's *Journal of a Residence in Sierra Leone* had further dissuaded him from African missionary work, and its commentary – mocking the local 'woolly-haired children', stating that 'all the Black people seem alike', observing that women did not wear shoes and that their gait 'is exactly that of a goose', and her descriptions of the dangerous climate, including bugs, termites, and fevers – was unlikely to inspire Europeans to migrate to West Africa. For his part, Clayton wrote that he was 'Somewhat dejected at the prospect of being one day sent thither', but he conceded that God would place him where 'I may best glorify Thee, – for Jesus' sake'.[30]

In 1848, Clayton offered prayers to the audience when Crummell gave a speech in the Cambridge Town Hall on the "Spiritual Condition of the Negro Race in the United States." Lecturing to an audience that included the Reverend Dr Alfred Ollivant, Regius Professor of Divinity, the Reverend J. Rowlands, a Queens' fellow, and the Reverend H. A. Marsh, Dean of Trinity, Crummell explained the nature and realities of enslavement in the United States. 'He stated', a newspaper reported, 'that physically, politically, intellectually, and spiritually, the negro race in the United States were in the most miserable and degraded condition'. The more than 3 million enslaved people, he declared, 'were bought and sold like cattle' – with a 'regular trade… kept up between the more northern slave states and the southern slave states'. The transatlantic trade in enslaved Africans may have ended in the British Empire and the United States, he feared, but the internal slave trade – with perhaps 835,000 enslaved trafficked between 1790 and 1860 to the cotton states – was thriving and profitable. The conditions on the plantations, Crummell argued, were atrocious: the enslaved were poorly fed, uneducated, overworked, and 'whipped and scourged'.[31]

Liberated African Americans were free in name only; their condition, he observed, was one of 'nominal freedom' – in contrast to the French and Spanish Caribbean, or even Brazil, where 'a negro became relieved from slavery, he rose immediately to a condition of equality'. Crummell compared the 'caste' system in the United States to British India, complaining that it was a system of 'perfect exclusion' where Black artisans were unable to be apprentices, Black schoolchildren could not attend white schools, and where Black parishioners were unable to sit or pray in the same pews as whites. Hoping to raise funds for a Black church in New York whilst in England, Crummell proclaimed that education was the pathway to equality. 'If they', he claimed, 'only had institutions from which they could send forth annually virtuous and capable men into all the avenues of life, slavery and caste would certainly recede, like mist beside the mountain before the glory of the morning sun'. Neither 'agitation' nor 'deep and ardent indignation', he argued, would end enslavement. New Black colleges and churches, for which he raised more than £16 from audience contributions, were the solution. Crummell was an important contributor to a longstanding strain of thought within African-descended communities, which stressed that Black self-reliance, not armed resistance, would end the white "slave power" in the United States.[32]

The spirit for Black education was felt amongst evangelical activists in the Caribbean. Nevertheless, the Oxford don William Charles Dowding's efforts to revive Berkeley's scheme for a Christian college in Bermuda, known as St Paul's College, was illustrative of post-emancipation racial animosities in that region. Dowding had cause for confidence – after all, religious organisations continued to receive money from university men, such as Robert Griffin Laing of Trinity's donation of £500 in consolidated government bonds to the SPCK, and the classicist Christopher Wordsworth's subscription to the Christian Faith Society (the successor to Porteus's mission for Black conversion). The Sir Peregrine Maitland essay prize was founded at Cambridge, too, in 1844 and promised £100 to the top student writing on 'the propagation of the Gospel, through missionary exertions, in India and in other parts of the heathen world.' General Maitland had supported missionary efforts whilst Lieutenant-Governor of Upper Canada (1818–1828), where he was an 'early proponent of [Indigenous] boarding schools'. Missionary schemes were ongoing in the Caribbean: since emancipation, the Cambridge Bible Association had, with the assistance of the Professors Scholefield and Farish and local women, aimed to free people 'from the slavery of Satan as well as man'; and sermons to that end had been preached in Cambridge churches with the profits from the sale of those addresses supporting the construction of chapels and schoolhouses for the formerly enslaved.[33]

As one of the preeminent British centers of learning, Dowding lobbied Trinity College, Cambridge, for support. Writing to William Whewell, the then-Master, in March 1852, Dowding hoped that his *'academical'* project would 'obtain the special sympathy of our great Universities' – and, in pursuit of that mission, he wanted the 'two Universities' to raise at least £25,000 for building work, fellowships, and scholarships that would attract students to the school. The document that Dowding enclosed with his initial letter may have been his *Africa in the West*. Declaring Africa to be the 'crux of philanthropy', the 1852 treatise was an exemplar of humanitarian intervention, yet – unlike abolitionist efforts to "civilise" Africans in Africa – Dowding claimed that 'this question is solving itself *on the other side [of] the Atlantic*. The future of Africa is to be looked for in the West'. For Dowding (as for Porteus and the former abolitionists), the Caribbean was a humanitarian laboratory to "civilise" Africans and, they hoped, raise them from a state of 'childhood' and 'fix the graft of refinement upon the stock of barbarism'. The warning signs for the project were clear: the education advocate Susette Harriet Lloyd, who sought to promote Black education on Bermuda, was concerned that, as emancipation approached, the 4,297 white Bermudans had instituted property requirements for voting to disenfranchise the around 4,898 free and enslaved Black inhabitants on the island.[34]

Cambridge had a starring role in this doomed endeavour, with exhibitioners at the Black college holding a position as a 'Bye-Fellow at Cambridge; ranking in all social respects as a Fellow, but having no voice in the College government'. Emancipation, Dowding's supporters claimed, would remain unfulfilled and unachieved without 'raising the Negro race in the West Indies in the scale of educated and intellectual beings'. The Master must have been supportive given that Dowding thanked him for the 'kind manner' in which he had responded and he hoped that – since Berkeley's original proposal had royal support – the Trinity fellow would entreat Queen Victoria to become patron because there was 'no name at Cambridge which she would more willing meet than one so well known to her as your own'. St Paul's had an illustrious group of academic supporters: Whewell, the masters of St John's, St Catharine's, and Peterhouse colleges, and the Regius Professor of Divinity. The Governor of Bermuda and former Protector of Slaves in British Guiana, Charles Elliot, also served as Vice-President. His support was, in an ominous sign, much more tentative – and he wrote in June 1851 that, if the scheme was going to be a success, it would be due to the 'exertions of Individuals, and I am not aware that there are any measures which it is at present in the power of H. M's: Govt. to adopt to promote its success'. St Paul's was established in 1853, surviving three years and offering a curriculum rooted in classical and modern languages, music, and history – but the reaction that the institution stirred in the British Caribbean was a lesson in the durability and malleability of anti-Black racism.[35]

The Bermuda barrister and Inspector of Schools, Samuel Brownlow Grey, condemned Dowding's project. Writing to John Bird Sumner, the Archbishop of Canterbury (and a supporter of Dowding's 'noble project'), Grey defended Bermudans, whose resistance to the plan had been incorrectly 'represented to your Grace, as another phase in the history of human error, the bigotry of ignorance, and the sad effects of slavery on the minds and hearts of all who have even lived within its atmosphere'. Having been denounced as the 'enemies of liberty and learning and of the coloured race', the barrister's ire was focused on the missionaries, and he questioned whether the 'wild and dangerous' proposals of 'great names' were intended to manufacture 'a fusion between the coloured people in this hemisphere and the fair daughters of their

English homes?' Disputing the structural racism in Bermudan politics, education, and society, Grey responded that racism (including his opposition to miscegenation) was based on 'distinctions of rank' and class, not on skin colour – a defense that white colonists had also applied in Jamaica. Addressing the universities, he pondered whether the 'same benevolent men [were] ready to favour a plan for putting Oxford and Cambridge within the reach of the same class of children who now pursue their humble studies in the National Society's school-rooms, or in village dame-schools?'[36]

Unlike these imperial schemes, Crummell did not fail at his goal – he was the first recorded Black graduate of the University of Cambridge. Still, his experiences at the university reflected the widespread racism in British society at the time. Racism had increased and deepened following emancipation in 1833, as Britons recalibrated their views on race as the problem of slavery became the problem of ensuring freedom for Black Britons. Considered one of the first female sociologists, Harriet Martineu was typical of British approaches to enslavement after emancipation, arguing in the independent liberal *Saturday Review* that slavery and subjugation had civilised African Americans. Although Crummell met with a warm reception before beginning his degree, breakfasting and dining with the fellows and masters of Caius and Trinity colleges, he encountered bigoted views at Cambridge. Joseph Romilly, the Trinity fellow, dismissed Crummell as the 'woolly-haired undergraduate' with a 'black wife [Sarah] and 3 black piccaninnies'. The local racism transcended distinctions of class: Romilly reported that the Crummells' Irish servant had, upon being dismissed from her position, attacked 'Mrs. Crummell' with the 'following words, "you are a black devil: you are a slave & the daughter of a slave & your heart is as black as your face!!!"' Some Irish servants in Cambridge believed that they were superior to Black people, and wielded racial epithets to make that chasm in social status known.[37]

Crummell's graduation at the Senate House was greeted with racist epithets too. There, one observer reported that 'A boisterous individual in the gallery called out "Three groans for the Queens" nigger'. In response, an undergraduate shouted 'Shame, shame! Three groans for you, Sir!' and 'Three Cheers for Crummell!' The American did not respond. He had a great deal of esteem for Cambridge, turning English ingenuity and scientific endeavour into a foil for the close-minded United States. On the university, Crummell later wrote that 'Perhaps no seat of learning in the world has done more, for human liberty and human well-being, than this institution'. Such sincerely held views were perhaps also trained on American universities, colleges, and educational institutions that had purchased and enslaved Africans.[38]

Cambridge men, of course, both entertained and challenged these racial ideologies. On race and racial difference, anatomists continued to argue that humans had diffused from one singular origin throughout the world, and that physical and cultural environment – not innate qualities – were the principal drivers and explanatory factors underpinning human development. Though the "Prichardian Paradigm" (named after the thesis in James Cowles Prichard's 1808 *De generis humani varietate*) was coming under sustained challenge, monogenism had adherents in Cambridge. Sir George Murray Humphry (1820–1896) was one of these theorists. Born into a high achieving and politically prominent Suffolk family (his elder brother was a Trinity fellow and another sibling was a barrister), Humphry exceeded even thosy lofty expectations: he was the youngest surgeon at Cambridge's local Addenbrooke's Hospital (which had been established in 1766), he was elected a fellow of the Royal College of Surgeons at such a young age that he had to wait to the statutory age to attain the honour, and in 1847 the Reverend William Clark, Cambridge's Professor of Anatomy, appointed him a lecturer in surgery and anatomy at the Medical School.[39]

Four years after attaining that post (during which time he was elected a fellow at Downing College), he published his *A Treatise on the Human Skeleton (Including the Joints)*, which benefitted from the expertise of his wife, Mary, who made the accurate drawings and illustrations for his published articles and books. Humphry's text contained an extensive discussion on the 'inferior races of mankind'. According to him, these ethnicities 'exhibit proportions' which were 'intermediate between the higher or European orders and the monkeys'. The 'stature' of Black people, he claimed, was 'less than in the European', their 'cranium... bears a smaller proportion to the face', and 'the foot is less well-formed in the Negro than in European... more nearly resembling the monkey's, between which and the European there is a marked difference in this particular'. Comparing the skulls of European and African peoples, Humphry concluded that a perfect anatomical frame (and not simply skull shape or size, as phrenologists had claimed) was the natural corollary of a powerful intellect. In fact, he noted that 'the ascent from the lower animals to the higher orders of mankind' was associated with both 'the actual size and capacity of the cranium' and the 'size of the whole [human] frame, and more particularly in the size, strength, and excellency of conformation of the lower extremities'. Utilising skulls held at Cambridge, including that of a Congolese person, he argued that African-descended people were closest to the earliest human beings, and that Europeans had achieved a higher state of 'growth' and 'further development'. Humphry, who advocated for the reconstruction of Addenbrooke's and the inclusion of the subject of human anatomy in the Cambridge Natural Science Tripos, remained fixated on a stadial developmental model that had Europeans at the pinnacle of civilisation, and Africans at the lowest level of human progress, effectively at the intellectual and physical level of white children.[40]

Those racial views were exhibited in the colleges, even as some fellows were determined to challenge these public and private prejudices. Henry Venn argued in November 1863 that, as a tutor at Queens' College, he had 'several negroes resident with me from time to time' – students, such as Alexander Crummell, who had never displayed 'any inferiority of natural ability'. The prevalence of such prejudicial views in Cambridge, however, can be inferred from Professor James Scholefield, who, upon hearing the first African Anglican bishop of West Africa Samuel Ajayi Crowther's answers to a series of questions on the philosopher William Paley, planned to read those answers 'to certain of my old Trinity friends' in the fellows common room who had contended that Black people and students do 'not possess a logical faculty'.[41]

Cambridge's members debated the contentious subject of race and racial difference, and that institution's financial interconnection with enslavers remained constant as well. Slave money continued to percolate through the fellowship. Forty years after Britain's five-year occupation of western Saint-Domingue, the Cockburn baronets claimed a yearly pension from the Santo Domingo Board, an effort from the British government to compensate French slavers who had supported its efforts to occupy the island. Inspired by the potential profits from seizing France's richest colony, British soldiers and thousands of German mercenaries had arrived in September 1793 (greeted with 'Long live the English!' by local whites). Falling victim to disease, the government mobilised 7,000 enslaved people for the war effort; still, they did little to dent the revolutionaries' progress under generals André Rigaud and Toussaint Louverture. Sir James Fellowes, a Caian fellow and doctor, accompanied Rear-Admiral Hugh Cloberry Christian's naval contingent, and he there observed the 'melancholy' and 'painful' epidemics of yellow fever that gripped the inhabitants and soldiers. Following the Revolution, the Cockburns enjoyed payments due to Alexander Cockburn's marriage to Yolande Vignier, the daughter of a Saint-Domingue slaveholder. Granted a pension in the 1799 Bounty, their son, Sir Alexander Cockburn, was a fellow at Trinity Hall for more than two decades and a much-respected jurist who would become the 12th Baronet and Lord Chief Justice of the Queen's Bench, where he served on a Royal Commission on international law in relation to fugitive slaves. The family received an annual payment of £130 (and had claimed an indemnity from the French government for their lost estates) between Yolande, Sir Alexander, and their daughter Louisa.[42]

Former enslavers and financial beneficiaries of compensation also subscribed funds for the construction of Cambridge's "New Library" (known at the time as the "Cockerell Building," and now the home of Caius College's library and archive). Built between 1837 and 1840, the benefactors included abolitionists, such as William Whewell and Thomas Spring Rice, and men who earned significant incomes and fortunes from the plantation economy, particularly Lawrence Dundas (who donated £105 and earned £8,135 in compensation), Sir Charles Long, Baron Farnborough (who provided £105 and had inherited a significant Jamaican fortune), the MP Henry Goulburn (who gave £105 and was compensated with £5,601 from the Act), George Neville Grenville (£105 and more than £6,630 in compensation), Adam Sedgwick (with £105 donated and £3,783 awarded as a trustee to a Jamaican plantation), and Sir Nicholas

Conyngham Tindal (who provided £105 and had been awarded two-thirds of a compensation claim as the trustee of an estate in British Guiana). Abolitionists who had inherited fortunes connected to enslavement, such as the Reverend George Craufurd (who donated £100), contributed to the construction efforts too. Even Charles Robert Cockerell, the architect and building's namesake, drew much of his fortune from his Jamaican plantation-owning relatives. Long after the dissolution of slave-trading companies, men with monetary connections to enslavement supported Cambridge.[43]

Struggling against the enduring wealth, privilege, and power of that enslaver class, Crummell's classics and religious education at Cambridge was an important foundation of his abolitionist thought. Soon after leaving Cambridge, Crummell published (as he often did) as a "BA" of "Queen's College, Cambridge" his *The Negro Race not under a Curse*. Attacking the Curse of Ham myth, which he had seen 'much used by the schools and universities of England', he argued that the 'severities' of the slave trade and the 'horrors' of the plantation were not Biblical, but 'entirely *modern* – confined to a short period in the history of the world, and therefore not a true exemplification of the *general* condition of the Negro race'. A student of history, Crummell noted that Europeans had first 'enslaved and overworked' Native Americans – and once they had been 'exterminated, the Negro was torn from his native land, brought across the water, and made to supply the red man's place'. Turning proslavery arguments against their proponents (enslavers had dismissed criticisms of enslavement by claiming its longstanding roots in history), he observed that the 'whole human family', including Anglo-Saxons, had participated in and enslaved each other, but he noted that the 'Negro family' had suffered 'greatly' for 'some high and important ends.' The New Yorker's education in Greek, Roman, and Hebrew texts refuted proslavery ideologues like John C. Calhoun, the Vice-President, who had reportedly claimed at a Washington party that only when 'a Negro who knew the Greek syntax' existed would he 'believe that the Negro was a human being and should be treated as a man.'[44]

Joining Thomas Clarkson and Frederick Douglass, who also deployed classical examples in their antislavery arguments, Crummell used his education in Euclid, Plato's *Apology* and *Crito*, and Tacitus to shape Britain's perception of West Africa. 'The very words in which Cicero and Tacitus describe the home and families of the Germanic tribes', he argued, 'can truly be ascribed to the people of the West Coast of Africa'. These venerable moral traits included their 'maidenly virtue, the instinct to chastity, is a marvel… in West Africa every female is a virgin to the day of her marriage'. He contrasted this 'generalization' of African virtue with a corrupted Europe: 'The harlot class', he wrote, 'is unknown in all the tribes. I venture the assertation that any one walking through Pall Mall, London, or Broadway, New York, for a week would see more indecency in look and act than he could discover in an African town in a dozen years'. Upon meeting newly liberated Africans in Liberia, he lamented that these virtuous people – 'fresh from the plantations' – had had their spirits crushed, 'their inner life, is gone' – 'And only shreds – the wreck of humanity remains to be seen, and to have one's heart broken when seen'. Crummell argued that Africans, not white Europeans, occupied the moral high ground.[45]

W. E. B. Du Bois, a fellow Pan-Africanist and intellectual, lauded Crummell as a prophet and mentor, and the latter's writings had a profound influence on African diasporic thought. After leaving Cambridge, Crummell relocated to Liberia to work with the Protestant Episcopal Church. Arriving in 1853, he came ashore at a time when Liberia's free American Black population, who had relocated there with the support of the American Colonisation Society, had seized control. Whilst Crummell was initially opposed to colonisation, he called for Black Americans to civilise Africans. In his 1862 work *The Future of Africa*, he wrote that the 'children of Africa' in America had first 'been called, in the Divine providence, to meet the demands of civilization, of commerce, and of nationality' and second to perform the 'solemn responsibility of establishing the Christian faith amid the rude forms of paganism'. Unlike white imperialists, whether from the United States or Britain, Crummell dreamed that Liberia would be a safe haven for African-descended peoples, not a location to export Black people and thereby stop slave insurrections. He called the Colony a 'refuge of the oppressed' – a land where, quoting a poet, there would be 'No slave-hunt in our borders, no pirate on our strand, No fetters in Liberia, no slave upon our land!' That nation would carry on the civilisation of Europe, he thought, without the miseries and barbarities perpetuated in European states and colonies, such as enslavement. Many whites believed that colonisation was the only avenue to forestall a race war, but Crummell became a convert to colonisation to create what he thought was a better future for West Africa.[46]

Unfortunately for Crummell, he would not witness this new world. Fearing his life was in danger after the President of Liberia was assassinated, Crummell returned to the United States and became the rector at St Luke's in Washington, D.C., and taught at Howard University, a Black college, from 1895 to 1897. There he continued to advocate for the Republic of Liberia. In the preface to his *Africa and America*, a collection of his essays, sermons, and speeches, Crummell defended Liberia from the charge that it had revealed 'the incapacity of the Negro Race for free government!' or that 'Liberia is a failure!' Contrary to that prejudiced and pessimistic charge from white Americans, he considered the Republic to be 'one of the marvels of modern history! Yea but little short of a miracle!' One area where Crummell was pessimistic – correctly, as it turned out – was in the prospect for colour-blind democracy in the US. Crummell declared that it was the 'nation which was on trial' – and that the problem of race was the problem of democracy, and without equality the nation would collapse because 'her every fundamental dogma' was based upon racial injustice. Though he passed away ten years after this address, Crummell perceptively noted that emancipation was but a small step in breaching the divide between white Americans and African Americans, who remained stripped of their civil and democratic rights in the nation they had helped to build.[47]

Following Crummell's death, the University of Cambridge's association with Africa continued. In fact, the centenary of the abolition of the slave trade in 1907 opened with a *Times* article hoping for the 'names and addresses' of Wilberforce's descendants, and those 'English friends who are interested in Africa from an evangelical standpoint, and Africans, Afro-Americans, and black West Indians now in the United Kingdom'. Building on the efforts of the Cambridge Bible Association, which (with the express involvement of Professor Scholefield and other Cambridge members) had planned forty years earlier to send a New Testament to every freed African, Trinity College hosted a meeting of the "Universities' Mission to Central Africa."[48]

With the Master holding the chair, the members hoped to build upon David Livingstone's address to Cambridge in 1857. The missionary, explorer, and abolitionist had called upon undergraduates to join him and 'go back to Africa to try and make an open path for commerce and Christianity'. Flying the banner of Christianity and commerce, Livingstone planned to open Africa's fertile soil to Christian commerce – arguing that the land was 'admirably fitted' for a 'rich harvest' in cotton, sugar, and coffee for prospective colonists. Joining adherents from Oxford and Cambridge, these men hoped to go forth 'as the soldiers of Christianity were also soldiers of that civilization which was the highest honour of every western nation'. The new colonists in Africa included Joseph Gedge, a Caius alumnus and doctor, who accompanied Sir Samuel Baker's Egyptian Exhibition to suppress the slave trade, and later donated £1,000 to fund a Professorship in Physiology. The London Hausa Association also offered Cambridge £100 per annum for a Lectureship in the Hausa language of Nigeria, which 'ranks by the side of Arabic and Suaheli as one of the three most important languages for the development of Africa, and especially that part of it which lies within the British sphere of influence on the West Coast'. For the Association, there was little doubt that a Cambridge education in languages would spur economic and moral development in West and Central Africa. If soft power was unsuccessful, then visiting lecturers and recent graduates of the University advocated the 'annexation' of countries through military power to ensure the gradual termination of enslavement.[49]

From its inception, the Mission envisioned a commercial project in Central Africa as an avenue to end American slavery and make restitution for European colonialism. The UCMA's members, at a meeting in Oxford's Sheldonian Theatre in May 1859, feted the participation of Cambridge, Dublin, Durham, and Oxford universities in introducing a more "civilised," Christian commerce to Africa. Celebrating Africa's heritage in theology, philosophy, and literature (perhaps no better encapsulated than in the 'heavenly [Saint] Augustine'), the Reverend Selwyn, the Lady Margaret Professor of Divinity at Cambridge, argued that the Mission had a responsibility to 'give the people freedom' and ensure that West Africans would not glide 'slowly to the grave in ignorance and unbelief'. The twin pillars of *Christianity* and *commerce* were an article of faith for Selwyn and his Oxford contemporaries, who thought that '20 millions of [slave compensation] money' did not 'wipe off the stain' of Britain's trading empire.[50]

From a potential base of operations in the Cape Colony, one attendee hoped that the 'great national debt' owed to Africa and its inhabitants could be paid and repaired through the 'opening' of Central Africa to 'free and legitimate commerce' and the abolition of the East African slave trade, which transported 20,000 captives annually. The cotton trade was discussed, too, because that market underpinned 'slavery now in America', and the cultivation of that fibre in Africa would 'cut away the second of these great evils, the existence of slavery in the Southern States of America'. African abolition and American antislavery were two pillars of this Anglican Church project. As in the Caribbean, the concern was to what extent these white humanitarians involved Africans in their plans or, as Crummell envisioned, allowed for the prospect of West African self-government in their homelands.[51]

During the American Civil War, Britain and Cambridge's divisions on the issue of American slavery became apparent. From the outbreak of the conflict, Britons recognised that the contest in North America – whether they supported the Union under President Abraham Lincoln or the Confederate States of America under Jefferson Davis – was over enslavement. In his "Cornerstone Speech," delivered at the Atheneum in Savannah, Georgia, on 21 March 1861, Alexander H. Stephens, the Vice President of the Confederacy, proposed that the rebel nation's 'foundations are laid… upon the great truth that the negro is not equal to the white man; that slavery – subordination to the superior [white] race – is his natural condition'. That 'great physical, philosophical, and moral truth' was the foundation of their white supremacist government. Cambridge newspapers soon informed domestic readers about American politics, and a May 1861 paper advertised a 'Tinted Map of the United States', containing 'a Map of the United and Confederates States of North America, printed in colour, distinguishing the Free from the Slaves States, and giving the boundaries of every State and Territory'. As seven Southern states seceded from the Union after Lincoln's election – South Carolina first, then Mississippi, Florida, Alabama, Georgia, Louisiana, and Texas – town and gown residents recognised that enslavement and its expansion was the 'immediate cause' of the Civil War.[52]

Many British elites took up the mantle of defending the Confederacy from charges of rebellion at home and in the United States. These views pervaded every part of Cambridge life, from the lecture hall to clubs and societies and into the wider public sphere, where alumni and dons fought Unionist opinion. An unknown correspondent recounted these views in a November 1863 edition of the *Christian Examiner*. Noting that Britons were largely pro-Union, the observer worried that the Confederacy's influence 'is nowhere greater than in the Universities'. Struggling to 'account for this overmastering influence', the writer attributed pro-Confederate opinion in Cambridge to excessive reading of *The Times* newspaper (an 'anti-abolitionist' paper that tended to favour the South), but there were deeper feelings at play than devotion to a London newspaper. Observing a Union Debate, he wrote that, whilst no speaker defended slavery, the 'object of all [speakers] on the Southern side was to prove that slavery had nothing to do with Secession; that the South had seceded because of protective tariffs; that the negro was hated more and treated worse in the North than in the South[.]' The pro-Confederate Cambridge students argued that the North was fighting to 'keep slavery *in* the Union' while the 'South were fighting to take it *out*'. Consequently, the 'triumph of the South' made 'emancipation much more probable than it would be in any other event'. The author found this swing in academic opinion – a shift in allegiance towards those 'gallantly fighting for their independence' – disturbing considering that the Cambridge Union had voted ten years prior that the 'immediate abolition of slavery in the United States is right, practicable, and politic' (despite some members hoping for a period of apprenticeship for 'education'). That measure had been unanimously agreed upon 'by all hands'.[53]

The Cambridge Union records, whilst light on the debates' contents, reveal that the Civil War's origins and morality were a point of contention throughout the conflict. Most of the debates ended with majority support for the South. A narrow majority of Union participants saw no cause for 'regret' that the United States was breaking apart in the first place. At the beginning of the war in December 1861, V. W. Hutton of Trinity moved, and the House agreed with a resounding 54 votes to 5, 'That the seizure of Messrs Slidell and Mason by the American Ship Jacinta [*San Jacinto*] was a breach of international law and demands immediate reparation'. (The "seizure" in question was the Union arrest of two Confederate envoys aboard a British mail steamer, causing an international incident before Lincoln intervened and freed the men.) In the new year, pro-Union motions were defeated with convincing margins. In the first debate of 1862, one brave undergraduate moved (and was defeated 117 to 33) 'That the Cause of the Northern States of America is the Cause of Humanity and progress: and that the widespread sympathy for the Confederates, is the result of ignorance & misrepresentation'. In the final year of the conflict, a Trinity Hall undergraduate proposed the motion (and was once again rejected 76 to 29) 'That this House would view with regret the Success of the Confederates in the present American War as a fatal blow to the cause of Freedom and to the Stability of all Government'. In all, the Cambridge Union debated at least ten Civil War and Reconstruction motions, and each of the votes came down on the side of the Confederacy or anti-Black policies.[54]

Cambridge fellows were divided on the Civil War, with some supportive of the Confederacy. Charles Kingsley, the Regius Professor of History, was the most prominent of the pro-Southern Cambridge men. Educated at Magdalene, Kingsley was descended from slaveholders (his grandfather, according to Kingsley, had married a 'West Indian heiress'). As he reminisced in 1857, the results of emancipation were not 'encouraging' as it 'regarded the material conditions of the islands'. Still, his enslaver background, Kingsley thought, made him sensitive to the claims of 'our Southern planters, and how it tended to close their ears to all antislavery argument'. (He lamented how his family had been 'ruined' after the financial loss of their Caribbean plantation.) Kingsley's attitude to enslavement, then, was shaped by his family's bitter experience of emancipation, and his resulting belief that slavery's most unjust features were not in its treatment of Black enslaved persons, but rather how it degraded white society by making enslavers less industrious, prone to leisure, and despotic. The belief that whites suffered more from enslavement than Black people was a common one at the time. The Confederate General Robert E. Lee, in a December 1856 letter, noted that African American slavery was 'a greater evil to the white man to the black race' because the 'painful discipline they [African Americans] are undergoing, is necessary for their instruction as a race, & I hope will prepare and lead them to better things'. Some historians have been unable to understand Kingsley's pro-Confederate beliefs given his abolitionism either. Many conservatives had no love for enslavement; nevertheless, British elites, even men like Kingsley who were friends to working-class education, supported the South because of a shared sense of heritage between the landed southern planters and the English aristocracy, and a collective anxiety in Victorian Britain of threats from below – from democratic movements and expanding manhood suffrage.[55]

In May 1860, the Lord Palmerston, the then-prime minister, nominated Kingsley to the Regius Professorship. Often dismissed as a political appointment, the Professorship was one available avenue to reward friends and supporters of the ruling government, and, as a result, had few required qualifications. A first in classics and a professed willingness to devote oneself to modern history was a must. Reading his oeuvre, Kingsley was one of the most underqualified candidates in the Professorship's history. His reputation was based on numerous novels such as *Yeast, Alton Locke, Hypatia, Westward Ho!*, and *Two Years Ago*. *Alton Locke* provided the inspiration for some authors, such as John C. Cobden, in their arguments against 'White Slavery' and the 'slavery of the workmen' in Britain, but the latter novel, *Two Years Ago*, outlined his views on the United States and the politics of African American enslavement.[56]

Though the previously mentioned correspondent who attended the Cambridge Union debates read *Two Years* as a work of abolitionism, Kingsley's views were more complicated. He was an advocate for the Free-Soil Party, a short-lived coalition that opposed the expansion of slavery into the western states and which later merged with the Republican Party. In Kingsley's novel, a moderate New Englander argues in dialogue with an Englishmen to 'Leave us to draw a *cordon sanitaire* round the tainted States, and leave the system [slavery] to die a natural death, as it rapidly will if it be prevented from enlarging its field'. The fictional American maintained that enslavement would eventually end with the march of human progress. Echoing proslavery activists, Kingsley cast abolitionists in the novel as 'too-benevolent philanthropists' whose policies would lead to the 'disruption of the Union, an invasion of the South by the North; and an internecine war, aggravated by the horrors of a general rising of the slaves, and such scenes as Hayti beheld sixty years ago'. The spectre of Haiti and an enslaved uprising, for Kingsley, were to be more dreaded than the most violent civil war.[57]

Kingsley's encouragement of the South was also born out of his strident anti-Americanism and avowed belief in Teutonic white supremacy. Like many elite Britons, Kingsley considered Southerners to be white, genteel, quasi-English aristocrats compared to the "melting pot" of "Yankees" in the north. For him, races were endowed with specific characteristics that were expressed over time in a nation's history and character. If whites were members of the 'family of Teutonic races', the opposite was true for 'negros', 'Turks', and 'Celts' (the latter of whom he derided as 'human chimpanzees'). Far from oppose the Civil War, Kingsley wrote to a friend in 1862 that it 'will be a gain to us, that the rapacity and insolence of these men [Americans] must be sternly checked'. Britons' arrogance attitude toward the United States, it appears, had not abated since the Declaration of Independence. Writing to his brother, Henry, that year, Kingsley went further, arguing that the war was 'a blessing for the whole world by breaking up an insolent and aggressive republic of rogues, and a blessing to the poor niggers, because the South once seceded, will be amenable to the public opinion of England, and also will, from very fear, be forced to treat its niggers better'. The South, for Kingsley, was an avenging force of white "Anglo-Saxons" struggling against a combustible, multicultural coalition of Irish Americans, German Americans, and African Americans – many of whom, he surmised, 'know not why' they fought. Kingsley was obsessed with "nobility" (a term that he used for any cause or person which he deemed respectable), and his romanticisation of the agrarian, aristocratic, "noble" South, and its struggle against the industrial, polyglot might of the North permeated his writings.[58]

The apotheosis of Kingsley's pro-Southern beliefs were his Cambridge lecture series. The first series were titled the *Roman and the Teuton*. Published in 1864, these lectures on the decline of Rome and its lessons for the present were delivered at the university four years prior in Michaelmas 1860. The lectures compared Roman with American slavery, arguing that the former was 'not to be described by the pen of an Englishmen', and that it filled him with 'sorrow' for people who compared them with 'Southern slaveholders'. 'God forbid!',

Kingsley denounced, 'Whatsoever may have been the sins of a Southern gentleman, he is at least a Teuton, and not a Roman'. As for the fall of the Goths, who had conquered the Romans, Kingsley ascribed their decline from greatness to the weaknesses inherent to slavery: they had no 'middle class' and found themselves 'a small army of gentlemen, chivalrous and valiant, as slaveholders of our race have always been; but lessening day by day from battle and disease' and the replacement of their numbers with 'helpless, unarmed, degraded' enslaved persons who 'must eat though their masters starve'. He blamed the empire's collapse on the enslaved, who had weakened the economy, culture, and society of their white masters whilst providing limited military support in return.[59]

Following these lectures, Kingsley's well-attended courses on the United States and the "Limits and Exact Science applied to History" addressed contemporaneous events. To Kingsley, the 'American question' was imperative – he considered it impossible to 'be a Professor of past Modern History without the most careful study of the history which is enacting itself around me' – a war that, he thought, 'will be a gain to us [Britain]'. Addressing a captive audience of 100 undergraduates, he discussed the 'future of that unique country'. The observer hoped that Kingsley would stem the tide of British pro-Southern opinion. However, according to Kingsley, the 'North herself ought to have broken up the Union in 1850, at the passage of the Fugitive Slave Law'. The South was not the aggressor. Rather, he claimed that 'any resistance, any [Union] effort even to recover the lost ground [in the South], was positively wrong' and that the South therefore had a 'moral right' to secede, and 'the whole guilt of the struggle rested upon the North'. 'Even for the interests of the negro himself', he claimed, 'it was better to yield, as there was at least a chance of rescuing some of the Territories from slavery by peaceful emigration, while the country and humanity would alike have been spared all these torrents of blood!'[60]

The lectures condemned abolitionists for 'going headlong into war' – a conflict that was 'a worse evil than all the slavery which ever existed since the world began'. Pleading for the 'fair judgment' and 'impartial hearing, on behalf of the slaveholders in the South', Kingsley concluded that 'the applause of the world was ready for the Confederates, if they would commence the work of emancipation. They had already taken a step in the right direction, by solemnly prohibiting the reopening of the slave-trade at the very commencement of their political existence!' The United States was not, in his eyes, destined to be one nation, but rather four 'great empires' of which the 'Southern Confederacy' was one. The students greeted these controversial arguments with rapturous applause. They 'cheered every word' in favour of the Confederacy and another observer wrote that 'Man after man comes here [from Eton] delighted with Kingsley'. Frances Kingsley, his wife, recollected that as the lectures concluded, the class erupted into cheers and the Professor 'almost sobbed as he sat down amidst the storm [of applause]'.[61]

Kingsley further publicised these pro-Confederate comments. Amidst an economic depression in Britain, the Regius Professor took a stand against the cotton barons who blamed the Civil War for the crisis of overproduction, as industrialists imported more cotton in the boom years than could be sold. By the beginning of the conflict, 77 per cent of cotton consumed in the United Kingdom had been shipped from the United States, including the Confederate ports of New Orleans and Charleston. With Union ships blockading the South, six per cent of British cotton factories had closed after a year of war. Kingsley, a Christian socialist who argued that capitalism was the root of much vice, blamed industrialists for the crisis. These 'very Lancashire men', he claimed in a letter to *The Times*'s editor, 'have directly helped to cause the present distress and the present war, by their determination to use exclusively slave-grown cotton; developing thereby, alike slavery itself, and the political power of the slave owners'. Even as he cautioned his students to sympathise with Confederate slaveholders, he recognised that Britain had become a pawn of the "slave power" through its reliance on enslaved-produced cotton. Utilising his contacts, Kingsley also implored a Manchester millowner to stop concealing 'the broad fact, that the present distress came not merely from the American war, but from the overproduction of the last few years, and must have happened, more or less, in any case'. These issues, he noted, were akin to the crimes that the industry had inflicted on the white working family. As children earned wages 'too nearly equal' to their parents, they were encouraged to become 'independent' – another sign that 'mill-labour effeminates the men' through making them profligate in their spending (or so he speculated). In contrast to the drudgery of industry, Kingsley wanted all men to 'emigrate… because the life of a colonist would, by calling out the whole man, raise them in body and mind enormously'. To him, the muscular Christian colonist was a model for British men.[62]

Kingsley's interest in the Americas did not end following his lectures. In 1865, Paul Bogle, an activist and preacher, arrived in front of a Morant Bay courthouse, with hundreds of fellow Jamaicans at his back protesting poverty, racism, and injustice – the legacies of enslavement. Without warning, the volunteer milita fired into the crowd, killing seven and triggering a revolt against white rule. The Governor Edward John Eyre declared martial law, resulting in the murder of 400 Jamaicans and the arrest of 300 others on trumped-up charges, including Bogle (who was later executed). For the prosecution, the philosopher John Stuart Mill and other Britons denounced Eyre and established a Jamaica Committee to investigate his crimes and call for his prosecution. For the defense, Kingsley and John Ruskin, a polymath who gave the inaugural lecture at the Cambridge School of Art (now Anglia Ruskin University) and philanthropist who provided twenty-five Turner portraits to the Fitzwilliam Museum, sided with the former governor and supported Thomas Carlyle's Eyre Defence Fund. Sir Roderick Impey Murchison, too, sent a letter to *The*

Times, denouncing the prosecution (or persecution, as he saw it) of Eyre, a 'distinguished friend'. Murchison, an eminent geologist and founder of the Murchison chair at Edinburgh University, was the nephew and legatee of William McKenzie of Saint Vincent, who owned the plantation "Tourama" with 385 enslaved workers. He inherited around £4,000 from the will after significant litigation.[63]

The continued support at Cambridge for the planters may appear strange given the abolitionist context, but it bears remembering that plantation regimes were expanding across the British Empire. Few men illustrate the empire's ebullition in coerced labour better than the anthropologist Henry Ling Roth, whose name adorns a research fund at the Cambridge School of Anthropology. Roth was well-travelled, having worked for six months in his youth on sugar plantations in British Guiana, at the heart of an immigrant indenture-based economy that one former justice of the colony, Joseph Beaumont, labelled 'a new slavery' – a 'monstrous, rotten system, rooted upon slavery, grown in its stale soil, emulating its worst abuses'. The fellow George Holmes Blakesley of King's, alongside Beaumont and the Anti-Slavery Society, soon met to debate measures to end the 'dangerous probability of a revival of the worst features of slavery, under the cloak of free and untrammelled industry'. Even a century after abolition, labourers recognised that indentureship was 'a form of forced labour'. Plantation labourers remembered that they had 'to run with the cane like a thief in the night'. One declared that he had seen people drop dead from 'exhaustion', and another labourer argued that the 'Estate Authorities like to have illiterate children to be stooges all the time, and to press them into doing what they want them to do'. Labourers, working for white elites (including Cambridge graduates), understood the means and ends of this coercive system: 'If you live on the estate', commented one man, 'you have to serve the estate and suit the Management. If they order you and say you should go about, you have to do it'. Racial enslavement had been reconstituted through indentureship, with workers trapped in cycles of abuse and economic exploitation.[64]

Following his experience in one coerced labour regime, Roth journeyed to other coerced labour economies. First, he travelled to the Russian Empire, where he observed the 'demoralising influence' of the emancipation of the serfs on the banking and landowning classes. By 1878, Roth had settled in Mackay, Queensland – one of Australia's most productive sugar-growing regions, which was worked in large measure by South Sea islanders, who were denigrated as "Kanakas." Around 63,000 labourers were brought to Australia between 1868 and 1906 in conditions that resembled enslavement, with exploitative traders kidnapping or tricking islanders to board vessels bound for the Australian plantations. There, the labourers were treated more akin to 'prison gangs' than 'free workers', with an average daily yield at one mill of forty tonnes. White racialized violence was common – and the newspapers acted as cheerleaders, stirring fears that the labourers had a crime rate more than two times the white population (with newspapermen dubbing Mackay a 'Murder Metropolis'). Roth, who English investors had contracted to investigate the industry, published a much-publicised report on sugar in 1880, and two papers on the climate in Mackay and the roots of the sugar cane. Living on Foulden plantation, Roth was an active member of the Mackay Planters and Farmers Association and defended the civilising potential of the region's coerced labour system. In a letter to the *Pall Mall Gazette*, Roth attacked a British author who had denounced whites for transforming the South Seas from a 'paradise' into a 'pandemonium'. Roth claimed that death rates amongst labourers were equal to whites, they had access to hospitals for medical care and could claim redress for injuries in courts, and the 'savage life' was no 'paradise' – in fact, the planters had 'saved' their workers from 'disgusting customs – infanticide, orgies, and other abominations unknown to the cultured nations'. Brought to Queensland to 'labor for the general welfare of the civilised world', he defended the planters' reprisals because the labourers' 'vile island habits are not tolerated on the plantations'. Roth, whose son, George Kingsley, became a Fijian colonial administrator, was proof that the plantation system had not regressed after emancipation.[65]

In Cambridge, Kingsley worked with a wealthy descendent of slave-traders to fund an American history professorship. Henry Yates Thompson, a Trinity undergraduate at the start of the Civil War, was the son of Samuel Henry Thompson, a millionaire Liverpool financier, and Elizabeth Yates, the eldest daughter of Joseph Brooks Yates, a Jamaican plantation owner, trader in enslaved persons, and merchant. Samuel Thompson was a long-term partner in Heywood & Co. (a predecessor of Barclays), a firm 'experienced in the African trade'. Frustrated with 'the general ignorance of America among Englishmen', Thompson, who lectured in England on the Civil War and was a fervent abolitionist, offered an endowment of $6,000 in American bonds to fund the post in October 1865, with the interest funding a lecturer every two years. (Supporting, in essence, a forerunner to the current Pitt Professor of American History and Institutions.) His plan to 'improve Anglo-American understanding' did not fail – on a vote of 110 to 82 – because of Thompson's economic connections, but in part because of Cambridge arrogance, with one fellow commenting that to accept Thompson's fortune would 'cast a slur upon our selves, and pander to that which is perhaps the worst vice inherent in the North-American character – namely – self-conceit'.[66]

Cambridge was still willing decades after this incident to beg for Thompson's earned and inherited riches, however. In 1907, Ernest Stewart Roberts, the Vice-Chancellor, made another offer to Thompson, which he politely refused, instead donating to Harrow and providing funding and manuscripts to Newnham College's library (Cambridge's first women's college), which was named in his honour. His donation was another example of Cambridge's financial connections to enslavement, as women's colleges earned money from both abolitionists and individuals with familial connections to slaveholding. The reformist Emily Davies, who founded Girton College in 1869, opposed slave-grown cotton but had some doubts as to whether rights could be seized by force. On enslavement, she commented to one interlocutor that Black 'freedom should be restored by the people who have stolen it' (namely the enslaver class) rather than 'extorted' via an 'insurrection of the slaves'. On the other hand, Jane Catherine Gamble, whose bequest funded buildings, land purchases, and helped discharge Girton's debts, was excluded from her father's significant fortune in Floridian plantations (which she blamed on her stepmother), but she gained properties, $50,000 in Virginia state bonds, and twenty-six shares in the slavery-linked Upper Appomattox Canal Company thanks to her maternal uncle and aunt, Nancy and James Dunlop.[67]

Aside from Kingsley and Davies, there were other Cambridge men and women who dwelled on the causes and consequences of the American Civil War. Over the course of 1863, John Jermyn Cowell, a Trinity graduate, and member of the Cambridge Apostles debating society, tried to convince Henry Sidgwick, the Knightbridge Professor of Moral Philosophy, co-founder of Newnham College, and member of the Apostles debating society, to side with the Confederate States. (Cowell was also a benefactor to the Southern Prisoners' Relief Fund, which aimed to publicise the conditions of Confederate prisoners.) Writing from the Royal Hotel in Kent on 15 September 1863, Cowell reflected 'on our difference of view as to the invasion and devastation of the Southern States'. Labelling the Civil War as a 'war of invasion', Cowell challenged Sidgwick's assumptions: first, that the rebel states were not sovereign and therefore unable to secede and, second, that it was 'Moral to Make War upon a People because it will not abolish slavery'. Cowell refuted the sovereignty question using the American Constitution, but he spent more time pondering the problem of slavery. Cowell, like Kingsley, argued that slavery 'injures the general prosperity of both masters & slaves, and of all communities related to them'. Nevertheless, a 'sudden liberation', he continued, 'demoralizes the slaves, who are unaccustomed to independent action, and their industry comes to an end'. Denouncing Lincoln, he argued that a 'sudden military emancipation' would result in untold misery for the white population, whereas the policy of Brazil in 'improving the condition of her slaves, and paving the way for emancipation 50 years hence' was preferable. Sidgwick's answer to this letter does not exist; still, the philosopher's biographer, Bart Schulz, argues that Cowell had 'softened' Sidgwick's position toward the South's right to secede from the Union (despite the Cambridge professor applauding the 'triumph of the Federal Cause' in a later letter to his mother). Jermyn Cowell lived to witness the fall of Richmond and the Confederacy's defeat, passing away two years later in 1867.[68]

Determined to make a stand against the Cambridge pro-Confederates, the Harvard and Trinity College graduate William Everett, the son of the American diplomat and former Secretary of State, Edward Everett, promoted the Union's cause and denounced the aristocratic students who supported the South. Reflecting on this divisive period, Everett's friends mentioned that his 'eloquence' was often 'fired by his patriotism' as when he gave an 'extemporised panegyric' about George Washington in the College Chapel. Standing before the Cambridge Union as its President, in the middle of a speech defending the Union in the Civil War, Everett also dramatically 'flung open his overcoat, and displayed a tie flaming with the stars and stripes'. Following University, Everett returned to Harvard and completed his law degree at the end of the Civil War in 1865, later taking up a teaching position there in 1870. Upon his return to the US, Everett lectured about his Cambridge experiences, titled *On the Cam*. Published whilst completing his legal training, the twelfth lecture elaborated on the "Relations of Cambridge, England, to America."[69]

Everett betrayed his frustration at how Americans were viewed in Cambridge, arguing that the 'question of slavery makes very little difference'. English elites, he complained, 'prefer the South' because enslavers 'are country gentlemen, with some notion of aristocracy and the predominance of the landed interest'. The real friends of America, according to Everett, were not the 'governing class' who he thought dominated Cambridge, but rather the manufacturing and literary classes. As it turned out, Everett had similar hopes for white domination as his Southern counterparts. As his lectures concluded, Everett hoped – echoing Kingsley's call for a Teutonic race – for the 'whole English race', including America and Britain, to unite in a special relationship.[70]

Outside the University's limits, prominent Cambridge alumni lobbied for the Confederacy as it desperately struggled to achieve diplomatic recognition in Europe. John Jermyn's father, John Welsford Cowell, was one such figure. The son of a London merchant and a former trustee for Jamaican plantation owners, Cowell matriculated at Trinity as a pensioner in 1814, graduating four years later. After his studies, Cowell was a founding member of the Political Economy Club, which supported free trade (and included supporters of the Caribbean enslaver class), and joined the Bank of England, successively working in its Bristol and Gloucester branches before travelling to the US in 1837 to manage the Bank's assets after numerous American financial firms collapsed in the wake of that year's speculative panics. There he met with John C. Calhoun, the former Vice President, ardent sectionalist, and slaveholder. After meeting Calhoun, who argued that slavery was a 'positive good' – a means of self-improvement for enslaved African Americans – Cowell became an ardent public supporter of the 'Cotton States'. As he later wrote, the 'communications of that eminent Statesman' had helped him 'understand how, in the fullness of time, their secession was an unavoidable necessity which nothing on earth could possibly prevent'.[71]

The involvement of bankers and financiers in arguing for the Confederate cause, it should be noted, was not unusual. Sir David Salomons, the Alderman of London and Parliamentarian who invested much of his political capital into supporting Jewish emancipation, was a supporter of the Confederacy whilst in Parliament and donated to a fund established to build a monument to the Confederate General "Stonewall" Jackson, who had become famed for his stone-walled resistance to a Union charge at the First Battle of Bull-Run (the first engagement of the conflict) but had then, two years later, become a victim to friendly fire on 10 May 1863.[72]

The bank that Salomons had helped to found, London and Westminster (a forerunner of NatWest), helped to finance Britain's imperial interests. On 22 October 1857, at the height of India's rebellion against British rule, the firm loaned half a million pounds to the ruling EIC for two years at ten per cent of the security of East India bonds, adding to a substantial investment that the bank held in East Indian Railway bonds. (Cambridge colleges continued to hold similar securities, with Benjamin Hall Kennedy's 1865 benefaction for the establishment of the Kennedy Professorship of Latin partly funded with £3,745 in East India bonds, and Trinity Hall owning £2,296 in India securities to fund building works and a repair fund.) Salomons was so involved in the Bank at this time that his non-attendance at a shareholder meeting in 1867 had to be explained. The East India loan was controversial amongst some careful bank investors, with one asking the board, 'on what principle so large an amount of money had been lent to the East India Company at a time when it looked as if India must fall from our grasp?' Fortunately for the Bank, the independence struggle failed, with estimates of Indian deaths in the conflict perhaps numbering 800,000. Salomons bequeathed his money and baronetcy to his nephew, David Lionel Salomons, who endowed the Salomons' Lectureship in Russian at Cambridge and generously provided £5,000 to his alma mater, Caius, for a new building site, £5,000 for construction purposes, and an engineering scholarship.[73]

As for Cowell, he continued with the Bank for two years, before turning his attention to financial activities in another hemisphere: New Zealand. Like many enterprising Britons who helped to establish the Canterbury Association in 1848 (which intended to establish a colony), Cowell facilitated colonisation efforts there. Directed by Earl Grey to assist in resolving disputed land transactions with the Māori, Cowell corresponded with William Wakefield, the New Zealand Company's principal agent in Wellington. Whilst involved in these affairs from afar, Cowell participated in a land purchase in Otago from the Māori, and he ensured that the Company had 'full and correct statistical information' on colonial settlements in Wellington, New Plymouth, and Nelson.[74]

Following his retirement and the outbreak of the Civil War, Cowell grew in stature from a retired civil servant to a Confederate lobbyist. Funded by Confederate agents, Cowell wrote three tracts in four years in support of the South: *Southern Secession* (1862), *Lancashire's Wrongs and Remedy* (1863), and *France and the Confederate States* (1865). The three pamphlets argued that the South did not secede because of slavery – the South had seceded, Cowell maintained, because the North's protectionist policies (namely tariffs) had damaged the plantation economy and helped to precipitate the war. He argued that what Britons knew about slavery 'is supplied to us by your Northern enemies, selected and distorted for the very object of fomenting our aversion to it, and to you [addressing Southerners], as slave-owners'. On slavery, he claimed that the best chance for the 'gradual elevation of that unfortune race to a higher degree of humanity' depended on 'your achieving absolute independence in the South'. In Cowell's telling, the North's protectionism meant that the South was waging a just war of self-defence against the Yankees' 'protectionist army' of 'monopolists' who aimed to throw a 'financial yoke' on their fellow-countrymen and women. The South was, in short, fighting a war of independence.[75]

Cowell compared slaveholders to noble aristocrats. The "cavalier myth," popular on both sides of the Atlantic, maintained that Virginia's aristocratic slaveholders were descended from old English gentlemanly stock who had left England following the execution of Charles I. That myth, which remained influential in the South before, during, and after the Civil War, featured in all of Cowell's writings. Striking fear into his readers with images of an impending race war, the former banker criticised the North for arming the 'black peasantry' to participate in a conflict 'so nefarious, so horrible, that history affords nowhere any parallel to its atrocity'. Cowell juxtaposed that image of Black-imposed terror with the noble, English gentility of the "plantocracy." He asked his readers in his earliest pamphlet, *Southern Secession*: 'What natural connection have you with New England, New York, and Pennsylvania'. Despite the English having colonised New England and Pennsylvania, the first state by the Puritans and the latter by William Penn and the Society of Friends, Cowell described Virginians and Carolinians as 'your proper fellow-countrymen' and he hoped that Englishmen and southern slavers would 'mutually acknowledge each other as such'. Contrasting the "Yankees," whom he denounced (like Kingsley) as an amalgamation of ethnicities, he argued in his writings that the 'noble English spirit' lived on in the South and the 'Cotton Operatives' had raised themselves to a greater degree of 'material comfort, social respectability, and morality' than any class before. These writings reveal the extent to which former enslavers, such as Cowell, had again become active participants in the defense of enslavement decades after emancipation had taken place in the British Caribbean.[76]

The pro-southern partisan Alexander Beresford-Hope, the MP for Maidstone and then Stoke-upon-Trent, had Cambridge roots too. Beresford-Hope was born into a family that had earned a fortune from finance, which included providing loans to plantation owners in St. Croix, St. Thomas, and St. John in the Danish Caribbean colonies. In time, the Harrow and Trinity alumnus eagerly enlisted his pen – which up till that point had been busy writing on subjects ranging from English Cathedrals to paganism to the Latin language – in service to the Confederate cause. His 1861 work, *A Popular View of the American Civil War*, observed that Southerners should not be blamed for the institution of slavery because Americans had 'inherited' that system from their British forbears. Beresford supported his words with actions: he was an active servant for Confederate causes in Britain, providing lectures, lobbying for the South in Parliament, serving on the committee of the Southern Independence Association of London, and he donated £20 to the Jackson Monumental Fund. In 1868, the university elected Beresford-Hope as one of the two men to represent the University of Cambridge constituency – and he joined a distinguished list of representatives for that seat with economic connections to the plantation system, including Henry Goulburn, William John Bankes (1822–1826), and Sir Nicholas Conyngham Tindal (1827–1829).[77]

Beresford-Hope's talents were in pamphleteering, though. Contrary to the more critical view of slavery contained in Harriet Beecher Stowe's bestselling *Uncle Tom's Cabin*, Beresford-Hope followed Kingsley, Cowell, and others in claiming that the 'ultra-abolitionists' exaggerated the cruelties of enslavement. Beresford-Hope argued that 'the best of the slaveowners make its chains as light as possible – they educate their blacks, they make them Christians, while in Africa they would have remained untaught and uncivilised'. In contrast, the North had imposed a 'cruel war' and inspired the enslaved 'to massacre and ravish the whites, and devastate the seceding States'. The politician and polemicist argued that the enslaved had remained loyal, however. Parroting the "Black Confederate" myth, the disproven notion that African Americans willingly fought for the Confederacy, he proclaimed that the enslaved 'are actually a right arm of strength to their owner working hard for the very men against whom it was supposed they would be the first to turn their hands'. In a public lecture a year later, Beresford-Hope advocated for a Black colony in South America and argued that enslaved people were unworthy of freedom and equality because they did not have the necessary 'principles of self-dependence' to make their way in the world. Calculated to draw a distinction between the righteous cause of the slaveholders and the Union-supporting abolitionists, Beresford-Hope drew crowds in Britain for his speeches, a reminder that his views were not isolated – whatever William Everett claimed – to British aristocrats.[78]

Henry Hotze, the Swiss-born journalist in charge of the Confederacy's propaganda efforts in Britain, was determined to inspire pro-Southern opinion as well. Born in 1833, Hotze emigrated to the United States and became a naturalised citizen, taking up residence in Mobile, Alabama, in 1855. Hotze's attitudes to race were best expressed in his translation of English Joseph Arthur de Gobineau's tract, *An Essay on the Inequality of the Human Races*, which argued that whites were intellectually and physically superior to African-descended peoples. Hotze was a dedicated supporter of the Confederacy, too, holding a clerkship in Richmond, Virginia, and L. P. Walker, the Confederate Secretary of War, then ordered him to travel to London and acquire much needed funds for Southern agents and munitions for the war effort. It was there that he realised the Confederacy required a European advocate. To that end, on 14 November

1861 Hotze was given the important task of influencing British opinion and, with a mere 750 dollars in his pocket from the Confederacy, he tried to capitalise on British anti-Union sentiment. Attempting to prove that support for the Confederacy did not rest on the continuation of the cotton trade, he paid journalists to write favourable columns in the *Morning Post* (a paper supportive of the then-Prime Minister, Lord Palmerston), the *London Standard*, and the *Herald*. In May 1862, Hotze realised that he needed to target opinion leaders more directly – politicians, business leaders, fellows and professors, and clergymen – so he founded *The Index* newspaper.[79]

Hotze employed educated university men to staff *The Index*. As he commented to Judah P. Benjamin, the Confederate Secretary of State, hundreds of newspaper articles had to be published to influence public opinion, and that task was best left to talented writers. On that topic, he wrote in February 1864 that he was 'now recruiting upon this same principle among the generation of rising university men, who, within the next 10 years, will give the tone to public opinion in this country'. The strategy was effective because of Cambridge's prominence in Britain's political, social, and cultural establishment, and, perhaps, the university's enduring significance to white abolitionists given that it had educated Peckard, Wilberforce, and Clarkson. The tide of the Civil War may have turned (in July 1863, the Union was victorious at Gettysburg, Pennsylvania, and had captured Vicksburg, Mississippi, and, with it, the entire Mississippi River), yet Hotze wrote again to Benjamin from Paris in July 1864 to inform him that he wanted 'the Index [to] take deep and permanent root in the great university bodies of this kingdom, not so much with a view to [the] present as to future results upon the public opinion of which these bodies are, so to speak, the subsoil'. Hoping to discuss and promote his 'university idea', Hotze claimed that his 'object' would 'be realized in the course of this month by intimately identifying with the editorial conduct of the Index two gentlemen who combine with a zealous devotion to our principles and our cause the highest academical distinction, well merited popularity and influence, and a social position as honorable in the present as it is promising for the future'. One of the men that he identified was John George Witt, a King's fellow – proving the integral role of universities to the Confederate cause.[80]

The Swiss-born Confederate sympathiser also attempted to influence members of the British scientific establishment. Founded in 1843 as a subsidiary of the Aborigines' Protection Society, the Ethnological Society of London (ESL) provided a forum to debate the origins and nature of human diversity. The ESL had abolitionist and liberal roots founded on a support for Darwinian monogenism, but the organisation split as the speech therapist Dr James Hunt, a Confederate sympathiser, and others were more supportive of polygenism, or the notion that human beings had multiple sources of origin (a distinction often used to scientifically support theories of Black inferiority). The Anthropological Society of London (ASL) was thus born in 1863, and Hotze accepted Hunt's invitation to join its fourteen-member council. The ASL lasted eight years and promoted a white supremacist approach to racial science. Hunt's paper on the "Negro's Place in Nature" set the Society's tone on race and slavery. He claimed that scientists could not deny that the 'improvement in mind and body, as well as the general happiness [of the Black population], which is seen in those parts of the world in which the Negro is working in his natural subordination to the European'. For Hunt, the Confederacy had the most developed Black population in the world, and there they were 'able to work with impunity, and [the enslaved] does himself and the world generally much good by his labour'. The speech therapist also repeated the disproved notion that Black people were immune to infectious diseases, including yellow fever – a well-entrenched theory that had long been used to justify racial slavery in the southern states.[81]

Hunt was also a prominent member of the Cannibal Club, which met near Leicester Square, close to the ASL's rooms. These men (the inner sanctum of the Society) 'dined in front of a mace, which represented the ebony head of a negro gnawing the ivory thig-bone of a man'. Thomas Bendyshe, a King's fellow, was a member of both that secretive Club and the ASL, and other Cambridge-affiliated men were members of the Society too: Charles Kingsley, the Reverend William Selwyn, Edward J. Routh (a Peterhouse fellow and famed Tripos mathematics coach), William Stephen Mitchell (then a student at Caius College), the Reverend Joseph Bosworth (who provided £10,000 for a professorship of Anglo-Saxon at Cambridge), Thomas George Bonney (a St John's fellow and prominent geologist), and Charles Cardale Babington (Cambridge's chair of botany). Alfred Russell Wallace recognised Bendyshe's talents, and the King's man was an effective publicist for the ASL, publishing an influential translation of Blumenbach's writings (which oversimplified the German's more nuanced ideas on race, introducing the naturalist to English audiences as a supporter of Black racial inferiority), a history of anthropology, and an article on the extinction of races.[82]

Witt, who also appears to have been a member of the ASL's council, devoted an entire chapter of his memoir, *A Life in the Law*, to "America." By America, he meant the South and he commented at length in the book about his relationships with Confederate officials and role with *The Index*. Witt was the crowning jewel in Hotze's appeal for university men. The son of a prosperous Cambridgeshire farmer and barrister, Witt attended Eton as a King's Scholar, becoming Captain of the School, and then matriculated at King's in 1856, winning the Hulsean Prize in 1860, graduated seventh in his class in classics that same year, and held a fellowship for twenty years until 1888. Whilst a student, Witt met Hotze and stated his opinions on the Civil War in a Union debate, arguing that the 'probable separation' of the United States was to be regretted. Witt's unionist instincts appeared to have shifted following southern secession. After graduating and training as a barrister, he entered the Hotze's powerful circle of acquaintances at his home in Savile Row, London: officers, merchants, purchasers of stores and ships, journalists, soldiers, managers of confederate loans, and politicians. Witt operated at the heart of the Confederate world in Britain.[83]

Pocketing £300 per annum, Witt became the *Index*'s associate editor in August 1864. His editorial responsibilities were undefined (and there is little evidence that Witt played a significant role in the newspaper's content), but Hotze looked upon him and the executive editor, J. B. Hopkins, as his 'most trusted & beloved ministers' responsible for spreading the 'highest ideal of that Southern civilization which is as yet only in its infancy'. Witt, as he admitted in the memoir, was a willing collaborator of the 'Southern cause'. (One article he authored was a hagiographic poem dedicated to the Confederate general J. E. B. Stuart.) As for Witt's views on slavery, he condemned the Emancipation Proclamation as an illegal act 'which set the slaves free off-hand without adequate preparation by wise education and just laws'. Furthermore, he quipped that Britons did not understand the problem of enslavement. In Britain, he mused that the issue of slavery was viewed in terms of 'property' – a belief which, he thought, was a mistake born of ignorance. Witt recognised that the Confederates regarded slavery as a social and political question: 'Their creed', he claimed, 'was to have a class without civil or political rights, devoted to labour, and there was the negro ready to hand'. In a slave society, the 'white community consisted [of] the governing class, all white men being deemed equal'; still, there was a 'defined line of demarcation across which no trespassers were to be permitted'. It was this 'creed', Witt noted, that had ultimately resulted in the Civil War. Slavery, he recognised, went to the heart of the Confederacy's society and politics – and he defended such a nation predicated on white supremacy.[84]

Witt's pro-Confederate activities continued after the guns fell silent in the American Civil War. After the fall of Richmond, the Confederate capital, on 2 April 1865 and Lee's surrender at Appomattox Court House seven days later, former rebels fled to England to avoid prosecution. Witt embraced these men. He remained in contact with Henry Hotze, even as the cause of that man's life crumbled (the latter later died in obscurity in a Swiss village). Aside from Hotze, he was on close terms with several Confederates following the conflict, including Slidell, George Eustis, Jr., Colin J. McRae, General Richard Taylor, Jefferson Davis, and Judah Benjamin. Witt's memoirs are filled with anecdotes about these men. He took Eustis and McRae to dinner with him at King's, and along with General Taylor, a former Louisiana slaveholder and Confederate general, he visited Sandringham and played cards with Queen Victoria, the Prince of Wales, and the King of Denmark. Witt remarked that he had 'capital fun' with Taylor, whose 'appearance, apart from his prowess, was bound to win many looks of admiration'. Witt's association with Jefferson Davis was no less important. After Davis's release from prison, he met the former Confederate president, invited him to tour Cambridge, and described him as 'a delightful man of the most simple manners'. Together with Benjamin, he showed Davis around Eton, met the provost, and took both Confederates on a tour of Windsor Castle and Runnymede, the location for the signing of the Magna Carta in 1215 (the liberties of which Witt believed 'are the rich inheritance of our race'). They had a good time all around. 'Now', said Benjamin, 'this is the first time he [Davis] has laughed since the fall of Fort Sumter'.[85]

Judah Benjamin was Witt's most enduring friend from his years serving the Confederacy. Witt recalled that he was the first Englishman to shake Benjamin's hands upon the latter entering the country. They remained firm friends until the Confederate politician's death. Like the other Confederates with whom he socialised, Witt introduced Benjamin to Britain's most illustrious legal figures, including the Lord Chancellor, Lord Halsbury, at the Inner Temple. Through this association, Benjamin became a Queen's Counsel 'and then persuaded the Lord Chancellor to grant him a Patent of Precedence under the Great Seal in the Courts of Westminster'. Witt defended and launched Benjamin's career even as the latter faced a federal indictment in Richmond (which was soon quashed) for waging war against the United States. Witt denounced this political charge, arguing in his memoir that 'we can hardly realise the possibility of the Government of the United States taking umbrage at honour being paid to an American citizen'. Respected for generations in the South as a leader of the Confederate cause, Benjamin died in Paris in 1884. On his deathbed, the old Confederate knew that he owed much of the security and success that he had attained following the war to his friend and one of his chosen executors – a Cambridge don.[86]

As British slavery ended in North America and a new era of indentureship began in the Caribbean, Cambridge students and academics remained attentive to the problem of American slavery. Aside from the permanence of racial attitudes, Cambridge's debates surrounding American slavery again reveal the essential role of British fellows as agents of empire. Although Alexander Crummell and Edward Strutt Abdy attacked the basis of African American enslavement, with Crummell in particular pushing for colonisation in West Africa, John George Witt and other prominent Cambridge figures were actively courted by Confederate sympathisers and used their culturally and intellectually respectable positions to become significant agents of white civilisation and empire in the nineteenth century. Cambridge men, as shown in Charles Kingsley's case, were true believers, too, in a southern empire predicated on white supremacy, and were willing promoters in spreading this message both to students and British society, providing Britons with lectures, novels, and pamphlets that sought to transform the image of the American South in the British mind. Slavery's permanence and pre-eminence in British intellectual life – and the continuing role of academics in these practices – would ensure that its accompanying racial mentalities would survive and thrive well into the twentieth century.

Conclusion

Torn, smudged, and stained with the passage of time, a county ball notice stands as testament to Cambridge's many entanglements with the age of Atlantic slavery. The Tharp family of Jamaica's papers contain a notice of a ball held at the Town Hall on 20 November 1833, around three months after the passage of the Slavery Abolition Act. The dancing commenced at half-past nine with Weippert's Band in attendance, and both town and gown would have been excited. (The Tharps were prominent in both the county and university since John and his son Joseph had attended Trinity College as fellow-commoners and had been Justices of Peace.) George Weippart's Band was a significant drawcard: they had recently performed for the February birthday celebrations of Prince Adolphus, the Duke of Cambridge, in St George's Hall at Windsor Castle, with 250 distinguished guests and numerous gentlemen in attendance from Eton College. Turn the invitation over, and one is confronted with a rather different world to quadrilles, punch, and town festivities. An unknown individual had pencilled on the back a 'list of the Tharp Estates & number of Negroes in 1817': Covey with 451 enslaved, Goodhope with 448, Lansquinet with 400, Merrywood with 218, Pontrepant with 358, Potosi with 306, Wales with 355, Chippenham Park Pen with 133, Top Hill Pen with 67, and Windsor Pen with 214 – in total, 2,950 people were enslaved on these estates. (Due to the Slave Registry Bill of 1815, Parliament required slavers to construct an accurate record of their labourers' names, skin colour, and whether they were African or creole.) Ink from the invitation had bled into the plantation inventory, providing a striking visual of how intrinsic enslavement had been to Cambridge social and cultural life.[1]

Almost 200 years have passed since abolition, and the pressure has grown for Britons to "turn the page" and recognise their entanglements with their own nation's slave empire. On the university's bicentenary celebration of the abolition of the transatlantic trade in enslaved Africans, held at St John's College (which had memorialised Wilberforce in 1887), Cambridge engaged in a weekend of festivities that involved Professor Ruth Simmons, the President of Brown University, who had initiated an investigation into that college's ties to enslavement in Rhode Island. Professor Simmons made a fascinating admission: 'You know', she commented, 'I am very intrigued by the fact that you can hold this celebration here. Right now in the United States I don't think it would be possible to celebrate the end of slavery on a national basis, even today'. In 2021, President Biden made Juneteenth, which commemorates the enforcement of the Emancipation Proclamation in the state of Texas, a federal holiday, but Britons continue to find it difficult to discuss enslavement. Abolitionism remains a powerful nationalistic rallying-cry for Britons who are, with some justification, proud that their ancestors were the second European nation to abolish the slave trade after Denmark in 1803 (the Danish no longer believing it economically expedient to defend that coercive trade). Cambridge has taken centre stage in that larger national narrative because it educated Clarkson and Wilberforce; still, public and historical discussions of that institution's many interconnections with enslavement and abolition are concentrated on the lives of two men. A more complicated and accurate recounting of Cambridge and, by extension, Britain's, imperial past would recognise the varieties of connections that many Britons had to enslavement and empire, rather than focus on the few who left vast record collections or the most prominent abolitionists whose ideas and ideals obviously inspire much more sympathy in modern times.[2]

The antidote to such monochrome histories or national memories is a consideration of Britain's involvement in and opposition to enslavement, particularly in spaces where African slavery was thought not to reach. These historical efforts in Britain are flourishing, and attention has been paid to the interconnections between Britain's major cities and industrial centers – whether Bristol, London, Liverpool, and Manchester – that depended upon the goods that were grown and produced by enslaved labourers to function. Yet that discussion remains, with some notable exceptions, focused on major metropolitan centres and port cities where those linkages are more self-evident than in rural spaces or market towns that were often established along arterial canals and rivers. The story of Cambridge, then, builds upon work on the history and legacies of enslavement and empire in provincial England, Scotland, and Wales (not to mention the interior of continental Europe). More local and regional histories could, in turn, provide insights into the global pervasiveness of slave-begotten wealth and, therefore, the preconditions for insurgent resistance to these oppressive systems. Britain's prominent position as a slave empire and its abolitionism are, in the public mind at least, presented as opposites when, in fact, antislavery activists acknowledged Britain's longstanding debt to enslavement and the prominence of wealth that was earned from colonial activities. One Cambridge man, as we have seen, agreed with other antislavery activists that England had become "enslaved" to its colonies. Historians have stressed that opposition to enslavement was grounded in concerns for the empire following the American Revolution, and abolition, it appears, was also forged through more local and regional contests around the nature and origins of wealth in Britain.

A full accounting of Britain's participation in and connections to Atlantic enslavement requires an investigation, too, of the involvement of institutional actors, including universities, in the processes of empire-building. Institutions and institutional actors received donations and proactively promulgated and defended systems of coerced labour, colonisation, and enslavement. Institutional studies, whether universities, museums, charities, or other cultural organisations, have focused on significant donors. That emphasis makes a great deal of sense; nevertheless, that focus is incomplete as Cambridge and other academic institutions highlight the more subtle social, intellectual, and cultural connections and partnerships that were (and remain) the lifeblood of colonial activities. The narrative here ends in the nineteenth century, with emancipation in North America and the Caribbean, yet the multitude of political, intellectual, and economic connections between middling and elite Britons and coerced labour systems provides a potential model for histories that examine both enslavement and the post-emancipation world in the late nineteenth and twentieth centuries. If institutions and nations, particularly former empires, are reticent to examine their past relationships to slavery, then the same is true of the era after emancipation, which saw renewed connections between Britons and the plantation economy in the Caribbean, East Africa, and the Pacific. To address that complicated past, historians and the public must again examine the involvement of institutions in defending, propagating, and opposing systems of coerced labour, racism, and inequality.[3]

Universities have an important contribution to make in that discussion of systemic racism, coerced labour, and enslavement. As spaces where sometimes-disparate actors from throughout the nation and empire interacted and mediated, universities were combustible melting pots for individuals from multiple social, political, and economic backgrounds. These institutions, therefore, reflected and resisted the currents in wider British society, providing a focal lens on the interconnections between Britain and its empire. The history of the university undermines artificial historiographical boundaries between "direct" and "indirect" connections to enslavement. Contemporaries would have recognised no explicit division between the women and men who invested in and propagated the Atlantic slave economy, and metropolitan Britons who bought and sold goods that enslaved Africans had grown, picked, trucked, bartered, and made for European production and consumption. If such distinctions are removed, then one's vision is turned to the vibrant spectrum of experiences and interactions that many Britons and Europeans had to the slave system, from exchange alley to dining rooms to museum collections to court rooms to coffeehouse debates to political groups. Historians have reconceptualised the British Empire as a slave imperium, that is an empire that was predicated on the profits from enslavement and then used civilising language and antislavery action as spearheads to inspire further imperial conquests in West Africa. This book has built upon that political economic viewpoint with a renewed emphasis on the social, cultural, and intellectual relations that Britons had to the slaving enterprise. That holistic perspective is necessary to form a more complete picture of the history and legacies of a global empire that shaped, and continues to shape, the modern world and the role of Britons, whether great or small, in making and unmaking that world.

APPENDIX A: CAMBRIDGE FAMILIES AND THE TRANSATLANTIC ECONOMY

The opening paragraphs in the first chapter discuss the prospographical methodology used to analyse the students who were admitted to the University of Cambridge from families with a wide variety of connections to and involvement in the transatlantic economy. The four tables below illustrate the findings on student birthplaces, familial involvement in that economic system, and the various colleges that these undergraduates attended. The sample has omitted South Sea and Royal African investors to focus on families who shaped these activities on the ground.

Table 1 illustrates the variety of overseas (outside of mainland Britain) and local locations from which 847 Cambridge students originated. The data is remarkably consistent with other studies in suggesting the significance of Barbados, Jamaica, London, and Liverpool to the emergence of a class who were actively engaged in the Atlantic economy.

Table 1 *Student Birthplaces*

Location	Number of Students	Location	Number of Students
Overseas Locations		**British Locations**	
Antigua	46	Bedfordshire	3
Bahamas	4	Berkshire	4
Barbados	140	Buckinghamshire	2
Bermuda	14	Isle of Bute	1
British Guiana	9	Cambridgeshire	5
Demerara	1	Cheshire	7
Dominica	5	Cornwall	1
Jamaica	113	Cumberland	3
Montserrat	10	Denbighshire	8
St Kitts	12	Derbyshire	2
St Lucia	1	Devonshire	5

Table 1 (cont.)

Location	Number of Students	Location	Number of Students
St Nevis	6	Dorset	1
St Vincent	3	Essex	8
Trinidad and Tobago	4	Edinburghshire	5
Virgin Islands	3	Fife	1
Connecticut	1	Flintshire	2
Virginia	33	Hampshire	3
Maryland	6	Hertfordshire	9
Massachusetts	3	Huntingdonshire	1
New York	9	Isle of Wight	1
Pennsylvania	2	Kent	6
Rhode Island	1	Kirkcudbrightshire	1
South Carolina	17	Lanarkshire	3
France	1	Lancashire	76
Ireland	12	Lincolnshire	2
Total	456	Middlesex	132
		Northamptonshire	7
		Northumberland	1
		Nottinghamshire	4
		Rutland	2
		Somerset	20
		Staffordshire	2
		Stirlingshire	1
		Suffolk	12
		Surrey	7
		Sussex	9
		Warwickshire	1
		Westmorland	1
		Wiltshire	2
		Worcestershire	1
		Yorkshire	20
		Total	391

In discussing student numbers at academic institutions, there is a tendency to either focus on plantation owners or merchants in the transatlantic trade in enslaved Africans. However, individuals and families were often both slave-traders and plantation owners or bankers and merchants involved in the carrying trade of goods to North America and the Caribbean. Table 2, which utilises data from the *Legacies of Slave-Ownership* database and other primary and secondary sources, accounts for the varieties of engagement in enslavement for 850 students and their families.

Cambridge reflected the hierarchical nature of wider British society. For 832 students in the sample, their college rank has been recorded, particularly if they changed statuses multiple times whilst at the University (Table 3).

Table 4 lists in alphabetical order the colleges that students attended. The numbers, which are double-counted, account for the fact that undergraduates often attended multiple institutions whilst at Cambridge.

Table 2 *Familial Involvement in the Atlantic Economy*

Occupation	Number of Students
Planter	629
Planter and Merchant	47
Banker and Planter	12
Planter and Slave-Trader	17
Banker	26
Banker and Merchant	7
Banker and Slave-Trader	2
Merchant	52
Merchant and Slave-Trader	10
Slave-Trader	44
Cotton Manufacturer	4

Table 3 *Student College Ranks*

Rank	Number of Students
Nobleman	8
Sizar	27
Sizar then Pensioner then Fellow-Commoner	1
Pensioner	571
Pensioner then Scholar	2
Pensioner then Fellow-Commoner	14
Pensioner then Nobleman	1
Fellow-Commoner	203
Scholar	5

Table 4 *Colleges Attended*

Colleges	Number of Students
Christ's	40
Clare	31
Corpus Christi	14
Downing	3
Emmanuel	29
Gonville and Caius	33
Jesus	19
King's	3
Magdalene	14
Pembroke	35
Peterhouse	35
Queens'	35
Sidney Sussex	12
St Catharine's	12
St John's	160
Trinity	329
Trinity Hall	53

NOTES

Introduction

1. For British slavery and abolition, see Eric Williams, *Capitalism and Slavery* (Chapel Hill: University of North Carolina Press, 1944); David Brion Davis, *The Problem of Slavery in the Age of Revolution, 1770–1823* (Ithaca, NY: Cornell University Press, 1975); John R. Oldfield, *Popular Politics and British Anti-Slavery: The Mobilisation of Public Opinion against the Slave Trade, 1787–1807* (Manchester: Manchester University Press, 1995); Philip Gould, *Barbaric Traffic: Commerce and Antislavery in the Eighteenth-Century Atlantic World* (Cambridge, MA: Harvard University Press, 2003); Christopher Leslie Brown, *Moral Capital: Foundations of British Abolitionism* (Chapel Hill: University of North Carolina Press, 2006); Gelien Matthews, *Caribbean Slave Revolts and the British Abolitionist Movement* (Baton Rouge: Louisiana State University Press, 2006); Seymour Drescher, *Abolition: A History of Slavery and Antislavery* (Cambridge: Cambridge University Press, 2009); Srividhya Swaminathan, *Debating the Slave Trade: Rhetoric of British National Identity, 1759–1815* (Abingdon: Routledge, 2009); Nicholas Draper, *The Price of Emancipation: Slave-Ownership, Compensation, and British Society at the End of Slavery* (Cambridge: Cambridge University Press, 2010); Nicholas Draper et al., eds., *Legacies of British Slave-Ownership: Colonial Slavery and the Formation of Victorian Britain* (Cambridge: Cambridge University Press, 2016); Andrea Major, *Slavery, Abolition, and Empire in India, 1772–1843* (Liverpool: Liverpool University Press, 2012); Richard Huzzey, *Freedom Burning: Anti-Slavery and Empire in Victorian Britain* (Ithaca, NY: Cornell University Press, 2012); Bronwen Everill, *Abolition and Empire in Sierra Leone and Liberia* (New York: Palgrave Macmillan, 2013); Bronwen Everill, *Not Made by Slaves: Ethical Capitalism in the Age of Abolition* (Cambridge, MA: Harvard University Press, 2020); Tom M. Devine, ed., *Recovering Scotland's Slavery Past: The Caribbean Connection* (Edinburgh: Edinburgh University Press, 2015); Paula E. Dumas, *Proslavery Britain: Fighting for Slavery in an Era of Abolition* (New York: Palgrave Macmillan, 2016); Padraic X. Scanlan, *Freedom's Debtors: British Antislavery in Sierra Leone in the Age of Revolution* (New Haven, CT: Yale University Press, 2017); Padraic X. Scanlan, *Slave Empire: How Slavery Made Modern Britain* (London: Robinson, 2020); Michael Taylor, *The Interest: How the British Establishment Resisted the Abolition of Slavery* (London: Bodley Head, 2020); Michael E. Jirik, 'Beyond Clarkson: Cambridge, Black Abolitionists, and the British Anti-Slave Trade Campaign', *Slavery & Abolition* 41 (2020), 748–771; and Simon Newman, *Freedom Seekers: Escaping from Slavery in Restoration London* (London: University of London Press, 2022). For enslavement and abolition in the United States, see, for example, Larry E. Tise, *Proslavery: A History of the Defense of*

Slavery in America, 1701–1840 (Athens: University of Georgia Press, 1987); Joanne Pope Melish, *Disowning Slavery: Gradual Emancipation and 'Race' in New England, 1780–1860* (Ithaca, NY: Cornell University Press, 1998); Don E. Fehrenbacher, *The Slaveholding Republic: An Account of the United States Government's Relations to Slavery* (New York: Oxford University Press, 2001); John Stauffer, *The Black Hearts of Men: Radical Abolitionists and the Transformation of Race* (Cambridge, MA: Harvard University Press, 2002); W. Caleb McDaniel, *The Problem of Democracy in the Age of Slavery: Garrisonian Abolitionists and Transatlantic Reform* (Baton Rouge: Louisiana State University Press, 2013); Manisha Sinha, *The Slave's Cause: A History of Abolition* (New Haven, CT: Yale University Press, 2016); Nicholas Guyatt, *Bind Us Apart: How Enlightened Americans Invented Racial Segregation* (Oxford: Oxford University Press, 2016); Matthew Karp, *This Vast Southern Empire: Slaveholders at the Helm of American Foreign Policy* (Cambridge, MA: Harvard University Press, 2017); David W. Blight, *Frederick Douglass: Prophet of Freedom* (London: Simon & Schuster, 2018); and Hannah-Rose Murray, *Advocates of Freedom: African American Transatlantic Abolitionism in the British Isles* (Cambridge: Cambridge University Press, 2020).

2. The connections between Britain's countryside and enslavement are discussed in Madge Dresser and Andrew Hann, eds., *Slavery and the British Country House* (Swindon: English Heritage, 2013); Corinne Fowler, *Green Unpleasant Land: Creative Responses to Rural England's Colonial Connections* (Leeds: Peepal Tree Press, 2021); Corinne Fowler, *Our Island Stories: Country Walks Through Colonial Britain* (London: Penguin, 2024); Richard C. Maguire, *Africans in East Anglia, 1467–1833* (Martlesham, Suffolk: Boydell & Brewer, 2021); and David Alston, *Slaves and Highlanders: Silenced Histories of Scotland and the Caribbean* (Edinburgh: Edinburgh University Press, 2021). The European hinterland's linkages to slavery are explored in Felix Brahm and Eve Rosenhaft, *Slavery Hinterland: Transatlantic Slavery and Continental Europe, 1680–1850* (London: Boydell & Brewer, 2016); and Heike Raphael-Hernandez and Pia Wiegmink, 'German Entanglements in Transatlantic Slavery: An Introduction', *Atlantic Studies* 14 (2017), 419–435. For the many methodologies of Atlantic history, see Bernard Bailyn, *Atlantic History: Concepts and Contours* (Cambridge, MA: Harvard University Press, 2005); Alison Games, 'Atlantic History: Definitions, Challenges, and Opportunities', *The American Historical Review* 111 (June 2006), 741–757; and David Armitage, 'The Atlantic World,' in David Armitage, Alison Bashford, and Sujit Sivasundaram, eds., *Oceanic Histories* (Cambridge: Cambridge University Press, 2017), 85–109.

3. Alan Taylor, 'Foreword', in Robert A. Gross, *The Minutemen and Their World* (New York: Hill and Wang, 2001, rev. ed.), xi ('broader'); 'Introduction', in Lawrence Stone ed., *The University in Society, Volume I: Oxford and Cambridge from the 14th to the Early 19th Century* (Princeton: Princeton University Press, 1974), v ('conservatism', 'pressures', and 'external conditions'). For enslavement through a local and regional lens, see, for example, Randy J. Sparks, *Where the Negroes Are Masters: An African Port in the Era of the Slave Trade* (Cambridge, MA: Harvard University Press, 2014); Richard S. Dunn, *A Tale of Two Plantations: Slave Life and Labor in Jamaica and Virginia* (Cambridge, MA: Harvard University Press, 2014); and, more recently, Stephen Mullen, *The Glasgow Sugar Aristocracy: Scotland and Caribbean Slavery, 1775–1838* (London: University of London Press, 2023).

4. Catherine Hall, Nicholas Draper, and Keith McClelland, 'Introduction', in Catherine Hall, Nicholas Draper, and Keith McClelland eds., *Emancipation and the Remaking*

of the British Imperial World (Manchester: Manchester University Press, 2015), 2 ('histories' and 'linked'). The significance of the empire in British metropolitan life is explored in Peter J. Cain and A. G. Hopkins, *British Imperialism, 1688–2015: Third Edition* (London and New York: Routledge, 2016); Catharine Hall, *Civilising Subjects: Metropole and Colony in the English Imagination, 1830–1867* (Cambridge: Polity Press, 2002); Kathleen Wilson, *The Island Race: Englishness, Empire, and Gender in the Eighteenth Century* (London: Routledge, 2003); Tom M. Devine, *Scotland's Empire and the Shaping of America, 1600–1815* (London: Allen Lane, 2003); S. D. Smith, *Slavery, Family, and Gentry Capitalism in the British Caribbean: The World of the Lascelles, 1648–1834* (Cambridge: Cambridge University Press, 2006); and Catherine Molineux, *Faces of Perfect Ebony: Encountering Atlantic Slavery in Imperial Britain* (Cambridge, MA: Harvard University Press, 2012).

5. J. A. Schumpeter, 'The Crisis of the Tax State', in Richard Swedberg ed. *Joseph A. Schumpeter: The Economics and Sociology of Capitalism* (Princeton, NJ: Princeton University Press, 1991), 108. For the middling sort, see Jonathan Barry and C. W. Brooks, *The Middling Sort of People: Culture, Society, and Politics in England, 1550–1800* (New York: St. Martin's Press, 1994); Margaret R. Hunt, *The Middling Sort: Commerce, Gender, and the Family in England, 1680–1780* Berkeley: University of California Press, 1996); Maxine Berg, *Luxury and Pleasure in Eighteenth-Century Britain* (Oxford: Oxford University Press, 2005); and Hannah Barker, *The Business of Women: Female Enterprise and Urban Development in Northern England, 1760–1830* (Oxford: Oxford University Press, 2006). For elites in the Atlantic world, see, for instance, H. V. Bowen, *Elites, Enterprise and the Making of the British Overseas Empire, 1688–1775* (Basingstoke: Palgrave Macmillan, 1996).

6. *The New Annual Register, or General Repository of History, Politics, and Literature, For the Year 1788* (London: J. and J. Robinson, 1789), 103 ('1788'); *Journals of the House of Commons. From January the 31st, 1792, In the Thirty-second Year of the Reign of King George the Third, to November the 15th, 1792, In the Thirty-third Year of the Reign of King George the Third* (London: House of Commons, 1803), 542 ('1792'). There are numerous histories of Cambridge University; see E. S. Leedham-Green, *A Concise History of the University of Cambridge* (Cambridge and New York: Cambridge University Press, 1996); Peter Searby, *A History of the University of Cambridge, Volume III: 1750–1870* (Cambridge: Cambridge University Press, 1997); Victor Morgan and Christopher Brooke, *A History of the University of Cambridge, Volume II: 1546–1750* (Cambridge: Cambridge University Press, 2004); and R. R. Neild, *The Financial History of Cambridge University* (London: Thames River Press, 2012).

7. For institutional research into the legacies of enslavement at British universities, see, for example, Véronique Mottier et al., 'Jesus College Legacy of Slavery Working Party: Interim Report (July-October 2019)', www.jesus.cam.ac.uk/sites/default/files/inline/files/legacy_slavery_working_party_interim_report_27_nov_2019%20%283%29.pdf, accessed 4 April 2022; Martin Millett et al., 'University of Cambridge Advisory Group on Legacies of Enslavement: Final Report', www.cam.ac.uk/about-the-university/history/legacies-of-enslavement/advisory-group-on-legacies-of-enslavement-final-report, accessed 22 September 2022; Stephen Mullen and Simon Newman, *Slavery, Abolition and the University of Glasgow: Report and Recommendations of University of Glasgow History of Slavery Steering Committee* (Glasgow: University of Glasgow, 2018); and Cassandra Gooptar, *University of Dundee Founders Project: Final Report* (Dundee: University of Dundee, 2022).

For enslavement at American universities, see, for instance, David Collins et al., eds., *Report of the Working Group on Slavery, Memory, and Reconciliation to the President of Georgetown University* (Washington, D.C.: Georgetown University, 2016); Marcus L. Martin et al., eds., *President's Commission on Slavery and the University: Report to President Teresa A. Sullivan* (Charlottesville: University of Virginia, 2018); Jody Allen et al., eds., *The Lemon Project: A Journey of Reconciliation: Report of the First Eight Years* (Williamsburg, VA: College of William and Mary, 2019); James Campbell et al., eds., *Brown University's Slavery and Justice Report with Commentary on Context and Impact* (Providence, RI: Brown University, 2021); Tomiko Brown-Nagin et al., eds., *Harvard & The Legacy of Slavery* (Cambridge, MA: Harvard University, 2022); Martha A. Sandweiss and Craig Hollander, 'Princeton and Slavery: Holding the Center', *The Princeton & Slavery Project*, https://slavery.princeton.edu/stories/princeton-and-slavery-holding-the-center, accessed 23 May 2022; and David Blight et al., *Yale and Slavery: A History* (New Haven, CT and London: Yale University Press, 2024).

8. Craig Steven Wilder, *Ebony & Ivy: Race, Slavery, and the Troubled History of America's Universities* (New York: Bloomsbury Press, 2013), 11. For more recent treatments of universities and empire, see Richard Symonds, *Oxford and Empire: The Last Lost Cause?* (Oxford: Clarendon Press, 1992); E. Kaye Tully and Clive Whitehead, 'Audacious Beginnings: The Establishment of Universities in Australasia, 1850–1900', *Education Research and Perspectives* 36 (2009), 1–44; Joseph Morgan Hodge and Brett M. Bennett, eds., *Science and Empire: Knowledge and Networks of Science in the British Empire, 1800–1970* (New York: Palgrave Macmillan, 2011); Tamson Pietsch, *Empire of Scholars: Universities, Networks and the British Academic World, 1850–1939* (Manchester: University of Manchester Press, 2015); Caitlin Harvey, 'Bricks and Mortar Boards: University-Building in the Settlement Empire, 1840–1920' (PhD dissertation, Princeton University, 2021); and Caitlin Harvey, 'Gold Rushes, Universities and Globalization, 1840–1910', *Past & Present* 26 (November 2023), 118–157; For enslavement and the history of North American universities, see in particular Alfred L. Brophy, 'The University and Its Slaves: Apology and Its Meaning', in Mark Gibney et al. ed., *The Age of Apology: Facing Up to the Past* (Philadelphia: University of Pennsylvania Press, 2009); Alfred L. Brophy, *University, Court, and Slave: Pro-slavery Thought in Southern Courts and Colleges and the Coming of the Civil War* (New York: Oxford University Press, 2016); Lindsey K. Walters, 'Slavery and the American University: Discourses of Retrospective Justice at Harvard and Brown', *Slavery & Abolition* 38 (2017), 719–744; and Leslie M. Harris et al., eds., *Slavery and the University: Histories and Legacies* (Athens: University of Georgia Press, 2019). On the governmental seizure of Native American land to fund universities, see Robert Lee and Tristan Ahtone, 'Land-Grab Universities', *High Country News* 52 (April 2020), 32–45.

9. For the language of "direct" and "indirect" connections to enslavement, see Joseph E. Inikori, *Africans and the Industrial Revolution in England: A Study in International Trade and Economic Development* (Cambridge: Cambridge University Press, 2002), 25; Major, *Slavery, Abolition, and Empire*, 233; Madge Dresser, *Slavery Obscured: The Social History of the Slave Trade in an English Provincial Port* (London: Bloomsbury Publishing, 2016), 111; Pat Hudson, 'Slavery, the Slave Trade and Economic Growth: A Contribution to the Debate', in Hall et al., eds., *Emancipation*, 37 and 40; J. J. Wright, '"A work purely local?" Narratives of Empire in George Benn's *A History of the Town of Belfast*', in Daniel Sanjiv Roberts and Jonathan Jeffrey Wright, eds.,

Ireland's Imperial Connections, 1775–1947 (London: Palgrave Macmillan, 2019), 154; Melinda Elder, *Slave Trade and the Economic Development of 18th-Century Lancaster* (Edinburgh: Edinburgh University Press 2019), 75; Jessica Moody, *The Persistence of Memory: Remembering Slavery in Liverpool, 'slaving capital of the world'* (Liverpool: Liverpool University Press, 2020), 191; Antoinette Burton, 'New Narratives of Imperial Politics in the Nineteenth Century', in Catherine Hall and Sonya Rose, eds., *At Home with the Empire: Metropolitan Culture and the Imperial World* (Cambridge: Cambridge University Press, 2011), 214; Antoinette Burton, *Empire in Question: Reading, Writing, and Teaching British Imperialism* (Durham, NC: Duke University Press, 2011), 259; and Kristin L. Gallas and James DeWolf Perry, 'Comprehensive Content and Contested Historical Narratives', in Kristin L. Gallas and James DeWolf Perry, eds., *Interpreting Slavery at Museums and Historic Sites* (Lanham, MD: Rowman & Littlefield, 2015), 4. For these terms in the United States, see Jennifer Oast, *Institutional Slavery: Slaveholding Churches, Schools, Colleges, and Businesses in Virginia, 1680–1860* (Cambridge: Cambridge University Press, 2016), 131, 201, and 237.

10. Medieval Cambridge is discussed in Alan B. Cobban, *The Medieval English Universities: Oxford and Cambridge to c. 1500* (London: Routledge, 1988); Damian Riehl Leader, ed., *A History of the University of Cambridge, Volume 1: The University to 1546* (Cambridge: Cambridge University Press, 1994); and Hastings Rashdall, *The Universities of Europe in the Middle Ages, Part 2, English Universities, Student Life* (Cambridge: Cambridge University Press, 2010).

11. Robert Anderson, *British Universities: Past and Present* (London: Hambledon Continuum, 2006), 2 ('legal rights').

12. J. C. P. Roach, ed., *The Victoria History of the County of Cambridge and the Isle of Ely: Volume 3, the City and University of Cambridge* (London: Published for the University of London Institute of Historical Research by the Oxford University Press, 1959), 86–101 ('rise to prominence', 'trade fairs', and 'population'); H. C. Darby, *The Draining of the Fens: Second Edition* (Cambridge: Cambridge University Press, 1940), 53 ('our river'); Rev. Edward Conybeare, *Highways and Byways in Cambridge and Ely* (London: Macmillan and Co., 1910), 164 ('music booths'). See also Eric H. Ash, *The Draining of the Fens: Projectors, Popular Politics, and State Building in Early Modern England* (Baltimore: Johns Hopkins University Press, 2017), 17–49.

13. Lilian M. Quiller Couch, ed., *Reminiscences of Oxford by Oxford Men, 1559–1850* (Oxford: Oxford Historical Society at the Clarendon Press, 1892), 118 ('present' and 'apprehension'); Edward Gibbon, *The Autobiography and Correspondence of Edward Gibbon, The Historian: Reprint of the Original Edition* (London: Alex Murray & Son, 1869), 25 ('schools'). For early modern Cambridge, see John Gascoigne, *Cambridge in the Age of the Enlightenment: Science, Religion and Politics from the Restoration to the French Revolution* (Cambridge: Cambridge University Press, 1988). The decline of "Oxbridge" admissions is examined in John Cannon, *Aristocratic Century: The Peerage of Eighteenth-Century England* (Cambridge: Cambridge University Press, 1984); John Venn, ed., *Biographical History of Gonville and Caius College*, vol. 4 (Cambridge: Cambridge University Press, 1897); Peter Linehan, ed., *St John's College, Cambridge: A History* (Woodbridge, Suffolk: Boydell Press, 2011), 163–164; George Macaulay Trevelyan, *Trinity College: An Historical Sketch* (Cambridge: Trinity College, 1972), 73–74; and Stone, ed., *The University in Society, Volume I*, vii. The intellectual vibrancy of the ancient universities in the face of that decline

in admissions is discussed in Nigel Aston, *Enlightened Oxford: The University and the Cultural and Political Life of Eighteenth-Century Britain and Beyond* (Oxford: Oxford University Press, 2023), esp. 15.

14. Wesley Frank Craven, *The Virginia Company of London, 1606–1624* (Williamsburg, VA: 350th Anniversary Celebration Corporation, 1957), 1–14 and Lorena S. Walsh, *Motives of Honor, Pleasure, & Profit: Plantation Management in the Colonial Chesapeake* (Chapel Hill: University of North Carolina Press, 2010), 29 ('latitude'); Larry Gragg, *Englishmen Transplanted: The English Colonization of Barbados, 1627–1660* (Oxford: Oxford University Press, 2003), 31 ('Courten') and 1 ('£285,000'). For the Virginia Company, see Jean de Chantal Kennedy, *Isle of Devils: Bermuda under the Somers Island Company, 1609–1685* (London: William Collins Sons & Co Ltd., 1971); James Honor, *A Land as God Made It: Jamestown and the Birth of America* (New York: Basic Books, 2005); and Karen Ordahl Kupperman, *The Jamestown Project* (Cambridge, MA: Harvard University Press, 2009). The emergence of the plantation regime is explored in Allan Kulikoff, *Tobacco & Slaves: The Development of Southern Cultures in the Chesapeake, 1680–1800* (Chapel Hill and London: University of North Carolina Press, 1986); Rachel N. Klein, *Unification of a Slave State: The Rise of the Planter Class in the South Carolina Backcountry, 1760–1808* (Chapel Hill: University of North Carolina Press, 1990); Richard S. Dunn, *Sugar and Slaves: The Rise of the Planter Class in the English West Indies, 1624–1713*, foreword by Gary B. Nash (Chapel Hill: University of North Carolina Press, 2000); David Eltis, *The Rise of African Slavery in the Americas* (Cambridge: Cambridge University Press, 2000); Anthony S. Parent, Jr., *Foul Means: The Formation of a Slave Society in Virginia, 1660–1740* (Chapel Hill and London: University of North Carolina Press, 2003); Betty Wood, *Slavery in Colonial America, 1619–1776* (Plymouth: Rowman & Littlefield, 2005); Ira Berlin, *Many Thousands Gone: The First Two Centuries of Slavery in North America* (Cambridge, MA: The Belknap Press of Harvard University Press, 2003); Russell R. Menard, *Sweet Negotiations: Sugar, Slavery, and Plantation Agriculture in Early Barbados* (Charlottesville: University of Virginia Press, 2006); Natalie Zacek, *Settler Society in the English Leeward Islands, 1670–1776* (Cambridge: Cambridge University Press, 2010); Michael Guasco, *Slaves and Englishmen: Human Bondage in the Early Modern Atlantic World* (Philadelphia: University of Pennsylvania Press, 2014); Simon P. Newman, *A New World of Labor: The Development of Plantation Slavery in the British Atlantic* (Philadelphia: University of Pennsylvania Press, 2016); Trevor Burnard, *Planters, Merchants, and Slaves: Plantation Societies in British America, 1650–1820* (Chicago: University of Chicago Press, 2015); Trevor Burnard and John Garrigus, *The Plantation Machine: Atlantic Capitalism in French Saint-Domingue and British Jamaica* (Philadelphia: University of Pennsylvania Press, 2016); Abigail L. Swingen, *Competing Visions of Empire: Labor, Slavery, and the Origins of the British Atlantic Empire* (New Haven, CT and London: Yale University Press, 2015); Christopher Petley, *White Fury: A Jamaican Slaveholder and the Age of Revolution* (Oxford: Oxford University Press, 2018); and Randy M. Browne, *The Driver's Story: Labor and Power in the World of Atlantic Slavery* (Philadelphia: University of Pennsylvania Press, 2024).

15. Burnard, *Planters, Merchants, and Slaves*, 3–6. Enslavement in antiquity is discussed in Orlando Patterson, *Slavery and Social Death* (Cambridge, MA: Harvard University Press, 1985); Sandra R. Joshel, *Slavery in the Roman World* (Cambridge: Cambridge University Press, 2010); and Peter Hunt, *Ancient Greek and Roman Slavery* (Chichester: Wiley Blackwell, 2018).

16. Burnard, *Planters, Merchants, and Slaves*, 18 ('average'), 159 ('three times'), and 169 ('ninety'); Colin G. Calloway, *The Indian World of George Washington: The First President, the First Americans, and the Birth of the Nation* (New York: Oxford University Press, 2018), 7 ('45,000'). For slaveholders and their accounting methods, see Caitlin Rosenthal, *Accounting for Slavery: Masters and Management* (Cambridge, MA: Harvard University Press, 2018).
17. Jill Lepore, *The Name of War: King Philip's War and the Origins of American Identity* (New York: Knopf, 1998), 170 ('Wampanoag'); 'Trans-Atlantic Slave Trade – Estimates', SlaveVoyages, www.slavevoyages.org/assessment/estimates, accessed 24 February 2023 ('12.5 million'). For the business of slave trading, see, for instance, David Hancock, *Citizens of the World: London Merchants and the Integration of the Atlantic Community, 1735-1785* (Cambridge: Cambridge University Press, 1995); Nicholas Radburn, *Traders in Men: Merchants and the Transformation of the Transatlantic Slave Trade* (New Haven, CT: Yale University Press, 2023); Nicholas Draper, 'The City of London and Slavery: Evidence from the First Dock Companies, 1795-1800', *The Economic History Review* 61 (May 2008), 432-466; Marcus Rediker, *The Slave Ship: A Human History* (New York: Viking, 2007); Gregory E. O'Malley, *Final Passages: The Intercolonial Slave Trade of British America, 1619-1807* (Chapel Hill: University of North Carolina Press, 2014); and Stephanie E. Smallwood, *Saltwater Slavery: A Middle Passage from Africa to America* (Cambridge, MA: Harvard University Press, 2007).
18. 'Trans-Atlantic Slave Trade – Estimates', SlaveVoyages, www.slavevoyages.org/assessment/estimates, accessed 24 February 2023 ('186,286'); Richard B. Allen, 'Satisfying the "Want for Labouring People": European Slave Trading in the Indian Ocean, 1500-1850', *Journal of World History* 21 (March 2010), 64 ('10 and 13,000'). For the RAC and its successors, see K. G. Davies, *The Royal African Company* (London: Longmans, 1957); and William A Pettigrew, *Freedom's Debt: The Royal African Company and the Politics of the Atlantic Slave Trade, 1672-1752* (Chapel Hill: University of North Carolina Press, 2013). The East India Company is discussed in, amongst others, H. V. Bowen, *The Business of Empire: The East India Company and Imperial Britain, 1756-1833* (Cambridge: Cambridge University Press, 2006); Miles Ogborn, *Indian Ink: Script and Print in the Making of the English East India Company* (Chicago: University of Chicago Press, 2007); Tillman W. Nechtman, *Nabobs: Empire and Identity in Eighteenth-Century Britain* (Cambridge: Cambridge University Press, 2010); Philip J. Stern, *The Company-State: Corporate Sovereignty and the Early Modern Foundations of the British Empire in India* (Oxford: Oxford University Press, 2011); Margot Finn and Kate Smith, eds., *The East India Company at Home, 1757-1857* (London: UCL Press, 2018); Rupali Mishra, *A Business of State: Commerce, Politics and the Birth of the East India Company* (Cambridge, MA: Harvard University Press, 2018); William Dalrymple, *The Anarchy: The East India Company, Corporate Violence, and the Pillage of an Empire* (London: Bloomsbury, 2019); and David Veevers, *The Origins of the British Empire in Asia, 1600-1750* (Cambridge: Cambridge University Press, 2020). For the East India Company and the Indian Ocean slave trade, see Frenise A. Logan, 'The British East India Company and African Slavery in Benkulen, Sumatra, 1687-1792', *Journal of Negro History* 41 (October 1956), 339-348; Major, *Slavery, Abolition, and Empire*; and Richard B. Allen, *European Slave Trading in the Indian Ocean, 1500-1850* (Athens: Ohio University Press, 2014). For synthetic approaches to English and British colonial companies, see William A. Pettigrew and David Veevers, eds., *The Corporation as a Protagonist in Global History, c. 1550-1750*

(Leiden: Brill, 2018); and Philip J. Stern, *Empire, Incorporated: The Corporations That Built British Colonialism* (Cambridge, MA: Harvard University Press, 2023).

19. Advantages to Britain of the Negro trade, undated, Papers relating to the South Sea Company and crisis; states of the stock, minutes of the Court of Directors, notes of the meetings of the Bank and the Company 1711–1739, Cholmondeley (Houghton) Papers, CUL, GBR/0012/MS Ch(H), Papers 88, 139 ('Negro trade'); Daniel Defoe, *A true account of the design, and advantages of the South-Sea trade; with answers to all the objections rais'd against it: a list of the commodities proper for that trade* (London: John Morphew, 1711), 29–30 ('marketed'); 'Enslavers – Database', *SlaveVoyages*, www.slavevoyages.org/past/enslavers, accessed 24 February 2023 ('75,000'); Helen J. Paul, *The South Sea Bubble: An Economic History of Its Origins and Consequences* (London: Routledge, 2013), 56 ('risk diversification' and 'lottery ticket'); A Proposal for the Enlarging and Establishing the Trade of Great Britain, Papers relating to the South Sea Company, Cholmondeley Papers, CUL, GBR/0012/MS Ch(H), Paper 127, 2 ('lessening' and 'Ingaging'); The particular Advantages that may arise to Great Britain by the Assiento for Negroes, *ibid.*, Paper 139 ('Advantages' and '£455,000'); Richard S. Dale, Johnnie E. V. Johnson, and Leilei Tang, 'Financial Markets can go Mad: Evidence of Irrational Behaviour during the South Sea Bubble', *Economic History Review* 58 (2005), 236 ('£1,050'). For the SSC as a popular investment strategy, see Julian Hoppit, 'The Myths of the South Sea Bubble', *Transactions of the Royal Historical Society* 12 (2002), 141–165; Donald L. Cherry, 'The South Sea Company, 1711–1855', *Dalhousie Review* 13 (1934), 61–68; John Carswell, *The South Sea Bubble* (Stanford, CA: Stanford University Press, 1960); Bruce G. Carruthers, *City of Capital: Politics and Markets in the English Financial Revolution* (Princeton, NJ: Princeton University Press, 1996); Richard Dale, *The First Crash: Lessons from the South Sea Bubble* (Princeton, NJ: Princeton University Press, 2004); and Peter Temin and Hans-Joachim Voth, *Prometheus Shackled: Goldsmith Banks and England's Financial Revolution after 1700* (Oxford and New York: Oxford University Press, 2013). For the SSC and the slave trade, see Victoria Gardner Sorsby, 'British Trade with Spanish America under the Asiento, 1713–1740' (PhD dissertation, University College, London, 1975); and Colin A. Palmer, *Human Cargoes: The British Slave Trade to Spanish America, 1700–1739* (Chicago: University of Illinois Press, 1981). The institutional ownership of South Sea securities at Cambridge is discussed in 'King's College Research into Slavery, Past and Present', *King's College, University of* Cambridge, www.kings.cam.ac.uk/news/2019/kings-college-research-slavery-past-and-present, accessed 11 April 2022; and Sabine Cadeau, 'Bonds and Bondage: Financial Capitalism and the Legacies of Atlantic Slavery at the University of Cambridge' unpublished manuscript, University of Cambridge, 2024.

20. Rediker, *Slave Ship*, 289 ('suicide'); Jerome S. Handler, 'The Middle Passage and the Material Culture of Captive Africans', *Slavery & Abolition* 30 (2009), 8 ('refreshment' and 'distributed') and 11 ('gaming'); Radburn, *Traders in Men*, 204 ('efficiency'). The origins, nature, extent, and consequences of enslaved resistance in the Atlantic world is explored in Marjoleine Kars, *Blood on the River: A Chronicle of Mutiny and Freedom on the Wild Coast* (New York: The New Press, 2020); Sylviane A. Diouf, *Fighting the Slave Trade: West African Strategies* (Athens: Ohio University Press, 2003); John Thornton, *Africa and Africans in the Making of the Atlantic World, 1400–1800* (Cambridge: Cambridge University Press, 1998); Gerald W. Mullin, *Flight and Rebellion: Slave Resistance in Eighteenth-Century Virginia* (New York: Oxford University Press, 1972); James Sidbury, *Ploughshares into*

Swords: Race, Rebellion, and Identity in Gabriel's Virginia, 1730–1810 (Cambridge: Cambridge University Press, 1997); Eric Robert Taylor, *If We Must Die: Shipboard Insurrections in the Era of the Atlantic Slave Trade* (Baton Rouge: Louisiana State University Press, 2006); Stephanie M. H. Camp, *Closer to Freedom: Enslaved Women and Everyday Resistance in the Plantation South* (Chapel Hill: University of North Carolina Press, 2004); Sally E. Hadden, *Slave Patrols: Law and Violence in Virginia and the Carolinas* (Cambridge, MA: Harvard University Press, 2003); Philip D. Morgan, *Slave Counterpoint: Black Culture in the Eighteenth-Century Chesapeake and Lowcountry* (Chapel Hill: University of North Carolina Press, 1998); Vincent Brown, *Tacky's Revolt: The Story of an Atlantic Slave War* (Cambridge, MA: Harvard University Press, 2020); Jill Lepore, *New York Burning: Liberty, Slavery, and Conspiracy in Eighteenth-Century Manhattan* (New York: Alfred A. Knopf, 2005); and Jennifer L. Morgan, *Labouring Women: Reproduction and Gender in New World Slavery* (Philadelphia: University of Pennsylvania Press, 2004).

21. Peter Garnsey, *Ideas of Slavery from Aristotle to Augustine* (Cambridge: Cambridge University Press, 1999), 82 ('God'); Bartolomé de las Casas, *A Short Account of the Destruction of the Indies*, ed. by Nigel Griffin and Anthony Pagden (London: Penguin, 2004) and Francisco Vittoria, *On the American Indians*, January 1539, in Anthony Pagden and Jeremy Lawrance, eds., *Vittoria: Political Writings* (Cambridge: Cambridge University Press, 1991) ('denounced'); Edward Cavanagh, 'Infidels in English Legal Thought: Conquest, Commerce and Slavery in the Common Law from Coke to Mansfield, 1603–1793', *Modern Intellectual History* 16 (2019), 380 ('Coke'); José Lingna Nafafé, *Lourenço Da Silva Mendonça and the Black Atlantic Abolitionist Movement in the Seventeenth Century* (Cambridge: Cambridge University Press, 2022), 43–44 ('Vatican'); Erin Woodruff Stone, *Slavery in the Early Modern Spanish Caribbean* (Philadelphia: University of Pennsylvania Press, 2021), 142 ('Domingo'). Spanish criticisms of Indigenous enslavement are discussed in Andres Resendez, *The Other Slavery: The Uncovered Story of Indian Enslavement in America* (Boston: Houghton Mifflin Harcourt, 2016), 13–16.

22. Timothy Cleaveland, 'Ahmad Bab al-Timbukti and his Islamic Critique of Racial Slavery in the Maghrib', *The Journal of North African Studies* 20 (January 2015), 42–64 ('neither Muslims'); John Hunwick, 'Islamic Law and Polemics over Race and Slavery in North and West Africa (16th–19th Century)', in Shaun E. Marmon, ed., *Slavery in the Islamic Middle East* (Princeton, NJ: Markus Wiener Publishers, 1999), 43–68 ('religion'); Ehud R. Toledano, *As If Silent and Absent: Bonds of Enslavement in the Islamic Middle East* (New Haven, CT: Yale University Press, 2007), 47 ('sociocultural'); David Brion Davis, 'Looking at Slavery from Broader Perspectives', *The American Historical Review* 105 (April 2000), 457 ('successive'). For the Islamic debates over enslavement, see W. G. Clarence-Smith, *Islam and the Abolition of Slavery* (Oxford: Oxford University Press, 2006).

23. Daniel K. Richter, *Before the Revolution: America's Ancient Pasts* (Cambridge, MA: The Belknap Press of Harvard University Press, 2011), 247 ('DY'); O'Malley, *Final Passages*, 219 ('Mark A'); Palmer, *Human Cargoes*, 69 ('little palm'); Case Watkins, *Palm Oil Diaspora: Afro-Brazilian Landscapes and Economies on Bahia's Dendê Coast* (Cambridge: Cambridge University Press, 2021), 64 ('common').

24. Trevor Burnard, *Mastery, Tyranny, & Desire: Thomas Thistlewood and His Slaves in the Anglo-Jamaican World* (Chapel Hill and London: University of North Carolina Press, 2004), 31 ('well-respected') and 191 ('starving'); 17 March 1777, St. George Tucker's Journal to Charleston, W&M, Folder 12 ('burnt'); Extracts from Anburey's

Travels through North America, in 'Travellers' Impressions of Slavery in America from 1750 to 1800', *The Journal of Negro History* 1 (October 1916), 408 ('white person'); 4 June 1774, Harold B. Gill, Jr. and George M. Curtis III, eds., *A Man Apart: Journal of Nicholas Creswell, 1774–1781* (Lanham, MD: Lexington Books, 2009), 12 ('chained'); Vincent Brown, 'Spiritual Terror and Sacred Authority in Jamaican Slave Society', *Slavery & Abolition* 24 (2010), 26 ('spectacular terror').

25. Alden T. Vaughan and Virginia Mason Vaughan, 'Before Othello: Elizabethan Representations of Sub-Saharan Africans', *WMQ* 54 (January 1997), 44 ('unattractive'); Michael Neil, ed., *William Shakespeare: Othello, the Moor of Venice* (Oxford: Oxford University Press, 2006), 233 ('than black'), and 203 ('ram' and 'the devil'); Anne MacVicar Grant, *Memoirs of an American Lady. With Sketches of Manners and Scenery in America, as they Existed Previous to the Revolution* (New York: George Dearborn, 1836), 44 ('hapless'). For Christianity and anti-African racism, see Travis Glasson, '"Baptism doth not bestow Freedom": Missionary Anglicanism, Slavery, and the Yorke-Talbot Opinion, 1701–30', *WMQ* 67 (April 2010), 279–318; David M. Whitford, *The Curse of Ham in the Early Modern Era: The Bible and Justifications for Slavery* (London and New York: Routledge, 2009); Katharine Gerbner, *Christian Slavery: Conversion and Race in the Protestant Atlantic World* (Philadelphia: University of Pennsylvania Press, 2018); Colin Kidd, *The Forging of Races: Race and Scripture in the Protestant Atlantic World, 1600–2000* (Cambridge: Cambridge University Press, 2006); and Rebecca Anne Goetz, *The Baptism of Early Virginia: How Christianity Created Race* (Baltimore: Johns Hopkins University Press, 2012).

26. Edward Long, *The History of Jamaica. Or, General Survey of the Antient and Modern State of that Island: with Reflections on its Situation, Settlements, Inhabitants, Climate, Products, Commerce, Laws, and Government*, vol. 2 (London: T. Lowndes, 1774), 401 ('savage[s]' and 'tamed'); Pierre Joseph Laborie, *The Coffee Planter of Saint Domingo; with An Appendix, Containing a View of the Constitution, Government, Laws, and State of that Colony, previous to the Year 1789* (London: T. Cadell, 1798), 158–159 ('creature' and 'prolong'). For the origins and development of racial science, see Katy L. Chiles, *Transformable Race: Surprising Metamorphoses in the Literature of Early America* (Oxford and New York: Oxford University Press, 2014); Raymond Phineas Stearns, *Science in the British Colonies of America* (Chicago and London: University of Illinois Press, 1970); Roxann Wheeler, *Categories of Difference in Eighteenth-Century British Culture* (Philadelphia: University of Pennsylvania Press, 2000); Andrew S. Curran, *The Anatomy of Blackness: Science & Slavery in an Age of Enlightenment* (Baltimore: Johns Hopkins University Press, 2011); Bruce R. Dain, *A Hideous Monster of the Mind: American Race Theory in the Early Republic* (Cambridge, MA: Harvard University Press, 2002); Suman Seth, *Difference and Disease: Medicine, Race, and the Eighteenth-Century British Empire* (New York and Cambridge: Cambridge University Press, 2018); Sharon Block, *Colonial Complexions: Race and Bodies in Eighteenth-Century America* (Philadelphia: University of Pennsylvania Press, 2018); Ibram X. Kendi, *Stamped from the Beginning: The Definitive History of Racist Ideas in America* (New York: Nation Books, 2016); Rana A. Hogarth, *Medicalizing Blackness: Making Racial Difference in the Atlantic World, 1780–1840* (Chapel Hill: University of North Carolina Press, 2017); Winthrop D. Jordan, *White over Black: American Attitudes toward the Negro, 1550–1812*, intro. by Christopher Leslie Brown and Peter H. Wood (Chapel Hill: University of North Carolina Press, 2012); and Saliha Belmessous,

Assimilation and Empire: Uniformity in French and British Colonies, 1541–1954 (Oxford: Oxford University Press, 2013).

27. Olaudah Equiano, *The Interesting Narrative of the Life of Olaudah Equiano, or Gustavus Vassa, the African Written by Himself*, intro. and ed. by Robert Reid-Pharr and Shelly Eversley (New York: Modern Library, 2004), 102 ('meagre' and 'lump'); 'Narrative of Charley Williams', *National Humanities Center*, http://nationalhumanitiescenter.org/pds/maai/enslavement/text3/plantationchwilliams.pdf, accessed 24 February 2023 ('Bells and horns'); 'Bell Continues to Support an Honest Approach to the Legacies of Enslavement', *St Catharine's College, Cambridge*, www.caths.cam.ac.uk/slavery-exhibition, accessed 24 February 2023 ('Catharina'); Bonnie Gordon, 'What Mr. Jefferson Didn't Hear', in Olivia Bloechl et al., eds., *Rethinking Difference in Musical Scholarship* (Cambridge: Cambridge University Press, 2014), 126 ('Drums').

28. Philip Morgan, 'The Caribbean Environment to 1850', in Philip Morgan et al., eds., *Sea & Land: An Environmental History of the Caribbean* (Oxford: Oxford University Press, 2022), 20–129 ('devastating'); Kenneth Pomeranz, *The Great Divergence: China, Europe, and the Making of the Modern World Economy* (Princeton, NJ: Princeton University Press, 2000), 313 ('ghost acres'); Maxine Berg and Pat Hudson, *Slavery, Capitalism and the Industrial Revolution* (London: Polity Press, 2023), unpaginated e-book edition ('formative'); Jennifer L. Anderson, *Mahogany: The Cost of Luxury in Early America* (Cambridge, MA: Harvard University Press, 2015), 4 ('Yoruba'); Receipted Bill for Tea, Coffee and Sugar for Bene't Combination, 2–25 January 1749/50, Bursar's and Other Financial Records, CCC, GBR/0268/CCCC02/B/54/39 ('sugar'); Bennitt Combination Bill, Quarter to Lady Day 1738, Bursar's and Other Financial Records, CCC, GBR/0268/CCCC02/B/51/3 ('tobacco'); An Inventory then taken of the Goods of the late Dr Chapman, Master of Magdalene College Cambridge, Thomas Chapman Papers, MC, 27–33 ('numerous' and 'Canisters'). For the impact of the plantation economy on the environment, see David Silkenat, *Scars on the Land: An Environmental History of Slavery in the American South* (Oxford: Oxford University Press, 2022), esp. 6–31. For slavery and the consumer economy, see Everill, *Not Made by Slaves*; Julie L. Holcomb, *Moral Commerce: Quakers and the Transatlantic Boycott of the Slave Labor Economy* (Ithaca, NY: Cornell University Press, 2016); Anderson, *Mahogany*; Shane White and Graham White, 'Slave Clothing and African-American Culture in the Eighteenth and Nineteenth Centuries', *Past & Present* 148 (August 1995), 149–186; Leland Ferguson, *Uncommon Ground: Archaeology and Early African America, 1650–1800* (Washington, D.C.: Smithsonian Institution, 1992); Kay Dian Kriz, *Slavery, Sugar, and the Culture of Refinement: Picturing the British West Indies, 1700–1840* (New Haven, CT: Yale University Press, 2008); Ann Smart Martin, *Buying into the World of Goods: Early Consumers in Backcountry Virginia* (Baltimore: Johns Hopkins University Press, 2008); Kathleen M. Hilliard, *Masters, Slaves, and Exchange: Power's Purchase in the Old South* (Cambridge: Cambridge University Press, 2014); and Roderick A. McDonald, *The Economy and Material Culture of Slavery: Goods and Chattels on the Sugar Plantations of Jamaica and Louisiana* (Baton Rouge: Louisiana University Press, 1993). The impact of slavery on British economic growth is considered and debated in Williams, *Capitalism and Slavery*; Inikori, *Africans and the Industrial Revolution in England*; David Eltis, *Economic Growth and the Ending of the Transatlantic Slave Trade* (Oxford: Oxford University Press, 1987); Patrick K. O'Brien and Stanley L. Engerman, 'Exports and the Growth of the

British Economy from the Glorious Revolution to the Peace of Amiens', in Barbara L. Solow, ed., *Slavery and the Rise of the Atlantic System* (Cambridge: Cambridge University Press, 1991), 177–209; Kenneth Morgan, *Slavery, Atlantic Trade and the British Economy, 1660–1800* (Cambridge: Cambridge University Press, 2001); David Eltis and Stanley L. Engerman, 'The Importance of Slavery and the Slave Trade to Industrializing Britain', *Journal of Economic History* 60 (March 2000), 123–144; C. K. Harley, 'Slavery, the British Atlantic Economy and the Industrial Revolution', in A. B. Leonard and David Pretel, ed., *The Caribbean and the Atlantic World Economy* (New York: Palgrave Macmillan, 2015), 161–183; and Klas Rönnbäck, 'On the Economic Importance of the Slave Plantation Complex to the British Economy during the Eighteenth Century: A Value-Added Approach', *Journal of Global History* 13 (2018), 309–327.

29. Robert G. Parkinson, *The Common Cause: Creating Race and Nation in the American Revolution* (Chapel Hill: University of North Carolina Press, 2016), 581 ('fear'); Thomas Jefferson to George Rogers Clark, 25 December 1780, in Julian P. Boyd et al., eds., *The Papers of Thomas Jefferson*, vol. 4 (Princeton, NJ: Princeton University Press, 1951), 237–238 ('Empire of Liberty'). For slavery and abolition during the American Revolution, see, for example, Gary B. Nash, *The Forgotten Fifth: African Americans and the Age of Revolution* (Cambridge, MA: Harvard University Press, 2006); Alan Taylor, *The Internal Enemy: Slavery and War in Virginia, 1772–1832* (New York: W. W. Norton & Company, 2013); Chernoh M. Sesay, 'The Revolutionary Black Roots of Slavery's Abolition in Massachusetts', *The New England Quarterly* 87 (March 2014), 99–131; Judith L. Van Buskirk, *Standing in their Own Light: African American Patriots in the American Revolution* (New York: Blackwell Publishing, 2017); Cassandra Pybus, *Epic Journeys of Freedom: Runaway Slaves of the American Revolution and Their Quest for Liberty* (Boston: Beacon, 2006); David Waldstreicher, *Slavery's Constitution: From Revolution to Ratification* (New York: Hill and Wang, 2009); Woody Holton, *Forced Founders: Indians, Debtors, Slaves, and the Making of the American Revolution in Virginia* (Chapel Hill: University of North Carolina Press, 1999); Michael A. McDonnell, *The Politics of War: Race, Class, and Conflict in Revolutionary Virginia* (Chapel Hill: University of North Carolina Press, 2007); and Sylvia R. Frey, *Water from the Rock: Black Resistance in a Revolutionary Age* (Princeton, NJ: Princeton University Press, 1991). For the Haitian Revolution and its aftermath, see, for instance, Julius S. Scott, *The Common Wind: Afro-American Currents in the Age of the Haitian Revolution* (London and New York: Verso Books, 2018); Sudhir Hazareesingh, *Black Spartacus: The Epic Life of Toussaint Louverture* (London: Penguin, 2020); Laurent Dubois, *Avengers of the New World: The Story of the Haitian Revolution* (Cambridge, MA: Harvard University Press, 2005); and Johnhenry Gonzalez, *Maroon Nation: A History of Revolutionary Haiti* (New Haven, CT: Yale University Press, 2019).

30. Anthony E. Kaye, 'The Second Slavery: Modernity in the Nineteenth-Century South and the Atlantic World', *The Journal of Southern History* 75 (August 2009), 628 ('second'); Federal Writers Project, *Slave Narratives: A Folk History of Slavery in the United States From Interviews with Former Slaves*, vol. 4, part 2 (Washington, D.C.: Library of Congress, 1936), 175 ('150'); Solomon Northup, *Twelve Years a Slave: Narrative of Solomon Northup, a Citizen of New-York, Kidnapped in Washington City in 1841, and Rescued in 1853, from a Cotton Plantation near the Red River, in Louisiana*, in Yuvan Taylor, ed., *I Was Born a Slave: An Anthology of Classic Slave Narratives*, vol. 2 (New York: Lawrence Hill Books, 1999), 238 ('fatigued'); Henry

Bibb, *Narrative of the Life and Adventures of Henry Bibb, an American Slave*, in *ibid.*, 60 ('cotton they pick'). The cotton economy is discussed in Sven Beckert, *Empire of Cotton: A New History of Global Capitalism* (London: Penguin Books, 2015); Sven Beckert and Seth Rockman, eds., *Slavery's Capitalism: A New History of American Economic Development* (Philadelphia: University of Pennsylvania Press, 2016); Joseph P. Reidy, *From Slavery to Agrarian Capitalism in the Cotton Plantation South: Central Georgia, 1800–1880* (Chapel Hill and London: University of North Carolina Press, 1992); Andrew J. Torget, *Seeds of Empire: Cotton, Slavery, and the Transformation of the Texas Borderlands, 1800–1850* (Chapel Hill: University of North Carolina Press, 2015); Edward E. Baptist, *The Half Has Never Been Told: Slavery and the Making of American Capitalism* (New York: Basic Books, 2014); Daina Ramey Berry, *The Price for Their Pound of Flesh: The Value of the Enslaved, from Womb to Grave, in the Building of a Nation* (Boston: Beacon Press, 2017); Walter Johnson, *River of Dark Dreams: Slavery and Empire in the Cotton Kingdom* (Cambridge, MA: The Belknap Press of the Harvard University Press, 2013); and Adam Rothman, *Slave Country: American Expansion and the Origins of the Deep South* (Cambridge, MA: Harvard University Press, 2005).

31. James Wiles to Ann Wiles, 9 April 1818, James Wiles letters in the Wiles Family correspondence and genealogical papers, CUL, GBR/0012/MS Add.7721/1-19 ('happy people', 'anxious', and 'rising price').

32. Paul E. Lovejoy, *Transformations in Slavery: A History of Slavery in Africa* (Cambridge: Cambridge University Press, 2000), 244–266 ('1843'); Catherine Hall et al., 'Introduction', in Hall et al., eds., *Legacies of British Slave-Ownership*, 6 ('£20 million'); Joseph Martin Mulhern, 'After 1833: British Entanglement with Brazilian Slavery' (PhD dissertation, University of Durham, 2018), 191–216 ('merchants'); Marshall C. Eakin *A British Enterprise in Brazil: The St. John d'el Rey Mining Company and the Morro Velho Gold Mine, 1830–1960* (Durham, NC: Duke University Press, 1989), 172–173 ('mining'); Kent Fedorowich, 'The British Empire on the Move, 1760–1914', in Sarah Stockwell, ed., *The British Empire: Themes and Perspectives* (Oxford: Blackwell Publishing, 2008), 63 ('2.5 million'). For a more recent overview of the indentured labour trade, see Jonathan Connolly, *Worthy of Freedom: Indenture and Free Labor in the Era of Emancipation* (Chicago: University of Chicago Press, 2024).

1 'The principal ingredient necessary to form a good planter': Education and the Making of a Transatlantic Elite

1. "The Cricketers," *National Portrait Gallery*, https://npg.si.edu/object/npg_UK990702, accessed 8 September 2020. For the students and their backgrounds, see Darold D. Wax, 'Robert Ellis, Philadelphia Merchant and Slave Trader', *The Pennsylvania Magazine of History and Biography* 88 (January 1964), 52; Tithable List of Ralph Wormeley, 25 May 1773, Wormeley Family Papers 1671-1944, VMHC; Gregory T. Massey, 'Izard, Ralph', *South Carolina Encyclopedia*, www.scencylopedia.org/sce/entries/izard-ralph/, accessed 18 November 2021; and Barbara Doyle, *Beyond the Fields: Slavery and Middleton Place* (Columbia: University of South Carolina Press, 2008), 21–30. Izard and Wormeley can be found in Trinity Hall's accounting records. (College Accounts for 1760 and 1762, Master's Books, 1664-1799, TH, GBR/1936/THAR/1/4/3.) For context on the *Cricketers* and its artist,

see John Caldwell et al., eds., *American Paintings in the Metropolitan Museum of Art*, vol. 1 (New York: Metropolitan Museum of Art, 1994), 57; Daniel Kilbride, *Being American in Europe, 1750–1860* (Baltimore: Johns Hopkins University Press, 2013); Carrie Rebora Barratt, 'Inventing American Stories, 1765–1830', in H. Barbara Weinberg and Carrie Rebora Barratt, eds., *American Stories: Paintings of Everyday Life, 1765–1915* (New Haven and London: Yale University Press, 2009), 3; and Julie Flavell, *When London Was the Capital of America* (New Haven, CT: Yale University Press, 2011), 24.

2. The problems and pitfalls with using college matriculation records are discussed in Hester Jenkins and D. Caradog Jones, 'Social Class of Cambridge University Alumni of the 18th and 19th Centuries', *The British Journal of Sociology* 1 (June 1950), 93–116; and John Cannon, *Aristocratic Century*, 44–45. The Cambridge Alumni Database compiles the list of names in John Venn and John Archibald Venn, *Alumni Cantabrigiensis: A Biographical List of all Known Students, Graduates and Holders of Office at the University of Cambridge, from the Earliest Times to 1900*, 4 vols. (Cambridge: Cambridge University Press, 1922–27); and A. B. Emden's *A Biographical Register of the University of Cambridge to 1500* (Cambridge: Cambridge University Press, 1963). For student connections to enslavement, see also David Pope, 'The Wealth and Social Aspirations of Liverpool's Slave Merchants of the Second Half of the Eighteenth Century', in David Richardson et al. eds., *Liverpool and Transatlantic Slavery* (Liverpool: Liverpool University Press, 2007), 164–226; and Hilary Perraton, *A History of Foreign Students in Britain* (London: Palgrave Macmillan, 2014). This chapter has also benefited from discussions with Christopher Jeppesen, whose forthcoming work on Jesus College examines students with slave-holding, mercantile, and East Indian connections through to the end of the nineteenth century. For Trinity students and their family's extensive ties to the North American and Caribbean slave economies, see Michael Banner, *Britain's Slavery Debt: Reparations Now!* (Oxford: Oxford University Press, 2024), 135–138.

3. Andrew Jackson O'Shaughnessy, *An Empire Divided: The American Revolution and the British Caribbean* (Philadelphia: University of Pennsylvania Press, 2000), xiii ('twenty-six') and 26 ('fewer'). See also Julie M. Flavell, 'The "School for Modesty and Humility": Colonial American Youth in London and Their Parents, 1755–1775', *HJ* 42 (1999), 377–403. For the colonial American colleges and their social and intellectual environment, see J. David Hoeveler, *Creating the American Mind: Intellect and Politics in the Colonial Colleges* (Lanham, MD: Rowman & Littlefield Publishers, 2002).

4. Stuart Anderson, *Pharmacy and the Professionalization of the British Empire, 1780–1970* (London: Palgrave Macmillan, 2021), 104 ('provisioning'); The Court of Directors of the South Sea Company, *A List of the Names of Such Proprietors of Annuities, Transferable at the South Sea House, as were Entitled to Dividends on or Before the 5th July, 1837, and which Remained Unpaid on the 10th October 1842* (London: H. Teape and Son, 1842), 10 ('Riddlesworth'); Thomas Nicholas, *Annals and Antiquities of the Counties and County Families of Wales: Containing a Record of all Ranks of the Gentry, their Lineage, Alliances, Appointments, Armorial Ensigns, and Residences*, vol. 1 (Baltimore: Genealogical Publishing Company, 1991), 392 ('Lleweni'); 'Sir Robert Salusbury Cotton, 5th Baronet', *Legacies*, www.ucl.ac.uk/lbs/person/view/1170816936, accessed 13 January 2022 ('Kitts and Nevis'); 'Edward Gray', *ibid.*, www.ucl.ac.uk/lbs/person/view/12855, accessed 13 January 2022 ('Blaise').

5. O'Shaughnessy, *An Empire Divided*, 26.

6. Mark Rothery and Henry French, ed., *Making Men: The Formation of Elite Male Identities in England, c. 1660–1900* (Basingstoke: Palgrave Macmillan, 2012), 15 ('polite' and 'inner'); Nathaniel Burwell to Lewis Burwell, 13 June 1718, 'Letter of Col. Nathaniel Burwell', *WMQ* 7 (July 1898), 44 ('unfit'); Richard and Elizabeth Ambler to Edward Ambler, 1 August 1748, in Lucille Griffith, ed., 'English Education for Virginia Youth: Some Eighteenth-Century Ambler Family Letters', *VMHB* 69 (January 1961), 15 ('common', 'lower', and 'preserve'). See also Carolyn D. Williams, *Pope, Homer and Manliness: Some Aspects of Eighteenth-Century Classical Learning* (London: Routledge, 1993); Henry French and Mark Rothery, '"Upon Your Entry into the World": Masculine Values and the Threshold of Adulthood among Landed Elites in England 1680–1800', *Social History* 33 (2008), 409–410; and Alexandra Shepard, 'Student Masculinity in Early Modern Cambridge, 1560–1640', in Barbara Krug-Richter and Ruth E. Mohrmann, eds., *Frühneuzeitliche Universitätskulturen: Kulturhistorische Perspektiven auf die Hochschulen in Europa* (Cologne: Böhlau, 2009), 53–74.

7. Alan Taylor, *Thomas Jefferson's Education* (New York: W. W. Norton & Company, 2019), 14 ('poor schooling'); 'Carter Papers', *VMHB* 6 (July 1898), 17 ('bred'); 'The Will of Charles Carter of Cleve', *VMHB* 31 (December 1923), 40, n. 2 ('perfect master'). Carter stipulated that the cost of his son's education would be 'born by my ex'tors and out of the interest of my Said son George's Bank stock'. ('Carter Papers', 17.) For the Fuller family's SSC investments, see John Fuller to John Lade, 25 July 1730, in David Crossley and Richard Saville, eds., *The Fuller Letters: Guns, Slaves and Finance, 1728–1755* (Lewes: Sussex Record Society, 1991), 24; and John Fuller, Accountant's Department: Old South Sea Company Annuities Ledgers, BE, AC27/6455, 518. John Fuller held £4,202 of these securities in 1728. For his East India bonds, see John Fuller to Mr Serocold, 30 October 1736, in Crossley and Saville, eds., *Fuller Letters*, 93.

8. Brown, *Tacky's Revolt*, 89 ('Akan'); Kevin J. Hayes, *The Library of William Byrd of Westover* (Madison, WI: Madison House, 1997), 90 ('smallpox'); Jane Tucker to St. George Tucker, 1 August 1816, St. George Tucker Papers, W&M, Box 35, Folder 7 ('sea air'); Richard B. Sheridan, 'Samuel Martin, Innovating Sugar Planter of Antigua 1750–1776', *Agricultural History* 34 (July 1960), 129 ('five editions'); Richard B. Sheridan, *Sugar and Slaves: An Economic History of the British West Indies, 1623–1775* (Jamaica: Canoe Press, 1994), 200–207 ('Young'); Samuel Martin, *An Essay Upon Plantership, Humbly Inscribed To his Excellency George Thomas, Esq.; Chief Governor of All the Leeward Islands, As a Monument to Antient Friendship* (London: Samuel Jones, 1765), v ('instruction') and vii ('captivated' and 'liberal'); Michal J. Rozbicki, 'The Curse of Provincialism: Negative Perceptions of Colonial American Plantation Gentry', *The Journal of Southern History* 63 (November 1997), 729–730 ('crudeness' and 'de-anglicize[d]'). Martin was a South Sea investor, owning £1,000 of annuities in July 1729 and £2,900 by September 1733. (Samuel Martin, Old South Sea Company Annuities Legers, BE, AC27/6457, 541.) Martin is mentioned in Janet Schaw, *Journal of a Lady of Quality: Being the Narrative of a Journey from Scotland to the West Indies, North Carolina, and Portugal, in the Years 1774 to 1776*, ed. by Evangeline Walker Andrews and Charles McLean Andrews (New Haven, CT: Yale University Press, 1921), 106. For Arthur Young, see Peter M. Jones, *Agricultural Enlightenment: Knowledge, Technology, and Nature, 1750–1840* (Oxford: Oxford University Press, 2016), 66.

9. Peter Peckard to James Beattie, 23 January 1789, Beattie Manuscripts, MC ('chagrin'); Morgan Godwyn, *The Negro's & Indians advocate, suing for their admission to the church, or, A persuasive to the instructing and baptizing of the Negro's and Indians in our plantations shewing that as the compliance therewith can prejudice no mans just interest, so the wilful neglecting and opposing of it, is not less than a manifest apostacy from the Christian faith* (London: J. D., 1680), 13 ('deity' and 'Profit'); Stephen Fuller to Benjamin Newton, 25 May 1756, Correspondence received by Stephen Fuller (at Sussex, London, and elsewhere) relating mainly to estate matters, 1731–1757, SHC, DD/DN/8/1/1/55 ('Mathematicians'); Robert Beverley Student Notebooks, 1787, Beverley Family Papers, VMHC, Mss1 B4678 a 4768[54] ('algebra'); Robert Beverley notes on logic, 1787, Robert Beverley Papers, NYPL, MssCol 282 ('logic').

10. Peter Peckard, *Piety, Benevolence, and Loyalty, recommended: A sermon preached before the University of Cambridge, January the 30th, 1784* (Cambridge: J. Archdeacon for J. & J. Merrill, 1784), 3 ('fashionable') and 1 ('firm' and 'Natural'). The Corpus Christi College library accounts, for instance, do not show any major purchases of abolition material. In Michaelmas 1787, the College purchased Richard Chandler's history of Greece, Clarendon's state papers, and Sir David Dalrymple's 1786 pamphlet on the propagation of Christianity, among other manuscripts. The tradition of purchasing histories, travel volumes, and legal texts continued throughout the late eighteenth century. (Expenses for Michaelmas 1787, Library Account, 1690–1818, CCC, GBR/0268/CCCC07).

11. Searby, *History of the University of Cambridge, Volume III*, 404 ('excluded'); Rebecca Zwick, *Fair Game? The Use of Standardized Admissions Tests in Higher Education* (New York: Routledge, 2002), ch. 1 ('standardised'); Stephen Fuller to Colonel Orgyll, 15 April 1756, Correspondence received by Stephen Fuller, 1731–1757, SHC, DD/DN/8/1/1/3 ('superintendency'); John Norton to John Hatley Norton, London, 21 April 1770, in Frances Norton Mason, ed., *John Norton & Sons, Merchants of London and Virginia: Being the Papers from Their Counting House for the Years 1750 to 1795* (Richmond, VA: Dietz Press, 1937), 132 ('Cozin' and 'answer').

12. John Witherspoon, *Address to the Inhabitants of Jamaica, and other West-India Islands, In Behalf of the College of New-Jersey*, 1772, in J. Witherspoon, *The Works of John Witherspoon, D. D. Sometime Minister of the Gospel at Paisley, and Late President of Princeton College, in New Jersey*, vol. 3 (Edinburgh: J. Ogle, 1815), 309 ('highest', 'activity', and 'opulence'); Philip V. Fithian to the Reverend Enoch Green, 1 December 1773, in Hunter Dickinson Farish, ed., *Journal & Letters of Philip Vickers Fithian 1773-1774: A Plantation Tutor of the Old Dominion* (Williamsburg, VA: Colonial Williamsburg, Incorporated, 1965), 26 ('Boy') and 27 ('course'); *Candid Remarks on Dr. Witherspoon's Address To the Inhabitants of Jamaica, And the other West-India Islands, &c. In a Letter to those Gentlemen* (Philadelphia, PA: William Goddard, 1772), 9 ('numerous' and 'Person'). From the colonisation of Virginia in 1607 to the start of the American Civil War in 1861, eighty per cent of colleges failed. (Craig Steven Wilder, '"Sons from the Southward & Some from the West Indies": The Academy and Slavery in the Revolutionary America', in Harris et al., eds., *Slavery and the University*, 21–45.)

13. Kevin Joel Berland, ed., *The Dividing Line Histories of William Byrd II of Westover* (Chapel Hill: University of North Carolina Press, 2013), 5 ('Perceval'); William Byrd

II to Sir Robert Southwell, 5 August 1701, William Byrd Papers, 1701–1745, VMHC, Mss2 B9964 b 3 ('colebatch', 'distinction', 'din'd', and 'discoverys'); 31 July 1701, in Mark R. Wenger, ed., *The English Travels of Sir John Percival and William Byrd II: The Percival Diary of 1701* (Columbia: University of Missouri Press, 1989), 73–74 ('Bentley'); Lee Ann Caldwell, ed., *The Journal of the Earl of Egmont: Abstract of the Trustees Proceedings for Establishing the Colony of Georgia, 1732–1738* (Athens: University of Georgia Press, 2021), xviii ('president'); Kathleen Brown, *Good Wives, Nasty Wenches, and Anxious Patriarchs: Gender, Race, and Power in Colonial Virginia* (Chapel Hill: University of North Carolina Press, 1996), 332 ('affairs').

14. William Gooch to Thomas Gooch, 4 April 1728, Thomas Gooch Letters and Correspondence, GCC, PPC/GOO ('Peace'); Stacy L. Lorenz, '"To Do Justice to His Majesty, the Merchant and the Planter": Governor William Gooch and the Tobacco Inspection Act of 1730', *VMHB* 108 (2000), 357 ('secure'); William Gooch to Thomas Gooch, 20 July 1733, Gooch Letters, GCC, PPC/GOO ('politicks'); William Gooch to Thomas Gooch, 28 October 1727, *ibid*. ('Horses', 'boy', and 'Caius'). For Gooch, see also Dan M. Hockman, 'William Dawson: Master and Second President of the College of William and Mary', *Historical Magazine of the Protestant Episcopal Church* 52 (September 1983), 199–214; Christopher Brooke, *A History of Gonville and Caius College* (Woodbridge, Suffolk: Boydell Press, 1996), 163–170; and Christopher Brooke, J. M. Horn, and N. L. Ramsay, 'A Canon's Residence in the Eighteenth Century: The Case of Thomas Gooch', *Journal of Ecclesiastical History* 39 (October 1988), 545–556.

15. William Gooch to Thomas Gooch, October 1732, Gooch Letters, GCC, PPC/GOO ('inn'); William Gooch to Thomas Gooch, 12 June 1731, *ibid*. ('young' and 'Colledge'); William Gooch to Thomas Gooch, 7 May 1733, *ibid*. ('Son', 'University', and 'encourage'); William Gooch to Thomas Gooch, 5 July 1733, *ibid*. ('Trinity Hall', 'dinner', and 'shew'). For enslaved people in the governor's household, see Graham Hood, *The Governor's Palace in Williamsburg: A Cultural Study* (Williamsburg, VA: University of North Carolina Press, 1991), 254.

16. A. H. John, 'The London Assurance Company and the Maritime Insurance Market of the Eighteenth Century', *Economica* 25 (May 1958), 134 ('Bosanquet'); 'Mapps Estate', *Legacies*, www.ucl.ac.uk/lbs/estate/view/441#:~:text=Samuel%20 Mapp's%20plantation%20was%20130,Hughes%2DQueree%20Index%20of%20 Plantations.&text=In%201764%20Richard%20Smith%20of,the%20owner%20 of%20Mapp's%20plantation, accessed 18 January 2022 ('Mapps'); Pope, 'Wealth and Aspirations', in Tibbles et al., eds., *Liverpool*, 179 ('Buddicom'); Andrew Kippis, *Biographica Britannica: Or, the Lives of the Most Eminent Persons, who Have Flourished in Great Britain and Ireland, from the Earliest Ages, Down to the Present Times*, vol. 6 (London: Unknown, 1763), 3930 ('correction', 'voyage', and 'sailor'); Madge Dresser, 'Bristol and the Transatlantic Slave Trade', *Bristol Museum & Art Gallery*, www.bristolmuseums.org.uk/stories/bristol-transatlantic-slave-trade/, accessed 4 July 2022 ('20,000'). The Rev. Smith's involvement in Mapps Estate is also mentioned in Charlotte Smith's letter to William Tyler, 9 August 1801, in Charlotte Turner Smith and Judith Philipps Stanton, eds., *The Collected Letters of Charlotte Smith* (Bloomington: Indiana University Press, 2003), 378.

17. Benefaction received by Mr Thomas Boughey, Merchant since the 22nd Decr. 1678, Library records: donors, c. 1680, WL, Add. MS a/106 ('£100'); Articles and Orders of the Company of Adventurers to the Bahama Islands, 1672, Indenture for the Settlement of Lands, BL, Add MS 15640, f. 1 ('Proprietors'); 'Dr George Sandby',

Legacies, www.ucl.ac.uk/lbs/person/view/2146650797, accessed 26 November 2021 and Lease for 13 and a half years of Triall plantation, 1762 Church Mission Society Unofficial Papers, CRL, CMS/ACC81 T11 ('Sandby'); 'Hon. George Neville Grenville', *Legacies*, wwwdepts-live.ucl.ac.uk/lbs/person/view/42697, accessed 26 November 2021 ('£20,000'). Christopher Monck was also a founding investor in the Hudson's Bay Company and was listed on their Royal Charter in May 1670. (Copy of the patent of Hudson's Bay Company, 2 May 1670, The Patent of the Hudson's Bay Company, BL, 2447.) The information on the various tutors at Cambridge has been compiled from *ACAD* and the Jamaican Family Research Library, which has digitised documents related to slavery in Jamaica.

18. 'Walter Pollard', *ACAD*, https://venn.lib.cam.ac.uk/cgi-bin/search-2018.pl?sur=pollard&suro=w&fir=walter&firo=c&cit=&cito=c&c=all&z=all&tex=&sye=&eye=&col=all&maxcount=50, accessed 7 July 2023 ('Harrow'); John Pollard to Walter Pollard, 29 November 1772, Correspondence of Walter Pollard, 1771–1788, BL, Add MS 35655 ('much disappointed', 'disapprobation', 'Tutor', 'large', 'Logick', and 'Essay'); John Pollard to Walter Pollard, 7 March 1773, *ibid.* ('Experimental' and 'insufficiency'); John Pollard to Walter Pollard, 21 March 1773, *ibid.* ('ever honoured' and 'considerable'); Rev. William Field, *Memoirs of the Life, Writings, and Opinions of the Rev. Samuel Parr, LL.D.; with Biographical Notices of Many of His Friends, Pupils, and Contemporaries*, vol. 2 (London: Henry Colburn, 1828), 394 ('ingenuous' and 'friendship'); Matthew Mulcahy, 'Weathering the Storms: Hurricanes and Risk in the British Greater Caribbean', *The Business History Review* 78 (Winter 2004), 659 ('hurricane' and 'properties').

19. Crossley and Saville, eds., *Fuller Letters*, xxiv ('380' and 'plantations') and x ('income' and 'landholdings'); Geoffrey Plank, *Atlantic Wars: From the Fifteenth Century to the Age of Revolution* (New York and Oxford: Oxford University Press, 2020), 92 ('imperial'); Walter Thornbury, ed., *The Life of J. M. W. Turner: Founded on Letters and Papers Furnished by His Friends and Fellow Academicians*, vol. 2 (Cambridge: Cambridge University Press, 2013), 47 ('patrons'); Joseph Jekyll to Marguerite Gardiner, 1833, in R. R. Madden, ed., *The Literary Life and Correspondence of the Countess of Blessington*, vol. 3 (London: T. C. Newby, 1855), 183 ('sponsors'). For imperial wars in the Caribbean, see Elena A. Schneider, *The Occupation of Havana: War, Trade, and Slavery in the Atlantic World* (Chapel Hill: University of North Carolina Press, 2018); and Brown, *Tacky's Revolt*, ch. 1. At the Royal Institution, "Mad Jack" Fuller founded a Professorship of Chemistry and a gold medal prize for the same subject.

20. John Fuller to Dr Rose Fuller, 1 January 1741/2, in Crossley and Saville, eds., *Fuller Letters*, 413 ('Chosen Fellow'); John Fuller, 'Part of a letter from Mr. Stephen Fuller, Fellow of Trinity College, Cambridge, to his father John Fuller, Esq; Senior, F. R. S. concerning a violent hurricane in Huntingtonshire, Sept. 8 1741. Communicated by Sir Hans Sloane, late Pr. R. S', *Philosophical Transactions* 41 (December 1740), 851 ('violent'); Stephen Whisson to Stephen Fuller, 19 March 1756, Correspondence received by Stephen Fuller, 1731–1757, SHC, DD/DN/8/1/1/53 ('offer', 'prospect', and 'pittances'); Stephen Fuller to Stephen Whisson, 25 May 1756, *ibid.* ('defray'); Stephen Whisson to Stephen Fuller, 26 May 1756, *ibid.* ('admitted' and 'entitle'). Fuller continued to be a member of the Royal Society into the 1760s. (11 June 1761, Journal Books of the Royal Society, Volume 25, RS, JBO/25/119.)

21. Venn, ed., *Biographical History*, vol. 1, xxiii.

22. Trevelyan, *Trinity College*, 71 ('silver'); Searby, *History of the University of Cambridge, Volume III*, 4 ('lax'); *Remarks on the Enormous Expence in the Education*

of Young Men in the University of Cambridge; with a Plan for the Better Regulation of the Discipline of that University (London: C. Stalker, 1788), 2 ('Concern'). Henry Pennant, who matriculated at Queens' College in 1732 and became a fellow-commoner two years later in December 1734, provided a set of four sauce tureens of neo-classical form. Two of these were engraved 'Coll: Regin: dederunt Henricus Pennant ex Insula Jamaica et Johan: Peploe Mosdey Arm: Soc: commensalis ann: 1736 & 1788'. ('Silverware, 1750-99', *Queens' College, University of Cambridge*, www.queens.cam.ac.uk/visiting-the-college/history/college-facts/silverware/silverware-1750-99, accessed 30 April 2020.)

23. Roach, ed., *Victoria History of the County of Cambridge and the Isle of Ely*, 235-265 ('tuition'); Accounts of Rose Fuller at Cambridge, Leiden, and Paris, 1728-32, Books, Plans, and Account Books of the Fuller Family, ES, SAS/RF/15/27 ('spent'); Charles Davenant, *Discourses on the Public Revenues and on the Trade of England*, vol. 2 (London: James Knapton, 1698), 96 ('rich'); *Some Considerations humbly offered to both Houses of Parliament, Concerning the Sugar Colonies, and Chiefly the Island of Barbadoes* (London: A. Baldwin, 1701), 4 ('50,000').

24. Stephen Fuller to Dr Aikenhead, April 1758, Correspondence received by Stephen Fuller, 1731-1757, SHC, DD/DN/8/1/16/13 ('200'); Denis Arthur Winstanley, *Unreformed Cambridge: A Study of Certain Aspects of the University in the Eighteenth Century* (Cambridge: Cambridge University Press, 2009), 209 ('lavish'); Peter Edwards, *Horse and Man in Early Modern England* (London: Hambledon Continuum, 2007), 116 ('integral'); Anthony Hinton to Rose Fuller, 12 October 1756, Papers of Rose Fuller, ES, SAS/RF/19/34 ('Races', 'cloaths', and 'me'); Stephen Fuller to Dr Gilbert Parker, 18 June 1766, Stephen Fuller Letterbooks in the Williams Ethnological Collection, JJBL, MS.2009.030 ('Ascot'); Thomas Katheder, *The Baylors of Newmarket: The Decline and Fall of a Virginia Planter Family* (New York: Bloomington, 2009), 1-2 ('honour'). For horse racing as a pastime in the southern colonies and states, see T. H. Breen, 'Horses and Gentlemen: The Cultural Significance of Gambling among the Gentry of Virginia', *WMQ* 34 (April 1977), 239-257; Rhys Isaac, *The Transformation of Virginia, 1740-1790* (Chapel Hill: University of North Carolina Press, 1982), 119; Bertram Wyatt-Brown, *Southern Honor: Ethics & Behavior in the Old South* (Oxford and New York: Oxford University Press, 2007); and Katherine C. Mooney, *Race Horse Men: How Slavery and Freedom Were Made at the Racetrack* (Cambridge, MA: Harvard University Press, 2014).

25. Richard Roderick, Old South Sea Annuities Ledgers, BE, AC27/6459, 220 ('annuities'); 'Richard Roderick', *ACAD*, https://venn.lib.cam.ac.uk/cgi-bin/search-2018.pl?sur=&suro=w&fir=&firo=c&cit=&cito=c&c=all&z=all&tex=RDBK728R&sye=&eye=&col=all&maxcount=50, accessed 9 May 2022 ('fellow at Magdalene'); John Mandevile (or Mandeville), Old South Sea Annuities Ledgers, BE, AC27/6446, 67 ('Corpus'); Zachary Pearce, *Epistolæ Duæ ad Celeberrimum Doctissimumque Virum F—V—Professorem Amestelodamensem Scriptæ* (London: Francis Clay, 1721), 2 ('thirst', 'educated', and 'desire'); Richard Monins, Old South Sea Annuities Ledgers, BE, AC27/6446, 541 ('Monins'); Richard Loving of Trinity College, Cambridge, Transfer Book for the Company of Royal Adventurers Trading with Africa, 9 January 1722 to 3 October 1723, TNA, T70/206, 111 ('Loving'); Dr. Richard Bentley, 'Angustam Amice Pauperiem Pati', 1722, in Charles Whibley, ed., *In Cap and Gown: Three Centuries of Cambridge Wit* (London: Kegan Paul, Trench, & Co., 1889), 17 ('rich'); Richard Bentley, D. D., Old South Sea Annuities Ledgers, BE, AC27/6437, 402 ('stock'); 'Past Fellows', *The Royal*

Society, https://catalogues.royalsociety.org/CalmView/Record.aspx?src=CalmView.Persons&id=NA8038, accessed 2 February 2024 ('lost' and 'South Seas'). The South Sea Company's stock ledgers do not survive, but historians can determine the stock holdings of many earlier investors because the account books mention "By Joynt Stock SSA" if that person held these securities before the government divided South Sea stockholdings evenly into annuities and stock to ensure the Company's survival after the Bubble. Put simply, if someone owned £100 in stock in 1720, the government-enforced division of these assets in 1723 meant that someone ended up with £50 in annuities and £50 trading capital. For a helpful explanation of these source material issues, see Andrew Odlyzko, 'Newton's Financial Misadventures in the South Sea Bubble', *Royal Society Journal of the History of Science* 73 (2019), 29–59; and Ellen T. Harris, '"Master of the Orchester with a Salary": Handel at the Bank of England', *Music & Letters* 101 (February 2020), 1–29.

26. Frances Walker Baylor to John Baylor, May 25 1770, George Daniel Baylor Papers, 1743–1964, VMHC, Mss1 B3445 d 9 ('hams'); John Fuller to Rose Fuller, 21 November 1759, Papers of Rose Fuller, ES, SAS/RF/19/171 ('boarding' and 'Confidence').

27. Accounts of John Fuller, *ibid.*, 189/1–2 ('seventy pounds' and 'services'); J. E. B. Mayor, *Cambridge under Queen Anne: Illustrated by Memoir of Ambrose Bonwicke and Diaries of Francis Burman and Zacharias Conrad von Uffenbach* (Cambridge: Deighton, Bell & Co., 1911), 132 ('professors' and 'pipe'); Christopher Wordsworth, *Social Life at the English Universities in the Eighteenth Century* (Cambridge: Cambridge University Press, 1874), 373 ('traded news'). For coffeehouse culture in Britain, see Brian Cowan, *The Social Life of Coffee: The Emergence of the British Coffeehouse* (New Haven, CT: Yale University Press, 2008).

28. 'Emmanuel College', *An Inventory of the Historical Monuments in the City of Cambridge* (London: Her Majesty's Stationary Office, 1959) ('earned'); 'Burch Hothersall', *Emmanuel College Paintings*, www.emma.cam.ac.uk/about/history/paintings/index.cfm, accessed 20 February 2021 ('donated'); 'Church and Organ Music', *The Musical Times* 49 (October 1908), 649 ('Joice'); 'William Long', ACAD, https://venn.lib.cam.ac.uk/cgi-bin/search-2018.pl?sur=long&suro=w&fir=william&firo=c&cit=&cito=c&c=all&z=all&tex=&sye=&eye=&col=all&maxcount=50, accessed 17 March 2021 ('Long'); Greg Dening, *The Death of William Gooch: A History's Anthropology* (Melbourne: Melbourne University Press, 1995), 97 ('two hundred'); Mr Byam's Legacies, Wills, 1800–1914, KCA, GBR/0272/KCHR/3/1/8, 76 ('£200'); Gavin Stamp, 'George Gilbert Scott, Jun., and King's College Chapel', *Architectural History* 37 (1994), 160 ('erecting'). The fire gutted the southern range of the Front Court at Emmanuel College.

29. Searby, *History of the University of Cambridge, Volume III*, 69 ('Gentlemen'); Wordsworth, *Social Life at the English Universities*, 109 ('entitled'); 25 October 1786, Master/Registry Gesta, 1784–1811, GCC, GC/GOV/03/01/07 ('plate'); Dr William Savage to the Master of Caius College, 15 December 1724, Papers concerning foundation and fellowships; and papers relating to the Mastership of Sir John Ellys, GCC, GC/MAS/01/01/01 ('Lustre' and 'proper').

30. Wordsworth, *Social Life at the English Universities*, 98 ('pensioner'); Searby, *History of the University of Cambridge, Volume III*, 142–143 ('sizars'); Roach, ed., *Victoria History of the County of Cambridge and the Isle of Ely: Volume 3*, 255–265 ('reformed'); Cannon, *Aristocratic Century*, 55 ('servants'); Venn and Venn, *Alumni Cantabrigiensis*, vol. 1, 399 ('Holt').

31. Edmund Berkeley, Jr., 'Carter, Robert (ca. 1664–1732)', in Sara B. Bearss, ed., *The Dictionary of Virginia Biography*, vol. 3 (Richmond: Library of Virginia, 2006),

84–86 ('owned'); Walsh, *Motives of Honor*, 240 ('Fairfield'); Festo Annunc. 1729 to Festum Mich. 1729, College Bursar Book, GCC, GC/BUR/F/88 ('appears'); Robert Carter to Lewis Burwell, 22 August 1727, Robert Carter Letterbook, 1701–1732, microfilm, VMHC ('Scholar'); Robert Carter to Lewis Burwell, 26 June 1729, *ibid.* ('Qualitys'); Robert Carter to Lewis Burwell, 12 August 1731, *ibid.* ('fairly'); Robert Carter to William Dawkins, 11 July 1732, *ibid.* ('denied'); Robert Carter to Micajah Perry, 11 July 1732, *ibid.* ('Effects'); William Hamilton Bryson, ed., 'A Letter of Lewis Burwell to James Burrough, July 8, 1734', *VMHB* 81 (1973), 409 ('Burrough') and 414 ('Master'); Robert Simpson, Old South Sea Annuities Ledgers, BE, AC27/6459, 719 ('investor').

32. Dr Henry Godolphin, List of Holders of East India Company Stock, 16 April 1694, Stocks and Bonds of the East India Company, BL, IOR/H/2, 10 ('EIC'); Dr Henry Godolphin, Dean of St. Pauls, Old South Sea Annuities Ledgers, BE, AC27/6442, 405 ('South Sea'); H. C. Maxwell Lyte, *A History of Eton College, 1440–1875* (London: Macmillan and Co., 1875), 284 ('own cost').

33. Ralph Izard to William Drayton, 26 October 1777, in Anne Izard Deas, ed., *Correspondence of Mr. Ralph Izard, of South Carolina, From the Year 1774 to 1804; with a Short Memoir* (New York: Charles S. Francis & Co., 1844), 368 ('good character', 'proper', and 'residence'); Petley, *White Fury*, 26 ('Eton'); Jonathan H. Poston, 'Ralph Wormeley V of Rosegill: A deposed Virginia aristocrat, 1774–1781' (MA Thesis, College of William and Mary, 1979), 15 ('friends' and 'companions'). There was a sixfold increase in the number of Caribbean enslaver children attending Eton. After leaving, these students remembered their time at school fondly. Eton received donations of books and prints from Anthony Morris Stoner, and several portraits from students remain at the College. (O'Shaughnessy, *An Empire Divided*, 20–21.) See also Sol Gamsu et al., 'Elite Schools and Slavery in the UK – Capital, Violence and Extractivism', *Discourse: Studies in the Cultural Politics of Education* 45 (2024), 325–345.

34. Christopher Reid, 'Whig Declamation and Rhetorical Freedom at Trinity College, Cambridge, 1770–1805', *The Review of English Studies* 64 (September 2013), 630 ('prestigious'); R. G. Thorne, ed., *The History of Parliament: The House of Commons, 1790–1820*, vol. 1 (London: Haynes Publishing, 1986), 293 ('peers'); 'Rt. Hon. Henry Goulburn', *Legacies*, www.ucl.ac.uk/lbs/person/view/21529, accessed 30 November 2021 ('Goulburn'). In May 1831, Goulburn became the MP for Cambridge University, a seat which he held until his death in January 1856. See Brian Jenkins, *Henry Goulburn, 1784–1856: A Political Biography* (Montreal and London: McGill-Queen's University Press, 1996), 173–174.

35. 'John Downman', *National Portrait Gallery*, www.npg.org.uk/collections/search/person/mp06903/john-downman, accessed 10 November 2021 ('Downman'); J. H. P., 'The Gorsuch and Lovelace Families (Continued)', *VMHB* 25 (July 1917), 316 ('mortarboard'); 'Ralph Wormeley V (1745–1806)', *Colonial Virginia Portraits*, https://colonialvirginiaportraits.org/portrait/ralph-wormeley-v-1745-1806-2/, accessed 9 September 2020 ('Trinity Hall'); 'John Carter', *Encyclopedia Virginia*, https://encyclopediavirginia.org/11631-6eb94a2f744480e/, accessed 9 September 2020 ('posed'); Sir Godfrey Kneller, Transfer Book, May-June 1720, TNA, T70/199/1, 40 ('investor'). Kneller held £1,000 in Royal African stock. Downman studied under Benjamin West and painted in Cambridge after a residence in Italy from 1773 to 1775. Though associated with Napoleon, the hand-in-waistcoat pose was popular in eighteenth-century England. See Arline Meyer, 'Re-dressing Classical Statuary: The

Eighteenth-Century "Hand-in-Waistcoat" Portrait', *The Art Bulletin* 77 (March 1995), 45–63.
36. 'Charles Crawford, "Earl of Crawford and Lindsay"', *Legacies*, www.ucl.ac.uk/lbs/person/view/2146639287, accessed 7 April 2022 ('son'); 'Alexander Crawford of Antigua and Devonshire Street', *ibid.*, www.ucl.ac.uk/lbs/person/view/2146659687, accessed 7 April 2022 ('brother'); Winstanley, *Unreformed Cambridge*, 219 ('drunk').
37. *Ibid.*, 220 ('take', 'self-preservation', and 'touch'); *The Scots Magazine*, 1773 ('West-Indians', 'discreet', 'expensive', and 'colder'); Lewis Leary, 'Charles Crawford: A Forgotten Poet of Early Philadelphia', *The Pennsylvania Magazine of History of Biography* 83 (July 1959), 294 ('abolitionist'); 'To the Printer', *The Public Advertiser*, 21 October 1773 ('Slave-Drivers'). For enslaver violence on campuses in the United States, see Jennifer Bridges Oast, 'Negotiating the Honor Culture: Students and Slaves at Three Virginia Colleges', in Harris et al., eds., *Slavery and the University*, 84–98; and Maurie D. McInnis, 'Violence', in. Maurie D. McInnis and Louis P. Nelson, eds., *Educated in Tyranny: Slavery at Thomas Jefferson's University* (Charlottesville: University of Virginia Press, 2019), unpaginated e-book edition.
38. Norma Myers, *Reconstructing the Black Past: Blacks in Britain, 1780–1830* (London and New York: Routledge, 2003), 20 ('10 to 15,000'); Vincent Caretta, ed., *Unchained Voices: An Anthology of Black Authors in the English-Speaking World of the 18th Century* (Lexington: University Press of Kentucky, 2004), 399 ('Born'); 'An Act to Prevent Slaves being Evidence against John Williams, a Free Negro', in *Acts of the Assembly, Passed in the island of Jamaica, from 1681, to 1737, inclusive* (London: John Baskett, 1789), 119 ('customs'); Caretta, *Unchained Voices*, 398–399 ('experiment') and 400–401 ('records' and 'member'); David Hume, 'Of National Characters', David Hume, *Essays Moral, Political and Literary* (Oxford: Oxford University Press, 1963), 213 ('man of parts'); *Gentleman's Magazine*, 1771, 595–596 ('dressed' and 'rejected'). These figures were subject to sensationalist debate – further highlighting white fears about Black immigration. In 1764, the *Gentleman's Magazine* claimed that there were '20,000 Negroe servants' in Britain, and, in 1772, Lord Mansfield, deciding whether James Somerset was to be freed, estimated that there were 15,000 African-descended people residing in the country.
39. Baptism of a 'Negro Christian in the house, the weather being extremely cold', 4 February 1710, Registers and Service of the Gamlingay Parish Church, CA KP76/1/1 ('Negro Christian'); 'A Black Servant', *Cambridge Chronicle and Journal*, 2 December 1797 ('Lady' and 'Jamaica'); 'Deaths', *The Royal Gazette* (Jamaica), 6 April 1793 ('Westmoreland'); 'Advertisements', *Cambridge Chronicle and Journal*, 5 August 1848 ('servant'); Chris Lloyd, 'The Richmond slave given his freedom after saving life of gamekeeper during moor's fire', 14 November 2019, *The Northern Echo*, www.thenorthernecho.co.uk/history/18036868.richmond-slave-given-freedom-saving-life-gamekeeper-moors-fire/, accessed 15 October 2021 ('Fish River' and 'Barker'); Venn and Venn, *Alumni Cantabrigiensis*, vol. 1, 442 ('alumnus'); Baptism of John Yorke, 1776, Copies of Entries of Marske Parish Register, NYCRO, ZAZ/70/22/24 ('catechism'); 'Timothy Hutton', ACAD, https://venn.lib.cam.ac.uk/cgi-bin/search-2018.pl?sur=hutton&suro=w&fir=timothy&firo=c&cit=&cito=c&c=all&z=all&tex=&sye=&eye=&col=all&maxcount=50, accessed 15 October 2021 ('donated'). Charles Ignatius Sancho was featured in a painting of Lady Mary Churchill, Duchess of Montagu, and Caesar Shaw, an enslaved African man in the employment of the Spencer family, was featured in two portraits of John Spencer. (Peter Fryer, *Staying Power: The History of Black People in Britain* [London: Pluto Press, 1984], 72–73.)

40. Venn and Venn, *Alumni Cantabrigiensis*, vol. 2, 158 ('matriculated'); James A. Rawley, 'Henry Laurens and the Atlantic Slave Trade', in James A. Rawley ed., *London: Metropolis of the Slave Trade* (Columbia: University of Missouri Press, 2003), 82–97 ('8,000'); Flavell, *London*, 43–44 ('Scipio'); Henry Laurens to John Paul Grimké, 3 October 1772, in Philip M. Harmer et al., eds., *The Papers of Henry Laurens*, vol. 8 (Columbia: University of South Carolina Press, 1980), 489 ('genteel' and 'preparative').
41. 'Hon. Samuel Alpress', *Legacies* www.ucl.ac.uk/lbs/person/view/2146650011, accessed 30 November 2021 ('father'); George Alpress's Letter of Introduction to Jesus College, 19 July 1754, Correspondence received by Stephen Fuller, 1731–1757, SHC, DD/DN/8/1/1 ('expended' and 'qualify'); Stephen Fuller to Benjamin Newton, 25 May 1756, *ibid.* ('intended').
42. Samuel Alpress to Stephen Fuller, 19 January 1757, *ibid.* ('Fence'); Samuel Alpress to Stephen Fuller, 26 January 1758, Correspondence received by Stephen Fuller (at Sussex and London) relating mainly to estate and business matters (including Jamaica), 1758–1762, SHC, 18 ('Estates', 'Circle', and 'Credit').
43. William Hawes to Stephen Fuller, 20 February 1757, Papers of Stephen Fuller, ES, DD/DN/503 ('Misfortune' and 'Expence'); Samuel Alpress to Stephen Fuller, 29 October 1758, Correspondence received by Stephen Fuller, 1758–1762, SHC, DD/DN/8/1/18 ('Curacy' and 'best living').
44. Samuel Alpress to Stephen Fuller, 13 February 1759, *ibid.* ('oblig'd'); Benjamin Newton to Stephen Fuller, 25 May 1759, *ibid.* ('frollick'); Benjamin Newton to Stephen Fuller, 28 May 1759, *ibid.* ('suffering'); Samuel Alpress to Stephen Fuller, 14 June 1759, *ibid.* ('Friends').
45. Robert Carter Nicholas to John Norton, 30 November 1772, in Mason, ed., *John Norton & Sons*, 285 ('Foundation'); William Nelson to John Norton, 27 February 1768, in *ibid.* ('Temptations'); 23 February 1770, in 'Extracts from Diary of Col. Landon Carter', *WMQ* 13 (July 1904), 47 ('priggishness'). In 1785, one parent forbade their children from associating with the Virginia gentry, many of whom had English educations, 'lest they should imbibe more exalted notions of their own importance than I could wish any child of mine to possess'. (Will of Thompson Mason, 1785, in Kate M. Rowland, ed., *Life of George Mason, 1725–1792*, vol. 2 [New York and London: G. P. Putnam's Sons, 1892], 77.)
46. *South Carolina Gazette and American General Advertiser*, 20 November 1769 ('Patriotick' and 'True'); Hugh Swinton Legaré, 'On Classical Learning', in Mary Legaré, ed., *Writings of Hugh Swinton Legaré, Late Attorney General and Acting Secretary of State of the United States: Consisting of a Diary of Brussels, and Journal of the Rhine; Extracts from his Private and Diplomatic Correspondence; Orations and Speeches; and Contributions to the New-York and Southern Reviews*, vol. 2 (Charleston, SC: Burges and James, 1845), 7 ('opulent' and 'scholarship'); Samuel Miller, *A Brief Retrospect of the Eighteenth century. Part First; In Two Volumes: Containing a Sketch of the Revolutions and Improvements in Science, Arts, and Literature, During that Period*, vol. 2 (New York: T. and J. Swords, 1803), 400 ('classics'); Michael O'Brien, *Conjectures of Order: Intellectual Life and the American South, 1810–1860*, vol. 1 (Chapel Hill: University of North Carolina Press, 2004), 91 ('travelled'). For another example of newspapers promoting the American colleges, see the *Connecticut Gazette* (New Haven), 2 August 1765.
47. 'John Collingwood Tarleton', *ACAD*, https://venn.lib.cam.ac.uk/cgi-bin/search-2018.pl?sur=tarleton&suro=w&fir=john&firo=c&cit=&cito=c&c=all&z=all&tex=&sye=&eye=&col=all&maxcount=50, accessed 1 December 2021

('fellow-commoner'); Jim Piecuch, *Three Peoples, One King: Loyalists, Indians, and Slaves in the Revolutionary South, 1775-1782* (Columbia: University of South Carolina Press, 2008), 239 ('massacring'); James A. Rawley and Stephen D. Behrendt, *The Transatlantic Slave Trade: A History* (Lincoln and London: University of Nebraska Press, 2005), 182-184 ('slave-trading operations'); John Tarleton to Clayton Tarleton, 5 February 1788, Tarleton family correspondence, including letters and papers of Clayton Tarleton (1762-1797) during his mayoralty, 1792-93, LRO, 920 TAR/4/5 ('minutely' and 'impending'); *The Times*, 13 September 1819 ('worth'). Between 1750 and 1799, Pope has identified nineteen sons of slave-traders who attended Cambridge, and the wealth from these operations persisted into the nineteenth century. ('Wealth and Social Aspirations of Liverpool's Slave Merchants', in Richardson et al., eds., *Liverpool*, 179.)

48. Greg Dening, *The Death of William Gooch: A History's Anthropology* (Melbourne: Melbourne University Press, 1995), 97 ('200'); 'Forby, Robert', Leslie Stephen, ed., *Dictionary of National Biography*, vol. 19 (New York: Macmillan and Co., 1889), 414 ('tutor'); Jerome Handler et al. *Searching for a Slave Cemetery in Barbados, West Indies: A Bioarchaeological and Ethnohistorical Investigation* (Southern Illinois University: Center for Archaeological Investigations, Research Paper No. 59, 1989), 38 ('tenure').

49. *Ibid.*, 37 ('consisted'); *Abridgment of the Minutes of the Evidence: Taken Before a Committee of the whole House, to whom it was referred to consider of the Slave Trade*, vol. 3 (London: Unknown, 1791), 129 ('same' and 'employed'); Martin Folkes to Robert Fellowes, 20 November 1789, Letters to Sir Martin Browne Folkes re. Sir John Berney's affairs, NRO, MC 50/45 ('Sugar works'); *The Norfolk Chronicle, or, the Norwich Gazette*, 22 June 1782 ('principal part'); Jonathan Worrell to Robert Fellowes, 15 February 1792, Letters re. Sir John Berney's affairs, NRO, MC 50/45 ('enhance', 'advantage', 'temporary', 'Domingo', 'peace', and 'produce'); Dubois, *Avengers of the New World*, 163 ('abolish'); Olaudah Equiano, *The Interesting Narrative of the Life of Olaudah Equiano, or Gustavus Vassa, the African. Written by Himself* (London: Printed by the Author, 1794), xviii ('subscriber'); 'To Be Sold', *Barbados Mercury and Bridge-Town Gazette*, 17 November 1810 ('1810'). For the names of the enslaved people on the plantation, see Journal of Hanson Plantation Accounts, 1792, NRO, FEL 884, 556X4. There are nine different references to the sale or lease of Hanson's plantation in the 1810 editions of the *Barbados Mercury*, perhaps illustrating the desire of Berney's executors to profit from the estate.

50. Josephine R. B. Wright, 'George Polgreen Bridgetower: An African Prodigy in England, 1789-99', *The Musical Quarterly* 66 (January 1980), 65-82 ('Bachelor'); Clifford D. Panton, *George Augustus Polgreen Bridgetower, Violin Virtuoso and Composer of Color in Late 18th Century Europe* (New York: Edwin Mellen Press, 2005), 5-6 ('father'); F. G. E., 'George P. Bridgetower and the Kreutzer Sonata', *The Musical Times* 49 (May 1908), 305 ('renowned') and 306 ('composed'); *The Times*, 2 July 1811 ('composition'); Vere Langford Oliver, *The History of the Island of Antigua, One of the Leeward Caribbees in the West Indies. From the First Settlement in 1635 to the Present Time*, vol. 3 (London: Mitchell and Hughes, 1896), 153 ('Royal African').

51. 'Thomas Hopkinson', *Legacies*, www.ucl.ac.uk/lbs/person/view/45307, accessed 3 March 2022 ('admitted'); *The Times*, 17 September 1828 ('man of colour'); Daniel Livesay, *Children of Uncertain Fortune: Mixed-Race Jamaicans in Britain and the Atlantic Family, 1733-1833* (Chapel Hill: University of North Carolina Press,

2018), unpaginated e-book edition ('shunned'); *The Times*, 25 August 1828 ('nobleman'); Emilia Viotti da Costa, *Crowns of Glory, Tears of Blood: The Demerara Slave Rebellion of 1823* (Oxford: Oxford University Press, 1994), 223 ('fired'); Joshua Bryant, *Account of an Insurrection of the Negro Slaves in the Colony of Demerara, which broke out on the 18th of August, 1823* (Demerara: A. Stevenson, 1824), 47 ('revolt'); Drescher, *Abolition*, 257 ('freeborn').
52. 'Robert Collymore', ACAD, https://venn.lib.cam.ac.uk/cgi-bin/search-2018.pl?sur=collymore&suro=w&fir=robert&firo=c&cit=&cito=c&c=all&z=all&tex=&sye=&eye=&col=all&maxcount=50, accessed 1 December 2021 ('matriculated'); Katherine Paugh, *The Politics of Reproduction: Race, Medicine, and Fertility in the Age of Abolition* (Oxford: Oxford University Press, 2017), 193–194 ('manumitted'); Kit Candlin and Cassandra Pybus, *Enterprising Women: Gender, Race, and Power in the Revolutionary Atlantic* (Athens: University of Georgia Press, 2015), 39 ('richest'); Jerome S. Handler, *The Unappropriated People: Freedmen in the Slave Society of Barbados* (Mona, Jamaica: University of the West Indies Press, 2009), 121 ('bequeathed'); 'Amaryllis Collymore', *Legacies*, www.ucl.ac.uk/lbs/person/view/2146639537, accessed 12 January 2022 ('will'); Michael Pike Mate to Alexander Gooden, 10 August 1841, in Jonathan Smith and Christopher Stray, eds., *Cambridge in the 1830s: The Letters of Alexander Chisolm Gooden, 1831–1841* (London: Boydell & Brewer, 2003), 210 ('Sugar Bichard'). For the significance of free Black women in slave societies, see also Erin Trahey, 'Among Her Kinswomen: Legacies of Free Women of Color in Jamaica', *WMQ* 76 (April 2019), 257–288.
53. 'Private Tuition', *The Barbadian*, 17 May 1825 ('advertisements' and 'instructing'); Peter Campbell Scarlett, ed., *A Memoir of the Right Honourable James, First Lord Abinger Chief Baron of Her Majesty's Court of Exchequer* (London: John Murray, 1877), 22 ('sensible', 'contamination', 'intercourse', and 'dialect').
54. 'Sir Lawrence Dundas, 1st Baronet', *Legacies*, www.ucl.ac.uk/lbs/person/view/2146656113, accessed 29 January 2023 ('career'); 'Sir Keith Alexander Jackson, 2nd Baronet, of Arsley', *ibid.*, www.ucl.ac.uk/lbs/person/view/2146664351, accessed 29 January 2023 ('Jackson'); 'Peter Isaac Thellusson, 1st Baronet Rendlesham', *ibid.*, www.ucl.ac.uk/lbs/person/view/2146641149, accessed 29 January 2023 ('heir'); Rev. Frederick Herbert Maberly, *The Melancholy and Awful Death of Lawrence Dundas, Esq.* (London: J. F. Dove, 1818), 4–5 ('resort', 'stripping', and 'glutton'). Marmaduke Lawson, a Magdalene fellow, responded with a scathing rejoinder; see *Strictures on the Rev. F. H. Maberly's Account of 'The Melancholy and Awful End of Lawrence Dundas, Esq. of Trinity College;' and His Appeal to the University on its Laxity of Discipline* (London: Bensley and Sons, 1818).
55. 'Stephen Fuller', *Legacies*, www.ucl.ac.uk/lbs/person/view/2146645307, accessed 30 September 2021 ('£10,000'); 'Francis Henry Dickinson', ACAD, https://venn.lib.cam.ac.uk/cgi-bin/search-2018.pl?sur=dickinson&suro=w&fir=francis&firo=c&cit=&cito=c&c=all&z=all&tex=&sye=&eye=&col=all&maxcount=9999, accessed 1 December 2021 ('1831'); 'Edmund Henry Dickinson', *ibid.* ('1838'); George Dickinson to Francis Henry Dickinson, 7 June 1838, Correspondence received by Francis Henry Dickinson (usually at Kingweston), 1833–1838, SHC, DD/DN/4/4/5 ('Club'); George Peacock to Francis Henry Dickinson, 23 June 1838, *ibid.* ('Astronomy'); Printed rules of the Association of Jamaica Proprietors, 1838, Listing the Names members of the Association's Select Committee for 1838–1839, *ibid.*, 9 ('Association'); Will of Thomas Lowndes of London, Prerogative Court of Canterbury and related Probate Jurisdictions: Will Registers, TNA, PROB 11/762/307 ('my estate'); The Memorial of

the Association of Jamaica Proprietors to the Viscount Melbourne and the Marquis of Normanby, 24 May 1838, in *Papers Relative to the West Indies. Part IV. Bahamas. Honduras. Mauritius. Cape of Good Hope* (London: House of Commons, 1839), 2 ('proportion'). Historians who have challenged this rise and fall narrative include Christopher Petley, ed., *Rethinking the Fall of the Planter Class* (London: Routledge, 2016); Nicholas Draper, 'The Rise of a New Planter Class? Some Countercurrents from British Guiana and Trinidad, 1807–33', *Atlantic Studies* 9 (January 2012), 65–83; and Nicholas Draper, *Price of Emancipation*, 341–346.

2 'The Highe Priest hath banished you forth': Missionary Protestantism and the Origins of the British Empire

1. John Peile, *Biographical Register of Christ's College, 1505–1905, and of the Earlier Foundation, God's House, 1448–1505*, vol. 2 (Cambridge: Cambridge University Press, 1910), 215 ('fellow'); *An Account of Two Missionary Voyages by the Appointment of the Society for the Propagation of the Gospel in Foreign Parts* (London: Benjamin Dod, 1758), 35–38 ('five years') and 43 ('Barbarians'). For Thompson's travel writings in North America, see *A Letter from New Jersey in America, Giving Some Account and Description of that Province* (London: M. Cooper, 1756). Thompson also published his *A Discourse Relating to the Present Times, Addressed to the Serious Consideration of the Public* (London: J. Oliver, 1757).
2. Newman, *A New World of Labor*, 39–41 ('Castle'); Thompson, *An Account of Two Missionary Voyages*, 37 ('Table'); Governor Thomas Melvil to African Committee, 11 June 1752, in Vincent Caretta and Ty M. Reese, eds., *The Life and Letters of Philip Quaque: The First African Anglican Missionary* (Athens and London: University of Georgia Press, 2010), 189 ('convert' and 'Prophets').
3. Travis Glasson, *Mastering Christianity: Missionary Anglicanism and Slavery in the Atlantic World* (Oxford: Oxford University Press, 2011), 174–175 ('Quaque'); Thomas Thompson, *The African Trade for Negro Slaves, Consistent with Humanity and Revealed Religion* (Canterbury: Simmons and Kirkby, 1772), 6 ('dedicated') and title page ('SOMETIME FELLOW'); Stephen J. Braidwood, *Black Poor and White Philanthropists: London's Blacks and the Foundation of the Sierra Leone Settlement 1786–1791* (Liverpool: Liverpool University Press, 1994), 267 ('African Company'). Thompson's arguments aligned with the views of the Royal African Company and its successor organisation, the African Company of Merchants: that African enslavement improved the lives of enslaved Africans because they were free from human sacrifices, cannibalism, and paganism in their homelands. (Pettigrew, *Freedom's Debt*, 196.) For Thompson's impact on proslavery discourse, see Tise, *Proslavery*, 24–25; Swaminathan, *Debating the Slave Trade*, 142–143; Jack P. Greene, *Evaluating Empire and Confronting Colonialism in Eighteenth-Century Britain* (Cambridge and New York: Cambridge University Press, 2013), 180–183; and Molly Oshatz, *Slavery & Sin: The Fight against Slavery and the Rise of Liberal Protestantism* (Oxford and New York: Oxford University Press, 2012), 27–29.
4. Thompson, *African Trade*, 8 ('necessity') and 30 ('natives').
5. Granville Sharp, *An Essay on Slavery, Proving from Scripture its Inconsistency with Humanity and Religion* (Burlington: Isaac Collins, 1776), 19 ('leisure') and 28 ('destroys'); Edmund Keene, *A Sermon Preached before the Incorporated Society for the Propagation of the Gospel in Foreign Parts; At Their Parish Church of St.*

Mary-Le-Bow On Friday February 18, 1757 (London: E. Owen and T. Harrison, 1757), 59-60 ('Distemper'); Letter of Thanks to the Master and Fellows of Christ's College, 8 March 1757, Letters from Thomas Thompson, CCMR ('Benefaction'). For Benezet's attack against Thompson, see also Jonathan D. Sassi, 'Anthony Benezet as Intermediary between the Transatlantic and Provincial: New Jersey's Antislavery Campaign on the Eve of the American Revolution', in Marie-Jeanne Rossignol and Betrand Van Ruymbeke, eds., *The Atlantic World of Anthony Benezet (1713–1784): From French Reformation to American Quaker Antislavery Activism* (Leiden: Brill 2017), 136. Furthermore, in a 22 August 1772 letter to Benezet Benjamin Franklin noted the 'great Effects' that the abolitionist had achieved in his attacks against Thompson's pamphlet. (Benjamin Franklin to Anthony Benezet, 22 August 1772, Founders Online, https://founders.archives.gov/documents/Franklin/01-19-02-0173, accessed 7 January 2022.) In 1776, Sharp lambasted slavery's 'advocates' who had 'palliate[d] the guilt [of enslavers], and have even ventured to appeal to Scripture' to justify their actions. (Granville Sharp, *The Just Limitation of Slavery in the Laws of God, Compared with the unbounded Claims of the African Traders and British American Slaveholders* [London: B. White, 1776], 2–3.)

6. For the spread of Christianity and the debates within its denominations about slavery and abolition, see Glasson, *Mastering Christianity*; Randy J. Sparks, *On Jordan's Stormy Banks: Evangelicalism in Mississippi, 1773–1876* (Athens: University of Georgia Press, 1994); Kenneth P. Minkema, 'Jonathan Edwards on Slavery and the Slave Trade', *WMQ* 54 (October 1997), 823–834; Mary Turner, *Slaves and Missionaries: The Disintegration of Jamaican Slave Society, 1787–1834* (Barbados: The Press University of the West Indies, 1998); Sylvia R. Frey and Betty Wood, *Come Shouting to Zion: African American Protestantism in the American South and British Caribbean to 1830* (Chapel Hill: University of North Carolina Press, 1998); Jon F. Sensbach, *Rebecca's Revival: Creating Black Christianity in the Atlantic World* (Cambridge, MA: Harvard University Press, 2006); Philip Hoffman, 'Christian Missionaries, Slavery, and the Slave Trade: The Third Order of Saint Francis in Eighteenth-Century Angola', *African Economic History* 51 (May 2023), 65–92; and Gerbner, *Christian Slavery*.

7. Andrew Fitzmaurice, *Humanism and America: An Intellectual History of English Colonisation, 1500–1625* (Cambridge: Cambridge University Press, 2003), 66–67 ('educated' and 'vigorous'); P. J. Wallis, 'The Library of William Crashawe', *Transactions of the Cambridge Bibliographical Society* 2 (1956), 223 ('Southampton').

8. 'The Names of the Adventurers, with their seuerall summes aduentured, paid to Sir *Thomas* Smith, Knight, late Treasurer of the Company for Virginia', 22 June 1620, in Susan Myra Kingsbury, ed., *The Records of the Virginia Company*, vol. 3 (Washington, D.C.: Government Printing Office, 1935), 322 ('shareholder'); William Crashaw, *A sermon preached in London before the right honorable the Lord Lavvarre, Lord Gouernour and Captaine Generall of Virginea, and others of his Maiesties Counsell for that kingdome, and the rest of the aduenturers in that plantation* (London: W. Hall, 1610), unnumbered ('soules', 'want', and 'richer'); Draft of open letter, c.1619, Nicholas Ferrar Papers, MC, FP 134 ('Schooles' and 'Civilitye').

9. 'Nicholas Ferrar', *ACAD*, https://venn.lib.cam.ac.uk/cgi-bin/search-2018.pl?sur=ferrar&suro=w&fir=&firo=c&cit=&cito=c&c=all&z=all&tex=&sye=&eye=&col=all&maxcount=50, accessed 2 December 2021 ('Clare Hall'); Peter Peckard, 'A Life of Nicholas Ferrar', in B. Blackstone, ed., *The Ferrar Papers: Containing a Life of Nicholas Ferrar, the Winding Sheet an Ascetic Dialogue, a Collection of Short Moral Histories, and a Selection of Family Letters* (Cambridge: Cambridge University

Press, 1938), 67 ('Raleigh'); Michael Leroy Oberg, *Dominion and Civility: English Imperialism and Native America, 1585–1685* (Ithaca, NY: Cornell University Press, 1999), 69 ('headright'); Allan Lawson Maycock, *Nicholas Ferrar of Little Gidding* (London: Society for Promoting Christian Knowledge, 1938), 167–168 ('iron'); Ben Marsh, *Unravelled Dreams: Silk and the Atlantic World, 1500–1840* (Cambridge: Cambridge University Press, 2020), 126–135 ('silkworks'); Alexander Whitaker, *Good newes from Virginia Sent to the Counsell and Company of Virginia, resident in England* (London: William Welby, 1613) ('Scholler'). See also Andrew Fitzmaurice, *Sovereignty, Property and Empire, 1500–2000* (Cambridge: Cambridge University Press, 2014), 60–62.

10. Newman, *A New World of Labor*, 82 ('tens'); Brendan Smith, *Crisis and Survival in Late Medieval Ireland: The English of Louth and Their Neighbours, 1330–1450* (Oxford: Oxford University Press, 2013), 82–83 ('*Visitation*'); Maeve Callan, 'Making Monsters Out of One Another in the Early Fourteenth-Century British Isles', *Eolas: The Journal of the American Society of Irish Medieval Studies* 12 (2019), 58 ('sacrilegious', 'crusade', 'wellbeing', and 'just war'); 'William Bedell', *ACAD*, https://venn.lib.cam.ac.uk/cgi-bin/search-2018.pl?sur=bedell&suro=w&fir=william&firo=c&cit=&cito=c&c=all&z=all&tex=&sye=&eye=&col=all&maxcount=50, accessed 29 June 2022 ('Bedell'); 'Sir Thomas Bendish (1607–1674)', *St John's College, Cambridge*, www.joh.cam.ac.uk/library/special_collections/early_books/bendish.htm, accessed 22 May 2023 ('books'); David Brown, *Empire and Enterprise: Money, Power and the Adventurers for Irish Land during the British Civil Wars* (Manchester: Manchester University Press, 2020), 235 ('East India', 'Muscovy', and '£250') and 239 ('£400'); Charles Saye, *Annals of Cambridge University Library* (Cambridge: University Library, 1916), 80 ('forty'); Robert Potts, *Liber Cantabrigiensis, an Account of the Aids Afforded to Poor Students, the Encouragements Offered to Diligent Students, and the Rewards Conferred on Successful Students, in the University of Cambridge* (Cambridge: Cambridge University Press, 1855), 365 ('ten'). Ash's benefaction to Emmanuel was made in 1654 following his speculation with the Adventurers. For the colonisation of Ireland, particularly the Ulster plantation, see Nicholas P. Canny, *Making Ireland British, 1580–1650* (Oxford: Oxford University Press, 2001); Audrey J. Horning, *Ireland in the Virginian Sea: Colonialism in the British Atlantic* (Chapel Hill: University of North Carolina Press, 2013); Gerard Farrell, *The 'Mere Irish' and the Colonisation of Ulster, 1570–1641* (London: Palgrave Macmillan, 2017); John Patrick Montaño, *The Roots of English Colonialism in Ireland* (Cambridge: Cambridge University Press, 2011); and Patricia Palmer, *Language and Conquest in Early Modern Ireland: English Renaissance Literature and Elizabethan Imperial Expansion* (Cambridge: Cambridge University Press, 2001).

11. John Strype, *The Life of the Learned Sir Thomas Smith, Kt. Doctor of the Civil Law, Principal Secretary of State to King Edward the Sixth, and Queen Elizabeth* (Oxford: Clarendon Press, 1820).

12. *Ibid.* ('thirteen-year'); Indenture and Patent of 5 October 1571, *ibid.*, 131–132 ('wicked'); Hiram Morgan, 'The Colonial Venture of Sir Thomas Smith in Ireland, 1571–1575', *HJ* 28 (June 1985), 261 ('enrichment').

13. *Ibid.*, 262 ('joint-stock') and 264 ('three'); Sir Thomas Smith, *A Letter sent by I. B. Gentleman unto his very frende Mayster R. C. Esquire, wherin is conteined a large discourse of the peopling and inhabiting the Cuntrie called the Ardes, and other adiacent in the North of Ireland, and taken in hand by Sir Thomas Smith, one of the Queens Maisties priuie counsel, and Thomas Smith Esquire, his sonne* (London: Henry

Binneman, 1572) ('godly'); Jonathan McMahon, 'The Humanism of Sir Thomas Smith' (MA dissertation, College of William and Mary, 1999), 63 ('playnting', 'barbarity', and 'profite'); Nicholas P. Canny, 'The Permissive Frontier: The Problem of Social Control in English Settlements in Ireland and Virginia, 1550-1650', in Nicholas P. Canny et al., eds., *The Westward Enterprise: English Activities in Ireland, the Atlantic, and America, 1480-1650* (Liverpool: Liverpool University Press, 1978), 24 ('Eutopia'); D. B. Quinn, 'Renaissance Influences in English Colonization', *Transactions of the Royal Historical Society*, vol. 26 (December 1976), 545 ('Eden's'); Pietro Martire d'Anghiera and Richard Eden, *The decades of the new worlde or west India conteynyng the nauigations and conquests of the Spanyardes, with the particular description of the most ryche and large landes and islandes lately founde in the west ocean perteynyng to the inheritaunce of the kings of Spayne* (London: Edwarde Sutton, 1555) ('cannibalistic'); Horning, *Ireland in the Virginian Sea*, 277 ('transferred').

14. Anne McLaren, 'Reading Sir Thomas Smith's *De Republica Anglorum* as Protestant Apologetic', *HJ* 42 (December 1999), 911-939 ('justified'); Sir Thomas Smith, *De Republica Anglorum: The maner of Gouernement or policie of the Realme of England, compiled by the Honorable man Thomas Smyth, Doctor of the civil lawes, Knight, and principall Secretarie unto the two most worthie Princes, King Edwarde the sixt, and Queene Elizabeth* (London: Henrie Midleton, 1583), 107 ('servi'), 10-11 ('free men' and 'instruments'); David Armitage, *The Ideological Origins of the British Empire* (Cambridge: Cambridge University Press, 2000), 51 ('Vagrancy Act'); Strype, *Life of the Learned Sir Thomas Smith*, 207 ('leaving'). See also Johann P. Somerville, 'English and Roman Liberty in the Monarchical Republic of Early Stuart England', in John F. McDiarmid, ed., *The Monarchical Republic of Early Modern England: Essays in Response to Patrick Collinson* (London and New York: Routledge, 2016), 212-213.

15. Kennedy, *Isle of Devils*, 174, 189, 206-211, 216-218, 237-238, 243, and 247 ('brought to the island'); Frederick Johnson Simmons, *Emmanuel Downing* (Montclair, NJ: Unknown Publisher, 1958), 82-86 ('scholar'); Emmanuel Downing to John Winthrop, August 1645, in Adam Winthrop, ed., *Winthrop Papers*, vol. 5 (Boston: The Massachusetts Historical Society, 1947), 38 ('pilladge'); Wendy Warren, *New England Bound: Slavery and Colonization in Early America* (New York: W. W. Norton & Company, 2017), 265-266 ('1,300'). According to Warren, enslaved Black and Indigenous people made up ten per cent of New England's population in the seventeenth century. (*Ibid.*, 266).

16. 'Letter from John Elliot Protesting against Selling Indians as Slaves, 13 August 1675', *Yale Indian Papers Project*, https://findit.library.yale.edu/yipp/catalog/digcoll:1018374, accessed 29 June 2022 ('sending', 'perpetual', 'extirpate', 'dangerous', 'condition', and 'destroying'); 'Epistle XLIII. *Mr. Mede's Answer to Dr.* Twisse *his Fourth Letter, touching the first Gentile Inhabitants, and the late Christian Plantations, in* America: *as also touching our Saviour's proof of the Resurrection from* Exod. 3. 6. *with an Answer to the Objection in the Postscript of the foregoing Letter*', in Joseph Mede, *The Works of the Pious and Profoundly-Learned Joseph Mede, B. D. Sometime Fellow of Christ's College in Cambridge. In Five Books: The Fourth Edition* (London: Roger Norton and Richard Royston, 1677), 799 ('well as' and 'grounds') and 800 ('barbarous', 'good', 'Christ', 'Mastives', 'hunt', 'worry', 'hideous', 'Army', and 'Kingdom'). For Native American enslavement, see Alan Gallay, *The Indian Slave Trade: The Rise of the English Empire in the American*

South, 1670–1717 (New Haven, CT: Yale University Press, 2002); Brett Rushforth, *Bonds of Alliance: Indigenous & Atlantic Slaveries in New France* (Chapel Hill: University of North Carolina Press, 2012); Reséndez, *Other Slavery*; Tiya Miles, *Ties that Bind: The Story of an Afro-Cherokee Family in Slavery and Freedom* (Berkeley and Los Angeles: University of California Press, 2005); and Christina Snyder, *Slavery in Indian Country* (Cambridge, MA: Harvard University Press, 2010).

17. John Thornton, 'The African Experience of the "20. and Odd Negroes" Arriving in Virginia in 1619', *WMQ* 55 (July 1988), 421 ('odd'); John Pory to Sir Dudley Carleton, 30 September 1619, in Kingsbury, ed., *Records of the Virginia Company*, vol. 3, 619–622 ('victualled'); William S. Powell, *John Pory, 1572–1636: The Life and Letters of a Man of Many Parts* (Chapel Hill: University of North Carolina Press, 1977), 9–19 ('Pory'); al-Hasan Muhammad al-Wazzan (or "Joannes Leo Africanus"), *A Geographical Historie of Africa, written in Arabicke and Italian by John Leo a More, borne in Grenada, and brought up in Barbarie* (London: George Bishop, 1600), title ('lately'), 6 ('Negros' and 'Noah'), and 36 ('hereditary'); Neill, ed., *Othello*, 223 ('influenced'). For Pory's translation and interpretation of al-Wazzan's work, see Whitford, *Curse of Ham*, 128–129. See also Engel Sluiter, 'New Light on the "20. and Odd Negroes" Arriving in Virginia, August 1619', *WMQ* 54 (April 1997), 395–398.

18. Kingsbury, ed., *Records of the Virginia Company*, vol. 3, 565–571 ('347'); 'Samuel Macocke', *ACAD*, https://venn.lib.cam.ac.uk/cgi-bin/search-2018.pl?sur=macock e&suro=w&fir=samuel&firo=c&cit=&cito=c&c=all&z=all&tex=&sye=&eye=&c ol=all&maxcount=50, accessed 2 December 2020 ('alumnus'); Alden T. Vaughan, '"Expulsion of the Salvages": English Policy and the Virginia Massacre of 1622', *WMQ* 35 (January 1978), 57–84 ('historians'); Edward Waterhouse and Henry Briggs, *A declaration of the state of the colony and affaires in Virginia With a relation of the barbarous massacre in the time of peace and league, treacherously executed by the native infidels upon the English, the 22 of March last* (London: Robert Mylbourne, 1622) ('conquering', 'Mastives', and 'wilde').

19. Henry Briggs, 'A Treatise of the Northwest Passage to the South Sea, through the Continent of Virginia and by *Fretum Hudson*', in Waterhouse and Briggs, *A Declaration of the State of the Colony*, 45 ('noble') and 50 ('ignorant' and 'publique'); Grants of Shares in Virginia, 30 January 1622, in Kingsbury, ed., *Records of the Virginia Company*, vol. 3, 592 ('shares'); Virginia Company to the Virginia Governor and Council, October 1622, in *ibid.*, 683 ('revenge'); Gregory Ablavsky, 'Making Indians "White": The Judicial Abolition of Native Slavery in Revolutionary Virginia and Its Racial Legacy', *University of Pennsylvania Law Review* 159 (April 2011), 1492 ('Native American'). The practice of Native American enslavement continued in Virginia until 1806. For the Powhatan and their allies, see Helen Rountree, *The Powhatan Indians of Virginia: Their Traditional Culture* (Norman: University of Oklahoma Press, 1989); James Axtell, *The Rise and Fall of the Powhatan Empire: Indians in Seventeenth-Century Virginia* (Williamsburg, VA: Colonial Williamsburg Foundation, 1995); and Frederic W. Gleach, *Powhatan's World and Colonial Virginia: A Conflict of Cultures* (Lincoln and London: University of Nebraska Press, 1997). For the pervasive anti-Indian sentiment in North America, see Wayne E. Lee, *Barbarians and Brothers: Anglo-American Warfare, 1500–1865* (New York and Oxford: Oxford University Press, 2011), 226; Peter Silver, *Our Savage Neighbors: How Indian War Transformed Early America* (New York: W. W. Norton & Company, 2008); and Parkinson, *Common Cause*.

240

NOTES TO PAGES 57–59

20. 'John Donne', *ACAD*, https://venn.lib.cam.ac.uk/cgi-bin/search-2018.pl?sur=don ne&suro=w&fir=john&firo=c&cit=&cito=c&c=all&z=all&tex=&sye=&eye=&col= all&maxcount=999, accessed 3 December 2021 ('rectorship'); Thomas Festa, 'The Metaphysics of Labor in John Donne's Sermon to the Virginia Company', *Studies in Philology* 106 (Winter 2009), 99 ('theoretical').
21. Sermon Preached to the Virginia Company, 13 November 1622, in John Carey, ed., *John Donne: The Major Works* (Oxford and New York: Oxford University Press, 1990), 321 ('Plantation'); William G. Hinkle, *A History of Bridewell Prison, 1553–1700* (New York: Edwin Mellen Press, 2006) ('Bridewell'); Festa, 'Metaphysics of Labor', 96 ('impoverished children'). For Donne's thought, see Tom Cain, 'John Donne and the Ideology of Colonization', *English Literary Renaissance* 31 (Autumn 2001), 440–476; and Achsah Guibbory, ed., *The Cambridge Companion to John Donne* (Cambridge: Cambridge University Press, 2006).
22. John Ray, *The Wisdom of God Manifested in the Works of the Creation* (London: Samuel Smith, 1691), 114 ('Improvement' and 'Industry') and 117–118 ('civil', 'thy Country', 'Merchandise', 'Wilderness', 'Scythia', 'unpolished', 'slothful', 'Cabans', and 'brute'); Brown, *Good Wives*, 57–58 ('indolent').
23. Shareholders in the Virginia Company from 1615 to 1623, in Kingsbury, ed., *Records of the Virginia Company*, vol. 3, 59 ('shareholder'); Copy of the Codicil of Lord Brooke's Will, 6 September 1628, Papers of the Regius Professor of Modern History, University registry guard books, 1327–2000, CUL, GBR/0265/UA/CUR 39.14 ('founding'); Charles Henry Cooper, *On an Early Autograph of Sir Henry Spelman, with Some New or not Generally Known Facts Respecting Him*, 13 May 1861, *ibid.* ('lectureship', 'MP', 'induced', and 'treasurer'); J. M. Svalastog, *Mastering the Worst of Trades: England's Early Africa Companies and their Traders, 1618–1672* (Brill: Leiden, 2021), 62 ('ambitions'); Gillian Weiss, *Captives and Corsairs: France and Slavery in the Early Modern Mediterranean* (Stanford, CA: Stanford University Press, 2011), 8–9 ('seized'); Quoted in C. W. W. Greenridge, *Slavery* (London: Allen and Unwin, 1958), 123 ('poor' and 'prisoners') For Spelman, see also Peter J. Lucas, 'A Conspectus of Letters to and from Sir Henry Spelman (1563/4–1641)', *The Antiquaries Journal* 102 (2022), 370–388.
24. Jacqueline Cox, 'Trials and Tribulations: The Cambridge University Courts, 1540–1660', *Transactions of the Cambridge Bibliographical Society* 15 (2015), 595–623 ('court of record'); *Lobspruch deß edlen/hochberühmten Krauts Petum oder Taback* (Nuremburg: Paul Fürst, 1658) ('noble herb'); John Swan, *Speculum Mundi or a Glasse Representing the Face of the World; Shewing both that it did begin, and must also end: The manner How, and time When being largely examined* (Cambridge: Printers to the University of Cambridge, 1635), 266 ('vertues', 'West *Indies*', 'helpeth', 'bitings', and 'mad'); Lucinda Cole, *Imperfect Creatures: Vermin, Literature, and the Sciences of Life, 1600–1740* (Ann Arbor: University of Michigan Press, 2016), 135 ('canines'); Office v. Whitney of Gonville and Caius College, 17 January 1611, Act Book, 18 January 1610 to October 1612, Vice-Chancellor's Court records, 1498–1957, CUL, GBR/0265/UA/VCCt.I 7, 184r ('puffing'); Interrogatories ex parte Henry Gooch, 25 January 1619/20, 1619 [Exhibita] coram Dre Scott, Procan:', 1616–1620, *ibid.*, VCCt.III 24, 46 ('expelled'); Vice-Chancellor's rules for behaviour of University members, '1623 [Exhibita] coram Dre Paske, Procan:'; 1624 [Exhibita] coram Dre Mansell, Procan:', 1610–1626, *ibid.*, 27, 112 ('attendance'); Seven licensed tobacconists promise to sell to innholders, shopkeepers, and the like, 17 June 1635, '1635 [Exhibita] coram Dre Smith, Procan'.; '1636 [Exhibita] coram Dre Comber,

Procan'., 1615–1638, *ibid.*, 34, 18–20 ('seven'); List of unlicensed retailers of tobacco, 19 January 1634/5, '1633 [Exhibita] coram Dre Love, Procan'.; 1634 [Exhibita] coram Dre Beale, Procan'., 1620–1635, *ibid.*, 33, 137b ('unlicensed').

25. Wesley Frank Craven, *Dissolution of the Virginia Company: The Failure of a Colonial Experiment* (Gloucester, MA: Peter Smith, 1964) ('substantial losses'); A Complete List in Alphabetical Order of the 'Adventurers to Virginia', With the Several Amounts of their Holdings, 1618, in Kingsbury, ed., *Records of the Virginia Company*, vol. 3, 83 ('£50') and 86 ('1618' and '£400'); The Names of the Adventurers, with the seueral summes adventured, 22 June 1620, in *ibid.*, 329 ('1620'); Howard Staunton, *The Great Schools of England* (London: Strahan and Co., Publishers, 1869), 426 ('property'); David L. Niddrie, 'An Attempt at Planned Settlement in St Kitts in the Early Eighteenth Century', *Caribbean Studies* 5 (January 1966), 3 ('grant'). See also Brian O'Farrell, *Shakespeare's Patron, William Herbert, Third Earl of Pembroke 1580–1630: Politics, Patronage and Power* (London: Bloomsbury, 2011), 143–158.

26. Larzer Ziff, *The Career of John Cotton: Puritanism and the American Experience* (Princeton: Princeton University Press, 1962), 3–35 ('matriculated'); John Cotton, *God's Promise to His Plantations* (London: John Bellamy, 1634), 8–9 ('plant', 'merchandize', and 'Arise'); Franklin Bowditch Dexter, *The Influence of the English Universities in the Development of New England* (Cambridge: Cambridge University Press, 1880), 5–6 ('exodus'). For Cotton and his career in New England, see also Warren, *New England Bound*, 22–24.

27. The Body of Liberties, 1641, in William H. Whitmore, ed., *The Colonial Laws of Massachusetts* (Boston: Rockwell and Churchill, 1890), 53 ('slaverie' and 'liberties'); Warren, *New England Bound*, 35 ('antislavery clause' and 'legalised').

28. Sargent Bush, *The Library of Emmanuel College, Cambridge, 1584–1637* (Cambridge: Cambridge University Press, 1986), 27 ('5,000'); Michael Edwards, 'Slavery and Charity: Tobias Rustat and the African Companies, 1662–94', *Historical Research* 97 (2024), 64 ('court') and 80–81 ('helped' and 'two fee-farms'); Transcript, made 1830, of Bishop Thomas Sherlock's collections on University customs, privileges, and property, mid 18th century, University Registry miscellanea, 1544–1988, CUL, GBR/0265/UA/Misc.Collect.18, 43–44 ('University Library' and 'Oxford'); *The Laws of Jamaica, Passed by the Assembly, And Confirmed by His Majesty in Council, April 17. 1684* (London: H. H. Jun., 1684), x ('seated', 'sweet', 'Cross', 'world', and 'serve') and xi ('Lyttleton'); Benjamin Justice, 'The Art of Coining Christians: Indians and Authority in the Iconography of British Atlantic Colonial Seals', *Journal of British Studies* 61 (January 2022), 118–119 ('barbarousness'); Matthew Kruer, *Time of Anarchy: Indigenous Power and the Crisis of Colonialism in Early America* (Cambridge, MA: Harvard University Press, 2022), 24–48 ('resistance'); Caroline Dodds Pennock, *On Savage Shores: How Indigenous Americans Discovered Europe* (New York: Alfred. A. Knopf, 2023), 51 ('diplomatic missions').

29. 'John Mapletoft', ACAD, https://venn.lib.cam.ac.uk/cgi-bin/search-2018.pl?sur=&suro=w&fir=&firo=c&cit=&cito=c&c=all&z=all&tex=MPLT648J&sye=&eye=&col=all&maxcount=50, accessed 29 January 2023 ('matriculated'); Articles of Agreement between the Lords Proprietors of the Bahama Islands and the Bahama Adventurers, 4 September 1672, in Larry J. Kreitzer, ed., *William Kiffen and His World (Part 1)*, foreword by Paul S. Fiddes (Oxford: Centre for Baptist History and Heritage Studies, Regent's Park College, 2010), 365–366 ('Association' and 'royalties'); Sir Peter Colleton to John Locke, in E. S. De Beer, ed., *The Correspondence of John Locke, Volume One* (Oxford: Clarendon Press, 1976), 379–380 ('planting').

For a helpful overview of Locke's investments in and perspective on slavery and the slave trade, see Holly Brewer, 'Slavery, Sovereignty, and "Inheritable Blood": Reconsidering John Locke and the Origins of American Slavery', *The American Historical Review* 122 (October 2017), esp. 1042–1043.

30. J. C. D. Clark, *English Society, 1660–1832: Religion, Ideology and Politics during the ancien régime* (Cambridge: Cambridge University Press, 2000), 27–28 ('bolstered'); Linda Colley, *Britons: Forging the Nation, 1707–1837* (New Haven, CT: Yale University Press, 2005), 11–54 ('distinctive'); Jeremy Gregory, 'Introduction', in Jeremy Gregory ed., *The Oxford History of Anglicanism, Volume II: Establishment and Empire, 1662–1829* (Oxford: Oxford University Press, 2017), 5 ('twin pillars'); E. R. Norman, *Church and Society in England, 1770–1970: An Historical Study* (Oxford: Oxford University Press, 1976), 19 ('upheld'); W. M. Jacob, *The Clerical Profession in the Long Eighteenth Century* (Oxford: Oxford University Press, 2007), 40–41 ('gentile') and 45 ('seventy-eight').

31. Tim Harris, 'Anti-Catholicism and Anti-Popery in Seventeenth-Century England', in Eran Haefli, ed., *Against Popery: Britain, Empire, and Anti-Catholicism* (Charlottesville: University of Virginia Press, 2020), 28 ('anti-English'); Jonathan Healey, *The Blazing World: A New History of Revolutionary England, 1603–1689* (New York: Vintage, 2023), 23–25 ('gunpowder') and 379 ('great'); Thomas Taylor, 'The Romish Furnace', in Thomas Taylor, *The Works of the Judicious and Learned Divine Thomas Taylor D. D. Late Pastor of Aldermanbury London*, vol. 2 (London: Thomas Ratcliffe, 1659), 231 ('Romish', 'effusion', 'seven', 'throwne', 'poore', 'hang', and 'dash'); J. Frederick Fausz, 'An "Abundance of Blood Shed on Both Sides": England's First Indian War, 1609–1614', *VMHB* 98 (January 1990), 32 ('deadliest') and 33 ('shoteinge').

32. Lisa Jardine, *Going Dutch: How England Plundered Holland's Glory* (London: Harper Press, 2008), 47–49 ('Torbay'); 13 December 1688, in J. E. Foster, ed., *The Diary of Samuel Newton Alderman of Cambridge (1662–1717)* (Cambridge: Cambridge Antiquarian Society, 1890), 96 ('2 *or* 300', 'pretence', 'seeke', 'ransack[ed]', and 'armes'); 14 December 1688, in *ibid.*, 97 ('Irish', 'cut', and 'escape'); Henry More to Lady Conway, March 1664–65, in Marjorie Hope Nicolson and Sarah Hutton, eds., *The Conway Letters: The Correspondence of Anne, Viscountess Conway, Henry More, and their Friends 1642–1684* (Oxford: Clarendon Press, 1992), 233 ('Irish beasts').

33. The Company to Doctors Connett, Owen, Goodwin, and Wilkinson at Oxford, and Doctors Tuckney and Arrowsmith at Cambridge, 13 February 1658, in Ethel Bruce Sainsbury and William Foster, eds., *A Calendar of the Court Minutes Etc. of the East India Company 1655–1659* (Oxford: Clarendon Press, 1916), 227 ('godly'); Roger Wood to Nathaniel Barnard, 1634, in John Henry Lefroy, ed., *Memorials of the Discovery and Early Settlement of the Bermudas or Somers Island, 1515–1685: Compiled from the Colonial Records and Other Original Sources*, vol. 1 (London: Longmans, Green, and Co., 1877), 541 ('help us').

34. Venn and Venn, ed., *Alumni Cantabrigiensis*, Part I, vol. 2, 95 ('Scholar'); Receipt for Money, 27 March 1700, Receipts for money paid to the College, 1441–1918, KCA, GBR/0272/KCA/242 ('three advowsons'); Rev. Robert Robinson, *A Letter to the Right Reverend the Lord Bishop of London, From An Inhabitant of His Majesty's Leeward-Caribbee-Islands* (London: J. Wilford, 1730), 76 ('Propagate', 'Thirty', 'none', and 'Divinity').

35. Reid, 'Whig Declamation', 635 ('declamation'); Will of John Craister, of Trinity College of Cambridge, Cambridgeshire, Prerogative Court of Canterbury and

related Probate Jurisdictions: Will Registers, TNA, PROB 11/684/201 ('Learning' and 'security'); Doctor John Craister's Legacy to the College Stated, Muniments, Senior Bursar's Audit Books, 1739–1756, WL ('Bonds' and '£80').

36. 8 May 1752, Magdalene College Register III, 1675–1814, MC, B/423, 751 ('repairs'); Due upon the Proby Fund, 17 December 1720, Audit Book, 1709–1734, College Accounts, JC, JCCA/JCAD/2/2/1/6 ('South Sea'); Dr Charles Proby, List of Holders of East India Company Stock, April 1707, Stocks and Bonds of the East India Company, BL, IOR/H/3, 179 ('£400'); Alfred William Winterslow Dale, ed., *Warren's Book* (Cambridge: Cambridge University Press, 1911), 303–304 ('Oxenden'); 3 January 1740–41, Chest Book, 1690–1794, TH, GBR/1936/THAR/2/2/5/1 ('Pinfold'); Will of John Andrews, Wills, *ibid*., 6/1/2/1 ('Andrews'); Exton Sayer, Old South Sea Annuities Ledgers, BE, AC27/6459, 432 ('South Sea'); 'Sayer, Exton (c. 1691–1731), of Doctors' Commons, London', *The History of Parliament*, www.historyofparliamentonline.org/volume/1715-1754/member/sayer-exton-1691-1731, accessed 29 June 2022 ('East India'). For more on the Proby fund and the South Sea losses, see also Dr Caryl's Book on Statutes, Trusts, &c., College Statutes, JC, JCCA/JCGB/4/3/8, 105. At Magdalene College, the principal and interest of the bond were calculated at over £113 in June 1752.

37. Venn and Venn, ed., *Alumni Cantabrigiensis*, Part I, vol 1, 171 ('fellow'); Probate will of Samuel Blythe, 1713, Blythe Benefaction (now Blythe Trust), CCA, GB 1114/CCAD/4/1/2/2/1 ('entirety'); Daniel Lysons and Samuel Lysons, *Magna Britannia; Being a Concise Topographical Account of the Several Counties of Great Britain*, vol. 2 (London: T. Cadell and W. Davies, 1810), 148 ('great'); George Measom, *The Official Illustrated Guide to the Great Eastern Railway (Cambridge Line): With Descriptions of Some of the Most Important Manufactories in the Towns on the Lines* (Cambridge: C. Griffin and Co., 1865), 138 ('principal'); 'The Samuel Blythe Society', Clare College, University of Cambridge, www.clarealumni.com/pages/supporting-clare/the-samuel-blythe-society, accessed 1 July 2022 ('continuing').

38. Accounts of Blythe Benefaction, Blythe Benefaction, CCA, GB 1114/CCAD/4/1/2/2/3, 4 ('East India') and 166 ('271'); Laurence Fowler and Helen Fowler, ed., *Cambridge Commemorated: An Anthology of University Life* (Cambridge: Cambridge University Press, 1989), 99 ('Perrott'); Gary Parks, ed., *Virginia Tax Records: From the Virginia Magazine of History and Biography, the William and Mary Quarterly, and Tyler's Quarterly* (Baltimore: Genealogical Publishing Company, 1983), 243 ('acre').

39. Accounts of Blythe Benefaction, Blythe Benefaction, CCA, GB 1114/CCAD/4/1/2/2/3, 166 ('windfall'), 186 ('£3,500'), 39 ('South Sea'), 44 ('interest'), and 116 ('sold'). See P. S. Gooddard to Charles Yorke, 10 November 1762, Correspondence of Charles Yorke Regarding Cambridge University, 1752–1770, BL, Add MS 35640/84.

40. Brooke, *History of Gonville & Caius*, 150–152 ('fellowship'); Charter Granted to the English Company, Trading to the East-Indies, 5 September 1698, in John Shaw, ed., *Charters Relating to the East India Company from 1600 to 1761* (Madras: R. Hill, 1887), 133 ('invested'), 145 ('five hundred'), and 151 ('last Will').

41. *Ibid*., 144 ('instruct'); Penelope Carson, *The East India Company and Religion, 1698–1858* (London: Boydell Press, 2012), 7–8 ('decent' and 'Gentoos'); Stern, *Company-State*, 22 ('Barbados'); Indenture Tripartite Between Her Majesty Queen Anne and the Two East-India Companies, For Uniting the Said Companies, 21 July 1702, in Shaw, ed., *Charters Relating to the East India Company*, 157 ('merge'). For independent traders 'interloping' in the transatlantic slave trade, see also Pettigrew, *Freedom's Debt*, 88–89.

42. Bartholomew Wortley, Old South Sea Annuities Ledgers, BE, AC27/6452, 775 ('stock'); An Account Taken of my Mortgages, Bonds and other Obligations then Due, 16 November 1741, Wortley Benefaction Account, GCC, GC/BUR/F/74 ('Villain', and 'Annihilated'); William Barbor to Thomas Gooch, 1 June 1749, Wortley Account, GCC, GC/BUR/F/74 ('Papers'); Will of Bartholomew Wortley, Clerk of Bratton Fleming, Devon, 7 June 1749, Prerogative Court of Canterbury, TNA, PROB 11/771/66 ('funded'). For Wortley's South Sea investments, see also Bartholomew Wortley, New South Sea Company Annuities Ledgers, BEAC27/6051/920.

43. Rev. John Fairfax, *Life of the Rev. Owen Stockton, M.A.* (London: Religious Tract Society, 1832), 3–5 ('schooling'); Brooke, *History of Gonville & Caius*, 134, n. 35 ('£500'); Will of Owen Stockton, 20 December 1678, Robert Woodberry Lovett, ed., *Documents from the Harvard University Archives, 1638–1750* (Boston: Colonial Society of Massachusetts, 1975), 137 ('reside'); 'An Account of the Fire at Harvard-College, in Cambridge; with the Loss sustained thereby', *Massachusetts-Gazette*, 2 February 1764 ('Old Testament' and 'oriental'); Lisa Tanya Brooks, *Our Beloved Kin: A New History of King Philip's War* (New Haven, CT: Yale University Press, 2018), 81 ('subjects'); David Silverman, *Faith and Boundaries: Colonists, Christianity, and Community among the Wampanoag Indians of Martha's Vineyard, 1600–1871* (New York and Cambridge: Cambridge University Press, 2005), 47–48 ('alliances'); Stockton Account Book, Stockton Benefaction Account, GCC, BUR/F/70 ('£300').

44. John Robertson, 'Empire and Union: Two Concepts of the Early Modern European Political Order', in John Robertson ed., *A Union for Empire: Political Thought and the British Union* (Cambridge: Cambridge University Press, 1996), 32–33 ('Panama'); 'List of subscribers to the Company of Scotland Trading to Africa and the Indies, 1696–1700', *NatWest Group Archive*, www.natwestgroup.com/heritage/companies/company-of-scotland-trading-to-africa-and-the-indies.html, accessed 16 September 2022 ('investors included'); 'George Mosman', *Edinburgh University Library Gallery of Benefactors*, www.docs.is.ed.ac.uk/docs/lib-archive/bgallery/Gallery/records/fifteen/mosman.html, accessed 16 September 2022 ('library donor'); C. P. Finlayson, 'Edinburgh University and the Darien Scheme', *The Scottish Historical Review* 34 (October 1955), 97 ('Scott') and 102 ('well-merited' and 'four-square'). See also Julie M. Orr, *Scotland, Darien and the Atlantic World* (Edinburgh: Edinburgh University Press, 2018).

45. Glasson, *Mastering Christianity*, 141 ('Codrington'); Subscription Book, 1698–1768, Subscriptions to the Society for the Promotion of Christian Knowledge, CUL, GBR/0012/MS SPCK/C1/1 ('list of college fellows'); 5 April 1726 and 23 June 1743, Master/Registry Gesta, 1849–1857, GCC, GOV/03/01/05; Festo Mich. 1726 to Festum Annunc. 1727 and Festo Michaelis 1752 to Festum Annunc. 1753, College Bursar Book, 1792–1810, GCC, GC/BUR/F/88 ('donations'); Dr. Spencer's Account, 1693–1929, CCC, GBR/0268/CCCC02/B/146 ('Society' and 'Propagation').

46. Henry Newman to the Marquis Duqueñe, 25 January 1723/24, Henry Newman's Jamaica Letter Books, 1722–1729, CUL, GBR/0012/MS SPCK/D4/44-45 ('elegantly', 'Bubble', and 'Adventure'); August 1720 Shares, Papers of the Royal Mines Company, Jamaica, Vol. 1, BL, MS Add. 43498 ('Supported with investments'); Henry Newman to Duke of Portland, Middle Temple, 17 August 1724, Newman's Jamaica Books, CUL, GBR/0012/MS SPCK/D4/44-45 ('Modern History').

47. Brent S. Sirota, *The Christian Monitors: The Church of England and the Age of Benevolence, 1680–1730* (New Haven, CT: Yale University Press, 2014), 139 ('Tranquebar'); Accounts of the Subscriptions and Expenditure, 1710–1719, Papers

of the Protestant Mission to the East Indies, 1710–1859, CUL, GBR/0012/MS SPCK/C12/1 ('Cash' and 'individual subscriptions'); 14 September and 26 November 1726, Cash Account Book, 1710–1732, CUL, GBR/0012/MS SPCK/C5/1 ('donation'); 10 May 1729, Accounts, 1719–1734, Papers of the Protestant Mission, CUL, GBR/0012/MS SPCK/C12/2 ('£4,000').

48. Dr. Bray's Feoffment, 15 January 1730, in Rodney M. Baine, ed., *Creating Georgia: Minutes of the Bray Associates 1730–1732 & Supplementary Documents* (Athens and London: University of Georgia Press, 1995), 5–6 ('£900'); *Abstract of the Proceeding of the Associates of Doctor Bray, For the Year 1785* (London: Unknown, 1785), 18 ('Heslop'); *An Account of the Designs of the Associates of the late Dr Bray; with an Abstract of Their Proceedings* (London: Unknown, 1768), 35–35 ('Lucasian' and 'Provision').

49. Meeting of the Trustees in Palace Court, 29 June 1732, in Baine, ed., *Creating Georgia*, 114 ('eighty'); Matthias Mawson, *A Sermon Preached before the Incorporated Society for the Propagation of the Gospel in Foreign Parts; at their Anniversary Meeting in the Parish-Church of St. Mary-Le-Bow, On Friday, February 18, 1742-3* (London: J. Roberts, 1743), 25 ('Labours'); Dr. Spencer's Account, 1693–1929, CCC, GBR/0268/CCCC02/B/146 ('Governor').

50. Charles Eden to the Society for the Propagation of the Gospel in Foreign Parts, 8 October 1714, in Robert J. Cain, ed., *The Colonial Records of North Carolina, Volume X: The Church of England in North Carolina: Documents, 1699–1741* (Raleigh: Division of Archives and History, North Carolina Department of Cultural Resources, 1999), 186 ('Tedious'); Chapter Book 3, 1709–1752', *Corpus Christi College, Cambridge*, www.corpus.cam.ac.uk/sites/default/files/downloads/chapter-book-3.pdf, accessed 30 March 2022 ('£250').

51. A Proposal, 1725, in Alexander Campbell Fraser, ed., *The Works of George Berkeley, Formerly Bishop of Cloyne. Collected and Edited with Prefaces and Annotations*, vol. 3 (Oxford: Clarendon Press, 1871), 229 ('reservoir' and 'purging'); List of Subscriptions for the Bermuda Scheme, 1724, Correspondence of Bishop Berkeley, 1710–1828, BL, Add MS 39311, f. 63 ('aided'); Tom Jones, *George Berkeley: A Philosophical Life* (Princeton, NJ: Princeton University Press, 2021), 150 ('Whitehall') and 353 ('Parliament').

52. Glasson, *Mastering Christianity*, 20 ('establish'); Gerbner, *Christian Slavery*, 132 ('SOCIETY' and 'mark'); 23 January 1712, Barbados Journal, vol. 1, BOD, X/14 ('keeping up'); 23 May 1716, *ibid*. ('purged'); 23 January 1712, *ibid*. ('Dawes' and 'chair'); 9 October 1713 and 19 February 1719, *ibid*. ('Gooch'); 9 October 1713, *ibid*. ('Gatford'); 18 August 1710, *ibid*. ('Moore'); Joseph Roper, *A Sermon Preach'd at the Anniversary Meeting of the Sons of Clergy, in the Cathedral-Church of St. Paul, on the 9th of December, 1725* (London: Jonah Bowyer, 1725), 27 ('exhibitions').

53. Donations and Legacies of £100 and Upwards, from 1702 to 1839, in *Incorporated Society for the Propagation of the Gospel in Foreign Parts. Report for the Year 1840. With the 139th Anniversary Sermon Preached Before the Society at the Cathedral Church of St. Paul* (London: Society for the Propagation of the Gospel in Foreign Parts, 1840), 20 ('£1,000'); Mortgage to Thomas Tenison, Archbishop of Canterbury, for £1,000 of lands in St Ives at 4%, 18 May 1710, Papers relating to Archbishop Thomas Tenison's Bequest, 1713–1723, CCC, GBR/0268/CCCC10/7/3/4 ('mortgaging'); 20 December 1745, Barbados Journal, vol 2, X/15, f. 144 ('Mathematicks'); Sheridan, *Sugar and Slavery*, 126 ('yellow fever'); Robert Forsyth Scott, *Admissions to the College of St John the Evangelist in the University of Cambridge*, Part III (Cambridge: Cambridge University Press, 1903), 500 ('died'). Dr Humphrey Gower, the Master of St John's College, donated £100 to the SPG too.

54. 26 May 1716, Barbados Journal, vol. 1, BOD, X/14 ('Barbados'); Williams, *Capitalism and Slavery*, 42 ('civil property'); Hilary M. Carey, *God's Empire: Religion and Colonialism in the British World, c. 1801–1908* (Cambridge: Cambridge University Press, 2011), 253 ('East India Company'); James B. Bell, *A War of Religion: Dissenters, Anglicans, and the American Revolution* (Houndmills, Basingstoke: Palgrave Macmillan, 2008), 63 ('proposal'); Thomas Sherlock, *The Lord Bishop of Bangor's Defence of His Assertion, Viz.* (London: J. Pemberton, 1718), title ('Example'), 19 ('Countrey'), and 19–20 ('*Negroes*').
55. 'William Fleetwood', *ACAD*, https://venn.lib.cam.ac.uk/cgi-bin/search-2018.pl?sur=fleetwood&suro=w&fir=william&firo=c&cit=&cito=c&c=all&z=all&tex=&sye=&eye=&col=all&maxcount=999, accessed 2 December 2021 ('fellow'); William Fleetwood to Charles Lockyer, 2 April 1722, William Fleetwood Manuscript Documents, HL, Volume 5, Part 5 ('South Sea'); William Fleetwood, *A Sermon Preached before the Society for the Propagation of the Gospel in Foreign Parts At the Parish-Church of St. Mary-le-Bow, On Friday the 16th of February, Being the Day of their Anniversary Meeting* (London: J. Downing, 1711), 16–17 ('losing', 'imagin'd', and '*English-Men*'). Charles Lockyer was an accountant for the South Sea Company.
56. Glasson, *Mastering Christianity*, 44 ('ethnic'); Stephen R. Haynes, *Noah's Curse: The Biblical Justification of American Slavery* (Oxford: Oxford University Press, 2002), 23 ('nakedness' and 'lowest'); Richard Kidder, *A Commentary on the Five Books of Moses: With a Dissertation Concerning the Author or Writer of the said Books; and a General Argument to each of them*, vol. 1 (London: J. Keptinstall, 1694), 46 ('servant'); Simon Patrick, *A Commentary Upon the First Book of Moses, Called Genesis* (London: Chiswell, 1695), 203 ('Four Sons'); Thomas Newton, *Dissertations on the Prophecies, Which Have Remarkably Been Fulfilled, and At This Time Are Fulfilling in the World*, vol. 1 (Perth: R. Morison Junior, 1790), 13 ('peopled') and 9 ('servant of servants'); Adam Elliot, 'A Narrative of My Travails, Captivity and Escape from Sallee, in the Kingdom of Fez', in Adam Elliot, *A Modest Vindication of Titus Oates the Salamanca-Doctor from Perjury: or an Essay to Demonstrate Him only Forsworn in several Instances* (London: Joseph Hindmarsh, 1682) and Simon Ockley, *An Account of South-West Barbary: Containing What is most Remarkable in the Territories of the King of Fez and Morocco* (London: J. Bowyer and H. Clements, 1713) ('captivity'). See also Lisa Voigt, *Writing Captivity in the Early Modern Atlantic: Circulations of Knowledge and Authority in the Iberian and English Imperial Worlds* (Chapel Hill: University of North Carolina Press, 2009).
57. 'David Humphreys', *ACAD*, https://venn.lib.cam.ac.uk/cgi-bin/search-2018.pl?sur=humphreys&suro=w&fir=david&firo=c&cit=&cito=c&c=all&z=all&tex=&sye=&eye=&col=all&maxcount=50, accessed 2 December 2021 ('fellow'); David Humphreys, *An Historical Account of the Incorporated Society for the Propagation of the Gospel in Foreign Parts* (London: Joseph Downing, 1730), 232–235 ('*Pagan*', 'Planters', and 'souls') and 241–242 ('most guilty'); Jill Lepore, 'The Tightening Vise: Slavery and Freedom in British New York', in Ira Berlin and Leslie M. Harris, eds., *Slavery in New York* (New York: The New Press, 2005), 78–79 ('1712'); John K. Thornton, 'African Dimensions of the Stono Rebellion', *The American Historical Review* 96 (October 1991), 1112–1113 ('sporadic').
58. 'Anthony Ellys', *ACAD*, https://venn.lib.cam.ac.uk/cgi-bin/search-2018.pl?sur=ellys&suro=w&fir=anthony&firo=c&cit=&cito=c&c=all&z=all&tex=&sye=&eye=&col=all&maxcount=9999, accessed 2 December 2021 ('pensioner'); Anthony Ellys, *A Sermon Preached before the Incorporated Society for the Propagation of the Gospel*

in Foreign Parts at their Anniversary Meeting in the Parish Church of St. Mary-le-Bow, On Friday February 23, 1759 (London: E. Owen and T. Harrison, 1754), 30–31 ('advantage', 'obstinacy', and 'guards').

59. James R. Hertzler, 'Slavery in the Yearly Sermons Before the Georgia Trustees', *The Georgia Historical Quarterly* 59 (1975), 119 ('supported those colonists'); George Harvest, *A Sermon Preach'd before the Honourable Trustees for Establishing the Colony of Georgia in America*, 1749, in George Harvest, *A Collection of Sermons, Preached Occasionally on Various Subjects* (London: J. and R. Tonson and S. Draper, 1754), 292 ('depopulate'), 299 ('auxiliaries'), 300 ('*Gibraltar*'), 301–302 ('Fitness' and 'industrious'), and 310–311 ('profane', 'released', 'free', 'abhors', and 'agree with me'); Ben Marsh, *Georgia's Frontier Women: Female Fortunes in a Southern Colony* (Athens: University of Georgia Press, 2007), 56–57 ('£28,125') Harvest was also listed as a subscriber of twelve copies to the third edition of John Wright's *The American Negotiator, or the Various Currencies of the British Colonies in America* (London: J. Smith, 1765), xlvii. For contemporary concerns around the 'dispeopling' of the British metropole, see also P. J. Marshall, *The Making and Unmaking of Empires: Britain, India, and America c. 1750–1783* (Oxford: Oxford University Press, 2005), 323.

60. Watson W. Jennison, *Cultivating Rice: The Expansion of Slavery in Georgia, 1750–1860* (Lexington: University Press of Kentucky, 2012), 19–20 ('population'); Thomas Francklin, *A Sermon Preached before the Honourable Trustees for Establishing the colony of Georgia in America, the Associates of the late Rev. Dr. Bray* (London: R. Francklin, 1750), 13 ('Force', 'Blood', 'design'd', and 'Equality') and 13–14 ('Necessity', 'Prudence', 'unhappy', and 'Happiness').

61. *Boston Gazette*, 25 July and 1 August 1737 ('slave trader'); John C. Shields, *The American Aeneas: Classical Origins of the American Self* (Knoxville: The University of Tennessee Press, 2001), 79 ('Jesus'); East Apthorp, *The Constitution of a Christian Church Illustrated in a Sermon at the Opening of Christ-Church, in Cambridge on Thursday 15 October, MDCCLXI* (Boston: Green and Russell, 1761), title page ('late Fellow'); Douglass Shand-Tucci and Richard Cheek, *Harvard University: An Architectural Tour* (Princeton: Princeton Architectural Press, 2001), 104 ('mansion'); East Apthorp, *Discourses on Prophecy: Read in the Chapel of Lincoln's Inn, at the Lecture Founded by the Right Reverend William Warburton Late Lord Bishop of Gloucester*, vol. 2 (London: J. F. and C. Rivington, 1786), 340 ('prelate' and 'freed').

3   'The Glory of their times': Natural Philosophy, the Law, and the Spoils of Empire

1. Peile, *Biographical Register of Christ's College*, vol. 1, 611–612 ('matriculating'); Mark Govier, 'The Royal Society, Slavery and the Island of Jamaica: 1660–1700', *Notes and Records of the Royal Society of London* 53 (May 1999), 203–217 ('investments'). Townes and his work are discussed in Stearns, *Science in the British Colonies*, 215–217; Cristina Malcolmson, *Studies of Skin Color in the Early Royal Society: Boyle, Cavendish, Swift* (London: Taylor & Francis, 2016), 66–69; and Sarah Irving, *Natural Science and the Origins of the British Empire* (London: Taylor & Francis. 2015), 99–100. For Lister, see Anna Marie Roos, *Web of Nature: Martin Lister (1639–1712), the First Arachnologist* (Leiden: Brill, 2011).

2. Thomas Townes to Martin Lister, ca. May 1674, in Anna Marie Roos, ed., *The Correspondence of Dr. Martin Lister (1639–1712). Volume One: 1662–1677* (Leiden and Boston: Brill, 2015), 700 ('goe' and 'commands'); Thomas Townes to Martin Lister, 26 March 1675, *ibid.*, 782 ('bottome').
3. *Ibid.* ('Sunne' and 'Latitude').
4. Martin Lister to Henry Oldenburg, 27 June 1675, *ibid.*, 795 ('correspondent'); Martin Lister to John Ray, July 1675, *ibid.*, 800 ('Blood'); Henry Oldenburg to Martin Lister, 10 June 1676, *ibid.*, 841 ('Ingenious', 'florid', and 'observation'); Martin Lister to Henry Oldenburg, 9 July 1676, *ibid.*, 851 ('Experiment'). In 1682 and 1696, the Society debated the nature of Black skin, with several correspondents agreeing that Blackness was innate. (Govier, 'Royal Society', 215.) See also John G. T. Anderson, *Deep Things Out of Darkness: A History of Natural History* (Berkeley: University of California Press, 2013), 52–72.
5. The imperial history of collecting is discussed in Margot C. Finn, 'Material Turns in British History: III. Collecting: Colonial Bombay, Basra, Baghdad and the Enlightenment Museum', *Transactions of the Royal Historical Society* 30 (2020), 1–28; Dan Hicks, *The Brutish Museums: The Benin Bronzes, Colonial Violence and Cultural Restitution* (London: Pluto Press, 2021); and Maya Jasanoff, *Edge of Empire: Conquest and Collecting in the East, 1750–1850* (London: Harper Perennial, 2006). For the imperial origins of natural history, see Leslie B. Cormack, *Charting an Empire: Geography at the English Universities, 1580–1620* (Chicago: University of Chicago Press, 1997); Richard Drayton, *Nature's Government: Science, Imperial Britain, and the "Improvement" of the World* (New Haven and London: Yale University Press, 2000); Londa Schiebinger, *Plants and Empire: Colonial Bioprospecting in the Atlantic World* (Cambridge, MA: Harvard University Press, 2004); Justin Roberts, *Slavery and the Enlightenment in the British Atlantic* (Cambridge: Cambridge University Press, 2013); Tracy-Ann Smith et al., *Slavery and the Natural World* (London: Natural History Museum, 2007); April G. Shelford, *A Caribbean Enlightenment: Intellectual Life in the British and French Colonial Worlds, 1750–1792* (Cambridge: Cambridge University Press, 2023); and Kathleen S. Murphy, *Captivity's Collections: Science, Natural History, and the British Transatlantic Slave Trade* (Chapel Hill: University of North Carolina Press, 2023).
6. Kathleen S. Murphy, 'Collecting Slave Traders: James Petiver, Natural History, and the British Slave Trade', *WMQ* 70 (October 2013), 638 ('expanded').
7. James Delbourgo, *Collecting the World: Hans Sloane and the Origins of the British Museum* (Cambridge, MA: Harvard University Press, 2019), 191 ('manati'); Robert Willis and John Willis Clark, *The Architectural History of the University of Cambridge and of the Colleges of Cambridge and Eton*, vol. 2 (Cambridge: Cambridge University Press, 1886), 210–212 ('£100' and 'built'); Catherine Ansorge, 'The Revd George Lewis: His Life and Collection', *Journal of the History of Collections* 32 (March 2020), 143–156 ('Lewis').
8. Inventory of Weapons, Utensils, and Manufactures of various kinds collected by Captn. Cook of His Majesty's ship the Endeavour in the Years 1768, 1769, 1770 & 1771, October 1771, Library records: donors, c. 1680, WL, Add. MS a/106 ('Weapons' and 'inventory'); An Inventory of all the Rarities & besides Books in Trinity, *ibid.* ('magick' and 'Quiver'); Edwin D. Rose, 'Empire and the Theology of Nature in the Cambridge Botanic Garden, 1760–1825', *Journal of British Studies* 62 (October 2023), 1016 ('1660s'); Thomas Salmon, *The Foreigner's Companion Through the Universities of Cambridge and Oxford, and the Adjacent Counties* (London: William Owen, 1748), 67 ('Coffee-shrub' and 'Torch-thistle').

9. 'Science', in Samuel Johnson, *A Dictionary of the English Language: In Which The Words are deduced from their Originals, Explained in their Different Meanings, and Authorized by the Names of the Writers in whose Works they are found* (Dublin: W. G. Jones, 1768) ('Knowledge'); Sara Landreth, 'Science in the Long Eighteenth Century', in Frans De Bruyn, ed., *The Cambridge Companion to Eighteenth-Century Thought* (Cambridge: Cambridge University Press, 2019), 58–97 ('defined').
10. Dr Woodward's Will with Remarks by Mr. Peck and Election of Mr. Green, 7 May 1778, Archives of the Department of Geology and the Woodwardian and Sedgwick Museums, 1731–1987, CUL, GBR/0265/UA/GEOL 1/1 ('ready money' and '£100'). For Woodward's life and times, see V. A. Eyles, 'John Woodward, F. R. S.', Nature 205 (1965), 868–870; Ken McNamara, 'Dr Woodward's 350-year legacy', *Geology Today* 31 (September–October 2015), 181–186; Roy Porter, 'John Woodward; "A Droll Sort of Philosopher"', *Geological Magazine* 116 (1978), 335–417; Roy Porter, *The Making of Geology: Earth Science in Britain, 1660–1815* (Cambridge: Cambridge University Press, 1977); and Joseph M. Levine, *Dr. Woodward's Shield: History, Science, and Satire in Augustan England* (Ithaca, NY and London: Cornell University Press, 1977).
11. John Woodward, Old South Sea Annuities Ledgers, BE, AC27/6452, 735 ('stock'); Dr. John Woodward, Transfer Book, May–June 1720, TNA, T70/199/1, 33 ('Royal African'); John Woodward, *The Natural History of the Earth, Illustrated, Inlarged, and Defended* (London: Thomas Edlin, 1726), 106 ('Stature') and 107 ('Nothing').
12. William Deringer, 'Compound Interest Corrected: The Imaginative Mathematics of the Financial Future in Early Modern England', *Osiris* 33 (2018), 109–110 ('owed' and 'logarithms'); William Deringer, *Calculated Values: Finance, Politics, and the Quantitative Age* (Cambridge, MA: Harvard University Press, 2018) ('pique'); Odlyzko, 'Newton's Financial Misadventures', 29–59 ('Newton's South Sea holdings'); Miscellaneous Papers on Compound Interest, c.1700 – c.1749, The Macclesfield Collection, CUL, GBR/0012/MS Add.9597/8/1 ('compound'); Amount of an Annuity at Compound Interest, c.1700 – c.1749, ibid., GBR/0012/MS Add.9597/8/2; Questions on Annuities, c.1700 – c.1750, ibid., 3 ('annuities'). See John Brewer, *The Sinews of Power: War, Money, and the English State, 1688–1783* (Cambridge, MA: Harvard University Press, 1989); Anne L. Murphy, *The Origins of English Financial Markets: Investment and Speculation before the South Sea Bubble* (Cambridge: Cambridge University Press, 2009); and Carl Wennerlind, *Casualties of Credit: The English Financial Revolution, 1620–1720* (Cambridge, MA: Harvard University Press 2011).
13. Woodward, *Natural History*, pref. ('promiscuous'); John Woodward, *Brief instructions for making observations in all parts of the world as also, for collecting, preserving, and sending over natural things: being an attempt to settle an universal correspondence for the advancement of knowledge both natural and civil* (London: Richard Wilkin, 1696), 16 ('Insects').
14. John Woodward, *An Attempt Towards a Natural History of the Fossils of England; In A Catalogue of the English Fossils in the Collection of J. Woodward, M. D.*, vol. 1 (London: F. Fayram, 1729), 112 ('Coasts' and 'Shores'); ibid., vol. 2, 5 ('Shell'). For enslaved diving, see Molly A. Warsh, 'Enslaved Pearl Divers in the Sixteenth Century Caribbean', *Slavery and Abolition* 31 (2010), 345–362; Burnard, *Mastery, Tyranny, & Desire*, 143; and Kathleen M. Brown, *Foul Bodies: Cleanliness in Early America* (New Haven and London: Yale University Press, 2009), 68. The collection was included in John Woodward, *An Attempt towards a Natural History of the Fossils of England*, 2 vols. (London, 1728–1729).

15. Delbourgo, *Collecting the World*, 97 ('bestow'); Woodward, *Natural History*, vol. 1, 29 ('Lump'); Niccolò Guicciardini, *The Development of Newtonian Calculus in Britain, 1700–1800* (Cambridge: Cambridge University Press, 1989), 16 ('Hayes'); Woodward, *Collection*, 30 ('Ounces'). Dr John Arbuthnot, Transfer Book, 2 May to 28 June 1720, TNA, T70/199/1, 41 ('Arbuthnot'); Dr. John Freind, *ibid.*, 23 ('Freind'); J. S. Rowlinson, 'John Freind: Physician, Chemist, Jacobite, and Friend of Voltaire's', *Notes and Records of the Royal Society of London* 61 (May 2007), 119 ('Readership'); Dr Thomas Pellett, Transfer Book, 2 May to 28 June 1720, TNA, T70/199/1, 10 ('Pellett'); Dr William King, *ibid.*, 99 ('King'). Charles Hayes published a letter in support of the RAC: *The Importance of effectually supporting the Royal African Company of England impartially consider'd;…in a Letter to a Member of the House of Commons* (London: M. Cooper, 1744).
16. Woodward, *Collection*, 24 ('*Vernon*'); George F. Frick et al., 'Botanical Explorations and Discoveries in Colonial Maryland, 1688 to 1753', *Huntia: A Journal of Botanical History*, 7 (1987), 23 ('befriended'); Christopher Wordsworth, *Scholae Academica* (Cambridge: Cambridge University Press, 1877), 207 ('improve'); Lindsay O'Neill, *The Opened Letter: Networking in the Early Modern British World* (Philadelphia: University of Pennsylvania Press, 2015), 58–59 ('sent to Virginia').
17. Conyers Middleton's certificate for sale of South Sea Stock, 29 September 1721, Records of and relating to academic officers, 1620–2014, CUL, GBR/0265/UA/O.XIV 262 ('sale document'); John A. Dussinger, 'Middleton, Conyers', *Oxford Dictionary of National Biography*, www.oxforddnb.com/view/10.1093/ref:odnb/9780198614128.001.0001/odnb-9780198614128-e-18669;jsessionid=F4144B18598FDED6BC9179ABA2AD3EB4, accessed 29 June 2022 ('fossils'); Conyers Middleton, *A Letter from Rome, shewing an exact conformity between popery and paganism, with the Prefatory Discourse, in answer to the objections of a popish writer, and a Postscript, in which Mr. Warburton's opinion concerning the paganism of Rome is considered*, in idem., *The Miscellaneous Works Of the late Reverend and Learned Conyers Middleton, D.D. Principal Librarian of the University of Cambridge*, vol. 5 (London: R. Manby and H. S. Cox, 1755), 111 ('black'); Vaughan and Vaughan, 'Before Othello', 19–44 ('sinfulness'); Isaac Barrow, 'Of Submission to the Divine Will', in John Tillotson, ed., *The Works of Isaac Barrow, D. D.*, vol. 3 (London: J. R., 1692), 38 ('*Negros*').
18. Gascoigne, *Cambridge*, 179 ('twenty-eight'); Reverend William Cole's Account of Mason, in John Willis Clark and Thomas McKenny Hughes, eds., *The Life and Letters of the Reverend Adam Sedgwick, LL.D., D.C.L., F.R.S., Fellow of Trinity College, Cambridge, Prebendary of Norwich, Woodwardian Professor of Geology, 1818–1873*, vol. 1 (Cambridge: Cambridge University Press, 1890), 190 ('unhewn'); William Smith, *A Natural History of Nevis, and the Rest of the English Leeward Charibee Islands in America with Many Other Observations on Nature and Art* (Cambridge: Cambridge University Press, 2014), i–ii ('Worthy', 'spiritual', and 'encouraged'), 3–4 ('cockles' and 'dogwood'), and 10–11 ('*Oxford*').
19. Frank N. Egerton, ed., 'Richard Bradley's Relationship with Sir Hans Sloane', *Notes and Records: The Royal Society Journal of the History of Science* 25 (June 1970), 60–61.
20. Richard Bradley to Sir Hans Sloane, circa 1727, in Egerton, ed., 'Bradley's Relationship with Sloane', 67 ('money' and 'Jamaica'); Richard Bradley, *A Philosophical Account of Works of Nature. Endeavouring to set forth the several Gradations Remarkable in the*

Mineral, Vegetable, and Animal Parts of the Creation Tending to the Composition of a Scale of Life (London: W. Mears, 1721), 75 ('*Flying Lizard*' and '*plates*'), 153–154 ('*Lanthorn*' and '*rareities*'), and 86 ('*Rat*'); Richard Bradley, *The History of Succulent Plants Containing, The Aloes, Ficoids (or Fig-Marygolds) Torch-Thistles, Melon-Thistles, and such others as are capable of an Hortus Siccus* (London: J. Hodges, 1739), 3 ('*growing*').

21. Richard Bradley, *A Survey of the Ancient Husbandry and Gardening, Collected from Cato, Varro, Columella, Virgil* (London: B. Motte, 1725), pref. ('*Physick*', 'Governors', 'Tun', 'Coffee', 'Plantations', and 'Use'); Richard Walker, *A Short Account of the late Donation of a Botanic Garden to the University of Cambridge By the Revd Dr. Walker, Vice-Master of Trinity College; with Rules and Orders for the Government of it* (Cambridge: J. Bentham, 1763), 1 ('Goodness'); Michel-Rolph Trouillot, 'Motion in the System: Coffee, Color, and Slavery in Eighteenth-Century Saint-Domingue', *Review* 5 (Winter 1982), 332 ('quadrupled'). For the coffee economy in North America, see also Michelle Craig McDonald, 'The Chance of the Moment: Coffee and the New West Indies Commodities Trade', *WMQ* 62 (July 2005), 441–472.

22. Richard Bradley, *The Weekly Miscellany For the Improvement of Husbandry, Trade, Arts, and Sciences*, 12 September 1727 ('pleased', 'good Number', 'Plantations', 'encouraged', 'fresher', and 'parcel'); Richard Bradley, *A Short Historical Account of Coffee; Containing the most remarkable Observations of the greatest Men in Europe concerning it, from the first Knowledge of it down to this present Time; with a more accurate Description of the Coffee-Tree than has yet been Publish'd* (London: E. Matthews, 1715), 21 ('medicinal') and 24 ('mercantile'); Richard Bradley, *Kalendarium Universale: or, the Gardiner's Universal Calendar.* (London: L James Lacy, 1726), 175–176 ('raising'). For Bradley's interest in coffee's medicinal properties, see also his *The Virtue and Use of Coffee, with regard to the plague, and other infectious distempers: containing the most remarkable observations of the greatest men in Europe concerning it* (London: E. Matthews and W. Mears, 1721).

23. Will of Claude Fonnereau, Merchant of Saint Antholin, City of London, Prerogative Court of Canterbury and related Probate Jurisdictions: Will Registers, TNA, PROB 11/701/472 ('EIC'); South Sea Company, *A List of the Names of the Corporation of the Governor and Company of Merchants of Great Britain Trading to the South-Seas, and other Parts of America, and for Encouraging the Fishery* (London: John Barber, 1720), 6 ('SSC'); Murphy, *Captivity's Collections*, 94–95 ('surgeon') and 97 ('fourteen'); Rose, 'Theology of Nature', 1022 ('Indigenous and enslaved'); John Martyn to William Houstoun, 22 May 1731, George Cornelius Gorham, ed., *Memoirs of John Martyn, F.R.S., and of Thomas Martyn, B.D., F.R.S., F.L.S., Professors of Botany in the University of Cambridge* (London: Hatchard and Son, 1830), 46–47 ('jealousy'); Raymond Phineas Stearns, 'Colonial Fellows of the Royal Society of London, 1661–1788', *WMQ* 3 (April 1946), 234–235 ('Search' and 'Skill'd'); John Martyn, *Historia Plantarum Rariorum* (London: Richard Reily, 1728), 9 and 22 ('Barbados'), 27 and 39 ('Dominica' and 'Jamaica').

24. 'Went away from his Master', *The Grub-Street Journal*, 25 May 1732 ('Named', 'heard', 'Livery', 'Strong', and 'English'); Newman, *Freedom Seekers*, 35 ('commodify'); 'Advertisements and Notices', *London Gazette*, 15 July 1732 ('Cheapside'); Monica L. Miller, *Slaves to Fashion: Black Dandyism and the Styling of Black Diasporic Identity* (Durham, NC: Duke University Press, 2009), 49 ('garish outfits').

25. Stuart Max Walters, *The Shaping of Cambridge Botany: A Short History of Whole-Plant Botany in Cambridge from the Time of Ray into the Present Century*

(Cambridge: Cambridge University Press, 1981), 39 ('numerous works') and 42–43 ('assisted as Curator' and 'teaching'); Gorham, ed., *Memoirs of John Martyn, F.R.S., and of Thomas Martyn*, 139 ('advantageous').

26. Thomas Martyn, *The Gardener's and Botanist's Dictionary; Containing the Best and Newest Methods of Cultivating and Improving the Kitchen, Fruit, and Flower Garden, and Nursery; or Performing the Practical Parts of Agriculture; of Managing Vineyards, and of Propagating all Sorts of Timber Trees*, vol. 1 (London: C. and J. Rivington, 1807), unpaginated.
27. Lorri Glover, *Eliza Lucas Pinckney: An Independent Woman in the Age of Revolution* (New Haven, CT: Yale University Press, 2020), 58–63 ('perfecting'); Julien Poydras to Mr. Marre, 6 August 1795, Julien Poydras Letterbook, LHC, RG 98, ff. 5–6 ('London' and 'insurance').
28. Martyn, *The Gardener's and Botanist's Dictionary*, vol. 1, unpaginated.
29. Derek Howse, *Nevil Maskelyne: The Seaman's Astronomer* (Cambridge: Cambridge University Press, 1989), 1–26.
30. Dalrymple, *Anarchy*, 133–134 ('fortune'); Lady Clive to Edmund Maskelyne, 16 May 1766, Letters Sent by Lady Clive, Vol. 1, 1762–1805, CUL, GBR.0180/RGO 218/9/1 ('instrument' and 'December'); Nevil Maskelyne to Edmund Maskelyne, 15 May 1766, Letters to Edmund Maskelyne, CUL, GBR/0180/RGO 35/32 ('India stock'); 'John Pate Rose (ne Pate)', *Legacies*, www.ucl.ac.uk/lbs/person/view/2146660545, accessed 10 July 2023 ('Mount Hindmost').
31. Howse, *Maskelyne*, 26–39 ('observe'); 3 July 1760, Minutes of a Meeting of the Council of the Royal Society, RS, CMO/4/105 ('Members', 'Settlements', 'Factories', and 'tools'); 2 June 1761, Confirmed minutes of the Board of Longitude, 1737–1779, Papers of the Board of Longitude, CUL, GBR/0180/RGO 14/5 ('Jamaica'); Nevil Maskelyne to Edmund Maskelyne, 8 September 1763, Letters to Edmund Maskelyne, CUL, GBR/0180/RGO 35/30 ('Portugal specie' and '8 months'). Two years later, the Reverend John Mitchell, a Queens' fellow, 'applied at the East India House in relation to the Transit of Venus over the Sun'. (Anonymous note about the Rev Mr Mitchell, 1762, Miscellaneous Manuscripts by, about or belonging to the Fellows of the Royal Society, RS, MM/10/150.)
32. Log Book of Voyage to Barbados, 1761–1764, Papers of Nevil Maskelyne, CUL, GBR/0180/RGO 4/321 ('15 Guns'); Nevil Maskelyne to Edmund Maskelyne, 29 December 1763, Letters to Edmund Maskelyne, CUL, GBR/0180/RGO 35/31 ('arrival', 'civilities', 'Constitution', 'somewhat', 'Sugar', and 'Garden'); 6 January 1764, Astronomical Observations made at the Island of Barbados, 1763–1764, Maskelyne Papers, CUL, GBR/0180/RGO 4/323 ('workmen'); Nevil Maskelyne, 'Astronomical Observations made at the Island of Barbadoes', in *Philosophical Transactions, Giving some Account of the Present Undertakings, Studies, and Labours, of the Ingenious, in many Considerable Parts of the World*, vol. 44 (London: L. Davis and C. Reymers, 1765), 389 ('Fellow'); 13 February 1805, A List of Nevil Maskelyne's Books, Maskelyne Papers, CUL, GBR/0180/RGO 218/4 ('Observations'); Jesse Foot *Observations Principally Upon the Speech of Mr. Wilberforce, on his Motion in the House of Commons, the 30th of May, 1804, for the Abolition of the Slave Trade* (London: T. Becket, 1805), 6 ('accusations').
33. 'Nathaniel Lloyd', *ACAD*, https://venn.lib.cam.ac.uk/cgi-bin/search-2018.pl?sur=lloyd&suro=w&fir=nathaniel&firo=c&cit=&cito=c&c=all&z=all&tex=&sye=&eye=&col=all&maxcount=50, accessed 30 January 2023 ('educated'); H. Helmholz, *The Profession of Ecclesiastical Lawyers: An Historical Introduction*

(Cambridge: Cambridge University Press, 2019), 18 ('masculine'); *Law Quibbles: Or, a Treatise of the Evasions, Tricks, Turns and Quibbles, Commonly Used in the Profession of the Law, to the Prejudice of Clients and Others* (London, 1724), 4 ('Laudable'); *A General Description of All the Trades, Digested in Alphabetical Order: By which Parents, Guardians, and Trustees, may, with greater Ease and Certainty, make choice of Trades agreeable to the Capacity, Education, Inclination, Strength, and Fortune of the Youth under their Care* (London: E. and R. Nutt, 1724), 6 ('worthy'); *Ignoramus: Or, The English Lawyer – A Comedy* (London: W. Feales, 1736), 39 ('stinking'); David Lemmings, *Professors of the Law: Barristers and English Legal Culture in the Eighteenth Century* (Oxford: Oxford University Press, 2000), 111 ('attractive' and 'national').

34. Jacob Youde William Lloyd, *The History of the Princes, the Lords Marcher, and the Ancient Nobility of Powys Fadog: And the Ancient Lords of Arwystli, Cedewen, and Meirionydd*, vol. 6 (London: Whiting & Co., 1887), 348 ('seat'); Will of Sir Richard Lloyd, Dean of the Arches, Records of the Prerogative Court of Canterbury, TNA, PROB 11/384/51 ('inheritance'); Lemmings, *Professors of the Law*, 112 ('Blackstone'); John H. Langbein et al., *History of the Common Law: The Development of Anglo-American Legal Institutions* (Frederick, MD: Aspen Publishing, 2009), 194–195 ('specialist' and 'employment').

35. Charles Crawley, *Trinity Hall: The History of a Cambridge College, 1350-1975* (Cambridge: Trinity Hall, 2007), 74–77 ('£63'); A Lease of ye Common Rooms in Drs Commons made to Dr Henchman and Dr Pinfold in trust, 1728, Leases of Doctors Commons, 1671–1765, CUL, Add.9266/DC6 ('Henchman'); Humphrey Henchman, Call of 5 per cent., 1722, Books Concerning Stock, TNA, T70/180 ('£3,500'); Paul C. Nigol, 'Discipline, Discretion and Control: The Private Justice System of the Hudson's Bay Company in Rupert's Land, 1670-1770' (PhD dissertation, University of Calgary, 2001), 51 ('Penfold'); Michael Lobban, 'English Approaches to International Law in the Nineteenth Century', in Matthew Craven et al., eds., *Time, History and International Law* (Leiden: Martinus Nijhoff Publishers, 2007), 67 ('462'); Brian P. Levack, *The Civil Lawyers in England, 1603-1641: A Political Study* (Oxford: Clarendon Press, 1973), 26 ('statesmanship'); Sir Nathaniel Lloyd's opinion on the boundaries of the British seas, William Mildmay Papers, 1748–1756, vol. 1, WLC, M-231 ('sovereignty').

36. David Waddell, 'Charles Davenant and the East India Company', *Economica* 23 (August 1956), 261–264 ('Davenant' and '£1,000'); Charles Davenant, *An Essay on the East-India Trade* (London: Unknown, 1696), 8 ('Wealth'); Charles Davenant, *Reflections Upon the Constitution and Management of the Trade to Africa, Through the Whole Course and Progress thereof, from the Beginning of the last Century, to this Time* (London: John Morphew, 1709), 2 ('Planters'). For Davenant and the RAC, see Pettigrew, *Freedom's Debt*, 49–50.

37. Lord Treasurer Godolphin to Sir Nathaniel Lloyd, 27 June 1710, *The Twenty-Eighth Annual Report of the Deputy Keeper of the Public Records* (London: George E. Eyre and William Spottiswoode, 1867), 483 ('advocate Generall'); Henry St John, Viscount Bolingbroke, to Sir Charles Hedges and Sir Nathaniel Lloyd, 17 March 1712, in Adrian Lashmore-Davies, ed., *The Unpublished Letters of Henry St John, First Viscount Bolingbroke*, vol. 2 (London: Routledge, 2013), 136 ('negotiating'); John Shovlin, *Trading with the Enemy: Britain, France, and the 18th-Century Quest for a Peaceful World Order* (New Haven, CT: Yale University Press, 2021), 49 ('nullified'); Alan L. Karras, *Smuggling: Contraband and Corruption in World History*

(Lanham, MD: Rowman & Littlefield, 2010), 54–70 ('illegal trade'); Manuscript from the Papers of Sir Nathaniel Lloyd on the Rules and Directions appointed by his Majesty in Council to be observed by the High Court of Admiralty in the Adjudication of Prizes, in Frederic Thomas Pratt, ed., *Law of Contraband of War: With a Selection of Cases from the Papers of the Right Hon. Sir George Lee, LL.D. Formerly Dean of the Arches, Etc. Etc. Etc.* (London: William G. Benning, 1856), 250 ('plantations').

38. Kate Hodgson, 'Franco-Irish Saint-Domingue: Family Networks, Trans-colonial Diasporas', *Caribbean Quarterly* 64 (November 2018), 434–451 ('families' and 'Stapleton'); Report to the queen from Sir Nathaniel Lloyd, concerning the petition of Hughes O'Kelly, 13 March 1712, State Papers Domestic, Queen Anne, TNA, SP 34/34/62, ff. 199–201 ('late Brother', 'judgment', and 'Practice'); Sir Nathaniel Lloyd to the Council of Trade and Plantations, 2 August 1715, in Cecil Headlam, ed., *Calendar of State Papers, Colonial Series, American and West Indies, August, 1714 – December, 1715, Preserved in the Public Record Office* (London: H. M. Stationary Office, 1928), 254 ('negroes' and 'fled').

39. David Wilson, *Suppressing Piracy in the Eighteenth Century: Pirates, Merchants and British Imperial Authority in the Atlantic and Indian Oceans* (Woodbridge, Suffolk: The Boydell Press, 2021), 155 ('attacked'); Trial of Pirates, 1720, in R. G. Marsden, ed., *Documents Relating to Law and Custom of the Sea*, vol. 1 (Union, NJ: The Lawbook Exchange, Ltd., 1999), 253–254 ('within' and 'pyrates').

40. A Petition of the Royal Africa Company of England concerning an allegation of piracy against Lieutenant James Massey [Mattey], 19 January 1723, State Papers Domestic, George I, TNA, SP 35/41/16 ('mutinous' and 'fairly'); Order in Council for a Commission to the captain of H. M. S. Kinsale and others to try pirates, 1725, in Marsden, ed., *Law and Custom of the Sea*, vol. 1, 262 ('coast'). See also M. J. Prichard and D. E. C. Yale, ed., *Hale and Fleetwood on Admiralty Jurisdiction* (London: Selden Society, 1993), 363–365. In Lloyd's time, the Admiralty Court was in decline and the Common law had 'absorbed much of this business'. (Warren Swain, *The Law of Contract, 1670–1870* [Cambridge: Cambridge University Press, 2015], 21–22.) For the Massey incident, see also J. M. Gray, *A History of the Gambia*, intro. by Sir Thomas Southorn (Cambridge: Cambridge University Press, 1940), 173–175.

41. *Weekly Journal or Saturday's Post*, 8 March 1718 ('committed'); *Weekly Journal or British Gazetteer*, 29 October 1720 ('Squirrel'); Samuel G. Margolin, 'Lawlessness on the Maritime Frontier of the Greater Chesapeake, 1650–1750' (PhD dissertation, College of William and Mary, 1992), 354 ('Whorwood'); *Weekly Journal or British Gazetteer*, 29 October 1720 ('Ship', 'dispose', and 'Criminal'); Mark Knights, *Trust and Distrust: Corruption in Office in Britain and Its Empire, 1600–1850* (Oxford: Oxford University Press, 2021), 329–330 ('controversial').

42. William Gerbing Wood, *The Annual Ships of the South Sea Company, 1711–1736* (Champaign: University of Illinois Press, 1938), 4 ('tons'); Case of implementation of Treaty of England with Spain, 1713 and 1717, re. tonnage and unloading of yearly ship to the West Indies, sent by South Sea Company, argued by Nathaniel Lloyd, 10 August 1722, NLJ, MS 1369 ('measurement', 'Frauds', and 'Convention'). See also Jean O. McLachlan, *Trade and Peace with Old Spain, 1667–1750: A Study of the Influence of Commerce on Anglo-Spanish Diplomacy in the First Half of the Eighteenth Century* (Cambridge: Cambridge University Press, 1940), 24.

43. Dr Nathaniel Lloyd and George Cooke, List of Holders of East India Company Stock, April 1707, Stocks and Bonds of the East India Company, BL, IOR/H/3,

173 ('£230'); East India Company, *A list of the names of all the adventurers in the stock of the honourable the East-India-Company, the 12th day of April, 1684 whereof those marked with a * are not capable (by their adventure) to be chosen committees* (London: A. Baldwin, 1699) ('1684'); Dame Elizabeth Lloyd and Sir Richard Lloyd decd., List of Holders of East India Company Stock, 18 April 1691, Stocks and Bonds of the East India Company, BL, IOR/H/2, 54; ('1691'); Dame Elizabeth Lloyd and Sir Richard Lloyd decd., April 1699, *Ibid.*, 90 ('holdings'); South Sea Company, *A List of the Names*, 9 ('separate holdings'); *A List of the Names of the Corporation of the Governor and Company of Merchants of Great Britain Trading to the South-Seas, and other Parts of America, and for Encouraging the Fishery* (London: Edward Symon, 1723), 9 and Sir Nathaniel Lloyd, Doctors Commons, Old South Sea Stock Ledgers, BE, AC27/6445, 571, and Sir Nathaniel Lloyd and Jacob Sawbridge, *ibid.* ('£6,000'); Sir Nathaniel Lloyd and Henry Wright, *ibid.*, 572 ('£12,080'); Sir Nathaniel Lloyd, Doctors Commons, *ibid.*, 6465, 367 and Sir Nathaniel Lloyd and Henry Wright, *ibid.* ('£9,158'); Sir Nathaniel Lloyd's Charity, *Further Report of the Commissioners Appointed in Pursuance of Two Several Acts of Parliament; The one, made and passed in the 58th Year of His late Majesty, c. 91, intituled, 'An Act for appointing Commissioners to inquire concerning Charities in England, for the Education of the Poor'* (London: House of Commons, 1831), 434 ('£600'). Both of Lloyd's parents stopped appearing in the stock ledgers after 1703, and Dame Elizabeth died on 16 August 1731. She was 'handsomely buried at St Bennet's Paul's-Wharf'. (*London Evening Post*, 21 August 1731). At Lloyd's death, the South Sea securities amounted to £600 16s. in stock and £2,623 16s. in annuities. He also appeared on lists of stockholders in both 1735 and 1747. See *A List of the Name of the Corporation of the Governor and Company of Merchants of Great Britain, Trading to the South-Seas, and other Parts of America, and for Encouraging the Fishery* (London: South Sea Company, 1747), 6.

44. *A List of the Names of the Adventurers of the Royal African Company of England* (London: Royal African Company, 1720), 3 ('appeared'); Sir Nathaniel Lloyd, Transfer Book, May-June 1720, TNA, T70/199/2, 42 ('£3,000'); E. I. Carlyle and S. J. Skedd, 'Smith, Joseph (1670-1756)', *ODNB*, www.oxforddnb.com/view/10.1093/ref:odnb/9780198614128.001.0001/odnb-9780198614128-e-25870?rskey=16RO4S&result=1, accessed 12 May 2022 ('£1,000'); Reverend Dr Joseph Smith, Transfer Book, May-June 1720, TNA, T70/199/2, 23 ('500'); His Grace the Duke of Chandos, *ibid.*, 1, 1 ('30,000'); John Kerr, *Scottish Education: School and University: From Early Times to 1908 with an Addendum 1908-1913* (Cambridge: Cambridge University Press, 1913), 222-223 ('chair'); Benefactors to the new building, n.d., Senate House, 1673-1899, University registry guard books, 1327-2000, CUL, GBR/0265/UA/CUR 46 ('£500'); Gary S. Shea, '(Re)financing the Slave Trade with the Royal African Company in the Boom Markets of 1720', *Centre for Dynamic Macroeconomic Analysis Working Paper Series*, CDMA11/14 (October 2011), 6 ('reinvigorate') and 43 ('quadrupling'); Nathaniel Day attorney to Sir Nathaniel Lloyd, Transfer Book, 1721-1722, TNA, T70/203, 98-99 ('dump').

45. Peregrine Horden and Simon J. D. Green, *All Soul's under the Ancien Régime: Politics, Learning, and the Arts, c. 1600-1850* (Oxford: Oxford University Press, 2008), 142 ('Codrington' and '£10,000'); Will of Christopher Codrington, 8 February 1711, Records of the Prerogative Court of Canterbury, TNA, PROB 20/540 ('guineas'); Sir Nathaniel Lloyd to Warden Gardiner, 3 March 1710, ASC, CTM, 352, no. 320 ('possession'); Sir Nathaniel Lloyd to Warden Gardiner, 13 September 1712,

ASC, CTM, 354, no. 343 ('Dead'); Birke Häcker, 'A Case Note on All Souls College v. Cod[d]rington (1720)', *Journal of Comparative and International Law* 76 (October 2012), 1059 ('refusing'); 18 August 1710, Barbados Committee Papers, Papers of the Society for the Propagation of the Gospel in Foreign Parts, BOD, USPG X/14, vol. 1 ('bequeathed' and 'counsel'); Dr Lloyd, 1709, An Account of Quarterly Payments & Benefactions to the Society, 1700–1735, Society for Promoting Christian Knowledge Archive, CUL, GBR/0012/MS SPCK/C1/3 ('SPCK'); Edward Waddington, *A Sermon preached before the Incorporated Society for the Propagation of the Gospel in Foreign Parts; at their Anniversary Meeting in the Parish-Church of St. Mary le Bow; on Friday the 17th of February, 1720* (London: John Downing, 1721), 67 ('SPG').

46. Häcker, 'Case Note on All Souls College', 1060, n. 52 ('overseers'); 2 June 1714, Account Books of Codrington's Legacy and Lloyd's Benefaction, ASC, CTM, 416 ('£2,300'); The General Stock, 14 April 1727, Books Concerning Stock, TNA, T70/214, 2 ('Royal African'); Peirce Dod, *Several cases in Physick: and one in particular, giving an account of a person who was inoculated for the small-pox, and had the small-pox upon the inoculation, and yet had it again* (London: Royal Society, 1746) ('dismissing'); 3 June 1715, Account Books of Codrington's Legacy and Lloyd's Benefaction, ASC, CTM, 416 ('coach'); 7 February 1715, *ibid*. ('name').

47. Häcker, 'Case Note on All Souls College', 1058 ('Retrieving'); The Wardens Colledge of All Souls in Oxford, Old South Sea Annuities Ledgers, BE, AC27/6459, 882 ('held'); 21 November 1728, Account Books of Codrington's Legacy and Lloyd's Benefaction, ASC, CTM, 416 ('£5,100'); The Wardens Fellows & Schollars of Wadham Colledge Oxon, Old South Sea Annuities Ledgers, BE, AC27/6452, 11 ('Wadham'); Peirce Dodd to Stephen Niblett, 22 May 1729, Papers Concerning the Building of the College, ASC, CTM 34, 293 ('Interest'). Dod possessed £1,000 of RAC stock. By 1725, William Baker, the Bishop of Bangor and Warden of Wadham College, had purchased £780 in annuities.

48. John Smail, 'The Culture of Credit in Eighteenth-Century Commerce: The Textile Industry', *Enterprise & Society* 4 (June 2003), 299 ('emotive'); Sir Nathaniel Lloyd to the Bursars, 1 November 1718, Papers Concerning the Building of the College, ASC, CTM, 297, no. 8 ('Discharge'); *Daily Journal*, 28 October 1726 ('resigned'); Bond of Warden and Fellows for Payment of 60l. per annum to Sir Nathaniel Lloyd, 3 March 1723, Papers Concerning the Building of the College, ASC, CTM, 297, no. 9 and Bond for Payment of 1,000l. to Sir Nathaniel Lloyd, 25 August 1729, *ibid.*, 298, no. 14 ('two bonds'); Sir Nathaniel Lloyd to Stephen Niblett, 19 July 1729, *ibid.*, no. 11 ('Creditour' and 'Benefaction'); John Guinness, 'Portraits of Sir Nathaniel Lloyd', *Oxoniensa* 25 (1960), 296 ('portrait').

49. Campbell R. Hone, *The Life of Dr. John Radcliffe, 1652–1714: Benefactor of the University of Oxford* (London: Faber and Faber Limited, 1950), 76–77 ('South Sea' and 'East India') and 118–126 ('worth around'); William Pittis, *The History of the Present Parliament and Convocation with the Debates at large relating to the Conduct of the War abroad, the Mismanagements of the Ministry at home, and the Reasons why some Offenders are not yet Impeached* (London: John Baker, 1711), 351 ('invested'); Ivor Guest, *Dr. John Radcliffe and His Trust* (London: The Radcliffe Trust, 1991), 67 ('£12,500') and 68 ('partly funded'); 'Radcliffe, John (1653–1714), of Wolverton, Bucks., and Carshalton, Surr.', *The History of Parliament*, www.histparl.ac.uk/volume/1690-1715/member/radcliffe-john-1653-1714#footnote1_b18puie, accessed 30 June 2022 ('£50'); 'Dr John Ratcliffe', List of Holders of East India Company Stock, 16 April 1694, Stocks and Bonds of the East India Company, BL, IOR/H/2, 37

('Company's stock'); Lord Finch to Charles Townshend, 25 June 1725, State Papers Domestic, George I, TNA,SP 35/56/59, f. 110 ('Master'). Radcliffe had £3,000 in EIC stock in 1694. The trustees for Radcliffe's estate had hoped to make windfall profits from the Bubble, which they believed would help to fund the construction in record time. The stock's collapse, however, soon dashed their hopes of strong returns from this security.

50. Wills of Sir Nathaniel Lloyd, 29 May 1739 and 1740, Papers Concerning the Building of the College, ASC, CTM, 299, no. 4 ('library', 'Regent's Walk', '£500', and 'Trinity'); Vivian Hubert Howard Green, *The Commonwealth of Lincoln College, 1427–1977* (Oxford: Oxford University Press, 1979), 400 ('remodel'); 'Founders & Benefactors of Lincoln College, with a birds eye view of the building', *Oxford Almanack*, 1743 ('Founders'); Crawley, *Trinity Hall*, 117 ('Hall'); Dale, ed., *Warren's Book*, 318–323 ('chapel' and 'Oswestry'); To the Master and Fellows of Trinity Hall in Cambridge a Proposal for Repairing and Beautifying their Chapel according to the Designs approved by the said Gentleman, 10 May 1729, Building Accounts, 1727–1730, TH, GBR/1936/THAR/4/1/2/5/1 ('extensive'); Thomas Wright and Rev. H. Longueville Jones, ed., *Memorials of Cambridge: A Series of Views of the College Halls, and Public Buildings, Engraved by J. Le Keux; with Historical and Descriptive Accounts*, vol. 1 (London: David Bogue, 1845), 8 ('almost rebuilt'); Memorandum on Nathaniel Lloyd in in the College's Account of Stock, Building Accounts, 1727–1730, TH, GBR/1936/THAR/4/1/2/5/1 ('£2,660'); 'Nathanael Lloyd Society', *Trinity Hall, University of Cambridge*, www.trinhall.cam.ac.uk/supporters/your-impact/recognition/nathanael-lloyd-society/., accessed 12 May 2022 ('fabric').

51. Crawley, *Trinity Hall*, 120–121.

52. Blight, *Yale and Slavery*, 55 ('forty'); William Wynne's opinion concerning granting registers to ships built in America, 1785, The Liverpool Papers, BL, Add MS 38346, 54 ('adjudicate', 'Plantation', and 'trading').

53. Parliamentary and Judicial Appendix, No. XV, in *Correspondence concerning Claims against Great Britain, Transmitted to the Senate of the United States in Answer to the Resolutions of December 4 and 10, 1867, and of May 27*, 1868, vol. 5 (Washington, D.C.: Philp & Solomons, 1869), 310.

54. John Gascoigne, 'Rutherforth, Thomas (1712–1771)', *ODNB*, www.oxforddnb.com/view/10.1093/ref:odnb/9780198614128.001.0001/odnb-9780198614128-e-24367, accessed 2 December 2021.

55. *Names of the Adventurers*, 1 ('investor'); Thomas Rutherforth, *Two Sermons Preached Before the University of Cambridge, One May XXIX: The Other June XI: MDCCXLVII* (London: W. Innys, 1747), 1–2 ('placing').

56. Gary L. McDowell, 'The Limits of Natural Law: Thomas Rutherforth and the American Legal Tradition', *The American Journal of Jurisprudence* 37 (1992), 59 and Jack P. Greene, *The Intellectual Heritage of the Constitutional Era: The Delegates' Library* (Philadelphia: Library Company of Philadelphia, 1986), 18 ('popular'); James Madison's List of Books for Congress, 1783, in William T. Hutchinson et al., eds., *The Papers of James Madison*, vol. 6 (Charlottesville: University of Virginia Press, 1969), 62–115 ('Madison'); Edmund Randolph to Thomas Jefferson, 14 May 1793, in John Catanzariti et al., eds., *The Papers of Thomas Jefferson*, vol. 26 (Princeton, NJ: Princeton University Press, 1995), 33 and Joseph Story, *Commentaries on the Constitution of the United States*, vol. 1 (Boston: Hilliard, Gray, and Company, 1833), 322 ('American statesmen'); Thomas Rutherforth, *Institutes of Natural Law: Being the substance of a Course of*

Lectures on Grotius de Jure Belli et Pacis Read in St. Johns College Cambridge, vol. 1 (Cambridge: J. Bentham, 1745), 475 ('good of the child' and 'parent'). For early modern natural law theory, see Timothy Hochstrasser, *Natural Law Theories in the Early Enlightenment* (Cambridge: Cambridge University Press, 2006); Knud Haakonssen, *Grotius, Pufendorf, and Modern Natural Law* (Brookfield: Ashgate, 1999); and Annabel Brett, *Changes of State: Nature and the Limits of the City in Early Modern Natural Law* (Princeton, NJ: Princeton University Press, 2011).

57. Rutherforth, *Institutes of Natural Law*, vol. 1, 475-476 ('Nature', 'judge', 'directed', 'obligation', and 'benefit') and 488 ('liberty'); Edmund S. Morgan, *American Slavery, American Freedom: The Ordeal of Colonial Virginia* (New York, NY and London: W. W. Norton & Company, 1975), 311 ('Grinstead'). For *partus sequitur ventrem*, see Sasha Turner, *Contested Bodies: Pregnancy, Childrearing, and Slavery in Jamaica* (Philadelphia: University of Pennsylvania Press, 2017); Jessica Marie Johnson, *Wicked Flesh: Black Women, Intimacy, and Freedom in the Atlantic World* (Philadelphia: University of Pennsylvania Press, 2020); Thomas D. Morris, *Southern Slavery and the Law, 1619-1860* (Chapel Hill: University of North Carolina Press, 1996); and Brewer, 'Slavery, Sovereignty, and "Inheritable Blood,"' 1049. For Jefferson and Hemings, see Annette Gordon-Reed, *The Hemingses of Monticello: An American Family* (New York, NY: W. W. Norton & Company, 2009).

58. Rutherforth, *Institutes of Natural Law*, vol. 1, 488-491 ('four justifications') and 492 ('debt', 'extraordinary', and 'gestation').

59. Samuel von Pufendorf, *Of the Law of Nature and Nations. Eight Books* (Oxford: L. Lichfield, 1703), 127 ('jurist'); Francis Hutcheson, *A System of Moral Philosophy. In Three Books*, vol. 2 (London: A. Millar, 1755), 81-82 ('posterity' and 'plainly'). Pufendorf's support for natural slavery and the enslavement of Africans is discussed in Kari Saastamoinen, 'Pufendorf on Natural Equality, Human Dignity, and Self-Esteem', *Journal of the History of Ideas* 71 (January 2010), esp. 43-44. For Hutcheson, see Wylie Sypher, 'Hutcheson and the 'Classical' Theory of Slavery', *The Journal of Negro History* 24 (1939), 263-280; Caroline Robbins, '"When It Is That Colonies May Turn Independent": An Analysis of the Environment and Politics of Francis Hutcheson (1694-1746)', *WMQ* 11 (April 1954), 214-251, esp. 244; and Michal J. Rozbicki, 'To Save Them from Themselves: Proposals to Enslave the British Poor, 1698-1755', *Slavery & Abolition* 22 (2001), 29-50.

60. Thomas Gilbert, *Poems on Several Occasions* (London: Charles Bathurst, 1747), 121 ('1738') and 141 ('Negro'); Michael H. Hoffheimer, 'The Common Law of Edward Christian', *The Cambridge Law Journal* 53 (March 1994), 140-163 ('Edward Christian'); Edward Christian, *Notes to Blackstone's Commentaries, Which are Calculated to Answer All the Editions* (Dublin: P. Byrne, 1797), 542-543 ('barbarous' and 'continue').

61. Rutherforth, *Institutes of Natural Law*, vol. 2, 389-390 ('judgment', 'security', and 'authority'); David Ramsay, *A Dissertation on the Manner of Acquiring the Character and Privileges of a Citizens of the United States* (Charleston: Unknown, 1789), 3 ('inhabitants'); Alan Watson, *Slave Law in the Americas* (Athens and London: University of Georgia Press, 1989), 158 ('Ruffin'). For enslaved soldiers, see Christopher Leslie Brown and Philip D. Morgan, eds., *Arming Slaves: From Classical Times to the Modern Age* (New Haven, CT: Yale University Press, 2006). Rutherforth was used as legal authority in a number of slave cases, including Mahoney vs. Ashton, May 1799, in Thomas Harris and John McHenry, eds., *Maryland Reports, Being a Series of the Most Important Law Cases Argued and Determined in the General Court*

and Court of Appeals of the State of Maryland, From May, 1797, to the End of 1799, vol. 4 (New York: I. Riley, 1818), 300; and Thomas Aves, *Case of the Slave-Child, Med: Report of the Arguments of Counsel, and of the Opinion of the Court, in the Case of Commonwealth vs. Aves* (Boston: Isaac Knapp, 1836), 17.

62. William Holdsworth, *A History of English Law*, vol. 12 (London: Methuen & Co., Sweet and Maxwell, 1938), 644 ('tutor'); John Taylor, *Elements of the Civil Law* (Cambridge: Charles Bathurst, 1755), 424 ('impotency'), 476 ('horses'), and 436 ('Romans' and 'West India').

63. E. Millicent Sowerby, ed., *Catalogue of the Library of Thomas Jefferson*, vol. 2 (Washington, D.C.: Library of Congress, 1953), 404 ('libraries'); Gilbert Francklyn, *An Answer to the Rev. Mr. Clarkson's Essay on the Slavery and Commerce of the Human Species, particularly the African; in a Series of Letters From a Gentleman in Jamaica, to His Friend in London: Wherein Many of the Mistakes and Misrepresentations of Mr. Clarkson are pointed out, Both with Regard to The Manner in which that Commerce is carried on in Africa, and The Treatment of the Slaves in the West Indies* (London: J. Walter, 1789), 66–67 ('proslavery'); Taylor, *Elements*, 435 ('Christianity'), 410 ('private family'), and 429 ('no persons' and 'beasts'); Rev. La Roy Sunderland, *Anti-Slavery Manual, Containing a Collection of Facts and Arguments on American Slavery* (New York: S. W. Benedict, 1837), 39 ('*cruelties*' and '*injustice[s]*'); Earl M. Maltz, *Dred Scott and the Politics of Slavery* (Lawrence: University Press of Kansas, 2007), 106 ('Lemmon'), 69 ('originates'), and 95 ('violation'). John Taylor's *Summary of the Roman Law* (London: T. Payne, 1772), a redacted version of *Civil Law*, was included in the first White House library established during Millard Fillmore's presidency (1850–1853). See Catherine M. Parisian, ed., *The First White House Library: A History and Annotated Catalogue* (University Park: Pennsylvania State University Press, 2010), 317. The many uses of John Taylor's jurisprudence are discussed in Thomas D. Morris, '"Villeinage… as It Existed in England, Reflects but Little Light on Our Subject": The Problem of the "Sources" of Southern Slave Law', *The American Journal of Legal History* 32 (April 1988), 95–137.

64. William Whyte, 'The Intellectual Aristocracy Revisited', *Journal of Victorian Culture* 10 (December 2011), 39.

4 'Several University Gentlemen, who have quite altered their Tone': The Problem of the British Slave Trade

1. Account of South Sea Stock Purchased on Behalf of George I, George II Papers, RA, GEO/MAIN/52842-52843 ('tens of thousands'); His Royal Highness George Prince of Wales, Old South Sea Annuities Ledgers, BE, AC27/6452, f. 38 ('owned stock'); William, Duke of Clarence, to Samuel Hawker, 1807, Daniell Papers, RA, GEO/ADD/44/10 ('weaken'); George III to Lord North, 11 June 1779, in William Bodham Donne, ed., *The Correspondence of King George the Third with Lord North From 1768 to 1783*, vol. 2 (London: J. Murray, 1867), 254 ('Jamaica'); David Armitage, 'George III and the Law of Nations', *WMQ* 79 (January 2022), 27 ('helpless' and 'dominion'). The Prince of Wales, whose patronage of the arts led to the commissioning of "Rule, Britannia" and helped to popularise the Rococo style of architecture and furniture, owned £2,176 in stock at the time of the Bubble (though his personal involvement in these transactions was unrecorded). (Colley, *Britons*, 206.) For George III and

the British Caribbean, see Andrew Jackson O'Shaughnessy, *The Men Who Lost America: British Command during the Revolutionary War and the Preservation of the Empire* (New Haven, CT: Yales University Press, 2013), 35.

2. Henry Venn, *The Life and a Selection from the Letters of the Late Rev. Henry Venn, M. A., Successively Vicar of Huddersfield, Yorkshire, and Rector of Yelling, Huntingdonshire, Author of 'The Complete Duty of Man, &c.* (London: John Hatchard and Son, 1839), 422 ('circles'); 'Henry William Coulthurst', *Legacies*, www.ucl.ac.uk/lbs/person/view/2146634732, accessed 1 February 2023 ('compensation'); 'Henry William Coulthurst', *ACAD*, https://venn.lib.cam.ac.uk/cgi-bin/search-2018.pl?sur=coulthurst&suro=w&fir=&firo=c&cit=&cito=c&c=all&z=all&tex=&sye=&eye=&col=all&maxcount=50, accessed 1 February 2023 ('tutor'); 'At a General Meeting of the Gentlemen, Clergy, Merchants, and principal Inhabitants of the Town and Parish of Halifax, previously called by public Advertisement, The Rev. Dr Coulthurst, in the Chair', *The Leeds Intelligencer*, 27 February 1792 ('Police', 'Population', and 'Importations from Africa').

3. Charles Farish, 'A Summary of the consequences of the abolition of the slave-trade', 1798, Letters, Papers, and Domestic Correspondence of George III, TNA, HO 42/42/109 ('happy effects', 'half its horrors', and 'Master'). Farish's petition is mentioned briefly in James Gregory, *Mercy and British Culture, 1760–1960* (London: Bloomsbury Academic, 2021), 225, n. 121.

4. Farish, 'A Summary of the consequences of the abolition of the slave-trade', 1798, Correspondence of George III, TNA, HO 42/42/109.

5. 'Appleby Gilpin', *Legacies*, www.ucl.ac.uk/lbs/person/view/2146632829, accessed 1 February 2023 ('Grenada'); T. W. Thompson and Robert Woof, ed., *Wordsworth's Hawkshead* (London: Oxford University Press, 1970), 134, n. 1 ('boarding lodge'); 'To a Friend & School-fellow', June 1784, in *ibid.*, 316 ('direful'); Henry Gunning, *Reminiscences of the University, Town and County of Cambridge, From the Year 1780*, vol. 2 (Cambridge: Cambridge University Press, 2012), 94 and Wordsworth, *Social Life at the English Universities*, 356 ('celibacy'); 11 October 1792, Book of Orders, 1787–1830, QC, unnumbered ('mundane'). Enslavement was a particularly fraught issue within the Society of Friends. See, for example, Jean R. Soderlund, *Quakers & Slavery: A Divided Spirit* (Princeton, NJ: Princeton University Press, 1985); Larry Gragg, *The Quaker Community on Barbados: Challenging the Culture of the Planter Class* (Columbia: University of Missouri Press, 2009); Brycchan Carey, *From Peace to Freedom: Quaker Rhetoric and the Birth of American Antislavery, 1657–1761* (New Haven, CT: Yale University Press, 2012); and Markus Rediker, *The Fearless Benjamin Lay: The Quaker Dwarf Who Became the First Revolutionary Abolitionist* (London: Verso, 2017).

6. Samuel Johnson, 'Taxation no Tyranny; An Answer to the Resolutions and Address of the American Congress', 1775, in Samuel Johnson, *Political Tracts* (London: W. Strahan and T. Cadell, 1776), 262 ('drivers'); Thomas Harwood, *Alumni Etoniensis; or, a Catalogue of the Provosts & Fellows of Eton College & King's College, Cambridge, from the Foundation in 1443, to the Year 1797; With an Account of their Lives & Preferments, Collected from Original Mss.* (Birmingham: T. Pearson, 1797), 329 ('solemnity'); Sir William Draper, *The Thoughts of a Traveller Upon Our American Disputes* (London: J. Ridley, 1774), 21 ('Proclame'); Prince Hoare, ed., *Memoirs of Granville Sharp, Esq.* (Cambridge: Cambridge University Press, 2014), 188 ('Spanish Regulations' and 'soften') and xvi ('*wages*', 'industry', and 'encouragement').

7. Brown, *Moral Capital*, 195 ('Hinchcliffe'); Keene, *A Sermon*, 22 ('Civil', 'Opportunity', 'Vicinity', and 'Dependence'). See also Oldfield, *Popular Politics and British Anti-Slavery*, 70–71.

8. Jirik, 'Beyond Clarkson', 2 ('most significant'); Peckard, *Piety, Benevolence, and Loyalty, recommended*, 3 ('treatment' and 'despotism'), 1 ('honour'), and 4 ('human' and 'complexion'). Peckard published numerous sermons, petitions, and pamphlets against the slave trade and slavery before his death in December 1797. See, for example, *The Nature and Extent of Civil and Religious Liberty* (Cambridge: J. Archdeacon 1783); and *Justice and Mercy recommended, particularly with reference to the Slave Trade* (Cambridge: J. Archdeacon, 1788). Jirik rightly argues that Peckard's influence on the antislavery cause at Cambridge has long been underappreciated.

9. Brown, *Moral Capital*, 435 ('topic') and 229 ('Spanish'); Micah Alpaugh, *Friends of Freedom: The Rise of Social Movements in the Age of Atlantic Revolution* (Cambridge: Cambridge University Press, 2021), 199 ('horses'); Thomas Clarkson, *The History of the Rise, Progress, and Accomplishment of the Abolition of the African Slave-Trade by the British Parliament*, vol. 1 (London: R. Taylor and Co., 1808), 205 ('*Anne*') and 210–212 ('awakening'); Members' Prizes, 1785, Registrum præmorium, 1752–1872, University scholarship awards and prizes records, 1649–2015, CUL, GBR/0265/UA/Char.I.1, f. 25 ('Heslop'). On the *Zong* massacre, see Vincent Brown, *The Reaper's Garden: Death and Power in the World of Atlantic Slavery* (Cambridge, MA: Harvard University Press, 2008), 158–160.

10. Clarkson, *History of the Rise, Progress, and Accomplishment*, vol. 1, 436 ('essay'); Thomas Clarkson, *An Essay on the Slavery and Commerce of the Human Species, Particularly the African, Translated from a Latin Dissertation, which was Honoured with the First Prize in the University of Cambridge, for the Year 1785, with Additions* (London: Re-Printed by Joseph Crukshank, 1786), xi–xii ('government', 'traffick', and 'planters').

11. Jirik, 'Beyond Clarkson', 2 ('forgotten') and 14–16 ('radicalize'); Olaudah Equiano, 'To the printer of the Cambridge Chronicle', *Cambridge Chronicle*, 1 August 1789 ('Gentlemen' and 'civility'); Peter Peckard to the Chairmen of the Committee for the Abolition of the Slave Trade, 26 May 1790, in Vincent Caretta, ed., *Olaudah Equiano: The Interesting Narrative and Other Writings* (London: Penguin, 1995), 8 ('advertise'); Thomas Clarkson to the Reverend Thomas Jones, 9 July 1789, Business Records of Cambridgeshire Manors, CA, K132/B/1B ('sell'); Peter Peckard, *The Neglect of a Known Duty is a Sin. A Sermon Preached before the University of Cambridge on Sunday, January 31, 1790* (Cambridge: J. Archdeacon, 1790), 26 ('yoke'). For Equiano's life and times, see Vincent Caretta, 'Olaudah Equiano or Gustavus Vassa? New Light on an Eighteenth-Century Question of Identity', *Slavery and Abolition* 20 (1999), 96–105; and Vincent Caretta, *Equiano the African: Biography of a Self-Made Man* (Athens and London: University of Georgia Press, 2005), xvi.

12. Everill, *Not Made by Slaves*, 85–86 ('Wedgwood'); *Am I Not a Man? and a Brother? With all Humility Addressed to the British Legislature* (Cambridge: J. Archdeacon, 1788), 1–2 ('Peckard', 'Rights', 'Traffick', and 'beast'), 7 ('inferior' and 'precision'), and 13 ('Kidneys'); Thomas Jefferson, *Notes on the State of Virginia*, 1788, in Merrill D. Peterson, ed., *Thomas Jefferson: Writings* (New York: The Library of America, 2011), 264–265 ('white skins'). The story of the 'white negroes' was publicised in newspaper articles, such as 'The History of White Negroes', *The New-Haven Gazette, and the Connecticut Magazine*, 13 April 1786. For the "white negroes" and Jefferson's discussions

NOTES TO PAGES 111–113

of race, see also Charles D. Martin, *The White African American Body: A Cultural and Literary Exploration* (New Brunswick, NJ: Rutgers University Press, 2002), 22; Dain, *A Hideous Monster of the Mind*, 26; and Jordan, *White Over Black*, 250.

13. "Tyro," 'For the Cambridge Chronicle on the Slave Trade Occasioned by the late sermon preached by P. Peckard D.D.', *Cambridge Chronicle*, 1 March 1788 ('Sons', 'Arrest', and 'patriot'); J. M. [signed from Magdalene College], 'For the Cambridge Chronicle. Occasioned by Dr. Peckard's sermon on the Slave Trade', *ibid*., March 1788 ('Moore' and 'groans').

14. Amy Garnai, 'An Exile on the Coast: Robert Merry's Transatlantic Journey, 1796–1798', *The Review of English Studies* 64 (February 2013), 90 ('Merry'); Gresdna Ann Doty, *The Career of Mrs. Anne Brunton Merry in the American Theatre* (Baton Rouge: Louisiana State University Press, 1971), 35 ('Hudson's Bay Company'); 'Della Crusca' [Robert Merry], 'For the Cambridge Chronicle. The Slaves. An Elegy.', *Cambridge Chronicle*, 8 March 1788 ('Stalks' and 'TEEMING'); 'Sir John Willes', *Legacies*, www.ucl.ac.uk/lbs/person/view/2146644091, accessed 6 February 2023 ('maternal grandfather').

15. *A List of the Society, Instituted in 1787, For the Purpose of effecting the Abolition of the Slave Trade* (London: Unknown, 1787) ('entire section of donors'); Jirik, 'Beyond Clarkson', 9 ('£161') and 10 ('six per cent').

16. Special Committee on 22 November 1787, Fair Minute Book of the Committee for the Abolition of the Slave Trade, 1787–1788, BL, Add Ms 21254, f. 20 ('Frend') and 25 ('Lambert' and 'Questions'); Committee on 5 March 1788, Fair Minute Book of the Committee for the Abolition of the Slave Trade, 1788–1790, BL, Add Ms 21255, f. 3 ('Coulthurst') and 53 ('Jones'); Clarkson, *History of the Rise, Progress, and Accomplishment*, vol. 1, 462 ('unhappy slaves'); Gascoigne, *Cambridge*, 226 ('reformist' and 'student'); A Speech on the Character and Memory of King William the Third, in Rev. Robert Tweddell, ed., *Remains of John Tweddell, Late Fellow of Trinity-College Cambridge Being a Selection of his Correspondence a Republication of his Prolusiones Juveniles an Appendix Containing Some Account of the Author's Collections Mss. Drawings &c.* (London: J. Mawman, 1816), 110 ('english', 'legalized', and 'sweets').

17. Festo. St. Michaelis 1787 to Festum Annunc. 1788 and Festo Annunc. 1792 to Festum St. Michaelis 1792, College Bursar Book, 1792–1810, GCC, GC/BUR/F/88 ('donations to end the slave trade'); 15 January 1789, Master/Registry Gesta, 1784–1811, GCC, GC/GOV/03/01/07 ('Poor'); 13 April 1796, *ibid* ('relief'); Disbursements for the Year ended at Michaelmas 1726, Dr Spencer's Account, 1693–1929, CCC, GBR/0268/CCCC02/B/146 ('Eastern'); Disbursements for the Year ended at Michaelmas 1759, *ibid*. ('British army'); Disbursements to Michaelmas 1793, *ibid*. ('emigrant'); Searby, *History of the University of Cambridge, Volume III*, 420 ('£7,000').

18. Vincent Caretta, 'Olaudah Equiano: African British Abolitionist and Founder of the African American Slave Narrative', in Audrey Fisch, ed., *The Cambridge Companion to the African American Slave Narrative* (Cambridge: Cambridge University Press, 2007), 55 ('number and status'); Christopher Wright, *The Irresistible Glory and Everlasting Freedom; or, Religious Liberty, Exempt from Slavery. Being an Entire New Work* (Birmingham: Mr. Brown, 1787), title page ('omitted' and 'speculate'); James Plumptre, *Four Discourses on Subjects Relating to the Amusement of the Stage: Preached at St. Mary's Church, Cambridge, on Sunday September 25, and Sunday October 2, 1808* (Cambridge: Francis Hodson, 1809), 41 ('public mind'); Rev. Thomas

Harwood, *The Noble Slave: A Tragedy* (Bury St Edmunds: J. Rackham, 1788), list of subscribers ('subscribed'), title page ('University College' and 'noble slave'), and 87 ('laws', 'encroach', and 'rights of man').

19. 15 December 1796, Diary of the Reverend Romaine Hervey, MC, F/OMP/IV/VII ('House of Commons'); 'Thomas Truebody Thomason', *ACAD*, https://venn.lib.cam.ac.uk/cgi-bin/search-2018.pl?sur=thomason&suro=w&fir=&firo=c&cit=&cito=c&c=all&z=all&tex=&sye=&eye=&col=all&maxcount=999, accessed 13 February 2023 ('East India'); Kenneth Morgan, *Slavery and the British Empire: From Africa to America* (Oxford: Oxford University Press, 2007), 162 ('163 votes').

20. Samuel Taylor Coleridge, 'A Greek Prize Ode on the Slave Trade', 1791, in Samuel Taylor Coleridge, *The Poetical Works of Samuel Taylor Coleridge*, vol. 1 (London: Macmillan and Company, 1880), 26–27 ('publickly', 'evil', and 'groans'); Legh Richmond, *Cum vincamur in omni Munere, sola Deos æquat Clementia nobis*, 1790, Tripos verses and lists, 1768–1802, CUL, GBR/0265/UA/Exam.L.3 ('labours'). Thomason was an opponent of the slave trade, writing in 1800 as a "Late Fellow of Queens' College" of his hopes that the 'disgrace of our age and nation' would end. (Rev. Thomas Truebody Thomason, *An Essay Tending to Shew that the Christian Religion Has in its Effects been Favourable to Human Happiness* [Cambridge: J. Burghes, 1800], 44). The treatise won the Norrisian Prize for an essay on Christian doctrine.

21. Jane Webster, 'Collecting the cabinet of freedom: the parliamentary history of Thomas Clarkson's chest', *Slavery & Abolition* 38 (December 2016), 135–154 ('visualise'); Coleridge, 'Lecture on the Slave Trade', 16 June 1795, in *ibid*, Coleridge, vol. 1, 233 ('Jesus College'), 235 ('artificial'), 236 ('useful'), 238 ('savage', 'nursery', and 'shadows'), and 251 ('rebelling').

22. Farish, 'Reverie on a Benguelinha or Angola Linnet, which was caught in Africa and carried successively to Brazil, to Botany-bay, to England, twice to the West-Indies, & finally to England again', 1798, Correspondence of George III, TNA, HO 42/42/109. For the "negral," see Richard Brookes, *The Natural History of Birds: With the Method of Bringing Up and Managing those of the Singing Kind*, vol. 2 (London: J. Newberry, 1763), 280.

23. Andrew Burnaby, *Travels Through the Middle Settlements in North-America* (Dublin: R. Marchbank, 1775), 199 ('cruel'); William Eddis, *Letters from America, Historical and Descriptive; Comprising Occurrences from 1769, to 1777, Inclusive* (London: C. Dilly, 1792), list of subscribers ('Hinchliffe'), 64 ('scarce'), and 65 ('white inhabitants').

24. William Smyth to Dr James Currie, 2 April 1792, Letters of William Smyth to Dr Currie, LRO, 920 CUR/46 ('Intention' and 'retreat'); *The Debate on a Motion for the Abolition of the Slave-Trade, in the House of Commons, on Monday and Tuesday April 18 and 19, 1791, Report in Detail* (London: W. Woodfall, 1791), 49 ('Providence').

25. Kenneth Morgan, 'Liverpool's Dominance in the British Slave Trade, 1740–1807', in Richardson et al, *Liverpool*, 15 ('£2.6 million'); K. J. Allison, ed., *A History of the County of York East Riding: Volume 1, the City of Kingston Upon Hull* (London: Victoria County History, 1969), 175 ('tobacco'); Berg and Hudson, *Capitalism*, unpaginated eBook edition ('per cent').

26. Gilbert Wakefield, *Memoirs of the Life of Gilbert Wakefield, B. A. Late Fellow of Jesus College, Cambridge* (London: E. Hodson, 1792), 176–177 ('mart', '*head-quarters*', 'aggravating', 'immoral', 'privateering', '*thunder*', and 'agitated') and 179 ('knockt' and 'sea').

27. Thomas Clarke, *A Sermon on the Injustice of the Slave Trade, Preached February 12th, 1792, in the Parish Church of the Holy Trinity, in Kingston-Upon-Hull* (Hull: J.

Ferraby, 1792), title ('Late-Fellow'), 6 ('Cause'), 8 ('Test' and 'Humanity'), 11 ('Labourers' and 'moistened'), 17 ('Seeds' and 'rapid'), 18 ('glaring', 'impressment', and 'INDIA'), and 19 ('domestic'); Denver Brunsman, *The Evil Necessity: British Naval Impressment in the Eighteenth-Century Atlantic World* (Charlottesville: University of Virginia Press, 2013), 6 ('250,000').

28. M. J. Smith, 'Benjamin Flower and the "Cambridge Intelligencer," 1793-1803', *Transactions of the Cambridge Bibliographical* Society 16 (2018), 417 ('syndicated'); 'To the Editor of the Cambridge Intelligencer', *Cambridge Intelligencer*, 17 November 1791 ('Wakefield'); 'Slave Trade', *ibid.*, July 1796 ('SALE'); 'The Willing Slave', *ibid.*, 20 February 1796 ('AFRICAN' and 'Gold'); 'Voluntary Contributions', *ibid.*, 17 March 1798 ('traffick'); Eve Tavor Bannet, *Eighteenth-Century Manners of Reading: Print Culture and Popular Instruction in the Anglophone Atlantic World* (Cambridge: Cambridge University Press, 2017), 46 ('school-dames'). Flower was also listed as a subscriber to Captain John Gabriel Stedman's *Narrative, of a five years' expedition, against the Revolted Negroes of Surinam, in Guiana, on the Wild Coast of South America; from the Year 1772, to 1777: elucidating the History of that Country, and describing its Productions*, 2 vols. (London: J. J. Johnson, 1796).

29. William Paley, *The Works of William Paley, D. D. Archdeacon of Carlisle. With a Life and Portrait of the Author. In Five Volumes*, vol. 1 (Edinburgh: John Fairbairn, 1825), vi ('lectures'); Niall O'Flaherty, *Utilitarianism in the Age of Enlightenment: The Moral and Political Thought of William Paley* (Cambridge: Cambridge University Press, 2019), 17 ('Christian utilitarian'); William Paley, *The Principles of Moral and Political Philosophy*, vol. 1 (London: R. Faulder, 1785), 268-270 ('obligation', 'proportioned', and 'brutality') and 272 ('emancipation' and 'diffusion'). Paley's arguments were influential in the United States too. (O'Brien, *Conjectures of Order*, vol. 1, 961.) For another contemporaneous statement questioning the relative cost of free and enslaved labour, see Sir Joseph Banks to Thomas Coltman giving his 'Opinions on the subject of the slave trade', Papers from a letter book belonging to Sir Joseph Banks, BOD, MSS.Brit.Emp.r.2.

30. Searby, *History of the University of Cambridge, Volume III*, 405 ('prominent'); George Dyer, *Memoirs of the Life and Writings of Robert Robinson, Late Minister of the Dissenting Congregation, in Saint Andrew's Parish, Cambridge* (London: G. G. and J. Robinson, 1796), 131-132 ('Randall'); Robert Robinson, *Slavery inconsistent with the Spirit of Christianity. A Sermon Preached at Cambridge, on Sunday, Feb. 10, 1788* (Cambridge: J. Archdeacon, 1788), 39 ('silver' and 'ambition').

31. Dyer, *Robert Robinson*, 193-195.

32. Roshan Allpress, *British Philanthropy in the Globalizing World: Entrepreneurs and Evangelicals, 1756-1840* (Oxford: Oxford University Press, 2023), 105 ('ideally positioned'); Leonard W. Cowie, 'Venn, Henry (1725-1797)', *ODNB*, www.oxforddnb.com/view/10.1093/ref:odnb/9780198614128.001.0001/odnb-9780198614128-e-28184;jsessionid=69C84D0C06C333025B9667856ACB310D, accessed 9 January 2021 ('Royal Navy'); Anne Stott, *Wilberforce: Family and Friends* (Oxford: Oxford University Press, 2012), 9-17 ('Cambridge')

33. Allpress, *British Philanthropy*, 106 ('credibility' and 'political influence'); Mary Milner, ed., *The Life of Isaac Milner, D.D., F.R.S., Dean of Carlisle, President of Queen's College, and Professor of Mathematics in the University of Cambridge; comprising a portion of his correspondence and other writings hitherto unpublished* (London: John W. Parker, 1842), 15-16 ('Milner') and 75 ('pivotal'); Hugh Evan Hopkins, *Charles Simeon of Cambridge* (Eugene, OR: Wipf and Stock, 2012), 198

('African Institution'); William Jowett, *Mercy for Africa. A Sermon Preached in Favour of the Endowment Fund for the Bishopric of Sierra Leone. With an Appendix* (London: Seeleys, 1851), 9 ('bodily' and 'spiritual').

34. Andrew Jackson O'Shaughnessy, 'The Formation of a Commercial Lobby: The West India Interest, British Colonial Policy and the American Revolution', *HJ* 40 (March 1997), 49 ('chief broker') and 78 ('amenability', 'case', 'direction', 'too much', and 'annual budget'); Roger Anstey, *The Atlantic Slave Trade and British Abolition, 1760–1810* (London: Humanities Press, 1975), 288 ('work').
35. Stephen Fuller to the Committee of Correspondence, 6 February 1788, in W. M. McCahill, ed., *The Correspondence of Stephen Fuller, 1788–1795: Jamaica, the West India Interest at Westminster and the Campaign to Preserve the Slave Trade* (Chichester: West Sussex, 2014), 71 ('Rights of Humanity' and 'impossibility').
36. O'Shaughnessy, *Men Who Lost America*, 314–317 ('Saintes'); Stephen Fuller to Lord Rodney, 12 March 1788, McCahill, ed., *Correspondence of Stephen Fuller*, 77 ('Plantation Office'); Paper received from Lord Rodney, March 1788, in *ibid.*, 77–78 ('prominent'). For the proslavery argument concerning the poorer conditions of white labourers relative to the enslaved, see also 'An Old Planter', Letter VII, *Letters to a Young Planter; Or, Observations on the Management of a Sugar-Plantation. To which is Added, The Planter's Kalendar* (London: Strachan, 1785), 36–37; and Martin, *Essay Upon Plantership*, xviii. For a stinging rebuke against this viewpoint, see Sharp, *Just Limitation of Slavery*, 36–38.
37. Srividhya Swaminathan, 'Developing the West Indian Proslavery Position after the Somerset Decision', *Slavery and Abolition* 24 (December 2003), 56 ('tyrannic' and 'savage'); Tise, *Proslavery*, 82–83 ('Bastille'); Frank O'Gorman, 'The Paine Burnings of 1792–1793', *Past & Present* 193 (November 2006), 120 ('412'); Clive Emsley, 'An Aspect of Pitt's "Terror": Prosecutions for Sedition during the 1790s', *Social History* 6 (May 1981), 155–156 ('twelve').
38. Gunning, *Reminiscences*, vol. 1, 277 ('burst', 'Masters', and 'Laudable'), 278 ('Republicans', 'every', 'rogue' and 'exhibited'), and 279 ('Paine' and 'America'); Henry Crabb Robinson to Thomas Robinson, 7 May 1852, in Thomas Saddler, ed., *Diary, Reminiscences, and Correspondence of Henry Crabb Robinson, Barrister-at-Law, F.S.A.*, vol. 3 (London: Macmillan and Co., 1869), 401 ('Frend'); Frida Knight, *University Rebel: The Life of William Frend (1757–1841)* (London: Victor Gollancz Ltd., 1971), 140 ('LIBERTY' and 'EQUALITY') and 141 ('Coleridge'); William Frend, *A Sequel to the Account of the Proceedings in the University of Cambridge, Against the Author of a Pamphlet, Entitled Peace and Union; Containing the Application to the Court of King's Bench, a Review of Similar Cases in the University, and Reflections on the Impolicy of Religious Persecution, and the Importance of Free Enquiry* (London: G. and J. Robinson, 1795), ix ('violence'); George Dyer, *Slavery and Famine, Punishments for Edition; or, an Account of the Miseries and Starvation at Botany Bay* (London: J. Ridgway, 1794), 41 ('FAMINE').
39. Stephen Fuller to the Committee of Correspondence, 2 April 1788, in McCahill, ed., *Fuller*, 80.
40. Stephen Fuller, *The New Act of Assembly of the Island of Jamaica, Intitled, An Act to repeal an Act, intitled, 'An Act to repeal several Acts, and Clauses of Acts, respecting Slaves, and for the better Order and Government of Slaves, and for other Purposes'* (London: B. White and Son, 1789), vii ('philanthropy'); Robert Bisset, *A Defence of the Slave Trade on the Grounds of Humanity, Policy and Justice* (London: J. Hales, 1804), 56 ('theophilanthropic' and 'revolutionary'). For amelioration, see, for

instance, Robert E. Luster, *The Amelioration of the Slaves in the British Empire* (New York: New York University Press, 1995); Christa Dierksheide, *Amelioration and Empire: Progress and Slavery in the Plantation Americas* (Charlottesville: University of Virginia Press, 2014); Trevor Burnard and Kit Candlin, 'Sir John Gladstone and the Debate over the Amelioration of Slavery in the British West Indies in the 1820s', *Journal of British Studies* 57 (October 2018), 760–782; and Carolina Quarrier Spence, 'Ameliorating Empire: Slavery and Protection in the British Colonies, 1783–1865' (PhD dissertation, Harvard University, 2014). See also Stephen Fuller, *Notes on the Two Reports from the Committee of the Honourable House of Assembly of Jamaica, Appointed To examine into, and to report to the House, the Allegations and Charges contained in the several Petitions which have been presented to the British House of Commons, on the Subject of the Slave Trade, and the Treatment of the Negroes, &c. &c. &c.* (London: J. Philips 1789).

41. John Henry Thomas and John Farquhar Fraser, eds., *The Reports of Sir Edward Coke, Knt. In Thirteen Parts: A New Edition*, vol. 4, parts 7–8 (London: Joseph Butterworth and Son, 1826), 373 ('eyes and soul'); Stephen Fuller to Lord Hawkesbury, 27 June 1788, in McCahill, ed., *Fuller*, 92 ('Petitions to Parliament'); Lord Hawkesbury to Stephen Fuller, 28 June 1788, *ibid.*, 92 ('Formality').

42. Stephen Fuller to the Committee of Correspondence, 6 May 1789, *ibid.*, 120 ('University Gentlemen'); Glasson, '"Baptism Doth Not Bestow Freedom"', 292 ('legality of African slavery'). The Right Rev. the Hon. James Yorke was a Doctor of Divinity and the Bishop of Ely from 1781 to 1808. In October 1952, the Right Rev. H. E. Wynn, the Lord Bishop of Ely, deposited Yorke's book collection in the University Library.

43. Miriam Elizabeth Burstein, 'A Forgotten Novel: John Riland's *Memoirs of a West-India Planter* (1827)', *Slavery & Abolition* 41 (July 2020), 582 ('creole' and 'abolitionist') and 583 ('Hall' and '1800'); 'The Gipsies', 1837, in *Oxford Prize Poems: Being a Collection of Such English Poems as Have at Various Times Obtained Prizes in the University of Oxford* (Oxford: J. H. Parker, 1839), 337 ('poems'); Thomas Coke, *A History of the West Indies, Containing the Natural, Civil, and Ecclesiastical History of each Island: with an Account of the Missions Instituted in Those Islands, from the Commencement of their Civilization; But more Especially of the Missions which have been Established in that Archipelago By the Society Late in Connexion with the Rev. John Wesley*, vol. 1 (London: T. Blanshard, 1808) ('histories'); George Barnett Smith, *The Life of the Right Honourable William Ewart Gladstone, M.P., D.C.L., &c.* (New York: G. P. Putnam's Sons, 1880), 26 ('public debates'); Clara Reeve, *The Progress of Romance, through Times, Countries, and Manners… In a Course of Evening Conversations*, vol. 1 (Colchester: W. Keymer, 1785), 111 ('real life'); Rev. John Riland, *Memoirs of a West-India Planter. Published from an Original MS. With a Preface and Additional Details* (London: Hamilton, Adams & Co., 1827), 35 ('domestic' and 'special'), 37 ('massa'), and 37–38 ('middle').

44. *Ibid.*, 38 ('Cambridge'), 39 ('fanatical' and 'sanctioned'), and 43 ('commercial', 'status', and 'intolerable'). For novels as historical sources in British imperial history, see Maya Jasanoff, *The Dawn Watch: Joseph Conrad in a Global World* (New York: Penguin, 2017).

45. George Randolph, *An Inquiry into the Medicinal Virtues of Bristol Waters* (Oxford: M. Cooper, 1745), title page ('Medicinal'); 'Francis Randolph', *ACAD*, https://venn.lib.cam.ac.uk/cgi-bin/search-2018.pl?sur=randolph&suro=w&fir=francis&firo=c&cit=&cito=c&c=all&z=all&tex=&sye=&eye=&col=all&maxcount=50, accessed 1

February 2023 ('upbringing'); Francis Randolph, *A Letter to the Right Honourable William Pitt, Chancellor of the Exchequer, &c. &c.* (London: T. Cadell, 1798), title ('Late'), 5–6 ('Mode and Manner'), and 8 ('Bitterness of Servitude').
46. *Ibid.*, 43–46.
47. Francis Randolph (or "Britannicus"), *A Letter to the Right Hon. William Pitt, Containing some New Arguments against the Abolition of the Slave Trade* (London: A. Macpherson, 1804), 2 ('*political existence*'), 5 ('*improve Africa*'), 9 ('father of the faithful'), 11 ('barbarity or refinement'), 13 ('*indebted*'), 15 ('Slave Commerce'), and 30 ('pockets'). Randolph is identified as "Britannicus" in William Cushing, *Initials and Pseudonyms: A Dictionary of Literary Disguises* (New York: Thomas Y. Crowell & Co., 1888), 20.
48. 'Samuel Hallifax', *ACAD*, https://venn.lib.cam.ac.uk/cgi-bin/search-2018.pl?sur=hallifax&suro=w&fir=samuel&firo=c&cit=&cito=c&c=all&z=all&tex=&sye=&eye=&col=all&maxcount=50, accessed 10 July 2023 ('fellowship'); Samuel Hallifax, *An Analysis of the Roman Civil Law; in which A Comparison is, occasionally, made between the Roman Laws and those of England: Being the Heads of a Course of Lectures, Publickly Read in the University of Cambridge* (Cambridge: J. Archdeacon, 1779), 9 ('Revival'); Samuel Hallifax, *A Sermon Preached before the Incorporated Society for the Propagation of the Gospel in Foreign Parts; at their Anniversary Meeting in the Parish Church of St. Mary-Le-Bow On Friday February 20, 1789* (London: T. Harrison and S. Brooke, 1789), xxvi–xxvii ('*civilizing*' and 'propose').
49. *Ibid.*, xxxiv ('Mitigation', 'due regard', 'annulled', and 'future'), xxix ('sober', 'incompatible', and 'affirm'), xxxi ('Roman'), and xxxiii ('virtual').
50. 'Marriott, Sir James', *History of Parliament*, https://www.historyofparliamentonline.org/volume/1790-1820/member/marriott-sir-james-1730-1803, accessed 1 July 2022 ('numerous positions'); 'Observations by the King's Advocate, Sir James Marriott, on enforcing residence at a living in Barbadoes, in the Case of the Rev. Mr. Barnard', 1764, in William Forsyth, ed., *Cases and Opinions on Constitutional Law, and Various Points of English Jurisprudence, Digested from Official Documents and other Sources* (London: Stevens & Haynes, 1869), 44–45 ('residence requirement'); 'America a Part of Kent', *Percy's Anecdotes: Original and Select* (London: T. Boys, 1822), 149 ('*knights*'); Sir James Marriott, 'Plan of a Code of Laws for the Province of Quebec', 1774, in Adam Shortt and Arthur G. Doughty, eds., *Documents Relating to the Constitutional History of Canada, 1759–1791: Second and Revised Edition* (Ottawa: J. de L. Taché, 1918), 445–483 ('Quebec').
51. 'Trial of Captain Kimber', *Sheffield Public Advertiser*, 15 June 1792 ('*Recovery*'); Isaac Cruikshank, 'The abolition of the slave trade', 1792, British Museum, www.britishmuseum.org/collection/object/P_1868-0808-6179, accessed 21 April 2022 ('Dealers' and 'modesty').
52. *The Trial of Captain John Kimber, for the Murder of Two Female Negro Slaves, on Board the Recovery, African Slave Ship* (London: C. Stalker, 1792), 36 ('William IV'); *The Whole of the Proceedings and Trial of Captain John Kimber for the wilful murder of a Negro girl: held at the Old Bailey on the 7th and 8th of June 1792 by virtue of his Majesty's commission; to which is added, an extract from Mr. Wilberforce's speech, which gave rise to the trial; also the charges to the juries; being the most complete edition published* (Edinburgh: John Elder, 1792), 9 ('government', 'security', 'absolute', and 'passions'); Nicholas Rogers, *Murder on the Middle Passage: The Trial of John Kimber* (London: Boydell and Brewer, 2020), 98 ('propertied') and 118–119 ('misleading').

53. *R. v. George Hindmarsh*, 168 E.R. 387 (1792) ('league'); Will of Sir James Marriott, Prerogative Court of Canterbury, NA, PROB 11/1391/29 ('Governor' and 'stone'); Will of Jacob Ricketts, Planter of Westmoreland, Island of Jamaica, West Indies, *ibid.*, 826/325 ('free Mulatto').
54. Members of Parliament with West India Connections, 1780 to 1796, in McCahill, ed., *Fuller*, 229–233 ('twenty'); 'Gilbert Francklyn', *Legacies*, www.ucl.ac.uk/lbs/person/view/2146632169, accessed 30 September 2021 ('partner'); Gilbert Francklyn, *An Answer to the Rev. Mr. Clarkson's Essay on the Slavery and Commerce of the Human Species, particularly the African* (London: Logographic Press, 1789), 2 ('ocular evidence') and 236–237 ('education').
55. Stephen Fuller to John Grant, 3 December 1788, in McCahill, ed., *Fuller*, 102–103.
56. Stephen Fuller to the Committee of Correspondence, 10 February 1789, *ibid.*, 112 ('twelve hundred'); Stephen Fuller to the Committee of Correspondence, 31 March 1789, *ibid.*, 118–119 ('Parliament'); Stephen Fuller to Henry Dundas, 30 October 1791, in *ibid.*, 170 ('struck' and 'seeds'); Herbert Marsh, *The History of the Politicks of Great Britain and France from the Time of the Conference at Pillnitz, to the Declaration of War against Great Britain*, vol. 1 (London: John Stockdale, 1800), 43 ('insurrection' and 'dreadful') and 44 ('state'); Stuart Semmel, 'British Radicals and "Legitimacy": Napoleon in the Mirror of History', *Past & Present* 167 (May 2000), 148 ('coal mine owner'); William Burdon, *The Life and Character of Bonaparte, From his Birth to the 15th of August, 1804* (Newcastle-Upon-Tyne: K. Anderson, 1804), 179 ('nobly', 'black', 'bred', and 'enlightened') and 185 ('tyrant' and 'disgrace').
57. Stephen Fuller to the Committee of Correspondence, 4 May 1791, in McCahill, ed., *Fuller*, 165 ('solidity'); Stephen Fuller, *The Colonization of the Island of Jamaica* (London: Unknown, 1792), 1 ('active industry') and 15 ('statistics').
58. Stephen Fuller's Copy of Robert Norris, *Memoirs of the Reign of Bossa Ahadee, King of Dahomey, An Inland Country of Guiney. To which are Added, the Author's Journey To Abomey, the Capital; and a Short Account Of the African Slave Trade* (London: W. Lowndes, 1799), CUL, 7500.c.17, 151 ('12,000'), 157 ('Negroland'), 161 ('26,500'), and 182 ('three million').
59. Brown, *Moral Capital*, 294 ('Londoners'); *The Public Advertiser*, 5 January 1786 ('Quartern'); *ibid.*, 27 January 1786 ('Persons').
60. Granville Sharp, *Free English Territory in Africa* (London: Unknown, 1790) ('Inspired'); C. B. Wadstrom, *An Essay on Colonization, Particularly Applied to the Western Coast of Africa, with Some Free Thoughts on Cultivation and Commerce; Also Brief Descriptions of the Colonies Already Formed, or Attempted, in Africa, including those of Sierra Leona and Bulama* (London: Darton and Harvey, 1794), 344–353 ('these men included'); Everill, *Abolition and Empire*, 9 ('desire' and 'promoted').
61. Wallace Brown, 'The Black Loyalists in Sierra Leone', in John W. Pulis, ed., *Moving On: Black Loyalists in the Afro-Atlantic World* (New York: Taylor & Francis, 2013), 131, n. 21 ('1,190'); Richard Anderson, 'Abolition's Adolescence: Apprenticeship as "Liberation" in Sierra Leone, 1808–1848', *The English Historical Review* 117 (June 2022), 763–764 ('99,000', 'age', and 'redemptions'), 768 ('trained'), and 773 ('twenty' and 'outlaw'); Harold Nuttall Tomlins, *A Digest of the Criminal Statute Law of England*, vol. 2 (London: A. Strahan, 1819), 937 ('Term'); Gareth Atkins, *Converting Britannia: Evangelicals and British Public Life, 1770–1840* (Woodbridge, Suffolk: The Boydell Press, 2019), 164–165 ('Thompson'). There is some dispute over the numbers. Thomas Clarkson provided the accepted figure of 1,190, but Thomas Winterbottom

mentioned 1,196 in his *An Account of the Native Africans in the Neighbourhood of Sierra Leone*, vol. 1 (London: C. Whittingham, 1803), 275. For the colonisation of Sierra Leone, see John Peterson, *Province of Freedom: A History of Sierra Leone, 1787–1870* (London: Faber and Faber, 1969); Everill, *Abolition and Empire*; Scanlan, *Freedom's Debtors*; Richard Peter Anderson, *Abolition in Sierra Leone: Re-building Lives and Identities in Nineteenth-Century West Africa* (Cambridge: Cambridge University Press, 2020); and Emma Christopher, *Freedom in White and Black: A Lost Story of the Illegal Slave Trade and Its Global Legacy* (Madison: University of Wisconsin Press, 2018). See also Maeve Ryan, '"A moral millstone"?: British Humanitarian Governance and the Policy of Liberated African Apprenticeship, 1808–1848', *Slavery & Abolition* 37 (January 2016), 399–422. For apprenticeship in a transatlantic context, see Jake Christopher Richards, 'Anti-Slave-Trade Law, "Liberated Africans" and the State in the South Atlantic World, c. 1839–1852', *Past & Present* 241 (November 2018), 179–219.

62. Captain Philip Beaver, *African Memoranda: Relative to an Attempt to Establish a British Settlement on the Island of Bulama, On the Western Coast of Africa, in the year 1792* (London: C. and R. Baldwin, 1805), 164 ('275'); Brown, *Moral Capital*, 272 ('Postlethwayt' and 'humane'); *Memorandum of Agreement, and Constitution of Government, for a Colony About to Be Established on or Near the Island of Bulama. In Africa. As Engrossed and Signed on the Ninth Day of March, 1792* (London: Unknown, 1792), Papers of the Bulama Association, CUL, GBR/0115/RCS/RCMS 113/15, 7–8 ('sixty pounds'); 'List of the Original Subscribers to the Association Formed in 1791, for Cultivating the Island of Bulama', in Wadstrom, *Essay on Colonization*, 359–361 ('alumni and officials'); Kalle Kananoja, *Healing Knowledge in Atlantic Africa: Medical Encounters, 1500–1850* (Cambridge: Cambridge University Press, 2021), 113 ('collections'); Tim Soriano, '"What Rascals!" Perceptions of Free Labor in the Bulama Settlement, 1792–1793', *African Economic History* 49 (November 2021), 173–191 ('colonial reality').

63. List of Members of the Association, Association for Promoting the Discovery of Interior Parts of Africa: Papers, CUL, GBR/0012/MS Add.7086. The initial list of subscribers who contributed at least fifty guineas did not include Comings, Winne, or Renouard. They were inducted as members in, respectively, the meetings of 20 March 1799, 18 June 1800, and 15 June 1829. Comings was listed as 'of Trinity College, Cambridge'.

64. Cormack, *Charting an Empire*, 55–57 ('centuries-long') and 246 (*'His Pilgrimage'*); Samuel Purchas, *Purchase His Pilgrimage* (London: William Stansby, 1613), 76 ('fittest'); Griffith Hughes, *The Natural History of Barbados* (London: Unknown, 1750), list of subscribers ('Library') and 17 ('little better'); 'Salmon, Thomas (1679–1767)', in Lee, ed., *DNB*, vol. 17, 697 ('coffeehouse'); Daniel Waterland, *Advice to a Young Student* (London: John Crownfield, 1730), 31 ('recommended to undergraduates').

65. Thomas Salmon, *Modern History: or, the Present State of All Nations*, vol. 3 (London: Bettesworth and Hitch, 1739), 43 ('Young' and 'profit') and 51 ('jumped', 'cruel', 'Planters', and 'much better'); Vincent Woodward, *The Delectable Negro: Human Consumption and Homoeroticism within U.S. Slave Culture*, ed. by Justin A. Joyce and Dwight A. McBride (New York: New York University Press, 2014), 31 ('Narrative').

66. Aims of the Association for Promoting the Discovery of the Interior Parts of Africa, Association Papers, Add. 7085, 4 ('blank') and 5 ('fund'); Jeremy Black, *Geographies of an Imperial Power: The British World, 1688–1815* (Bloomington: Indiana

University Press, 2018), 20 ('Houghton'); 25 May 1793, Association Papers, CUL, GBR/0012/MS Add.7087, 9 ('lucrative' and 'European'); 6 March 1796, *ibid.*, Add.7085 ('Million', 'East Indies', and 'Mercantile'); 31 March 1794, *ibid.* ('Fort'); 25 May 1799, *ibid.*, Add.7087 ('ignorant', 'assert', and 'Rival').

67. Barry Boubacar, *Senegambia and the Atlantic Slave Trade* (Cambridge: Cambridge University Press, 1998), 62 and 66 ('five hundred'); 5 July 1790, Association Papers, CUL, GBR/0012/MS Add.7085 ('Negro Nations'); Sparks, *Where the Negroes Are Masters*, 17 ('conduits'); 6 March 1796, Association Papers, CUL, GBR/0012/MS Add.7085 ('free', 'noxious', and 'factory'); 4 June 1804, *ibid.* ('reputation'); 31 May 1794, *ibid.*, Add.7087 ('Missionary'); 31 May 1806, *ibid.* ('great Men').

68. Johann Friedrich Blumenbach, *On the Natural Varieties of Mankind* (New York: Bergman Publishers, 1969), 264–265 ('monogenism'); 3 June 1796, Association Papers, CUL, GBR/0012/MS Add.7085 ('instruction')

69. *Ibid.* ('tutelage'); George Bancroft, *Ancient Greece. From the German of Arnold H. L. Heeren* (Boston: Charles C. Little and James Brown, 1842), 187 ('nobility', 'labors', and 'introduction'); E. W. Bovill, ed., *Missions to the Niger, I: The Journal of Friedrich Hornemann's Travels and The Letters of Alexander Gordon Laing* (Cambridge: Cambridge University Press, 1964), unpaginated eBook edition ('Niger').

70. Lovejoy, *Transformations in Slavery*, 68 ('warlordism'), 72 ('Hausa'), and 84–85 ('inability'), and 88 ('twenty').

71. 3 June 1796, Association Papers, CUL, GBR/0012/MS Add.7085 ('Slave Trade'); Lovejoy, *Transformations in Slavery*, 105 ('gold'); 18 December 1790, Association Papers, CUL, GBR/0012/MS Add.7085 ('Dealers' and 'frequent'); 22 June 1804, *ibid.* ('remuneration'); 2 August 1804, *ibid.* ('English'); 11 August 1804, *ibid.* ('conciliate' and 'principal').

72. Johann Ludwig Burckhardt, *Travels of M. Burckhardt in Egypt and Nubia* (London: Sir Richard Phillips and Co., 1819), 3 ('Cambridge educations'); William Otter, *The Life and Remainings of the Rev. Edward Daniel Clarke, LL.D.* (London: J. F. Dove, 1824), 44 ('Jesus') and 54 ('balloon'); Jennifer Speake, ed., *Literature of Travel and Exploration: An Encyclopedia, Volume One: A To F* (London and New York: Routledge, 2003), 144 ('Petra' and 'Abu Simbel'); Jacob Lewis Burckhardt, *Travels in Nubia; By the Late John Lewis Burckhardt* (London: John Murray, 1819), 360 ('merchandize', 'slave boy', 'useful', and 'afforded'); Jacob Lewis Burckhardt, *Travels in Arabia, Comprehending an Account of those Territories in Hedjaz which the Mohammedans Regard as Sacred*, vol. 1 (London: Henry Colburn, 1829), 4 ('sell my slave', 'faithful', 'defray', 'possession', and 'equal') and 5 ('forty-eight'); Otter, *Life and Remainings*, 428 ('faithful slave'); George Michael La Rue, '"My Ninth Master Was a European": Enslaved Blacks in European Households in Egypt, 1798–1848', in Terence Walz and Kenneth M. Cuno, eds., *Race and Slavery in the Middle East: Histories of Trans-Saharan Africans in Nineteenth-Century Egypt, Sudan, and the Ottoman Mediterranean* (Cairo: American University in Cairo Press, 2010), 100–101 and 114 ('oppose'); Warwick William Wroth, 'Clarke, Edward Daniel', in Leslie Stephen and Sidney Lee, eds., *DNB*, vol. 10, 422 ('two principal'); 'The man who discovered a "lost" wonder of the world', *University of Cambridge*, www.cam.ac.uk/research/news/the-man-who-discovered-a-lost-wonder-of-the-world, accessed 17 January 2023 ('manuscripts').

73. Jeremy Black, *Europe and the World, 1650–1830* (London and New York: Routledge, 2002), 17 ('Timbuktu' and 'three editions'); Mungo Park, *Travels in the Interior District of Africa: Performed Under the Direction and Patronage of the African Association in the Years 1795, 1796, and 1797* (London: W. Bulmer and Company,

1799), 319 ('salt water'); Folarin Shyllon, *Edward Long's Libel of Africa: The Foundations of British Racism* (Newcastle: Cambridge Scholar Publishing, 2021), 101 ('revise') and 102 ('tenor' and 'conviction'); 9 July 1831, Association Papers, CUL, GBR/0012/MS Add.7085 ('merger').

74. Richard Watson, Bishop of Llandaff, to William Pitt, 14 May 1800, in Richard Watson, Jr., ed., *Anecdotes of the Life of Richard Watson, Bishop of Llandaff* (London: T. Cadell and W. Davies, 1817), 349 ('rear'); St. George Tucker, *Dissertation on Slavery: With A Proposal for the Gradual Abolition of It, in the State of Virginia* (Philadelphia: Mathew Carey, 1796), 95 ('compensate'); Speech in the House of Lords, 1807, in Watson, Jr., ed., *Life of Richard Watson*, 458 ('recompense', 'twenty', and 'reasonably'); Anstey, *Slave Trade and British Abolition*, 407–408 ('France'). For Tucker's struggle with the problem of enslavement, see also Philip Hamilton, 'Revolutionary Principles and Family Loyalties: Slavery's Transformation in the St. George Tucker Household of Early National Virginia', *WMQ* 55 (October 1998), 531–556.

5 'Those who wish to see the Slave System decline, and at length gradually and safely': The Ambitions of Cambridge Abolitionism

1. Petition to the two Houses of Parliament for the abolition of the slave trade, 4 July 1814 and 16 April 1823, Representatives in Parliament, 1614–1934, CUL, GBR/0265/UA/CUR 50, f. 8 ('Chancellor'); 'Slave Trade Felony Bill, March 1811', *Hansard*, https://api.parliament.uk/historic-hansard/commons/1811/mar/05/slave-trade-felony-bill#column_233, accessed 7 July 2023 ('contrary' and 'capital'); Dubois, *Avengers of the New World*, 285–286 ('re-establish enslavement').
2. *Journals of the House of Lords, Beginning Anno Quinquagesimo Tertio Georgii Tertii*, 1812, vol. 49 (London: H. M. Stationary Office, 1812), 1043 ('cities'); Petition to the two Houses of Parliament, 4 July 1814 and 16 April 1823, Representatives, 1614–1934, CUL, GBR/0265/UA/CUR 50, f. 8 ('total', 'forward', 'Foreign', 'regret', 'Settlements', 'Guardians', 'abhorrence', 'Sentiments', and 'promoting'); Denys Arthur Winstanley, *Early Victorian Cambridge* (Cambridge: Cambridge University Press, 1955), 98 ('on account').
3. Petition to the two Houses of Parliament, 4 July 1814 and 16 April 1823, Representatives, 1614–1934, CUL, GBR/0265/UA/CUR 50, f. 8. ('Sound', 'effectual', Debasing', and 'infrequent'); T. C. Hansard, *The Parliamentary Debates: Forming a Continuation of the Work Entitled 'The Parliamentary History of England, From the Earliest Period to the Year 1803'*, vol. 9 (London: T. C. Hansard, 1824), 312 ('attack').
4. Dumas, *Proslavery Britain*, 30 ('co-founder'); Thomas Clarkson, *Thoughts on the Necessity of Improving the Condition of the Slaves in the British Colonies: With a View to the Ultimate Emancipation, and on the Practicability, Safety, and the Advantages of the Latter Measure* (London: Society for the Mitigation and Gradual Abolition of Slavery throughout the British Dominions, 1824), 2 ('materially') and 3 ('*resume*'); Adam Hochschild, *Bury the Chains: Prophets and Rebels in the Fight to Free an Empire's Slaves* (Boston: Houghton Mifflin, 2005), 324 ('Everywhere People').
5. Elizabeth Heyrick, *Immediate, Not Gradual Abolition; Or, An Inquiry into the Shortest, Safest, and Most Effectual Means of Getting Rid of West Indian Slavery* (London: Hatchard and Son, 1824), 17.
6. Coleridge, 'Ode on the Slave Trade', 1791, in Samuel Taylor Coleridge, *Poetical Works of Coleridge*, vol. 1, 27 ('burning'); Barbara Taylor Paul-Emile, 'Samuel

Taylor Coleridge as Abolitionist', *ARIEL* 5 (1974), 62 ('Susquehanna'); Samuel Taylor Coleridge, 'Lectures on Shakespeare and Other Dramatists', 1812, in W. G. T. Shedd, ed., *The Complete Works of Samuel Taylor Coleridge: With an Introductory Essay Upon His Philosophical and Theological Opinions*, vol. 4 (New York: Harper & Brothers, 1884), 178 ('Moor'); Samuel Taylor Coleridge, 'Table Talk', 8 June 1833, *ibid.*, vol. 6, 457 ('condemn' and 'brethren'). For the cultural malleability of the epithet "Moor" and the meaning of "Moorishness" in early modern Britain, see Emily C. Bartels, *Speaking of the Moor: From Alcazar to Othello* (Philadelphia: University of Pennsylvania Press, 2008).

7. L. G. Mitchell, *Lord Melbourne, 1779–1848* (Oxford: Oxford University Press, 1997), 48 ('Charles James Fox'); Lloyd C. Sanders, ed., *Lord Melbourne's Papers: With a Preface by the Earl Cowper, K. G.* (London: Longmans, Green, and Co., 1889), 375 ('folly') and 376 ('posts' and 'civilising'); William Lamb, *Essay on the Progressive Improvement of Mankind* (London: William Clowes and Sons, 1860), 15 ('civilize') and 16 ('strike'); Alison Bashford and Joyce Chaplin, *The New Worlds of Thomas Robert Malthus: Rereading the Principle of Population* (Princeton, NJ: Princeton University Press, 2016), 198–199 ('notably silent').

8. These individuals and their respective donations and investments can be found in the subscriber lists in the *Sixteenth Report of the Directors of the African Institution, Read at the Annual General Meeting, Held on the 10th Day of May, 1822* (London: Ellerton and Henderson, 1822); and *Account of the Receipts & Disbursements of the Anti-Slavery Society for the Years 1823, 1824, 1825 & 1826: with a list of the subscribers* (London: Bagster and Thomas, 1827). For the Rev. Venn's involvement on the Anti-Slavery Society committee, see, for instance, the Meeting of 9 April 1823, Minute book of the Committee on Slavery, 31 January 1823 to 9 February 1825, Archive of the Anti-Slavery Society, BOD, MSS. Brit. Emp. s. 20/E2/1, f. 9.

9. The Declaration of Independence, 1 January 1804, in David Geggus, ed., *The Haitian Revolution: A Documentary History* (Indianapolis: Hackett Publishing, 2014), 179 ('State of Haiti' and 'independent'); Christina Cecelia Davidson, 'Mission, Migration, and Contested Authority: Building an AME Presence in Haiti in the Nineteenth Century', in John Corrigan et al. eds., *Global Faith, Worldly Power: Evangelical Internationalism and U.S. Empire* (Chapel Hill: University of North Carolina Press, 2022), 76 ('wave'); Leslie John Griffiths, 'A History of Methodism in Haiti, 1817–1916' (PhD dissertation, School of Oriental and African Studies, 1986), 31 ('Wilberforce') and 33 ('attend' and 'stopped'); William Woodis Harvey, *Sketches of Hayti; from the Expulsion of the French, to the Death of Christophe* (London: L. B. Seeley and Son, 1827), 308 ('infidel'); *The Missionary Register For MDCCCXXIV* (London: R. Watts, 1824), 520 ('mob').

10. Charles Valentine Le Grice, *Analysis of Paley's Principles of Moral and Political Philosophy* (Cambridge: Benjamin Flower, 1799) ('Paley critic'); 9 December 1823, Minute Book of Union Society, Papers of the Cambridge Union, CUL, USOC 1/1/1/1, unnumbered ('£20'); 24 February 1824, *ibid.* ('*Jamaica Chronicle*'); *ibid.*, 11 ('*Voice*'); 15 March 1824, *ibid*, 35 ('*Appeal*'); 30 March 1824, *ibid.*, 42 ('*Stephens*'); 25 November 1823, *ibid.*, unnumbered ('*Negro Slavery*'); James Townley, 'Abolition of Slavery, 1833', *JSTOR Primary Sources*, www.jstor.org/stable/60227882, accessed 16 June 2023 ('Saxon', 'entries', 'manumissions', and 'unhappily'). Townley drew from the Biblical commentaries of the Rev. Adam Clarke. See his *The New Testament of Our Lord and Saviour Jesus Christ; containing the Text, Taken from the Most Correct Copies of the Present Authorised Translation, including the Marginal Readings and*

Parallel Texts with a Commentary and Critical Notes, vol. 2 (London: J. Butterworth & Son, 1817), I. Corinthians, 40.
11. 9 March 1824, Minute Book of Union Society, Papers of the Cambridge Union, CUL, USOC 1/1/1/1, 26–27 ('condition' and 'defeated'); 8 May 1825, *ibid.*, USOC 1/1/1/2, unnumbered ('conduct' and 'negative').
12. *Report of the Proceedings of the Great Anti-Slavery Meeting, Held at the Town Hall, Birmingham, on Wednesday, October 14th, 1835* (Birmingham: B. Hudson, 1835) ('Birmingham'); 'The Greek Cause', *The Times*, 19 December 1823 ('Liberty'); 'Town Meeting for the Abolition of Slavery', *Cambridge Chronicle*, 26 November 1830 ('borne', 'speedy', 'burthen', 'desirable', 'slavish', and 'cruelty'); *The Fifth Report of the Colchester and East Essex Association, in Aid of the Church Missionary Society for Africa and the East, 10th of April, 1821; and a List of Benefactors, Subscribers, and Collectors* (Colchester: W. Keymer, 1821), 4 ('passionate'). For a recent treatment of the international reaction to the Greek Revolution, see Mark Mazower, *The Greek Revolution: 1821 and the Making of Modern Europe* (New York: Penguin, 2021).
13. Harvey, *Sketches of Hayti*, vii–viii ('still' and 'knowledge'), xii ('excesses'), 3 ('contended'), 23 ('waste'); 31 ('uneducated'), and 37 ('superior'); Dubois, *Avengers of the New World*, 270–271 ('massacre'). For Harvey and Haiti, see also Karen Salt, *The Unfinished Revolution: Haiti, Black Sovereignty and the Nineteenth-Century Atlantic World* (Liverpool: Liverpool University Press, 2019), 68.
14. "A Member of the University of Cambridge," *Suggestions on the Abolition of Slavery in the British Colonies; or, Slavery Gradually Starved to Death Upon a Low Diet, V: Strangulation* (Cambridge: J. J. Deighton, T. Stevenson, and R. Newby, 1831), title ('Member'), iv ('feed'), v–vi ('invasion', 'constrain', and 'dependence'); Everill, *Not Made by Slaves*, 48 ('sixty').
15. *Ibid.*, 49 ('70,000' and 'Barbarities'); Gunning, *Reminiscences*, vol. 2, 39 ('held meetings').
16. "Member," *Slavery Gradually Starved to Death*, 1 ('Question'), 2–3 ('wantonly'), and 5–6 ('Slave owner' and 'least expenditure'). The mention of England being "enslaved" to her colonies was perhaps a reference to James Stephen, *England Enslaved by Her Own Slave Colonies* (London: Hatchard and Son, 1826).
17. Richard Bourke, *Empire and Revolution: The Political Life of Edmund Burke* (Princeton: Princeton University Press, 2015), 647–663 ('Burke'); Major, *Slavery, Abolitionism and Empire*, 314 ('reproduced').
18. "Member," *Slavery Gradually Starved to Death*, 7 ('Adam Smith' and 'travel narratives'), 21–22 ('emancipated' and 'Hayti'), and 23 ('economising'); J. R. Ward, 'The Profitability of Sugar Planting in the British West Indies, 1650–1834', *Economic History Review* 31 (May 1978), 209 ('annual profits').
19. "Member," *Slavery Gradually Starved to Death*, 29 ('opiate', 'melioration', and 'stupefy') and 26 ('volcano', 'bedlam', 'carnage', and 'lawless'); *A List of the Names of the Proprietors of East-India Stock who Appear, By the Books of the East-India Company, Qualified to Vote at the General Election, 12th April 1837* (London: Cox and Sons, 1836), 92 ('invest'); Charles Henry Cooper and John William Cooper, eds., *Annals of Cambridge, Volume V: 1850–1856 with Additions and Corrections to Volumes I–IV and Index to the Complete Work* (Cambridge: Cambridge University Press, 1908), 107 ('college prize').
20. 'Sir Alexander Craufurd', *Legacies*, www.ucl.ac.uk/lbs/person/view/2146660847, accessed 6 February 2023 ('Grenville'); 'George William Gregan Craufurd', *ACAD*,

https://venn.lib.cam.ac.uk/cgi-bin/search-2018.pl?sur=craufurd&suro=w&fir=george&firo=c&cit=&cito=c&c=all&z=all&tex=&sye=&eye=&col=all&maxcount=50, accessed 6 February 2023 ('fellowship'); Will of George William Craufurd, Wills, 1800–1914, KCA, GBR/0272/KCHR/3/1/8, 33–38 ('Divinity Lectureship'); Adam Sedgwick to Bishop Wilberforce, 16 July 1848, in Clark and Hughes, eds., *Life and Letters of the Reverend Adam Sedgwick*, vol. 2, 143 ('slave-grown'); Adam Sedgwick to Mrs Norton, in *ibid.*, 394 ('sucked'); 'Rev. Adam Sedgwick', *Legacies*, www.ucl.ac.uk/lbs/person/view/24026, accessed 4 March 2022 ('trustee'). Sedgwick, who taught the famed naturalist Charles Darwin, supported the Union during the American Civil War, and advocated in his private letters for the conflict to be a 'war for the abolition of slavery'. (Adrian Desmond and James Moore, *Darwin's Sacred Cause: How a Hatred of Slavery Shaped Darwin's Views on Human Evolution* [Boston and New York: Houghton Mifflin Harcourt, 2009], 327.)

21. George W. Craufurd, 'The Impolicy of Slave Labour', *Tourist: A Literary and Anti-Slavery Journal, under the Superintendence of the Agency of the Anti-Slavery Society*, 10 December 1832 ('mankind', 'liberally', 'direct tax', 'loss to the British economy', and 'system'); Lawrence Goldman, *Victorians and Numbers: Statistics and Society in Nineteenth Century Britain* (Oxford: Oxford University Press, 2022), 33–34 ('Statistical Section'); Rev. Richard Jones, *An Introductory Lecture on Political Economy, Delivered at King's College, London, 27th February, 1833* (London: John Murray, 1833), 59 ('Evils'). For abolitionists and the profitability of free labour, see Seymour Drescher, *The Mighty Experiment: Free Labor versus Slavery in British Emancipation* (Oxford: Oxford University Press, 2002), 149–152.

22. Jeremy C. Mitchell and James Cornford, 'The Political Demography of Cambridge 1832–1868', *Albion: A Quarterly Journal Concerned with British Studies* 9 (Autumn 1977), 251 ('1,400'); Searby, *History of the University of Cambridge, Volume III*, 386–387 ('held elections') and 390 ('uncontested'); '1832 General Election – Cambridge', *UK General Election Results, 1832–2019*, https://api.parliament.uk/uk-general-elections/elections/53, accessed 12 September 2023 ('contest' and 'victorious'); George Pryme, *An Introductory Lecture and Syllabus, to a Course Delivered in the University of Cambridge, on the Principles of Political Economy* (Cambridge: Deighton & Sons, 1823), 13 ('dearer') and 18 ('scarcity', 'slavery', 'plunder', and 'neglected'). The Senate named Pryme as a Professor, but the chair was not endowed until 1863 (after Pryme's retirement). (Professor Pryme to the Rev. the Master of Trinity, 11 May 1863, in Alicia Bayne, ed., *Autobiographic Recollections of George Pryme, Esq. M.A.* [Cambridge: Deighton, Bell, and Co., 1870], 348–349.)

23. "Fair Play," *To the Electors of Cambridgeshire. Economy, Independence, and Truth* (Cambridge: H. Talbot, 1832), Election Broadsides, CA, KAR89/82/11 ('declares'); Michael J. Turner, *Independent Radicalism in Early Victorian Britain* (London: Bloomsbury Publishing, 2004), 195 ('sceptic'); George Pryme, *To the Electors of the Town of Cambridge* (Cambridge: W. Hatfield, 1832), Election Broadsides, CA, KAR89/82/53 ('condition'); "An Abolitionist," *Slavery! To the Electors Of the County of Cambridge and Isle of Ely* (Cambridge: Hodson & Brown, 1832), *ibid.*, 136 ('FRIEND' and 'excerpts'); Charles Philip Yorke, *To the Electors of the County of Cambridge and Isle of Ely* (Cambridge: Hodson and Brown, 1832), *ibid.*, 138 ('humanity' and 'common justice').

24. *A Full Report of the Proceedings at the Cambridge County Election, Commencing Tuesday, August 10, 1830* (Cambridge: Matfield, 1830), 50 ('interest', 'sincere',

'faithful', and 'management') and 56 ('common'); 'Diamond', *Legacies*, www.ucl.ac .uk/lbs/estate/view/3500, accessed 27 September 2022 ('trustee'); David R. Fisher, 'Cambridgeshire', *History of Parliament*, www.historyofparliamentonline.org/ volume/1820-1832/constituencies/cambridgeshire#footnoteref18_3kjxjcw, accessed 27 September 2022 ('white' and 'distresses').
25. George W. Craufurd, *Slavery! Captain Yorke's Views, on the Subject of Colonial Slavery, Refuted, In Two Letters, Together with Captain Yorke's Attempted Defence* (Cambridge: Weston Hatfield, 1832), 3 ('placards' and 'emancipation'), 5 ('clothing', 'sudden', and 'equitable'), 6 ('cattle'), and 8 ('*industry*'); Thomas Seccombe, 'Charles Philip Yorke (1764–1834)', in Stephen and Lee, eds., *DNB*, vol. 63, 341 ('Tory'). See, for example, "A Well Wisher to All Parties," *Negro Slavery Exposed* (Cambridge: W. Hatfield, 1824); Rev. William Cuttriss, *Slavery Inconsistent with Christianity* (Cambridge: Johnson, 1825); Charles Telfair and Thomas Jackson, *An Appeal to the Freeholders of the County of Cambridge and Isle of Ely, on the Subject of Colonial Slavery* (Cambridge: W. Metcalfe, 1832); Charles Telfair and Thomas Jackson, *Britain's Burden, or, The Intolerable Evils of Colonial Slavery Exposed* (Cambridge: W. Metcalfe, 1832); and *The Mauritius: an Exemplification of Colonial Policy; Addressed to the Electors of Cambridge and Devonport* (Birmingham: B. Hudson, 1837). In 1840, a Cambridge publisher reprinted Robert Robinson's *Slavery inconsistent with the spirit of Christianity* for 'gratuitous distribution'.
26. J. Kent McGaughy, *Richard Henry Lee of Virginia: Portrait of an American Revolutionary* (Oxford: Rowman & Littlefield Publishers, Inc., 2004), 24 ('owner'); R. B. Harraden, Jr., *History of the University of Cambridge Illustrated by a Series of Engravings Representing the Most Picturesque and Interesting Edifices in the University and the Most Striking Parts of the Town* (Cambridge: J. Smith, 1814), 155 ('college fellow'). Two years before his death, Porteus transferred government stock worth £1,200 to Christ's to fund three gold medal prizes for students. (*Cambridge University Commission: Report of Her Majesty's Commissioners Appointed to Inquire into the State, Discipline, Studies, and Revenues of the University and Colleges of Cambridge: Together with the Evidence, and an Appendix* [London: W. Clowes and Sons, 1852], 382.)
27. J. C. S. Mason, *The Moravian Church and the Missionary Awakening in England, 1760–1800* (Woodbridge, Suffolk: The Boydell Press, 2001), 92 ('unwilling'); William Knox to the Lord Chancellor (Thurlow), 26 May 1789, 'The manuscripts of Captain H. V. Knox', in *Report on Manuscripts in Various* Collections, vol. 6 (Dublin: John Falconer, 1909), 203 ('prevented'); Brown, *Moral Capital*, 346 ('reformation').
28. Brown, *Moral Capital*, 240 ('means') and 352–364 ('awakening'); Beilby Porteus, *The Cultivation, improvement, and conversion of the Negro-slaves in the British West-India islands recommended*, 23 February 1783, in Beilby Porteus, *Sermons on Several Subjects by the Right Reverend Beilby Porteus, D. D. Bishop of London* (London: T. Payne, T. Cadell, and W. Davies, 1808), 396 ('human' and 'saved'), 397 ('knowledge'), and 403 ('improvement').
29. *Ibid.*, 406 ('failed'), 410 ('blessings'), and 411 ('emoluments').
30. Mason, *Moravian Church*, 127 ('Christians'); 1789 report, in Sessional Papers, LXIX, 1 ('State'); *Address of Incorporated Society for the Conversion and Religious Instruction and Education of the Negro Slaves in the British West India Islands* (London: The Society, 1824), 3–5 ('founded' and 'amelioration').
31. *Selected Parts of the Holy Bible, For the Use of the Negro Slaves, in the British West-India Islands* (London: Law and Gilbert, 1807) ('Exodus'); William Greenfield,

A Defence of the Surinam Negro-English Version of the New Testament (London: Samuel Bagster, 1830), 5 ('Austen').
32. *Address of Incorporated Society*, list of governors ('members'), 14 ('Planters'), 7 ('Byam'), and 11 ('Ireland').
33. Beilby Porteus, *A Letter to the Governors, Legislatures, and Proprietors of Plantations, in the British West-India Islands* (London: T. Cadell and W. Davies, 1808), 3 ('blessings'), 5–6 ('natural', 'fatal', and 'moral'), and 12–13 ('enormous'); Joyce E. Chaplin, 'Slavery and the Principle of Humanity: A Modern Idea in the Early Lower South', *Journal of Social History* 24 (Winter 1990), 311 ('souls').
34. Richard Burgh Byam to William Howley, 4 December 1820, Papers of the Bishop of London: Correspondence and papers on the church overseas, LPL, FP Howley 2, 23–26.
35. 'Rev. John Hothersall Pinder', *Legacies*, www.ucl.ac.uk/lbs/person/view/2146652643, accessed 9 July 2021 ('ordained'); 17 January 1797, Barbados Journal, BOD, vol. 4, X23, 72276x23, ff. 19–20 ('Nicholson'); John Hothersall Pinder to William Howley, 12 May 1821, Papers of the Bishop of London: Correspondence and papers on the church overseas, LPL, FP Howley 2, 599 ('instruct', 'afternoon', and 'Creed'); *The Christian Remembrancer; or, The Churchman's Biblical, ecclesiastical & literary miscellany*, vol. 6 (London, 1824), 151–152 ('thanksgiving' and 'servant').
36. Richard Burgh Byam, *Suggestions for Promoting (Under the Patronage of the Church) Such Measures in the West Indies, as may Reasonably be Expected to Produce the Rapid Decline of Slavery, By a Member of the Senate, Who is also a Clergyman of the Church of England an Owner of West India Property, and a Member of His Majesty's Council in one of the Colonies*, 1825, Papers of the Bishop of London: Correspondence and papers on the church overseas, LPL, FP Howley 2, 91–94.
37. 'Henry Nelson Coleridge', ACAD, https://venn.lib.cam.ac.uk/cgi-bin/search-2018.pl?sur=coleridge&suro=w&fir=henry&firo=c&cit=&cito=c&c=all&z=all&tex=&sye=&eye=&col=all&maxcount=50, accessed 17 January 2022 ('distinguished'); Sehon Sylvester Coleridge, *Facing the Challenge of Emancipation: A Study of the Ministry of William Hart Coleridge, First Bishop of Barbados, 1824–1842* (London: Canoe Press, 2014) ('advocate'); Henry Nelson Coleridge, *Six Months in the West Indies, in 1825* (London: John Murray, 1826), 7 ('Polar'), 8 ('Planters'), and 72 ('turn'); Henry Nelson Coleridge, *Six Months in the West Indies: Fourth Edition* (London: Thomas Tegg, 1841), preface to the third edition ('Abolitionists', 'hacked', and 'domestic treason').
38. *Ibid.*, title page ('Late Fellow'); Simon P. Newman, 'Hidden in Plain Sight: Escaped Slaves in Late-Eighteenth- and Early-Nineteenth Century Jamaica', *WMQ*, https://oireader.wm.edu/open_wmq/hidden-in-plain-sight/hidden-in-plain-sight-escaped-slaves-in-late-eighteenth-and-early-nineteenth-century-jamaica/, accessed 1 December 2022 ('Hakewill' and 'vibrancy'); Jay B. Haviser, *African Sites: Archaeology in the Caribbean* (Princeton, NJ: Markus Weiner Publishers, 1999), 205 ('coarse').
39. Coleridge, *Six Months*, 45 ('mass'), 53 ('violent'), 169 ('feudal'), 72 ('noble plant'), 109 ('sublime' and 'lovely'), 183 ('verdant'), 52 ('beautiful'), 123 ('delightful'), and 221 ('country villages'); Johnson, *River of Dark Dreams*, 209 ('carceral'); Daniel McKinnen, *A Tour Through the British West Indies, in the Years 1802 and 1803, Giving a Particular Account of the Bahama Islands* (London: J. White, 1804), 69 ('tone and argument'). For these Caribbean travellers, see also John R. Oldfield, *Transatlantic Abolitionism in the Age of Revolution: An International History of Anti-slavery, c. 1787–1820* (Cambridge: Cambridge University Press, 2013), 141–142.

40. Coleridge, *Six Months*, 84 ('disgusting' and 'correct'), 136 ('naked', 'sucking', 'pleasure', and 'gratitude'), 84–85 ('passion' and 'intensity'), 76 ('delightful', 'negro girls', and 'massa'), 92 ('external'), 88 ('new comforts'), and 104 ('stimulus' and 'improvement').
41. *Ibid.*, 102 ('Castle'), 239 ('education' and 'tempers'), 315–316 ('Oxford or Cambridge' and 'monsters'), 239 ('scarcely' and 'protection'), 314 ('refused'), 299 ('model of England', 'equality', and 'restlessness'), 302 ('interference' and 'tyranny'), 303 ('every age'), 304 ('spirit'), and 312 ('exception').
42. B. W. Higman, *Slave Populations of the British Caribbean, 1807–1834* (Mona, Jamaica: University of the West Indies Press, 1995), 72 ('665,000'); Coleridge, *Six Months*, 118 ('churches', 'tread-wheel', 'chained slave', and 'Brixton'), 326 ('insurrections'), 185 ('observant race'); David H. Shayt, 'Stairway to Redemption: America's Encounter with the British Prison Treadmill', *Technology and Culture* 30 (October 1989), 909–910 ('1779'); Diana Paton, *No Bond but the Law: Punishment, Race, and Gender in Jamaican State Formation, 1780–1870* (Durham, NC: Duke University Press, 2004), 93 ('amongst other reformers').
43. Coleridge, *Six Months*, 308 ('Planters and Slaves'), 318 ('hardly at present', 'equality', and 'citizens'), 319 ('*moral*'), 327 ('protection'), 320 ('market'), 321 ('sudden' and 'fit').
44. Coleridge, *Six Months*, 1 ('rheumatism'); 'Literature', *The Morning Post*, 20 December 1832 ('newspapers'); 'Mode of Dressing a Turtle', *The Charleston Mercury*, 22 August 1826 ('excerpts'); 'New Books for Christmas Gifts, &c.', *The Sydney Morning Herald*, 18 December 1837 ('New South Wales'); Charles Lamb to Samuel Taylor Coleridge, 22 March 1826, in Alfred Ainger, ed., *The Letters of Charles Lamb Newly Arranged, with Additions*, vol. 2 (New York: A. C. Armstrong & Son, 1894), 144 ('excellent sense'); *The Young Logicians; or School-Boy Conceptions of Rights and Wrongs. With a Particular Reference to 'Six Months in the West Indies'. Part the Second* (Birmingham: B. Hudson, 1828), 31–32 ('licentiousness', 'tenth', 'filthy', and 'readers'); Kathleen Coburn and Merton Christensen, eds., *The Notebooks of Samuel Taylor Coleridge*, vol. 4 (London: Routledge, 2003), 558 ('flippancy', 'vulgarity', and 'enormity').
45. Ralph Bernal, *Substance of the Speech of Ralph Bernal, Esq.* (London: J. Moyes, 1826), 3 ('general body') and 5 ('case').
46. Rev. Stephen Isaacson, *A Vindication of the West-India Proprietors, In a Speech Delivered at Mansion House Chapel, Camberwell, August 18, 1832, With an Appendix* (London: J. Fraser, 1832), 4 ('crowded'), 7 ('prosperous'), and 8 ('last').
47. Rev. Richard Bickell, *The West Indies as They Are; or A Real Picture of Slavery: But more particularly as it Exists in the Island of Jamaica* (London: J. Hatchard and Son, 1825), title page ('Member'); 'Rev. Richard Bickell', *Legacies*, www.ucl.ac.uk/lbs/person/view/2146636055, accessed 10 February 2023 ('five-year'); Venn and Venn, *Alumni Cantabrigiensis*, vol. 2, 256 ('Sidney'); 'John Anderson', *Legacies*, www.ucl.ac.uk/lbs/person/view/2146642899, accessed 10 February 2023 ('Anderson').
48. Bickell, *West Indies as They Are*, 146–147 ('working' and 'handsome income'); 'Excerpts from Jamaican Records and Anglican Parish Registers', *Jamaican Family Search*, www.jamaicanfamilysearch.com/Members/Rw_j-y.htm, accessed 10 February 2023 ('quadroon').
49. '"A West Indian Proprietor" to the Rev. Dr. Lambe', *Grenada Free Press, and Public Gazette*, 27 August 1828.
50. Ralph Davis, *The Industrial Revolution and British Overseas Trade* (Leicester: Leicester University Press, 1979), 43 ('most valuable'); Copy of lease to Robert Sacker

of Haverhill, 5 May 1609, Cambridge, St Edward's Parish deeds, CCC, GBR/0268/CCCC09/09/49D, Copy of a lease to Robert Tavan, tailor, 10 May 1624, Cambridge, St Bene't (St Benedict's) parish, *ibid.*, 18/202J, Copy of a lease to Robert Sacker of Offord Darcy, 8 January 1630, Cambridge, St. Edward's parish, *ibid.*, 09/122F, Counterpart of lease to Elizabeth Sadler of a tenement, 27 May 1786, Cambridge, St Bene't (St Benedict's) parish, *ibid.*, 18/223, Counterpart of lease to Mary Harrison of a tenement, 31 March 1800, *ibid.*, 223b, Lease to John Bicheno of property in Bene't Street, 4 March 1814, Deeds relating to the college tenement in Bene't Street, *ibid.*, 18/236, Lease to John Bicheno of premises, *ibid.*, 236.1, and Counterpart of lease to George Salmon, gent., 1 June 1838, Cambridge, St. Edward's parish, deeds, *ibid.*, 09/191 ('good Barbary'); Theodore B. Leinwand, *Theatre, Finance and Society in Early Modern England* (Cambridge: Cambridge University Press, 2004), 24 ('Thomas Gresham'); Chouki El Hamel, *Black Morocco: A History of Slavery, Race, and Islam* (Cambridge: Cambridge University Press, 2014), 144–145 ('al-Mansur'), 152 ('pyramids' and 'gold'), and 154 ('Caribbean').

51. John Gilmore, *The Poetics of Empire: A Study of James Grainger's The Sugar Cane (1764)* (New Brunswick, NJ: The Athlone Press, 2000), 9 ('patronage'); Susan Clair Imbarrato, *Sarah Gray Cary from Boston to Grenada: Shifting Fortunes of an American Family, 1764–1826* (Baltimore: Johns Hopkins University Press, 2018), 29–30 ('undergraduate'); M. J. Chapman, *Barbadoes, and Other Poems* (London: J. Moyes, 1833), vii–viii ('colonies and empire') and 42 ('infuriate'). John Bourryau, whose father owned property on Saint Kitts, was Grainger's patron and may have also assisted with translation work for the poem.

52. *Ibid.*, 101–102 ('Polygamy'); Sharon Block, *Rape and Sexual Power in Early America* (Philadelphia: University of Pennsylvania Press, 2006), 208–209 ('sexual violence'); Sarah M. S. Pearsall, *Polygamy: An Early American History* (New Haven, CT: Yale University Press, 2019), 119 ('shorthand') and 120 ('unfit').

53. 'John Pollard Mayers', *Legacies*, www.ucl.ac.uk/lbs/person/view/41310, accessed 10 January 2022 ('matriculated'); Bruce M. Taylor, 'Our Man in London: John Pollard Mayers, Agent for Barbados, and the British Abolition Act, 1832–1834', *Caribbean Studies* 16 (October 1976), 75–76 ('testimonies and statistics'), 83–84 ('reluctant', 'conciliation', and 'attaining'), and 74 ('indemnity').

54. 25 April 1834, in John Patrick Tuer Bury, ed., *Romilly's Cambridge Diary, 1832–42: Selected Passages from the Diary of the Rev. Joseph Romilly, Fellow of Trinity College and Registrar of the University of Cambridge* (Cambridge: Cambridge University Press, 2011), 56 ('grand quarterly feast'); Matthew Gregory Lewis, *Journal of a West India Proprietor, Kept during a Residence in the Island of Jamaica* (Cambridge: Cambridge University Press, 2010) ('volume'); 'Matthew Gregory Lewis', *Legacies*, www.ucl.ac.uk/lbs/person/view/-1890542757, 12 January 2022 ('five hundred').

55. 'Sir Alexander Cray Grant, 8th Baronet', *ibid.*, www.ucl.ac.uk/lbs/person/view/19810, accessed 12 January 2022 ('£14,000'); 29 June 1841, in Bury, ed., *Romilly's Cambridge Diary, 1832–42*, 219 ('Banner'); 'The Cambridge Election', *Cambridge Independent Press*, 23 May 1840 ('respectable' and 'human').

56. 'The Slavery Question and the Cambridge Constituency', *ibid.*, 26 June 1841 ('monopoly', 'dear', and 'foreign'); Thomas Perronet Thompson, *Catechism on the Corn Laws; with a List of Fallacies and the Answers. Twelfth Edition* (London: Robert Heward, 1829), 55 ('unity'); Philip Harling, 'Sugar Wars: The Culture of Free Trade versus the Culture of Anti-Slavery in Britain and the British

Caribbean, 1840–50', in Barry Crosbie and Mark Hampton, eds., *The Cultural Construction of the British World* (Manchester: Manchester University Press, 2015), 59 ('Brazilian').

6 'We presume that its influence is nowhere greater than in the Universities': Ending and Defending American Slavery

1. Bishop Green of Mississippi to the Rev. Dr. William Hepworth Thompson, 8 June 1868, Letters received from various dignitaries, 1613–1868, CUL, GBR/0265/UA/Lett.17/30 ('thanked' and 'pleasure'); Books 'presented by the University of Cambridge to The Library of the University of the Southern States of America, 26 March 1868', University of Cambridge Book Collection, WRL ('volumes included'); William Clark, *Catalogue of the Osteological Portions of Specimens Contained in the Anatomical Museum of the University of Cambridge* (Cambridge: Cambridge University Press, 2010), 106 ('Negroes' and 'Budd').
2. George Rainsford Fairbanks, *History of the University of the South, at Sewanee, Tennessee: From Its Founding by the Southern Bishops, Clergy, and Laity of the Episcopal Church in 1857 to the Year 1905* (Jacksonville, FL: The H. & W. B. Drew Company, 1905), 7 ('theological'); Woody Register and Benjamin King, 'A Research Summary on Slavery at the University of the South and in the Community of Sewanee', *The University of the South*, https://new.sewanee.edu/roberson-project/learn-more/research-summary/#:~:text=While%20other%20universities%20have%20documented,itself%20ever%20owned%20enslaved%20people, accessed 10 February 2023 ('native' and 'go forth'); W. Brown Patterson, *The Liberal Arts at Sewanee* (Sewanee, TN: The University of the South, 2009), 16 ('Sewanee Mining Company').
3. Kate Parrish, 'Ghosts of Lone Rock', *University of the South*, https://new.sewanee.edu/features/ghosts-of-lone-rock/, accessed 10 February 2023 ('convicts'); Charles Todd Quintard, *The Confederate Soldier's Pocket Manual of Devotions* (Charleston: Evans & Cogswell, 1863), title page ('compile') and 29–30 ('servant').
4. Charles Reagan Wilson, *Baptized in Blood: The Religion of the Lost Cause, 1865–1920* (Athens: University of Georgia Press, 2009), 147 ('five trips'); Richard J. M. Blackett, *Divided Hearts: Britain and the American Civil War* (Baton Rouge: Louisiana State University Press, 2001), 104 ('thirty-nine'); Benjamin J. King, 'Church, Cotton, and Confederates; What Bishop Charles Todd Quintard's Fundraising Trips to Great Britain Reveal about Some Nineteenth-Century Anglo-Catholics', *Anglican and Episcopal History* 90 (June 2021), 112 ('University Church'); 'Charles Todd Quintard', *ACAD*, https://venn.lib.cam.ac.uk/cgi-bin/search-2018.pl?sur=quintard&suro=w&fir=&firo=c&cit=&cito=c&c=all&z=all&tex=&sye=&eye=&col=all&maxcount=50, accessed 13 February 2023 ('doctorate'); 'University of the South (Sewanee, Tennessee, U.S.A.)', in Carol Summerfield and Mary Elizabeth Devine, ed., *International Dictionary of University Histories* (London and New York: Routledge, 1998), 640 ('£2,500'); An Offering from English Churchmen to the American Bishops Towards the Re-Establishment of their University for the South and South-West Dioceses, Charles Todd Quintard Papers, WRL, Box 3, Folder 4 ('Joining' and 'donors'); 'Hope, Alexander Beresford', *ACAD*, https://venn.lib.cam.ac.uk/cgi-bin/search-2018.pl?sur=&suro=w&fir=&firo=c&cit=&cito=c&c=all&z=all&tex=HP837AJ&sye=&eye=&col=all&maxcount=50, accessed 17 January 2022 ('honorary'); Patterson, *Liberal Arts*, 16 ('first-class' and 'civilized world').

5. Bishop Green to Thompson, 8 June 1868, Letters from various dignitaries, 1613–1868, CUL, GBR/0265/UA/Lett.17/30.
6. 'Caskie Harrison', *ACAD*, https://venn.lib.cam.ac.uk/cgi-bin/search-2018.pl?sur=harrison&suro=w&fir=caskie&firo=c&cit=&cito=c&c=all&z=all&tex=&sye=&eye=&col=all&maxcount=50, accessed 14 February 2023 ('Harrison'); Wilson, *Baptized in Blood*, 197 ('Gothic'); Rev. William Mercer Green and Rev. Telfair Hodgson, *The University of the South: Papers relating to Christian Education at this University, and the necessity of this Institution to the country, especially to the South and Southwest, etc.* (Sewanee, TN: James Pott & Co., Church Publishers, 1882), 34 ('plainer'); Register and King, 'A Research Summary on Slavery at the University of the South and in the Community of Sewanee' ('portals').
7. 'Edward Strutt Abdy', *ACAD*, https://venn.lib.cam.ac.uk/cgi-bin/search-2018.pl?sur=abdy&suro=w&fir=edward&firo=c&cit=&cito=c&c=all&z=all&tex=&sye=&eye=&col=all&maxcount=50, 11 January 2022 ('educated'); 'Sir William Abdy, 7th Baronet', *Legacies*, www.ucl.ac.uk/lbs/person/view/293, accessed 13 January 2022 ('£13,404'); Sir Bernard Burke and Ashworth Peter Burke, *A Genealogical and Heraldic History of the Peerage and Baronetage, the Privy Council, Knightage and Companions* (London: Harrison, 1910), 1393–1394 ('Rutherforth').
8. Edward Strutt Abdy, *Journal of a Residence and Tour in the United States of North America, From April, 1833, to October, 1834*, vol. 1 (London: John Murray, 1835), ch. 8. ('travelled'); Alexis de Tocqueville, *De la Démocratie en Amérique*, 2 vols. (Brussels: C. Gosselin, 1835 and 1840) ('journeyed'); Abdy, *Journal of a Residence and Tour in the United States*, vol. 3, 85 ('less than whites'), 207 ('hardly safe' and 'stones and racist epithets'), and 118 ('Chatham Street').
9. *Ibid.*, vol. 2, 180–181 ('disdain') and 97 ('frozen'); *ibid.*, vol. 1, 375 ('disgraceful'), 378 ('Spartacus'), 391 ('plunder and oppression'), and vi ('civil or servile').
10. Andrew Jackson O'Shaughnessy, *The Illimitable Freedom of the Human Mind: Thomas Jefferson's Idea of a University* (Charlottesville: University of Virginia Press, 2021), 187 ('Key' and 'Cottrell'); *The Alumni Bulletin of the University of Virginia* (Charlottesville: University of Virginia, 1894), 33 ('$250'); *The History of the College of William and Mary: From Its Foundation, 1660, to 1874* (Richmond, VA: J. W. Randolph & English, 1874), 69 ('Potts'); 'Advertisement', *The Evening Post* (New York), 23 August 1842 ('late Fellow'); 31 May 1849, in Thomas Fitzhugh, ed., *Letters of George Long* (Charlottesville: University of Virginia Press, 1917), 18 ('professor') and 23 ('friend'); George Long, *The Geography of America and the West Indies* (London: Society for the Diffusion of Useful Knowledge, 1841), 223–224 ('degraded', 'produces', and 'superiority').
11. Abdy, *Journal of a Residence and Tour in the United States*, vol. 3, 274–275 ('indifference', 'pure love', and 'obloquy'); *First Annual Report of the Board of Managers of the New-England Anti-Slavery Society, Presented Jan. 9, 1833* (Boston: Garrison and Knapp, 1833), 22–23 ('life member' and 'unrighteously'); Wilder, *Ebony & Ivy*, 277–278 ('Egypt' and 'merchant').
12. 'The United States', *Leigh Hunt's London Journal* (London: Charles Knight and Henry Hooper, 1834), 262 ('*Leigh*'); 'Abdy's Tour in the United States', *The Monthly Review, From May to August Inclusive*, vol. 2 (London: G. Henderson, 1835), 326 ('*Monthly*' and 'tiresome'); 'Abdy's Journal in the United States', *The Westminster Review* (New York: Theodore Foster, 1835), 1836 ('*Westminster*'); 'Abdy's Journal and Residence of a Tour in the United States', in W. J. Fox, ed., *The Monthly Repository for 1835*, vol. 9 (London: Charles Fox, 1835), 729 ('*Repository*'); 'Tours in America, by Latrobe, Abdy, &c.', *The Quarterly Review*, vol. 54 (London: John

Murray, 1835), 392 ('*Quarterly*' and 'Latrobe'); 'Review. – Abdy's Tour in the United States', *The Baptist Magazine*, vol. 27 (London: George Wightman, 1835), 373 ('*Baptist*'); *Catalogue of Books Added to the Library of the Library Company of Philadelphia, Since the Large Catalogue of 1835 to January, 1844* (Philadelphia: C. Sherman, 1844), 134 ('Library Company'); 'E. S. Abdy', in Julius Rubens Ames, ed., *'Liberty': The Image and Superscription on Every Coin Issued by the United States of America* (New York, NY: American Anti-Slavery Society, 1837), 202 ('*Liberty*'); *The Legion of Liberty and Force of Truth, Containing the Thoughts, Words, and Deeds, of Some Prominent Apostles, Champions and Martyrs* (New York, NY: American Anti-Slavery Society, 1857), 230 ('*Legion of Liberty*').

13. Iain Whyte, *Scotland and the Abolition of Black Slavery, 1756–1838* (Edinburgh: Edinburgh University Press, 2006), 234–235 ('floggings'); Edward Strutt Abdy to William Tait, 2 September 1835, African American History Collection, 1729–1966, WLC ('flattering', 'wounded', and 'republican').

14. *Second Annual Report of the American Anti-Slavery Society; with the Speeches Delivered at the Anniversary Meeting, Held in the City of New-York, On the 12th May, 1835, and the Minutes of the Meetings of the Society for Business* (New York, NY: William S. Dorr, 1835), 58 ('abolitionist') and 15 ('friends').

15. Thomas F. Harwood, 'Prejudice and Antislavery: The Colloquy between William Ellery Channing and Edward Strutt Abdy, 1834', *American Quarterly* 18 (Winter 1966), 699 ('racial prejudice'); Abdy, *Journal of a Residence and Tour in the United States*, vol. 3, 228 ('distinction'); E. S. Abdy, *American Whites and Blacks, In Reply to a German Orthodermist* (London: Charles Gilpin, 1842), 22 ('racial mixing'), 5–6 ('immigration'), and 39 ('pure religion').

16. Abdy, *Journal of a Residence and Tour in the United States*, vol. 1, xii ('craniology') and 341 ('thicker').

17. Johann Gaspar Spurzheim, *Examination of the Objections Made in Britain against the Doctrines of Gall and Spurzheim* (Boston: Marsh, Capen & Lyon, 1833), 42 ('botanical', 'favor', and 'increased'); 'The Present State of Phrenology in the University of Cambridge', *The Phrenological Journal and Miscellany*, vol. 10 (Edinburgh: Clachlan and Stewart, and John Anderson, 1837), 706–709 ('attended', 'perusing', 'leading', 'theme', and 'casts'); Alan Richardson, *British Romanticism and the Science of the Mind* (Cambridge: Cambridge University Press, 2001), 23–25 ('Spurzheim').

18. Abdy, *American Whites and Blacks*, 45 ('blessings') and 44 ('war for America'); Walter M. Merrill, ed., *The Letters of William Lloyd Garrison, Volume III: No Union With Slavers, 1841–1849* (Cambridge, MA: The Belknap Press of Harvard University Press, 1973), 401 ('Garrison'); Boston Julie Winch, *A Gentleman of Color: The Life of James Forten* (Oxford: Oxford University Press, 2003), 122 ('Forten'); *The Third Annual Report of the British and Foreign Anti-Slavery Society, for the Abolition of Slavery and the Slave-Trade Throughout the World; Presented to the General Meeting Held in Exeter Hall, On Friday, May 13th, 1842* (London: Thomas Ward and Co., 1842), 183 ('donated'); 'Abdy, Edward Strutt (1791–1846)', in Junius Rodriguez, ed., *Encyclopedia of Emancipation and Abolition in the Transatlantic World*, vol. 1 (London and New York: Routledge, 2015), 4 ('American' and '£500'). The debate within Black abolition circles over whether violence would be required to abolish slavery in the United States is discussed in Kellie Carter Jackson, *Force and Freedom: Black Abolitionists and the Politics of Violence* (Philadelphia: University of Pennsylvania Press, 2019); and Blight, *Frederick Douglass*, 242.

19. John R. Oldfield, ed., *Civilization and Black Progress: Selected Writings of Alexander Crummell on the South* (Charlottesville: University Press of Virginia, 1995), 2–3 ('New York'); Gene Dattel, *Cotton and Race in the Making of America: The Human Costs of Economic Power* (New York: Rowman & Littlefield, 2009), 86 ('forty'); Jacqueline Bacon, *Freedom's Journal: The First African-American Newspaper* (New York, NY: Lexington Books, 2007), 38–39 ('*Journal*').
20. Oldfield, ed., *Civilization and Black Progress*, 3–4 ('England') and 6 ('success'); Wilson Jeremiah Moses, *Alexander Crummell: A Study of Civilization and Discontent* (New York and Oxford: Oxford University Press, 1989), 57 ('Queens'); Alexander Crummell to John Jay, 9 August 1848, in C. Peter Ripley, ed, *The Black Abolitionist Papers*, vol. 1 (Chapel Hill: University of North Carolina Press, 1985), 143 ('superior', 'lively', 'standard', 'advantages', and 'my people'). For Pan-Africanism, see Brandon R. Byrd, *The Black Republic: African Americans and the Fate of Haiti* (Philadelphia: University of Pennsylvania Press, 2019); and Sinha, *Slave's Cause*, 131–132.
21. Anna B. Roderick, *Lecturing the Victorians: Knowledge-Based Culture and Participatory Citizenship* (London: Bloomsbury Publishing, 2024), 5 ('culture') and 89 ('international'); 'Cambridge Anti-Slavery Meeting', *Cambridge Independent Press*, 25 July 1840 ('instrumentality', 'heartfelt', 'rescued', and 'fetters').
22. Audrey Fisch, 'Uncle Tom and Harriet Beecher Stowe in England', in Cindy Weinstein, ed., *The Cambridge Companion to Harriet Beecher Stowe* (Cambridge: Cambridge University Press, 2004), 96 ('million'); 'Lecture on Slavery', *Cambridge Chronicle*, 15 September 1855 ('thrilling', 'Craft', 'slave', and 'buying'); Barbara McCaskill, 'William and Ellen Craft in Transatlantic Literature and Life', in Barbara McCaskill ed., *William Craft & Ellen Craft: Running a Thousand Miles for Freedom* (Athens: University of Georgia Press, 1999), ix. ('mother'); Blight, *Frederick Douglass*, 171 ('£150'); 'Slave Education', *Cambridge Independent Press*, 29 March 1856 ('late' and 'testimony'); 'American Slavery', *Cambridge Independent Press*, 5 June 1858 ('escaped' and 'cruelty').
23. Marty Gould, *Nineteenth-Century Theatre and the Imperial Encounter* (London: Routledge, 2011), 3–8 ('three hundred'); '*Negro Life! in Freedom and in Slavery*', *The Cambridge Chronicle and University Journal, Isle of Ely Herald, and Huntingdonshire Gazette*, 18 March 1854 ('Series', 'African Village', and 'Slave Sale'); Henry Russell, 'The African Village', in John Diprose, *Diprose's Comic and Sentimental Song Book* (London: David Bryce, 1856), 44 ('savage').
24. Lewis Defrates, '"Showing Up America": Performing Race and Nation in Britain Before the First World War', *The Journal of the Gilded Age and Progressive Era* 21 (2022), 319 ('culture' and 'Wells') and 323 ('Fisk'); 'The Jubilee Singers', *The Cambridge Chronicle and University Journal, Isle of Ely Herald, and Huntingdonshire Gazette*, 10 June 1876 ('Days of Slavery' and 'Swing Low'); Frederick Douglass, *Narrative of the Life of Frederick Douglass, an American Slave* (Boston: Anti-Slavery Office, 1845), 14 ('feeble comprehension').
25. Lawrence Goldman, *Science, Reform, and Politics in Victorian Britain: The Social Science Association, 1857–1886* (Cambridge: Cambridge University Press, 2002), 239 ('middle-class'); Heather Ellis, *Generational Conflict and University Reform: Oxford in the Age of Revolution* (Leiden and Boston: Brill, 2012), 187–217 ('Royal Commission' and 'stranglehold'); *A Collection of Cambridge Senate-House Papers, In Homer, Virgil, Locke and Paley's Philosophy and Evidences, As Given At the Examination for B.A. Degrees* (Cambridge: J. Hall and J. Hankin, 1832), 54 ('favour of Slavery' and 'Define') and 24 ('what causes' and 'arise').

26. *Cambridge Examination Papers: Being A Supplement to the University Calendar for the Year 1856* (Cambridge: Deighton, Bell and Co., 1856), 83 ('always wrong'); *Cambridge University Examination Papers*, vol. 8 (Cambridge: Cambridge University Press, 1879), 462 ('circumstances'); 'Subjects for the University Prizes for the Year 1857', *The Times*, 17 December 1856 ('poetry'); Churchill Babington, *The Influence of Christianity in Promoting the Abolition of Slavery in Europe* (Cambridge: J. & J. J. Deighton, 1846), 163–164 ('medieval'); C. M. Kennedy, *The Influence of Christianity upon International Law* (Cambridge: Macmillan and Co., 1856), 122–125 ('international laws').
27. 'Charles Clayton', *ACAD*, https://venn.lib.cam.ac.uk/cgi-bin/search-2018.pl?sur=clayton&suro=w&fir=charles&firo=c&cit=&cito=c&c=all&z=all&tex=&sye=&eye=&col=all&maxcount=50, accessed 14 February 2023 ('admitted'); J. M. Gray, *A History of the Perse School Cambridge* (Cambridge: Bowes & Bowes, 1921), 13–14 ('founded'); 7 April 1848, Private Diary of Charles Clayton, GCC, Claytonia ('from New York'); 9 April 1848, *ibid*. ('tour'); 14 April 1848, *ibid*. ('religious education'); 8 May 1850, *ibid*. ('missionary'); 13 April 1848, 29 October 1849, 24 November 1849, and 10 November 1850, *ibid*. ('walking'); 22 May 1849, *ibid*. ('boat').
28. Isaiah. 6. v. 8, *ibid*. ('knowledge'); 'Church Pastoral-Aid Society', *The Ecclesiastical Gazette; or, Monthly Register of the Affairs of the Church of England and of its Religious Societies and Institutions*, vol. 1 (London: Charles Cox, 1839), 118 ('door'); 10 November 1835, Private Diary of Charles Clayton, GCC, Claytonia ('Chieftain'); 23 May 1836, *ibid*. ('stations' and 'unhealthy').
29. *Ibid*. ('dejected'); 18 August 1839, *ibid*. ('abolitionist figures' and 'cruelties'); 23 August 1850, *ibid*. ('men's'); 24 April 1849, *ibid*. ('merchant'); 15 January 1849, *ibid*. ('see').
30. 31 May 1849, *ibid*. ('dissuaded' and 'dejected at the prospect'); Elizabeth Melville, *A Residence at Sierra Leone. Described from a Journal Kept on the Spot, and from Letters written to Friends at Home* (London: John Murray, 1849), 7 ('woolly-haired'), 22 ('all Black'), 21 ('goose'), and 45 ('termites').
31. 'Spiritual Condition of the Negro in the United States', *Cambridge Chronicle and University Journal, Isle of Ely Herald, and Huntingdonshire Gazette*, 15 April 1848 ('physically', 'cattle', and 'regular'); Jonathan B. Pritchett, 'Quantitative Estimates of the United States Interregional Slave Trade, 1820–1860', *The Journal of Economic History* 61 (June 2001), 467 ('835,000').
32. 'Spiritual Condition', *Cambridge* Chronicle, 15 April 1848. For self-reliance in Crummell's thought is noted in Moses, *Alexander Crummell*, 9.
33. Robert Griffin Laing, Legacies absolute/contingent and reversionary, summary volume, 1735–1904, CUL, GBR/0012/MS SPCK/C25/6 ('Laing'); Christopher Wordsworth, Register of Subscriptions and Donations, LPL, CFS E/13 ('Wordsworth'); 'Foundation of New Theological Prize in the University of Cambridge', *Port Philip Gazette*, 10 May 1845 ('heathen'); Elizabeth Elbourne, *Empire, Kinship and Violence: Family Histories, Indigenous Rights and the Making of Settler Colonialism, 1770–1842* (Cambridge: Cambridge University Press, 2022), 171 ('boarding'); 'Cambridge Bible Association', *Cambridge Chronicle and Journal*, 8 August 1834 ('Satan'); 'Emancipated Negroes', *Cambridge Chronicle and Journal*, 11 September 1835 ('construction').
34. William Charles Dowding to William Whewell, 10 March c. 1852, William Whewell, Letters received by William Whewell, WL, Add. MS a/203/37-38 ('*academical*', 'Universities', '£25,000', 'kind', and 'name'); William Charles Dowding, *Africa in the West: Its State; Prospects; and Educational Needs: With Reference to Bishop Berkeley's Bermuda College* (Oxford and London: John Henry Parker, 1852), 4–5 ('crux' and 'solving'), 12 ('childhood'), and 14 ('graft'); Sarah Hannon and Neil Kennedy,

'"Slavery wears the mildest Aspect": Imagining Mastery and Emancipation in Bermuda's House of Assembly', The *Journal of Caribbean History* 53 (2019), 74, n. 9 ('4,297' and '4,898'); Susette Harriet Lloyd, *Sketches of Bermuda* (London: James Cochrane and Co., 1835), 245 ('disenfranchise').

35. Dowding, *Africa in the West*, 25 ('Cambridge'); John Gregory to William Charles Dowding, 26 July 1852, in *Accounts and Papers: Forty-Eight Volumes. Colonies. Auckland Islands; Ceylon; West Indies; Africa, &c.*, vol. 65 (London: H. M. Stationary Office, 1859), 4 ('fix'); Dowding, *Africa in the West*, 31–32 ('academic supporters'); Extract from Governor Charles Elliot, 2 June 1851, Despatches from Charles Elliot, governor of Bermuda, TNA, CO 37/135, f. 263 ('exertions'); 'The Seal of St. Paul's College, c. 1853', *National Museum of Bermuda*, https://nmb.bm/collection/the-seal-of-st-pauls-college-c-1853/, accessed 11 July 2023 ('curriculum'); Bishop of Newfoundland to Charles Elliot, 17 April 1851, Despatches from Charles Elliot, governor of Bermuda, TNA, CO 37/135, f. 264 ('noble').

36. Samuel Brownlow Gray, *The Revival of Bp. Berkeley's Bermuda College: A Letter to His Grace the Archbishop of Canterbury, Primate of all England, &c.* (London: Whitaker and Co., 1853), 3–4 ('human' and 'enemies'), 8 ('dangerous' and 'great names'), 12 ('fusion'), and 16 ('distinctions' and 'Oxford and Cambridge'); Thomas C. Holt, *The Problem of Freedom: Race, Labor, and Politics in Jamaica and Britain, 1832–1938* (Baltimore: Johns Hopkins University Press, 1991), 190 ('applied in Jamaica').

37. *Ibid.*, 284 ('racism'); Dubrulle, *Ambivalent Nation*, 100 ('Martineau'); Moses, Alexander Crummell, 57 ('warm reception') and 70–71 ('woolly' and 'following words').

38. A. C. Benson, *The Life of Edward White Benson: Sometime Archbishop of Canterbury*, vol. 1 (London: Macmillan and Co., 1899), 109 ('Three groans' and 'Three cheers'); Alexander Crummell, 'Eulogium on the Life and Character of Thomas Clarkson, Esq. of England', 26 December 1846, in Alexander Crummell, *Africa and America: Addresses and Discourses* (Springfield, MA: Wiley & Co., 1891), 208 ('no seat of learning').

39. Suman Seth, 'Race, Specificity, and Statistics in Victorian Medicine', *Journal of Victorian Culture* 27 (April 2022), 377 ('Prichardian'); Sir Humphry Rolleston, 'Sir George Murray Humphry, M.D., F.R.S.', *Annals of Medical History* 9 (Spring 1927), 1–3 ('exceeded expectations') and 4–7 ('advocated').

40. George Murray Humphry, *A Treatise on the Human Skeleton (Including the Joints)* (Cambridge: Macmillan and Co., 1858), 91 ('inferior', 'exhibit', 'intermediate', 'stature', 'less', 'cranium', and 'foot'), 93 ('ascent', 'actual size', and 'conformation'), 298 ('Congolese'), 98 ('growth' and 'development'), and 99 ('children').

41. George Moore, *The First Man and His Place in Creation* (London: Longmans, 1866), 334 ('several' and 'natural ability'); Jesse Page, *The Black Bishop: Samuel Adjai Crowther* (London: Hodder and Stoughton, 1908), 71 ('certain' and 'logical').

42. Dubois, *Avengers of the New World*, 166 ('Long live'); Sir James Fellowes, *Reports of the Pestilential Disorder of Andalusia, which Appeared at Cadiz in the Year 1800, 1804, 1810, and 1813* (London: Longman, Hurst, Rees, Orme, and Brown, 1815), title page ('Caian'), x ('melancholy'), and xi ('painful'); Payments made by Thomas Crafer for Allowances to St: Domingo Sufferers, between the 31st March 1839 and the 31st March 1840, Expired Commissions: Santo Domingo Claims Committee, West Indies Accounts, TNA, PRO 57/766 ('yearly pension' and '£130'); 'Sir Alexander Cockburn Obituary Notice, Monday, November 22, 1880', *Eminent Persons Biographies: Reprinted from The Times*, vol. 2 (London: Macmillan and Co., 1893), 222 ('marriage') and 223 ('Trinity Hall'); Summary of Bounty recommended, of Payments on Account, of Extra Payments; Receipts; and

General Balance, 14 October 1799, Santo Domingo Claims Commission: Minutes and Papers, TNA, T 81/18 ('1799'); Hersch Lauterpacht, ed., *Annual Digest and Reports of Public International Law Cases: Being a Selection from the Decisions of International and National Courts and Tribunals Given during the Years 1938-1940*, vol. 9 (Cambridge: Grotius Publications Ltd., 1988), 267 ('fugitive'); Oliver Gliech, 'Cockburn, comte' de', *Plantation and House Owners of St. Domingue, 1750-1803*, www.domingino.de/stdomin/index_colons_a_z_engl.html, accessed 16 October 2023 ('indemnity'). The Vigniers, according to a Cockburn family history, had 'suffered great misfortunes in the Revolution'. (Sir Robert Cockburn and Harry A. Cockburn, *The Records of the Cockburn Family* [London and Edinburgh: T. N. Foulis, 1913], 68.) See also David Geggus, *Slavery, War, and Revolution: The British Occupation of Saint Domingue, 1793-1798* (Oxford: Clarendon Press, 1982).

43. The names and amounts of donations can be found in *Subscriptions for Building a New Library, &c. &c. in the University of Cambridge* (Cambridge: Pitt Press, 1836), 9-39. These subscribers were then cross-referenced with the UCL slave-ownership database. For Cockerell's slaver connections, see J. Q. Davies, *Creatures of the Air: Music, Atlantic Spirits, Breath, 1817-1913* (Chicago: The University of Chicago Press, 2023), 110-111.

44. Alexander Crummell, *The Negro Race not under a Curse, an Examination of Genesis IX. 25* (London: Wertheim, Macintosh & Hunt, 1853), 7 ('used'), 21 ('severities', 'horrors' and '*modern*'), and 30 ('human'); 25 ('overworked' and 'exterminated'); Crummell, 'The Race-Problem in America', 20 November 1888, in Crummell, *Africa and America*, 54-55 ('syntax').

45. Tessa Roynon, *Toni Morrison & The Classical Tradition: Transforming American Culture* (Oxford: Oxford University Press, 2013), 81 ('classical examples'); Alexander Crummell, *Destiny and Race: Selected Writings, 1840-1898*, ed., by Wilson Jeremiah Moses (Amherst: University of Massachusetts Press, 1992), unpaginated e-book edition ('Cicero and Tacitus', 'maidenly', 'harlot', and 'inner life').

46. W. E. B. Du Bois, *The Souls of Black Folk*, ed. and intro. by Brent Hayes Edwards (Oxford: Oxford University Press, 2008), 145 and David Levering Lewis, *W. E. B. Du Bois: A Biography, 1868-1963* (New York: Henry Holt and Company, 2009), 118-121 ('lauded'); Oldfield, ed., *Civilization and Black Progress*, 7-9 ('relocated'); Alexander Crummell, *The Future of Africa: Being Addresses, Sermons, Etc., Etc., Delivered in the Republic of Liberia* (New York: Charles Scribner, 1862), 3-4 ('responsibility') and 53 ('slave-hunt').

47. Oldfield, ed., *Civilization and Black Progress*, 9-13 ('taught'); Crummell, *Africa and America*, v ('incapacity'), vii ('miracle'), and 53 ('fundamental dogma').

48. 'The Abolition of the African Slave Trade', *The Times*, 13 March 1907.

49. 'Universities' Mission to Central Africa', *The Cambridge Chronicle and University Journal, Isle of Ely Herald, and Huntingdonshire Gazette*, 11 November 1892 ('back to Africa' and 'soldiers of Christianity'); David Livingstone, *Dr Livingstone's Cambridge Lectures, Together with a Prefatory Letter By the Rev. Professor Sedgwick, M.A., F.R.S., &c.* (Cambridge: Deighton, Bell and Co., 1858), xxxiv ('admirably') and 78 ('harvest'); John Willis Clark, ed., *Endowments of the University of Cambridge* (Cambridge: Cambridge University Press, 1904), 429-430 ('Gedge'); Hausa Association to the Vice-Chancellor, 16 May 1896, *ibid.*, 278 ('Hausa language'); Samuel W. Baker, 'Slavery and the Slave Trade', *Macmillan's Magazine*, 30 (July 1874), 194 ('visiting lecturers' and 'annexation'); William Stone, *Shall We Annex Egypt: Remarks upon the Present Aspect of the Egyptian Question, Founded upon Observations made in the Country whilst Travelling in the Delta and in the Soudan* (London: Sampson Low, Marston, Searle, and Rivington, 1884), 12 ('recent

graduates'). Stone later donated £10,000 to Peterhouse – the largest post-foundation benefaction in its history. (William Stone, *The Squire of Piccadilly: Memories of William Stone in Conversation with Henry Baerlein* [London: Jarrolds, 1951], 17.)
50. 'Oxford and Cambridge Mission to Central Africa', *Oxford University Herald*, 21 May 1859.
51. *Ibid.* ('debt', 'opening', 'commerce', 'slavery', and 'Southern'); D. E. Nwulia, 'The Role of Missionaries in the Emancipation of Slaves in Zanzibar', *The Journal of Negro History* 60 (1975), 247, n. 22 ('20,000'). See also Andrew Porter, *Religion versus Empire? British Protestant Missionaries and Overseas Expansion, 1700–1914* (Manchester: Manchester University Press, 2004), 225–234.
52. Alexander H. Stephens, 'Cornerstone Address, March 21, 1861', in Frank Moore, ed., *The Rebellion Record: A Diary of American Events with Documents, Narratives, Illustrative Incidents, Poetry, etc.*, vol. 1 (New York: O. P. Putnam, 1862), 45–46 ('natural condition' and 'immediate'); 'Advertisements', *Cambridge Chronicle and University Journal, Isle of Ely Herald, and Huntingdonshire Gazette*, 25 May 1861 ('Tinted'). For the British pro-Confederates, see Duncan Andrew Campbell, *English Public Opinion and the American Civil War* (London: Boydell Press, 2003), esp. ch. 5; Amanda Foreman, *A World on Fire: Britain's Crucial Role in the American Civil War* (New York: Random House, 2012); Alfred Grant, *The American Civil War and the British Press* (London: McFarland and Company, 2000); Dubrulle, *Ambivalent Nation*; and John D. Bennett, *The London Confederates: The Officials, Clergy, Businessmen and Journalists Who Backed the American South during the Civil War* (London: McFarland and Company, 2008). For the secession crisis in the United States, see also William W. Freehling and Craig M. Simpson, eds., *Secession Debated: Georgia's Showdown in 1860* (New York: Oxford University Press, 1992); and Russell McClintock, *Lincoln and the Decision for War: The Northern Response to Secession* (Chapel Hill: University of North Carolina Press, 2008).
53. Cambridge and Kingsley on American Affairs, *Christian Examiner*, November 1863 ('nowhere greater', 'overmastering', 'tariffs', 'triumph', and 'all hands'); Richard D. Fulton, '"Now Only the Times is on our Side": The London Times and America Before the Civil War', *Victorian Review* 16 (Summer 1990), 50 ('anti-abolitionist'). In 1863, *The Times* publicly opposed the Emancipation Proclamation of 1 January that year, which stated that all enslaved persons held within the Confederate states were free. The paper described it as 'measure which is not freedom to the blacks, but is, as far as possible, massacre to the women and children of the whites'. (*The Times*, 5 March 1863). The *Times*'s pro-Southern approach had earned a stinging rebuke from Samuel R. Calthrop, who wrote a letter in February 1863 to the *Daily News* in London from Marblehead, Massachusetts, as a man 'late of Trinity College, Cambridge'. He wrote that the *Times* was out of touch with American public opinion on enslavement and had misunderstood the origins of the 'great American contest', which had broken out, he claimed, because of 'slavery, and slavery alone'. ('The American War', *The Daily News*, 2 March 1863.)
54. 12 February 1862, Minute Book of Cambridge Union Society, CUL, USOC 1/1/1/17 ('regret'); 9 December 1861, *ibid.* ('seizure'); 28 and 29 October 1862, *ibid.* ('misrepresentation'); 14 February 1865, *ibid.*, 18 ('Stability of all Government'). See also the debates on 26 November 1861, 9 December 1861, 11 February 1862, 12 February 1862, 28 October 1862, 24 February 1863, 27 October 1863, 17 February 1864, 14 February 1865, and 14 November 1865, *ibid.*, 17–18.
55. Ellis Yarnall, *Wordsworth and the Coleridges: With Other Memories, Literary and Political* (London: Macmillan and Co., 1899), 187 ('heiress', 'encouraging', and

'Southern'); Robert E. Lee to Mary Anna Randolph Custis Lee, 27 December 1856, *Lee Family Digital Archive*, https://leefamilyarchive.org/9-family-papers/339-robert-e-lee-to-mary-anna-randolph-custis-lee-1856-december-27, accessed 6 December 2021 ('instruction'). John O. Waller argues that his opinions 'defy prediction and are still relatively resistant to rational explanation'. ('Charles Kingsley and the American Civil War', *Studies in Philology* 60 [July 1963]: 554.) Owen Chadwick writes that it was 'odd' to find him 'on the Confederate side in the American Civil War'. ('Charles Kingsley at Cambridge', *HJ* 18 [June 1975], 317.)

56. Chadwick, 'Kingsley at Cambridge', 304 ('first in classics') and 322 ('novels'); John C. Cobden, *The White Slaves of England* (Auburn: Derby and Miller, 1853), 193 ('White Slavery').

57. American Affairs, *Christian Examiner*, November 1863 ('abolitionism'); Waller, 'Kingsley and the American Civil War', 557 ('Free-Soil'); Charles Kingsley, *Two Years Ago*, vol. 1 (London: Macmillan and Co., 1857), ii–iii ('tainted', 'philanthropists', and 'disruption').

58. Charles Kingsley, *The Roman and the Teuton: A Series of Lectures Delivered Before the University of Cambridge* (London: Macmillan and Co., 1864), 305 ('Teutonic'); Jonathan Conlin, 'An Illiberal Descent: Natural and National History in the Work of Charles Kingsley', *History* 96 (April 2011), 186–187 ('family of Teutonic races'); Francis Kingsley, ed., *Charles Kingsley: His Letters and Memories of His Life*, vol. 2 (New York: Charles Scribner's Sons, 1885), 107 ('chimpanzees'); Robert Bernard Martin, *The Dust of Combat: A Life of Charles Kingsley* (New York: Macmillan, 1960), 257 ('rapacity'); Margaret Farrand Thorp, *Charles Kingsley, 1819–1875* (Princeton, NJ: Princeton University Press, 1937), 150 ('amenable'); Charles Kingsley, *The Gospel of the Pentateuch: A Set of Parish Sermons* (London: Parker, Son, and Bourn, 1863), 18 ('know not'); Waller, 'Kingsley and the American Civil War', 562 ('noble').

59. *Ibid.*, 561 ('lectures'); Kingsley, *Roman and the Teuton*, 20 ('domestic' and 'gentleman') and 169 ('chivalrous', 'unarmed', and 'masters').

60. Charles Kingsley, *The Limits of Exact Science as Applied to History: An Inaugural Lecture, Delivered Before the University of Cambridge* (Cambridge and London: Macmillan and Co., 1860) ('*Limits*'); Charles Kingsley to Sir Charles Bunbury, 31 December 1861, in Kingsley, ed., *Charles Kingsley*, vol. 1, 319 ('American', 'Professor', and 'gain to us'); *ibid.*, vol. 2, 311 ('captive'); 'American Affairs', *Christian Examiner*, November 1863 ('unique country', 'fugitive', 'moral', and 'torrents').

61. *Ibid.*, ('worse evil', 'political existence', 'Confederacy', and 'Man after man'); Kingsley, ed., *Charles Kingsley*, vol. 2, 150–151 ('sobbed').

62. Beckert, *Empire of Cotton*, 243 ('77') and 247 ('six'); Charles Kingsley to the Editor of *The Times*, undated, in Kingsley, ed., *Charles Kingsley*, vol. 2, 137 ('very Lancashire' and 'distress'); Charles Kingsley to a Millowner, undated, *ibid.*, 137–138 ('broad', 'nearly', 'independent', 'effeminates', and 'emigrate').

63. Gad J. Heuman, *'The Killing Time': The Morant Bay Rebellion in Jamaica* (Knoxville: University of Tennessee Press, 1994) ('400' and '300'); Jake Subryan Richards, 'Political Thought and the Emotion of Shame: John Stuart Mill and the Jamaica Committee during the Governor Eyre Controversy', *Modern Intellectual History* (2022), 1–21 ('investigate'); George Gawler, 'Governor Edward John Eyre', *The Times*, 5 December 1865 ('Kingsley'); 'Eyre Defence and Aid Fund', *The Times*, 12 September 1866 ('Ruskin'); John Ruskin, *Cambridge School of Art. Mr. Ruskin's Inaugural Address* (Cambridge: Deighton, Bell, and Co. 1858) ('School of Art'); Clark, *Endowments*, 498 ('Fitzwilliam'); Roderick Murchison, 'The Prosecution of

Ex-Governor Eyre', *The Times*, 23 May 1868 ('distinguished'); 'Sir Roderick Impey Murchison', *Legacies*, www.ucl.ac.uk/lbs/person/view/2146644333, accessed 1 March 2023 ('Tourama').

64. Helga M. Griffin, 'Henry Ling Roth (1855–1925)', *Australian Dictionary of Biography*, https://adb.anu.edu.au/biography/roth-henry-ling-8278, accessed 16 January 2024 ('Guiana'); Joseph Beaumont, *The New Slavery: An Account of the Indian and Chinese Immigrants in British Guiana* (London: W. Ridgway, 1871), 6 ('new slavery'); Sheldon Amos, *The Existing Laws of Demerara for the Regulation of Coolie Immigration* (London: Social Science Association, 1871), 2 ('revival') and 18 ('Blakesley'); 14 January 1949, Minutes of Meetings, Labour Situation in British Guiana, TNA, CO 946/1 ('form of forced labour' and 'Estate'); 17 January 1949, *ibid*. ('thief' and 'serve'); Edward Jenkins, *The Coolie: His Rights and Wrongs* (New York: George Routledge and Sons, 1871), 25 ('Cambridge graduates').

65. Henry Ling Roth Research Fund, 1972–1988, University Registry subject files, 1896–2019, CUL, GBR/0265/UA/R188/1972, Box 1332 ('research fund'); Russell McDougall and Iain Davidson, 'Introduction', in Russell McDougall and Iain Davidson eds., *The Roth Family, Anthropology, and Colonial Administration* (London and New York: Routledge, 2008), 13 ('Guiana'); Henry Ling Roth, *A Sketch of the Agriculture and Peasantry of Eastern Russia* (London: Baillière, Tindall, & Cox, 1878), 82 ('demoralizing'); Tracey Banivanua-Mar, 'The Contours of Agency: Women's Work, Race, and Queensland's Indentured Labor Trade', in Carol Williams, ed., *Indigenous Women and Work: From Labor to Activism* (Urbana, Chicago: University of Illinois Press, 2012), 74 ('63,000'); Tracey Banivanua-Mar, *Violence and Colonial Dialogue: The Australian-Pacific Indentured Labour Trade* (Honolulu: University of Hawaii Press, 2007), 53 ('prison' and 'free'), 55 ('forty'), and 248 ('Metropolis'); Griffin, 'Roth' ('contracted', 'report', and 'two papers'); 'Meeting of the Mackay Planters and Farmers Association', *Mackay Mercury*, 5 April 1884, in Henry Ling Roth's Cuttings on the Queensland sugar industry, CUL, GBR/0115/RCS/RCMS 294 ('active member'); Henry Ling Roth, 'To the Editor of the *Pall Mall Gazette*', 6 April 1883, in *ibid*. ('paradise', 'pandemonium', 'death rates', 'hospitals', 'savage life', 'disgusting', and 'general welfare'); Russell McDougall and Julian Croft, 'Henry Ling Roth's and George Kingsley Roth's Pacific Anthropology', *The Journal of Pacific History* 40 (September 2005), 149 ('Fijian').

66. Ged Martin, 'The Cambridge Lectureship of 1866: A False Start in American Studies', *Journal of American Studies* 7 (April 1973), 22 ('Kingsley' and '$6,000') and 27–28 ('self-conceit'); 'Joseph Brooks Yates', *Legacies*, www.ucl.ac.uk/lbs/person/view/21522, accessed 16 April 2022 ('plantation'); Nicholas Draper, 'British Universities and Caribbean Slavery', in Jill Pellew and Lawrence Goldman, eds., *Dethroning Historical Reputations: Universities, Museums, and the Commemoration of Benefactors* (London: Institute of Historical Research, 2018), 98 ('experienced'); Christopher Chancellor, ed., *An Englishman in the American Civil War: The Diaries of Henry Yates Thompson* (New York: New York University Press, 1971), 14 ('abolitionist' and 'understanding').

67. Emily Davies to Barbara Bodichon, 12 March 1863, in Ann B. Murphy and Deidre Raftery, eds., *Emily Davies: Collected Letters, 1861–1875* (Charlottesville: University of Virginia Press, 2004), 42 ('slave-grown cotton'); Emily Davies to Henry Tomkinson, 14 November 1865, in *ibid*., 162 ('restored', 'extorted', and 'insurrection'); 'Henry and Elizabeth Yates Thompson', *Newnham College, University of Cambridge*, https://newn.cam.ac.uk/about/history/biographies/, accessed 4 April 2022 ('funding'); 'Glimpses of Girton: Catherine Gamble', 22 April 2018, *Girton*

College, Cambridge, www.girton.cam.ac.uk/news/glimpses-girton-jane-catherine-gamble, accessed 15 June 2023 ('bequest funded'); Last Will and Testament of John G. Gamble, 6 December 1852, Florida County Judge's Court (Leon County) Probate Records, 1827–1887, microfilm, GSU, 167–177 and 'Lands of Col. John G. Gamble', *Floridian & Journal*, 2 October 1858 ('Floridian'); Journal: 'Fragments of a Life', 1876–1879, Personal Papers of Jane Catherine Gamble, 1783–1884, GCA, GBR/0271/GCPP Gamble 1/35, 7–8 ('pernicious influence'); Account of the estate of the late James and N. G. Dunlop, 1847, *ibid.*, 2/5 ('bonds' and 'Canal'). Thompson also donated to the British Museum, but his Cambridge benefaction was more impactful in Newnham's early history, providing the College with a Library in 1897 and then in 1907 donating funds to double its capacity.

68. Charles Priestley, ed., 'A Philosopher's Defense of the Confederacy: Jermyn Cowell to Henry Sidgwick, September 1863', *North & South* 9 (May 2006), 82–88 ('Trinity graduate'); *The Index*, 3 September 1863 ('Relief Fund'); John Jermyn Cowell to Henry Sidgwick, 15 September 1863, Letters Received by Henry Sidgwick, WL, Add. MS c/93/93 ('devastation', 'rebel states', 'injuries', 'sudden liberation', and 'emancipation'); Bart Schultz, *Henry Sidgwick – Eye of the Universe: An Intellectual Biography* (Cambridge: Cambridge University Press, 2004), 647 ('softened'); Henry Sidgwick to Mary Sidgwick, 15 May 1865, Letters Received by Henry Sidgwick, WL, Add. MS c/99/46 ('federal'). The Cowells were close to the British educationalist, historian, and King's fellow Oscar Browning too. John Jermyn became acquainted with Browning through the Union. (Oscar Browning, *Memories of Sixty Years at Eton, Cambridge and Elsewhere* [London: John Lane, 1910], 39). See also John Jermyn Cowell to Oscar Browning, 6 June 1860 and 21 July 1860, John Jermyn and John Welsford Cowell Letters to Oscar Browning, KCA, GBR/0272/OB/1/412/A.

69. W. C. Lubenow, *The Cambridge Apostles, 1820–1914: Liberalism, Imagination, and Friendship in British Intellectual and Professional Life* (Cambridge: Cambridge University Press, 1998), 310–311 ('Union's virtues'); Henry Jackson, 'The Hon. William Everett', *Cambridge Review*, 3 March 1910, 316 ('panegyric' and 'tie flaming').

70. William Everett, *On the Cam: Lectures on the University of Cambridge in England* (Cambridge, MA: Harvard University Press, 1865), 371 ('difference' and 'landed interest'), 362 ('governing'), 377 ('literary'), and 380 ('whole English race'). For race, ethnicity, and the special relationship, see also Duncan Bell, *Dreamworlds of Race: Empire and the Utopian Destiny of Anglo-America* (Princeton, NJ: Princeton University Press, 2020).

71. 'John Welsford Cowell', *Legacies*, www.ucl.ac.uk/lbs/person/view/11832, accessed 4 August 2021 ('trustee'); Michael Taylor, 'Conservative Political Economy and the Problem of Colonial Slavery, 1823–1833', *HJ* 57 (2014), 986 ('Political Economy Club'); Bennett, *London Confederates*, 39 ('branches'); Jessica M. Lepler, *The Many Panics of 1837: People, Politics, and the Creation of a Transatlantic Financial Crisis* (Cambridge: Cambridge University Press, 2013), 57 ('panics'); John Welsford Cowell, *France and the Confederate States* (London: Robert Hardwicke, 1865), 11–12 ('Calhoun') and 12 ('cotton' and 'unavoidable necessity'); John C. Calhoun, 'Speech on the Reception of Abolition Petitions', February 1837, in *Speeches of John C. Calhoun: Delivered in the Congress of the United States from 1811 to the Present Time* (New York: Harper & Brothers, 1843), 225 ('positive good').

72. T. E. Gregory, *The Westminster Bank: Through a Century*, pref. by the Hon. Rupert E. Beckett, vol. 2 (London: Westminster Bank Limited, 1936), 188–202 ('Alderman'

and 'emancipation'); Thomas E. Sebrell II, *Persuading John Bull: Union and Confederate Propaganda in Britain, 1860-65* (New York, NY: Lexington Books, 2014), 212 ('supporter'); 'British Jackson Monumental Fund', *The Index*, 23 July 1863 ('donated').

73. 22 October 1857, Minute book of the board of directors of London & Westminster Bank, NatWest, LWB/234/3, 462 ('loan'); 21 June 1854, *ibid.*, 288 ('Railway'); *Reports from Commissioners: Oxford and Cambridge*, vol. 20, 7 ('building works'); Gregory, *Westminster Bank*, vol. 2, 188 ('non-attendance'); *ibid.*, vol. 1, 264-265 ('fall from our grasp'); Douglas M. Peers, *India under Colonial Rule: 1700-1885* (London and New York: Routledge, 2006), 64 ('800,000'); 'David Lionel Salomons', *ACAD*, https://venn.lib.cam.ac.uk/cgi-bin/search-2016.pl?sur=&suro=w&fir=&firo=c&cit=&cito=c&c=all&z=all&tex=SLMS870DL&sye=&eye=&col=all&maxcount=50, accessed 11 April 2022 ('alma mater').

74. Original Correspondence from John W. Cowell, February 1840 to 1852, New Zealand Company Original Correspondence, TNA, CO 208/11 ('corresponded'); 'Terms of a Purchase of Land in the Settlement of Otago', in Cuthbert W. Johnson and William Shaw, ed., *The Farmers' Almanac and Calendar*, vol. 3 (London: James Ridgway, 1847-48), 158-161 ('land purchase'); Colonial William Wakefield to John Welsford Cowell, 10 November 1842, New Zealand Company, TNA, CO 208/11 ('statistical'). See also John W. Cowell to Charles Cox, 1 November 1853, in *A Letter from J. W. Cowell, Esq., to Sir George Grey, K.C.B. Late Governor of New Zealand, On the Mode of the Freeing that Colony from the Tax Imposed Upon it of Paying £268,000 to the New Zealand Company* (London: Raynell and Wight, 1854), 7-8. Though it was involved in sending the first four ships to New Zealand, the Association was not a success, and its business was concluded in 1855. See *Canterbury Papers: Information Concerning the Principles, Objects, Plans, & Proceedings of the Founders of the Settlement of Canterbury, in New Zealand*, 10 vols. (London: John W. Parker, 1850).

75. J. F. Jameson, 'The London Expenditures of the Confederate Secret Service', *The American Historical Review* 35 (July 1930), 816 ('Confederate agents'); John Welsford Cowell, *Southern Secession* (London: Robert Hardwicke, 1862), 33 ('very object' and 'absolute independence'); John Welsford Cowell, *Lancashire's Wrongs and the Remedy: Two Letters Addressed to the Cotton Operatives of Great Britain* (London: Robert Hardwicke, 1863), 29 ('protectionist'); Cowell, *France*, 8 ('monopolists') and 18 ('yoke').

76. Cowell, *Lancashire's Wrongs*, 33 ('peasantry') and 5 ('Operatives'); Cowell, *Southern Secession*, 18-19 ('natural' and 'mutually') and 32 ('noble'); Catherine Hall, 'Reconfiguring Race: The Stories the Slave-Owners Told', in Hall et al., eds., *Legacies of British Slave-Ownership*, 163-202 ('participants'). See Ritchie D. Watson, Jr., *The Cavalier in Virginia Fiction* (Baton Rouge: Louisiana State University Press, 1985).

77. Martin G. Buist, *At Specs Non Fracta: Hope & Co. 1770-1815: Merchant Bankers and Diplomats at Work* (The Hague: Nijhoff, 1974), 20 ('loans'); Alexander Beresford Hope, *Essays* (London: Francis & John Rivington, 1844) and Alexander Beresford Hope, *The English Cathedral of the Nineteenth Century* (London: John Murray, 1861) ('busy'); Alexander Beresford Hope, *A Popular View of the American Civil War* (London, James Ridgway, 1861), 11 ('inherited'); Bennett, *London Confederates*, 167-170 ('Fund'); 'Hope, Alexander Beresford', *ACAD*, https://venn.lib.cam.ac.uk/cgi-bin/search-2018.pl?sur=&suro=w&fir=&firo=c&cit=&cito=c&c=all&z=all&tex=HP837AJ&sye=&eye=&col=all&maxcount=50, accessed 17 January 2022 ('1868'). See

also 'William John Bankes', *Legacies*, www.ucl.ac.uk/lbs/person/view/2146645443, accessed 9 July 2021; and 'Sir Nicholas Conyngham Tindal', *Legacies*, www.ucl.ac.uk/lbs/person/view/7212, accessed 9 July 2021.

78. Hope, *Popular View*, 10–11 ('ultra-abolitionists' and 'untaught'), 35 ('cruel war'), 28 ('massacre'), and 36 ('right arm of strength'); Alexander Beresford Hope, *The Results of the American Disruption: The Substance of a Lecture Delivered by Request Before the Maidstone Literary & Mechanics' Institution, In Continuation of A Popular View of the American Civil War, and England, the North, and the South* (London: James Ridgway, 1862), 16 ('principles of self-dependence'). For the Black Confederate myth, see Kevin M. Levin, *Searching for Black Confederates: The Civil War's Most Persistent Myth* (Chapel Hill: University of North Carolina Press, 2019).

79. Stephen B. Oates, 'Henry Hotze: Confederate Agent Abroad', *The Historian* 27 (February 1965), 133–134 ('emigrated'); Dubrulle, *Ambivalent Nation*, 108 ('Gobineau'); Charles M. Hubbard, *The Burden of Confederate Diplomacy* (Knoxville: The University of Tennessee Press, 1998), 100 ('seven hundred'); Lonnie A. Burnett, ed., *Henry Hotze, Confederate Propagandist: Selected Writings on Revolution, Recognition, and Race* (Tuscaloosa: The University of Alabama Press, 2008), 19 ('paid journalists') and 20–22 ('opinion').

80. Henry Hotze to Hon. J. B. Benjamin, 13 February 1864, in Colonel Harry Kidder White, ed., *Official Records of the Union and Confederate Navies in the War of the Rebellion*, vol. 3 (Washington, D.C.: Naval War Records Office 1922), 1025 ('locality'); Henry Hotze to Hon. J. B. Benjamin, 29 July 1864, *ibid.*, 1178 ('permanent root' and 'two gentlemen'); Oates, 'Henry Hotze', 151 ('idea'); Richard Barksdale Harwell, ed., 'The Creed of a Propagandist: Letter from a Confederate Editor', *Journalism Quarterly* 28 (Spring 1951), 215 ('identified').

81. Zoë Laidlaw, *Protecting the Empire's Humanity: Thomas Hodgkin and British Colonial Activism, 1830–1870* (Cambridge: Cambridge University Press, 2021), 81 ('Ethnological'); Seth, 'Race, Specificity, and Statistics', 379 ('polygenism'); James Hunt, 'On the Negro's Place in Nature', in *Memoirs Read Before the Anthropological Society of London, 1863–4* (London: Trübner and Co., 1865), 55 ('improvement' and 'impunity') and 56 ('diseases'); Kathryn Olivarius, *Necropolis: Disease, Power, and Capitalism in the Cotton Kingdom* (Cambridge, MA: Harvard University Press, 2022), 81 ('immune').

82. Barbara Black, *A Room of His Own: A Literary-Cultural Study of Victorian Clubland* (Athens: Ohio University Press, 2012), 170 ('Cannibal Club'); Edmund Gosse, *Books on the Table* (New York, NY: Charles Scribner's Sons, 1921), 64 ('dined') and 65 ('Bendyshe'); 'Twelfth List of the Foundation Fellows of the Anthropological Society of London', in Thomas Bendyshe, ed., *The Anthropological Treatises of Johann Friedrich Blumenbach, Late Professor at Göttingen and Court Physician to the King of Great Britain* (London: Longman, Roberts, & Green, 1865), 3–16 ('Cambridge-affiliated men'); John S. Michael, 'Nuance Lost in Translation: Interpretations of J. F. Blumenbach's Anthropology in the English Speaking World', *NTM: International Journal of History & Ethics of Natural Sciences Technology & Medicine* 25 (July 2017), 291 ('oversimplified'); Thomas Bendyshe, 'On the Extinction of Races', *Journal of the Anthropological Society of London* 2 (1864), xcix–cxiii ('extinction').

83. James Hunt, *Anniversary Address Delivered Before the Anthropological Society of London, January 5th, 1864* (London: Anthropological Society of London, 1864), 21 ('ASL'); 'John George Witt', *ACAD*, https://venn.lib.cam.ac.uk/cgi-bin/search-2018

.pl?sur=&suro=w&fir=&firo=c&cit=&cito=c&c=all&z=all&tex=WT856JG&sye=&eye=&col=all&maxcount=50, accessed 17 January 2022 ('matriculated'); John George Witt, *Life in the Law* (London: T. Werner Laurie, 1906), 141 ('met') and 143 ('entered'); 12 February 1861, Minute Book of Cambridge Union Society, CUL, USOC 1/1/1/17 ('probable').

84. Henry Hotze to John George Witt, 11 August 1864, Henry Hotze Letter and Dispatch Book, LARC, 90 ('highest ideal'); Witt, *Life*, 144 ('Southern cause') and 156 ('free off-hand', 'property', 'creed', and 'demarcation'); John George Witt, 'In Ducem Illustrissimum', *The Index*, 2 June 1864 ('poem'). Hotze's attention to the universities was not unusual or unprecedented. One southern enslaver identified Oxford University as the 'eye' and 'telescope' of 'British policy'. (Samuel A. Cartwright, 'The Education, Labor, and Wealth of the South', in E. N. Elliott, ed., *Cotton is King, and Pro-Slavery Arguments* [Augusta, GA: Pritchard, Abbott & Loomis, 1860], 893).

85. Witt, *Life*, 146 and 148 ('remained in contact'), 154 ('dinner'), 157 ('many looks'), 158–159 ('rich inheritance', 'laughed', and 'delightful'); Jefferson Davis to John George Witt, 4 December 1868, in Lynda Lasswell Crist et al., *The Papers of Jefferson Davis*, vol. 12 (Baton Rouge: Louisiana State University Press, 2008), 331 ('Cambridge'). These exiles settled in many countries, including Brazil, Mexico, and Britain. See Michael L. Conniff and Cyrus B. Dawsey, eds., *The Confederados: Old South Immigrants in Brazil* (Auburn: University of Alabama Press, 1987); William Clark Griggs, *The Elusive Eden: Frank McMullan's Confederate Colony in Brazil* (Austin: University of Texas Press, 1987); and Daniel E. Sutherland, 'Exiles, Emigrants, and Sojourners: The Post-Civil War Confederate Exodus in Perspective', *Civil War History* 31 (September 1985), 237–256.

86. Witt, *Life*, 160 ('introduced') and 166–167 ('Great Seal' and 'American citizen'). Thanks, in part, to Witt's efforts, Benjamin did not die a poor man. His executors, including Witt and Lindsay Middleton Appland (another London barrister), appraised the estate at over £60,221. From 1867 to 1882, Benjamin had earnt more than £143,900 from his work at the English bar. (Pierce Butler, *Judah P. Benjamin* [Philadelphia: George W. Jacobs & Company, 1906], 419 ['appraised'] and 441 ['work'].)

Conclusion

1. List of Tharp Estates & Number of Slaves in 1817, Tharp Papers, CA, R55/7/123/16 ('Weippart' and 'list'); Sarah M. S. Pearsall, *Atlantic Families: Lives and Letters in the Later Eighteenth Century* (Oxford: Oxford University Press, 2008), 213, n. 12 ('Trinity'); 'Splendid Entertainment at Windsor Castle', *The Court Journal. From January to December 1833* (London: Henry Colburn, 1833), 212 ('birthday'); Robert Livingston Schuyler, 'The Constitutional Claims of the British West Indies: The Controversy over the Slave Registry Bill of 1815', *Political Science Quarterly* 40 (March 1925), 6 ('Registry').

2. Ruth Simmons, 'Hidden in Plain Sight: Slavery and Justice in Rhode Island', *The Eagle*, 2007, 54 ('intrigued'); Lauren Egan, 'Biden Signs into Law Bill Establishing Juneteenth as Federal Holiday', *NBC News*, www.nbcnews.com/politics/whitehouse/biden-signs-law-bill-establishing-juneteenth-federal-holiday-n1271213, accessed 17 June 2021 ('Juneteenth'); John R. Oldfield and Mary Wills, 'Remembering

1807: Lessons from the Archives', *History Workshop Journal* 90 (Autumn 2020), 253–272 ('nationalistic'); Erik Gøbel, *The Danish Slave Trade and Its Abolition* (Leiden: Brill, 2016), 177 ('1803').

3. The interconnections between British society and culture and the empire to the present have been more recently discussed in Sathnam Sanghera, *Empireland: How Imperialism Has Shaped Modern Britain* (New York: Pantheon Books, 2023); and Charlotte Lydia Riley, *Imperial Island: An Alternative History of the British Empire* (Cambridge, MA: Harvard University Press, 2024).

BIBLIOGRAPHY

Archival Material

All Souls College Archive, University of Oxford

Account Books of Codrington's Legacy and Lloyd's Benefaction
Papers Concerning the Building of the College

Bank of England, London

Accountant's Department: Old South Sea Company Annuities Ledgers
New South Sea Company Annuities Ledgers

Bodleian Library, University of Oxford

Archive of the Anti-Slavery Society
Papers from a letter book belonging to Sir Joseph Banks
Papers of the Society for the Propagation of the Gospel in Foreign Parts

British Library, London

Correspondence of Bishop Berkeley, 1710–1828
Correspondence of Charles Yorke Regarding Cambridge University, 1752–1770
Correspondence of Walter Pollard, 1771–1788
Fair Minute Books of the Committee for the Abolition of the Slave Trade
Indenture for the Settlement of Lands
The Liverpool Papers
Papers of the Royal Mines Company, Jamaica
The Patent of the Hudson's Bay Company
Stocks and Bonds of the East India Company

Cadbury Research Library, University of Birmingham

Church Mission Society Unofficial Papers

Cambridgeshire Archive, Ely

Business Records of Cambridgeshire Manors
Election Broadsides
Registers and Service of the Gamlingay Parish Church
Tharp Family Papers

Cambridge University Library

Archives of the Department of Geology and the Woodwardian and Sedgwick Museums, 1731–1987
Association for Promoting the Discovery of Interior Parts of Africa: Papers
Cholmondeley (Houghton) Papers
Henry Ling Roth's Cuttings on the Queensland sugar industry
Leases of Doctors Commons, 1671–1765
Legacies absolute/contingent and reversionary, summary volume, 1735–1904
Letters received from various dignitaries, 1613–1868
The Macclesfield Collection
Nevil Maskelyne: Personal and Family Papers
Papers of the Board of Longitude
Papers of the Bulama Association
Papers of the Cambridge Union
Records of and relating to academic officers, 1620–2014
Representatives in Parliament, 1614–1934
Society for Promoting Christian Knowledge Archive
Tripos verses and lists, 1768–1802
University registry guard books, 1327–2000
University Registry miscellanea, 1544–1988
University Registry subject files, 1896–2019
University scholarship awards and prizes records, 1649–2015
Vice-Chancellor's Court records, 1498–1957
Wiles Family correspondence and genealogical papers

Christ's College Muniments Room, University of Cambridge

Letters from Thomas Thompson

Clare College Archive, University of Cambridge

Blythe Benefaction

Corpus Christi College Archives, University of Cambridge

Bursar's and Other Financial Records
Cambridge, St Edward's Parish deeds

Deeds relating to the college tenement in Bene't Street
Dr Spencer's Account, 1693–1929
Papers relating to Archbishop Thomas Tenison's Bequest, 1713–1723

Earl Gregg Swem Library, College of William and Mary, Williamsburg

St George Tucker Papers

East Sussex Record Office, Brighton, UK

Books, Plans, and Account Books of the Fuller Family
Papers of Rose Fuller
Papers of Stephen Fuller

Genealogical Society of Utah, Salt Lake City, Utah

Florida County Judge's Court (Leon County) Probate Records, 1827–1887

Girton College Archive, University of Cambridge

Personal Papers of Jane Catherine Gamble, 1783–1884

Gonville and Caius College Lower Library, University of Cambridge

College Bursar Books
Master/Registry Gesta, 1849–1857
Papers concerning foundation and fellowships; and papers relating to the Mastership of Sir John Ellys
Private Diary of Charles Clayton
Stockton Benefaction Account
Thomas Gooch Letters and Correspondence
Wortley Benefaction Account

Houghton Library, Harvard University, Cambridge, Massachusetts

William Fleetwood Manuscript Documents

Jesus College Archive, University of Cambridge

Dr Caryl's Book on Statutes, Trusts, &c., College Statutes

John J. Burns Library, Boston College, Massachusetts

Stephen Fuller Letterbooks in the Williams Ethnological Collection

King's College Archive Center, University of Cambridge

John Jermyn and John Welsford Cowell Letters to Oscar Browning
Receipts for money paid to the College, 1441–1918
Wills, 1800–1914

Lambeth Palace Library, London

Papers of the Bishop of London: Correspondence and papers on the church overseas
Register of Subscriptions and Donations

Lancashire Archives, Preston, United Kingdom

W. J. Dickson & Sons, Solicitors, Kirkham

Liverpool Record Office, Liverpool, UK

Letters of William Smyth to Dr Currie
Tarleton family correspondence, including letters and papers of Clayton Tarleton (1762–1797) during his mayoralty, 1792–93

Louisiana Historical Center, Louisiana State Museums, New Orleans

Julien Poydras Letterbook

Louisiana Research Collection, Tulane University, New Orleans

Henry Hotze Letter and Dispatch Book (Original in Library of Congress)

Magdalene College Archive, University of Cambridge

Magdalene College Register III, 1675–1814
Nicholas Ferrar Papers
Thomas Chapman Papers

The National Archives, Kew, London

Books Concerning Stock in the Royal African Company
Despatches from Charles Elliot, governor of Bermuda

Expired Commissions: Santo Domingo Claims Committee, West Indies Accounts
Letters, Papers, and Domestic Correspondence of George III
Minutes of Meetings, Labour Situation in British Guiana
New Zealand Company Original Correspondence
Prerogative Court of Canterbury and related Probate Jurisdictions: Will Registers
Santo Domingo Claims Commission: Minutes and Papers
State Papers Domestic, George I
State Papers Domestic, Queen Anne
Transfer Books for the Company of Royal Adventurers Trading with Africa

National Library of Jamaica, Kingston

Case of implementation of Treaty of England with Spain, 1713 and 1717, re. tonnage and unloading of yearly ship to the West Indies, sent by South Sea Company, argued by Nathaniel Lloyd

NatWest Group Archives, Edinburgh, UK

Minute book of the board of directors of London & Westminster Bank

New York Public Library, New York

Robert Beverley Papers

Norfolk Record Office, Norwich, UK

Journal of Hanson Plantation Accounts, 1792
Letters to Sir Martin Browne Folkes re. Sir John Berney's affairs, his estate having been put in trust for the payment of his debts, mostly from Robert Fellowes of Shotesham and Lord Abergavenny Folkes' fellow trustees and Berney himself

North Yorkshire County Record Office, Northallerton, UK

Copies of Entries of Marske Parish Register

Queens' College Presidential Lodge, University of Cambridge

Book of Orders, 1787–1830

The Royal Archives, Windsor Castle, Windsor

Daniell Papers
George II Papers

The Royal Society, London

Journal Book of the Royal Society
Minutes of a Meeting of the Council of the Royal Society
Miscellaneous Manuscripts by, about or belonging to the Fellows of the Royal Society

Somerset Heritage Centre, Taunton, UK

Correspondence received by Francis Henry Dickinson (usually at Kingweston), 1833–1838
Correspondence received by Stephen Fuller (at Sussex, London, and elsewhere) relating mainly to estate matters, 1731–1757
Correspondence received by Stephen Fuller (at Sussex and London) relating mainly to estate and business matters (including Jamaica), 1758–1762

Trinity Hall Archive, University of Cambridge

Building Accounts, 1727–1730
Chest Book, 1690–1794
Master's Books, 1664–1799

Virginia Museum of History and Culture, Richmond

George Daniel Baylor Papers, 1743–1964
Robert Carter Letterbook, 1701–1732
Wormeley Family Papers 1671–1944

William L. Clements Library, University of Michigan, Ann Arbor

African American History Collection, 1729–1966
William Mildmay Papers, 1748–1756

William R. Laurie University Archives and Special Collections, University of the South, Sewanee, Tennessee

Charles Todd Quintard Papers
University of Cambridge Book Collection

Wren Library, Trinity College, University of Cambridge

Letters Received by Henry Sidgwick
Letters received by William Whewell
Library records: donors, c. 1680
Senior Bursar's Audit Books, 1739–1756

Newspapers, Magazines, and Periodicals

The Anti-Slavery Reporter
The Baptist Magazine
The Barbadian
Barbados Mercury and Bridge-Town Gazette
Boston Gazette
Cambridge Chronicle & Journal
Cambridge Independent Press
Cambridge Intelligencer
Cambridge Review
The Charleston Mercury
Christian Examiner
The Christian Remembrancer; or, The Churchman's Biblical, ecclesiastical & literary miscellany
Connecticut Gazette (New Haven)
Daily Journal
The Daily News
The Eagle
The Evening Post (New York)
Floridian & Journal
Gentleman's Magazine
Grenada Free Press, and Public Gazette
The Grub-Street Journal
The Index
The Leeds Intelligencer
Leigh Hunt's London Journal
London Evening Post
London Gazette
Massachusetts-Gazette
The Monthly Repository for 1835
The Monthly Review, From May to August Inclusive
The Morning Post
The New-Haven Gazette, and the Connecticut Magazine
The Norfolk Chronicle, or, the Norwich Gazette
Oxford Almanack
Oxford University Herald
The Phrenological Journal and Miscellany
Port Philip Gazette
The Public Advertiser
The Quarterly Review
The Royal Gazette (Jamaica)
The Scots Magazine
Sheffield Public Advertiser

South Carolina Gazette and American General Advertiser
The Sydney Morning Herald
The Times
Weekly Journal or British Gazetteer
Weekly Journal or Saturday's Post
The Weekly Miscellany For the Improvement of Husbandry, Trade, Arts, and Sciences
The Westminster Review

Databases

Dawson, J. L., *ACAD: A Cambridge Alumni Database*, https://venn.lib.cam.ac.uk/, accessed 3 March 2020.
Oxford English Dictionary, www.oed.com/, accessed 2 October 2020.
Legacies of British Slavery, www.ucl.ac.uk/lbs/search/, accessed 2 March 2020.
SlaveVoyages, www.slavevoyages.org/voyage/database, accessed 7 July 2023.

Legal Cases

R. v. George Hindmarsh, 168 E.R. 387 (1792).

Published Primary Sources

'1832 General Election – Cambridge', *UK General Election Results, 1832–2019*, https://api.parliament.uk/uk-general-elections/elections/53, accessed 12 September 2023.
Abdy, Edward Strutt, *American Whites and Blacks, In Reply to a German Orthodermist*. London: Charles Gilpin, 1842.
Journal of a Residence and Tour in the United States of North America, From April, 1833, to October, 1834, 3 vols. London: John Murray, 1835.
Abridgment of the Minutes of the Evidence: Taken Before a Committee of the whole House, to whom it was referred to consider of the Slave Trade, 4 vols. London: Unknown, 1789–91.
Abstract of the Proceeding of the Associates of Doctor Bray, For the Year 1785. London: Unknown, 1785.
Account of the Receipts & Disbursements of the Anti-Slavery Society for the Years 1823, 1824, 1825 & 1826: with a list of the subscribers. London: Bagster and Thomas, 1827.
Accounts and Papers: Forty-Eight Volumes. Colonies. Auckland Islands; Ceylon; West Indies; Africa, &c. Session 4 November 1852–20 August 1853, 48 vols. London: H. M. Stationary Office, 1859.
A Collection of Cambridge Senate-House Papers, In Homer, Virgil, Locke and Paley's Philosophy and Evidences, As Given At the Examination for B.A. Degrees. Cambridge: J. Hall and J. Hankin, 1832.

Acts of the Assembly, Passed in the island of Jamaica, from 1681, to 1737, inclusive. London: John Baskett, 1789.

Address of Incorporated Society for the Conversion and Religious Instruction and Education of the Negro Slaves in the British West India Islands. London: The Society, 1824.

A Full Report of the Proceedings at the Cambridge County Election, Commencing Tuesday, August 10, 1830. Cambridge: Matfield, 1830.

A General Description of All the Trades, Digested in Alphabetical Order: By which Parents, Guardians, and Trustees, may, with greater Ease and Certainty, make choice of Trades agreeable to the Capacity, Education, Inclination, Strength, and Fortune of the Youth under their Care. London: T. Waller, 1747.

Ainger, Alfred, ed., *The Letters of Charles Lamb Newly Arranged, with Additions*, 2 vols. New York: A. C. Armstrong & Son, 1894.

A Letter from J. W. Cowell, Esq., to Sir George Grey, K. C. B. Late Governor of New Zealand, On the Mode of the Freeing that Colony from the Tax Imposed Upon it of Paying £268,000 to the New Zealand Company. London: Raynell and Wight, 1854.

A List of the Society, Instituted in 1787, For the Purpose of effecting the Abolition of the Slave Trade. London: Unknown, 1787.

The Alumni Bulletin of the University of Virginia. Charlottesville: University of Virginia, 1894.

al-Wazzan, al-Hasan Muhammad, *A Geographical Historie of Africa, written in Arabicke and Italian by John Leo a More, borne in Grenada, and brought up in Barbarie. Wherein he Hath at Large Described, Not Onely the Qualities, Situations, and True Distances of the Regions, Cities, Townes, Mountaines, Rivers, and other Places Throughout all the North and Principall Partes of Africa; But also the Descents and Families of their Kings, the Causes and Events of their Warres, with their Manners, Customes, Religions, and Civile Government, and many other Memorable Matters: Gathered Partly out of his Owne Diligent Observations, and partly out of the Ancient Records and Chronicles of the Arabians and Mores. Before which, out of the Best Ancient and Moderne Writers, is Prefixed a Generall Description of Africa, and also a Particular Treatise of all the Maine Lands and Islands described by John Leo. And after the same is annexed a relation of the great Princes, and the Manifold Religions in that Part of the World. Translated and collected by John Pory, lately of Gonevill and Caius College in Cambridge.* London: George Bishop, 1600.

"A Member of the University of Cambridge," *Suggestions on the Abolition of Slavery in the British Colonies; or, Slavery Gradually Starved to Death Upon a Low Diet, V: Strangulation.* Cambridge: J. J. Deighton, T. Stevenson, and R. Newby, 1831.

Ames, Julius Rubens, ed., *'Liberty': The Image and Superscription on Every Coin Issued by the United States of America. Proclaim Liberty Throughout all the Land Unto all the Inhabitants Thereof.* New York: American Anti-Slavery Society, 1837.

Am I Not a Man? and a Brother? With all Humility Addressed to the British Legislature. Cambridge: J. Archdeacon, 1788.

Amos, Sheldon, *The Existing Laws of Demerara for the Regulation of Coolie Immigration*. London: Social Science Association, 1871.

An Account of the Designs of the Associates of the late Dr Bray; with an Abstract of Their Proceedings. London: Unknown, 1768.

Apthorp, East, *The Constitution of a Christian Church Illustrated in a Sermon at the Opening of Christ-Church, in Cambridge on Thursday 15 October, MDCCLXI*. Boston: Green and Russell, 1761.

　Discourses on Prophecy: Read in the Chapel of Lincoln's Inn, at the Lecture Founded by the Right Reverend William Warburton Late Lord Bishop of Gloucester, 2 vols. London: J. F. and C. Rivington, 1786.

Aubrey, John, *Letters Written by Eminent Persons… and Lives of Eminent Men*, 2 vols. London: Longman, 1813.

Aves, Thomas, *Case of the Slave-Child, Med: Report of the Arguments of Counsel, and of the Opinion of the Court, in the Case of Commonwealth vs. Aves; Tried and Determined in the Supreme Judicial Court of Massachusetts*. Boston: Isaac Knapp, 1836.

"A Well Wisher to All Parties," *Negro Slavery Exposed*. Cambridge: W. Hatfield, 1824.

Babington, Churchill, *The Influence of Christianity in Promoting the Abolition of Slavery in Europe. A Dissertation which Obtained the Hulsean Prize for the Year 1845*. Cambridge: J. & J. J. Deighton, 1846.

Baine, Rodney M., ed., *Creating Georgia: Minutes of the Bray Associates 1730–1732 & Supplementary Documents*. Athens and London: University of Georgia Press, 1995.

Baker, Samuel W., 'Slavery and the Slave Trade', *Macmillan's Magazine*, 30 (July 1874): 185–195.

Baldwin, Joseph G., *The Flush Times of Alabama and Mississippi: A Series of Sketches*. New York: D. Appleton and Co., 1854.

Bancroft, George, *Ancient Greece. From the German of Arnold H. L. Heeren*. Boston: Charles C. Little and James Brown, 1842.

Bayne, Alicia, ed., *Autobiographic Recollections of George Pryme, Esq. M.A.* Cambridge: Deighton, Bell, and Co., 1870.

Beaumont, Joseph, *The New Slavery: An Account of the Indian and Chinese Immigrants in British Guiana*. London: W. Ridgway, 1871.

Beaver, Captain Philip, *African Memoranda: Relative to an Attempt to Establish a British Settlement on the Island of Bulama, On the Western Coast of Africa, in the year 1792. With a Brief Notice of the Neighbouring Tribes, Soil, Productions, &c. and Some Observations on The facility of Colonizing that part of Africa, with a View to Cultivation; and the Introduction of Letters and Religion to its Inhabitants; But More Particularly as the Means of Gradually Abolishing African Slavery*. London: C. and R. Baldwin, 1805.

Bendyshe, Thomas, ed., *The Anthropological Treatises of Johann Friedrich Blumenbach, Late Professor at Göttingen and Court Physician to the King of Great Britain*. London: Longman, Roberts, & Green, 1865.

'On the Extinction of Races', *Journal of the Anthropological Society of London* 2 (1864): xcix-cxiii.

'Benjamin Franklin to Anthony Benezet, 22 August 1772', *Founders Online*, https://founders.archives.gov/documents/Franklin/01-19-02-0173, accessed 7 January 2022.

Benson, A. C., *The Life of Edward White Benson: Sometime Archbishop of Canterbury*, 2 vols. London: Macmillan and Co., 1899.

Berland, Kevin Joel, ed., *The Dividing Line Histories of William Byrd II of Westover*. Chapel Hill: University of North Carolina Press, 2013.

Bernal, Ralph, *Substance of the Speech of Ralph Bernal, Esq. In the Debate in the House of Commons, On the 19th May, 1826, Upon Mr. Brougham's Motion 'For Taking into Consideration Early in the Next Session of Parliament such Measures as may appear to be Necessary for giving effect to the Resolution of the House of Commons of the 25th May, 1823, Touching the Condition of Slaves'*. London: J. Moyes, 1826.

Bickell, Rev. Richard, *The West Indies as They Are; or A Real Picture of Slavery: But more particularly as it Exists in the Island of Jamaica. In Three Parts. With Notes*. London: J. Hatchard and Son, 1825.

Bisset, Robert, *A Defence of the Slave Trade on the Grounds of Humanity, Policy and Justice*. London: J. Hales, 1804.

Blackstone, B., ed., *The Ferrar Papers: Containing a Life of Nicholas Ferrar, the Winding Sheet An Ascetic Dialogue, a Collection of Short Moral Histories, and a Selection of Family Letters*. Cambridge: Cambridge University Press, 1938.

Blumenbach, Johann Friedrich, *On the Natural Varieties of Mankind*. New York: Bergman Publishers, 1969.

Bovill, E. W., ed., *Missions to the Niger, I: The Journal of Friedrich Hornemann's Travels and The Letters of Alexander Gordon Laing*. Cambridge: Cambridge University Press for The Hakluyt Society, 1964.

Boyd, Julian P., Charles T. Cullen, John Catanzariti, Barbara B. Oberg, and James P. McClure, eds., *The Papers of Thomas Jefferson*, 46 vols. Princeton, NJ: Princeton University Press, 1950–2022.

Bradley, Richard, *A Philosophical Account of Works of Nature. Endeavouring to set forth the several Gradations Remarkable in the Mineral, Vegetable, and Animal Parts of the Creation Tending to the Composition of a Scale of Life. To which is added, An Account of the State of Gardening, as it is now in Great Britain, and other Parts of Europe: Together with several new Experiments relating to the Improvement of Barren Ground, and the Propagating of Timber-Trees, Fruit-Trees, &c*. London: W. Mears, 1721.

A Short Historical Account of Coffee; Containing the most remarkable Observations of the greatest Men in Europe concerning it, from the first Knowledge of it down to this present Time; with a more accurate Description of the Coffee-Tree than has yet been Publish'd. London: E. M. Matthews, 1715.

A Survey of the Ancient Husbandry and Gardening, Collected from Cato, Varro, Columella, Virgil. And others the most eminent Writers among the Greeks and Romans: Wherein many of the most difficult Passages in those Authors are explain'd, and the whole render'd familiar to our Climate; with Variety of new Experiments. Adorn'd with Cuts. With a Preface, shewing the Use of Husbandry, and the Necessity of erecting Publick Gardens. London: B. Motte, 1725.

The History of Succulent Plants Containing, The Aloes, Ficoids (or Fig-Marygolds) Torch-Thistles, Melon-Thistles, and such others as are capable of an Hortus Siccus. Engraved, from the Originals, on Copper-Plates. With their Descriptions, and Manner of Culture. Second Edition. London: J. Hodges, 1739.

Kalendarium Universale: or, the Gardiner's Universal Calendar. Containing An Account of the several Monthly Operations in the Kitchen-Garden, Flower-Garden, and Parterre throughout the Year. And also, Experimental Directions for performing all manner of Works in Gardening, whether relating to Sowing, Planting, Pruning, Herbs, Flowers, Shrubs, Trees, Evergreens, &c. with the Products of each Month. On a Method wholly New. Taking in the whole Business of Gardening and Horticulture. London: L James Lacy, 1726.

The Virtue and Use of Coffee, with regard to the plague, and other infectious distempers: containing the most remarkable observations of the greatest men in Europe concerning it… To which is prefix'd an exact figure of the tree, flower, and fruit. London: E. Matthews and W. Mears, 1721.

Brookes, Richard, *The Natural History of Birds: With the Method of Bringing Up and Managing those of the Singing Kind*, 4 vols. London: J. Newbery, 1763.

Browning, Oscar, *Memories of Sixty Years at Eton, Cambridge and Elsewhere*. London: John Lane, 1910.

Bryant, Joshua, *Account of an Insurrection of the Negro Slaves in the Colony of Demerara, which broke out on the 18th of August, 1823*. Demerara: A. Stevenson, 1824.

Bryson, William Hamilton, ed., 'A Letter of Lewis Burwell to James Burrough, July 8, 1734', *The Virginia Magazine of History and Biography* 81 (1973): 405–414.

'Burch Hothersall', *Emmanuel College Paintings*, www.emma.cam.ac.uk/about/history/paintings/index.cfm, accessed 20 February 2021.

Burckhardt, Johann Ludwig, *Travels in Arabia, Comprehending an Account of those Territories in Hedjaz which the Mohammedans Regard as Sacred. By the Late John Lewis Burckhardt. Published By Authority of the Association for Promoting the Discovery of the Interior of Africa*, 2 vols. London: Henry Colburn, 1829.

Travels in Nubia; By the Late John Lewis Burckhardt. Published By the Association for Promoting the Discovery of the Interior Parts of Africa. London: John Murray, 1819.

Travels of M. Burckhardt in Egypt and Nubia. From the Calcutta Journal. London: Sir Richard Phillips and Co., 1819.

Burdon, William, *The Life and Character of Bonaparte, From his Birth to the 15th of August, 1804*. Newcastle-Upon-Tyne: K. Anderson, 1804.

Burnaby, Andrew, *Travels Through the Middle Settlements in North-America. In the Years 1759 and 1760. With Observations upon the State of the Colonies.* Dublin: R. Marchbank, 1775.

Burnett, Lonnie A., ed., *Henry Hotze, Confederate Propagandist: Selected Writings on Revolution, Recognition, and Race.* Tuscaloosa: The University of Alabama Press, 2008.

Bury, John Patrick Tuer, ed., *Romilly's Cambridge Diary, 1832–42: Selected Passages from the Diary of the Rev. Joseph Romilly, Fellow of Trinity College and Registrar of the University of Cambridge.* Cambridge: Cambridge University Press, 2011.

Cain, Robert J., ed., *The Colonial Records of North Carolina, Volume X: The Church of England in North Carolina: Documents, 1699–1741.* Raleigh: Division of Archives and History, North Carolina Department of Cultural Resources, 1999.

Caldwell, Lee Ann, ed., *The Journal of the Earl of Egmont: Abstract of the Trustees Proceedings for Establishing the Colony of Georgia, 1732–1738.* Athens: University of Georgia Press, 2021.

Calhoun, John C., *Speeches of John C. Calhoun: Delivered in the Congress of the United States from 1811 to the Present Time.* New York: Harper & Brothers, 1843.

Cambridge Examination Papers: Being A Supplement to the University Calendar for the Year 1856. With Lists of Ordinary Degrees, and of those who have passed the Previous and Theological Examinations. Cambridge: Deighton, Bell and Co., 1856.

Cambridge University Commission: Report of Her Majesty's Commissioners Appointed to Inquire into the State, Discipline, Studies, and Revenues of the University and Colleges of Cambridge: Together with the Evidence, and an Appendix. London: W. Clowes and Sons, 1852.

Cambridge University Examination Papers. Michaelmas Term, 1878, to Easter Term, 1879. Cambridge: Cambridge University Press, 1879.

Candid Remarks on Dr. Witherspoon's Address To the Inhabitants of Jamaica, And the other West-India Islands, &c. In a Letter to those Gentlemen. Philadelphia, PA: William Goddard, 1772.

Canterbury Papers: Information Concerning the Principles, Objects, Plans, & Proceedings of the Founders of the Settlement of Canterbury, in New Zealand, 10 vols. London: John W. Parker, 1850.

Caretta, Vincent, ed., *Olaudah Equiano: The Interesting Narrative and Other Writings.* London: Penguin, 1995.

Unchained Voices: An Anthology of Black Authors in the English-Speaking World of the 18th Century. Lexington: University Press of Kentucky, 2004.

and Ty M. Reese, eds., *The Life and Letters of Philip Quaque: The First African Anglican Missionary.* Athens and London: University of Georgia Press, 2010.

Carey, John, ed., *John Donne: The Major Works.* Oxford and New York: Oxford University Press, 1990.

Caruthers, William Alexander, *The Cavaliers of Virginia; or, The Recluse of Jamestown. An Historical Romance of the Old Dominion,* 2 vols. New York: Harper & Brothers, 1834.

Catalogue of Books Added to the Library of the Library Company of Philadelphia, Since the Large Catalogue of 1835 to January, 1844. Philadelphia: C. Sherman, 1844.

Chancellor, Christopher, ed., *An Englishman in the American Civil War: The Diaries of Henry Yates Thompson*. New York: New York University Press, 1971.

Chapman, M. J., *Barbadoes, and Other Poems*. London: J. Moyes, 1833.

'Chapter Book 3, 1709–1752', *Corpus Christi College, Cambridge*, www.corpus.cam.ac.uk/sites/default/files/downloads/chapter-book-3.pdf, accessed 30 March 2022.

Christian, Edward, *Notes to Blackstone's Commentaries, Which are Calculated to Answer All the Editions*. Dublin: P. Byrne, 1797.

Clark, John Willis, ed., *Endowments of the University of Cambridge*. Cambridge: Cambridge University Press, 1904.

Clark, John Willis, and Thomas McKenny Hughes, eds., *The Life and Letters of the Reverend Adam Sedgwick, LL.D., D.C.L., F.R.S., Fellow of Trinity College, Cambridge, Prebendary of Norwich, Woodwardian Professor of Geology, 1818–1873*, 2 vols. Cambridge: Cambridge University Press, 1890.

Clark, William, *Catalogue of the Osteological Portions of Specimens Contained in the Anatomical Museum of the University of Cambridge*. Cambridge: Cambridge University Press, 2010.

Clarke, Adam, *The New Testament of Our Lord and Saviour Jesus Christ; containing the Text, Taken from the Most Correct Copies of the Present Authorised Translation, including the Marginal Readings and Parallel Texts with a Commentary and Critical Notes*, 3 vols. London: J. Butterworth & Son, 1817.

Clarke, Thomas, *A Sermon on the Injustice of the Slave Trade, Preached February 12th, 1792, in the Parish Church of the Holy Trinity, in Kingston-Upon-Hull*. Hull: J. Ferraby, 1792.

Clarkson, Thomas, *An Essay on the Slavery and Commerce of the Human Species, Particularly the African, Translated from a Latin Dissertation, which was Honoured with the First Prize in the University of Cambridge, for the Year 1785, with Additions*. London: Re-Printed by Joseph Crukshank, 1786.

The History of the Rise, Progress, and Accomplishment of the Abolition of the African Slave-Trade by the British Parliament, 2 vols. London: R. Taylor and Co., 1808.

Thoughts on the Necessity of Improving the Condition of the Slaves in the British Colonies: With a View to the Ultimate Emancipation, and on the Practicability, Safety, and the Advantages of the Latter Measure. London: Society for the Mitigation and Gradual Abolition of Slavery throughout the British Dominions, 1824.

Cobden, John C., *The White Slaves of England. Compiled from Official Documents. With Twelve Spirited Illustrations*. Auburn: Derby and Miller, 1853.

Coburn, Kathleen, and Merton Christensen, eds., *The Notebooks of Samuel Taylor Coleridge*, 4 vols. London: Routledge, 2003.

Cockburn, Sir Robert, and Harry A. Cockburn, *The Records of the Cockburn Family*. London and Edinburgh: T. N. Foulis, 1913.

Coke, Thomas, *A History of the West Indies, Containing the Natural, Civil, and Ecclesiastical History of each Island: with an Account of the Missions Instituted in Those Islands, from the Commencement of their Civilization; But more Especially of the Missions which have been Established in that Archipelago By the Society Late in Connexion with the Rev. John Wesley*, 3 vols. London: T. Blanshard, 1808–11.

Coleridge, Henry Nelson, *Six Months in the West Indies, in 1825*. London: John Murray, 1826.

Six Months in the West Indies: Fourth Edition. London: Thomas Tegg, 1841.

Coleridge, Samuel Taylor, *The Poetical Works of Samuel Taylor Coleridge*, 2 vols. London: Macmillan and Company, 1880.

Cooke, John Esten, *Henry St. John, Gentleman, of 'Flowers of Hundred', In the County of Prince George, Virginia. A Tale of 1774–'75*. New York: Harper & Brothers, 1859.

Cooper, Charles Henry, and John William Cooper, eds., *Annals of Cambridge, Volume V: 1850–1856 with Additions and Corrections to Volumes I–IV and Index to the Complete Work*. Cambridge: Cambridge University Press, 1908.

Correspondence concerning Claims against Great Britain, Transmitted to the Senate of the United States in Answer to the Resolutions of December 4 and 10, 1867, and of May 27, 1868, 7 vols. Washington, D.C.: Philp & Solomons, 1869–71.

Couch, Lilian M. Quiller, ed., *Reminiscences of Oxford by Oxford Men, 1559–1850*. Oxford: Oxford Historical Society at the Clarendon Press, 1892.

The Court Journal. From January to December 1833. London: Henry Colburn, 1833.

The Court of Directors of the South Sea Company, *A List of the Names of Such Proprietors of Annuities, Transferable at the South Sea House, as were Entitled to Dividends on or Before the 5th July, 1837, and which Remained Unpaid on the 10th October 1842*. London: H. Teape and Son, 1842.

Cowell, John Welsford, *France and the Confederate States*. London: Robert Hardwicke, 1865.

Lancashire's Wrongs and the Remedy: Two Letters Addressed to the Cotton Operatives of Great Britain. London: Robert Hardwicke, 1863.

Southern Secession. A Letter Address to Captain M. T. Maury, Confederate Navy, on His Letter to Admiral Fitzroy. London: Robert Hardwicke, 1862.

Crashaw, William, *A sermon preached in London before the right honorable the Lord Lavvarre, Lord Gouernour and Captaine Generall of Virginea, and others of his Maiesties Counsell for that kingdome, and the rest of the aduenturers in that plantation*. London: W. Hall, 1610.

Craufurd, George W., *Slavery! Captain Yorke's Views, on the Subject of Colonial Slavery, Refuted, In Two Letters, Together with Captain Yorke's Attempted Defence*. Cambridge: Weston Hatfield, 1832.

'The Cricketers', *National Portrait Gallery*, https://npg.si.edu/object/npg_UK990702, accessed 8 September 2020.

Crossley, David, and Richard Saville, eds., *The Fuller Letters: Guns, Slaves and Finance, 1728–1755*. Lewes: Sussex Record Society, 1991.

Cruikshank, Isaac, 'The abolition of the slave trade', 1792, *British Museum*, www.britishmuseum.org/collection/object/P_1868-0808-6179, accessed 21 April 2022.

Crummell, Alexander, *Africa and America: Addresses and Discourses*. Springfield, MA: Wiley & Co., 1891.

Destiny and Race: Selected Writings, 1840–1898, ed. by Wilson Jeremiah Moses. Amherst: University of Massachusetts Press, 1992.

The Future of Africa: Being Addresses, Sermons, Etc., Etc., Delivered in the Republic of Liberia. New York: Charles Scribner, 1862.

The Negro Race not under a Curse, an Examination of Genesis IX. 25. London: Wertheim, Macintosh & Hunt, 1853.

Cushing, William, *Initials and Pseudonyms: A Dictionary of Literary Disguises*. New York: Thomas Y. Crowell & Co., 1888.

Cuttriss, Rev. William, *Slavery Inconsistent with Christianity*. Cambridge: Johnson, 1825.

Dale, Alfred William Winterslow, ed., *Warren's Book*. Cambridge: Cambridge University Press, 1911.

Dallaway, James, ed., *Letters of the Late Thomas Rundle, LL.D. Lord Bishop of Derry in Ireland, To Mrs. Barbara Sandys, of Miserden, Gloucestershire. With Introductory Memoirs*. Dublin: P. Byrne, J. Moore, J. Jones, Grueber and McAllister, and W. Jones, 1789.

d'Anghiera, Pietro Martire, and Richard Eden, *The decades of the new worlde or west India conteynyng the nauigations and conquests of the Spanyardes, with the particular description of the most ryche and large landes and islandes lately founde in the west ocean perteynyng to the inheritaunce of the kings of Spayne. Wrytten in the Latine tounge by Peter Martyr of Angleria, and translated in Englysshe by Rycharde Eden*. London: Edwarde Sutton, 1555.

Davenant, Charles, *An Essay on the East-India Trade*. London: Unknown, 1696.

Discourses on the Public Revenues and on the Trade of England, 2 vols. London: James Knapton, 1698.

Reflections Upon the Constitution and Management of the Trade to Africa, Through the Whole Course and Progress thereof, from the Beginning of the last Century, to this Time. Wherein the Nature and uncommon Circumstances of that Trade are particularly consider'd; and all the Arguments urg'd alternately by the Two contending Parties here, touching the different Methods now proposed by them, for carrying on the same to a National Advantage, impartially stated and consider'd. By all which, A clear View is given of such a Constitution, as (if establish'd by Act of Parliament) would, in all Probability, render the African Trade a permanent, creditable and advantageous Trade to Britain. London: John Morphew, 1709.

Deas, Anne Izard, ed., *Correspondence of Mr. Ralph Izard, of South Carolina, From the Year 1774 to 1804; with a Short Memoir*. New York: Charles S. Francis & Co., 1844.

The Debate on a Motion for the Abolition of the Slave-Trade, in the House of Commons, on Monday and Tuesday April 18 and 19, 1791, Report in Detail. London: W. Woodfall, 1791.

De Beer, E. S., ed., *The Correspondence of John Locke, Volume One*. Oxford: Clarendon Press, 1976.

Defoe, Daniel, *A true account of the design, and advantages of the South-Sea trade; with answers to all the objections rais'd against it: a list of the commodities proper for that trade: and the progress of the subscription towards the South-Sea Company*. London: John Morphew, 1711.

de las Casas, Bartolomé, *A Short Account of the Destruction of the Indies*, ed. by Nigel Griffin and Anthony Pagden. London: Penguin, 2004.

de Tocqueville, Alexis, *De la Démocratie en Amérique*, 2 vols. Brussels: C. Gosselin, 1835 and 1840.

Diprose, John, *Diprose's Comic and Sentimental Song Book. New Edition*. London: David Bryce, 1856.

Dod, Peirce, *Several cases in Physick: and one in particular, giving an account of a person who was inoculated for the small-pox, and had the small-pox upon the inoculation, and yet had it again. To which is added, a letter to Dr. Lee, giving him an account of a letter of Dr. Friend's*. London: Royal Society, 1746.

Donne, William Bodham, ed., *The Correspondence of King George the Third with Lord North From 1768 to 1783*, 2 vols. London: J. Murray, 1867.

Douglass, Frederick, *Narrative of the Life of Frederick Douglass, an American Slave. Written by Himself*. Boston: Anti-Slavery Office, 1845.

Dowding, William Charles, *Africa in the West: Its State; Prospects; and Educational Needs: With Reference to Bishop Berkeley's Bermuda College*. Oxford and London: John Henry Parker, 1852.

Draper, Sir William, *The Thoughts of a Traveller Upon Our American Disputes*. London: J. Ridley, 1774.

Du Bois, W. E. B., *The Souls of Black Folk*, ed. and intro. by Brent Hayes Edwards. Oxford: Oxford University Press, 2008.

Dyer, George, *Memoirs of the Life and Writings of Robert Robinson, Late Minister of the Dissenting Congregation, in Saint Andrew's Parish, Cambridge*. London: G. G. and J. Robinson, 1796.

Slavery and Famine, Punishments for Edition; or, an Account of the Miseries and Starvation at Botany Bay. London: J. Ridgway, 1794.

East India Company, *A list of the names of all the adventurers in the stock of the honourable the East-India-Company, the 12th day of April, 1684 whereof those marked with a *are not capable (by their adventure) to be chosen committees*. London: A. Baldwin, 1699.

East India Company, *A List of the Names of the Proprietors of East-India Stock who Appear, By the Books of the East-India Company, Qualified to Vote at the General Election, 12th April 1837*. London: Cox and Sons, 1836.

The Ecclesiastical Gazette; or, Monthly Register of the Affairs of the Church of England and of its Religious Societies and Institutions. From July 1838 to June 1839. London: Charles Cox, 1839.

Eddis, William, *Letters from America, Historical and Descriptive; Comprising Occurrences from 1769, to 1777, Inclusive*. London: C. Dilly, 1792.

Egerton, Frank N., ed., 'Richard Bradley's Relationship with Sir Hans Sloane', *Notes and Records: The Royal Society Journal of the History of Science* 25 (June 1970): 59–77.

Elliot, Adam, *A Modest Vindication of Titus Oates the Salamanca-Doctor from Perjury: or an Essay to Demonstrate Him only Forsworn in several Instances*. London: Joseph Hindmarsh, 1682.

Elliott, E. N., ed., *Cotton is King, and Pro-Slavery Arguments: Comprising the Writings of Hammond, Harper, Christy, Stringfellow, Hodge, Bledsoe, and Cartwright, on this Important Subject*. Augusta, GA: Pritchard, Abbott & Loomis, 1860.

Ellys, Anthony, *A Sermon Preached before the Incorporated Society for the Propagation of the Gospel in Foreign Parts at their Anniversary Meeting in the Parish Church of St. Mary-le-Bow, On Friday February 23, 1759*. London: E. Owen and T. Harrison, 1754.

Equiano, Olaudah, *The Interesting Narrative of the Life of Olaudah Equiano, or Gustavus Vassa, the African. Written by Himself*. London: Printed by the Author, 1794.

The Interesting Narrative of the Life of Olaudah Equiano, or Gustavus Vassa, the African Written by Himself, intro. and ed. by Robert Reid-Pharr and Shelly Eversley. New York: Modern Library, 2004.

Everett, William, *On the Cam: Lectures on the University of Cambridge in England*. Cambridge, MA: Harvard University Press, 1865.

'Excerpts from Jamaican Records and Anglican Parish Registers', *Jamaican Family Search*, www.jamaicanfamilysearch.com/Members/Rw_j-y.htm, accessed 10 February 2023.

'Extracts from Diary of Col. Landon Carter', *The William and Mary Quarterly* 13 (July 1904): 45–53.

Fairbanks, George Rainsford, *History of the University of the South, at Sewanee, Tennessee: From Its Founding by the Southern Bishops, Clergy, and Laity of the Episcopal Church in 1857 to the Year 1905*. Jacksonville, FL: The H. & W. B. Drew Company, 1905.

Fairfax, Rev. John, *Life of the Rev. Owen Stockton, M.A.* London: Religious Tract Society, 1832.

Farish, Hunter Dickinson, ed., *Journal & Letters of Philip Vickers Fithian 1773–1774: A Plantation Tutor of the Old Dominion*. Williamsburg, VA: Colonial Williamsburg, Incorporated, 1965.

Federal Writers Project, *Slave Narratives: A Folk History of Slavery in the United States From Interviews with Former Slaves*, 17 vols. Washington, D.C.: Library of Congress, 1936–38.

Fellowes, Sir James, *Reports of the Pestilential Disorder of Andalusia, which Appeared at Cadiz in the Year 1800, 1804, 1810, and 1813*. London: Longman, Hurst, Rees, Orme, and Brown, 1815.

Field, Rev. William, *Memoirs of the Life, Writings, and Opinions of the Rev. Samuel Parr, LL.D.; with Biographical Notices of Many of His Friends, Pupils, and Contemporaries*, 2 vols. London: Henry Colburn, 1828.

The Fifth Report of the Colchester and East Essex Association, in Aid of the Church Missionary Society for Africa and the East, 10th of April, 1821; and a List of Benefactors, Subscribers, and Collectors. Colchester: W. Keymer, 1821.

First Annual Report of the Board of Managers of the New-England Anti-Slavery Society, Presented Jan. 9, 1833. With an Appendix. Boston: Garrison and Knapp, 1833.

Fitzhugh, Thomas, ed., *Letters of George Long*. Charlottesville: University of Virginia Press, 1917.

Fleetwood, William, *A Sermon Preached before the Society for the Propagation of the Gospel in Foreign Parts At the Parish-Church of St. Mary-le-Bow, On Friday the 16th of February, Being the Day of their Anniversary Meeting*. London: J. Downing, 1711.

Fletcher, Reginald J., ed., *The Pension Book of Gray's Inn*, 2 vols. London: Chiswick Press, 1901.

Foot, Jesse, *Observations Principally Upon the Speech of Mr. Wilberforce, on his Motion in the House of Commons, the 30th of May, 1804, for the Abolition of the Slave Trade*. London: T. Becket, 1805.

Forsyth, William, ed., *Cases and Opinions on Constitutional Law, and Various Points of English Jurisprudence, Digested from Official Documents and other Sources*. London: Stevens & Haynes, 1869.

Foster, J. E., ed., *The Diary of Samuel Newton Alderman of Cambridge (1662–1717)*. Cambridge: Cambridge Antiquarian Society, 1890.

Fowler, Laurence, and Helen Fowler, ed., *Cambridge Commemorated: An Anthology of University Life*. Cambridge: Cambridge University Press, 1989.

Francklyn, Gilbert, *An Answer to the Rev. Mr. Clarkson's Essay on the Slavery and Commerce of the Human Species, particularly the African; in a Series of Letters From a Gentleman in Jamaica, to His Friend in London: Wherein Many of the Mistakes and Misrepresentations of Mr. Clarkson are pointed out, Both with Regard to The Manner in which that Commerce is carried on in Africa, and The Treatment of the Slaves in the West Indies. Shewing, at the same time, the Antiquity, Universality, and Lawfulness of Slavery, as ever having been one of the States and Conditions of Mankind*. London: J. Walter, 1789.

Fraser, Alexander Campbell, ed., *The Works of George Berkeley, Formerly Bishop of Cloyne. Collected and Edited with Prefaces and Annotations*, 4 vols. Oxford: Clarendon Press, 1871.

Frend, William, *A Sequel to the Account of the Proceedings in the University of Cambridge, Against the Author of a Pamphlet, Entitled Peace and Union; Containing the Application to the Court of King's Bench, a Review of Similar Cases in the University, and Reflections on the Impolicy of Religious Persecution, and the Importance of Free Enquiry*. London: G. and J. Robinson, 1795.

Fuller, John, 'Part of a letter from Mr. Stephen Fuller, Fellow of Trinity College, Cambridge, to his father John Fuller, Esq; Senior, F. R. S. concerning a violent hurricane in Huntingtonshire, Sept. 8 1741. Communicated by Sir Hans Sloane, late Pr. R. S', *Philosophical Transactions* 41 (December 1740): 851–855.

Fuller, Stephen, *The Colonization of the Island of Jamaica*. London: Unknown, 1792.

The New Act of Assembly of the Island of Jamaica, Intitled, An Act to repeal an Act, intitled, 'An Act to repeal several Acts, and Clauses of Acts, respecting Slaves, and for the better Order and Government of Slaves, and for other Purposes:' And also to repeal the several Acts, and Clauses of Acts, which were repealed by the Act intitled as aforesaid; and for consolidating and bringing into One Act the several Laws relating to Slaves, and for giving them further Protection and Security; for altering the Mode of Trial of Slaves charged with capital Offences; and for other Purposes; Commonly Called, The New Consolidated Act, Which was passed by the Assembly on the 6th of November – by the Council on the 5th Day of December – and by the Lieutenant Governor on the 6th Day of December, 1788; Being the Present Code Noir of that Island. London: B. White and Son, 1789.

Notes on the Two Reports from the Committee of the Honourable House of Assembly of Jamaica, Appointed To examine into, and to report to the House, the Allegations and Charges contained in the several Petitions which have been presented to the British House of Commons, on the Subject of the Slave Trade, and the Treatment of the Negroes, &c. &c. &c. London: J. Philips 1789.

Geggus, David, ed., *The Haitian Revolution: A Documentary History*. Indianapolis: Hackett Publishing, 2014.

Gibbon, Edward, *The Autobiography and Correspondence of Edward Gibbon, The Historian: Reprint of the Original Edition*. London: Alex Murray & Son, 1869.

Gilbert, Thomas, *Poems on Several Occasions*. London: Charles Bathurst, 1747.

Gill, Harold B., Jr., and George M. Curtis III, eds., *A Man Apart: Journal of Nicholas Creswell, 1774–1781*. Lanham, MD: Lexington Books, 2009.

Godwyn, Morgan, *The Negro's & Indians advocate, suing for their admission to the church, or, A persuasive to the instructing and baptizing of the Negro's and Indians in our plantations shewing that as the compliance therewith can prejudice no mans just interest, so the wilful neglecting and opposing of it, is not less than a manifest apostacy from the Christian faith: to which is added, a brief account of religion in Virginia*. London: J. D., 1680.

Gorham, George Cornelius, ed., *Memoirs of John Martyn, F.R.S., and of Thomas Martyn, B.D., F.R.S., F.L.S., Professors of Botany in the University of Cambridge*. London: Hatchard and Son, 1830.

Grant, Anne MacVicar, *Memoirs of an American Lady. With Sketches of Manners and Scenery in America, as they Existed Previous to the Revolution*. New York: George Dearborn, 1836.

Gray, Samuel Brownlow, *The Revival of Bp. Berkeley's Bermuda College: A Letter to His Grace the Archbishop of Canterbury, Primate of all England, &c. &c. &c. One of the Vice-Patrons of the Scheme, On the Plan which has been Lately Promulgated with the Above Title*. London: Whitaker and Co., 1853.

Green, Rev. William Mercer, and Rev. Telfair Hodgson, *The University of the South: Papers relating to Christian Education at this University, and the necessity *of this Institution to the country, especially to the South and Southwest, etc.* Sewanee, TN: James Pott & Co., Church Publishers, 1882.

Greenfield, William, *A Defence of the Surinam Negro-English Version of the New Testament: Founded on the History of the Negro-English Version, a View of the Situation, Population, and History of Surinam, a Philological Analysis of the Language, and a Careful Examination of the Version*. London: Samuel Bagster, 1830.

Griffith, Lucille, ed., 'English Education for Virginia Youth: Some Eighteenth-Century Ambler Family Letters', *The Virginia Magazine of History and Biography* 69 (January 1961): 7-27.

Gunning, Henry, *Reminiscences of the University, Town and County of Cambridge, From the Year 1780*, 2 vols. Cambridge: Cambridge University Press, 2012.

Hallifax, Samuel, *An Analysis of the Roman Civil Law; in which A Comparison is, occasionally, made between the Roman Laws and those of England: Being the Heads of a Course of Lectures, Publickly Read in the University of Cambridge. Third Edition*. Cambridge: J. Archdeacon, 1779.

A Sermon Preached before the Incorporated Society for the Propagation of the Gospel in Foreign Parts; at their Anniversary Meeting in the Parish Church of St. Mary-Le-Bow On Friday February 20, 1789. London: T. Harrison and S. Brooke, 1789.

Hansard, T. C., *The Parliamentary Debates: Forming a Continuation of the Work Entitled 'The Parliamentary History of England, From the Earliest Period to the Year 1803'*, vol. 9. London: T. C. Hansard, 1824.

Harmer, Philip M., George C. Rogers, Jr., and David R. Chesnutt, eds., *The Papers of Henry Laurens*, 16 vols. Columbia: University of South Carolina Press, 1968-2003.

Harraden, R. B., Jr., *History of the University of Cambridge Illustrated by a Series of Engravings Representing the Most Picturesque and Interesting Edifices in the University and the Most Striking Parts of the Town*. Cambridge: J. Smith, 1814.

Harris, Thomas, and John McHenry, eds., *Maryland Reports, Being a Series of the Most Important Law Cases Argued and Determined in the General Court and Court of Appeals of the State of Maryland, From May, 1797, to the End of 1799. With an Appendix of Cases Argued and Determined in the Late Provincial Court*, 4 vols. New York: I. Riley, 1812-18.

Harvest, George, *A Collection of Sermons, Preached Occasionally on Various Subjects*. London: J. and R. Tonson and S. Draper, 1754.

Harvey, William Woodis, *Sketches of Hayti; from the Expulsion of the French, to the Death of Christophe*. London: L. B. Seeley and Son, 1827.

Harwell, Richard Barksdale, ed., 'The Creed of a Propagandist: Letter from a Confederate Editor', *Journalism Quarterly* 28 (Spring 1951): 213-218.

Harwood, Thomas, *Alumni Etoniensis; or, a Catalogue of the Provosts & Fellows of Eton College & King's College, Cambridge, from the Foundation in 1443, to the Year 1797; With an Account of their Lives & Preferments, Collected from Original Mss. And Authentic Biographical Works*. Birmingham: T. Pearson, 1797.

The Noble Slave: A Tragedy. Bury St Edmunds: J. Rackham, 1788.

Hayes, Charles, *The Importance of effectually supporting the Royal African Company of England impartially consider'd;...in a Letter to a Member of the House of Commons*. London: M. Cooper, 1744.

Headlam, Cecil, ed., *Calendar of State Papers, Colonial Series, American and West Indies, August, 1714 – December, 1715, Preserved in the Public Record Office*. London: H. M. Stationary Office, 1928.

Heyrick, Elizabeth, *Immediate, Not Gradual Abolition; Or, An Inquiry into the Shortest, Safest, and Most Effectual Means of Getting Rid of West Indian Slavery*. London: Hatchard and Son, 1824.

The History of the College of William and Mary: From Its Foundation, 1660, to 1874. Richmond, VA: J. W. Randolph & English, 1874.

Hoare, Prince, ed., *Memoirs of Granville Sharp, Esq. Composed from His Own Manuscripts and Other Authentic Documents in the Possession of His Family and of the African Institution*. Cambridge: Cambridge University Press, 2014.

Hope, Alexander Beresford, *A Popular View of the American Civil War*. London, James Ridgway, 1861.

The English Cathedral of the Nineteenth Century. London: John Murray, 1861.

Essays. London: Francis & John Rivington, 1844.

The Results of the American Disruption: The Substance of a Lecture Delivered by Request Before the Maidstone Literary & Mechanics' Institution, In Continuation of A Popular View of the American Civil War, and England, the North, and the South. London: James Ridgway, 1862.

Hughes, Griffith, *The Natural History of Barbados. In Ten Books*. London: Unknown, 1750.

Hume, David, *Essays Moral, Political and Literary*. Oxford: Oxford University Press, 1963.

Humphreys, David, *An Historical Account of the Incorporated Society for the Propagation of the Gospel in Foreign Parts. Containing their Foundation, Proceedings, and the Success of their Missionaries in the British Colonies, to the Year 1728*. London: Joseph Downing, 1730.

Humphry, George Murray, *A Treatise on the Human Skeleton (Including the Joints)*. Cambridge: Macmillan and Co., 1858.

Hunt, James, *Anniversary Address Delivered Before the Anthropological Society of London, January 5th, 1864*. London: Anthropological Society of London, 1864.

Hutcheson, Francis, *A System of Moral Philosophy. In Three Books*, 3 vols. London: A. Millar, 1755.

Hutchinson, William T., William M. E. Rachal, and William Munford Ellis, eds., *The Papers of James Madison*, 17 vols. Charlottesville: University of Virginia Press, 1962–1991.

Ignoramus: Or, The English Lawyer – A Comedy. As it was Acted at the Theatre-Royal in Drury-Lane. London: W. Feales, 1736.

Incorporated Society for the Propagation of the Gospel in Foreign Parts. Report for the Year 1840. With the 139th Anniversary Sermon Preached Before the Society at the Cathedral Church of St. Paul. London: Society for the Propagation of the Gospel in Foreign Parts, 1840.

Isaacson, Rev. Stephen, *A Vindication of the West-India Proprietors, In a Speech Delivered at Mansion House Chapel, Camberwell, August 18, 1832, With an Appendix*. London: J. Fraser, 1832.

Jenkins, Edward, *The Coolie: His Rights and Wrongs*. New York: George Routledge and Sons, 1871.

Johnson, Cuthbert W., and William Shaw, ed., *The Farmers' Almanac and Calendar*, 18 vols. London: James Ridgway, 1844–1876.

Johnson, Samuel, *A Dictionary of the English Language: In Which The Words are deduced from their Originals, Explained in their Different Meanings, and Authorized by the Names of the Writers in whose Works they are found*. Dublin: W. G. Jones, 1768.

Political Tracts. London: W. Strahan and T. Cadell, 1776.

Jones, Rev. Richard, *An Introductory Lecture on Political Economy, Delivered at King's College, London, 27th February, 1833*. London: John Murray, 1833.

Journals of the House of Commons. From January the 31st, 1792, In the Thirty-second Year of the Reign of King George the Third, to November the 15th, 1792, In the Thirty-third Year of the Reign of King George the Third. London: House of Commons, 1803.

Journals of the House of Lords, Beginning Anno Quinquagesimo Tertio Georgii Tertii, 49 vols. London: H. M. Stationary Office, 1812.

Jowett, William, *Mercy for Africa. A Sermon Preached in Favour of the Endowment Fund for the Bishopric of Sierra Leone. With an Appendix*. London: Seeleys, 1851.

Keene, Edmund, *A Sermon Preached before the Incorporated Society for the Propagation of the Gospel in Foreign Parts; At Their Parish Church of St. Mary-Le-Bow On Friday February 18, 1757*. London: E. Owen and T. Harrison, 1757.

Kennedy, C. M., *The Influence of Christianity upon International Law. The Hulsean Prize Essay in the University of Cambridge, for the Year 1854*. Cambridge: Macmillan and Co., 1856.

Kidder, Richard, *A Commentary on the Five Books of Moses: With a Dissertation Concerning the Author or Writer of the said Books; and a General Argument to each of them*, 2 vols. London: J. Keptinstall, 1694.

Kingsbury, Susan Myra, ed., *The Records of the Virginia Company*, 4 vols. Washington, D.C.: Government Printing Office, 1906–1935.

Kingsley, Charles, *The Gospel of the Pentateuch: A Set of Parish Sermons*. London: Parker, Son, and Bourn, 1863.

The Limits of Exact Science as Applied to History: An Inaugural Lecture, Delivered Before the University of Cambridge. Cambridge and London: Macmillan and Co., 1860.

The Roman and the Teuton: A Series of Lectures Delivered Before the University of Cambridge. London: Macmillan and Co., 1864.

Two Years Ago, 2 vols. London: Macmillan and Co., 1857.

Kingsley, Francis, ed., *Charles Kingsley: His Letters and Memories of His Life*, 2 vols. New York: Charles Scribner's Sons, 1885.

Kippis, Andrew, *Biographica Britannica: Or, the Lives of the Most Eminent Persons, who Have Flourished in Great Britain and Ireland, from the Earliest Ages, Down to the Present Times*, 6 vols. London: Unknown, 1763.

Laborie, Pierre Joseph, *The Coffee Planter of Saint Domingo; with An Appendix, Containing a View of the Constitution, Government, Laws, and State of that Colony, previous to the Year 1789. To which are Added, Some Hints on the Present State of the Island, Under the British Government*. London: T. Cadell, 1798.

Lamb, William, *Essay on the Progressive Improvement of Mankind. Delivered in the Chapel of Trinity College, Cambridge, On the Day of Commemoration, Monday, Dec. 17, 1798*. London: William Clowes and Sons, 1860.

Lashmore-Davies, Adrian, ed., *The Unpublished Letters of Henry St John, First Viscount Bolingbroke*, 5 vols. London: Routledge, 2013.

Lauterpacht, Hersch, ed., *Annual Digest and Reports of Public International Law Cases: Being a Selection from the Decisions of International and National Courts and Tribunals given during the Years 1938–1940*, 6 vols. Cambridge: Grotius Publications Ltd., 1988.

Law Quibbles: Or, a Treatise of the Evasions, Tricks, Turns and Quibbles, Commonly Used in the Profession of the Law, to the Prejudice of Clients and Others. London: E. and R. Nutt 1724.

The Laws of Jamaica, Passed by the Assembly, And Confirmed by His Majesty in Council, April 17. 1684. London: H. H. Jun., 1684.

Lawson, Marmaduke, *Strictures on the Rev. F. H. Maberly's Account of 'The Melancholy and Awful End of Lawrence Dundas, Esq. of Trinity College;' and His Appeal to the University on its Laxity of Discipline*. London: Bensley and Sons, 1818.

Lefroy, John Henry, ed., *Memorials of the Discovery and Early Settlement of the Bermudas or Somers Island, 1515–1685: Compiled from the Colonial Records and Other Original Sources*, 2 vols. London: Longmans, 1877.

Legaré, Mary, ed., *Writings of Hugh Swinton Legaré, Late Attorney General and Acting Secretary of State of the United States: Consisting of a Diary of Brussels, and Journal of the Rhine; Extracts from his Private and Diplomatic Correspondence; Orations and Speeches; and Contributions to the New-York and Southern Reviews*, 2 vols. Charleston, SC: Burges and James, 1845.

The Legion of Liberty and Force of Truth, Containing the Thoughts, Words, and Deeds, of Some Prominent Apostles, Champions and Martyrs. Pictures and Poetry. New York: American Anti-Slavery Society, 1857.

Le Grice, Charles Valentine, *Analysis of Paley's Principles of Moral and Political Philosophy*. Cambridge: Benjamin Flower, 1799.

'Letter from John Elliot Protesting against Selling Indians as Slaves', 13 August 1675, *Yale Indian Papers Project*, https://findit.library.yale.edu/yipp/catalog/digcoll:1018374, accessed 29 June 2022.

'Letter of Col. Nathaniel Burwell', *The William and Mary Quarterly* 7 (July 1898): 43–45.

Letters to a Young Planter; Or, Observations on the Management of a Sugar-Plantation. To which is Added, The Planter's Kalendar. London: Strachan, 1785.

Lewis, Matthew Gregory, *Journal of a West India Proprietor, Kept during a Residence in the Island of Jamaica.* Cambridge: Cambridge University Press, 2010.

'List of subscribers to the Company of Scotland Trading to Africa and the Indies, 1696–1700', *NatWest Group Archive*, www.natwestgroup.com/heritage/companies/company-of-scotland-trading-to-africa-and-the-indies.html, accessed 16 September 2022.

Livingstone, David, *Dr Livingstone's Cambridge Lectures, Together with a Prefatory Letter By the Rev. Professor Sedgwick, M.A., F.R.S., &c. Vice-Master of Trinity College, Cambridge, Edited with Introduction, Life of Dr Livingstone, Notes and Appendix, By the Rev. William Monk, M.A. F.R.A.S. &c. of St John's College, and Curate of Christ's Church, Cambridge. With a Portrait and Map.* Cambridge: Deighton, Bell and Co., 1858.

Lloyd, Jacob Youde William, *The History of the Princes, the Lords Marcher, and the Ancient Nobility of Powys Fadog: And the Ancient Lords of Arwystli, Cedewen, and Meirionydd*, 6 vols. London: Whiting & Co., 1887.

Lloyd, Susette Harriet, *Sketches of Bermuda*. London: James Cochrane and Co., 1835.

Lobspruch deß edlen/hochberühmten Krauts Petum oder Taback. Nuremburg: Paul Fürst, 1658.

Long, Edward, *The History of Jamaica. Or, General Survey of the Antient and Modern State of that Island: with Reflections on its Situation, Settlements, Inhabitants, Climate, Products, Commerce, Laws, and Government*, 3 vols. London: T. Lowndes, 1774.

Long, George, *The Geography of America and the West Indies.* London: Society for the Diffusion of Useful Knowledge, 1841.

Lovett, Robert Woodberry, ed., *Documents from the Harvard University Archives, 1638–1750.* Boston: Colonial Society of Massachusetts, 1975.

Lysons, Daniel, and Samuel Lysons, *Magna Britannia; Being a Concise Topographical Account of the Several Counties of Great Britain*, 6 vols. London: T. Cadell and W. Davies, 1810.

Maberly, Rev. Frederick Herbert, *The Melancholy and Awful Death of Lawrence Dundas, Esq. An Under Graduate of Trinity College, Cambridge: With an Address to the Younger Members of the University on the Evil Nature, Tendency, and Effects of Drunkenness & Fornication: Followed by an Appeal to the University on the Laxity of its Discipline and Licentiousness; Pointing out Means Whereby it may be Prevented, and Shewing the Necessity of Making An Example on the Present Occasion, &c.* London: J. F. Dove, 1818.

Madden, R. R., ed., *The Literary Life and Correspondence of the Countess of Blessington*, 3 vols. London: T. C. Newby, 1855.

Marsden, R. G., ed., *Documents Relating to Law and Custom of the Sea*, 2 vols. Union, NJ: The Lawbook Exchange, Ltd., 1999.

Marsh, Herbert, *The History of the Politicks of Great Britain and France from the Time of the Conference at Pillnitz, to the Declaration of War against Great Britain*, 2 vols. London: John Stockdale, 1800.

Martin, Samuel, *An Essay Upon Plantership, Humbly Inscribed To his Excellency George Thomas, Esq.; Chief Governor of All the Leeward Islands, As a Monument to Antient Friendship*. London: Samuel Jones, 1765.

Martyn, John, *Historia Plantarum Rariorum*. London: Richard Reily, 1728.

Martyn, Thomas, *The Gardener's and Botanist's Dictionary; Containing the Best and Newest Methods of Cultivating and Improving the Kitchen, Fruit, and Flower Garden, and Nursery; or Performing the Practical Parts of Agriculture; of Managing Vineyards, and of Propagating all Sorts of Timber Trees*, 2 vols. London: C. and J. Rivington, 1807.

Mason, Frances Norton, ed., *John Norton & Sons, Merchants of London and Virginia: Being the Papers from their Counting House for the Years 1750 to 1795*. Richmond: Dietz Press, 1937.

The Mauritius: an Exemplification of Colonial Policy; Addressed to the Electors of Cambridge and Devonport. Birmingham: B. Hudson, 1837.

Mawson, Matthias, *A Sermon Preached before the Incorporated Society for the Propagation of the Gospel in Foreign Parts; at their Anniversary Meeting in the Parish-Church of St. Mary-Le-Bow, On Friday, February 18, 1742–3*. London: J. Roberts, 1743.

Mayor, J. E. B., *Cambridge Under Queen Anne: Illustrated by Memoir of Ambrose Bonwicke and Diaries of Francis Burman and Zacharias Conrad von Uffenbach*. Cambridge: Deighton, Bell & Co., 1911.

McCahill, W. M., ed., *The Correspondence of Stephen Fuller, 1788–1795: Jamaica, the West India Interest at Westminster and the Campaign to Preserve the Slave Trade*. Chichester: West Sussex, 2014.

McKinnen, Daniel, *A Tour Through the British West Indies, in the Years 1802 and 1803, Giving a Particular Account of the Bahama Islands*. London: J. White, 1804.

Measom, George, *The Official Illustrated Guide to the Great Eastern Railway (Cambridge Line): With Descriptions of Some of the Most Important Manufactories in the Towns on the Lines*. Cambridge: C. Griffin and Co., 1865.

Mede, Joseph, *The Works of the Pious and Profoundly-Learned Joseph Mede, B. D. Sometime Fellow of Christ's College in Cambridge. In Five Books: The Fourth Edition*. London: Roger Norton and Richard Royston, 1677.

Melville, Elizabeth, *A Residence at Sierra Leone. Described from a Journal Kept on the Spot, and from Letters written to Friends at Home*. London: John Murray, 1849.

Memoirs Read Before the Anthropological Society of London, 1863–4. London: Trübner and Co., 1865.

Merrill, Walter M., ed., *The Letters of William Lloyd Garrison, Volume III: No Union with Slavers, 1841–1849*. Cambridge, MA: The Belknap Press of Harvard University Press, 1973.

Middleton, Conyers, *The Miscellaneous Works Of the late Reverend and Learned Conyers Middleton, D.D. Principal Librarian of the University of Cambridge*, 8 vols. London: R. Manby and H. S. Cox, 1755.

Miller, Samuel, *A Brief Retrospect of the Eighteenth century. Part First; In Two Volumes: Containing a Sketch of the Revolutions and Improvements in Science, Arts, and Literature, During that Period*, 2 vols. New York: T. and J. Swords, 1803.

Milner, Mary, ed., *The Life of Isaac Milner, D.D., F.R.S., Dean of Carlisle, President of Queen's College, and Professor of Mathematics in the University of Cambridge; comprising a portion of his correspondence and other writings hitherto unpublished*. London: John W. Parker, 1842.

The Missionary Register For MDCCCXXIV. Containing the Principal Transactions of the Various Institutions for Propagating the Gospel: with the Proceedings, at Large, of the Church Missionary Society. London: R. Watts, 1824.

Moll, Herman, *A view of the coasts, countrys & islands within the limits of the South-Sea Company: Containing A Relation of the Discoveries, Settlements, and present State; the Bays, Ports, Harbours, Rivers, &c. the Product, People, Manufactures, Trade, and Riches of the several Places: With an Account of Former Projects in England for a Settlement, and the Accomplishment of the Last in the Present Company. As also Lists of the Commissioners, Governours, and Directors Names appointed by Her Majesty. With Some Useful Observations on the several Voyages hitherto publish'd*. London: John Morphew, 1712.

Moore, Frank, ed., *The Rebellion Record: A Diary of American Events with Documents, Narratives, Illustrative Incidents, Poetry, etc.*, 11 vols. New York: O.P. Putnam, 1861–68.

Moore, George, *The First Man and His Place in Creation*. London: Longmans, Green, and Co., 1866.

Murphy, Ann B., and Deidre Raftery, eds., *Emily Davies: Collected Letters, 1861–1875*. Charlottesville: University of Virginia Press, 2004.

Neil, Michael, ed., *William Shakespeare: Othello, the Moor of Venice*. Oxford: Oxford University Press, 2006.

The New Annual Register, or General Repository of History, Politics, and Literature, For the Year 1788. London: J. and J. Robinson, 1789.

Newton, Thomas, *Dissertations on the Prophecies, Which Have Remarkably Been Fulfilled, and At This Time Are Fulfilling in the World*, 3 vols. Perth: R. Morison Junior, 1790.

Nicolson, Marjorie Hope, and Sarah Hutton, eds., *The Conway Letters: The Correspondence of Anne, Viscountess Conway, Henry More, and Their Friends 1642–1684*. Oxford: Clarendon Press, 1992.

Ockley, Simon, *An Account of South-West Barbary: Containing What is most Remarkable in the Territories of the King of Fez and Morocco. Written by a Person who had been a Slave there a considerable Time; and Published from his Authentick Manuscript. To which are Added, Two Letters: One from the Present King of Morocco to Colonel Kirk; The Other to Sir Cloudesly Shovell: With Sir Cloudesly's Answer, &c.* London: J. Bowyer and H. Clements, 1713.

Oldfield, John R., ed., *Civilization and Black Progress: Selected Writings of Alexander Crummell on the South*. Charlottesville and London: University Press of Virginia, 1995.

Otter, William, *The Life and Remainings of the Rev. Edward Daniel Clarke, LL.D. Professor of Mineralogy in the University of Cambridge*. London: J. F. Dove, 1824.

Oxford Prize Poems: Being a Collection of Such English Poems as Have at Various Times Obtained Prizes in the University of Oxford. Oxford: J. H. Parker, 1839.

Pagden, Anthony, and Jeremy Lawrance, eds., *Vittoria: Political Writings*. Cambridge: Cambridge University Press, 1991.

Paley, William, *The Principles of Moral and Political Philosophy*, 2 vols. London: R. Faulder, 1785.

The Works of William Paley, D. D. Archdeacon of Carlisle. With a Life and Portrait of the Author. In Five Volumes, 5 vols. Edinburgh: John Fairbairn, 1825.

Papers Relative to the West Indies. Part IV. Bahamas. Honduras. Mauritius. Cape of Good Hope. London: House of Commons, 1839.

Parisian, Catherine M., ed., *The First White House Library: A History and Annotated Catalogue*. University Park, PA: Pennsylvania State University Press, 2010.

Park, Mungo, *Travels in the Interior District of Africa: Performed Under the Direction and Patronage of the African Association in the Years 1795, 1796, and 1797*. London: W. Bulmer and Company, 1799.

Parks, Gary, ed., *Virginia Tax Records: From the Virginia Magazine of History and Biography, the William and Mary Quarterly, and Tyler's Quarterly*. Baltimore: Genealogical Publishing Company, 1983.

Patrick, Simon, *A Commentary Upon the First Book of Moses, Called Genesis*. London: Chiswell, 1695.

Pearce, Zachary, *Epistolæ Duæ ad Celeberrimum Doctissimumque Virum F—V— Professorem Amestelodamensem Scriptæ*. London: Francis Clay, 1721.

Peckard, Peter, *Justice and Mercy recommended, particularly with reference to the Slave Trade. A Sermon Preached Before the University of Cambridge*. Cambridge: J. Archdeacon, 1788.

The Nature and Extent of Civil and Religious Liberty. A Sermon Preached Before the University of Cambridge, November the 5th 1783. Cambridge: J. Archdeacon 1783.

The Neglect of a Known Duty is a Sin. A Sermon Preached before the University of Cambridge on Sunday, January 31, 1790. Cambridge: J. Archdeacon, 1790.

Piety, Benevolence, and Loyalty, recommended: A sermon preached before the University of Cambridge, January the 30th, 1784. Published at the request of the Vice-Chancellor and Heads of Colleges. Cambridge: J. Archdeacon for J. & J. Merrill, 1784.

Percy's Anecdotes: Original and Select. London: T. Boys, 1822.

Peterson, Merrill D., ed., *Thomas Jefferson: Writings*. New York: The Library of America, 2011.

Pittis, William, *The History of the Present Parliament and Convocation with the Debates at large relating to the Conduct of the War abroad, the Mismanagements of the Ministry at home, and the Reasons why some Offenders are not yet Impeached. Interspers'd with several Speeches and Representations of Grievances, in Matters Religious as well as Civil; together with the Motives that induc'd the B----ps not to consent to the Representation agreed to by the Committee of both Houses of Convocation. To which is added an exact List of the Parliament and Convocation, as also an Abstract of the South Sea Act; with a List of the Commissioners Names*. London: John Baker, 1711.

Plumptre, James, *Four Discourses on Subjects Relating to the Amusement of the Stage: Preached at St. Mary's Church, Cambridge, on Sunday September 25, and Sunday October 2, 1808*. Cambridge: Francis Hodson, 1809.

Porteus, Beilby, *A Letter to the Governors, Legislatures, and Proprietors of Plantations, in the British West-India Islands*. London: T. Cadell and W. Davies, 1808.

Porteus, Beilby, *Sermons on Several Subjects by the Right Reverend Beilby Porteus, D.D. Bishop of London*. London: T. Payne, T. Cadell, and W. Davies, 1808.

Pratt, Frederic Thomas, ed., *Law of Contraband of War: With a Selection of Cases from the Papers of the Right Hon. Sir George Lee, LL.D. Formerly Dean of the Arches, Etc. Etc. Etc. And An Appendix Containing Extracts from Treaties, Miscellaneous Papers, and Forms of Proceedings. With the Cases to the Present Time*. London: William G. Benning, 1856.

Prichard, M. J., and D. E. C. Yale, ed., *Hale and Fleetwood on Admiralty Jurisdiction*. London: Selden Society, 1993.

Priestley, Charles, ed., 'A Philosopher's Defense of the Confederacy: Jermyn Cowell to Henry Sidgwick, September 1863', *North & South* 9 (May 2006): 82–88.

Pryme, George, *An Introductory Lecture and Syllabus, to a Course Delivered in the University of Cambridge, on the Principles of Political Economy*. Cambridge: Deighton & Sons, 1823.

Purchas, Samuel, *Purchase His Pilgrimage. Or Relations of the World and the Religions Observed in all Ages and Places discouered, from the Creation unto this Present*. London: William Stansby, 1613.

Quintard, Charles Todd, *The Confederate Soldier's Pocket Manual of Devotions*. Charleston, SC: Evans & Cogswell, 1863.

'Ralph Wormeley V (1745–1806)', *Colonial Virginia Portraits*, https://colonialvirginiaportraits.org/portrait/ralph-wormeley-v-1745-1806-2/, accessed 9 September 2020.

Ramsay, David, *A Dissertation on the Manner of Acquiring the Character and Privileges of a Citizens of the United States*. Charleston: Unknown, 1789.

Randolph, Francis, *A Letter to the Right Honourable William Pitt, Chancellor of the Exchequer, &c. &c. On the Proposed Abolition of the African Slave Trade*. London: T. Cadell, 1798.

A Letter to the Right Hon. William Pitt, Containing some New Arguments against the Abolition of the Slave Trade. London: A. Macpherson, 1804.

Randolph, George, *An Inquiry into the Medicinal Virtues of Bristol Waters*. Oxford: M. Cooper, 1745.

Ray, John, *The Wisdom of God Manifested in the Works of the Creation. Being the Substance of some common Places delivered in the Chappel of Trinity-College, in Cambridge*. London: Samuel Smith, 1691.

Recorde, Robert, *The Whetstone of Witte: whiche is the seconde parte of arithmetike; containyng the extraction of rootes: the cossike practise, with the rule of equation: and the woorkes of surde nombers*. London: Robert Recorde, 1557.

Reeve, Clara, *The Progress of Romance, through Times, Countries, and Manners… In a Course of Evening Conversations*, 2 vols. Colchester: W. Keymer, 1785.

Remarks on the Enormous Expence in the Education of Young Men in the University of Cambridge; with a Plan for the Better Regulation of the Discipline of that University. London: C. Stalker, 1788.

Report of the Proceedings of the Great Anti-Slavery Meeting, Held at the Town Hall, Birmingham, on Wednesday, October 14th, 1835; with an Appendix, containing Notices of the Condition of the Apprenticed Labourers in the West Indies under the Act for the Abolition of Slavery in the British Colonies. Birmingham: B. Hudson, 1835.

Report on Manuscripts in Various Collections, 6 vols. Dublin: John Falconer, 1901–14.

Reports from Commissioners: Twenty-One Volumes. Universities of Oxford and Cambridge, 21 vols. London: Parliament, 1873.

Riland, Rev. John, *Memoirs of a West-India Planter. Published from an Original MS. With a Preface and Additional Details*. London: Hamilton, Adams & Co., 1827.

Ripley, C. Peter, ed, *The Black Abolitionist Papers*, 5 vols. Chapel Hill: University of North Carolina Press, 1985–1992.

'Robert E. Lee to Mary Anna Randolph Custis Lee, 27 December 1856', *Lee Family Digital Archive*, https://leefamilyarchive.org/9-family-papers/339-robert-e-lee-to-mary-anna-randolph-custis-lee-1856-december-27, accessed 6 December 2021.

Robertson, Rev. Robert, *A Letter to the Right Reverend the Lord Bishop of London, From An Inhabitant of His Majesty's Leeward-Caribbee-Islands. Containing some Considerations on His Lordship's Two Letters of May 19, 1727. The First to the Masters and Mistresses of Families in the English Plantations abroad; The Second to the Missionaries There. In which is Inserted, A Short Essay concerning the conversion of the Negro-Slaves in our Sugar-Colonies: Written in the Month of June, 1727, by the same Inhabitant*. London: J. Wilford, 1730.

Robinson, Robert, *Slavery inconsistent with the Spirit of Christianity. A Sermon Preached at Cambridge, on Sunday, Feb. 10, 1788*. Cambridge: J. Archdeacon, 1788.

Roos, Anna Marie, ed., *The Correspondence of Dr. Martin Lister (1639–1712). Volume One: 1662–1677*. Leiden and Boston: Brill, 2015.

Roper, Joseph, *A Sermon Preach'd at the Anniversary Meeting of the Sons of Clergy, in the Cathedral-Church of St. Paul, on the 9th of December, 1725*. London: Jonah Bowyer, 1725.

Roth, Henry Ling, *A Sketch of the Agriculture and Peasantry of Eastern Russia*. London: Baillière, Tindall, & Cox, 1878.

Rowland, Kate M., ed., *Life of George Mason, 1725–1792*, 2 vols. New York and London: G. P. Putnam's Sons, 1892.

Royal African Company, *A List of the Names of the Adventurers of the Royal African Company of England. Whereof those Marked ++, are Qualified by their Adventure, to be Elected Governor, Sub-Governor, or Deputy-Governor; those Marked +, are Qualified to be Elected of the Court of Assistants, and have Five Votes each. And those who are not Mark'd, have each Five Votes*. London: Royal African Company, 1720.

Ruskin, John, *Cambridge School of Art. Mr. Ruskin's Inaugural Address. Delivered at Cambridge, Oct. 29, 1858*. Cambridge: Deighton, Bell, and Co. 1858.

Rutherforth, Thomas, *Institutes of Natural Law: Being the substance of a Course of Lectures on Grotius de Jure Belli et Pacis Read in St. Johns College Cambridge*, 2 vols. Cambridge: J. Bentham, 1745–46.

Two Sermons Preached Before the University of Cambridge, One May XXIX: The Other June XI: MDCCXLVII. London: W. Innys, 1747.

Saddler, Thomas, ed., *Diary, Reminiscences, and Correspondence of Henry Crabb Robinson, Barrister-at-Law, F.S.A.*, 3 vols. London: Macmillan and Co., 1869.

Sainsbury, Ethel Bruce, and William Foster, eds., *A Calendar of the Court Minutes Etc. of the East India Company 1655–1659*. Oxford: Clarendon Press, 1916.

Salmon, Thomas, *The Foreigner's Companion Through the Universities of Cambridge and Oxford, and the Adjacent Counties. Describing the Several Colleges, and other Public Buildings. With An Account of their respective Founders, Benefactors, Bishops, and other Eminent Men educated in them*. London: William Owen, 1748.

Modern History: or, the Present State of All Nations, 3 vols. London: Bettesworth and Hitch, 1739.

Scarlett, Peter Campbell, ed., *A Memoir of the Right Honourable James, First Lord Abinger Chief Baron of Her Majesty's Court of Exchequer*. London: John Murray, 1877.

Schaw, Janet, *Journal of a Lady of Quality: Being the Narrative of a Journey from Scotland to the West Indies, North Carolina, and Portugal, in the Years 1774 to 1776*, ed. by Evangeline Walker Andrews and Charles McLean Andrews. New Haven, CT: Yale University Press, 1921.

'The Seal of St. Paul's College, c. 1853', *National Museum of Bermuda*, https://nmb.bm/collection/the-seal-of-st-pauls-college-c-1853/, accessed 11 July 2023.

Second Annual Report of the American Anti-Slavery Society; with the Speeches Delivered at the Anniversary Meeting, Held in the City of New-York, On the 12th May, 1835, and the Minutes of the Meetings of the Society for Business. New York: William S. Dorr, 1835.

Selected Parts of the Holy Bible, For the Use of the Negro Slaves, in the British West-India Islands. London: Law and Gilbert, 1807.

Sewall, Samuel, *The Selling of Joseph: A Memorial*. Boston: Bartholomew Green and John Allen, 1700.

Sharp, Granville, *An Essay on Slavery, Proving from Scripture its Inconsistency with Humanity and Religion*. Burlington: Isaac Collins, 1776.
Free English Territory in Africa. London: Unknown, 1790.
The Just Limitation of Slavery in the Laws of God, Compared with the unbounded Claims of the African Traders and British American Slaveholders. London: B. White, 1776.
Shaw, John, ed., *Charters Relating to the East India Company from 1600 to 1761*. Madras: R. Hill, 1887.
Shedd, W. G. T., ed., *The Complete Works of Samuel Taylor Coleridge: With an Introductory Essay Upon His Philosophical and Theological Opinions*, 7 vols. New York: Harper & Brothers, 1884.
Sherlock, Thomas, *The Lord Bishop of Bangor's Defence of His Assertion, Viz. That the Example of our Lord is much more peculiarly fit to be urged to Slaves than to Subjects, Considered*. London: J. Pemberton, 1718.
Shortt, Adam, and Arthur G. Doughty, eds., *Documents Relating to the Constitutional History of Canada, 1759–1791: Second and Revised Edition*. Ottawa: J. de L. Taché, 1918.
'Silverware, 1750–99', *Queens' College, University of Cambridge*, www.queens.cam.ac.uk/visiting-the-college/history/college-facts/silverware/silverware-1750-99, accessed 30 April 2020.
Sir Nathaniel Lloyd's Charity, *Further Report of the Commissioners Appointed in Pursuance of Two Several Acts of Parliament; The one, made and passed in the 58th Year of His late Majesty, c. 91, intituled, 'An Act for appointing Commissioners to inquire concerning Charities in England, for the Education of the Poor;' And the other, made and passed in the 59th Year of His late Majesty, c. 81, intituled, 'An Act to amend an Act of the last Session of Parliament, for appointing Commissioners to inquire concerning Charities in England, for the Education of The Poor, and to extend the Powers thereof to other Charities in England and Wales:' And both of which Acts have been continued by an Act passed in the 5th Year of His present Majesty, c. 58; And by another Act passed in the 10th Year of His present Majesty, c. 57*. London: House of Commons, 1831.
Sixteenth Report of the Directors of the African Institution, Read at the Annual General Meeting, Held on the 10th Day of May, 1822. With an Account of the Proceedings of the Annual Meeting, and an Appendix. London: Ellerton and Henderson, 1822.
'Slave Trade Felony Bill, March 1811', *Hansard*, https://api.parliament.uk/historic-hansard/commons/1811/mar/05/slave-trade-felony-bill#column_233, accessed 7 July 2023.
Smith, Jonathan, and Christopher Stray, eds., *Cambridge in the 1830s: The Letters of Alexander Chisolm Gooden, 1831–1841*. London: Boydell & Brewer, 2003.
Smith, Sir Thomas, *A Letter sent by I. B. Gentleman unto his very frende Mayster R. C. Esquire, wherin is conteined a large discourse of the peopling and inhabiting the Cuntrie called the Ardes, and other adiacent in the North of Ireland, and*

taken in hand by Sir Thomas Smith, one of the Queens Maisties priuie counsel, and Thomas Smith Esquire, his sonne. London: Henry Binneman, 1572.

De Republica Anglorum: The maner of Gouernement or policie of the Realme of England, compiled by the Honorable man Thomas Smyth, Doctor of the civil lawes, Knight, and principall Secretarie unto the two most worthie Princes, King Edwarde the sixt, and Queene Elizabeth. London: Henrie Midleton, 1583.

Smith, William, *A Natural History of Nevis, and the Rest of the English Leeward Charibee Islands in America With Many Other Observations on Nature and Art*. Cambridge: Cambridge University Press, 2014.

Some Considerations humbly offered to both Houses of Parliament, Concerning the Sugar Colonies, and Chiefly the Island of Barbadoes. London: A. Baldwin, 1701.

South Sea Company, *A List of the Names of the Corporation of the Governor and Company of Merchants of Great Britain Trading to the South-Seas, and other Parts of America, and for Encouraging the Fishery; Who are Qualified to Vote at the ensuing Election for Governor, Sub-Governor, and Deputy-Governor, to be made on the Thirty First of January; and of Directors on the Second Day of February next: Together with Part of the 7th By-Law concerning Elections.* London: John Barber, 1720.

A List of the Names of the Corporation of the Governor and Company of Merchants of Great Britain Trading to the South-Seas, and other Parts of America, and for Encouraging the Fishery; Who are Qualified to Vote at the ensuing Election for Governor, Sub-Governor, and Deputy-Governor, to be made on the Third, and of Directors on the fifth Day of February next; Together with Part of the 7th By-Law concerning Elections. London: Edward Symon, 1723.

A List of the Name of the Corporation of the Governor and Company of Merchants of Great Britain, Trading to the South-Seas, and other Parts of America, and for Encouraging the Fishery; Who are Qualified to Vote at the ensuing Election for Governor, Sub-Governor, and Deputy-Governor, to be made on Tuesday the 3d. and of Director on Thursday the 5th Day of February next: Together with Part of the 7th By-Law concerning Elections. London: Edward Symon, 1735.

A List of the Names of the Corporation of the Governor and Company of Merchants of Great Britain, Trading to the South-Seas, and other Parts of America and for Encouraging the Fishery. Who are Qualified to Vote at the ensuing Election for Governor, Sub-Governor, and Deputy-Governor, to be made on Tuesday the Second, and of Directors on Thursday the Fourth Day of February next: Together with Part of the Seventh By-Law concerning Elections. London: South Sea Company, 1747.

Sowerby, E. Millicent, ed., *Catalogue of the Library of Thomas Jefferson*, 5 vols. Washington, D.C.: Library of Congress, 1953.

Speake, Jennifer, ed., *Literature of Travel and Exploration: An Encyclopedia, Volume One: A To F*. London and New York: Routledge, 2003.

Spurzheim, Johann Gaspar, *Examination of the Objections Made in Britain against the Doctrines of Gall and Spurzheim*. Boston: Marsh, Capen & Lyon, 1833.

Stedman, John Gabriel, *Narrative, of a five years' expedition, against the Revolted Negroes of Surinam, in Guiana, on the Wild Coast of South America; from the Year 1772, to 1777: elucidating the History of that Country, and describing its Productions*, 2 vols. London: J. J. Johnson, 1796.

Stephen, James, *England Enslaved by Her Own Slave Colonies. An Address to the People and Electors of England*. London: Hatchard and Son, 1826.

Stone, William, *Shall We Annex Egypt: Remarks upon the Present Aspect of the Egyptian Question, Founded upon Observations made in the Country whilst Travelling in the Delta and in the Soudan*. London: Sampson Low, Marston, Searle, and Rivington, 1884.

Story, Joseph, *Commentaries on the Constitution of the United States*, 3 vols. Boston: Hilliard, Gray, and Company, 1833.

Strype, John, *The Life of the Learned Sir Thomas Smith, Kt. Doctor of the Civil Law, Principal Secretary of State to King Edward the Sixth, and Queen Elizabeth*. Oxford: Clarendon Press, 1820.

Subscriptions for Building a New Library, &c. &c. in the University of Cambridge. Cambridge: Pitt Press, 1836.

Sunderland, Rev. La Roy, *Anti-Slavery Manual, Containing a Collection of Facts and Arguments on American Slavery*. New York: S. W. Benedict, 1837.

Swan, John, *Speculum Mundi or a Glasse Representing the Face of the World; Shewing both that it did begin, and must also end: The manner How, and time When being largely examined*. Cambridge: Printers to the University of Cambridge, 1635.

Taylor, John, *Elements of the Civil Law*. Cambridge: Charles Bathurst, 1755.

Summary of the Roman Law, Taken from Dr. Taylor's Elements of the Civil War. To which is Prefixed a Dissertation on Obligation. London: T. Payne, 1772.

Taylor, Thomas, *The Works of the Judicious and Learned Divine Thomas Taylor D. D. Late Pastor of Aldermanbury London*, 2 vols. London: Thomas Ratcliffe, 1659.

Taylor, Yuvan, ed., *I Was Born a Slave: An Anthology of Classic Slave Narratives*, 2 vols. New York: Lawrence Hill Books, 1999.

Telfair, Charles, and Thomas Jackson, *An Appeal to the Freeholders of the County of Cambridge and Isle of Ely, on the Subject of Colonial Slavery*. Cambridge: W. Metcalfe, 1832.

Britain's Burden, or, The Intolerable Evils of Colonial Slavery Exposed. Cambridge: W. Metcalfe, 1832.

The Third Annual Report of the British and Foreign Anti-Slavery Society, for the Abolition of Slavery and the Slave-Trade Throughout the World; Presented to the General Meeting Held in Exeter Hall, On Friday, May 13th, 1842. London: Thomas Ward and Co., 1842.

Thomas, John Henry, and John Farquhar Fraser, eds., *The Reports of Sir Edward Coke, Knt. In Thirteen Parts: A New Edition*, 6 vols. London: Joseph Butterworth and Son, 1826.

Thomason, Rev. Thomas Truebody, *An Essay Tending to Shew that the Christian Religion Has in its Effects been Favourable to Human Happiness*. Cambridge: J. Burghes, 1800.

Thompson, Thomas, *A Discourse Relating to the Present Times, Addressed to the Serious Consideration of the Public*. London: J. Oliver, 1757.

The African Trade for Negro Slaves, Consistent with Humanity and Revealed Religion. Canterbury: Simmons and Kirkby, 1772.

A Letter from New Jersey in America, Giving Some Account and Description of that Province. London: M. Cooper, 1756.

An Account of Two Missionary Voyages by the Appointment of the Society for the Propagation of the Gospel in Foreign Parts. This one to New Jersey in North America, the other from America to the Coast of Guiney. London: Benjamin Dod, 1758.

Thompson, Thomas Perronet, *Catechism on the Corn Laws; with a List of Fallacies and the Answers. Twelfth Edition*. London: Robert Heward, 1829.

Thompson, T. W., and Robert Woof, ed., *Wordsworth's Hawkshead*. London: Oxford University Press, 1970.

Thornbury, Walter, ed., *The Life of J. M. W. Turner: Founded on Letters and Papers Furnished By His Friends and Fellow Academicians*, 2 vols. Cambridge: Cambridge University Press, 2013.

Thorne, R. G., ed., *The History of Parliament: The House of Commons, 1790–1820*, 5 vols. London: Haynes Publishing, 1986.

Tillotson, John, ed., *The Works of Isaac Barrow, D. D.*, 4 vols. London: J. R., 1686–1692.

Tomlins, Harold Nuttall, *A Digest of the Criminal Statute Law of England. Alphabetically and Analytically Arranged*, 2 vols. London: A. Strahan, 1819.

Townley, James, 'Abolition of Slavery, 1833', *JSTOR Primary Sources*, www.jstor.org/stable/60227882, accessed 16 June 2023.

'Travellers' Impressions of Slavery in America from 1750 to 1800', *The Journal of Negro History* 1 (October 1916): 399–435.

The Trial of Captain John Kimber, for the Murder of Two Female Negro Slaves, on Board the Recovery, African Slave Ship. London: C. Stalker, 1792.

Tucker, St. George, *Dissertation on Slavery: With A Proposal for the Gradual Abolition of It, in the State of Virginia*. Philadelphia: Mathew Carey, 1796.

Tweddell, Rev. Robert, ed., *Remains of John Tweddell, Late Fellow of Trinity-College Cambridge Being a Selection of his Correspondence a Republication of his Prolusiones Juveniles an Appendix Containing Some Account of the Author's Collections Mss. Drawings &c*. London: J. Mawman, 1816.

The Twenty-Eighth Annual Report of the Deputy Keeper of the Public Records. London: George E. Eyre and William Spottiswoode, 1867.

'Virginia Gleanings in England', *The Virginia Magazine of History and Biography* 25 (October 1917): 389–399.

von Pufendorf, Samuel, *Of the Law of Nature and Nations. Eight Books. Written in Latin by the Baron Pufendorf, Counsellor of State to His late Swedish Majesty, and to the present King of Prussia*. Oxford: L. Lichfield, 1703.

Waddington, Edward, *A Sermon preached before the Incorporated Society for the Propagation of the Gospel in Foreign Parts; at their Anniversary Meeting in the Parish-Church of St. Mary le Bow; on Friday the 17th of February, 1720*. London: John Downing, 1721.

Wadstrom, C. B., *An Essay on Colonization, Particularly Applied to the Western Coast of Africa, with Some Free Thoughts on Cultivation and Commerce; Also Brief Descriptions of the Colonies Already Formed, or Attempted, in Africa, including those of Sierra Leona and Bulama*. London: Darton and Harvey, 1794.

Wakefield, Gilbert, *Memoirs of the Life of Gilbert Wakefield, B. A. Late Fellow of Jesus College, Cambridge*. London: E. Hodson, 1792.

Walker, Richard, *A Short Account of the late Donation of a Botanic Garden to the University of Cambridge By the Revd Dr. Walker, Vice-Master of Trinity College; with Rules and Orders for the Government of it*. Cambridge: J. Bentham, 1763.

Waterhouse, Edward, and Henry Briggs, *A declaration of the state of the colony and affaires in Virginia With a relation of the barbarous massacre in the time of peace and league, treacherously executed by the native infidels upon the English, the 22 of March last. Together with the names of those that were then massacred; that their lawfull heyres, by this notice giuen, may take order for the inheriting of their lands and estates in Virginia. And a treatise annexed, written by that learned mathematician Mr. Henry Briggs, of the Northwest passage to the South Sea through the continent of Virginia, and by Fretum Hudson. Also a commemoration of such worthy benefactors as have contributed their Christian charitie towards the advancement of the colony. And a note of the charges of necessary provisions fit for every man that intends to goe to Virginia. Published by authoritie*. London: Robert Mylbourne, 1622.

Waterland, Daniel, *Advice to a Young Student. With a Method of Study for the Four First Years*. London: John Crownfield, 1730.

Watson, Richard, Jr., ed., *Anecdotes of the Life of Richard Watson, Bishop of Llandaff. Written By Himself at Different Intervals, and Revised in 1814*. London: T. Cadell and W. Davies, 1817.

Wenger, Mark R., ed., *The English Travels of Sir John Percival and William Byrd II: The Percival Diary of 1701*. Columbia: University of Missouri Press, 1989.

Whibley, Charles, ed., *In Cap and Gown: Three Centuries of Cambridge Wit*. London: Kegan Paul, Trench, & Co., 1889.

Whitaker, Alexander, *Good newes from Virginia Sent to the Counsell and Company of Virginia, resident in England. From Alexander Whitaker, the minister of Henrico in Virginia. Wherein also is a narration of the present state of that countrey, and our colonies there. Perused and published by direction from that Counsell. And a preface prefixed of some matters touching that plantation, very requisite to be made knowne* London: William Welby, 1613.

White, Colonel Harry Kidder, ed., *Official Records of the Union and Confederate Navies in the War of the Rebellion*, 27 vols. Washington, D.C.: Naval War Records Office 1894–1922.

Whitmore, William H., ed., *The Colonial Laws of Massachusetts. Reprinted from the Edition of 1672, With the Supplements through 1686. Containing also, a Bibliographical Preface and Introduction Treating of all the Printed Laws from 1649 to 1686. Together with the Body of Liberties of 1641, and the Records of the Court of Assistants, 1641–1644*. Boston: Rockwell and Churchill, 1890.

The Whole of the Proceedings and Trial of Captain John Kimber for the wilful murder of a Negro girl: held at the Old Bailey on the 7th and 8th of June 1792 by virtue of his Majesty's commission; to which is added, an extract from Mr. Wilberforce's speech, which gave rise to the trial; also the charges to the juries; being the most complete edition published. Edinburgh: John Elder, 1792.

Wilcocks, Joseph, *A Sermon Preached Before the Incorporated Society for the Propagation of the Gospel in Foreign Parts; at their Anniversary Meeting in the Parish-Church of St. Mary-le-Bow; on Friday the 18th of February, 1725*. London: Joseph Downing, 1726.

'The Will of Charles Carter of Cleve', *The Virginia Magazine of History and Biography* 31 (December 1923): 39–69.

Winterbottom, Thomas, *An Account of the Native Africans in the Neighbourhood of Sierra Leone*, 2 vols. London: C. Whittingham, 1803.

Winthrop, Adam, ed., *Winthrop Papers*, 4 vols. Boston: The Massachusetts Historical Society, 1944–47.

Witherspoon, John, *The Works of John Witherspoon, D. D. Sometime Minister of the Gospel at Paisley, and Late President of Princeton College, in New Jersey*, 5 vols. Edinburgh: J. Ogle, 1815.

Witt, John George, *Life in the Law*. London: T. Werner Laurie, 1906.

Woodward, John, *An Attempt Towards a Natural History of the Fossils of England; In A Catalogue of the English Fossils in the Collection of J. Woodward, M. D. Containing A Description and Historical Account of each; with observations and Experiments, made in order to discover, as well the Origin and Nature of them, as their Medicinal, Mechanical, and other Uses*, 2 vols. London: F. Fayram, 1729.

Brief instructions for making observations in all parts of the world as also, for collecting, preserving, and sending over natural things: being an attempt to settle an universal correspondence for the advancement of knowledge both natural and civil. London: Richard Wilkin, 1696.

The Natural History of the Earth, Illustrated, Inlarged, and Defended. London: Thomas Edlin, 1726.

Wordsworth, Christopher, *Scholae Academica*. Cambridge: Cambridge University Press, 1877.

Wright, Christopher, *The Irresistible Glory and Everlasting Freedom; or, Religious Liberty, Exempt from Slavery. Being an Entire New Work*. Birmingham: Mr. Brown, 1787.

Wright, John, *The American Negotiator, or the Various Currencies of the British Colonies in America*. London: J. Smith, 1765.

Wright, Thomas, and Rev. H. Longueville Jones, ed., *Memorials of Cambridge: A Series of Views of the College Halls, and Public Buildings, Engraved by*

J. Le Keux; with Historical and Descriptive Accounts, 2 vols. London: David Bogue, 1845.

Yarnall, Ellis, *Wordsworth and the Coleridges: With Other Memories, Literary and Political*. London: Macmillan and Co., 1899.

The Young Logicians; or School-Boy Conceptions of Rights and Wrongs. With a Particular Reference to 'Six Months in the West Indies'. Part the Second. Birmingham: B. Hudson, 1828.

SECONDARY SOURCES

Ablavsky, Gregory, 'Making Indians "White": The Judicial Abolition of Native Slavery in Revolutionary Virginia and its Racial Legacy', *University of Pennsylvania Law Review* 159 (April 2011): 1457–1531.

Alexander, Leslie M., *Fear of a Black Republic: Haiti and the Birth of Black Internationalism in the United States*. Champaign, IL: University of Illinois Press, 2023.

Allen, Jody, Stephanie Blackmon, David Brown, Kelley Deetz, Leah Glenn, Chon Glover, Artisia Green, Susan A. Kearn, Arthur Knight, Terry Meyers, Neil Norman, Sarah Thomas, and Alexandra Yeumeni, eds., *The Lemon Project: A Journey of Reconciliation: Report of the First Eight Years*. Williamsburg, VA: College of William and Mary, 2019.

Allen, Richard B., *European Slave Trading in the Indian Ocean, 1500–1850*. Athens: Ohio University Press, 2014.

⸻ 'Satisfying the "Want for Labouring People": European Slave Trading in the Indian Ocean, 1500–1850', *Journal of World History* 21 (March 2010): 45–73.

Allison, K. J., ed., *A History of the County of York East Riding: Volume 1, the City of Kingston Upon Hull*. London: Victoria County History, 1969.

Allpress, Roshan, *British Philanthropy in the Globalizing World: Entrepreneurs and Evangelicals, 1756–1840*. Oxford: Oxford University Press, 2023.

Alpaugh, Micah, *Friends of Freedom: The Rise of Social Movements in the Age of Atlantic Revolution*. Cambridge: Cambridge University Press, 2021.

Alston, David, *Slaves and Highlanders: Silenced Histories of Scotland and the Caribbean*. Edinburgh: Edinburgh University Press, 2021.

Anderson, Jennifer L., *Mahogany: The Cost of Luxury in Early America*. Cambridge, MA: Harvard University Press, 2015.

Anderson, John G. T., *Deep Things Out of Darkness: A History of Natural History*. Berkeley: University of California Press, 2013.

Anderson, Richard, 'Abolition's Adolescence: Apprenticeship as "Liberation" in Sierra Leone, 1808–1848', *The English Historical Review* 137 (June 2022): 763–793.

Anderson, Richard Peter, *Abolition in Sierra Leone: Re-building Lives and Identities in Nineteenth-Century West Africa*. Cambridge: Cambridge University Press, 2020.

Anderson, Robert, *British Universities: Past and Present*. London: Hambledon Continuum, 2006.

Anderson, Stuart, *Pharmacy and the Professionalization of the British Empire, 1780–1970*. London: Palgrave Macmillan, 2021.
An Inventory of the Historical Monuments in the City of Cambridge. London: Her Majesty's Stationary Office, 1959.
Ansorge, Catherine, 'The Revd George Lewis: His Life and Collection', *Journal of the History of Collections* 32 (March 2020): 143–156.
Anstey, Roger, *The Atlantic Slave Trade and British Abolition, 1760–1810*. London: Humanities Press, 1975.
Araujo, Ana Lucia, ed., *Politics of Memory: Making Slavery Visible in the Public Space*. New York: Routledge, 2012.
Armitage, David, 'George III and the Law of Nations', *The William and Mary Quarterly* 79 (January 2022): 3–30.
  The Ideological Origins of the British Empire. Cambridge: Cambridge University Press, 2000.
Alison Bashford, and Sujit Sivasundaram, eds., *Oceanic Histories*. Cambridge: Cambridge University Press, 2017.
Ash, Eric H., *The Draining of the Fens: Projectors, Popular Politics, and State Building in Early Modern England*. Baltimore: Johns Hopkins University Press, 2017.
Aston, Nigel, *Enlightened Oxford: The University and the Cultural and Political Life of Eighteenth-Century Britain and Beyond*. Oxford: Oxford University Press, 2023.
Atkins, Gareth, *Converting Britannia: Evangelicals and British Public Life, 1770–1840*. Woodbridge, Suffolk: The Boydell Press, 2019.
Axtell, James, *The Rise and Fall of the Powhatan Empire: Indians in Seventeenth-Century Virginia*. Williamsburg, VA: Colonial Williamsburg Foundation, 1995.
Bacon, Jacqueline, *Freedom's Journal: The First African-American Newspaper*. New York: Lexington Books, 2007.
Bailyn, Bernard, *Atlantic History: Concepts and Contours*. Cambridge, MA: Harvard University Press, 2005.
Banivanua-Mar, Tracey, *Violence and Colonial Dialogue: The Australian-Pacific Indentured Labour Trade*. Honolulu: University of Hawaii Press, 2007.
Banner, Michael, *Britain's Slavery Debt: Reparations Now!* Oxford: Oxford University Press, 2024.
Bannet, Eve Tavor, *Eighteenth-Century Manners of Reading: Print Culture and Popular Instruction in the Anglophone Atlantic World*. Cambridge: Cambridge University Press, 2017.
Baptist, Edward E., *The Half Has Never Been Told: Slavery and the Making of American Capitalism*. New York: Basic Books, 2014.
Barker, Hannah, *The Business of Women: Female Enterprise and Urban Development in Northern England, 1760–1830*. Oxford: Oxford University Press, 2006.
Barry, Jonathan, and C. W. Brooks, *The Middling Sort of People: Culture, Society, and Politics in England, 1550–1800*. New York: St Martin's Press, 1994.

Bartels, Emily C., *Speaking of the Moor: From Alcazar to Othello*. Philadelphia: University of Pennsylvania Press, 2008.

Bashford, Alison, and Joyce Chaplin, *The New Worlds of Thomas Robert Malthus: Rereading the Principle of Population*. Princeton, NJ: Princeton University Press, 2016.

Bearss, Sara B., ed., *The Dictionary of Virginia Biography*, 3 vols. Richmond: Library of Virginia, 2006.

Beckert, Sven, *Empire of Cotton: A New History of Global Capitalism*. London: Penguin Books, 2015.

— and Seth Rockman, eds., *Slavery's Capitalism: A New History of American Economic Development*. Philadelphia: University of Pennsylvania Press, 2016.

'Bell continues to support an honest approach to the legacies of enslavement', *St Catharine's College, Cambridge*, www.caths.cam.ac.uk/slavery-exhibition, accessed 24 February 2023.

Bell, Duncan, *Dreamworlds of Race: Empire and the Utopian Destiny of Anglo-America*. Princeton, NJ: Princeton University Press, 2020.

Bell, James B., *A War of Religion: Dissenters, Anglicans, and the American Revolution*. Houndmills, Basingstoke: Palgrave Macmillan, 2008.

Belmessous, Saliha, *Assimilation and Empire: Uniformity in French and British Colonies, 1541–1954*. Oxford: Oxford University Press, 2013.

Bennett, John D., *The London Confederates: The Officials, Clergy, Businessmen and Journalists Who Backed the American South During the Civil War*. London: McFarland and Company, 2008.

Bennett, Martyn, Raymond Gillespie, and Scott Spurlock, eds., *Cromwell and Ireland: New Perspectives*. Liverpool: Liverpool University Press, 2021.

Berg, Maxine, *Luxury and Pleasure in Eighteenth-Century Britain*. Oxford: Oxford University Press, 2005.

— and Pat Hudson, *Slavery, Capitalism and the Industrial Revolution*. London: Polity Press, 2023.

Berlin, Ira, *Many Thousands Gone: The First Two Centuries of Slavery in North America*. Cambridge, MA: The Belknap Press of Harvard University Press, 2003.

— and Leslie M. Harris, eds., *Slavery in New York*. New York: The New Press, 2005.

Berry, Daina Ramey, *The Price for Their Pound of Flesh: The Value of the Enslaved, from Womb to Grave, in the Building of a Nation*. Boston: Beacon Press, 2017.

Berry, Mary Frances, *My Face Is Black Is True: Callie House and the Struggle for Ex-slave Reparations*. New York: Knopf, 2005.

Black, Barbara, *A Room of His Own: A Literary-Cultural Study of Victorian Clubland*. Athens: Ohio University Press, 2012.

Black, Jeremy, *Europe and the World, 1650–1830*. London and New York: Routledge, 2002.

— *Geographies of an Imperial Power: The British World, 1688–1815*. Bloomington: Indiana University Press, 2018.

Blackett, Richard J. M., *Divided Hearts: Britain and the American Civil War*. Baton Rouge: Louisiana State University Press, 2001.

Blackmon, Douglas A., *Slavery by Another Name: The Re-enslavement of Black Americans from the Civil War to World War II*. New York: Random House, 2008.

Blight, David W., *Frederick Douglass: Prophet of Freedom*. London: Simon & Schuster, 2018.

and the Yale and Slavery Research Project, *Yale and Slavery: A History*. New Haven, CT and London: Yale University Press. 2024.

Block, Sharon, *Colonial Complexions: Race and Bodies in Eighteenth-Century America*. Philadelphia: University of Pennsylvania Press, 2018.

Rape and Sexual Power in Early America. Philadelphia: University of Pennsylvania Press, 2006.

Bloechl, Olivia, Melanie Lowe, and Jeffrey Kallberg, eds., *Rethinking Difference in Musical Scholarship*. Cambridge: Cambridge University Press, 2014.

Boubacar, Barry, *Senegambia and the Atlantic Slave Trade*. Cambridge: Cambridge University Press, 1998.

Boucher, M., *The University of the Cape of Good Hope and the University of South Africa, 1873-1946: A Study in National and Imperial Perspective*. Pretoria: The Government Printer, 1974.

Bourke, Richard, *Empire and Revolution: The Political Life of Edmund Burke*. Princeton, NJ: Princeton University Press, 2015.

Bowen, H. V., *The Business of Empire: The East India Company and Imperial Britain, 1756-1833*. Cambridge: Cambridge University Press, 2006.

Elites, Enterprise and the Making of the British Overseas Empire, 1688-1775. Basingstoke: Palgrave Macmillan, 1996.

Brahm, Felix, and Eve Rosenhaft, *Slavery Hinterland: Transatlantic Slavery and Continental Europe, 1680-1850*. London: Boydell & Brewer, 2016.

Braidwood, Stephen J., *Black Poor and White Philanthropists: London's Blacks and the Foundation of the Sierra Leone Settlement 1786-1791*. Liverpool: Liverpool University Press, 1994.

Breen, T. H., 'Horses and Gentlemen: The Cultural Significance of Gambling among the Gentry of Virginia', *The William and Mary Quarterly* 34 (April 1977): 239-257.

Brett, Annabel, *Changes of State: Nature and the Limits of the City in Early Modern Natural Law*. Princeton. NJ: Princeton University Press, 2011.

Brewer, Holly, 'Slavery, Sovereignty, and "Inheritable Blood": Reconsidering John Locke and the Origins of American Slavery', *The American Historical Review* 122 (October 2017): 1038-1078.

Brewer, John, *The Sinews of Power: War, Money, and the English State, 1688-1783*. Cambridge, MA: Harvard University Press, 1989.

Brooke, Christopher, *A History of Gonville and Caius College*. Woodbridge, Suffolk: Boydell Press, 1996.

J. M. Horn, and N. L. Ramsay, 'A Canon's Residence in the Eighteenth Century: The Case of Thomas Gooch', *Journal of Ecclesiastical History* 39 (October 1988): 545-556.

Brooks, Lisa Tanya, *Our Beloved Kin: A New History of King Philip's War*. New Haven, CT: Yale University Press, 2018.

Brophy, Alfred L., *University, Court, and Slave: Pro-slavery Thought in Southern Courts and Colleges and the Coming of the Civil War*. New York: Oxford University Press, 2016.

Brown, Christopher Leslie, *Moral Capital: Foundations of British Abolitionism*. Chapel Hill: University of North Carolina Press, 2006.

and Philip D. Morgan, eds., *Arming Slaves: From Classical Times to the Modern Age*. New Haven, CT: Yale University Press, 2006.

Brown, David, *Empire and Enterprise: Money, Power and the Adventurers for Irish Land during the British Civil Wars*. Manchester: Manchester University Press, 2020.

Brown, Kathleen M., *Foul Bodies: Cleanliness in Early America*. New Haven, CT and London: Yale University Press, 2009.

Good Wives, Nasty Wenches, and Anxious Patriarchs: Gender, Race, and Power in Colonial Virginia. Chapel Hill: University of North Carolina Press, 1996.

Browne, Randy M., *The Driver's Story: Labor and Power in the World of Atlantic Slavery*. Philadelphia: University of Pennsylvania Press, 2024.

Brown-Nagin, Tomiko, Sven Beckert, Nancy F. Koehn, Meira Levinson, Tiya Miles, Martha Minow, Maya Sen, Daniel Albert Smith, David R. Williams, William Julius Wilson, and Paul Farmer, eds., *Harvard & The Legacy of Slavery*. Cambridge, MA: Harvard University, 2022.

Brown, Peter, *The Body and Society: Men, Women, and Sexual Renunciation in Early Christianity*. New York: Columbia University Press, 1988.

Brown, Vincent, *The Reaper's Garden: Death and Power in the World of Atlantic Slavery*. Cambridge, MA: Harvard University Press, 2008.

'Spiritual Terror and Sacred Authority in Jamaican Slave Society', *Slavery & Abolition* 24 (2010): 24–53.

Tacky's Revolt: The Story of an Atlantic Slave War. Cambridge, MA: Harvard University Press, 2020.

Brunsman, Denver, *The Evil Necessity: British Naval Impressment in the Eighteenth-Century Atlantic World*. Charlottesville: University of Virginia Press, 2013.

Buist, Martin G., *At Specs Non Fracta: Hope & Co. 1770–1815: Merchant Bankers and Diplomats at Work*. The Hague: Nijhoff, 1974.

Burke, Sir Bernard, and Ashworth Peter Burke, *A Genealogical and Heraldic History of the Peerage and Baronetage, the Privy Council, Knightage and Companions*. London: Harrison, 1910.

Burnard, Trevor, *Mastery, Tyranny, & Desire: Thomas Thistlewood and His Slaves in the Anglo-Jamaican World*. Chapel Hill and London: University of North Carolina Press, 2004.

Planters, Merchants, and Slaves: Plantation Societies in British America, 1650–1820. Chicago: University of Chicago Press, 2015.

and John Garrigus, *The Plantation Machine: Atlantic Capitalism in French Saint-Domingue and British Jamaica*. Philadelphia: University of Pennsylvania Press, 2016.

and Kit Candlin, 'Sir John Gladstone and the Debate over the Amelioration of Slavery in the British West Indies in the 1820s', *Journal of British Studies* 57 (October 2018): 760–782.

Burstein, Miriam Elizabeth, 'A Forgotten Novel: John Riland's *Memoirs of a West-India Planter* (1827)', *Slavery & Abolition* 41 (July 2020): 582–598.

Burton, Antoinette, *Empire in Question: Reading, Writing, and Teaching British Imperialism*. Durham, NC: Duke University Press, 2011.

Bush, Sargent, *The Library of Emmanuel College, Cambridge, 1584–1637*. Cambridge: Cambridge University Press, 1986.

Butler, Pierce, *Judah P. Benjamin*. Philadelphia: George W. Jacobs & Company, 1906.

Byrd, Brandon R., *The Black Republic: African Americans and the Fate of Haiti*. Philadelphia: University of Pennsylvania Press, 2019.

Cadeau, Sabine, 'Bonds and Bondage: Financial Capitalism and the Legacies of Atlantic Slavery at the University of Cambridge'. Unpublished manuscript, University of Cambridge, 2024.

Cain, Tom, 'John Donne and the Ideology of Colonization', *English Literary Renaissance* 31 (Autumn 2001): 440–476.

Caldwell, John, Oswaldo Rodriguez Roque, Dale T. Johnson, Kathleen Luhrs, Carrie Rebora, and Patricia R. Windels, eds., *American Paintings in the Metropolitan Museum of Art*, 3 vols. New York: Metropolitan Museum of Art, 1994.

Callan, Maeve, 'Making Monsters Out of One Another in the Early Fourteenth-Century British Isles', *Eolas: The Journal of the American Society of Irish Medieval Studies* 12 (2019): 43–63.

Calloway, Colin G., *The Indian World of George Washington: The First President, the First Americans, and the Birth of the Nation*. New York: Oxford University Press, 2018.

Campbell, Duncan Andrew, *English Public Opinion and the American Civil War*. London: Boydell Press, 2003.

Campbell, Gwyn, Suzanne Miers, and Joseph C. Miller, eds., *Women and Slavery: The Modern Atlantic*, 2 vols. Athens: Ohio University Press, 2008.

Campbell, James, Brenda A. Allen, Paul Armstrong, Farid Azfar, Omer Bartov, Anthony Bogues, Ross E. Cheit, Steven R. Cornish, Neta C. Crawford, Evelyn Hu-DeHart, Vanessa Huang, Arlene R. Keizer, Seth Magaziner, Marion Orr, Kerry Smith, William Tucker, and Michael Vorenberg, eds., *Brown University's Slavery and Justice Report with Commentary on Context and Impact*. Providence, RI: Brown University, 2021.

Camp, Stephanie M. H., *Closer to Freedom: Enslaved Women and Everyday Resistance in the Plantation South*. Chapel Hill: University of North Carolina Press, 2004.

Candlin, Kit, and Cassandra Pybus, *Enterprising Women: Gender, Race, and Power in the Revolutionary Atlantic*. Athens: University of Georgia Press, 2015.

Cannon, John, *Aristocratic Century: The Peerage of Eighteenth-Century England*. Cambridge: Cambridge University Press, 1984.

Canny, Nicholas P., *Making Ireland British, 1580–1650*. Oxford: Oxford University Press, 2001.
 and Kenneth R. Andrews, Paul Edward Hedley Hair, David B. Quinn, eds., *The Westward Enterprise: English Activities in Ireland, the Atlantic, and America, 1480–1650*. Liverpool: Liverpool University Press, 1978.
Caretta, Vincent, *Equiano the African: Biography of a Self-Made Man*. Athens and London: University of Georgia Press, 2005.
 'Olaudah Equiano or Gustavus Vassa? New Light on an Eighteenth-Century Question of Identity', *Slavery and Abolition* 20 (1999): 96–105.
Carey, Brycchan, *From Peace to Freedom: Quaker Rhetoric and the Birth of American Antislavery, 1657–1761*. New Haven, CT: Yale University Press, 2012.
Carey, Hilary M., *God's Empire: Religion and Colonialism in the British World, c. 1801–1908*. Cambridge: Cambridge University Press, 2011.
Carruthers, Bruce G., *City of Capital: Politics and Markets in the English Financial Revolution*. Princeton, NJ: Princeton University Press, 1996.
Carson, Jane, *Colonial Virginians at Play*. Williamsburg, VA: Colonial Williamsburg Foundation, 1965.
Carson, Penelope, *The East India Company and Religion, 1698–1858*. London: Boydell Press, 2012.
Carswell, John, *The South Sea Bubble*. Stanford, CA: Stanford University Press, 1960.
Cavanagh, Edward, 'Infidels in English Legal Thought: Conquest, Commerce and Slavery in the Common Law from Coke to Mansfield, 1603–1793', *Modern Intellectual History* 16 (2019): 375–409.
Chadwick, Owen, 'Charles Kingsley at Cambridge', *The Historical Journal* 18 (June 1975): 303–325.
Chaplin, Joyce, 'Slavery and the Principle of Humanity: A Modern Idea in the Early Lower South', *Journal of Social History* 24 (Winter 1990): 299–315.
Cherry, Donald L., 'The South Sea Company, 1711–1855', *Dalhousie Review* 13 (1934): 61–68.
Chiles, Katy L., *Transformable Race: Surprising Metamorphoses in the Literature of Early America*. Oxford and New York: Oxford University Press, 2014.
Chou, Meng-Hsuan, Isaac Kamola, and Tamson Pietsch, eds., *The Transnational Politics of Higher Education: Contesting the Global/Transforming the Local*. Abingdon: Routledge, 2016.
Christopher, Emma, *Freedom in White and Black: A Lost Story of the Illegal Slave Trade and Its Global Legacy*. Madison: University of Wisconsin Press, 2018.
'Church and Organ Music', *The Musical Times* 49 (October 1908): 647–650.
Clarence-Smith, W. G., *Islam and the Abolition of Slavery*. Oxford: Oxford University Press, 2006.
Clark, J. C. D., *English Society, 1660–1832: Religion, Ideology and Politics during the Ancien Régime*. Cambridge: Cambridge University Press, 2000.
Cleaveland, Timothy, 'Ahmad Bab al-Timbukti and his Islamic critique of racial slavery in the Maghrib', *The Journal of North African Studies* 20 (January 2015): 42–64.

Cobban, Alan B., *English University Life in the Middle Ages*. London: UCL Press, 1999.
The King's Hall within the University of Cambridge in the Later Middle Ages. Cambridge: Cambridge University Press, 1969.
The Medieval English Universities: Oxford and Cambridge to c. 1500. London: Routledge, 1988.
'The Codrington Legacy', *All Soul's College, University of Oxford*, www.asc.ox.ac.uk/codrington-legacy, accessed 5 April 2022.
Coleridge, Sehon Sylvester, *Facing the Challenge of Emancipation: A Study of the Ministry of William Hart Coleridge, First Bishop of Barbados, 1824–1842*. London: Canoe Press, 2014.
Cole, Lucinda, *Imperfect Creatures: Vermin, Literature, and the Sciences of Life, 1600–1740*. Ann Arbor: University of Michigan Press, 2016.
Colley, Linda, *Britons: Forging the Nation, 1707–1837*. New Haven, CT: Yale University Press, 2005.
Captives: Britain, Empire and the World, 1600–1850. London: Pimlico, 2002.
Collins, David, Ayodele Aruleba, Matthew Carnes, Marcia Chatelain, Haben Fecadu, Carolyn Forché, Maurice Jackson, Rosemary Kilkenny, Connor Maytnier, Kevin O'Brien, Matthew Quallen, Adam Rothman, Daviree Velázquez, Chris Wadibia, Crystal Walker, Eric Woods, eds., *Report of the Working Group on Slavery, Memory, and Reconciliation to the President of Georgetown University*. Washington, D.C.: Georgetown University, 2016.
Conniff, Michael L., and Cyrus B. Dawsey, eds., *The Confederados: Old South Immigrants in Brazil*. Auburn: University of Alabama Press, 1987.
Connolly, Jonathan, *Worthy of Freedom: Indenture and Free Labor in the Era of Emancipation*. Chicago: University of Chicago Press, 2024.
Conybeare, Rev. Edward, *Highways and Byways in Cambridge and Ely*. London: Macmillan and Co., 1910.
Cormack, Leslie B., *Charting an Empire: Geography at the English Universities, 1580–1620*. Chicago: University of Chicago Press, 1997.
Corrigan, John, Melani McAlister, and Axel R. Schäfer, eds., *Global Faith, Worldly Power: Evangelical Internationalism and U.S. Empire*. Chapel Hill: University of North Carolina Press, 2022.
Cowan, Brian, *The Social Life of Coffee: The Emergence of the British Coffeehouse*. New Haven, CT: Yale University Press, 2008.
Cox, Jacqueline, 'Trials and Tribulations: The Cambridge University Courts, 1540–1660', *Transactions of the Cambridge Bibliographical Society* 15 (2015): 595–623.
Craven, Matthew, Malgosia Fitzmaurice, and Maria Vogiatzi, eds., *Time, History and International Law*. Leiden: Martinus Nijhoff Publishers, 2007.
Craven, Wesley Frank, *Dissolution of the Virginia Company: The Failure of a Colonial Experiment*. Gloucester, MA: Peter Smith, 1964.
The Virginia Company of London, 1606–1624. Williamsburg, VA: 350th Anniversary Celebration Corporation, 1957.
Crawley, Charles, *Trinity Hall: The History of a Cambridge College, 1350–1975*. Cambridge: Trinity Hall, 2007.

Crosbie, Barry, and Mark Hampton, eds., *The Cultural Construction of the British World*. Manchester: Manchester University Press, 2015.

Curran, Andrew S., *The Anatomy of Blackness: Science & Slavery in an Age of Enlightenment*. Baltimore: Johns Hopkins University Press, 2011.

da Costa, Emilia Viotti, *Crowns of Glory, Tears of Blood: The Demerara Slave Rebellion of 1823*. Oxford: Oxford University Press, 1994.

Dain, Bruce R., *A Hideous Monster of the Mind: American Race Theory in the Early Republic*. Cambridge, MA: Harvard University Press, 2002.

Dale, Richard S., Johnnie E. V. Johnson, and Leilei Tang, 'Financial Markets can go Mad: Evidence of Irrational Behaviour during the South Sea Bubble', *Economic History Review* 58 (2005): 233–271.

Dale, Richard S., *The First Crash: Lessons from the South Sea Bubble*. Princeton, NJ: Princeton University Press, 2004.

Dalrymple, William, *The Anarchy: The East India Company, Corporate Violence, and the Pillage of an Empire*. London: Bloomsbury, 2019.

Darby, H. C., *The Draining of the Fens: Second Edition*. Cambridge: Cambridge University Press, 1940.

Dattel, Gene, *Cotton and Race in the Making of America: The Human Costs of Economic Power*. New York: Rowman & Littlefield, 2009.

Davies, J. Q., *Creatures of the Air: Music, Atlantic Spirits, Breath, 1817–1913*. Chicago: University of Chicago Press, 2023.

Davies, K. G., *The Royal African Company*. London: Longmans, 1957.

Davis, David Brion, *Inhuman Bondage: The Rise and Fall of Slavery in the New World*. Oxford and New York: Oxford University Press, 2006.

'Looking at Slavery from Broader Perspectives', *The American Historical Review* 105 (April 2000), 452–466.

The Problem of Slavery in the Age of Revolution, 1770–1823. Ithaca, NY: Cornell University Press, 1975.

Davis, Ralph, *The Industrial Revolution and British Overseas Trade*. Leicester: Leicester University Press, 1979.

De Bruyn, Frans, ed., *The Cambridge Companion to Eighteenth-Century Thought*. Cambridge: Cambridge University Press, 2019.

Defrates, Lewis, '"Showing Up America": Performing Race and Nation in Britain Before the First World War', *The Journal of the Gilded Age and Progressive Era* 21 (2022): 319–341.

Delbourgo, James, *Collecting the World: Hans Sloane and the Origins of the British Museum*. Cambridge, MA: Harvard University Press, 2019.

Dening, Greg, *The Death of William Gooch: A History's Anthropology*. Melbourne: Melbourne University Press, 1995.

Deringer, William, *Calculated Values: Finance, Politics, and the Quantitative Age*. Cambridge, MA: Harvard University Press, 2018.

'Compound Interest Corrected: The Imaginative Mathematics of the Financial Future in Early Modern England', *Osiris* 33 (2018): 109–129.

Desmond, Adrian, and James Moore, *Darwin's Sacred Cause: How a Hatred of Slavery Shaped Darwin's Views on Human Evolution*. Boston and New York: Houghton Mifflin Harcourt, 2009.

Devine, Tom M., ed., *Recovering Scotland's Slavery Past: The Caribbean Connection*. Edinburgh: Edinburgh University Press, 2015.
Dexter, Franklin Bowditch, *The Influence of the English Universities in the Development of New England*. Cambridge: Cambridge University Press, 1880.
Dierksheide, Christa, *Amelioration and Empire: Progress and Slavery in the Plantation Americas*. Charlottesville: University of Virginia Press, 2014.
Diouf, Sylviane A., *Fighting Slave Trade: West African Strategies*. Athens: Ohio University Press, 2003.
Doty, Gresdna Ann, *The Career of Mrs. Anne Brunton Merry in the American Theatre*. Baton Rouge: Louisiana State University Press, 1971.
Downs, Jim, *Maladies of Empire: How Colonialism, Slavery, and War Transformed Medicine*. Cambridge, MA: Harvard University Press, 2021.
Doyle, Barbara, *Beyond the Fields: Slavery and Middleton Place*. Columbia: University of South Carolina Press, 2008.
Draper, Nicholas, 'The City of London and Slavery: Evidence from the First Dock Companies, 1795–1800', *The Economic History Review* 61 (May 2008): 432–466.
  The Price of Emancipation: Slave-Ownership, Compensation and British Society at the End of Slavery. Cambridge: Cambridge University Press, 2010.
  'The Rise of a New Planter Class? Some Countercurrents from British Guiana and Trinidad, 1807–33', *Atlantic Studies* 9 (January 2012): 65–83.
  and Catherine Hall, Keith McClelland, eds., *Legacies of British Slave-Ownership: Colonial Slavery and the Formation of Victorian Britain*. Cambridge: Cambridge University Press, 2016.
Drayton, Richard, *Nature's Government: Science, Imperial Britain, and the 'Improvement' of the World*. New Haven, CT and London: Yale University Press, 2000.
Drescher, Seymour, *Abolition: A History of Slavery and Antislavery*. Cambridge: Cambridge University Press, 2009.
  The Mighty Experiment: Free Labor versus Slavery in British Emancipation. Oxford: Oxford University Press, 2002.
  Capitalism and Antislavery: British Mobilization in Comparative Perspective. New York: Oxford University Press, 1987.
Dresser, Madge, 'Bristol and the Transatlantic Slave Trade', *Bristol Museum & Art Gallery*, www.bristolmuseums.org.uk/stories/bristol-transatlantic-slave-trade/, accessed 4 July 2022.
  Slavery Obscured: The Social History of the Slave Trade in an English Provincial Port. London: Bloomsbury Publishing, 2016.
  and Andrew Hann, eds., *Slavery and the British Country House*. Swindon: English Heritage, 2013.
Dubois, Laurent, *Avengers of the New World: The Story of the Haitian Revolution*. Cambridge, MA: Harvard University Press, 2005.
Dubrulle, Hugh, *Ambivalent Nation: How Britain Imagined the American Civil War*. Baton Rouge: Louisiana State University Press, 2018.

Dumas, Paula E., *Proslavery Britain: Fighting for Slavery in an Era of Abolition*. New York: Palgrave Macmillan, 2016.
Dunn, Richard S., *A Tale of Two Plantations: Slave Life and Labor in Jamaica and Virginia*. Cambridge, MA: Harvard University Press, 2014.
  Sugar and Slaves: The Rise of the Planter Class in the English West Indies, 1624–1713, foreword by Gary B. Nash. Chapel Hill: University of North Carolina Press, 2000.
Durden, Robert F., *The Gray and the Black: The Confederate Debate on Emancipation*. Baton Rouge: Louisiana State University Press, 1972.
Eakin, Marshall C., *A British Enterprise in Brazil: The St. John d'el Rey Mining Company and the Morro Velho Gold Mine, 1830–1960*. Durham, NC: Duke University Press, 1989.
Edwards, Michael, 'Slavery and Charity: Tobias Rustat and the African Companies, 1662–94', *Historical Research* 97 (2024): 63–82.
Edwards, Peter, *Horse and Man in Early Modern England*. London: Hambledon Continuum, 2007.
Egan, Lauren, 'Biden Signs into Law Bill Establishing Juneteenth as Federal Holiday', *NBC News*, www.nbcnews.com/politics/white-house/biden-signs-law-bill-establishing-juneteenth-federal-holiday-n1271213, 17 June 2021.
Eisenstadt, Peter, *Black Conservatism: Essays in Intellectual and Political History*. New York: Taylor & Francis, 2013.
Elbourne, Elizabeth, *Empire, Kinship and Violence: Family Histories, Indigenous Rights and the Making of Settler Colonialism, 1770–1842*. Cambridge: Cambridge University Press, 2022.
Elder, Melinda, *Slave Trade and the Economic Development of 18th-Century Lancaster*. Edinburgh: Edinburgh University Press 2019.
El Hamel, Chouki, *Black Morocco: A History of Slavery, Race, and Islam*. Cambridge: Cambridge University Press, 2014.
Ellis, Heather, *Generational Conflict and University Reform: Oxford in the Age of Revolution*. Leiden and Boston: Brill, 2012.
Eltis, David, *Economic Growth and the Ending of the Transatlantic Slave Trade*. Oxford: Oxford University Press, 1987.
  The Rise of African Slavery in the Americas. Cambridge: Cambridge University Press, 2000.
  and Stanley L. Engerman, 'The Importance of Slavery and the Slave Trade to Industrializing Britain', *Journal of Economic History* 60 (March 2000): 123–144.
Emden, A. B., *A Biographical Register of the University of Cambridge to 1500*. Cambridge: Cambridge University Press, 1963.
Eminent Persons Biographies: Reprinted from The Times, 6 vols. London: Macmillan and Co., 1892–97.
Emmer, P. C., ed., *Colonialism and Migration; Indentured Labour Before and After Slavery*. Leiden: Brill, 1986.
Emsley, Clive, 'An Aspect of Pitt's 'Terror': Prosecutions for Sedition during the 1790s', *Social History* 6 (May 1981): 155–184.

Engerman, Stanley L., 'The Slave Trade and British Capital Formation: A Comment on the Williams Thesis', *The Business History Review* 46 (Winter 1972): 430–443.

Everill, Bronwen, *Abolition and Empire in Sierra Leone and Liberia*. New York: Palgrave Macmillan, 2013.

Not Made by Slaves: Ethical Capitalism in the Age of Abolition. Cambridge, MA: Harvard University Press, 2020.

Eyles, V. A., 'John Woodward, F. R. S.', *Nature* 205 (1965): 868–870.

Farrell, Gerard, *The 'Mere Irish' and the Colonisation of Ulster, 1570–1641*. London: Palgrave Macmillan, 2017.

Fausz, J. Frederick, 'An "Abundance of Blood Shed on Both Sides": England's First Indian War, 1609–1614', *Virginia Magazine of History and Biography* 98 (January 1990), 3–56.

Fehrenbacher, Don E., *The Slaveholding Republic: An Account of the United States Government's Relations to Slavery*. New York: Oxford University Press, 2001.

Fergus, Claudius, *Revolutionary Emancipation: Slavery and Abolitionism in the British West Indies*. Baton Rouge: Louisiana State University Press, 2013.

Ferguson, Leland, *Uncommon Ground: Archaeology and Early African America, 1650–1800*. Washington, D.C.: Smithsonian Institution, 1992.

Festa, Thomas, 'The Metaphysics of Labor in John Donne's Sermon to the Virginia Company', *Studies in Philology* 106 (Winter 2009): 76–99.

F. G. E., 'George P. Bridgetower and the Kreutzer Sonata', *The Musical Times* 49 (May 1908): 302–308.

Finlayson, C. P., 'Edinburgh University and the Darien Scheme', *The Scottish Historical Review* 34 (October 1955): 97–102.

Finn, Margot, 'Material Turns in British History: III. Collecting: Colonial Bombay, Basra, Baghdad and the Enlightenment Museum', *Transactions of the Royal Historical Society* 30 (2020): 1–28.

and Kate Smith, eds., *The East India Company at Home, 1757–1857*. London: UCL Press, 2018.

Fisch, Audrey, ed., *The Cambridge Companion to the African American Slave Narrative*. Cambridge: Cambridge University Press, 2007.

Fisher, David R., 'Cambridgeshire', *The History of Parliament*, www.historyofparliamentonline.org/volume/1820-1832/constituencies/cambridgeshire#footnoteref18_3kjxjcw, accessed 27 September 2022.

Fitzmaurice, Andrew, *Humanism and America: An Intellectual History of English Colonisation, 1500–1625*. Cambridge: Cambridge University Press, 2003.

Sovereignty, Property and Empire, 1500–2000. Cambridge: Cambridge University Press, 2014.

Flavell, Julie, *When London Was the Capital of America*. New Haven, CT: Yale University Press, 2011.

Foreman, Amanda, *A World on Fire: Britain's Crucial Role in the American Civil War*. New York: Random House, 2012.

Fowler, Corinne, *Green Unpleasant Land: Creative Responses to Rural England's Colonial Connections*. Leeds: Peepal Tree Press, 2021.

Our Island Stories: Country Walks through Colonial Britain. London: Penguin, 2024.
Freehling, William W., and Craig M. Simpson, eds., *Secession Debated: Georgia's Showdown in 1860*. New York: Oxford University Press, 1992.
French, Henry, and Mark Rothery, '"Upon Your Entry into the World": Masculine Values and the Threshold of Adulthood among Landed Elites in England 1680–1800', *Social History* 33 (2008): 402–422.
Frey, Sylvia R., *Water from the Rock: Black Resistance in a Revolutionary Age*. Princeton, NJ: Princeton University Press, 1991.
  and Betty Wood, *Come Shouting to Zion: African American Protestantism in the American South and British Caribbean to 1830*. Chapel Hill: University of North Carolina Press, 1998.
Frick George F., James L. Reveal, C. Rose Broome, and Melvin L. Brown, 'Botanical Explorations and Discoveries in Colonial Maryland, 1688 to 1753', *Huntia: A Journal of Botanical History* 7 (1987): 5–60.
Fryer, Peter, *Staying Power: The History of Black People in Britain*. London: Pluto Press, 1984.
Fulton, Richard D., '"Now Only the Times Is on Our Side": The London Times and America before the Civil War', *Victorian Review* 16 (Summer 1990): 48–58.
Gallas, Kristin L., and James DeWolf Perry, eds., *Interpreting Slavery at Museums and Historic Sites*. Lanham, MD: Rowman & Littlefield, 2015.
Gallay, Alan, *The Indian Slave Trade: The Rise of the English Empire in the American South, 1670–1717*. New Haven, CT: Yale University Press, 2002.
Games, Alison, 'Atlantic History: Definitions, Challenges, and Opportunities', *The American Historical Review* 111 (June 2006): 741–757.
Gamsu, Sol, Stephen Ashe, and Jason Arday, 'Elite Schools and Slavery in the UK – Capital, Violence and Extractivism', *Discourse: Studies in the Cultural Politics of Education* 45 (2024): 325–345.
Garnai, Amy, 'An Exile on the Coast: Robert Merry's Transatlantic Journey, 1796–1798', *The Review of English Studies* 64 (February 2013): 87–104.
Garnsey, Peter, *Ideas of Slavery from Aristotle to Augustine*. Cambridge: Cambridge University Press, 1999.
Gascoigne, John, *Cambridge in the Age of the Enlightenment: Science, Religion and Politics from the Restoration to the French Revolution*. Cambridge: Cambridge University Press, 1988.
Geggus, David, *Slavery, War, and Revolution: The British Occupation of Saint Domingue, 1793–1798*. Oxford: Clarendon Press, 1982.
Genovese, Eugene D., and Elizabeth Fox-Genovese, *Fatal Self-Deception: Slaveholding Paternalism in the Old South*. New York and Cambridge: Cambridge University Press, 2011.
'George Mosman', *Edinburgh University Library Gallery of Benefactors*, www.docs.is.ed.ac.uk/docs/lib-archive/bgallery/Gallery/records/fifteen/mosman.html, accessed 16 September 2022.
Gerbner, Katharine, *Christian Slavery: Conversion and Race in the Protestant Atlantic World*. Philadelphia: University of Pennsylvania Press, 2018.

Gibney, Mark, Rhoda E. Howard-Hassmann, Jean-Marc Coicaud, and Niklaus Steiner, ed., *The Age of Apology: Facing Up to the Past*. Philadelphia: University of Pennsylvania Press, 2009.
Gilmore, John, *The Poetics of Empire: A Study of James Grainger's The Sugar Cane (1764)*. New Brunswick, NJ: The Athlone Press, 2000.
Glasson, Travis, '"Baptism doth not bestow Freedom": Missionary Anglicanism, Slavery, and the Yorke-Talbot Opinion, 1701-30', *The William and Mary Quarterly* 67 (April 2010): 279-318.
  Mastering Christianity: Missionary Anglicanism and Slavery in the Atlantic World. Oxford: Oxford University Press, 2011.
Gleach, Frederic W., *Powhatan's World and Colonial Virginia: A Conflict of Cultures*. Lincoln and London: University of Nebraska Press, 1997.
Gliech, Oliver, 'Cockburn, comte' de', *Plantation and House owners of St. Domingue, 1750-1803*, www.domingino.de/stdomin/index_colons_a_z_engl.html, accessed 16 October 2023.
Glover, Lorri, *Eliza Lucas Pinckney: An Independent Woman in the Age of Revolution*. New Haven, CT: Yale University Press, 2020.
Gøbel, Erik, *The Danish Slave Trade and Its Abolition*. Leiden: Brill, 2016.
Goetz, Rebecca Anne, *The Baptism of Early Virginia: How Christianity Created Race*. Baltimore: Johns Hopkins University Press, 2012.
Goldman, Lawrence, *Science, Reform, and Politics in Victorian Britain: The Social Science Association, 1857-1886*. Cambridge: Cambridge University Press, 2002.
  Victorians and Numbers: Statistics and Society in Nineteenth Century Britain. Oxford: Oxford University Press, 2022.
Gonzalez, Johnhenry, *Maroon Nation: A History of Revolutionary Haiti*. New Haven, CT: Yale University Press, 2019.
Gooptar, Cassandra, *University of Dundee Founders Project: Final Report*. Dundee: University of Dundee, 2022.
Gordon-Reed, Annette, *The Hemingses of Monticello: An American Family*. New York: W. W. Norton & Company, 2009.
Gosse, Edmund, *Books on the Table*. New York: Charles Scribner's Sons, 1921.
Gould, Marty, *Nineteenth-Century Theatre and the Imperial Encounter*. London: Routledge, 2011.
Gould, Philip, *Barbaric Traffic: Commerce and Antislavery in the Eighteenth-Century Atlantic World*. Cambridge, MA: Harvard University Press, 2003.
Govier, Mark, 'The Royal Society, Slavery and the Island of Jamaica: 1660-1700', *Notes and Records of the Royal Society of London* 53 (May 1999): 203-217.
Gragg, Larry, *Englishmen Transplanted: The English Colonization of Barbados, 1627-1660*. Oxford: Oxford University Press, 2003.
  The Quaker Community on Barbados: Challenging the Culture of the Planter Class. Columbia: University of Missouri Press, 2009.
Grant, Alfred, *The American Civil War and the British Press*. London: McFarland and Company, 2000.

Gray, J. M., *A History of the Gambia*, intro. by Sir Thomas Southorn. Cambridge: Cambridge University Press, 1940.
A History of the Perse School Cambridge. Cambridge: Bowes & Bowes, 1921.
Green, Vivian Hubert Howard, *The Commonwealth of Lincoln College, 1427–1977*. Oxford: Oxford University Press, 1979.
Greene, Jack P., *Evaluating Empire and Confronting Colonialism in Eighteenth-Century Britain*. Cambridge and New York: Cambridge University Press, 2013.
The Intellectual Heritage of the Constitutional Era: The Delegates' Library. Philadelphia: Library Company of Philadelphia, 1986.
Greenridge, C. W. W., *Slavery*. London: Allen and Unwin, 1958.
Gregory, James, *Mercy and British Culture, 1760–1960*. London: Bloomsbury Academic, 2021.
Gregory, Jeremy, ed., *The Oxford History of Anglicanism, Volume II: Establishment and Empire, 1662–1829*. Oxford: Oxford University Press, 2017.
Gregory, T. E., *The Westminster Bank: Through a Century*, pref. by the Hon. Rupert E. Beckett, 2 vols. London: Westminster Bank Limited, 1936.
Griffin, Helga M., 'Henry Ling Roth (1855–1925)', *Australian Dictionary of Biography*, https://adb.anu.edu.au/biography/roth-henry-ling-8278, accessed 16 January 2024.
Griggs, William Clark, *The Elusive Eden: Frank McMullan's Confederate Colony in Brazil*. Austin: University of Texas Press, 1987.
Gross, Robert A., *The Minutemen and Their World*. New York: Hill and Wang, 2001, rev. ed.
Guasco, Michael, *Slaves and Englishmen: Human Bondage in the Early Modern Atlantic World*. Philadelphia: University of Pennsylvania Press, 2014.
Guest, Ivor, *Dr. John Radcliffe and His Trust*. London: The Radcliffe Trust, 1991.
Guibbory, Achsah, ed., *The Cambridge Companion to John Donne*. Cambridge: Cambridge University Press, 2006.
Guicciardini, Niccolò, *The Development of Newtonian Calculus in Britain, 1700–1800*. Cambridge: Cambridge University Press, 1989.
Guinness, John, 'Portraits of Sir Nathaniel Lloyd', *Oxoniensa* 25 (1960): 96–103.
Guyatt, Nicholas, *Bind Us Apart: How Enlightened Americans Invented Racial Segregation*. Oxford: Oxford University Press, 2016.
Haakonssen, Knud, *Grotius, Pufendorf, and Modern Natural Law*. Brookfield: Ashgate, 1999.
Häcker, Birke, 'A Case Note on All Souls College v. Cod[d]rington (1720)', *Journal of Comparative and International Law* 76 (October 2012): 1051–1077.
Hadden, Sally E., *Slave Patrols: Law and Violence in Virginia and the Carolinas*. Cambridge, MA: Harvard University Press, 2003.
Haefli, Eran, ed., *Against Popery: Britain, Empire, and Anti-Catholicism*. Charlottesville: University of Virginia Press, 2020.
Haglund, David G., *The US 'Culture Wars' and the Anglo-American Special Relationship*. London: Palgrave Macmillan, 2019.

Hall, Catherine, and Sonya Rose, eds., *At Home with the Empire: Metropolitan Culture and the Imperial World*. Cambridge: Cambridge University Press, 2011.

and Nicholas Draper, Keith McClelland, eds., *Emancipation and the Remaking of the British Imperial World*. Manchester: Manchester University Press, 2015.

Hamilton, Philip, 'Revolutionary Principles and Family Loyalties: Slavery's Transformation in the St. George Tucker Household of Early National Virginia', *The William and Mary Quarterly* 55 (October 1998): 531–556.

Hancock, David, *Citizens of the World: London Merchants and the Integration of the Atlantic Community, 1735–1785*. Cambridge: Cambridge University Press, 1995.

Handler, Jerome S., 'The Middle Passage and the Material Culture of Captive Africans', *Slavery & Abolition* 30 (2009): 1–26.

The Unappropriated People: Freedmen in the Slave Society of Barbados. Mona, Jamaica: University of the West Indies Press, 2009.

and Michael David Conner, Keith P. Jacobi, *Searching for a Slave Cemetery in Barbados, West Indies: A Bioarchaeological and Ethnohistorical Investigation*. Southern Illinois University: Center for Archaeological Investigations, Research Paper No. 59, 1989.

Hannon, Sarah, and Neil Kennedy, '"Slavery wears the mildest Aspect": Imagining Mastery and Emancipation in Bermuda's House of Assembly', *The Journal of Caribbean History* 53 (2019): 60–81.

Harris, Ellen T., '"Master of the Orchester with a Salary": Handel at the Bank of England', *Music & Letters* 101 (February 2020): 1–29.

Harris, Leslie M., James T. Campbell, and Alfred L. Brophy, eds., *Slavery and the University: Histories and Legacies*. Athens: University of Georgia Press, 2019.

Harvey, Caitlin, 'Gold Rushes, Universities and Globalization, 1840–1910', *Past & Present* 26 (November 2023): 118–157.

Harvey, Mark, 'Slavery, Indenture and the Development of British Industrial Capitalism', *History Workshop Journal* 88 (Autumn 2019): 66–88.

Harwood, Thomas F., 'Prejudice and Antislavery: The Colloquy between William Ellery Channing and Edward Strutt Abdy, 1834', *American Quarterly* 18 (Winter 1966): 697–700.

Haviser, Jay B., *African Sites: Archaeology in the Caribbean*. Princeton, NJ: Markus Weiner Publishers, 1999.

Hayes, Kevin J., *The Library of William Byrd of Westover*. Madison, WI: Madison House, 1997.

Haynes, Stephen R., *Noah's Curse: The Biblical Justification of American Slavery*. Oxford: Oxford University Press, 2002.

Hazareesingh, Sudhir, *Black Spartacus: The Epic Life of Toussaint Louverture*. London: Penguin, 2020.

Healey, Jonathan, *The Blazing World: A New History of Revolutionary England, 1603–1689*. New York: Vintage, 2023.

Helmholz, R. H., *The Profession of Ecclesiastical Lawyers: An Historical Introduction*. Cambridge: Cambridge University Press, 2019.

Hertzler, James R., 'Slavery in the Yearly Sermons before the Georgia Trustees', *The Georgia Historical Quarterly* 59 (1975), 118–126.

Heuman, Gad J., '*The Killing Time*': *The Morant Bay Rebellion in Jamaica*. Knoxville: University of Tennessee Press, 1994.

Hicks, Dan, *The Brutish Museums: The Benin Bronzes, Colonial Violence and Cultural Restitution*. London: Pluto Press, 2021.

Higman, B. W., *Slave Populations of the British Caribbean, 1807–1834*. Mona, Jamaica: University of the West Indies Press, 1995.

Hilliard, Kathleen M., *Masters, Slaves, and Exchange: Power's Purchase in the Old South*. Cambridge: Cambridge University Press, 2014.

Hinkle, William G., *A History of Bridewell Prison, 1553–1700*. New York: Edwin Mellen Press, 2006.

Hochshild, Adam, *Bury the Chains: Prophets and Rebels in the Fight to Free an Empire's Slaves*. Boston: Houghton Mifflin, 2005.

Hochstrasser, Timothy, *Natural Law Theories in the Early Enlightenment*. Cambridge: Cambridge University Press, 2006.

Hockman, Dan M., 'William Dawson: Master and Second President of the College of William and Mary', *Historical Magazine of the Protestant Episcopal Church* 52 (September 1983): 199–214.

Hodge, Joseph Morgan, and Brett M. Bennett, eds., *Science and Empire: Knowledge and Networks of Science in the British Empire, 1800–1970*. New York: Palgrave Macmillan, 2011.

Hodgson, Kate, 'Franco-Irish Saint-Domingue: Family Networks, Trans-colonial Diasporas', *Caribbean Quarterly* 64 (November 2018): 434–451.

Hoeveler, J. David, *Creating the American Mind: Intellect and Politics in the Colonial Colleges*. Lanham, MD: Rowman & Littlefield Publishers, 2002.

Hoffeimer, Michael H., 'The Common Law of Edward Christian', *The Cambridge Law Journal* 53 (March 1994): 140–163.

Hoffman, Philip, 'Christian Missionaries, Slavery, and the Slave Trade: The Third Order of Saint Francis in Eighteenth-Century Angola', *African Economic History* 51 (May 2023): 65–92.

Hogarth, Rana A., *Medicalizing Blackness: Making Racial Difference in the Atlantic World, 1780–1840*. Chapel Hill: University of North Carolina Press, 2017.

Holcomb, Julie L., *Moral Commerce: Quakers and the Transatlantic Boycott of the Slave Labor Economy*. Ithaca, NY: Cornell University Press, 2016.

Holdsworth, William, *A History of English Law*, 16 vols. London: Methuen & Co., Sweet and Maxwell, 1938.

Holt, Thomas C., *The Problem of Freedom: Race, Labor, and Politics in Jamaica and Britain, 1832–1938*. Baltimore: Johns Hopkins University Press, 1991.

Holton, Woody, *Forced Founders: Indians, Debtors, Slaves, and the Making of the American Revolution in Virginia*. Chapel Hill: University of North Carolina Press, 1999.

Hone, Campbell R., *The Life of Dr. John Radcliffe, 1652-1714: Benefactor of the University of Oxford*. London: Faber and Faber Limited, 1950.
Honor, James, *A Land as God Made It: Jamestown and the Birth of America*. New York: Basic Books, 2005.
Hood, Graham, *The Governor's Palace in Williamsburg: A Cultural Study*. Williamsburg, Virginia: Distributed by the University of North Carolina, Chapel Hill, for the Colonial Williamsburg Foundation, 1991.
Hopkins, Hugh Evan, *Charles Simeon of Cambridge*. Eugene, OR: Wipf and Stock, 2012.
Hoppit, Julian, 'The Myths of the South Sea Bubble', *Transactions of the Royal Historical Society* 12 (2002): 141-165.
Horden, Peregrine, and Simon J. D. Green, *All Soul's under the Ancien Régime: Politics, Learning, and the Arts, c. 1600-1850*. Oxford: Oxford University Press, 2008.
Horning, Audrey J., *Ireland in the Virginian Sea: Colonialism in the British Atlantic*. Chapel Hill: University of North Carolina Press, 2013.
Howse, Derek, *Nevil Maskelyne: The Seaman's Astronomer*. Cambridge: Cambridge University Press, 1989.
Hubbard, Charles M., *The Burden of Confederate Diplomacy*. Knoxville: The University of Tennessee Press, 1998.
Hunt, Margaret R., *The Middling Sort: Commerce, Gender, and the Family in England, 1680-1780*. Berkeley: University of California Press, 1996.
Hunt, Peter, *Ancient Greek and Roman Slavery*. Chichester: Wiley Blackwell, 2018.
Imbarrato, Susan Clair, *Sarah Gray Cary from Boston to Grenada: Shifting Fortunes of an American Family, 1764-1826*. Baltimore: Johns Hopkins University Press, 2018.
Inikori, Joseph E., *Africans and the Industrial Revolution in England: A Study in International Trade and Economic Development*. Cambridge: Cambridge University Press, 2002.
Irving, Sarah, *Natural Science and the Origins of the British Empire*. London: Taylor & Francis, 2015.
Isaac, Rhys, *Landon Carter's Uneasy Kingdom: Revolution and Rebellion on a Virginia Plantation*. Oxford: Oxford University Press, 2005.
  The Transformation of Virginia, 1740-1790. Chapel Hill: University of North Carolina Press, 1982.
Jackson, Kellie Carter, *Force and Freedom: Black Abolitionists and the Politics of Violence*. Philadelphia: University of Pennsylvania Press, 2019.
Jacob, W. M., *The Clerical Profession in the Long Eighteenth Century*. Oxford: Oxford University Press, 2007.
Jameson, J. F., 'The London Expenditures of the Confederate Secret Service', *The American Historical Review* 35 (July 1930): 811-824.
Jardine, Lisa, *Going Dutch: How England Plundered Holland's Glory*. London: Harper Press, 2008.
Jasanoff, Maya, *The Dawn Watch: Joseph Conrad in a Global World*. New York: Penguin, 2017.

Edge of Empire: Conquest and Collecting in the East, 1750–1850. London: Harper Perennial, 2006.

Jenkins, Brian, *Henry Goulburn, 1784–1856: A Political Biography*. Montreal and London: McGill-Queen's University Press, 1996.

Jenkins, Hester, and D. Caradog Jones, 'Social Class of Cambridge University Alumni of the 18th and 19th Centuries', *The British Journal of Sociology* 1 (June 1950): 93–116.

J. H. P., 'The Gorsuch and Lovelace Families (Continued)', *The Virginia Magazine of History and Biography* 25 (July 1917): 302–323.

Jirik, Michael E., 'Beyond Clarkson: Cambridge, Black Abolitionists, and the British Anti-Slave Trade Campaign', *Slavery & Abolition* 41 (2020): 748–771.

John, A. H., 'The London Assurance Company and the Maritime Insurance Market of the Eighteenth Century', *Economica* 25 (May 1958): 126–141.

'John Carter', *Encyclopedia Virginia*, https://encyclopediavirginia.org/11631-6eb94a2f744480e/, accessed 9 September 2020.

'John Downman', *National Portrait Gallery*, www.npg.org.uk/collections/search/person/mp06903/john-downman, accessed 10 November 2021.

Johnson, Jessica Marie, *Wicked Flesh: Black Women, Intimacy, and Freedom in the Atlantic World*. Philadelphia: University of Pennsylvania Press, 2020.

Johnson, Walter, *River of Dark Dreams: Slavery and Empire in the Cotton Kingdom*. Cambridge, MA: The Belknap Press of the Harvard University Press, 2013.

Jones, Tom, *George Berkeley: A Philosophical Life*. Princeton, NJ: Princeton University Press, 2021.

Jordan, Winthrop D., *White over Black: American Attitudes toward the Negro, 1550–1812*, intro. by Christopher Leslie Brown and Peter H. Wood. Chapel Hill: University of North Carolina Press, 2012.

Joshel, Sandra R., *Slavery in the Roman World*. Cambridge: Cambridge University Press, 2010.

Justice, Benjamin, 'The Art of Coining Christians: Indians and Authority in the Iconography of British Atlantic Colonial Seals', *Journal of British Studies* 61 (January 2022), 105–137.

Kananoja, Kalle, *Healing Knowledge in Atlantic Africa: Medical Encounters, 1500–1850*. Cambridge: Cambridge University Press, 2021.

Karp, Matthew, *This Vast Southern Empire: Slaveholders at the Helm of American Foreign Policy*. Cambridge, MA: Harvard University Press, 2017.

Karras, Alan L., *Smuggling: Contraband and Corruption in World History*. Lanham, MD: Rowman & Littlefield, 2010.

Kars, Marjoleine, *Blood on the River: A Chronicle of Mutiny and Freedom on the Wild Coast*. New York: The New Press, 2020.

Katheder, Thomas, *The Baylors of Newmarket: The Decline and Fall of a Virginia Planter Family*. New York: Bloomington, 2009.

Kaye, Anthony E., 'The Second Slavery: Modernity in the Nineteenth-Century South and the Atlantic World', *The Journal of Southern History* 75 (August 2009): 627–650.

Kendi, Ibram X., *Stamped from the Beginning: The Definitive History of Racist Ideas in America*. New York: Nation Books, 2016.
Kennedy, Jean de Chantal, *Isle of Devils: Bermuda under the Somers Island Company, 1609–1685*. London: William Collins Sons & Co Ltd., 1971.
Kerr, John, *Scottish Education: School and University: From Early Times to 1908 with an Addendum 1908–1913*. Cambridge: Cambridge University Press, 1913.
Kidd, Colin, *The Forging of Races: Race and Scripture in the Protestant Atlantic World, 1600–2000*. Cambridge: Cambridge University Press, 2006.
Kilbride, Daniel, *Being American in Europe, 1750–1860*. Baltimore: Johns Hopkins University Press, 2013.
King, Benjamin J., 'Church, Cotton, and Confederates; What Bishop Charles Todd Quintard's Fundraising Trips to Great Britain Reveal about Some Nineteenth-Century Anglo-Catholics', *Anglican and Episcopal History* 90 (June 2021): 109–133.
'King's College Research into Slavery, Past and Present', *King's College, University of Cambridge*, www.kings.cam.ac.uk/news/2019/kings-college-research-slavery-past-and-present, accessed 11 April 2022.
Klein, Rachel N., *Unification of a Slave State: The Rise of the Planter Class in the South Carolina Backcountry, 1760–1808*. Chapel Hill: University of North Carolina Press, 1990.
Knight, Frida, *University Rebel: The Life of William Frend (1757–1841)*. London: Victor Gollancz Ltd., 1971.
Knights, Mark, *Trust and Distrust: Corruption in Office in Britain and Its Empire, 1600–1850*. Oxford: Oxford University Press, 2021.
Kopelson, Heather Miyano, *Faithful Bodies: Performing Religion and Race in the Puritan Atlantic*. New York: New York University Press, 2014.
Krauthammer, Barbara, *Black Slaves, Indian Masters: Slavery, Emancipation, and Citizenship in the Native American South*. Chapel Hill: University of North Carolina Press, 2013.
Kriz, Kay Dian, *Slavery, Sugar, and the Culture of Refinement: Picturing the British West Indies, 1700–1840*. New Haven, CT: Yale University Press, 2008.
Kruer, Matthew, *Time of Anarchy: Indigenous Power and the Crisis of Colonialism in Early America*. Cambridge, MA, Harvard University Press, 2022.
Krug-Richter, Barbara, and Ruth E. Mohrmann, eds., *Frühneuzeitliche Universitätskulturen: Kulturhistorische Perspektiven auf die Hochschulen in Europa*. Cologne: Böhlau, 2009.
Kulikoff, Allan, *Tobacco & Slaves: The Development of Southern Cultures in the Chesapeake, 1680–1800*. Chapel Hill and London: University of North Carolina Press, 1986.
Kupperman, Karen Ordahl, *The Jamestown Project*. Cambridge, MA: Harvard University Press, 2009.
Laidlaw, Zoë, *Protecting the Empire's Humanity: Thomas Hodgkin and British Colonial Activism, 1830–1870*. Cambridge: Cambridge University Press, 2021.
Lamb, Jonathan, *Preserving the Self in the South Seas*. Chicago and London: University of Chicago Press, 2001.

Langbein, John H., Renee Lettow Lerner, and Bruce P. Smith, *History of the Common Law: The Development of Anglo-American Legal Institutions*. Frederick, MD: Aspen Publishing, 2009.
Leader, Damian Riehl, ed., *A History of the University of Cambridge, Volume 1: The University to 1546*. Cambridge: Cambridge University Press, 1994.
Leary, Lewis, 'Charles Crawford: A Forgotten Poet of Early Philadelphia', *The Pennsylvania Magazine of History of Biography* 83 (July 1959): 293–306.
Leedham-Green, E. S., *A Concise History of the University of Cambridge*. Cambridge and New York: Cambridge University Press, 1996.
Lee, Robert, and Tristan Ahtone, 'Land-Grab Universities', *High Country News* 52 (April 2020): 32–45.
Lee, Wayne E., *Barbarians and Brothers: Anglo-American Warfare, 1500–1865*. New York and Oxford: Oxford University Press, 2011.
Leinwand, Theodore B., *Theatre, Finance and Society in Early Modern England*. Cambridge: Cambridge University Press, 2004.
Lemmings, David, *Professors of the Law: Barristers and English Legal Culture in the Eighteenth Century*. Oxford: Oxford University Press, 2000.
Leonard, A. B., and David Pretel, ed., *The Caribbean and the Atlantic World Economy*. New York: Palgrave Macmillan, 2015.
Lepler, Jessica M., *The Many Panics of 1837: People, Politics, and the Creation of a Transatlantic Financial Crisis*. Cambridge: Cambridge University Press, 2013.
Lepore, Jill, *The Name of War: King Philip's War and the Origins of American Identity*. New York: Knopf, 1998.
  New York Burning: Liberty, Slavery, and Conspiracy in Eighteenth-Century Manhattan. New York: Alfred A. Knopf, 2005.
Levack, Brian P., *The Civil Lawyers in England, 1603–1641: A Political Study*. Oxford: Clarendon Press, 1973.
Levin, Kevin M., *Searching for Black Confederates: The Civil War's Most Persistent Myth*. Chapel Hill: University of North Carolina Press, 2019.
Levine, Joseph M., *Dr. Woodward's Shield: History, Science, and Satire in Augustan England*. Ithaca, NY and London: Cornell University Press, 1977.
Lewis, David Levering, *W. E. B. Du Bois: A Biography, 1868–1963*. New York: Henry Holt and Company, 2009.
Linehan, Peter, ed., *St John's College, Cambridge: A History*. Woodbridge, Suffolk: Boydell Press, 2011.
Livesay, Daniel, *Children of Uncertain Fortune: Mixed-Race Jamaicans in Britain and the Atlantic Family, 1733–1833*. Chapel Hill: University of North Carolina Press, 2018.
Lloyd, Chris, 'The Richmond Slave Given His Freedom after Saving Life of Gamekeeper during Moor's Fire', 14 November 2019, *The Northern Echo*, www.thenorthernecho.co.uk/history/18036868.richmond-slave-given-freedom-saving-life-gamekeeper-moors-fire/, accessed 15 October 2021.
Logan, Frenise A., 'The British East India Company and African Slavery in Benkulen, Sumatra, 1687–1792', *Journal of Negro History* 41 (October 1956): 339–348.

Lorenz, Stacy L., '"To Do Justice to His Majesty, the Merchant and the Planter": Governor William Gooch and the Tobacco Inspection Act of 1730', *The Virginia Magazine of History and Biography* 108 (2000): 345–392.

Lovejoy, Paul E., *Transformations in Slavery: A History of Slavery in Africa*. Cambridge: Cambridge University Press, 2000.

Lubenow, W. C., *The Cambridge Apostles, 1820–1914: Liberalism, Imagination, and Friendship in British Intellectual and Professional Life*. Cambridge: Cambridge University Press, 1998.

Lucas, Peter. J., 'A Conspectus of Letters to and from Sir Henry Spelman (1563/4–1641)', *The Antiquaries Journal* 102 (2022): 370–388.

Luster, Robert E., *The Amelioration of the Slaves in the British Empire*. New York: New York University Press, 1995.

Lyte, H. C. Maxwell, *A History of Eton College, 1440–1875*. London: Macmillan and Co., 1875.

Maguire, Richard C., *Africans in East Anglia, 1467–1833*. Martlesham, Suffolk: Boydell & Brewer, 2021.

Major, Andrea, *Slavery, Abolition, and Empire in India, 1772–1843*. Liverpool: Liverpool University Press, 2012.

Malcolmson, Cristina, *Studies of Skin Color in the Early Royal Society: Boyle, Cavendish, Swift*. London: Taylor & Francis, 2016.

Maltz, Earl M., *Dred Scott and the Politics of Slavery*. Lawrence: University Press of Kansas, 2007.

'The Man who Discovered a 'lost' Wonder of the World', *University of Cambridge*, www.cam.ac.uk/research/news/the-man-who-discovered-a-lost-wonder-of-the-world, accessed 17 January 2023.

Marmon, Shaun E., ed., *Slavery in the Islamic Middle East*. Princeton, NJ: Markus Wiener Publishers, 1999.

'Marriott, Sir James', *The History of Parliament*, www.historyofparliamentonline.org/volume/1790-1820/member/marriott-sir-james-1730-1803, accessed 1 July 2022.

Marsh, Ben, *Georgia's Frontier Women: Female Fortunes in a Southern Colony*. Athens: University of Georgia Press, 2007.

—— *Unravelled Dreams: Silk and the Atlantic World, 1500–1840*. Cambridge: Cambridge University Press, 2020.

Marshall, P. J., *The Making and Unmaking of Empires: Britain, India, and America c. 1750–1783*. Oxford: Oxford University Press, 2005.

Martin, Ann Smart, *Buying into the World of Goods: Early Consumers in Backcountry Virginia*. Baltimore: Johns Hopkins University Press, 2008.

Martin, Charles D., *The White African American Body: A Cultural and Literary Exploration*. New Brunswick, NJ: Rutgers University Press, 2002.

Martin, Ged, 'The Cambridge Lectureship of 1866: A False Start in American Studies', *Journal of American Studies* 7 (April 1973): 17–29.

Martin, Marcus L., Kirt von Daacke, Meghan S. Faulkner, Derrick P. Alridge, Andrea Douglas, Ishraga Eltahir, Tierney Temple Fairchild, Dorrie Fontaine,

Benjamin P. Ford, Gertrude Fraser, Gary W. Gallagher, Patrice P. Grimes, Walter F. Heinecke, Mary Hughes, Petrina Jackson, Alex M. Johnson Jr., eds., *President's Commission on Slavery and the University: Report to President Teresa A. Sullivan*. Charlottesville: University of Virginia, 2018.

Martin, Robert Bernard, *The Dust of Combat: A Life of Charles Kingsley*. New York: Macmillan, 1960.

Mason, J. C. S., *The Moravian Church and the Missionary Awakening in England, 1760–1800*. Woodbridge, Suffolk: The Boydell Press, 2001.

Massey, Gregory T., 'Izard, Ralph', *South Carolina Encyclopedia*, www.scencylopedia.org/sce/entries/izard-ralph/, accessed 18 November 2021.

Matthews, Gelien, *Caribbean Slave Revolts and the British Abolitionist Movement*. Baton Rouge: Louisiana State University Press, 2006.

Maycock, Allan Lawson, *Nicholas Ferrar of Little Gidding*. London: Society for Promoting Christian Knowledge, 1938.

Mazower, Mark, *The Greek Revolution: 1821 and the Making of Modern Europe*. New York, NY: Penguin, 2021.

McCaskill, Barbara, ed., *William Craft & Ellen Craft: Running a Thousand Miles for Freedom*. Athens: University of Georgia Press, 1999.

McClintock, Russell, *Lincoln and the Decision for War: The Northern Response to Secession*. Chapel Hill: University of North Carolina Press, 2008.

McCurry, Stephanie, *Confederate Reckoning: Power and Politics in the Civil War South*. Cambridge, MA: Harvard University Press, 2012.

McDaniel, W. Caleb, *The Problem of Democracy in the Age of Slavery: Garrisonian Abolitionists and Transatlantic Reform*. Baton Rouge: Louisiana State University Press, 2013.

McDiarmid, John F., ed., *The Monarchical Republic of Early Modern England: Essays in Response to Patrick Collinson*. London and New York: Routledge, 2016.

McDonald, Michelle Craig, 'The Chance of the Moment: Coffee and the New West Indies Commodities Trade', *The William and Mary Quarterly* 62 (July 2005): 441–472.

McDonald, Roderick A., *The Economy and Material Culture of Slavery: Goods and Chattels on the Sugar Plantations of Jamaica and Louisiana*. Baton Rouge: Louisiana University Press, 1993.

McDonnell, Michael A., *The Politics of War: Race, Class, and Conflict in Revolutionary Virginia*. Chapel Hill: University of North Carolina Press, 2007.

McDougall, Russell, and Iain Davidson, ed., *The Roth Family, Anthropology, and Colonial Administration*. London and New York: Routledge, 2008.

and Julian Croft, 'Henry Ling Roth's and George Kingsley Roth's Pacific Anthropology', *The Journal of Pacific History* 40 (September 2005), 149–170.

McDowell, Gary L., 'The Limits of Natural Law: Thomas Rutherforth and the American Legal Tradition', *The American Journal of Jurisprudence* 37 (1992): 57–81.

McGaughy, J. Kent, *Richard Henry Lee of Virginia: Portrait of an American Revolutionary*. Oxford: Rowman & Littlefield Publishers, Inc., 2004.

McInnis, Maurie D., and Louis P. Nelson, eds., *Educated in Tyranny: Slavery at Thomas Jefferson's University*. Charlottesville: University of Virginia Press, 2019.

McLachlan, Jean O., *Trade and Peace with Old Spain, 1667–1750: A Study of the Influence of Commerce on Anglo-Spanish Diplomacy in the First Half of the Eighteenth Century*. Cambridge: Cambridge University Press, 1940.

McLaren, Anne, 'Reading Sir Thomas Smith's *De Republica Anglorum* as Protestant Apologetic', *The Historical Journal* 42 (December 1999): 911–939.

McNamara, Ken, 'Dr Woodward's 350-Year legacy', *Geology Today* 31 (September–October 2015): 181–186.

Melish, Joanne Pope, *Disowning Slavery: Gradual Emancipation and 'Race' in New England, 1780–1860*. Ithaca, NY: Cornell University Press, 1998.

Mellafe, Roland, *Negro Slavery in Latin America*. Berkeley: University of California Press, 1975.

Menard, Russell R., *Sweet Negotiations: Sugar, Slavery, and Plantation Agriculture in Early Barbados*. Charlottesville: University of Virginia Press, 2006.

Meyer, Arline, 'Re-dressing Classical Statuary: The Eighteenth-Century "Hand-in-Waistcoat" Portrait', *The Art Bulletin* 77 (March 1995): 45–63.

Michael, John S., 'Nuance Lost in Translation: Interpretations of J. F. Blumenbach's Anthropology in the English-Speaking World', *NTM: International Journal of History & Ethics of Natural Sciences Technology & Medicine* 25 (July 2017): 281–309.

Miles, Tiya, *Ties that Bind: The Story of an Afro-Cherokee Family in Slavery and Freedom*. Berkeley and Los Angeles: University of California Press, 2005.

Miller, Monica L., *Slaves to Fashion: Black Dandyism and the Styling of Black Diasporic Identity*. Durham, NC: Duke University Press, 2009.

Millett, Martin, Ash Amin, Adam Branch, Mark Elliott, Toni Fola-Alade, Mónice Moreno Figueroa, Nicholas Guyatt, Mark Purcell, Sujit Sivasundaram, Ángel Gurría-Quintana, Sabine Cadeau, and Nicolas Bell-Romero, 'University of Cambridge Advisory Group on Legacies of Enslavement: Final Report', www.cam.ac.uk/about-the-university/history/legacies-of-enslavement/advisory-group-on-legacies-of-enslavement-final-report, 22 September 2022.

Minkema, Kenneth P., 'Jonathan Edwards on Slavery and the Slave Trade', *The William and Mary Quarterly* 54 (October 1997): 823–834.

Mishra, Rupali, *A Business of State: Commerce, Politics and the Birth of the East India Company*. Cambridge, MA: Harvard University Press, 2018.

Mitchell, Jeremy C., and James Cornford, 'The Political Demography of Cambridge 1832–1868', *Albion: A Quarterly Journal Concerned with British Studies* 9 (Autumn 1977): 242–272.

Money, John, 'Taverns, Coffee Houses and Clubs: Local Politics and Popular Articulacy in the Birmingham Area, in the Age of the American Revolution', *The Historical Journal* 14 (1971): 15–47.

Montaño, John Patrick, *The Roots of English Colonialism in Ireland*. Cambridge: Cambridge University Press, 2011.
Moody, Jessica, *The Persistence of Memory: Remembering Slavery in Liverpool, 'slaving capital of the world'*. Liverpool: Liverpool University Press, 2020.
Mooney, Katherine C., *Race Horse Men: How Slavery and Freedom Were Made at the Racetrack*. Cambridge, MA: Harvard University Press, 2014.
Morgan, Edmund S., *American Slavery, American Freedom: The Ordeal of Colonial Virginia*. New York and London: W. W. Norton & Company, 1975.
Morgan, Hiram, 'The Colonial Venture of Sir Thomas Smith in Ireland, 1571–1575', *The Historical Journal* 28 (June 1985): 261–278.
Morgan, Jennifer L., *Labouring Women: Reproduction and Gender in New World Slavery*. Philadelphia: University of Pennsylvania Press, 2004.
Morgan, Kenneth, *Slavery and the British Empire: From Africa to America*. Oxford: Oxford University Press, 2007.
  Slavery, Atlantic Trade and the British Economy, 1660–1800. Cambridge: Cambridge University Press, 2001.
Morgan, Philip D., *Slave Counterpoint: Black Culture in the Eighteenth-Century Chesapeake and Lowcountry*. Chapel Hill: University of North Carolina Press, 1998.
  and J. R. McNeill, Matthew Mulcahy, Struart B. Schwartz, eds., *Sea & Land: An Environmental History of the Caribbean*. Oxford: Oxford University Press, 2022.
Morgan, Victor, and Christopher Brooke, *A History of the University of Cambridge, Volume II: 1546–1750*. Cambridge: Cambridge University Press, 2004.
Morris, Thomas D., *Southern Slavery and the Law, 1619–1860*. Chapel Hill: University of North Carolina Press, 1996.
  '"Villeinage… as It Existed in England, Reflects but Little Light on Our Subject": The Problem of the "Sources" of Southern Slave Law', *The American Journal of Legal History* 32 (April 1988): 95–137.
Moses, Wilson Jeremiah, *Alexander Crummell: A Study of Civilization and Discontent*. New York and Oxford: Oxford University Press, 1989.
Mottier, Véronique, Elly Robson, Julius Grower, Claire Fenton-Glynn, Renaud Morieux, Shailaja Fennell, Chris Jeppesen, Rohan Clarke, Sorcha Keenan, Nabil Haque, Michael Edwards, Robert Athol, Preti Taneja, and Verene Shepherd, 'Jesus College Legacy of Slavery Working Party: Interim Report (July–October 2019)', www.jesus.cam.ac.uk/sites/default/files/inline/files/legacy_slavery_working_party_interim_report_27_nov_2019%20%283%29.pdf, accessed 4 April 2022.
Mulcahy, Matthew, 'Weathering the Storms: Hurricanes and Risk in the British Greater Caribbean', *The Business History Review* 78 (Winter 2004): 635–663.
Mullen, Stephen, and Simon Newman, *Slavery, Abolition and the University of Glasgow: Report and Recommendations of University of Glasgow History of Slavery Steering Committee*. Glasgow: University of Glasgow, 2018.
Mullin, Gerald W., *Flight and Rebellion: Slave Resistance in Eighteenth-Century Virginia*. New York: Oxford University Press, 1972.

Murphy, Anne L., *The Origins of English Financial Markets: Investment and Speculation before the South Sea Bubble*. Cambridge: Cambridge University Press, 2009.
Murphy, Kathleen S., *Captivity's Collections: Science, Natural History, and the British Transatlantic Slave Trade*. Chapel Hill: University of North Carolina Press, 2023.
  'Collecting Slave Traders: James Petiver, Natural History, and the British Slave Trade', *The William and Mary Quarterly* 70 (October 2013): 637–670.
Murray, Hannah-Rose, *Advocates of Freedom: African American Transatlantic Abolitionism in the British Isles*. Cambridge: Cambridge University Press, 2020.
Myers, Norma, *Reconstructing the Black Past: Blacks in Britain, 1780–1830*. London and New York: Routledge, 2003.
Nafafé, José Lingna, *Lourenço Da Silva Mendonça and the Black Atlantic Abolitionist Movement in the Seventeenth Century*. Cambridge: Cambridge University Press, 2022.
Nash, Gary B., *The Forgotten Fifth: African Americans and the Age of Revolution*. Cambridge, MA: Harvard University Press, 2006.
'Nathanael Lloyd Society', Trinity Hall, University of Cambridge, www.trinhall.cam.ac.uk/supporters/your-impact/recognition/nathanael-lloyd-society/, accessed 12 May 2022.
Nechtman, Tillman W., *Nabobs: Empire and Identity in Eighteenth-Century Britain*. Cambridge: Cambridge University Press, 2010.
Neild, R. R., *The Financial History of Cambridge University*. London: Thames River Press, 2012.
Newman Simon P., *A New World of Labor: The Development of Plantation Slavery in the British Atlantic*. Philadelphia: University of Pennsylvania Press, 2016.
  Freedom Seekers: Escaping from Slavery in Restoration London. London: University of London Press, 2022.
  'Hidden in Plain Sight: Escaped Slaves in Late-Eighteenth- and Early-Nineteenth Century Jamaica', *The William and Mary Quarterly*, https://oireader.wm.edu/open_wmq/hidden-in-plain-sight/hidden-in-plain-sight-escaped-slaves-in-late-eighteenth-and-early-nineteenth-century-jamaica/, accessed 1 December 2022.
Nicholas, Thomas, *Annals and Antiquities of the Counties and County Families of Wales: Containing a Record of all Ranks of the Gentry, Their Lineage, Alliances, Appointments, Armorial Ensigns, and Residences*, 2 vols. Baltimore: Genealogical Publishing Company, 1991.
Niddrie, David L., 'An Attempt at Planned Settlement in St. Kitts in the Early Eighteenth Century', *Caribbean Studies* 5 (January 1966): 3–11.
Norman, E. R., *Church and Society in England, 1770–1970: An Historical Study*. Oxford: Oxford University Press, 1976.
Nwulia, D. E., 'The Role of Missionaries in the Emancipation of Slaves in Zanzibar', *The Journal of Negro History* 60 (1975): 268–287.

Oast, Jennifer, *Institutional Slavery: Slaveholding Churches, Schools, Colleges, and Businesses in Virginia, 1680–1860*. Cambridge: Cambridge University Press, 2016.
Oberg, Michael Leroy, *Dominion and Civility: English Imperialism and Native America, 1585–1685*. Ithaca, NY: Cornell University Press, 1999.
O'Brien, Michael, *Conjectures of Order: Intellectual Life and the American South, 1810–1860*, 2 vols. Chapel Hill: University of North Carolina Press, 2004.
Odlyzko, Andrew, 'Newton's Financial Misadventures in the South Sea Bubble', *Royal Society Journal of the History of Science* 73 (2019): 29–59.
O'Farrell, Brian, *Shakespeare's Patron, William Herbert, Third Earl of Pembroke 1580–1630: Politics, Patronage and Power*. London: Bloomsbury, 2011.
Office of the President, 'Reexamining the History of Our Founder', *Johns Hopkins University*, https://president.jhu.edu/meet-president-daniels/speeches-articles-and-media/reexamining-the-history-of-our-founder/, accessed 23 May 2022.
O'Flaherty, Niall, *Utilitarianism in the Age of Enlightenment: The Moral and Political Thought of William Paley*. Cambridge: Cambridge University Press, 2019.
Ogborn, Miles, *Indian Ink: Script and Print in the Making of the English East India Company*. Chicago: University of Chicago Press, 2007.
O'Gorman, Frank, 'The Paine Burnings of 1792–1793', *Past & Present* 193 (November 2006): 111–155.
Oldfield, John R., *Popular Politics and British Anti-Slavery: The Mobilisation of Public Opinion against the Slave Trade, 1787–1807*. Manchester: Manchester University Press, 1995.
  Transatlantic Abolitionism in the Age of Revolution: An International History of Anti-slavery, c. 1787–1820. Cambridge: Cambridge University Press, 2013.
  and Mary Wills, 'Remembering 1807: Lessons from the Archives', *History Workshop Journal* 90 (Autumn 2020): 253–272.
Olivarius, Kathryn, *Necropolis: Disease, Power, and Capitalism in the Cotton Kingdom*. Cambridge, MA: Harvard University Press, 2022.
Oliver, Vere Langford, *The History of the Island of Antigua, One of the Leeward Caribbees in the West Indies. From the First Settlement in 1635 to the Present Time*, 3 vols. London: Mitchell and Hughes, 1896.
O'Malley, Gregory E., *Final Passages: The Intercolonial Slave Trade of British America*. Chapel Hill: University of North Carolina Press, 2014.
O'Neill, Lindsay, *The Opened Letter: Networking in the Early Modern British World*. Philadelphia: University of Pennsylvania Press, 2015.
Oshatz, Molly, *Slavery & Sin: The Fight against Slavery and the Rise of Liberal Protestantism*. Oxford and New York: Oxford University Press, 2012.
O'Shaughnessy, Andrew Jackson, *An Empire Divided: The American Revolution and the British Caribbean*. Philadelphia: University of Pennsylvania Press, 2000.
  'The Formation of a Commercial Lobby: The West India Interest, British Colonial Policy and the American Revolution', *The Historical Journal* 40 (March 1997): 71–95.

The Illimitable Freedom of the Human Mind: Thomas Jefferson's Idea of a University. Charlottesville: University of Virginia Press, 2021.

The Men Who Lost America: British Command during the Revolutionary War and the Preservation of the Empire. New Haven, CT: Yales University Press, 2013.

Oswald, P. H., and C. D. Preston, *John Ray's Cambridge Catalogue (1660)*. London: The Ray Society, 2011.

Pagden, Anthony, *The Fall of Natural Man: The American Indian and the Origins of Comparative Ethnology*. Cambridge: Cambridge University Press, 1982.

Page, Jesse, *The Black Bishop: Samuel Adjai Crowther*. London: Hodder and Stoughton, 1908.

Palmer, Colin A., *Human Cargoes: The British Slave Trade to Spanish America, 1700–1739*. Chicago: University of Illinois Press, 1981.

Palmer, Patricia, *Language and Conquest in Early Modern Ireland: English Renaissance literature and Elizabethan imperial expansion*. Cambridge: Cambridge University Press, 2001.

Panton, Clifford D., *George Augustus Polgreen Bridgetower, Violin Virtuoso and Composer of Color in Late 18th Century Europe*. New York: Edwin Mellen Press, 2005.

Parent, Anthony S., Jr., *Foul Means: The Formation of a Slave Society in Virginia, 1660–1740*. Chapel Hill and London: University of North Carolina Press, 2003.

Parkinson, Robert G., *The Common Cause: Creating Race and Nation in the American Revolution*. Chapel Hill: University of North Carolina Press, 2016.

Parrish, Kate, 'Ghosts of Lone Rock', *University of the South*, https://new.sewanee.edu/features/ghosts-of-lone-rock/, accessed 10 February 2023.

'Past Fellows', *The Royal Society*, https://catalogues.royalsociety.org/CalmView/Record.aspx?src=CalmView.Persons&id=NA8038, accessed 2 February 2024.

Paton, Diana, *No Bond but the Law: Punishment, Race, and Gender in Jamaican State Formation, 1780–1870*. Durham, NC: Duke University Press, 2004.

Patterson, Brown, *The Liberal Arts at Sewanee*. Sewanee, TN: The University of the South, 2009.

Patterson, Orlando, *Slavery and Social Death*. Cambridge, MA: Harvard University Press, 1985.

Paugh, Katherine, *The Politics of Reproduction: Race, Medicine, and Fertility in the Age of Abolition*. Oxford: Oxford University Press, 2017.

Paul, Helen J., *The South Sea Bubble: An Economic History of Its Origins and Consequences*. London: Routledge, 2013.

Paul-Emile, Barbara Taylor, 'Samuel Taylor Coleridge as Abolitionist', *ARIEL* 5 (1974): 59–75.

Pearsall, Sarah M. S., *Atlantic Families: Lives and Letters in the Later Eighteenth Century*. Oxford: Oxford University Press, 2008.

Polygamy: An Early American History. New Haven, CT: Yale University Press, 2019.

Peers, Douglas M., *India under Colonial Rule: 1700–1885*. London and New York: Routledge, 2006.
Peile, John, *Biographical Register of Christ's College, 1505–1905, and of the Earlier Foundation, God's House, 1448–1505*, 2 vols. Cambridge: Cambridge University Press, 1910.
Pellew, Jill, and Lawrence Goldman, eds., *Dethroning Historical Reputations: Universities, Museums, and the Commemoration of Benefactors*. London: Institute of Historical Research, 2018.
Pennock, Caroline Dodds, *On Savage Shores: How Indigenous Americans Discovered Europe*. New York: Alfred. A. Knopf, 2023.
Perraton, Hilary, *A History of Foreign Students in Britain*. London: Palgrave Macmillan, 2014.
Pestana, Carla Gardina, *The English Conquest of Jamaica: Oliver Cromwell's Bid for Empire*. Cambridge, MA: Harvard University Press, 2017.
Peterson, John, *Province of Freedom: A History of Sierra Leone, 1787–1870*. London: Faber and Faber, 1969.
Petley, Christopher, ed., *Rethinking the Fall of the Planter Class*. London: Routledge, 2016.
  White Fury: A Jamaican Slaveholder and the Age of Revolution. Oxford: Oxford University Press, 2018.
Pettigrew, William A., *Freedom's Debt: The Royal African Company and the Politics of the Atlantic Slave Trade, 1672–1752*. Chapel Hill: University of North Carolina Press, 2013.
  and David Veevers, eds., *The Corporation as a Protagonist in Global History, c. 1550–1750*. Leiden: Brill, 2018.
Piecuch, Jim, *Three Peoples, One King: Loyalists, Indians, and Slaves in the Revolutionary South, 1775–1782*. Columbia: University of South Carolina Press, 2008.
Pietsch, Tamson, *Empire of Scholars: Universities, Networks and the British Academic World, 1850–1939*. Manchester: Manchester University Press, 2015.
Pinarbasi, Sami, 'Manchester Antislavery, 1792–1807', *Slavery & Abolition* 41 (2020): 349–376.
Plank, Geoffrey, *Atlantic Wars: From the Fifteenth Century to the Age of Revolution*. New York and Oxford: Oxford University Press, 2020.
Pomeranz, Kenneth, *The Great Divergence: China, Europe, and the Making of the Modern World Economy*. Princeton, NJ: Princeton University Press, 2000.
Porter, Andrew, *Religion versus Empire? British Protestant Missionaries and Overseas Expansion, 1700–1914*. Manchester: Manchester University Press, 2004.
Porter, Roy, 'John Woodward; "A Droll Sort of Philosopher"', *Geological Magazine* 116 (1978): 335–417.
  The Making of Geology: Earth Science in Britain, 1660–1815. Cambridge: Cambridge University Press, 1977.
Potts, Robert, *Liber Cantabrigiensis, an Account of the Aids Afforded to Poor Students, the Encouragements Offered to Diligent Students, and the Rewards*

Conferred on Successful Students, in the University of Cambridge. Cambridge: Cambridge University Press, 1855.
Powell, William S., *John Pory, 1572–1636: The Life and Letters of a Man of Many Parts*. Chapel Hill: University of North Carolina Press, 1977.
Pritchett, Jonathan B., 'Quantitative Estimates of the United States Interregional Slave Trade, 1820–1860', *The Journal of Economic History* 61 (June 2001): 467–475.
Pulis, John W., ed., *Moving On: Black Loyalists in the Afro-Atlantic World*. New York: Taylor & Francis, 2013.
Pybus, Cassandra, *Epic Journeys of Freedom: Runaway Slaves of the American Revolution and Their Quest for Liberty*. Boston: Beacon, 2006.
Quinn, D. B., 'Renaissance Influences in English Colonization', *Transactions of the Royal Historical Society* 26 (December 1976): 73–93.
Radburn, Nicholas, *Traders in Men: Merchants and the Transformation of the Transatlantic Slave Trade*. New Haven, CT: Yale University Press, 2023.
'Radcliffe, John (1653–1714), of Wolverton, Bucks., and Carshalton, Surr.', *The History of Parliament*, www.histparl.ac.uk/volume/1690-1715/member/radcliffe-john-1653-1714#footnote1_b18puie, accessed 30 June 2022.
Raphael-Hernandez, Heike, and Pia Wiegmink, 'German Entanglements in Transatlantic Slavery: An Introduction', *Atlantic Studies* 14 (2017): 419–435.
Rashdall, Hastings, *The Universities of Europe in the Middle Ages, Part 2, English Universities, Student Life*. Cambridge: Cambridge University Press, 2010.
Raven, Charles E., *John Ray, Naturalist: His Life and Works*. Cambridge: Cambridge University Press, 1950.
Rawley, James A., ed., *London: Metropolis of the Slave Trade*. Columbia: University of Missouri Press, 2003.
 and D. Behrendt, *The Transatlantic Slave Trade: A History*. Lincoln and London: University of Nebraska Press, 2005.
Rediker, Marcus, *The Fearless Benjamin Lay: The Quaker Dwarf Who Became the First Revolutionary Abolitionist*. London: Verso, 2017.
 The Slave Ship: A Human History. New York: Viking, 2007.
Register, Woody, and Benjamin King, 'A Research Summary on Slavery at the University of the South and in the Community of Sewanee', *The University of the South*, https://new.sewanee.edu/roberson-project/learn-more/research-summary/#:~:text=While%20other%20universities%20have%20documented,itself%20ever%20owned%20enslaved%20people, accessed 10 February 2023.
Reid, Christopher, 'Whig Declamation and Rhetorical Freedom at Trinity College, Cambridge, 1770–1805', *The Review of English Studies* 64 (September 2013): 630–650.
Reidy, Joseph P., *From Slavery to Agrarian Capitalism in the Cotton Plantation South: Central Georgia, 1800–1880*. Chapel Hill and London: University of North Carolina Press, 1992.
Resendez, Andres, *The Other Slavery: The Uncovered Story of Indian Enslavement in America*. Boston: Houghton Mifflin Harcourt, 2016.

Richards, Jake Christopher, 'Anti-Slave-Trade Law, "Liberated Africans" and the State in the South Atlantic World, c. 1839–1852', *Past & Present* 241 (November 2018): 179–219.
  'Political Thought and the Emotion of Shame: John Stuart Mill and the Jamaica Committee during the Governor Eyre Controversy', *Modern Intellectual History* 20 (June 2023): 417–437.
Richardson, Alan, *British Romanticism and the Science of the Mind*. Cambridge: Cambridge University Press, 2001.
Richardson, David, Suzanne Schwarz, and Anthony Tibbles, eds., *Liverpool and Transatlantic Slavery*. Liverpool: Liverpool University Press, 2007.
Richter, Daniel K., *Before the Revolution: America's Ancient Pasts*. Cambridge, MA: The Belknap Press of Harvard University Press, 2011.
Riley, Charlotte Lydia, *Imperial Island: An Alternative History of the British Empire*. Cambridge, MA: Harvard University Press, 2024.
Roach, J. C. P., ed., *The Victoria History of the County of Cambridge and the Isle of Ely: Volume 3, the City and University of Cambridge*. London: Published for the University of London Institute of Historical Research by the Oxford University Press, 1959.
Robbins, Caroline, '"When It Is That Colonies May Turn Independent": An Analysis of the Environment and Politics of Francis Hutcheson (1694–1746)', *The William and Mary Quarterly* 11 (April 1954): 214–251.
Roberts, Daniel Sanjiv, and Jonathan Jeffrey Wright, eds., *Ireland's Imperial Connections, 1775–1947*. London: Palgrave Macmillan, 2019.
Roberts, Justin, *Slavery and the Enlightenment in the British Atlantic*. Cambridge: Cambridge University Press, 2013.
Robertson, John, ed., *A Union for Empire: Political Thought and the British Union*. Cambridge: Cambridge University Press, 1996.
Roderick, Anna B., *Lecturing the Victorians: Knowledge-Based Culture and Participatory Citizenship*. London: Bloomsbury Publishing, 2024.
Rodriguez, Junius, ed., *Encyclopedia of Emancipation and Abolition in the Transatlantic World*, 3 vols. London and New York: Routledge, 2015.
Rogers, Nicholas, *Murder on the Middle Passage: The Trial of John Kimber*. London: Boydell and Brewer, 2020.
Rolleston, Sir Humphry, 'Sir George Murray Humphry, M.D., F.R.S.', *Annals of Medical History* 9 (Spring 1927): 1–11.
Rönnbäck, Klas, 'On the Economic Importance of the Slave Plantation Complex to the British Economy during the Eighteenth Century: A Value-Added Approach', *Journal of Global History* 13 (2018): 309–327.
Roos, Anna Marie, *Martin Lister and His Remarkable Daughters: The Art of Science in the Seventeenth Century*. Oxford: Bodleian Library, 2018.
  Web of Nature: Martin Lister (1639–1712), the First Arachnologist. Leiden: Brill, 2011.
Rose, Edwin D., 'Empire and the Theology of Nature in the Cambridge Botanic Garden, 1760–1825', *Journal of British Studies* 62 (October 2023), 1011–1042.

Rosenthal, Caitlin, *Accounting for Slavery: Masters and Management*. Cambridge, MA: Harvard University Press, 2018.

Rossignol, Marie-Jeanne, and Betrand Van Ruymbeke, eds., *The Atlantic World of Anthony Benezet (1713-1784): From French Reformation to American Quaker Antislavery Activism*. Leiden: Brill 2017.

Rothery, Mark, and Henry French, ed., *Making Men: The Formation of Elite Male Identities in England, c. 1660-1900*. Basingstoke: Palgrave Macmillan, 2012.

Rothman, Adam, *Slave Country: American Expansion and the Origins of the Deep South*. Cambridge, MA: Harvard University Press, 2005.

Rountree, Helen, *The Powhatan Indians of Virginia: Their Traditional Culture*. Norman: University of Oklahoma Press, 1989.

Rowlinson, J. S., 'John Freind: Physician, Chemist, Jacobite, and Friend of Voltaire's', *Notes and Records of the Royal Society of London* 61 (May 2007): 109-127.

Roynon, Tessa, *Toni Morrison & The Classical Tradition: Transforming American Culture*. Oxford: Oxford University Press, 2013.

Rozbicki, Michal J., 'The Curse of Provincialism: Negative Perceptions of Colonial American Plantation Gentry', *The Journal of Southern History* 63 (November 1997): 727-752.

'To Save Them from Themselves: Proposals to Enslave the British Poor, 1698-1755', *Slavery & Abolition* 22 (2001): 29-50.

Rüegg, Walter, and H. De Ridder-Symoens, ed., *A History of the University in Europe, Volume 1: Universities in the Middle Ages*. Cambridge: Cambridge University Press, 1992.

Ryan, Maeve, '"A moral millstone"?: British Humanitarian Governance and the Policy of Liberated African Apprenticeship, 1808-1848', *Slavery & Abolition* 37 (January 2016): 399-422.

Saastamoinen, Kari, 'Pufendorf on Natural Equality, Human Dignity, and Self-Esteem', *Journal of the History of Ideas* 71 (January 2010): 39-62.

Salt, Karen, *The Unfinished Revolution: Haiti, Black Sovereignty and the Nineteenth-Century Atlantic World*. Liverpool: Liverpool University Press, 2019.

'The Samuel Blythe Society', *Clare College, University of Cambridge*, www.clarealumni.com/pages/supporting-clare/the-samuel-blythe-society, accessed 1 July 2022.

Sandweiss, Martha A., and Craig Hollander, 'Princeton and Slavery: Holding the Center', *The Princeton & Slavery Project*, https://slavery.princeton.edu/stories/princeton-and-slavery-holding-the-center, accessed 23 May 2022.

Sanghera, Sathnam, *Empireland: How Imperialism Has Shaped Modern Britain*. New York: Pantheon Books, 2023.

Saye, Charles, *Annals of Cambridge University Library*. Cambridge: University Library, 1916.

'Sayer, Exton (c. 1691-1731), of Doctors' Commons, London', *The History of Parliament*, www.historyofparliamentonline.org/volume/1715-1754/member/sayer-exton-1691-1731, accessed 29 June 2022.

Scanlan, Padraic X., *Freedom's Debtors: British Antislavery in Sierra Leone in the Age of Revolution*. New Haven, CT: Yale University Press, 2017.
  Slave Empire: How Slavery Made Modern Britain. London: Robinson, 2020.
Schiebinger, Londa, *Plants and Empire: Colonial Bioprospecting in the Atlantic World*. Cambridge, MA: Harvard University Press, 2004.
Schneider, Elena A., *The Occupation of Havana: War, Trade, and Slavery in the Atlantic World*. Chapel Hill: University of North Carolina Press, 2018.
Schultz, Bart, *Henry Sidgwick – Eye of the Universe: An Intellectual Biography*. Cambridge: Cambridge University Press, 2004.
Schuyler, Robert Livingston, 'The Constitutional Claims of the British West Indies: The Controversy over the Slave Registry Bill of 1815', *Political Science Quarterly* 40 (March 1925): 1–36.
Scott, Julius S., *The Common Wind: Afro-American Currents in the Age of the Haitian Revolution*. London and New York: Verso Books, 2018.
Scott, Robert Forsyth, *Admissions to the College of St John the Evangelist in the University of Cambridge*, 4 vols. Cambridge: Cambridge University Press, 1893–1931.
Searby, Peter, *A History of the University of Cambridge, Volume III: 1750–1870*. Cambridge: Cambridge University Press, 1997.
Sebrell II, Thomas E., *Persuading John Bull: Union and Confederate Propaganda in Britain, 1860–65*. New York: Lexington Books, 2014.
Semmel, Stuart, 'British Radicals and "Legitimacy": Napoleon in the Mirror of History', *Past & Present* 167 (May 2000): 140–175.
Sensbach, Jon F., *Rebecca's Revival: Creating Black Christianity in the Atlantic World*. Cambridge, MA: Harvard University Press, 2006.
Sesay, Chernoh M., 'The Revolutionary Black Roots of Slavery's Abolition in Massachusetts', *The New England Quarterly* 87 (March 2014): 99–131.
Seth, Suman, *Difference and Disease: Medicine, Race, and the Eighteenth-Century British Empire*. New York and Cambridge: Cambridge University Press, 2018.
  'Race, Specificity, and Statistics in Victorian Medicine', *Journal of Victorian Culture* 27 (April 2022): 370–383.
Shand-Tucci, Douglass, and Richard Cheek, *Harvard University: An Architectural Tour*. Princeton, NJ: Princeton Architectural Press, 2001.
Shayt, David H., 'Stairway to Redemption: America's Encounter with the British Prison Treadmill', *Technology and Culture* 30 (October 1989): 908–938.
Shea, Gary S., '(Re)financing the Slave Trade with the Royal African Company in the Boom Markets of 1720', *Centre for Dynamic Macroeconomic Analysis Working Paper Series*, CDMA11/14 (October 2011): 1–54.
Shelford, April G., *A Caribbean Enlightenment: Intellectual Life in the British and French Colonial Worlds, 1750–1792*. Cambridge: Cambridge University Press, 2023.
Sheridan, Richard B., 'Samuel Martin, Innovating Sugar Planter of Antigua 1750–1776', *Agricultural History* 34 (July 1960): 126–139.

Sugar and Slaves: An Economic History of the British West Indies, 1623–1775. Jamaica: Canoe Press, 1994.

Shields, John C., *The American Aeneas: Classical Origins of the American Self*. Knoxville: The University of Tennessee Press, 2001.

Shovlin, John, *Trading with the Enemy: Britain, France, and the 18th-Century Quest for a Peaceful World Order*. New Haven, CT: Yale University Press, 2021.

Shyllon, Folarin, *Edward Long's Libel of Africa: The Foundations of British Racism*. Newcastle: Cambridge Scholar Publishing, 2021.

Sidbury, James, *Ploughshares into Swords: Race, Rebellion, and Identity in Gabriel's Virginia, 1730–1810*. Cambridge: Cambridge University Press, 1997.

Silkenat, David, *Scars on the Land: An Environmental History of Slavery in the American South*. Oxford: Oxford University Press, 2022.

Silver, Peter, *Our Savage Neighbors: How Indian War Transformed Early America*. New York: W. W. Norton & Company, 2008.

Silverman, David, *Faith and Boundaries: Colonists, Christianity, and Community among the Wampanoag Indians of Martha's Vineyard, 1600–1871*. New York and Cambridge: Cambridge University Press, 2005.

Simmons, Frederick Johnson, *Emmanuel Downing* (Montclair, NJ: Unknown Publisher, 1958)

Sinha, Manisha, *The Slave's Cause: A History of Abolition*. New Haven, CT: Yale University Press, 2016.

Sirota, Brent S., *The Christian Monitors: The Church of England and the Age of Benevolence, 1680–1730*. New Haven, CT: Yale University Press, 2014.

'Sir Thomas Bendish (1607–1674)', *St John's College, Cambridge*, www.joh.cam.ac.uk/library/special_collections/early_books/bendish.htm, accessed 22 May 2023.

Sluiter, Engel, 'New Light on the "20. and Odd Negroes" Arriving in Virginia, August 1619', *The William and Mary Quarterly* 54 (April 1997): 395–398.

Smail, John, 'The Culture of Credit in Eighteenth-Century Commerce: The Textile Industry', *Enterprise & Society* 4 (June 2003): 299–325.

Smallwood, Stephanie E., *Saltwater Slavery: A Middle Passage from Africa to American Diaspora*. Cambridge, MA: Harvard University Press, 2007.

Smith, Brendan, *Crisis and Survival in Late Medieval Ireland: The English of Louth and their Neighbours, 1330–1450*. Oxford: Oxford University Press, 2013.

Smith, Edmond, *Merchants: The Community That Shaped England's Trade and Empire*. New Haven, CT: Yale University Press, 2021.

Smith, M. J., 'Benjamin Flower and the "Cambridge Intelligencer", 1793–1803', *Transactions of the Cambridge Bibliographical Society* 16 (2018): 415–454.

Smith, Tracy-Ann, Katherine Hann, Katherine Prior, and Mabintu Mustapha, *Slavery and the Natural World*. London: Natural History Museum, 2007.

Snader, Joe, *Caught Between Worlds: British Captivity Narratives in Fact and Fiction*. Lexington: University Press of Kentucky, 2000.

Snyder, Christina, *Slavery in Indian Country*. Cambridge, MA: Harvard University Press, 2010.

Soderlund, Jean R., *Quakers & Slavery: A Divided Spirit*. Princeton, NJ: Princeton University Press, 1985.
Solow, Barbara L., Barbara L. Solow, 'Caribbean Slavery and British Growth', *Journal of Development Economics* 17 (1985): 99–115.
  ed., *Slavery and the Rise of the Atlantic System*. Cambridge: Cambridge University Press, 1991.
Soriano, Tim, '"What Rascals!" Perceptions of Free Labor in the Bulama Settlement, 1792–1793', *African Economic History* 49 (November 2021): 173–191.
Sparks, Randy J., *On Jordan's Stormy Banks: Evangelicalism in Mississippi, 1773–1876*. Athens: University of Georgia Press, 1994.
  Where the Negroes Are Masters: An African Port in the Era of the Slave Trade. Cambridge, MA: Harvard University Press, 2014.
Speake, Jennifer, ed., *Literature of Travel and Exploration: An Encyclopedia, Volume One: A To F*. London and New York: Routledge, 2003.
Stamp, Gavin, 'George Gilbert Scott, Jun., and King's College Chapel', *Architectural History* 37 (1994): 153–164.
Stauffer, John, *The Black Hearts of Men: Radical Abolitionists and the Transformation of Race*. Cambridge, MA: Harvard University Press, 2002.
Staunton, Howard, *The Great Schools of England*. London: Strahan and Co., Publishers, 1869.
Stearns, Raymond Phineas, 'Colonial Fellows of the Royal Society of London, 1661–1788', *WMQ* 3 (April 1946), 269–274.
  Science in the British Colonies of America. Chicago and London: University of Illinois Press, 1970.
Stephen, Leslie, ed., *Dictionary of National Biography*, 63 vols. New York: Macmillan and Co., 1889.
Philip J. Stern, *The Company-State: Corporate Sovereignty and the Early Modern Foundations of the British Empire in India*. Oxford: Oxford University Press, 2011.
  Empire, Incorporated: The Corporations That Built British Colonialism. Cambridge, MA: Harvard University Press, 2023.
Stockwell, Sarah, ed., *The British Empire: Themes and Perspectives*. Oxford: Blackwell Publishing, 2008.
Stone, Erin Woodruff, *Slavery in the Early Modern Spanish Caribbean*. Philadelphia: University of Pennsylvania Press, 2021.
Stone, Lawrence, ed., *The University in Society, Volume I: Oxford and Cambridge from the 14th to the Early 19th Century*. Princeton, NJ: Princeton University Press, 1974.
Stone, William, *The Squire of Piccadilly: Memories of William Stone in Conversation with Henry Baerlein*. London: Jarrolds, 1951.
Stott, Anne, *Wilberforce: Family and Friends*. Oxford: Oxford University Press, 2012.
Strype, John, *The Life of the Learned Sir Thomas Smith, Kt. Doctor of the Civil Law, Principal Secretary of State to King Edward the Sixth, and Queen Elizabeth*. Oxford: Clarendon Press, 1820.

Summerfield, Carol, and Mary Elizabeth Devine, ed., *International Dictionary of University Histories*. London and New York: Routledge, 1998.
Sutherland, Daniel E., 'Exiles, Emigrants, and Sojourners: The Post-Civil War Confederate Exodus in Perspective', *Civil War History* 31 (September 1985): 237–256.
Svalastog, J. M., *Mastering the Worst of Trades: England's Early Africa Companies and Their Traders, 1618–1672*. Brill: Leiden, 2021.
Swain, Warren, *The Law of Contract, 1670–1870*. Cambridge: Cambridge University Press, 2015.
Swaminathan, Srividhya, *Debating the Slave Trade: Rhetoric of British National Identity, 1759–1815*. Abingdon: Routledge, 2009.
  'Developing the West Indian Proslavery Position after the Somerset Decision', *Slavery and Abolition* 24 (December 2003): 40–60.
Swedberg, Richard, ed. *Joseph A. Schumpeter: The Economics and Sociology of Capitalism*. Princeton, NJ: Princeton University Press, 1991.
Swingen, Abigail L., *Competing Visions of Empire: Labor, Slavery, and the Origins of the British Atlantic Empire*. New Haven, CT and London: Yale University Press, 2015.
Symonds, Richard, *Oxford and Empire: The Last Lost Cause?* Oxford: Clarendon Press, 1992.
Sypher, Wylie, 'Hutcheson and the "Classical" Theory of Slavery', *The Journal of Negro History* 24 (1939): 263–280.
Taylor, Alan, *American Colonies*. New York: Penguin, 2002.
  The Internal Enemy: Slavery and War in Virginia, 1772–1832. New York: W. W. Norton & Company, 2013.
  Thomas Jefferson's Education. New York: W. W. Norton & Company, 2019.
Taylor, Bruce M., 'Our Man in London: John Pollard Mayers, Agent for Barbados, and the British Abolition Act, 1832–1834', *Caribbean Studies* 16 (October 1976): 60–84.
Taylor, Eric Robert, *If We Must Die: Shipboard Insurrections in the Era of the Atlantic Slave Trade*. Baton Rouge: Louisiana State University Press, 2006.
Taylor, Michael, 'Conservative Political Economy and the Problem of Colonial Slavery, 1823–1833', *The Historical Journal* 57 (2014): 973–995.
  The Interest: How the British Establishment Resisted the Abolition of Slavery. London: Bodley Head, 2020.
Temin, Peter, and Hans-Joachim Voth, *Prometheus Shackled: Goldsmith Banks and England's Financial Revolution after 1700*. Oxford and New York: Oxford University Press, 2013.
Thornton, John, *Africa and Africans in the Making of the Atlantic World, 1400–1800*. Cambridge: Cambridge University Press, 1998.
  'African Dimensions of the Stono Rebellion', *The American Historical Review* 96 (October 1991), 1101–1113.
  'The African Experience of the "20. and Odd Negroes" Arriving in Virginia in 1619', *The William and Mary Quarterly* 55 (July 1988): 421–434.

Thorp, Margaret Tharrand, *Charles Kingsley, 1819–1875*. Princeton, NJ: Princeton University Press, 1937.
Tise, Larry E., *Proslavery: A History of the Defense of Slavery in America, 1701–1840*. Athens: University of Georgia Press, 1987.
Toledano, Ehud R., *As If Silent and Absent: Bonds of Enslavement in the Islamic Middle East*. New Haven, CT: Yale University Press, 2007.
Torget, Andrew J., *Seeds of Empire: Cotton, Slavery, and the Transformation of the Texas Borderlands, 1800–1850*. Chapel Hill: University of North Carolina Press, 2015.
Trahey, Erin, 'Among Her Kinswomen: Legacies of Free Women of Color in Jamaica', *The William and Mary Quarterly* 76 (April 2019): 257–288.
Trevelyan, George Macaulay, *Trinity College: An Historical Sketch*. Cambridge: Trinity College, 1972.
Trouillot, Michel-Rolph, 'Motion in the System: Coffee, Color, and Slavery in Eighteenth-Century Saint-Domingue', *Review* 5 (Winter 1982): 331–388.
Tully, Kaye, and Clive Whitehead, 'Audacious Beginnings: The Establishment of Universities in Australasia, 1850–1900', *Education Research and Perspectives* 36 (2009): 1–44.
Turner, Mary, *Slaves and Missionaries: The Disintegration of Jamaican Slave Society, 1787–1834*. Barbados: The Press University of the West Indies, 1998.
Turner, Michael J., *Independent Radicalism in Early Victorian Britain*. London: Bloomsbury Publishing, 2004.
Turner, Sasha, *Contested Bodies: Pregnancy, Childrearing, and Slavery in Jamaica*. Philadelphia: University of Pennsylvania Press, 2017.
Van Buskirk, Judith L., *Standing in their Own Light: African American Patriots in the American Revolution*. New York: Blackwell Publishing, 2017.
Vaughan, Alden T., '"Expulsion of the Salvages": English Policy and the Virginia Massacre of 1622', *The William and Mary Quarterly* 35 (January 1978): 57–84.
  and Virginia Mason Vaughan, 'Before Othello: Elizabethan Representations of Sub-Saharan Africans', *The William and Mary Quarterly* 54 (January 1997): 19–44.
Veevers, David, *The Origins of the British Empire in Asia, 1600–1750*. Cambridge: Cambridge University Press, 2020.
Venn, John, E. S. Roberts, E. J. Gross, F. E. A. Trayes, F. J. M. Stratton, M. J. Prichard, J. B. Skemp, Joachim Whaley, and Christopher Brooke, eds., *Biographical History of Gonville and Caius College*, 8 vols. Cambridge: Cambridge University Press, 1912.
  and John Archibald Venn, *Alumni Cantabrigiensis: A Biographical List of all Known Students, Graduates and Holders of Office at the University of Cambridge, from the Earliest Times to 1900*, 4 vols. Cambridge: Cambridge University Press, 1922–27.
Voigt, Lisa, *Writing Captivity in the Early Modern Atlantic: Circulations of Knowledge and Authority in the Iberian and English Imperial Worlds*. Chapel Hill: University of North Carolina Press, 2009.

Waddell, David, 'Charles Davenant and the East India Company', *Economica* 23 (August 1956): 261–264.
Waldstreicher, David, *Slavery's Constitution: From Revolution to Ratification*. New York: Hill and Wang, 2009.
Waller, John O., 'Charles Kingsley and the American Civil War', *Studies in Philology* 60 (July 1963): 554–568.
Wallis, P. J., 'The Library of William Crashawe', *Transactions of the Cambridge Bibliographical Society* 2 (1956): 213–228.
Walsh, Lorena S., *Motives of Honor, Pleasure, & Profit: Plantation Management in the Colonial Chesapeake*. Chapel Hill: University of North Carolina Press, 2010.
Walters, Lindsey K., 'Slavery and the American University: Discourses of Retrospective Justice at Harvard and Brown', *Slavery & Abolition* 38 (2017): 719–744.
Walters, Stuart Max, *The Shaping of Cambridge Botany: A Short History of Whole-Plant Botany in Cambridge from the Time of Ray into the Present Century*. Cambridge: Cambridge University Press, 1981.
Walz, Terence, and Kenneth M. Cuno, eds., *Race and Slavery in the Middle East: Histories of Trans-Saharan Africans in Nineteenth-Century Egypt, Sudan, and the Ottoman Mediterranean*. Cairo: American University in Cairo Press, 2010.
Ward, J. R., 'The Profitability of Sugar Planting in the British West Indies, 1650–1834', *Economic History Review* 31 (May 1978): 197–213.
Warren, Wendy, *New England Bound: Slavery and Colonization in Early America*. New York: W. W. Norton & Company, 2017.
Warsh, Molly A., 'Enslaved Pearl Divers in the Sixteenth Century Caribbean', *Slavery and Abolition* 31 (2010): 345–362.
Watkins, Case, *Palm Oil Diaspora: Afro-Brazilian Landscapes and Economies on Bahia's Dendê Coast*. Cambridge: Cambridge University Press, 2021.
Watson, Alan, *Slave Law in the Americas*. Athens and London: University of Georgia Press, 1989.
Watson, Ritchie D., Jr., *The Cavalier in Virginia Fiction*. Baton Rouge: Louisiana State University Press, 1985.
Wax, Darold D., 'Robert Ellis, Philadelphia Merchant and Slave Trader', *The Pennsylvania Magazine of History and Biography* 88 (January 1964): 52–69.
Weinberg, H. Barbara, and Carrie Rebora Barratt, eds., *American Stories: Paintings of Everyday Life, 1765–1915*. New Haven, CT and London: Yale University Press, 2009.
Weinstein, Cindy, ed., *The Cambridge Companion to Harriet Beecher Stowe*. Cambridge: Cambridge University Press, 2004.
Weiss, Gillian, *Captives and Corsairs: France and Slavery in the Early Modern Mediterranean*. Stanford, CA: Stanford University Press, 2011.
Wenham, Leslie P., *The History of Richmond School, Yorkshire*. Arbroath: The Herald Press, 1958.

Wennerlind, Carl, *Casualties of Credit: The English Financial Revolution, 1620–1720*. Cambridge, MA: Harvard University Press 2011.

Wheeler, Roxann, *Categories of Difference in Eighteenth-Century British Culture*. Philadelphia: University of Pennsylvania Press, 2000.

White, Shane, and Graham White, 'Slave Clothing and African American Culture in the Eighteenth and Nineteenth Centuries', *Past & Present* 148 (August 1995): 149–186.

Whitford, David M., *The Curse of Ham in the Early Modern Era: The Bible and Justifications for Slavery*. London and New York: Routledge, 2009.

Whyte, Iain, *Scotland and the Abolition of Black Slavery, 1756–1838*. Edinburgh: Edinburgh University Press, 2006.

Whyte, William, 'The Intellectual Aristocracy Revisited', *Journal of Victorian Culture* 10 (December 2011): 15–45.

and Mishka Sinha, 'St John's and the Colonial Past', *St John's College, University of Oxford*, www.sjc.ox.ac.uk/discover/about-college/st-johns-and-colonial-past/, accessed 4 April 2022.

Wilder, Craig Steven, *Ebony & Ivy: Race, Slavery, and the Troubled History of America's Universities*. New York: Bloomsbury Press, 2013.

Williams, Carol, ed., *Indigenous Women and Work: From Labor to Activism*. Urbana, Chicago: University of Illinois Press, 2012.

Williams, Carolyn D., *Pope, Homer and Manliness: Some Aspects of Eighteenth-Century Classical Learning*. London: Routledge, 1993.

Williams, Eric, *Capitalism and Slavery*. Chapel Hill: University of North Carolina Press, 1944.

Willis, Robert, and John Willis Clark, *The Architectural History of the University of Cambridge and of the Colleges of Cambridge and Eton*, 4 vols. Cambridge: Cambridge University Press, 1886.

Wilson, Charles Reagan, *Baptized in Blood: The Religion of the Lost Cause, 1865–1920*. Athens: University of Georgia Press, 2009.

Wilson, David, *Suppressing Piracy in the Eighteenth Century: Pirates, Merchants and British Imperial Authority in the Atlantic and Indian Oceans*. Woodbridge, Suffolk: The Boydell Press, 2021.

Winch, Boston Julie, *A Gentleman of Color: The Life of James Forten*. Oxford: Oxford University Press, 2003.

Winstanley, Denis Arthur, *Early Victorian Cambridge*. Cambridge: Cambridge University Press, 1955.

Unreformed Cambridge: A Study of Certain Aspects of the University in the Eighteenth Century. Cambridge: Cambridge University Press, 2009.

Wood, Alfred C., *A History of the Levant Company*. Oxford: Oxford University Press, 1964.

Wood, Betty, *Slavery in Colonial America, 1619–1776*. Plymouth: Rowman & Littlefield, 2005.

Wood, Peter H., *Black Majority: Negroes in Colonial South Carolina from 1670 through to the Stono Rebellion*. New York: W. W. Norton & Company, 1996.

Wood, William Gerbing, *The Annual Ships of the South Sea Company, 1711–1736*. Champaign: University of Illinois Press, 1938.
Woodward, Vincent, *The Delectable Negro: Human Consumption and Homoeroticism within U.S. Slave Culture*, ed. by Justin A. Joyce and Dwight A. McBride. New York: New York University Press, 2014.
Wordsworth, Christopher, *Social Life at the English Universities in the Eighteenth Century*. Cambridge: Cambridge University Press, 1874.
Wright, Josephine R. B., 'George Polgreen Bridgetower: An African Prodigy in England, 1789-99', *The Musical Quarterly* 66 (January 1980): 65–82.
Wyatt-Brown, Bertram, *Southern Honor: Ethics & Behavior in the Old South*. Oxford and New York: Oxford University Press, 2007.
Zacek, Natalie, *Settler Society in the English Leeward Islands, 1670–1776*. Cambridge: Cambridge University Press, 2010.
Ziff, Larzer, *The Career of John Cotton: Puritanism and the American Experience*. Princeton, NJ: Princeton University Press, 1962.
Zwick, Rebecca, *Fair Game? The Use of Standardized Admissions Tests in Higher Education*. New York: Routledge, 2002.

Unpublished Dissertations

Griffiths, Leslie John, 'A History of Methodism in Haiti, 1817–1916'. Ph.D. dissertation, School of Oriental and African Studies, 1986.
Harvey, Caitlin, 'Bricks and Mortar Boards: University-Building in the Settlement Empire, 1840–1920'. Ph.D. dissertation, Princeton University, 2021.
Margolin, Samuel G., 'Lawlessness on the Maritime Frontier of the Greater Chesapeake, 1650–1750'. Ph.D. dissertation, College of William and Mary, 1992.
McMahon, Jonathan, 'The Humanism of Sir Thomas Smith'. M.A. dissertation, College of William and Mary, 1999.
Mulhern, Joseph Martin, 'After 1833: British Entanglement with Brazilian Slavery'. Ph.D. dissertation, University of Durham, 2018.
Nigol, Paul C., 'Discipline, Discretion and Control: The Private Justice System of the Hudson's Bay Company in Rupert's Land, 1670–1770'. Ph.D. dissertation, University of Calgary, 2001.
Poston, Jonathan H., 'Ralph Wormeley V of Rosegill: A Deposed Virginia aristocrat, 1774–1781'. M.A. dissertation, College of William and Mary, 1979.
Sorsby, Victoria Gardner, 'British Trade with Spanish America under the Asiento, 1713–1740'. Ph.D. dissertation, University College, London, 1975.
Spence, Carolina Quarrier, 'Ameliorating Empire: Slavery and Protection in the British Colonies, 1783–1865'. Ph.D. dissertation, Harvard University, 2014.

INDEX

Abdy, Edward Strutt
  education and background of, 166
  opinions on race, 170–171
  reception of the Journal, 169–170
  support for abolition
    organisations, 171
  travels in the United States, 168–170
Abdy, Sir William, 166
Academia della Crusca, 111
Addenbrooke's Hospital, 180
Adeane, John, 148
Adventurers for Irish Land, 53
African Company of Merchants,
  49–50, 133, 235
African Institution, 119, 131, 141, 155, 157
Afzelius, Adam, 131
Alabama, 14, 185, 197
All Souls College, Oxford, 90, 95–97, 132
Allen, Andrew, 19
Allen, James, 19
Alpress, George, 40
Alpress, Samuel, 23, 40–42
Alston, Charles, 64
al-Timbukti, Ahmad Baba, 11
al-Wazzan, al-Hasan Muhammad, 56
American Anti-Slavery Society, 170–172
American Civil War
  British support for the Confederacy,
    185–189, 193–200
  British support for the Union, 194, 286
  causes of, 14
  Confederate lobbying efforts, 197–198
  Confederate religious revival, 165
  consequences for the University of
    the South, 165
  impact on the British economy, 190
  Juneteenth, 203
  Secession, 185
  surrender of the Confederacy, 18
  Trent Affair, 186
American Colonisation Society, 183
American Revolution
  Battle of Waxhaws, 43
  Black loyalists in, 130
  British defense of their Caribbean
    colonies during, 104
  consequences for American
    merchants, 98
  Declaration of Independence, 19, 59
  effect on colonial colleges, 42
  effect on enslavement, 13
  impact on abolition movement, 107,
    151, 203
  imperial crisis, 126
  Liverpool and American Prisoners
    of War, 115
  rise of proslavery movement
    during, 119
  Treaty of Paris, 4
Anderson, John, 159
Andrews, John, 64
Angola, 56, 95, 114, 117, 132
Anthropological Society of London,
  198–199
Antigua
  Abdy plantations in, 166
  Cambridge fellowship
    connections to, 45
  Coleridge's travels in, 157
  Elizabeth Pinckney's birth in, 88
  missionary activity in, 153
  Samuel Martin's plantation, 22
  student connections to
    plantations in, 20, 28, 38, 111
Appland, Lindsay Middleton, 292
Apthorp, Charles, 74

371

Apthorp, East, 74–75
Aquinas, Thomas, 5
Arbuthnot, John, 81
Archer, Gabriel, 51
Aristotle, 5–6, 23, 259
Associates of Dr Bray, 68–69, 86
Association for Promoting the Discovery of the Interior Parts of Africa, 131–136
Australian-Pacific indentured labour trade, 191–192
Ayerst, William, 68

Babington, Charles Cardale, 199
Backhouse, James, 27
Bacon, Anthony, 128
Bahamas, 27, 47, 61
Baker, Sir Samuel, 184
Baker, William, 256
Balliol College, Oxford, 91
Bamana Empire, 136
Banister, John, 81
Bank of England, 64–65, 127, 130, 194–195
Bankers
   Banking in Cambridge, 141
   Byam's abolition scheme at Goslings and Sharpe Bank, 155
   fellowship connections to, 27, 115
   Harford banking family, 20
   impact of Russian Emancipation on, 191
   involvement in South Sea Company, 95
   links to the abolition movement, 118
   student connections to, 21, 47
   support for British rule in India, 195
   support for the Confederacy, 194, 196
Bankes, William John, 197
Banks, Sir Joseph, 131, 135
the Baptist War, 172
Barbados
   Chapman's poem, 161
   Charles Pinfold's governorship of, 64
   coffee production in, 85
   Coleridge's travels in, 156–157
   English colonisation of, 7
   fellowship connections to plantations in, 27, 32, 44–45
   Fellowship connections to slave trading in, 27
   Friedrich de August's escape from, 45
   Hughes's *Natural History*, 132
   Irish indentured servitude in, 52
   John Martyn's specimens from, 86
   legal cases about, 126
   Maskelyne's journey to, 89–90
   missionary activity in, 23, 95, 152, 154
   plantation tutors in, 47
   proposed college in, 70
   proslavery lobby in, 161–162
   Ricketts family in, 127
   Robert Lowther's governorship in, 93–94
   scientific collecting in, 81
   ships impounded in, 98
   slave code, 60
   student connections to plantations in, 20, 28, 32, 44, 46, 76, 161
   support for coffee plantations in, 85
   Townes's scientific experiments, 76–77
Barbary slave trade, 58, 72, 160
Barbor, William, 66
Barker, Hannah, 40
Barnes, Rev. Francis, 113
Barrett, Edward, 172–173
Barwick, Peter, 79
Baylor, John III, 31
Baylor, John IV, 24, 31, 37
Beaumont, Joseph, 191
Beaver, Philip, 131
Bedell, William, 53
Bendish, Sir Thomas, 53
Bendyshe, Thomas, 199
Benezet, Anthony, 50, 109, 236
Benjamin, Judah P., 198, 200–201, 292
Bentinck, Henry, 1st Duke of Portland, 68
Bentley, Richard, 25, 31, 82
Beresford-Hope, Alexander, 165, 196–197
Berkeley, Anne Forster, 69
Berkeley, George, 69, 75
Bermuda
   Captain Roger Wood's governorship of, 63
   Charles Elliot's governorship of, 178

Earl of Pembroke's designs on, 59
proposed college in, 25, 69, 75
religious dissidents
 banished from, 61
Somers Island Company rule in, 55
St Paul's College in, 177–179
student connections to
 plantations in, 20
Bernal, Ralph, 158–159
Berney, John, 32, 44
Berney, Sir Hanson, 44
Berney, Sir John, 44
Berney, Sir Thomas, 44
Beverley, Robert, 23
Bickell, Rev. Richard, 158–159
Biden, Joseph R., 203
Bigland, Edward, 39
Bigland, Elizabeth, 39
Birmingham, 143
Blackstone, William, 91, 101
Blake, Sir Patrick, 128
Blakesley, George Holmes, 191
Bland, Henry, 68
Blumenbach, Johann Friedrich,
 134, 199
Blythe, Samuel, 64
Bogle, Paul, 190
Bologna, University of, 5
Bonaparte, Napoleon, 14, 129, 138, 230
Bonney, Thomas George, 199
Borthwick, Peter, 158
Bosworth, Rev. James, 199
Botany Bay, 114, 121
Bourryau, John, 278
Boyle, Sir Robert, 152
Boynton, Sir Griffith, 113
Bradley, Richard, 83, 85–86
Brazil, 15, 114, 163, 176, 193
Bridges, George Wilson, 142
Bridgetower, Friedrich Augustus, 45
Bridgetower, George Polgreen, 45
Bridgetower, Mary Ann, 45
Briggs, Henry, 56
Bristol
 abolition movement in, 114
 banking in, 194
 medicinal practices in, 124
 merchant support for Kimber, 127
 merchants in, 47, 85

 slave traders from, 126
 Thomas Tenison's schooling in, 27
British and Foreign Bible Society, 152
British Association for the
 Advancement of Science, 147
British Guiana, 13, 46–47, 178, 182, 191
Brougham, Henry Peter, 1st Baron
 Brougham and Vaux, 148
Browne, Rev. William, 46
Browning, Oscar, 289
Brydges, James, 1st Duke of Chandos, 95
Buchanan, Francis, 145
Budd, George, 164
Buddicom, Robert Pedder, 27
Bulama Association, 131
Burckhardt, Johann Ludwig, 135
Burdon, William, 129
Burke, Edmund, 145
Burnaby, Andrew, 115
Burrell, Peter, 99
Burrough, Sir James, 34
Burwell, Lewis, 34
Burwell, Nathaniel, 21
Butler, Joseph, 117
Buxton, Sir Thomas Fowell, 141
Byam, Richard Burgh, 32, 153–155
Byrd, William II, 25, 82

Cabot, Samuel, Jr., 169
Calabar, 127, 133, 135
Calamet, Augustin, 72
Calhoun, John C., 182, 194
Calthrop, Samuel R., 286
Calvin, John, 59
Cambridge Apostles, 193
Cambridge Bible
 Association, 177, 184
Cambridge Chronicle, 111, 116, 143, 162
Cambridge Elections, 148, 150, 162
Cambridge Independent Press, 162
Cambridge Intelligencer, 117–118
Cambridge School of Art, 190
Cambridge Society for Constitutional
 Information, 118
Cambridge Union Society, 142–144,
 186, 194, 199
Cambridge University Library, 40, 60,
 78, 97, 123, 266
Cambridge University Press, 168

Campbell, Elizabeth, 40
Cannibal Club, 199
Canterbury Association, 195
Cape Coast Castle, 10, 49, 81
Carlyle, Thomas, 190
Carter, George, 22, 26
Carter, John, 26, 38
Carter, Landon, 22, 42
Carter, Robert, 22, 34–35
Carteret, John, 2nd Earl Granville, 102
Cartwright, Rev. Thomas, 49
Cartwright, Samuel A., 292
Cary, Robert, 26
Cecil, Sir William, 53
Chafy, William, 138
Chamberlyn, Elizabeth, 68
Chandler, Richard, 225
Channing, William, 170
Chapman, M. J., 161
Chapman, Thomas, 13, 67
Charles I, 59
Charles II, 38, 62, 79
Charles, Thomas, 152
Charterhouse School, 29, 36
Chetwode, John, 64
Chiesly, Sir Robert, 67
Christ Church, Oxford, 123, 162
Christian Faith Society, 177
Christian, Edward, 101
Christian, Rear-Admiral Hugh Cloberry, 181
Christophe, Henri, 144
Christ's College, Cambridge
    alumni involvement in the proslavery movement, 158
    Beilby Porteus's benefaction, 275
    donors to the abolition movement, 111
    Henry Finch's donation to, 69
    John Covel's donation to, 78
    members' donations to the Sierra Leone Company, 130
    Owen Stockton's education at, 66
    Paley's fellowship at, 117
    students with connections to plantations, 33, 40, 76
    students with connections to the transatlantic economy, 37
    Thomas Thompson, 49, 51

Church Missionary Society, 175
Church of England, 23, 49, 61, 128, 157, 165
Church of Scotland, 170
Church Pastoral Aid Society, 175
Churchill, Lady Mary, Duchess of Montagu, 231
Cicero, Marcus Tullius, 6, 23
Clapham Sect, 118–119
Clare College, Cambridge
    alumni support for the proslavery movement, 128
    fellowship involvement in the SPG, 73
    fellowship involvement in the Virginia Company, 52
    Samuel Blythe's benefaction, 64–65
    support for the abolition movement, 115–116
Clark, Rev. William, 180
Clarke, Edward Daniel, 135
Clarke, Rev. Adam, 272
Clarke, Rev. Thomas, 116
Clarke, Samuel, 117
Clarkson, Thomas
    abolitionist thought of, 109, 123, 140, 182
    Cambridge essay on enslavement, 109
    campaign chest of, 113
    involvement in Sierra Leone, 268
    proslavery attacks on, 128
    recognition of, 143
Clathrop, Samuel Robert, 186
Clayton, Charles, 175–177
Clive, Robert, 1st Baron Clive, 89
Cockburn, Alexander, 181
Cockburn, Sir Alexander, 181
Cockerell Building, 181–182
Codrington, Christopher, 67, 95
Codrington College, 67, 70, 125, 152, 154–155
Coffee, 32, 83, 85–86, 114, 136, 184
Coke, Sir Edward, 10, 122
Colebatch, John, 25
Coleridge, Hartley, 158
Coleridge, Henry Nelson, 155–158
Coleridge, Samuel Taylor, 113–114, 140–141, 158
Coleridge, William Hart, 155

INDEX

College of William and Mary, 22, 25, 70, 82, 136, 152, 169
Colleton, Sir Peter, 61
Collins, John, 80
Collymore, Amaryllis, 46
Collymore, Robert, 46
Collymore, Robert, Jr., 46
Colton, John, 53
Comings, Thomas Gray, 132
Committee for the Abolition of the Slave Trade, 112
Committee for the Relief of the Black Poor, 130
Company of Adventurers to the Bahama Islands, 61
Company of Scotland Trading to Africa and the Indies, 66
Cook, Capt. James, 78, 131
Coolidge, Ellen Randolph, 169
Corn Laws, 163
Corpus Christi College, Cambridge
    alumni support for the proslavery movement, 128
    donations to the SPG, 67
    donors to the abolition movement, 111–112
    fellows and the abolition movement, 160
    fellowship donations to the SPCK, 67
    fellowship involvement in the University of the South, 165
    fellowship involvement in the SPCK, 68
    fellowship support for the SPG, 69
    library accounts of, 143, 225
    Matthias Mawson as Master, 68–69
    student ownership of South Sea Company securities, 31
    sugar and property leasing, 160
    Thomas Tenison's benefaction to, 70
Corpus Christi College, Oxford, 124
Cosins, John, 58
Cotton
    British support for plantations trading in, 194
    British support for traders in, 196
    impact of scarcity on British economy, 190
    missionary attacks on the trade in, 185
    missionary support for plantations in Africa, 184
    New York trade in, 172
    plantations, 170
    sale and distribution of, 115
    slave trafficking to cotton states, 176
Cotton, John, 59–60
Cottrell, Sally, 169
Coulthurst, William, 112
Coulthurst, William Henry, 104–105
Courten, Sir William, 7
Covel, John, 78
Cowell, John Jermyn, 193
Cowell, John Welsford, 194–196
Cowie, Samuel Burnie, 127
Craft, Ellen, 173
Craft, William, 173
Craister, John, 63
Crashaw, William, 51–52
Craufurd, James, 147
Craufurd, Rev. George W., 146–147, 150, 182
Craufurd, Sir Alexander, 147
Craufurd, Thomas, 147
Crawford, Alexander, 38
Crawford, Charles, 38
Cromwell, Oliver, 52
Crosse, Thomas, 82
Crowther, Samuel Ajayi, 181
Cruikshank, Isaac, 127
Crummell, Alexander
    abolitionist thought, 182–183
    commentary on Black civil rights, 184
    education and background of, 171–172, 180
    friendship with Charles Clayton, 175
    racism experienced in Cambridge, 179, 181
    reasons for attending Cambridge, 172
    speech at the Cambridge Town Hall, 176–177
    support for Liberia, 176, 183
Crummell, Boston, 171
Crummell, Sarah, 179
Cuba, 163
Cust, Brownlow, 128

Dahomey, 129
d'Alonne, Abel Tassin, 68
Dalrymple, Sir David, 225
d'Anghiera, Peter Martyr, 54
D'Arcy, Robert, 37
Darwin, Charles, 274
Davenant, Charles, 91–92
Davenant, William, 30
Davers, Sir Charles, 128
Davies, Emily, 193
Davis, Jefferson, 165, 200
de Gobineau, Joseph Arthur, 197
de Jussieu, Antoine Laurent, 86
de La Condamine, Charles-Marie, 78
de Secondat, Charles Louis, Baron de La Brède et de Montesquieu, 104
de Tocqueville, Alexis, 168
Decker, Sir Matthew, 69
Demerara, 27, 43, 46, 104
Denmark, 196, 203
Denne, John, 68
Dessalines, Jean-Jacques, 144
Devaynes, William, 49
d'Iberville, Pierre Le Moyne, 93
Dickinson, Francis, 48
Dickinson, William, 48
Doctors' Commons, 90–92, 96, 101
Dod, Peirce, 96
Dolben Act of 1788, 10
Dominica, 47, 86
Donne, John, 57
Douglas, Philip, 138
Douglass, Frederick, 173–174, 182
Dowding, William Charles, 177–179
Downing, Emmanuel, 55
Downman, John, 37, 230
Draining of the Fens, 6
Draper, Lieut. Gen. Sir William, 107
Du Bois, W. E. B., 183
Dublin (enslaved rebel), 46
Dulany, Daniel, 37
Dundas, Henry, 1st Viscount Melville, 152
Dundas, Lawrence, 1st Earl of Zetland, 47, 181
Dunlop, James, 193
Dunlop, Nancy, 193
Dutch West India Company, 9
Dyer, George, 121

East India Company
  abolitionist support for sugar production under, 147
  college investments in, 63–64, 243
  enslavement and coerced labour under, 145–146
  indentureship, 15
  individual investments in, 59, 64–65, 86, 89, 94, 97, 257
  loans to, 195
  missionary activity for, 63, 65, 70, 78, 113
  political support for, 64, 91
  Robert Clive's governorship, 89
  Royal Society's investment in, 76
  scientific research for, 89
  Sir Matthew Decker's directorship, 69
  slave-trading, 9
Eddis, William, 115
Eden, Charles, 69
Eden, Richard, 54
Edinburgh, University of, 67, 191
Edward, James Francis, 62
Edward VI, 53
Edwards, Bryan, 123, 135–136
Eliot, Rev. John, 55
Elizabeth I, 53–54
Elliot, Charles, 178
Elliott, Richard, 63
Ellys, Anthony, 73, 152
Elyott, Adam, 72
Emancipation of the Serfs, 191
Emancipation Proclamation, 200, 203, 286
Emery, William, 165
Emmanuel College, Cambridge
  alumni connections to Ireland, 53
  attitude to protests, 121
  donations from enslavers, 32
  fellows and the Haitian Revolution, 129
  former fellows and racial thought, 71–72
  fire, 229
  involvement in the abolition of the slave trade, 111
  members' support for American colonisation, 51, 59–60
  members' support for the SPCK, 67
  students and enslavement, 28

Equafo, 9
Equiano, Olaudah, 13, 45, 110, 112, 132
Erasmus, 6, 68
Ethnological Society of London, 198
Eton College
   Henry Nelson Coleridge's education at, 155
   Jefferson Davis's visit to, 201
   John George Witt's attendance at, 199
   Richard Elliott's attendance at, 63
   students with connections to the plantation economy, 28, 36–37, 147, 230
   alumni support for Charles Kingsley, 189
   Thomas Smith's tenure as provost, 53
Eustis, George, Jr., 200
Everett, Edward, 193
Everett, William, 193–194
Eyre, Edward John, 190–191

Farish, Charles, 104–106, 114–115
Farish, Rev. William, 130, 141, 143–144, 177
Farmer, Richard, 121
Fattatenda, Gambia, 133
Fellowes, Sir James, 181
Ferrar, Nicholas, 52, 55–56, 59
Ferrar, Virginia, 52
Fiji, 192
Fillmore, Millard, 259
Finch, Daniel, 2nd Earl of Nottingham, 69
Finch, Henry, 69
Fisk Jubilee Singers, 174
Fisk University, 174
Fleetwood, William, 71
Florida, 73, 185, 193
Flower, Benjamin, 117
Folkes, Elizabeth, 44
Follen, Charles, 169
Fonnereau, Claude, 86
Foot, Jesse, 90
Forby, Robert, 44
Forten, James, 171
Foster, Richard, 172
Fothergill, John, 131

Fox, Charles James, 37, 141
Fox, William, 145
Francklin, Thomas, 74
Franklin, Benjamin, 78, 236
Franklyn, Gilbert, 128
Frederick, Prince of Wales, 99, 104, 259
Free Soil Party, 187
Freedom's Journal, 172
Freind, John, 81
French Revolution, 112, 116, 120–121
Frend, Rev. William, 130
Frend, William, 112, 121
Fugitive Slave Act, 189
Fuller, Henry, 28
Fuller, John 'Mad Jack', 227
Fuller, John, Jr., 28, 31–32
Fuller, John, Sr., 29, 224
Fuller, Rose, 28, 30, 32, 41, 86
Fuller, Stephen
   dealings with Samuel Alpress, 40–42
   education at Cambridge, 28
   fellowship at Trinity College, 29
   guidance of students, 23–24, 29, 31
   involvement in the proslavery lobby, 119–123, 128–129
   last will and testament, 48
   membership of the Royal Society, 227
Fuller, Thomas, 29, 40
Fuller Rose, 31

Gale, Thomas, 69
Galen, 76
Galusha, Rev. Elon, 172
Gamble, Jane Catherine, 193
Garrison, William Lloyd, 171, 176
Gedge, Joseph, 184
General Theological Seminary, 172
George I, 38, 68, 82, 92, 104
George II, 37, 72, 99, 102, 104
George III, 45, 104–105, 114, 151
George IV, 125
Georgia, 68–69, 73–74, 86, 165, 173, 185
Gibbon, Edward, 7
Gibson, Thomas, 97
Giffard, Hardinge, 1st Earl of Halsbury, 201
Girton College, Cambridge, 193

INDEX

Gisborne, Thomas, 132
Gladstone, William, 103
Glasgow, University of, 7, 100
Glorious Revolution of 1688, 62
Glover, Thomas, 77
Godfrey, Rev. Henry, 141
Godolphin, Henry, 36
Godwyn, Morgan, 23
Gonville and Caius College, Cambridge
   alumni in Africa, 184
   alumni in the early Virginia colony, 56
   alumni support for missionary work, 154
   alumni support for the proslavery movement, 128
   alumni who were enslaved, 72
   Clayton's fellowship at, 175
   Cockerell building, 181
   college donations to the SPCK, 67
   college donations to the SPG, 67
   Crummell dining at, 179
   donations to other charitable causes, 112
   donations to the abolition movement, 111
   enslaved man named Caius, 26
   Fellows and Saint-Domingue, 181
   Fellows' involvement in phrenology, 164
   Fellows' involvement in the SPCK, 67
   Fellows with connections to the plantation economy, 32, 44
   Gooch's mastership, 25–26
   members' involvement in the colonisation of Ireland, 53
   Salomons benefaction, 195
   Stockton's benefaction, 66
   students and the ASL, 199
   students with connections to the plantation economy, 31, 34, 37, 44–45
   Tobacco case, 58
   Wortley's benefaction, 66
Gooch, Sir Thomas, 25–26, 35–36, 44, 66, 70
Gooch, William, 25–26, 35
Goslings and Sharpe Bank, 155
Gottingen, University of, 134
Goulburn, Henry, 37, 181, 197, 230

Gower, Dr Humphrey, 245
Grainger, James, 161
Grant, Alexander, 46
Grant, John, 128
Grant, Sir Alexander Cray, 162–163
Grant, Ulysses S., 18
Gray, Robert, 51
Green, John, 67
Green, William Mercer, 164
Greene, Henry, 130
Gregory, David, 67
Gregory, James, 66
Grenada, 47, 106, 127
Grenville, George Neville, 27, 181
Gresham College, 61
Gresham, Thomas, 160
Greville, Fulke, 1st Baron Brooke, 57
Grey, Samuel Brownlow, 178–179
Grigg, William, 65
Grimké, John Faucheraud, 40
Grinstead, Elizabeth Kay, 100
Grotius, Hugo, 99
Grymes, John I, 26
Grymes, John II, 26
Grymes, John Randolph, 37
Guadeloupe, 95, 138–139
Guinea Company, 58–59
Gunpowder Plot, 62

Hackwood, William, 110
Hague, Charles, 45
Hakewill, James, 155
Hall, Thomas Kirkpatrick, 27
Hallifax, Samuel, 125–126
Hamilton, Alexander, 99
Hamilton, John James, 28
Hammond, Arthur Atherley, 130
Hancorn, Richard, 131
Hanson, Samuel, 44
Hare, Sir Ralph, 58
Harley, Robert, 1st Earl of Oxford and Earl Mortimer, 9
Harper & Brothers, 170
Harrison, Caskie, 166
Harrison, John, 78
Harrow School, 28, 36, 192
Harvard University, 66, 75, 169, 193–194

Harvest, George, 73–74
Harvey, William Woodis, 142, 144
Harwood, Sir Busick, 121, 132
Harwood, Thomas, 113
Hawes, William, 41
Hay, James, 2nd Earl of Carlisle, 59
Hayes, Charles, 81, 250
Heeren, Arnold Hermann Ludwig, 134
Hemings, Sarah 'Sally', 100
Henchman, Humphrey, 91
Henry III, 5
Henry VIII, 6–7, 53
Henslow, John Stevens, 141
Herbert, William, 3rd Earl of Pembroke, 59
Heslop, John, 68
Heslop, Robert, 109
Heyne, Christian Gottlob, 134
Heyrick, Elizabeth, 140
Heywood & Co., 192
Hibbert, George, 136
Hicks, Charity, 171
Hinchcliffe, John, 108–109
Hinchliffe, Henry, 115
Hindmarsh, George, 127
Hoadly, Benjamin, 67
Hodgson, Francis, 116
Holt, Arthur, 33
Hooker, Thomas, 60
Hopkins, J. B., 200
Hopkinson, John, 46
Hopkinson, Thomas, 46
Hornemann, Friedrich Conrad, 134
Hornsby, Thomas, 28
Horse racing, 31
Hothersall, Burch, 32
Hotze, Henry, 17, 197–200
Houghton, Daniel, 133
Houstoun, William, 86
Howard University, 183
Howley, William, 153
Hubbard, Henry, 67
Hudson's Bay Company, 91, 111, 227
Hughes, Rev. Griffith, 132
Hull, 115–116, 120
Hume, David, 39
Humphreys, David, 72
Humphry, Mary, 180

Humphry, Sir George Murray, 180
Hunt, Dr James, 198–199
Hutcheson, Samuel, 100
Hutton, John, 40
Hutton, V. W., 186

Île de Gorée, Senegal, 133
The Index, 198, 200
India and the Indian subcontinent, 15, 63, 68, 89, 91, 116, 144–146, 176, 195
Inns of Court, 19, 22, 25, 31, 36, 39, 75, 201
Ireland, 16, 52–54, 63, 69
Ireland, John, 153
Isaacson, Rev. Stephen, 158–159
Islamic slave trade, 11, 134–135, 184
Izard, Ralph, 19, 36

Jackson, Keith Alexander, 47
Jackson, Thomas Jonathan 'Stonewall', 195
Jamaica
  abolition, 15, 162
  artistic depictions of, 155
  Association of Jamaican Proprietors, 48
  battles in, 120
  benefactor connections to, 192
  Bickell family, 159
  Bigland family, 39
  Board of Longitude plans in, 89
  Cowell family, 194
  Duke of Albemarle, 27
  enslaved revolts in, 114, 172
  fellowship connections to plantations in, 27, 29, 147, 181
  free Black people in, 39
  free protests in, 190
  Fulke Rose, 28, 78
  Fuller family, 28
  indentureship, 15, 192
  Long family, 28
  missionary activity in, 67–68, 159
  Monk Lewis's account of, 162
  prison labour in, 157
  proslavery lobby, 119–120, 122, 128–129
  racism following abolition, 179
  Rev. John Riland's novel, 123–124

380　　　　　　　　　　　　INDEX

Jamaica (cont.)
  Ricketts family, 128
  Rose family, 89–90
  scientific collecting in, 81, 83
  Seal of, 60–61
  slave advertisements, 117
  student connections to plantations in, 23, 27, 29, 37, 40–42, 46–47, 117, 202
  student familial connections to, 47, 75
  sugar exports, 145
  Tharp family, 202
  Thistlewood, 12
  wealth, 8
  Yorke Family, 39
James I, 7, 57, 59
James II, 11, 60, 62
Jefferson, Thomas, 14, 100, 102, 110, 169–170
Jeffrey, Francis, 148
Jenkinson, Charles, 1st Earl of Liverpool, 122, 152
Jenkinson, Robert, 2nd Earl of Liverpool, 138
Jesus College, Cambridge
  alumni and the trans-Saharan slave trade, 135
  alumni who supported the abolition movement, 117
  alumni who supported the proslavery movement, 158
  Coleridge's address in Bristol, 114
  college investments in the South Sea Company, 64
  Fellows who supported the abolition movement, 112, 115, 166
  Fellows with familial connections to the slave trade, 75
  members' support for Sierra Leone Company, 130
  Rustat's benefaction, 60
  students with connections to the plantation economy, 23, 40
  students with connections to the slave trade, 75
  subscribers to abolitionist literature, 113
  Thomas Robert Malthus and, 14
  William Frend's expulsion from, 121

Jesus College, Oxford, 98
Johnson, Samuel, 79, 107
Jones, Hugh, 82
Jones, Rev. Richard, 147
Jones, Rev. Thomas, 130
Jones, Thomas, 110, 112
Jones, William, 80
Jowett, Rev. Joseph, 130
Jowett, Rev. William, 119

Keene, Edmund, 75, 108
Kennedy, Benjamin Hall, 195
Key, Thomas Hewitt, 168
Kidder, Richard, 71
Kimber, John, 126–128
King, William, 81
King's College, Cambridge
  Byam's bequest, 32
  Draper's fellowship and donation, 107
  Elliott's benefaction, 63
  Fellows and opposition to indentured labour, 191
  Fellows and students with connections to the plantation economy, 146
  Fellows and the SPG, 71
  Fellows who supported amelioration, 155
  Fellowship investments in the EIC, 146
  former Confederates attend dinner at, 200
  Jermyn Cowell's friendship with Oscar Browning, 289
  member donations to the SPCK, 67
  members' involvement in the Anthropological Society of London, 199
  Randolph's support for the proslavery movement, 124
  subscribers to abolitionist literature, 113
  Witt's support for the Confederacy, 198–199
King's College, London, 173
Kingsley, Charles, 187–190, 192, 199, 201
Kingsley, Frances, 189
Kneller, Sir Godfrey, 38, 230
Knox, William, 151

Komenda Wars, 9
Kościuszko, Tadeusz, 168
Ksar-el-Kebir, Battle of, 160
Kynaston, Edward, 96

Laing, Robert Griffin, 177
Lamb, Charles, 158
Lamb, John, 160
Lamb, William, 2nd Viscount Melbourne, 141
Lambert, James, 112
Lascelles, Edward, 76
Latrobe, Charles Joseph, 169
Laughton, Richard, 65
Laurens, Henry, 40
Laurens, Robert Scipio, 40
Le Grice, Rev. Charles Valentine, 142
Leahy, Col. John, 46
Leclerc, Charles, 138
Lee, Robert E., 18, 187
Legaré, Hugh Swinton, 43
Legh, George J., 111
Leiden, University of, 30
Leman, Rev. Robert, 67
Lemmon Slave Case, 102
Levant Company, 78
Lewis, George, 78
Lewis, Matthew Gregory, 162
Liberia, 176, 182–184
Library Company of Philadelphia, 169
Lightfoot, John, 66
Lincoln, Abraham, 185
Lincoln College, Oxford, 97
Linneaus, Carl, 87
Lister, Martin, 76–77, 247
Liverpool
    abolitionist activism in, 115–116
    banking in, 115, 192
    Fellows with connections to the transatlantic slave economy, 27
    novels mention, 123
    proslavery lobby in, 153
    Sir Thomas Smith as the Member of Parliament for, 53
    students with connections to the transatlantic slave economy from, 20, 43
Livingstone, David, 184
Lloyd, Dame Elizabeth, 94

Lloyd, Sir Nathaniel
    advice to the South Sea Company, 94
    benefactions and loans to various causes, 96–98
    Codrington benefaction, 95–96
    Education of, 90
    election of Thomas Tenison to a fellowship, 27
    investments in the East India Company, 94
    investments in the Royal African Company, 95
    investments in the South Sea Company, 94–95, 255
    John Radcliffe donation, 97
    Nevis legal advice, 93
    piracy cases, 93–94
    Saint-Domingue plantation case, 92
    work on the law of contraband, 92
Lloyd, Sir Richard, 90–91, 94–95
Locke, John, 28, 61, 117
Lockyer, Charles, 246
London and Westminster Bank, 195
London Assurance Company, 27
London Hausa Association, 184
London Missionary Society, 46
The London Society of West India Planters and Merchants, 119, 153
Long, Beeston, 32
Long, Edward, 12
Long, George, 169
Long, Sir Charles, 181
Long, William, 32
Louis XIV, 122
Louisiana, 13–14, 73, 88, 165, 185, 200
Louverture, Toussaint, 129, 181
Lovell, Michael, 38
Loving, Richard, 31
Lowndes, Thomas, 48
Lowther, George, 93
Lowther, Robert, 93–94

Maberly, Rev. Frederick Herbert, 47, 150
Macaulay, Zachary, 130, 142
Macocke, Rev. Samuel, 56
Madagascar, 9
Madden, R. R., 169

INDEX

Magdalene College, Cambridge
  college investments in the EIC, 243
  fellowship connections to the plantation economy, 27
  Colony of Georgia, 73–74
  fellowship investments in the SSC, 31
  members' support for the SPCK, 67
  Peckard's antislavery views, 23, 108
  student support for abolition, 111, 113
Magdalene College, Oxford, 123
Magna Carta, 120, 201
Mahogany, 13, 114
Malden, Daniel, 78
Malthus, Thomas Robert, 141
Mandell, Rev. William, 141
Mandeville, John, 31
Manners-Sutton, Charles, 28
Mapletoft, John, 61, 67
Marriott, Sir James, 126–128
Marsh, Herbert, 129
Marsh, Rev. H. A., 176
Martin, Samuel, 22, 224
Martineu, Harriet, 179
Martyn, John, 86–87
Martyn, Thomas, 86–88
Mary I, 53
Maryland, 14, 37
Maskelyne, Edmund, 89
Maskelyne, Nevil, 88–90
Mason, Rev. Charles, 82–83
Massachusetts, 55
Massachusetts Anti-Slavery Society, 169
Massey, John, 93
Mawson, Matthias, 68–69
May, Samuel, 38
Mayer, Tobias, 89
Mayers, John Pollard, 158, 161–162
McCabe, W. Gordon, 168
McKenzie, William, 191
McRae, Colin J., 200
Melvil, Thomas, 49
Melville, Elizabeth, 176
Member of the University of Cambridge, 144–146
Merchants
  advice to student families, 36
  Apthorp's dealings with, 75
  chaperoning students, 29, 38, 40
  fellowship connections to, 45
  fellowship support for the children of, 99
  Hull traders, 116
  impact of the American Revolution on, 98
  involvement in missionary enterprises, 152
  involvement in the proslavery movement, 119
  Manchester support for the Bulama Association, 131
  participation in the colonisation of Barbados, 7
  Saint-Domingue traders, 92
  significance of enslaved people as commodities, 154
  student connections to, 21, 32, 47
  support for the Confederacy, 200
  tobacco traders, 24, 26, 36
  tutor connections to, 104
  West African elites, 134–135
Merry, Robert, 111
Metacom and Weetamoo's War, 8, 55
Mickleburgh, John, 82
Middleton, Arthur, 19
Middleton, Conyers, 82
Mill, John Stuart, 190
Miller, Charles, 87
Miller, Philip, 87
Miller, Samuel, 43
Milner, Isaac, 119
Mississippi, 185, 198
Mitchell, William Stephen, 199
Monck, Christopher, 2nd Duke of Albermarle, 27, 227
Monins, Richard, 31
Montagu, John, 2nd Duke of Montagu, 39
Montagu, John, 4th Earl of Sandwich, 78
Montaigne, George, 59
Moore, James, 111
Moore, Richard, 111
Morant Bay Rebellion, 190, 192
More, Sir Thomas, 54
Morland, Samuel, 78
Morocco, 160

Morris, Sarah, 82
Mortlock, John, 141
Morton, Thomas, 51
Mosman, George, 66
Murchison, Sir Roderick
    Impey, 190
Murray, John II, 168
Murray, William, 1st Earl of Mansfield,
    50, 125, 231
Musgrave, Thomas, 145

Native Americans, 62
  collections of objects in
      Cambridge, 78
  colonial attempts to educate and
      evangelise, 52, 66, 69, 72, 108
  English concerns about
      enslavement of, 55
  impact of Spanish colonisation on,
      62
  involvement in natural scientific
      discoveries, 78
  resistance to white colonisers, 11
  universities and dispossession
      of, 4, 57
  white enslavement of, 8, 10, 23, 55, 57, 60
  white racism toward, 12, 14, 54, 56–57
Nelson, Thomas, 42
Nelson, William, 42
Nevis, 20, 82–83, 93, 124
New England, 59, 60, 115, 168–169,
    188, 196
New Jersey, 49
New York, 28, 72–73, 102, 168, 170, 172,
    175, 177, 182, 196
New York Conspiracy of 1741, 73
New York Slave Revolt
    of 1712, 72–73
New Zealand, 165, 175, 195, 290
Newman, Henry, 67
Newmarket, 31
Newnham College, Cambridge,
    192–193
Newton, Benjamin, 23, 41–42
Newton, Henry, 92
Newton, Rev. John, 124
Newton, Sir Isaac, 23, 78, 80, 85
Newton, Thomas, 72
Nicholl, Sir John, 98

Norris, Robert, 129
North Carolina, 101
North, Brownlow, 132
Norton, John, 24, 42
Norton, John Hatley, 24

Oates, Titus, 62
Ockley, Simon, 72
Oglethrope, James, 68
O'Kelly, Cornelius, 92
O'Kelly, Hughes, 92
Oldenburg, Henry, 77
Ollivant, Rev. Alfred, 176
Oriel College, Oxford, 81
Oswestry, Shropshire, 91, 97
Otey, James Hervey, 164–165
Oxenden, George, 64
Oxford, University of, 5, 7, 56, 59,
    165, 177
Oxford (enslaved man), 83
Oxford and Cambridge University
    Club, 48

Padua, University of, 5, 53
Paine, Thomas, 121
Paley, William, 104, 117–118, 140, 142,
    174, 264
Palmer, Thomas Fyshe, 121
Panell, George, 173
Paris, Rev. John, 64
Paris, University of, 5, 24
Park, Mungo, 135–136
Parker, Robert, 111
Patrick, Simon, 72
Peacock, George, 48
Pearce, Zachary, 31
Peckard, Peter
  antislavery thought of, 108–109
  Cambridge essay question on
      slavery, 109
  conversations with Equiano, 110
  donation to the Sierra Leone
      Company, 130
  reaction to his antislavery thought, 111
  recognition of, 143
  support for education reform, 23
Pelham-Holles, Thomas, 1st Duke of
    Newcastle, 25
Pellett, Thomas, 81

Pelling, Edward, 69
Pembroke College
    Cambridge, 37–38, 60
    Oxford, 59
Penfold, Sir Thomas, 91
Penn, William, 196
Pennant, Henry, 228
Pennsylvania, 19, 38, 140, 196, 198
Pequot War, 55
Perceval, Sir John, 25
Perkins, Thomas H., 169
Perrott, Henry, Jr., 64
Perry, Micajah, 36
The Perse School, 175
Peterhouse, Cambridge
    donors to the abolition movement, 111
    Fellows and the Anthropological Society of London, 199
    Fellows visiting parliamentary debates, 115
    fellowship support for St Paul's College in Bermuda, 178
    Keene's ameliorationist views, 75, 108
    members' support for the Sierra Leone Company, 130
    Some's mastership, 59
    students with connections to the transatlantic economy, 37
    Vernon and natural science, 81
Petiver, James, 83, 85
The Phrenological Journal, 171
Pinckney, Elizabeth, 88
Pinder, Rev. John Hothersall, 154
Pine, Robert Edge, 37
Pinfold, Charles, 64
Pitcairn, Archibald, 67
Pitt, William (the Younger), 28, 43, 114, 119, 121, 125–126, 136
Planters
    Abdy's attacks on, 170
    advice for plantation owners, 22
    Australian sugar estates, 191–192
    Berkeley's ownership of a plantation, 69
    British compensation for Saint-Domingue slaveholders, 181
    Byrd family, 25
    Codrington's donation to the SPG, 95, 154
    compensation to enslavers, 15
    contributions to missionary causes, 153–154
    diversification of income streams, 8
    donations to Edinburgh University, 191
    donations to the Cockerell Building, 181–182
    Earl of Liverpool's trusteeship of a plantation, 138
    enslaved people brought to Britain, 39
    fellowship connections to, 27, 44, 104, 106, 128, 147, 150, 166
    Fuller family, 28
    Gamble family and Florida, 193
    Gilbert Franklyn's ownership of estates, 128
    Henry Nelson Coleridge's support for, 155–156
    hiring of plantation tutors, 46
    impact of Haitian Revolution on, 45
    integrated plantation system, 7–8
    interest in mathematics, 23
    interest in natural science, 78
    involvement in the abolition movement, 162
    involvement in the proslavery movement, 159
    Irish on Saint-Domingue, 92
    Kingsley's concerns about abolition, 187
    loans to, 196
    Maskelyne's marriage into the Rose family, 89
    MP connections to, 197
    Newmarket plantation, 31
    proposals for planting in Virginia, 57
    proposals to plant coffee in the British Caribbean, 85
    registration of enslaved people, 202
    resistance to enslaved revolts, 46
    social contacts in Britain, 24
    soundscape of the plantation, 13
    student connections to, 19–21, 32, 37–38, 40, 43, 47–48, 64, 111, 162, 192, 194
    support for the abolition of the slave trade, 15

Thomas Thistlewood's treatment of
    enslaved people, 12
tutors who educated children
    connected to, 27
Plowden, Sir Edmund, 32
Political Economy Club, 194
Pollard, John, 28
Pollard, Walter, 28
Porteus, Beilby, 130, 150–153,
    177, 275
Porteus, Robert, 150
Pory, John, 56
Postlethwaite, Rev. Thomas, 130
Postlethwayt, Malachy, 131
Postlewhaite, Thomas, 27
Potts, Robert, 169
Powhatan, 52, 56
Poydras, Julien de Lallande, 88
Prichard, James Cowles, 180
Prince Adolphus, Duke of
    Cambridge, 202
Prince William Frederick, Duke of
    Gloucester, 104, 138
Princess Augusta, 99
Princeton Theological Seminary, 43
Princeton University, 24
Proby, Charles, 64
Pryme, George, 148, 274
Purchas, Samuel, 51, 132

Quaque, Philip, 49
Québec, 126
Queens' College
    Cambridge, 6, 27, 31, 37–38, 53–54,
        59, 68, 72, 78, 81, 104, 106, 113, 115,
        119, 121, 131, 141–142, 152, 172, 176,
        180, 228, 263
    Oxford, 28, 95
Quintard, William, 164–165

Radcliffe, John, 97, 257
Raleigh, Sir Walter, 52
Ramsay, David, 101
Ramsay, James, 151
Randall, John, 118
Randolph, Francis, 124–125
Randolph, John, 26
Randolph, Thomas, 124
Rawlinson, John Job, 143

Ray, John, 57, 77, 82
Recorde, Robert, 23
Reepe, John, 67
Reform Act of 1832, 147
Renouard, George Cecil, 132
Republican Party, 188
Reve, Clare, 123
Rice, Thomas Spring, 1st Baron
    Monteagle, 148, 181
Richard II, 53
Ricketts, George Poyntz, 127
Ricketts, Jacob, 128
Ricketts, Sophia, 127
Rigaud, Andre, 181
Riggs-Miller, Sir John, 131
Riland, Rev. John, 123–124
Roberts, Ernest Stewart, 192
Robinson, F. J., 1st Viscount
    Goderich, 162
Robinson, Rev. Robert, 118, 275
Roderick, Richard, 31
Rodney, George Brydges, 1st Baron
    Rodney, 120
Romilly, Joseph, 162, 179
Rose, Elizabeth Langley, 78
Rose, Fulke, 28
Rose, John Pate, 89
Rose, Laetitia, 89
Rose, Sophia, 89
Roth, George Kingsley, 192
Roth, Henry Ling, 191–192
Rousseau, Jean Jacques, 87
Routh, Edward J., 199
Rowlands, Rev. J., 176
Royal Academy of Music, 81
Royal African Company, 9, 11, 28, 31,
    38, 45, 49, 60, 76, 80–81, 91, 93, 95,
    230, 235, 247, 250
Royal College of Physicians, 76, 81, 132
Royal College of Surgeons, 180
Royal Commission of 1850, 174
Royal Geographical Society, 136, 169
Royal Institution, 29, 227
Royal Mines Company, 67
Royal Navy, 119–120, 130
Royal Society, 25, 29, 39, 76–77, 79, 82,
    85–86, 89, 99, 227
Ruffin, Thomas, 101
Rule, Alexander, 67

Ruskin, John, 190
Russel, Richard, 86
Russell, Henry, 173
Rustat, Tobias, 60
Rutherforth, Thomas, 99–101, 104, 166, 259

Saint Kitts, 20, 150
Saint Vincent, 157, 166, 191
Saint-Domingue/Haiti, 12
   British invasion of, 181
   coffee exports from, 85
   fellowship connections to plantations in, 285
   French attempt to recapture, 138
   Haitian Declaration of Independence, 142
   Haitian Revolution, 14, 44, 105, 129, 146, 158–159, 161, 188
   Irish plantations in, 92
   Kingdom of Haiti, 144
   plantation manuals from, 12
   Santo Domingo Board, 181
   Wesleyan mission to, 142
Saintes, Battle of the, 120
Salmon, Thomas, 132
Salomons, David Lionel, 195
Salomons, Sir David, 194–195
Sancho, Charles Ignatius, 231
Sancroft, William, 60–61
Sandy, George, 27
Sandys, Sir Edwin, 52
Santo Domingo, 11
Savage, William, 32
Sawbridge, Jacob, 95
Sayer, Exton, 64
Scarlett, James, 47, 111
Scholefield, Rev. James, 143–144, 160, 175, 177, 181, 184
Scipio (enslaved man), 86–87
Scott, Sir William, 98
Secker, Thomas, 151
Sedgwick, Rev. Adam, 147, 181, 274
Selwyn, George, 165
Selwyn, Rev. William, 199
Selwyn, William, 165, 184–185
Selwyn College, Cambridge, 165
Sewanee Mining Company, 164

Seymour, Edward, 1st Duke of Somerset, 53
Seymour, John, 53
Shakespeare, William, 12, 56, 140
Sharp, Granville, 50, 108, 116, 123, 130, 236
Sharpe, Samuel, 173
Shaw, Caesar, 231
Sherlock, Thomas, 70
Sibbald, Sir Robert, 66
Sidgwick, Henry, 193
Sidney Sussex College, Cambridge, 52, 68, 87, 104, 109, 111–112, 138, 158
Siena, University of, 5
Sierra Leone
   abolitionist support for colonisation in, 130, 143, 146
   apprenticeship in, 130–131
   Clayton's support for mission in, 175, 177
   Devaynes's support for colonisation, 50
   proposal for a bishopric in, 119
   subscriptions to the Sierra Leone Company, 130
Simeon, Charles, 119
Simmons, Ruth, 202
Simpson, Robert, 36
Skerret, Helen, 92
Slave Compensation Act, 162, 181
Slave Registry Bill of 1815, 202
Slave Trade Felony Act, 138
Slavery Abolition Act, 15, 173, 202
Slidell, John, 186, 200
Sloane, Sir Hans, 78, 82–83, 85–86
Smallpox, 8, 10, 16, 22, 96
Smith, Adam, 7, 146
Smith, Andrew, 86–87
Smith, Rev. John, 46
Smith, Rev. Joseph, 95
Smith, Rev. Richard, 27
Smith, Rev. William, 82
Smith, Sir Thomas, 53–54
Smyth, William, 115
Society for Effecting the Abolition of the Slave Trade, 4, 111–112
Society for the Mitigation and Gradual Abolition of Slavery Throughout the British Dominions, 140–141

Society for the Promotion of Christian Knowledge, 67–68, 96, 177
Society for the Propagation of the Gospel in Foreign Parts, 49–50
　Barbados Committee, 50, 95–96
　Codrington donation, 67, 95, 152
　donations to, 67, 96–97
　intellectual support for, 69, 72–73, 108, 126, 151
　ministers in Massachusetts, 75
　Thomas Thompson's work for, 49–50
Society for the Religious Instruction and Education of the Negro Slaves in the British West Indies, 152–153
Society of Friends, 106, 109, 168, 173, 196
Some, Robert, 59
Somers Island Company, 55, 59
Somerset Decision, 40, 125
South Carolina, 8, 19–20, 28, 40, 48, 73, 88, 101, 185
South Sea Company
　abolitionist attacks on, 118
　college investments in, 64–66, 69, 96–97
　history of, 9, 11
　individual investments in, 31, 36, 64–65, 71, 79, 80, 82, 86, 97, 104, 224–255, 257
　officials of, 69, 95, 99, 246
　scarcity of stock records, 229
　scientific collecting for, 86
　SPCK investments in, 68
　trading problems in the Spanish Americas, 94
Southern Prisoners' Relief Fund, 193
Southwell, Sir Robert, 25
Spanish colonisation of Hispaniola, 62
Spelman, Sir Henry, 58
Spotswood, Alexander, 150
Spurzheim, Johann Gaspar, 171
St Andrews, University of, 95
St Catharine's College, Cambridge, 13, 66–67, 70, 88, 178
St Helena, 65, 89, 97
St John's College, Cambridge
　alumni as tutors in the Caribbean, 46
　alumni teaching in the United States, 168
　alumni who supported the proslavery movement, 128, 158, 161
　Crashaw's donation, 51
　donations from men connected to the colonisation of Ireland, 53
　donations to the abolition movement, 141
　donors who supported African exploration projects, 132
　education of Rutherforth at, 99
　Fellows and racial science, 76–77
　fellowship donations to the SPG, 245
　fellowship donations to the SSC, 31
　fellowship participation in the abolition movement, 119
　fellowship support for St Paul's College in Bermuda, 178
　Henry Venn's education at, 118
　Marsh's discussion of the Haitian Revolution, 129
　members' subscriptions to the Sierra Leone Company, 130
　members' support for dissenters, 121
　members' support for the Virginia Company, 51–52, 56
　memorialisation of Wilberforce, 202
　Sir Ralph Hare's donation to, 58
　student connections to the plantation economy, 47, 104, 162
　student connections to the transatlantic economy, 37, 51
　students and the ASL, 199
　students with connections to the transatlantic economy, 37
　Thomas Clarkson's attendance at, 109
　Wilberforce's education at, 119
St John's College, Oxford, 60
Stanton, Henry Brewster, 175
Stapleton, John, 92
Stephens, Alexander H., 185
Stephens, William, 69
Stevenson, Sir Archibald, 67
Stockton, Owen, 75
Stoner, Anthony Morris, 230
The Stono Rebellion, 73

Stourbridge Fair, 6
Stowe, Harriet Beecher, 173, 197
Stuart, J. E. B., 200
Sudan, 134
Sugar
  abolitionist attacks on, 145
  abolitionist support
    for, 144, 146–147
  Agricultural Society
    dedicated to, 156
  Australian plantations growing,
    191–192
  consumption of, 13, 32, 114
  duties on, 162
  efforts to ameliorate plantations
    producing, 146
  enslaved people eating, 12
  exporting of, 145
  fluctuating price of, 15, 44
  missionary support for plantations
    in Africa, 184
  plantations producing, 8, 13, 15,
    37, 44, 90
  poems concerning, 161
  production in Morocco, 160
  proslavery support for, 119, 129
  student name-calling, 46
  threat of foreign imports, 163
  use in property leasing
    arrangements, 160
  wealth from producing, 20
Sugar Duties Act, 163
Sumatra, 87
Sumner, John Bird, 178
Surinam, 83, 85, 152
Swedish Africa Company, 49

Tacky's Revolt, 114
Taíno, 62
Tait, William, 170
Tarleton, Banastre, 43
Tarleton, John, 43
Tarleton, John Collingwood, 43
Taylor, John, 101–102
Taylor, Richard, 200
Taylor, Simon, 37
Taylor, Thomas, 62
Temple, Henry John, 3rd Viscount
  Palmerston, 37, 187, 198

Tenison, Edward, 27
Tenison, Rev. Thomas, 27, 69, 79
Tenison, Thomas, 27
Texas, 14, 185, 203
Thackeray, Martin, 146
Tharp, John, 117, 202
Tharp, Joseph, 202
Thellusson, Peter Isaac, 1st Baron
  Rendlesham, 47
Thellusson, William, 47
Thirty Years' War, 99
Thistlewood, Thomas, 11
Thomason, Thomas Truebody, 113, 263
Thompson, Henry Yates, 192, 289
Thompson, Samuel Henry, 192
Thompson, Thomas, 49–50, 75, 114
Thompson, Thomas Perronet, 131, 163
Thompson, William Hepworth, 164
Thornton, Samuel, 130
Timbuktu, 133, 136
The Times, 186, 190, 286
Tindal, Sir Nicholas Conyngham,
  182, 197
Tobacco
  consumption of, 32, 58–59
  distribution on slave ships, 10
  Inspection Act, 25
  plantations growing, 8, 14, 57
  students with familial connections to
    plantations producing, 19
  traders, 24, 26, 36, 76, 115
  Virginia Company and, 52, 56
Tobago, 128
Tobin, James, 124
Townes, Thomas, 76, 109
Townley, James, 142–143
Townshend, Charles, 2nd Viscount
  Townshend, 97
Townshend, Thomas, 1st Viscount
  Sydney, 120
Transatlantic traders of enslaved
  Africans, 132
  Abolitionists campaign
    against, 116
  brandings, 11
  British abolition of, 138
  collaboration with African
    explorers, 134
  fellowship connections to, 27, 75

insurance arrangements, 27
involvement in natural science, 81, 83
legal cases involving, 92, 98, 126–127
Massachusetts and the legalistion of the slave trade, 60
student connections to, 21, 24, 43, 233
Tarleton family, 43
Thomas Salmon's attacks against, 132
Treaty of Utrecht, 9, 93
Trinidad, 47, 155–156
Trinity College, Cambridge
  alumni support for the proslavery movement, 128
  alumni teaching in the United States, 168
  attendance at Crummell's speech, 176
  collections of curiosities, 78–79
  consumption of tobacco, 58
  Cotton's education at, 59
  Craister's benefaction, 63
  Crummell dining at, 179
  donations to the abolition movement, 111, 130, 141
  donations to the SPCK, 67, 177
  donations to the Wren Library, 27
  donors who supported African exploration, 132
  Farish's education at, 106
  Fellows and correspondence with anti-slave-trade activists, 112
  Fellows opposed to investing, 31
  Fellows who invested in the SSC, 31, 80, 82
  Fellows with familial ties to the plantations, 27, 29
  Fellows with natural scientific interests in the Caribbean, 82–83
  fellowship opinions on emancipation, 162
  former members and Berkeley's scheme, 69
  founding of Statistical Section at, 147
  Hinchcliffe's support for amelioration, 108
  individual investments in the RAC, 31
  involvement in the Universities' Mission to Central Africa, 184
  Jones selling copies of Equiano's slave narrative, 110
  Mapletoft's investments in the Company of Adventurers, 61
  Maskelyne's education and fellowship at, 88–89
  member support for the SPG, 72
  members' attitudes to the American Civil War, 186, 193
  members involved in the Virginia Company, 52
  Subscriptions to the Sierra Leone Company, 130
  Support for the Union, 286
  racial attitudes of the fellowship, 181
  Ray's lectures supporting American colonisation, 57
  student poetry in support of slavery, 161
  students with familial ties to the plantations, 22–23, 26–28, 31, 37, 40, 46–47, 192, 202
  subscribers to abolitionist literature, 113
  subscribers to American travel literature, 115
  support for St Paul's College in Bermuda, 178
  support for the Colony of Georgia, 74
  Thomas Newton's support for the Curse of Ham myth, 72
Trinity College, Dublin, 53
Trinity College, Oxford, 97
Trinity Hall, Cambridge
  alumni support for Native American slavery, 55
  Bridgetower's education at, 45
  Cockburn and Saint-Domingue, 181
  donations to the abolition movement, 111
  Fellows debating enslavement, 125
  Fellows who invested in the EIC, 64
  Fellows with ties to slave trading, 27
  Lloyd's benefaction, 97
  Marriott's adjudication of the Kimber case, 126

Trinity Hall, Cambridge (cont.)
  members' donations to the Sierra Leone Company, 130
  ownership of East India securities, 195
  student opposition to the Confederacy, 186
  students with connections to the plantations, 26, 37–38
  ties to the Doctors' Commons, 91–92
  Wynne's donation to, 98
  Wynne's education at, 98
Tucker, St George, 136
Tudway, Thomas, 45
Turner, J. M. W., 29
Tweddell, John, 112
Tyschen, Thomas Christian, 134

Universities' Mission to Central Africa, 184–185
University College, Oxford, 97, 113
University of Cambridge Petitions to the House of Commons, 3, 115, 122, 138–139
University of the South, 164–166
University of Virginia, 168
Upper Appomattox Canal Company, 193
Uppsala University, 131

van Beethoven, Ludwig, 45
Venn, Henry (Church Missionary Society), 119, 176, 180
Venn, Rev. Henry, 118, 141
Vernon, William, 81
Victoria I, 178, 200
Vienna, University of, 171
Vignier, Yolande, 181
Virginia
  academic support for colonisation in, 56
  alumni and former fellows who emigrated to, 169
  Black experimentation in, 77
  Byrd's visit from, 25
  Cavalier myth, 196
  end of Company rule, 59
  First Anglo-Powhatan War, 62
  Gamble benefaction, 193
  General Assembly of, 56
  Gooch's governorship, 25–26
  Irish indentured servitude in, 52
  missionary activity in, 23
  Native American enslavement in, 8
  opposition to English educations, 42, 232
  origins of African enslavement in, 55
  parental wills, 22
  Pollard family, 28
  Porteus family, 150
  Samuel Purchas's writings about, 132
  scientific collections from, 81
  scientists travelling to, 82
  significance of Irish colonisation to, 54
  Slave Codes of 1705, 60
  slavery challenged in, 100
  students from, 19–21, 26, 28, 33–34, 37, 64
  transportation of impoverished children to, 57
  Tucker's proposals for gradual abolition, 136
  William Byrd II's visit to Cambridge, 25
Virginia Company
  1622 massacre, 56
  Cambridge support for, 51, 54
  investments in, 58–59
  proposals for the education of Native Americans, 52
  Sir Edward Coke's role in, 10
  trading activities of, 7
  transportation of impoverished children, 57
von Humboldt, Alexander, 78
von Pufendorf, Samuel, 100

Wadham College, Oxford, 96, 256
Wakefield, Gilbert, 115–117
Wakefield, William, 195
Walker, Jacob, 169
Walker, L. P., 197
Walker, Richard, 78, 85
Wallace, Alfred Russell, 199
Walpole, Robert, 97
Wampanoag, 8
War of the Spanish Succession, 92–94

Ward, Nathaniel, 60
Waring, Edward, 68
Warren, John, 128
Washington, D.C., 168, 182–183
Washington, George, 8, 38
Waterhouse, Edward, 56
Waterloo, Battle of, 147
Watson, Richard, 108, 132–133, 135–136
Watson, William, 173
Wedgwood, Josiah, 110
Wells, Ida B., 174
West, Benjamin, 19, 37, 230
West India Lobby, 119–120, 122, 128, 161
Westminster School, 36, 88
Whewell, William, 141, 177–178, 181
Whisson, Stephen, 29, 67
Whitaker, Alexander, 52
Whitaker, William, 52
Whitmore, Rev. George, 121
Whitney, Eli, 14
Wilberforce, William
  antislavery advocacy in Parliament, 113, 136
  antislavery thought, 140
  correspondence with Matthew Gregory Lewis, 162
  founding of the British and Foreign Bible Society, 152
  funding of Crummell's attendance at Cambridge, 172
  integral role in the Clapham Sect, 119
  involvement in Thompson's dismissal, 131
  Jesse Foot's opposition to, 90
  opposition to vice and immorality, 151
  recognition of, 111, 184
  role in Kimber's trial, 127
  support for African exploration, 132
  support for Haiti mission, 142
William IV, 104, 114
Williams, Charley, 13
Williams, Francis, 39
Williams, John, 39
Williams, Roger, 60
Winne, Luttrell, 132
Winthrop, John, 60
Witherspoon, John, 24
Witt, John George, 198, 200–201, 292
Wollaston, Francis, 130
Wood, Capt. Roger, 63
Woodward, John, 16, 79–82
Wordsworth, Christopher, 177
Wordsworth, William, 106
Wormeley, Ralph V, 19, 37
Wortley, Bartholomew, 65, 75
Wriothesley, Henry, 3rd Earl of Southampton, 51
Wynn, Rev. H. E., 266
Wynne, John, 98
Wynne, Sir William, 98

Yates, Elizabeth, 192
Yates, Joseph Brooks, 192
Yorke, Charles Philip, 148, 150
Yorke, John, 39–40
Yorke, Philip, 1st Earl of Hardwicke, 93, 123
Yorke, Rev. James, 123, 266
Yorkshire, 20
Young, Arthur, 22
Young, Sir William, 128
Young, Thomas, 66

Zong massacre, 109, 114